Spanish Colonial
Women and the Law

Spanish Colonial Women and the Law

Complaints, Lawsuits, and Criminal Behavior

*Documents from the Spanish Colonial Archives
of New Mexico, 1697—1749*

SPANISH/ENGLISH EDITION

Linda Tigges, Editor
J. Richard Salazar, Transcriber and Translator

✣ ✣ ✣ ✣
© 2016 by Linda Tigges
All Rights Reserved.
No part of this book may be reproduced in any form or by any electronic or mechanical means including information storage and retrieval systems without permission in writing from the publisher, except by a reviewer who may quote brief passages in a review.

Sunstone books may be purchased for educational, business, or sales promotional use.
For information please write: Special Markets Department, Sunstone Press,
P.O. Box 2321, Santa Fe, New Mexico 87504-2321.
Body typeface › Minion Pro
Printed on acid-free paper

Library of Congress Cataloging-in-Publication Data

Names: Tiggs, Linda, editor.
Title: Spanish colonial women and the law : documents from the 18th century / Linda Tigges, editor ; J. Richard Salazar, transcriber and translator.
Description: Santa Fe : Sunstone Press, [2016] Includes bibliographical references and index.
Indentifiers: LCCN 2015044710
 ISBN 9781632931054 (hardcover : alk. paper) -- ISBN 9781632931047 (softcover : alk. paper)
 Subjects: LCSH: New Mexico--History--To 1848. Women-- New Mexico--History--Sources. New Mexico--History--To 1848--Sources.
 New Mexico--History--To 1848--Biography. Spain--Colonies--America--History--Sources.
Classification: LCC F799 .L59 2016 DDC 305.40978909/032--dc23
LC record available at http://lccn.loc.gov/2015044710

WWW.SUNSTONEPRESS.COM
SUNSTONE PRESS / POST OFFICE BOX 2321 / SANTA FE, NM 87504-2321 /USA
(505) 988-4418 / ORDERS ONLY (800) 243-5644 / FAX (505) 988-1025

CONTENTS

LIST OF ILLUSTRATIONS / 7
ABBREVIATIONS IN TEXT AND NOTES / 7
FOREWORD / 9
PREFACE / 11
HISTORICAL INTRODUCTION / 13

DOCUMENTS

1 / Sisters Throw Rocks at Rival, Governor Threatens Banishment 51
2 / Jacinto Sánchez Granted Permission to Search for a Bar of Lost Spanish Silver........................60
3 / Gossip Creates Domestic Violence; Josefa Sedaño Fears Loss of Reputation 64
4 / Family Killed in 1696 Pueblo Revolt; Female Survivors Ask Permission to Leave the Colony 71
5 / Soldier Agustín de la Palma Accused of Rape; Takes Sanctuary in the Parroquia 76
6 / Francisca Gómez de Torres Asks Governor for Protection from Abusive Husband.....................110
7 / Cristóbal de Góngora Claims Divorce from Wife; She Resists..142
8 / Battered Woman Walks From Atrisco to Santa Fe in Fear of Husband and Mother-in-Law........158
9 / Couple Punished for Cohabitation..171
10 / Inheritance of Two Cows Demanded by Orphaned Daughter Catalina de Villalpando 174
11 / Two Male Servants Fight over Woman on the Other Side of the Santa Fe River....................178
12 / Presidio Soldier Killed in Action; Wife Requests Money from Insurance Fund............................187
13 / Mistress of Deceased Governor Cuervo y Valdés Searches for Promised Financial
   Guarantee of 10,000 Pesos..205
14 / Ana María Romero [Villalpando] Spreads Scandal; Sentenced to Humiliating Punishment........218
15 / New Mexican Ranchers Lucía Hurtado and Luis García de Noriega End Court Case
   with Embrace; Cow Recovered..223
16 / Pedro Montes Vigil Accuses Ana María Romero of Gossip and Father-in-Law of Reneging
   on Marriage Portion..227
17 / Father Demands Marriage of Presidio Soldier to Seduced Pregnant Daughter.........................238
18 / Bigamy Case Heard by Inquisition Tribunal Against Agustín de la Palma; Severe Punishment
   Imposed..261
19 / Prickly Pear Cactus Cause of Altercation between Santa Fe Neighbors.................................270
20 / Isidro Sánchez Confesses to Robbing Presidio Storehouse; Lieutenant-Governor Villasur
   Investigates 284
21 / Mother Accuses Daughter and Son-in-Law of Ongoing Affair...299
22 / Bigamy Case Dropped When Murder of Wife Discovered..322
23/ Juana de Anaya Almazán Claims La Cieneguilla Inheritance...360
24 / Fight between Chimayó Cousins Results in Head Injury; Mother Complains............................387
25 / Mother of Soldier Slapped by Santa Fe Trader; Son Intervenes...408
26 / Wife Complains about Husband's Fifteen-Year Affair to Governor 427
27 / Santiago Resident Asks for Help with Incorrigible Wife; Couple Escorted to Valencia
   by Soldiers 443
28 / Isidro Sánchez Gives Legal Advice to Jilted Presidio Soldier..453
29 / Isidro Sánchez Ordered to Stop Giving Legal Advice by Alcalde and Governor........................460
30 / Lovers Flee Santa Cruz to Outside the Kingdom; Woman Returned to Husband 464
31 / Rosalia García de Noriega Claims Inheritance; Rescinds Husband's Power of Attorney 478

GLOSSARY / 485

MAPS
1. New Mexico in the early and mid-eighteenth century. / 490
2. Central and northern New Spain in the eighteenth century. / 491
3. Santa Fe in the early eighteenth century. / 492
4. New Spain Borderland presidios in the mid-eighteenth century. / 493

BIBLIOGRAPHY / 494
INDEX / 513

LIST OF ILLUSTRATIONS

1. *Las Siete Partidas* (title page).
2. *Recopilacion de Indias*, 1681 (title page).
3. *Pulcheria* in Mexico, 1763.
4. Don Juan Fernando de la Cueba y Henriquez, Duque de Alburquerque, Marquez de Cuellar Condé de Ledesma y de Huelma, Viceroy (1702–1710).
5. Don Gaspar de la Serda, Condé de Galvé, Viceroy (1688–1696).
6. Santa Fe Parroquia and Convento in 1776.
7. Church at San Ildefonso Pueblo.
8. Signature of Christóbal de Góngora.
9. Women working in a *cocina* in Mexico, 1793.
10. Equestrian Soldiers of New Spain, 1793.
11. Plan of García de la Riva property at La Ciénega, 1601–1704.
12. Seal of the Mexican Tribunal of the Spanish Inquisition.
13. *Collegio de Propaganda Fide* at Querétaro, Mexico.
14. Signatures of don Pedro Villasur, Isidro Sanchez, and Miguel Tenorio de Alba.
15. Map of Hapsburg Spain showing the locations of Toledo and Cuidad Real.
16. Plan of Anaya Almazán Property at Cieneguilla, 1714.
17. *Carreta* at Las Golondrinas, near Santa Fe, New Mexico.
18. Making Adobe Bricks, Santa Fe, New Mexico.
19. Adobe Bricks Drying, Santa Fe, New Mexico.
20. Signature of Nicolas de Aragon.
21. Signature of Isidro Sánchez Bañares y Tagle.

Abbreviations in Text and Notes

AGN: Archivo General de la Nación
DM: Diligencias Matrimoniales
OLD: Oxford Latin Dictionary
SANM: Spanish Archives of New Mexico
NMSA: New Mexico Statutes, Annotated
NMGS: New Mexico Genealogical Society
WPA: Works Progress Administration

FOREWORD

There are periods within the New Mexico history that are vague or unknown and some just have not been written about—especially when it comes to women. The early 18th century is one of those periods. Fortunately for us, Linda Tigges, an independent historian, and J. Richard Salazar, transcriber and translator, have prepared a "women in history" book pertaining to New Mexico. They used primary documents and some of the best secondary sources available to tell stories of the Spanish Colonial women who were founders and settlers in the Post Revolt era. After reading many chapters you can see how tough and resilient these women were in the early pioneer days. Without these women there would be no descendants of generations of New Mexico families as we know them.

At first you might feel sorry for them or want for a better outcome for their situations. But in reading the documents, you can see that these women successfully sought for their rights within the laws and government of New Mexico, and made a better life for themselves and their children. The results are generations of New Mexican women who held land grants, homesteads, government office, were leaders within their communities, and so much more.

This is an important piece of work in that Linda Tigges and Richard Salazar deal in the genre of early eighteenth century women in history. It is an account of the existing historical documents, the Spanish legal system, and the outcomes of the public complaints and petitions made by New Mexican women to their alcaldes and the governors. In whatever way their cases were decided, these Spanish Colonial women were successful in the legacy they left for the future generations. If you are a twelfth generation New Mexican or a newcomer, you will find this work priceless.

—Henrietta Martinez Christmas

PREFACE

Women in eighteenth-century Spanish Colonial New Mexico had legal rights that women in the English colonies of the Americas could only dream about. Along with these legal rights came the responsibility to speak up for themselves and to challenge those who impinged upon them. As a result, eighteenth-century New Mexico did not lack for legal actions, or lawsuits as we would call them, pertaining to women residents. In fact, the Spanish Colonial Archives of New Mexico is replete with petitions and complaints made by women or about women involving inheritance, property intrusions, rape, insults, assaults, breach of marriage promises, or sometimes just for "*mala vida*"—a bad life—with their husbands. Most of the women were town dwellers, a few were wealthy property owners, and a couple of them were servants. No matter what their background was, these women not did not hesitate to send petitions to the governors asking them to make things right, which, for the most part, the governors tried to do.

Most women in New Mexico today—whether they have ancestors who lived in the province centuries ago or are newcomers to the region—are not aware that Spanish Colonial women had these legal rights. Once the court cases relating to women in the Spanish Colonial archives are transcribed and translated, as they are here, no further explanation is necessary—the documents speak for themselves.

Published here are thirty-one cases that were either presented by women directly to the alcaldes and governors or they were about women's concerns and presented by male settlers. They were selected from cases held in the years spanning 1697 (a few years after the Spanish Reconquest) through 1749. Included are the complete transcriptions and translations available in the archives for each case. The Spanish is included because translations differ depending on the background of the translator, and by including the transcripts here any Spanish-speaking readers have a chance to translate the documents themselves.

Most of the documents are drawn from the Spanish Archives of New Mexico, though a small number are from the Archivo General de la Nación (in the Center for Southwest Studies at the University of New Mexico) and the Archives of the Archdiocese in Santa Fe. Richard Salazar translated nearly all of them, but a few were translated by Aaron Taylor, Dorothy Mazon, and Rick Hendricks, New Mexico State Historian. We all took a try at some of the more difficult documents.

This book also received support from the following group of people, all of whom are well informed about and care about original Spanish Colonial-era documents: Cordelia Thomas Snow, Toni Griego Jones, Nancy Brown Martinez, Elinore Barrett, Malcolm Ebright, Robert Martinez, Emily Stovel, Samantha West of the University of New Mexico Classics Department, and Henrietta Christmas, as well as the staff of the New Mexico State Records Center and Archives and the University of New Mexico

Center for Southwest Research and Special Collections. The legal section was reviewed by attorney Margaret Kegel and the images were prepared by Jason Bache.

Special thanks to Margaret Moore Booker, copyeditor and indexer. In addition, we are grateful for the encouragement of Jim Smith and Carl Condit at Sunstone Press, both of whom were always ready to discuss problems and suggest alternatives.

Note to reader: Editorial policy

To assist the reader, the following changes were made when transcribing and translating the original documents: paragraph indentations were added to both the English and Spanish texts; basic punctuation, such as periods, were added to the English translations; paragraph headings in brackets were added to the English translations (indicating that these headings do not appear in the original text); and the English system of capital letters was followed in the translations.

When it seemed helpful or interesting, Spanish words were retained in the translations and defined there in parentheses, in a note, or in the glossary. Although accents in names and places were not used in eighteenth-century texts, they were added here. The spelling of Spanish names varies, even within a single document. In an effort to make the names consistent, Fray Angélico Chávez's *Origins of New Mexico Families* was followed. If the names did not appear in Chávez's book, other sources were consulted, including the current Santa Fe and Albuquerque telephone books, in which about 95 percent of the Spanish family names of historic New Mexico can be found.

To provide context, biographical information was provided for all names. For additional genealogical information, see the excellent resources of the New Mexico Genealogical Society, the Hispanic Genealogical Research Center of New Mexico, and, of course, the internet. The author's Internet address is www.lindatigges.com.

HISTORICAL INTRODUCTION

In 1748, in order to defend her property against intrusions by Domingo de Luna,[1] María de la Candelaria[2] petitioned the governor of New Mexico, Tomás Vélez Cachupín,[2] for relief.[3] María was the daughter of a founding family of Albuquerque and the granddaughter of Ana de Sandoval y Manzanares, the former owner of the San Clemente land grant located in the Río Abajo area. Luna was a prominent New Mexican citizen, who, in 1746, became the owner of the San Clemente grant, the area in which María's property was located.

María testified that when her sister died the land owned by her sister and her was divided in two—half of which went to María and the other half was to be inherited by her sister's husband and his children.[4] Before that transaction was complete, however, her brother-in-law had the land surveyed so that he could sell his portion to Domingo de Luna. But María then found that her brother-in-law, with the assistance of Alcalde Mayor Joseph Baca, had included some of her own land in the survey and also sold that to Luna. When queried about this, the brother-in-law stated that the land was added to help out his minor children. María protested to the *alcalde mayor*,[5] but the latter, according to her, "did absolutely nothing." After the property was sold, María discovered that the new owner, Domingo de Luna, had moved the wooden cross marking the boundary between his property and María's, thus taking even more of her land.

Receiving no support from the alcalde, María de la Candelaria submitted a complaint to Governor Vélez Cachupín, who assigned Lieutenant-Governor Bernardo Antonio de Bustamante[6] to investigate the case. Bustamante's first step was to order the boundaries resurveyed by Eusebio Rael,[7] with María agreeing to pay the cost of twelve pesos. Upon completing the survey, Rael found that one-sixth of Luna's land actually belonged to María. Governor Vélez Cachupín then ordered boundary markers "made of rock and dirt, high and thick, with a cross on top" be installed by Domingo de Luna and fined him twelve pesos. Although this portion of the document is barely legible, it appears that Vélez Cachupín then gave those twelve pesos to María.[8]

María de la Candelaria may not have been aware of it, but by bringing a lawsuit against Domingo de Luna she was taking advantage of centuries-old Spanish law. Unlike England and many European countries, Spanish law allowed women to inherit and own property in their own name, as well as to bring lawsuits, attend legal proceedings, and give testimony on their own and without receiving permission from anyone. María may have been "distressingly poor," as she said, but that did not prevent her from boldly appearing before Governor Vélez Cachupín and explaining to him that he "will be well served to hear my plea and to see me as a poor person who deserves justice." He and Lieutenant-Governor Bustamante did as she directed and decided the case in her favor.

Other New Mexican women also took advantage of the Spanish laws. From 1692 to 1749, women submitted more than thirty complaints and petitions to the alcaldes and governors of New Mexico. The cases included charges of physical abuse, breach of marriage promise, adultery, rape, theft, spreading scandalous gossip, and non-payment of dowries and inheritances. In most cases, women submitted petitions on their own, without the aid of a husband, brother, or other male relative. When submitting their cases, many stated they were doing so "in the best and most proper form I know and according to my legal right that I am given."[9]

Even though the documents in this book are only a portion of the many cases that are available to us, it is clear that New Mexican Spanish Colonial women not only spoke their minds but also understood that they were legally allowed to do so. Eighteenth-century New Mexican men did not always support a woman's case or the charges made against them, but they did not question a woman's right to submit petitions. Nor did they challenge a woman's right to act as a witness, accept a dowry or inheritance, own and administer property, or defend herself against charges made by others. Under Spanish law, women were considered separate legal entities with their own legal rights—and their society recognized them as such.

Spain and the New World colonies were a legalistic society. This included New Mexico, even though it had limited resources and was far away from the urban centers of New Spain. In New Mexico, the significance of the law and a defined legal process was understood by provincial officials and the men who represented themselves as legal authorities. The settlers may not have been particularly law abiding, but they had a sense of being a part of the Spanish empire where property and personal rights were upheld by the law and through the viceroys, governors, and alcaldes. More importantly for this book, New Mexicans accepted the independent status of the women in its province and were willing to support their legal rights, privileges, and restrictions.

LEGAL BACKGROUND

The explanation of why Spain was such a legalistic country begins, as it does for most western European countries, when the country became a part of the Roman empire.[10] The influence of Rome was profound: it gave Spain the Latin language, Roman law, the concept of empire, and, eventually, Christianity. Rome, however, could not hold back the invasions of tribes from the north and the east; in the sixth-century, most of Spain was overrun by these tribes.

The Visigoths emerged as the dominant group of invaders and by the late seventh century had developed their own legal code in which they modified Roman law to fit their own militaristic society. This code was usually called the *Fuero Juzgo*—also known as the Visigothic Code—and combined Roman, canon, and Germanic (Gothic) law. The Roman legal elements dealt with the relations between individuals such as inheritance and contracts. In variance to this were the laws based on Germanic laws and customs that were related to marriage, family relationships, and conjugal property. It recognized women as separate legal entities with their own rights, privileges, and protections.[11] This was different from Roman law in which women were treated as dependents of their fathers, or other male relatives, and were perpetually under male guardianship.

The Visigothic Code was known and respected by other countries. In the seventh century, Emperor Justinian and his staff in Constantinople looked to the west and used the Visigothic Code when preparing the *Corpus Juris Civilis* law code. The Visigothic Code was also an influence on the laws of the Franks, then located to the north and west of Spain. At that time, they were the enemies of the Visigoths, but later the Franks would enter Spain and assist the remaining Christians in conquering the Moors.[12]

In 712, Toledo, the Visigothic capital of Spain, was taken by the Moors and much of the country was soon under Moorish rule. Perhaps realizing that they could not easily impose their customs on such a large area, the Moors allowed the Christian towns in Spain to operate under their old laws as long as they paid the head and land taxes. As a result, portions of the older Visigothic law survived.[13]

In the early tenth century, the Christian reconquest of Spain began in a disorderly way with Christians fighting Moors and sometimes joining the Moors to fight each other.[14] The reconquest was facilitated by the influx of Frankish soldiers from the north. Under the leadership of Ferdinand III, who reigned from 1217 to 1252, the Moors were expelled from much of Spain and Castile was reunited with Leon, Asturias, and Galicia. Within a century, the Moors were defeated in Aragon, Valencia, and other principalities, until only the Moorish kingdom of Granada remained. During this period of uneasy coexistence, the Moors, Christians, and Jews lived together; for instance, they worked on the translation into Latin of Arabic translations of classical Greek authors.[15]

By the mid-1200s the Castilian king, Ferdinand III, faced the challenge of dealing with the newly conquered lands. These lands were divided by a variety of languages. The kingdom had towns governed by ancient and jealously guarded privileges and charters and barons who expected rewards for their part in the reconquest. By carefully balancing opposing interests, Ferdinand worked toward creating a set of unified laws. In the struggle to do so, Ferdinand and successive monarchs were assisted by the renewal of interest in Roman and Justinian law in the Italian universities, particularly Bologna, and by university scholars who came to Spain. Ferdinand contributed to this interest by establishing a law faculty at the University of Salamanca in Castile.[16]

Promising the town folk and military that he would maintain their privileges, Ferdinand prepared a statement of the law called the *Fuero Real*. It was based on Roman and canon law, old laws and charters of the Castilian cities, and the principles of the *Fuero Juzgo*. More importantly for this book, the *Fuero Real* set forth the principles of domestic relations and property rights for women—it assumed women had their own legal status, privileges, and rights. Restrictions and protections, such as the Roman and Justinian concept of the dowry, were included, but adult women were not considered chattel or legal dependents of men. While not promulgated as law, for centuries the *Fuero Real* served as a guide for the interpretation of Spanish laws and charters.[17]

Ferdinand's son, Alfonso X, also known as the Learned, who reigned from 1251 to1284, pushed for greater acceptance of the *Fuero Real* and for the preparation and adoption of a more comprehensive law code. The result was the much-praised code that we know as *Las Siete Partidas*, written between 1256 and 1265.

Las Siete Partidas, title page.

Although the names of the authors of the new code are debated, it is known that they included Castilian and Jewish jurists, scholars from Italian universities (particularly in Bologna), and church canons.[18] Whether Alfonso X wrote a part of it is unknown, though he certainly was involved with the process. Whoever the authors were, it is clear that they were familiar with Roman law, Justinian's *Corpus Juris Civilis* (after which *Las Siete Partidas* was modeled), the *Fuero Real*, the *Fuero Juzgo*, and canon law.

As with the *Fuero Real*, *Las Siete Partidas* gained only partial acceptance among the Castilian townspeople and barons. It served, however, as a model and a basis for legal interpretation in Spain. It addressed all aspects of Castilian society: property and domestic law, wills and inheritances, dowries, and the rights and privileges of women. *Las Siete Partidas* also set forth procedures for court cases and strengthened royal power by giving the king's court the right to appeal decisions based on local laws. The code was so extensive and carefully prepared that Spanish jurists referred to it throughout the eighteenth and nineteenth centuries. Familiar to the administrators of Spanish law in New Spain and elsewhere, *Las Siete Partidas* was occasionally cited in eighteenth-century New Mexican lawsuits.[19] In 2000, it became available in a seven-volume English translation.[20]

Alfonso X was, unfortunately, less able than his father in convincing the nobles and townspeople the value of a unified law code. In attempting to promulgate *Las Siete*

Partidas, he threatened the loss of legal privileges for both the nobles and townspeople. As a result, they united against him, and, in 1272, removed him from the throne.[21] His successors continued to support the preparation of legal codes, creating such codes as the *Fuero Viejo* and the *Ordenamiento de Alcalá de Henares*. But, like *Las Siete Partidas*, they were only used for interpretation of the law and for its implementation by the royal courts. As a result, the legal system continued to have tangled and overlapping laws that served as an obstacle to Spanish unity and economic growth.

The 1469 marriage of Isabella of Castile and Ferdinand of Aragon brought a measure of unity to Spain, which in turn provided an opportunity for replacing, or at least sorting out, the old laws. With the support (and probably insistence) of Queen Isabella, it was determined that the newly united kingdom would operate under the laws of Castile, rather than the laws of Aragon. Queen Isabella supported (and perhaps ordered) the preparation of the *Ordenamiento Real,* a compendium of relevant laws dating back to the *Fuero Real*.[22] Following this, the *Leyes de Toro* (named for the town of Toro, Spain) was prepared in order to reconcile the old laws with the new and to fill gaps in the statutes.[23] The *Leyes de Toro* was brief compared to *Las Siete Partidas*. It contained eighty statutes, many of which dealt with legal procedures and with laws regarding the rights and safeguards for women. As such, it was concerned with women's role in legal transactions, appearances in court, community property, inheritance, dowries, marriages, transfer of land, and guardianship.[24] In 1505, a few years after Queen Isabella's death, the court at Toledo in Castile, Spain, adopted the *Leyes de Toro* as statutory law.

The laws of the earlier compilations were, however, not rescinded and ambiguities remained. Unhappy with this situation, both King Charles V (who reigned from 1516 to 1556) and King Philip II (who reigned from 1556 to1598) ordered a complete compilation of the Spanish laws. The result was the *Nueva Recopilación de Todas las Leyes de Castilla*, which was completed in 1567.[25] The latter restated the *Leyes de Toro* and gave precedence to it. Local laws were to be applied next, followed by *Las Siete Partidas*, Roman law, and Justinian's code.[26] This explains why some two hundred years later, court cases in New Mexico, especially those relating to dowries and women's inheritances, included the *senatus consultus Velleianum* (or *Velayano*), the *Corpus Juris Civilis* of Justinian, *Las Siete Partidas*, and the *Leyes de Toro*.[27]

With the Spanish discovery of the New World, the Spanish Crown again faced a problem of governance—this time of a vast amount of land and thousands of indigenous people. Castilian laws were those applied to the New World rather than the laws of Aragon or other provinces. The New World belonged to the Crown of Castile, as the funding and organization of the colonies had been provided by Queen Isabella.

Soon, however, it became apparent that these laws were inadequate. And so, following the Castilian legalistic tradition, new sets of laws were compiled. The most well-known was the *Recopilación de Leyes de los Reinos de las Indias*—more commonly known as the Laws of the Indies. The *Recopilación* mostly focused on the rights and treatment of the Indians, granting of land, founding of towns, setting of military limits, governance, and matters not found in the old Castilian law codes. Work on this set of laws began as early as 1614, but was not promulgated until 1681.

Recopilacion de Indias, 1681, title page.

The *Recopilación* took precedence in the colonies, but the older, existing laws of Castile also applied when no applicable rules were found in the *Recopilación*. Certainly, in New Mexico, the *Leyes de Toro* and other older law codes continued to be referenced and applied in court cases for many years following the promulgation of the *Recopilación*.

WOMEN AND SPANISH COLONIAL LAW

As early as the 1200s, the Castilian Crown held a belief that law acted as a civilizing element in a divided and sometimes violent society, where war had been ongoing for centuries. The monarchs believed that law was the best way to ensure justice for everyone, including women. Imbedded in the accumulation of laws that guided and interpreted the Spanish legal system was the concept that stability was fostered by family and community and that women were an important part of both. The concept of women having their own identity and own standing under the law was of profound significance for Spanish women and, by extension, for women in eighteenth-century New Mexico. It gave them direct access to the laws and procedures of the legal system and allowed them the right to act independently.

Today, women in America and elsewhere take for granted the concept of women as separate legal entities. However, until the late nineteenth and early twentieth century, women in England, the United States, and other western European countries had no such legal distinction. Unmarried women were considered chattel and the property of their fathers or other male members of their families. When married, women became a dependent of their husbands. As William Blackstone explained, in his 1763 *Commentaries on the Laws of England*, "Husband and wife are one person in law, that is, the very being or legal existence of the woman is suspended during the marriage."[28] The four volumes of Blackstone's *Commentaries* were considered a primary source for the study of common law in England and the United States throughout the eighteenth and nineteenth centuries.

It is difficult to believe that up until one hundred and fifty years ago (or even one hundred years ago), women in many parts of the Old and New Worlds, with the exception of Spain and its colonies, were not legally separate entities. In the United States, some individual states had different laws for inheritance and property ownership.[29] Generally, however, women needed permission to petition or speak in court, make a will, or to bring a lawsuit in her own name; and, in most cases, she could not own personal property. Upon marriage, she lost her surname. Any personal property she brought to the marriage belonged to her husband, and therefore she needed his permission to sell it. And, because a woman was not a separate legal entity, her husband was responsible for her debts and wrongful acts and she was liable for his. Even when a woman was widowed, her legal rights were limited, with her affairs managed by a father (if living), a son, brother, or some other male.[30]

The situation was different under Spanish law. This is not to say that women had the same rights as men, for Spanish law did not accept the concept that all people were equal under the law. Instead, it recognized people as belonging to different categories. For example, single, married, and widowed women had different rights, privileges, and restrictions as did different categories of men.

The Spanish legal system was concerned with both civil and criminal law. Civil law was mostly concerned with property rights including inheritance, while criminal law was concerned with crimes against persons or the public welfare and with morals. In New Mexico, both types of law were implemented by the alcaldes and governors, thus the distinction between the two types was often blurred. In some cases, (see, for example, cases 5 and 17) the complainants, apparently wishing to make sure they did the correct thing, submitted their petitions as both civil and criminal complaints. This combination of civil and criminal law continued into the twentieth century. For example, in 1913 when lawyer Ralph Emerson Twitchell sorted through the existing documents in the Spanish Archives of New Mexico (SANM) and gave each one a caption, he divided them into two volumes: SANM I consisting of property records and inheritance records and SANM II consisting of civil and criminal law cases, treated as one and the same.[31]

Property Rights and Inheritance Laws

Laws relating to property rights, inheritance, and dowries were perhaps the most complicated among the Spanish laws relating to women, especially married women.[31] Some of the laws gave husbands the right to manage their wife's property, but other laws, particularly those related to dowries, were intended to protect wives from a spendthrift or otherwise incompetent husband. These protections were set forth in the ancient Roman and Justinian laws as stated above.

Under Spanish law, an unmarried, married, or widowed woman was the owner of the property she had inherited or purchased and was free to sell or bequeath such property as she pleased. The property was referred to as "*bienes parafernales.*"[32] The husband could manage and spend the income from the property, but the property was not to be used to pay his debts. If there was evidence that he was mismanaging the property, the wife could (and was even expected to) submit a lawsuit against him. If a woman's husband wished to sell or make contracts for the property, he had to receive his wife's official consent as set forth in a power of attorney.[33] If her husband died first, then the financial assets she brought to the marriage—the bienes parafernales—was subtracted from the estate first before the execution of her husband's will and division of the estate. If the wife died first, her bienes parafernales property was subtracted from the estate and set aside for her children.

Another aspect of property law relevant to women was the *bienes gananciales* (community property). This consisted of the increase in a couple's assets accumulated during a marriage. Under Spanish law, the increase was the property of both the husband and the wife. Upon the death of either spouse, half of the increase went to the surviving spouse and the other half was divided equally among the children. (This concept of community property was one of the few aspects of Spanish law incorporated into New Mexico Territorial law after the American conquest in 1846.)[34]

In regard to dowries, in more prosperous families or those of a higher rank, a dowry agreement was made as part of the betrothal prior to the marriage.[35] Several studies have been written about dowries in New Spain in which the purpose and variations in law and in practice of dowries are described.[36] Generally, the dowry was seen as a gift by the bride's family to support the new household. It could include currency, goods, land, and livestock.

In practice, the inheritance and dowry laws are similar to those of bienes parafernales, probably a reason for confusing the two. One difference was that if the wife died first, the dowry was divided among only her daughters; or, if she had no daughters, the dowry was given back to the wife's family, but not to her husband. The law also allowed the wife to bequeath her dowry (and her bienes parafernales) to her daughters before she died.

As documents in the Spanish Colonial archives indicate, the collection of dowry and inheritance goods by the daughter was an ongoing problem. It often involved petitions, frequently by disappointed husbands, to the governor complaining about non-payment. For instance, in 1716, Pedro Montes Vigil came before the Santa Fe alcalde claiming that his father-in-law, Mateo Trujillo, had not paid the marriage portion. Trujillo responded by strongly stating that he had given Montes Vigil a parcel of land which Montes Vigil had then sold and that if he gave all that Montes Vigil had asked for, his other children would have nothing. In another case, of 1733, Francisco de Silva, submitted a petition claiming that his wife's dowry had not been given to her by her father, Nicolás Chávez. Further testimony showed that Silva had, in fact, received twenty-seven sheep but, he said, they were so old he was "afraid within a short time they would die without my having a profit."[37] As with most financial transactions in eighteenth-century New Mexico, the dowry and inheritance were usually paid in goods, not cash.

As stated above, the alcaldes, governors, and scribes referred to the ancient Spanish laws, particularly in cases of dowries for and inheritance by women. For example, in 1716, when María Canseco asked that her daughter's inheritance be paid to María, instead of being held in trust until her daughter came of age, as she had first agreed, the presiding judge, Alfonso Rael de Aguilar, pointed out that in making this request she was renouncing the laws of *"Justiniano Auxilio de Vellano Senatus Consultos*, which speak in favor of women and state that they are not be taken advantage of now nor at any time." The laws that he conflated in his statement were those that protected dowries and women's inheritance as found in Justinian's *Corpus Juris Civilis* and the Roman *Senatus Consultus Velleianum*—a law written by, or at least presided over by, Consul Velleian and adopted by the Roman Senate sometime before 3 AD.[38]

Another example of a reference to the old Spanish laws occurred in New Mexico in 1746, when Rosalia García de Noriega gave her husband, Salvador Martínez, the power of attorney allowing him control of her dowry and inheritance. The presiding judge, Antonio de Ulibarrí, cautioned her that in doing so she was renouncing "the law codes of *Senatus Consultus, [Leyes de] Toro, Madrid* and *[Las Siete] Partidas*, and those of the *Velleyano* [sic], along with others favorable to women." She apparently considered his warning, because she later renounced the power of attorney, taking back control of her property.[39]

Criminal Law

Spanish criminal law protected and at the same time restricted Spanish colonial women in New Mexico. Most of the petitions submitted to the alcaldes and governors about women were criminal law cases relating to seduction and breach of promise, adultery, cohabitation, illegitimate children, spreading rumors or scandal, *mala vida* (spousal abuse), prostitution, rape, and murder. Some marriage and *divorcio* (legal separation) cases were handled by the priests, as addressed in a following section.

Seduction and Breach of Promise of Marriage

Under Spanish law, a woman could submit a lawsuit claiming she was seduced with a promise of marriage but the promise had not been kept.[40] The woman had a stronger case if she could prove the loss of her virginity, if she had a written promise of marriage (or a verbal promise recalled by witnesses), or if she had a gift given to her by the accused. If the woman was pregnant, she had to prove not only seduction and breach of promise but also that the pregnancy was the result of sexual activity with the accused and not another man (which was sometimes difficult to do). In a 1716 seduction and breach of promise case, brought by Juan de Leon Brito for his daughter Margarita Brito, Antonio de Abeytia confessed that he had promised to marry her and agreed there was sexual intimacy between them, but he denied that he was the father of her child. In an attempt to clear Abeytia, his legal representative, Antonio Durán de Armijo, tried to show that Margarita Brito had also had sexual relations with a soldier from El Paso and that Abeytia was therefore not the father of her child. The document ended with no final determination, suggesting that it was settled out of court, perhaps with financial compensation for the complainant.[41]

Breach of promise for marriage cases were not always initiated by women. In a 1744 case, Joseph Varela Jaramillo said that after promising marriage, giving gifts, and having sexual relations with his intended she changed her mind, denied having sexual relations with him, and agreed to marry someone else. She was supported by the ecclesiastical judge who stated that there had been no sexual intimacy.[42]

The preferred sentence for the seduction and break of promise was a forced marriage to the complainant. If one of the couple was already married, the judge could require financial compensation or community service such as the making of adobes for a public building. When a woman petitioned this type of case and won, she typically received compensation, her reputation may have been somewhat restored, and she at least had a dowry that might make a future marriage more likely.[43]

Adultery

In eighteenth-century New Mexico, adultery was defined as the situation when a married person voluntarily had sexual relations outside of marriage. It was taken more seriously than seduction or a breach of promise because it violated the sacrament of marriage and was considered a mortal sin (other mortal sins included incest, rape, abduction, sins against nature, and sacrilege).[44] It was also considered grounds for a *divorcio* (legal separation).[44] For a single man or woman, the penalty was typically banishment for one of the guilty parties, or, less often, imprisonment or a fine. In some instances, several penalties were incurred. For example, in 1744, as a result of Juana Martín's complaint about her husband's fifteen-year affair with

Gertrudes de Segura, Governor Codallos y Rabal banished Gertrudes to Santa Cruz and threatened Juana's husband with paying both the court and travel costs.[45]

The penalty for married women who committed adultery could be more severe, involving losing her dowry and her share of common property. One explanation for this could be that the offense confused the question of inheritance.[46] In other words, in a situation where bloodlines were important adultery made it impossible to determine if a woman's children had the right to inherit from her husband.

While adultery was clearly defined, in the documents discussed in this book it is not obvious as to why one complaint was called "cohabitation" while another was considered adultery, a much more serious offense. For example, in the 1744 case mentioned above, Juana Martín's complaint was about the relationship between her husband and Gertrudes de Segura, a single woman, who lived together for a period of time. Governor Joachín Codallos y Rabal dealt with the case as cohabitation. In another case, however, which lasted intermittently from 1705 to at least 1712, Cristóbal de Góngora claimed that his wife was committing adultery because she was having an affair with Joseph Antonio Romero, a single man, which Góngora declared was grounds for divorce.[47]

The difference as to whether or not it was considered adultery or cohabitation may have had to do with residence, whether it was the husband or wife who was the adulterer, and the type of scandal involved. In the Martín-Segura cohabitation case, a married man and a single woman were living together parttime in an established residence. While in the Góngora case, a married woman was the adulterer, the couple did not live together, and the woman was associated with scandal because of her husband's claims that she participated in witchcraft.

Volatile situations involving adultery could lead to the death of one of the parties involved. In eighteenth-century New Spain, the murder of a husband or wife without evidence of adultery was punishable by death. The laws also provided that if a man killed his wife, even if he found her committing adultery, he could not inherit her property.[48]

However, in some instances, it was acceptable for the husband to kill his wife's lover for adultery, but not his wife. In other cases, the husband apparently had the right to kill his wife, but not the lover.[49] For instance, in the bigamy investigation of Juan García de la Mora, the Holy Office determined that de la Mora was not a bigamist because his wife was already dead before he married a second time.[50] The fact that he murdered his wife for adultery was known and discussed in the community in which it happened, but it was apparently not a concern of the Holy Office. In another instance, disaster was averted by the intervention of the lieutenant-alcalde. In a 1746 case, when Nicolás de Aragon (along with the lieutenant-alcalde) found Aragon's wife and her lover in bed together, the lieutenant-alcalde cautioned Nicolás not to react but to let him handle the situation. This suggests that the alcalde feared a violent and lethal reaction from Nicolás, probably a reasonable concern.[51] What was acceptable during this period apparently depended on the rank and economic status of the people involved and on local custom.

Abduction

Although abduction was named in the Catholic Church's list of sexually prohibited behaviors and mortal sins, such cases were handled by the secular court. Generally, abduction was defined as the forced removal and sexual assault of a woman. The attempt by the twenty-five-year-old soldier Francisco Mondragón and the married, nineteen-year-old María de Olguín to flee the province in 1745 was a case of abduction. When questioned, María said she had not consented to the plan to flee (although others testified she had agreed to it). Governor Codallos y Rabal dealt leniently with both of them: he fined Mondragón and sent María back to her fifty-year-old husband. He also cautioned María's husband to "live in peace" with her,[52] which suggests that the governor was warning the husband against committing violence against her or Mondragón.

Cohabitation

Both secular and church law in eighteenth-century New Mexico prohibited "*amancebamiento*"—or cohabitation, sometimes called "concubinage" or "consensual union." It referred to a man and a woman living together outside the benefit of marriage. As shown by Juana Martín's complaint described above, cohabitation by itself was not considered adultery, nor was it among the list of grounds for divorce shown in studies of other areas, including Mexico City.[53] In New Spain, and certainly in New Mexico, amancebamiento did not lead to serious consequences unless the husband had not made provisions for the wife, it brought shame upon the wife or on her household, or the husband was physically abusing his wife. In any of these instances, the wife could go before the alcalde or governor and make a complaint, though it was more likely for *mala vida* (as described below) than for cohabitation. The penalty in these cases was typically banishment for the other woman and a fine or community work for the man. Judges of this period seemed to understand that in the New World, where geographic distances were so great and where the men were often gone from home for long periods of time (working as traders or soldiers), cohabitation was likely to be a common occurrence.

In some cases, cohabitation may have been the only way a widow or married and abandoned wife could survive. For instance, in 1715, Juan López Grande, a servant, claimed that the woman he lived with was married to a man who had been gone for six years and that he was trying to assist the woman as much as he could. In this case, Grande was ordered to leave Santa Fe to a place outside the kingdom with his master.[54]

Rape

Although rape was considered a forbidden sexual behavior and a mortal sin by the Catholic Church, charges of rape (like those of adultery and seduction) were heard by the alcalde and the governor rather than by a priest.[55] For example, in 1711, when Petrona de Carvajal accused Agustín de la Palma of raping her daughter, she made the charge before Governor don José Chacón, Marqués de la Peñuela, and not a priest.[56] Generally, after a charge of rape, a midwife was called to determine if the woman was no longer a virgin and if there were any injuries. The victim was also asked about her relationship with the rapist and if force and malice were involved. For some reason, in the Agustín de la Palma case, there was no inspection by a midwife, in spite of his request for one and his offer to pay for it. Because the document ends abruptly with no determination included, we do not know what effect this had on Petrona de Carvajal's case.

Proving a case of rape was difficult if there were no witnesses. When guilt could be shown, the penalty for the accused varied depending on the age of the victim, her reputation, and her social status. The penalty ranged from financial reparation to banishment to public shaming to whipping. In some cases, the victim was simply placed in another, safer home or, when available, a religious institution.[57]

In addition to the aforementioned de la Palma case, two other instances of rape were located in the Spanish Colonial archives. The first occurred in 1748 with the woman claiming rape and breach of marriage promise. For that case, Governor Codallos y Rabal fined the participants for fighting and referred the rape case to the ecclesiastical judge, Father Santiago de Roybal. The outcome was not recorded.[58] In the second case, in 1750, Margarita García Jurado charged a man for raping her. The case was heard, but the man was proven not guilty.[59]

Prostitution

According to historian Karen Vieira Powers, the Spanish Crown supported licensed houses of prostitution in urban centers. The prostitutes, or "public women" as they were known, were by law to be orphaned or abandoned women—women without any family that would experience shame. Though some women did work as prostitutes outside a public house, they could be arrested for doing so and could face dishonor and loss of their dowry and inheritance. Paying a woman for sex was not considered illegal for men.[60] During the eighteenth century, in large urban areas like Mexico City, the law required that prostitutes be contained in separate areas of the city.[61]

No prostitution cases were included in this book, although the terms *puta* (prostitute) and *puta alcagueta* or *puta alcahueta* (sexual intermediary or procuress) sometimes appear. For instance, in 1697, two sisters called a woman named Juana de Argüello a "puta alcagueta."[62] In another case, Catalina de Villalpando says that a boy, Manuel Domínguez, called her a "puta" for pulling up the cactus that he had planted in a walkway. When the context is examined, it becomes clear that these terms were intended more as an insult than as a statement of fact.[63]

Scandal and Spreading of Rumor

Given the precarious nature of the New Mexico colony, which was surrounded by hostile Indian tribes and constantly threatened by warfare, unity and peace among the inhabitants was essential. This made scandal and the spreading of rumors among settlers a matter of grave concern for the governors. This is evident in several cases, including the 1697 case, mentioned above, in which two women spread a rumor that Juana de Argüello was a puta alcagueta and insult her in other ways, as well as throw rocks at her. It was resolved when Juana approached the alcalde and the two women apologized.[64] In other court cases, charges were made against women spreading rumors about a married woman entertaining men in her home, about a woman having a brother-in-law as a lover, and about a man beating his wife.[65] In these instances, a complaint was made before the alcalde and a sentence of banishment or public shaming was handed down as a sentence for the accused. For example, when a complaint was made against Ana María Romero [Villalpando] in 1716 for spreading gossip, she was threatened with a sentence consisting of riding around the plaza naked from the waist up, in the chilly month of January.[66] We do not know if the penalty was imposed.

Mala Vida

A woman who was a victim of mistreatment by her husband could petition the court claiming that her life was *mala vida* (a bad life).[68] This usually meant the woman suffered from physical and verbal abuse, lack of financial support, or abandonment. It also could mean the woman's husband was having an affair with and/or living with another woman, or the woman was being treated like a servant by her husband. Today, we would call it "spousal abuse." In reading the eighteenth-century documents, one gets a sense that the term "mala vida" was used when a husband's abusive treatment of his wife went well beyond what was acceptable in the community and that it involved a woman fearing for her life.

Church and secular authorities in 1700s New Mexico allowed a husband to chastise or "correct" his wife, but if the correction was too severe and put the woman's life at risk then it was considered a mortal sin and a crime under the law.[69] As a result, when women complained about abuse, they often stated that they were "afraid of being killed" even when it may not have been the case. For instance, María de Castro, Josefa Sedaño, and Juana Montaño de Sotomayor each testified that their husbands were going to kill them.[70] However, when Francisca Gómez de Torres claimed she was afraid that her husband might kill her,[71] she truly had good reason for thinking that—in 1713, her husband's brother had been convicted for murdering his wife.[72]

If a husband was found guilty of mistreating his wife, he could face the threat of a fine, be required to repair public buildings, or go to prison, but rarely faced banishment. Generally, the governors preferred that the couple be reconciled in some way and keep their family intact.[73]

Illegitimate Children

As might be expected, the consequence of illicit relationships were illegitimate children.[74] If the children were recognized by their fathers, they had certain legal rights including the possibility of inheritance. When a father was wealthy and of a high rank, his child could be made legitimate by a petition to the viceroy or king. If the couple married after the child was born, the child was considered legitimate.[75] The latter may have been the intention of former New Mexico governor Francisco Cuervo y Valdés concerning the two children he had with María Francisca García de la Riva.[76] Unfortunately, he died before the two could marry.

In New Mexico, and probably elsewhere in New Spain, the birth of a "*hijo natural*" child to an unmarried woman of lower social status does not appear to have been an obstacle to community acceptance or social advancement for either the mother or the child. For example, Josefa Baca, who never married, had six children who later went on to marry well and at least two of them, Antonio and Joseph, became alcaldes.[77]

Honor

Underlying the laws and procedures described above, was the Spanish concept of "honor."[78] When applied to women in eighteenth-century New Mexico, the word usually referred to a woman's sexuality. Historian Sylvia Marina Arrom explains that honor occurred for an unmarried woman if she remained a virgin; for a married woman if she was monogamous; and for a widow if she was chaste. On the other hand, dishonor meant the loss of a woman's status in her community.[79]

In New Mexico, the question of honor was sometimes included as part of an accusation. For instance, in 1704, when Josefa Sedaño appeared in court against a woman who accused her of entertaining men in her home, Josefa claimed that the gossip resulted in her dishonor and loss of reputation in the community.[80] In a 1713 case, the servant of Francisca Gómez de Torres falsely claimed that her mistress was having an affair with her brother-in-law and subsequently was reprimanded by the governor for spreading rumors that tarnished Francisca's honor.[81] And, in 1716, Juan de León Brito petitioned the governor with a breach of promise of marriage and pregnancy lawsuit claiming that his daughter was dishonored. This was partly because she lost her virginity and also because of the insult to her honor resulting from the breach of promise.[82]

In those cases where the presiding judge upheld a woman's claim that she had behaved properly but the man had not, the complainant sometimes received financial compensation. This gave her a dowry and made her more eligible for a future marriage. In some instances, however, a woman's honor could not be restored. Women who had sex with a servant or a slave, or who were prostitutes or procuresses, were considered to have lost their honor permanently. These women could also lose their legal and property rights.

Though less common, a man could also claim loss of honor. In 1744, when Joseph Varela Jaramillo was jilted by Feliciana Chávez, as described above, his legal advisor, Isidro Sánchez, sued, claiming that Jaramillo had lost his honor.[83] Generally, however, loss of honor for a man occurred when he did not keep his word, did not behave in a socially acceptable way, or by acting in a cowardly fashion. Historian Karen Vieira Powers suggests that for men honor was something they gained through their behavior and so if they lost honor they could regain it by being courageous or other acts of exemplary behavior. For women, on the other hand, it was harder for them to regain honor because it was so closely tied to their sexual behavior.[84] Apparently, one of their best chances to regain honor was to go to court, as some eighteenth-century New Mexican women did.

Murder

Cases of murder by Spanish Colonial women were rare in early eighteenth-century New Mexico. There were, however, two cases concerning men who murdered their wives. The earliest was the 1713 murder of Catalina de Valdes by her husband Miguel Luján. Evidence submitted in the lengthy trial (forty-two folios, or eighty-four pages of documents) showed that Miguel was guilty. Because the punishment for this was a death sentence, he was sent to Mexico City for a final judgement, though on the way he escaped and took sanctuary in a church.[85] Another murder case occurred in 1741, when María Magdalena Baca was allegedly killed by her husband, Juan Marqués, assisted by Francisco Xavier, both soldiers. The final determination in that case was a four-year-long sentence of banishment for both of them.[86]

Legal Procedures of Alcaldes and Governors[87]

The Spanish concept of "justice for all" was not only reflected in the laws described above, but also found in the Spanish legal process. In Spain, the legal procedures were, as in most western European countries, derived from Roman and ecclesiastical law and were intended to give equal treatment for both the petitioner and the accused.

The concept of fair treatment under the law was not unique to the Spanish. In the late eighteenth century, Americans, referring to the concept as "due process," included it in the United States Constitution as the Fifth Amendment. Language in the amendment states that no one should be "deprived of life, liberty or property without the due process of law." Due process has been described as including such items as: the right to an unbiased judge; notice of the charge; opportunity to present evidence for defense and hear opposing evidence and question the opposing party; be represented by counsel; public attendance; and availability of a record of the trial.[88] Many of these rights are included in the Spanish legal procedures discussed below.

Although New Mexico was far from the courts of Chihuahua and Mexico City, the alcaldes and governors of the colony attempted to follow the established legal process. Even in the years of rebellion and famine, following the Reconquest in 1692, the alcaldes and governors asked questions, listened to testimony, made judgements about guilt and innocence, and imposed sentences following established procedures. To be sure, some presiding judges were less conscientious than others; some skipped over what seemed to be important steps and others called on what seemed to be an unnecessary number of witnesses, all of whom said essentially the same thing. Still, there was a sense that no matter how humble, each person had the right to approach the judge and have the case handled in a more or less predictable fashion. The colonists seemed aware of this, and, in fact, sometimes complained that procedures were not being correctly followed. In 1733, for instance, when Salvador Martínez was imprisoned for hitting another person's servant and giving them a bloody face, he complained the proper procedures had not been followed by Alcalde González Bas. He even instructed the alcalde on what he should have done: order a *curandero* to inspect the injury and then send the case to the governor.[89] The alcalde's response is not included in the document.

Court procedures were written into each document by the court or by the secretary of the governor (who were subject to certain standards themselves). For each case, the scribe transcribed the proceedings and gave or read copies to both parties involved. Spanish law required that a licensed notary transcribe court cases; however, because such a person was rarely available on the frontier, the law allowed for the substitution of a scribe and two *testigos* (witnesses). The testigos were to be literate, or at least be able to sign their names. Court documents were to be written on official stamped paper—though New Mexicans rarely had such paper on hand, as noted by the scribe in nearly every document. The propensity of the Spanish for writing everything down is the reason that despite floods, rodents, and careless humans, so many documents remain from the Spanish Colonial period.

Legal handbooks, or *guías* (guides), were available to assist alcaldes, governors, scribes, and legal representatives in court cases. There were also registers of court cases called *protocolos*.[90] Many of these publications provided fill-in-the-blank forms and examples of legal documents such as wills, apprenticeship contracts, donations, powers of attorney, and contracts for the sale or lease of property. When a comparison is made between the language used in eighteenth-century New Mexican court cases and the Spanish protocolos and guías of the same period, it becomes evident that some New Mexican governors and legal representatives had access to these publications (or at least remembered some aspects of them).[91] There were also specific handbooks for scribes. We know, for instance, that Governor Antonio de Valverde, a former scribe, owned two copies of *Examen and Practica de Escribanos*, which were listed in his estate when he died.[92]

Descriptions of the legal procedures used in eighteenth-century New Mexico are known from Charles Cutter's 1995 study, *The Legal Culture of Northern New Spain*.[93] As his study indicates, the large number and formality of the procedures were daunting. Given the difficult conditions of life on the frontier, it is impressive that so many were actually followed. The following are drawn from Cutter's book.

Querella de Parte or Acusación

A case usually began when a petitioner submitted a written accusation or complaint against another person to the alcalde. The complaint was signed by the petitioner, except in cases where the petitioner was unable to write and then a scribe, who had probably written the document, signed the plaintiff's name. Therefore, the petitioner's signature at the end of the document does not necessarily mean that it was written out by that person.

Summaria

This was an umbrella term for the fact-finding part of the case.[94] The term is rarely found in eighteenth-century New Mexican documents, but nearly all of the elements of the summaria were found in the cases cited in this book.

La cabeza del proceso. This was a statement of the complaint placed at the cabeza (head) of the written proceedings. Identifying a complaint as a "cabeza del proceso" was similar to making an indictment, indicating that the alcalde intended to investigate the complaint. Not all the alcaldes formally named the cabeza as such;[95] sometimes the petitioner's complaint as written in the petition counted as the cabeza.

Fé de heridas. In cases that involved a *heridas* (physical injury), the alcalde asked a local healer—a *curandero/curandera*, *barbero*, or *cirujano*—to describe the injury in detail and then treat the wound. For example, in describing a cut, the healer would indicate its length and depth and the number of *puntas* (stitches) that were needed. If there was a question of rape or pregnancy, a *partera* (midwife) was called to inspect the woman.[96]

Declaraciónes. Much of the time spent in court proceedings was taken up by the declaraciónes—statements of the opposing parties and of the witnesses who were called to give testimony. Sometimes, the witnesses ended their statements by saying that the "*generales de la ley*" did not apply to them. This meant that the witnesses were not related to the plaintiff or the accused and therefore had no prejudicial connection to the case.[97]

Auto de prisión. After the witness statements, the alcalde might issue an auto de prisión (similar to an arrest warrant) and order the accused taken to a secure place. In Santa Fe, this was referred to as either the *cárcel*, *prisión* of the *casas reales*, or the presidio guardhouse, all of which may, in fact, have been the same thing. In places where there was no cárcel or guardhouse, the accused was usually confined in the home of the alcalde. Women accused of crimes were most often placed in the alcalde's house or the house of a respected woman. There were some exceptions to this; for instance, in 1716, Ana María Romero [Villalpando] was threatened with confinement in the presidio guardhouse (though she may not have actually been sent there), and, in 1728, Antonia de Moraga was ordered confined in the casas reales in Santa Cruz, or at least a building called that by the alcalde.[98]

The accused, if aware of an impending arrest, might escape to a church and claim asylum or "*sanctuario*." The medieval process of sanctuario was used in New Mexico as early as 1613. When seeking sanctuary, the accused stayed either in the church itself or in the *convento* (the priests' living and working area). Sometimes, just to be on the safe side, the accused stayed in the most sacred part of the church, as near as possible to the altar or a crucifix.[99]

In order to question an accused person in sanctuary, the alcalde was required to ask permission from the priest. In the turbulent 1600s, however, some New Mexican officials simply ordered the removal of the accused. For instance, in 1626, Governor

Sotelo Osorio ordered a soldier to be removed from refuge, even if he was found "clinging to the crucifix itself." In 1663, after don Pedro Durán y Chávez escaped arrest and took refuge in the Santo Domingo Pueblo church, Governor Peñalosa ordered him removed by force.[100] No cases of forced removal have been found in eighteenth century records, although there may have been some.

It was understood that the accused could only stay in sanctuario a limited amount of time, though the acceptable amount of time seemed to vary. In some cases, the accused left one church to seek refuge in another. For example, in 1713, Felix Luján, after first finding sanctuary in the Santa Clara Pueblo church, left after a few weeks and then took refuge in the church at San Ildefonso Pueblo.[101] While sanctuary was used mostly by soldiers and male civilians, in 1764, a woman accused of being an accessory to a theft of presidio supplies took sanctuary in the Santa Fe parish church.[102]

Embargo de bienes. Following arrest and imprisonment, the alcalde carried out the embargo de bienes, the confiscation of the accused's goods and property taken to ensure payment of court costs and fines. For example, in a Chimayó case, the alcalde confiscated the meager goods of Nicolás Martín consisting of "a house with one room, an adobe mold, a planted cornfield, and one *almud* of corn."[103] The court costs were supposed to be based on a judicial fee schedule called an *arancel*, though most likely the alcalde decided the fee on his own. In 1715, in another case in Chimayó, the accused, Diego Martín, was charged thirty pesos to compensate the governor and his secretary, a healer, the alcalde, and a scribe for their time spent on the case, and an additional two pesos for the paper used.[104] If Diego actually paid these fees, it was likely that he, like most New Mexicans of this period, paid with goods, not cash.

Confesión. Finally, the accused had a chance to make a statement, sometimes called a confesión. It was not necessarily a confession in the modern sense, instead it was more often a defense of the accused's position, including a description of mitigating circumstances.

Juicio plenario. Juicio plenario was the name given by Spanish law to the second stage of the case. Cutter states that this term was not used in New Mexico in the eighteenth century. Instead, any additional procedures were included as part of the summaria. These procedures were the following:

Auto de cargo. After hearing testimony, the alcalde, or more likely the governor, announced the "auto de cargo," an official restatement of the charges. At this point, the accused person could request the help of a *procurador*—a person with some legal background. When presidio soldiers were charged, they were usually provided with a procurador; with civilians, it occurred less often. As stated above, there is a sense that the presidio had persons on call for the legal defense of their soldiers. The use of legal jargon and Latin phrases by the procurador in both civilian and military cases suggests that they were following a legal handbook (or at least using the legal phrases they recalled from such a handbook). In the cases included in this book, Juan Manuel de Chirinos, Antonio Durán de Armijo, and Isidro Sánchez acted as procuradores.[105] In a case dating from 1751, Ramón García Jurado described himself as the procurador for the Villa of Albuquerque.[106]

Interrogatorio. In this step, the accused and the plaintiff were allowed to call additional witnesses. Sometimes, the alcalde asked additional questions of witnesses who had already been heard.

Ratificación. At some point near the end of the document, the alcalde read back the testimony of the witnesses and asked each one of them to ratify it. Depending on the significance of the case or the preference of the presiding judge, ratification could be a separate step in the process. At other times, witnesses were asked to ratify what they said as part of their testimony.[107]

Remisión. The alcalde sometimes made a formal statement that the written documents prepared for the case had been remitted to the governor.[108] More often, the remission was just understood.

Governor's hearing. After receiving the documents from the alcalde, the governor heard the case, restated the charge, and sometimes asked for additional testimony. The governor might allow a face-to-face confrontation between the petitioner and the accused. With the two protagonists both in the courtroom, this confrontation would likely have involved additional complaints, strongly worded accusations, and probably, if we could but hear them, raised voices. For example, in the inheritance cases of Pedro Montes Vigil and of Juana de Anaya Almazán, charges of lying were exchanged between the petitioner and the accused. In other cases, negative responses involved claiming that the other person was a *puta* or "nothing but a dog."[109]

Occasionally, in cases where an ecclesiastical judge or a previous governor had heard the case, no witnesses were called and the case was concluded with a final determination by the governor or the alcalde.[110]

Sentencia. The sentencia was the last formal part of the case. It could include a punishment, but the governor could also order a compromise or reconciliation. Spanish law did not provide a list of prescribed sentences. The governor decided each case as it was presented to him, as he saw the intent of the law, and as he understood local custom. This meant that sometimes the governor ordered physical punishment, the two parties were required to compromise, or in the case of feuding married couples or neighbors they were instructed to just get along with each other. For instance, in 1704, the presiding judge, Juan Páez Hurtado, ordered two feuding women to "remain on a friendly basis, speaking to each other with all the love of close friends." When property damages were involved, the guilty party was sometimes ordered to pay compensation. Charles Cutter suggests that this view of justice was influenced by the Germanic "concept of compensation" rather than the Roman "concept of physical constraint or pain."[111]

The type of punishment varied by gender. For women, the sentence was frequently banishment to another town in New Mexico, usually for a period of several years. Once there, the women were ordered to reside with a respectable woman who could "correct" their behavior. Although not stated, the banished person was probably required to work for that woman. *Vergüenza* (in this context, public shaming) was also a sentence women sometimes received. In one case, the public shaming for spreading scandal was partial public nudity while riding a horse around the plaza.[112] In cases of complaints by women about their husband or other men, the governors tended to be supportive of the women and reprimanded the men involved.[113] In other instances, such as those found in Cases 6, 27, and 30, the governors supported the reconciliation of husband and wife.

Punishment for men was usually banishment, financial charges, or community service. In only a few cases was incarceration ordered,[114] probably because of the cost of feeding prisoners and the lack of secure jails. Imprisonment, often in the presidio guardhouse, was more often for confining prisoners while they waited for trial. In one instance, the governor reduced the final penalty, taking in account the amount of time the prisoner had already spent in jail.[115]

For more severe crimes, such as causing a serious injury, the sentence could be flogging or enforced servitude. For instance, in 1715, Governor Felix Martínez, following a viceroy's royal order, declared any resident found carrying weapons such as knives, guns, or swords would be condemned to two hundred lashes and four years of work on an ore crusher.[116] In 1736, Governor Marín de Valle, irate over cattle and horse losses because of lack of diligence by Albuquerque ranchers, declared that if any more livestock was lost, the owner, if *español*, would be punished by a fine of twenty pesos and two months imprisonment. If the owner was *mestizo*, the punishment would be twenty lashes and three months of imprisonment.[117] As the latter suggests, Governor Marín de Valle based the sentence on the perceived financial ability and caste of the accused.

Capital punishment in eighteenth-century Spanish Colonial court cases was rare. When the accused was found guilty of a serious crime, the sentence was determined by a superior authority outside New Mexico. For instance, in 1713, when Miguel Luján was convicted of the murder of his wife, he was sent to Mexico City so that legal advisors there could review his case.[118]

Notificación. Notification involved giving copies of court documents to the opposing parties. It was a significant part of the Spanish justice system because it allowed access to information by which both parties could better defend themselves (or at least be well informed about the accusation and the defense). Though not a dramatic part of the legal system, it nevertheless provided part of the due process. This aspect separates Spanish secular law from that of the Inquisition; the latter kept the denunciations of witnesses, accusations by the Inquisitors, the process of the trial, and even the location of the accused's cell secret.

Under Spanish law, both the petitioner and the accused were notified in writing or verbally of the charge, the testimony of the opposing party, and the final determination by the governor. Not all alcaldes gave notification of all the court procedures and sometimes when they did it was executed in a haphazard manner. Generally, though, notification of the guilty party of the sentence was almost always carried out, usually by the efforts of the alcalde or his assistant. For instance, in 1727, Lieutenant-Alcalde Juan Moya was ordered to ride to the house of Nicolás de Aragon and his wife, Margarita Gallegos, and deliver the governor's order that she was to move to Valencia with her husband. To make sure that she understood the order and was willing to comply, Moya escorted both of them to Valencia, noting in writing that she agreed to stay there with her husband.[119]

Real amparo

Although not a legal procedure, this term refers to the request of the special protection of the king ("real amparo") through the governor and appears in several eighteenth-century New Mexico cases. Apparently, it was a kind of backup to the Spanish legal process. Mention of real amparo was made in a 1733 assault case when Josefa de la Asención approached the governor and stated: "We prostrate ourselves at the feet of your honor (the governor) so that he may give us the real amparo of his majesty (the king)."[120] Another example occurred in 1715, when Catalina de Villalpando asked the governor to support her request for the return of her inheritance. In her petition, she stated that because she was an orphan he should favor her because he was "the father of this kingdom [as appointed by the King] and as such you worry about all the poor people and particularly the orphans."[121] When María Canseco asked for help from Governor Flores Mogollón in receiving presidio insurance money after her husband's death, she stated she was "requesting assistance through the *real auxilio* (royal kindness) of your honor which I hope will be favorable."[122] These women were aware of the legal process, but they also believed that the governor, as the representative of the "King and of God on earth," was responsible for helping the meek and downtrodden, and more to the point, the widows, orphans, and poor persons among whom they included themselves.

Sexually explicit language

Although by no means considered a crime, the sexually explicit language in many of the documents deserves from consideration. Fray Angélico Chávez, in his introduction to *New Mexico Roots*, refers to the explicit way in which New Mexicans publicly discussed their sexual lives. He explained that it was not embarrassing for people at that time and much of the information would have been well-known by most everyone anyway because people lived so close to each other and everyone knew everyone else's business. Similarly, Richard Boyer suggests that when persons testified in local courts they were speaking to fellow members of their community and thus had fewer inhibitions about what they said.[123]

Another point of view has been put forth by historian Michel Foucault. He states that in the mid-1500s, after the Council of Trent, the Catholic Church placed greater emphasis on penance for sins of the flesh. The latter included fornication, seduction, adultery, incest, sacrilege, and "acts against nature." Preaching from the pulpit, priests named these sexual sins and warned the congregation against them. In order to assign penance, the priests also ordered that these sins be admitted in the confessional. Because of this, sins having to do with sex were spoken about, or, as Foucault states, sex was "put into discourse" into the "endless mill of speech."[124] So, it is not surprising that in early eighteenth-century New Mexico explicit language describing sexual activity (or the lack of it) was found in court testimony and in marriage investigations.

Legal Procedures in Military Cases

The legal proceedings in court cases for soldiers were similar to those used for civilians, not surprising since the governor—as *el governador y capitán general*—acted as the presiding judge for both. One difference, as stated above, was that soldiers were often defended by a procurador, and, because the alcalde was not part of military justice, military cases were only heard by the governor. In addition, soldiers' crimes were somewhat different and seemed to occur more often than those of the civilian population. For example, soldiers were frequently charged with theft of presidio property, insubordination to officers, gambling, and, because of the weapons they carried, fights with serious injuries. When accused of a crime, soldiers more often than not took sanctuary in churches, probably because they were aware of the discomfort of the leg irons and stocks in which they might be confined in the presidio guardhouse. (Or, perhaps because in the churches, they had access to the royal horse herd and a horse would allow them a quick getaway.)

After proven guilty, soldiers were typically punished by flogging, especially for more serious crimes. For example, in 1745, Governor Codallos y Rabal threatened Francisco Mondragón with one hundred lashes for the attempted abduction of María de Olguín (the final sentence was only a fine).[125] Other punishments for soldiers were imprisonment in the presidio guardhouse in leg irons or stocks, enforced servitude at another presidio (see Map 4), a fine, or they were forced to guard the royal horse herd. In at least one case a soldier was drummed out of the military for insubordination,[126] but probably only as a last resort—given the frequent Indian raids in eighteenth-century New Mexico, every soldier was needed whether he was insubordinate or not.

THE CHURCH AND WOMEN: MARRIAGE AND *DIVORCIO*

In addition to the Spanish law, the lives of New Mexicans were regulated by canon or church law through the Franciscan friars. For the first half of the eighteenth century, Franciscans were the primary religious personnel in the colony. In addition to serving the mission Indians, they acted as priests for the colonial settlers: they held mass, undertook premarital marriage investigations, and conducted marriages, baptisms, and burials, and recorded all of these events. In New Mexico, the Franciscans were in the jurisdiction of the Custody of the Conversion of St. Paul. The head of the custody was called the *custos*. The Franciscans were also the agents for the Holy Office of the Inquisition.

Premarital Investigations and Marriage

In New Spain, as elsewhere in the Catholic World,[127] marriage was considered a holy sacrament carried out in a church by a priest and with witnesses. The process began with a verbal or written promise from the man, often accompanied by a gift and sometimes by the sexual union of the couple. Among the more prosperous settlers, the promise of marriage would be followed with a dowry agreement from the woman's family. A breach of the marriage promise could result in a lawsuit in the court of the ecclesiastical judge or governor.[128]

If all went well, bans were read by the priest on three festival days following the betrothal, with the priest allowing persons with an impediment against the marriage to come forward. If no one did, the marriage could proceed. If an impediment arose, the priest would hold an investigation to identify it and resolve it. Examples of impediments were kinship between the couple within a prescribed degree, previous betrothals, previous sexual unions (especially with persons closely related to either party), past imprisonment, impotence, disease, or insanity. Results of the investigations were transcribed into the church records as the *diligencias matrimoniales*.[129]

If the priest determined that a dispensation was needed, he ordered a penance. For example, when Antonio Durán y Chávez's first wife died, he wished to marry Antonia Baca, who was fifteen years old and who did not know who her parents were.[130] In the investigation, it was established that Antonio was related to Antonia in the "fourth degree" and had "illicit coupling" with one of her relatives. The priest granted a dispensation but only after ordering a stiff penance. Antonio was required to work one day a week for four months at the church, beg for alms, and donate one thousand adobes for the building of the Albuquerque church.[131] Despite the lengthy list of penances, Antonio managed to satisfy the priest and the marriage took place.

It was not uncommon for a woman to appear before the priest claiming that the prospective groom had had sexual relations with her. For instance, in 1702, Juana Luján claimed that Ventura de Esquivel promised marriage, had sexual relations with her, and gave her a gift. So when Ventura approached the priest asking for an investigation of marriage with another woman, Juana went before the priest to protest the breach of Ventura's promise, claiming loss of honor. Perhaps realizing that marriage with Ventura was unlikely or maybe less attractive than she thought, she agreed to accept compensation instead. The priest then ordered Ventura to pay Juana two hundred pesos (a good horse could be bought for fifteen pesos) as a dispensation before he married the other women.[132] It appears to have been a profitable decision for Juana Luján. With the money she was able to buy livestock and land, both of which she continued to accumulate throughout her life. A 1762 inventory of goods and property made after her death, showed that she died a wealthy woman.[133]

Divorcio

Because marriage was a sacrament, the Catholic Church required that married persons stay together until one of them died, and only then the remaining partner could remarry. In rare instances, marriage could be dissolved by what the church records referred to as a divorcio—it was not the same as the divorce of today, rather it was what we would call a legal separation. Reasons for considering a divorcio were: adultery; extreme physical or spiritual danger (such as the threat of murder by a spouse); being forced into heresy, witchcraft, or paganism by a partner; insanity; impotence; and an unconsummated marriage.[134]

If a divorcio was granted, the individuals were allowed to live apart and the woman received her dowry and inheritance and half of the assets acquired during the marriage. Requests for a divorcio were submitted to the provincial custos or ecclesiastical judge. Though there are not many eighteenth-century divorce cases in New Mexico, one such case occurred in 1705. In that case, Inez Aspitia submitted a petition to the ecclesiastical judge claiming that her husband, Cristóbal de Góngora, did not provide for her and she did not know why. Cristóbal argued that a certain Custos Álvarez had given him a divorce because of Inez's witchcraft and adultery. Other friars, who reviewed subsequent complaints by Inez insisted that Cristóbal support her, but had differing opinions among themselves on whether or not Cristóbal was, in fact, divorced. Though the document is not complete, it appears that Góngora forwarded the case to the Inquisition. And, he appears to have left New Mexico (with or without Inez) in 1715.[135] The case was handled under ecclesiastical law, which followed some secular court procedures such as: a statement of the complaint, testimony by the accused and witnesses, and notification.

THE CHURCH AND WOMEN: HOLY OFFICE OF THE INQUISITION

The Inquisition first appeared in Spain in 1478, when Queen Isabella, in an effort to unify Spain under one language, one law, and one religion, asked for permission from Pope Sixtus IV to establish a Holy Office of the Inquisition under the Spanish Crown. The pope gave his approval with the condition that it be funded by the monarch. Investigations and trials were to be held by tribunals, with the most prestigious located in Toledo. One of the primary purposes of the Holy Office was to "correct" or restore the beliefs of converted Jews and Moors who secretly still practiced their own religion and Lutherans who were former Catholics. Correction meant bringing these groups back into the Catholic Church through confession and penance. In 1569, King Philip II of Spain—fearing that heretics were fleeing Spain for the colonies and that non-Catholic foreigners were influencing New Spain—established the Holy Office with a tribunal in Mexico City. The tribunal was responsible for trials and the penance of persons found guilty of heresy in New Spain. In 1570, a royal decree removed the native population of the newly conquered area from the jurisdiction of the Holy Office.[136]

By the late 1600s, having eliminated or at least contained the major heresies in Spain and the New World, the Inquisition began to concern itself with minor heresies. Meaning, the Holy Office became focused on the correction and instruction of parishioners who committed transgressions against the Catholic faith and morality. These included bigamy, blasphemy, "sins against nature," superstitions (such as witchcraft and magical practices), immorality of the clergy (such as solicitation of women in the confessional), cohabitation by priests, sacrilegious behavior, and crimes against the Inquisition. Unlike other European countries, Inquisition officials in Spain found the practice of witchcraft and magic to be due to ignorance and superstition. They generally did not become involved in witchcraft unless there was evidence of a pact with the devil, a priest was involved, or if it was part of another matter, for example bigamy, over which the Inquisition did have jurisdiction.[137]

The Inquisition in New Mexico

In New Mexico, the work of the Inquisition was administered by the Franciscan friars. The chief official for the *comisario* was usually the same person as the provincial head (custos) of the Franciscan order. In the seventeenth-century, this combination of the two jurisdictions gave the Franciscans in New Mexico extraordinary authority that resulted in an ongoing and sometimes violent competition with the governors, who also claimed authority over the province. The competition resulted in the 1642 murder of one governor (Luís de Rosas), the 1643 beheading of eight prominent citizens by the succeeding governor (Alonso Pacheco y Heridias), and the 1676 Inquisition arrest of Governor Bernardo López de Mendizábal (who died in a Tribunal cell in Mexico City).[137a] After the Pueblo Revolt of 1680 and the Spanish Reconquest of the 1690s in New Mexico, and the installation of the Bourbon dynasty in Spain, the influence of the Inquisition was diminished, though they continued to be an active force in the colony.[138]

Inquisition Procedures

In some ways, the Inquisition procedures were similar to those of secular Spanish law. For instance, an Inquisition case was usually initiated by one person making a complaint (or denunciation, in the language of the Holy Office) against another person. However, Inquisition procedures required that persons who made denunciations were sworn to secrecy. For example, in the 1733 bigamy case against Juan García de la Mora (Case 22), when four New Mexicans voluntarily denounced García la Mora, Fray Guerrero ordered them not to discuss their denunciations or any aspect of the case. He then solicited information from the persons named in these denunciations and also swore them to secrecy.[139]

Following a denunciation, the inquisitors reviewed the evidence and determined whether it merited an assumption of guilt. If so, they embargoed the goods of the accused and then isolated the accused in a secret cell of the Tribunal. The prisoners were not told the names of their denouncers. The inquisitors then gathered additional evidence and interrogated witnesses and the accused. They did not accept hearsay evidence, instead relying on confession (called the "queen of proof") as the best evidence of guilt.[140] As with secular law enforcement of the period, a confession could be solicited through torture.[141] Finally, after a public trial in which the accused confessed, the inquisitors prescribed a penance. A chilling illustration of a confession and assignment of penance is found in the Inquisition's bigamy case against Agustín de la Palma.[142]

Edicts of Faith and Denunciations

The Holy Office of the Inquisition made its presence and purpose felt through regular visits of Holy Office officials. These officials scheduled readings of Edicts of

Faith—sometimes also called Edicts of Anathema—made before parishioners at church services or festivals.[143] For instance, we know that such edicts were read in Santa Fe in 1694 and 1716, and in El Paso in 1693.[144] Examples of seventeenth-century edicts show that they sometimes warned parishioners of the major heresies of Jews, Lutherans, and Moors, and, more often, the edicts read in New Spain were about the minor heresies, such as blasphemy, bigamy, misconduct by friars, invoking the devil, and the reading of prohibited books.[145]

As part of the edict, parishioners were ordered to come forward and denounce persons suspected of heresy. If a denunciation of a suspected person was not made, then those persons who knew about the heresy could themselves be denounced and face excommunication or a penance. When voluntarily making a denunciation, the statement usually began with the phrase: "I wish to clear my conscience." A clear example of this is found in the García de la Mora case mentioned above.[146]

Bigamy

The Holy Office in New Mexico was particularly concerned with the minor heresy of bigamy. This was defined as when a married man or married woman entered into a second marriage. Perhaps because marriage was considered a holy, indissoluble sacrament, Inquisition officials were diligent in ferreting out cases of bigamy. In many cases, the punishment was severe, involving public humiliation, flogging, and penal servitude. For instance, in 1717, convicted bigamist Agustín de la Palma was sentenced to two hundred and fifty lashes and four years of forced labor.[147] The ferocity with which some persons were punished for bigamy has been addressed by several scholars, including Richard Boyer and Sara McDougal,[148] and is further discussed in the Agustín de la Palma documents (See Case 18).

ENVIRONMENT

Economy

The potential for Spanish colonists to prosper in New Mexico was not promising, with few known mineral deposits and little fertile land available for farming. Much of the agricultural land was located along the Río Grande and its tributaries, with the limited amount uneasily shared between the Pueblo Indians and the colonists.

Despite this, a generation or so after the Spanish Reconquest, some colonists (both men and women) managed to thrive. They did so through reclaiming properties owned before the Pueblo Revolt, by acquiring land through land grants or purchase, and by successfully trading with Pueblo Indians, nomad Indians, Chihuahua merchants, and each other. Wealthier settlers—like Juan Páez Hurtado[149] and José Reaño[150]—owned both a house in Santa Fe and additional lands elsewhere, for example outside Santa Fe in La Cieneguilla. Others—like Sebastián Martín Serrano at La Soledad in northern New Mexico[151] and Fernando Durán y Chávez at Atrisco[152]—had large ranches with extended households. Most settlers described in the documents included in this book, however, were of more modest means and yet lived respectably—they owned some land, did some trading, and some worked at the Santa Fe presidio or in the casas reales (government offices). Others, less fortunate, lived on the margins of the economy and society.

Because of the information in the petitions and complaints in this book, submitted by or about women, we know that these women came from a variety of economic backgrounds. Only a few had the honorific of *doña*, which indicated they were from the elite. Among them were Micaela de Velasco, Lucía Hurtado y Salas, and Rosalia Gárcia de Noriega,[153] all of whom had wealth and position, owned and managed property, and carried out legal transactions on their own. Some petitioners were women from well-known families or were daughters of provincial officials (but they were not called doña). Among the latter were Juana de Anaya Almazán, daughter of Sergeant Major Francisco de Anaya Almazán II, and Francisca Gómez de Torres, daughter of Alcalde Cristóbal de Torres.[154] A few women petitioners are known to have bought and sold land and accumulated property on their own. Among them were Juana Luján,[155] who owned land near San Ildefonso Pueblo, and Antonia de Moraga, who held land in Santa Fe and Chimayó.[156] Respectable women, married or widowed, who lived in their own houses and were of modest means, were also heard by the alcaldes and governors, for example Josefa Sedaño, María Canseco, and Juana de Argüello.[157] Two complainants in this book, Ana María Romero [Villalpando] and her daughter Catalina de Villalpando, belong in a category by themselves. Sometimes complaining and sometimes complained about, we know that they each appeared at least twice before the alcalde or governor.[158]

Most women without family connections or inherited wealth had a more difficult time surviving in the province, but still were able to petition the alcalde or appear in court. Among them were Petrona de Carvajal (Case 5) and an unnamed woman (Case 10), whose husband had abandoned her for six years; both of these women had children.[158] There were few economic opportunities for women of limited means. Some acquired jobs at the Santa Fe presidio as cooks or laundresses, or were hired as servants at the larger residences of the more prosperous, though the latter role was largely filled by Indian women. Some women survived, at least temporarily, by cohabitating with men. These women, especially those with children, may have discovered it was beneficial to "grant their favors" to men who were not their husbands. The men with whom they cohabitated were married or single, civilians or Santa Fe presidio soldiers, or soldiers or travelers from El Paso and elsewhere.

Most of the New Mexico women who submitted petitions lived in Santa Fe, Santa Cruz, Chimayó, or the Río Abajo region (Bernalillo, Santiago, Alameda, Atrisco, Valencia, and Fuenclara/Tomé). It may be that women living in more isolated areas did not have the means or opportunity to make their complaints known to the alcaldes, usually located in towns some distance away.

Overall, the documents show that women of this period, whether literate or not, property owners or poor widows, made frequent appearances in court. Whatever their station in life, they were quite ready and willing to protect or further themselves (and their children) by using the New Mexico legal system.

The Santa Fe Presidio

The presidio was an important part of New Mexico's environment throughout its Spanish colonial history. It was there to protect the colonists from the raids of hostile, nomadic Indian tribes and to buffer the silver mines in Chihuahua and Zacatecas from raids by the Indians or from aggressive Europeans. In spite of its widespread responsibility, the presidio at full strength (which it rarely was) had only about one hundred to one hundred and twenty soldiers. More often, there were no more than sixty to eighty soldiers in Santa Fe at one time. The rest would have been on campaigns or serving as escorts to soldiers and civilians traveling outside the kingdom, or acting as mail carriers or horse-herd guards. Ten presidio soldiers were assigned to Albuquerque and, at times, to Santa Cruz.

The presidio was a major contributor to the economy. While most presidio supplies came up from the south, some were purchased locally. The presidio soldiers gave protection to the New Mexico settlers who traded with the Indians and the Chihuahua merchants, a major source of income for many residents. The salaries of the soldiers (even though the soldiers tended to be often in debt to the presidio store) were also an economic contribution to the region. In addition, despite repeated prohibitions by the governors, presidio soldiers and settlers participated in gambling, impacting the economy and providing a lucky few with additional goods. The testimony from the 1720 Palace of the Governors' robbery case identified alcaldes, blacksmiths, government officials, scribes, merchants, medics, and procuradors as participating in gambling at Juan de León Brito's house. Another case from, occurring over the years 1711 to 1712, described an afternoon gambling group as including a rancher, merchant, soldier, and the Frenchman Juan Archibeque.[160]

The presidio impacted lives of Spanish Colonial women because many of them were married to, widows of, cohabitated with, or lovers of presidio soldiers. The soldiers had wives and families who lived outside the presidio barracks; some of the soldiers owned houses, agricultural land, and livestock and traded with the Pueblo Indians, nomadic Indians, and with each other. Though many women depended on soldiers for economic support, this did not prevent women from submitting complaints to the governor against the soldiers for various charges, including rape, seduction and breach of marriage promise, cohabitation, lack of support, and abduction. Among the women who did so, in eighteenth-century New Mexico, were Petrona de Carvajal, María Canseco, Margarita Brito, and María de Olguín.[161]

In addition to the Santa Fe presidio, soldiers from El Paso, Janos, and other southern presidios visited the city on military business (see Map 4). In particular, there was a strong connection between the Santa Fe presidio and El Paso, where many of the Santa Fe soldiers' relatives remained after the 1692 Spanish Reconquest of New Mexico. As Spanish colonial-era documents indicate, soldiers from these different presidios frequently traveled to and from Santa Fe, and some were charged, correctly or not, with seducing women in the city. For example, see the cases of Agustín de la Palma and Cristóbal Lucero.[162]

Warfare

Because of the constant raids on the settlements by nomadic Indians, warfare was a part of life for New Mexicans. Navajos, Apaches, Utes, and later the Comanches stole goods and livestock from Spanish and Pueblo settlements. In particular, they raided these communities for cattle, sheep, and horses, as well as for women and children to use as slaves or for ransom at regional trade fairs.[163]

Because of the limited number of presidio soldiers, all New Mexican men were expected to join the militia and participate in the military campaigns against the Indians, leaving their families behind to fare as best as they could.[164] In the men's absence, New Mexican women took on the role of caring for and protecting their large households. As the Spanish colonial period documents suggest, these women not only dealt with hostile Indians but also with predatory neighbors who moved boundary markers, purposely misread livestock brands, and used more than their fair share of the precious water supply for irrigation.[164] Given this situation, it is no wonder that women in New Mexico during this period were seen as important members of society, and when they brought their complaints and petitions to the alcaldes and governors, they were listened to with respect.

Health

Illness and disease were a continual and serious threat to the New Mexico colony. Records kept by the Franciscan friars show that the colonists, as well as the Indians, died from infectious diseases such as smallpox, measles, and dysentery. Franciscan death records show that these diseases struck the Indian population the hardest, but the Spanish were not immune.[166] Venereal diseases were also known at this time in Latin America and Spain. Historian Susan Socolow, for instance, states that syphilis appeared to have been endemic for women of all social classes in late eighteenth-century Mexico City, but was particularly rampant among the urban poor.[167] Venereal diseases were not listed as the cause of death in the Franciscan records for New Mexico colonists, though these diseases probably did exist among the settlers.[167] Given the large number of soldiers and traders going back and forth between the southern presidios, mining districts, and towns, it would be surprising if such diseases did not occur in New Mexico.

Complications relating to pregnancy and childbirth were a common cause of death among women in New Spain.[169] A review of the many entries in Chávez's *Origins of New Mexico Families*[170] indicates that families with five to seven living children were common; there were also many cases of families with nine, ten, twelve, and even fifteen children. For some women, these constant pregnancies brought ill health and sometimes death.

CONCLUSION

Life for women in the harsh environment of early eighteenth-century New Mexico was clearly difficult. But, throughout this time, Spanish Colonial women had an ally in the law system that treated them with respect and as independent, legal entities with recognized rights and privileges. In fact, these women enjoyed rights beyond those held by their sisters in England and its colonies in North America. In particular, Spanish Colonial women had the right to present petitions, appear in court, and use the law to defend themselves, their property, and their families. In the eighteenth-century, the documents show that women were as effective and competent as men in utilizing these legal rights.

Notes

1. María de la Candelaria was the daughter of Feliciano de la Candelaria and Josefa Varela, both of whom were from founding families of Albuquerque. Maria's grandmother was Ana de Sandoval y Manzanares, owner of the San Clemente land grant. By 1734 her son, also named Feliciano, inheritor of the grant, had sold it to Bernabé Baca. The latter sold the land in 1746 to Nicolás Durán de Chávez, who in turn sold it to Domingo Luna. In 1750, a census showed María de la Candelaria living at the Sitio de Gutiérrez near Isleta with Juan Antonio de la Cruz, a niece Felipa de la Cruz, and Felipa's daughter, María Manuela. It is not known if the property that is the subject of María de Candelaria's petition was part of the San Clemente property. (SANM II #505; Chávez, *Origins*: 155-56; Sisneros, "Ana de Sandoval": 82–84; NMGS, *Aquí*: 116-17.)
2. Tomás Vélez Cachupín was a native of the Santander province in northwestern Spain, the second son of a landed family. He began his career in Cuba, and then served Viceroy the Conde de Revellagigedo (Horcasitas) in Mexico City. He served two full terms as governor of New Mexico 1749–1754 and from 1762–1767. He was known being well versed the law, in particular the *Recopilación de Leyes de los Reinos de las Indias*. He was also known for his success in dealing with the genizaros, Pueblo Indians, and nomadic tribes. (Ebright, *Witches of Abiquiu*: 63-7.)
3. Domingo Luna was the son of Antonio de Luna and Jacinta Peláez. As stated above, he purchased the San Clemente land grant in 1746. He married Josefa Lucero in 1745, and upon her death, sometime around 1758, he married María Baca. (Chávez, *Origins*: 214.)
4. The names of these family members are unknown. Records indicate that Feliciano de la Candelaria had two daughters, both named María. Possibly the sister mentioned in this case was the second-born María. (Chávez, *Origins*: 155-56.)
5. Joseph Baca was the son of Josefa Baca; his wife was Josefa Gallegos. He was shown as being a captain on the list of original petitioners for the Tomé grant. In 1745, he was alcalde of Fuenclara/Tomé, and in 1747, he was alcalde of Albuquerque. He wrote his will in 1766. (NMGS, *Aquí*: 243; Alexander, *Cottonwoods*: 32; SANM II #463; SANM I #117, WPA translation.)
6. Bernardo Antonio de Bustamante [y Tagle] was the lieutenant governor under Juan Domingo de Bustamante (1722 to 1731); Bernardo was a relative of the governor, possibly a nephew. Bernardo held the same position under Governor Codallos y Rabal (1743 to 1749) and Governor Vélez Cachupín. Bernardo, like Governor Valverde (1717 to 1722) and Governors Bustamante and Vélez Cachupín, came from the province of Santander, Spain. Bernardo was in New Mexico in 1745, when he traveled to Navajo country with fray Miguel Menchero. (Ebright, *Witches of Abiquiu*: 54.)
7. Eusebio Real [de Aguilar] was a son of the well-known Alfonso Real de Aguilar—who came to New Mexico with General don Diego de Vargas in 1692 and served as secretary of government and war, protector of the Indians, and alcalde of Santa Fe. Eusebio's mother was Josefa García de Noriega. In 1716, Eusebio was an alférez with the Santa Fe Presidio; and, in that same year, Eusebio was involved in a fight with Francisco de Tamaris. In trying to protect him, his brother Alonso killed Tamaris. (Chávez, *Origins*: 263; Tigges and Salazar, *Spanish Colonial Lives*: 221-34.)
8. The case referred to, SANM II #516, is not included in this book.
9. See Case 23. Another example is found in Case 12: "I, María Canseco . . . appear prostrated at the feet of your honor in my best and most proper form which my legal right allows me" ("*paresco postrada a los pies de Vuestra Señoria en la mas bastante forma y derecho que me combenga*"). And, in Case 13: "I, doña Micaela de Velasco . . . appear before your honor in the best form possible that is allowed to me according to my legal right" ("*paresco ante Vuestra Señoria en la mejor forma que el derecho me consede*").

10. Important studies on the history of Castilian and Spanish law and how it addressed domestic issues and the status of women are: Cutter, *Legal Culture*; Cutter, "Administration of Law in Colonial New Mexico;" Van Kleffens, *Hispanic Law*; Kagan, *Lawsuits and Litigants in Castile*; and Vance, *The Background of Hispanic-American Law*. Important sources on Spanish law are Arrom, *Women of Mexico City*; Couturier, "Women and the Family in Eighteenth-Century Mexico: Law and Practice"; Gauderman, *Women's Lives in Colonial Quito*; Lavrin, *Sexuality and Marriage in Colonial Latin America*; Powers, *Women in the Crucible of Conquest*; Stuntz, *Hers, His, and Theirs*; Socolow, *Women of Colonial Latin America*; and Twinam, *Public Lives, Private Secrets*. These and other helpful sources are included in the bibliography. For more on the identification of of Spanish officials with the Roman empire, see Pagden, *Lords of all the World*: 6–21.
11. See Korth and Flusche, "Dowry and Inheritance": 395; Van Kleffens, *Hispanic Law*: 79.
12. See Van Kleffens, *Hispanic Law*: 62, 66.
13. See Kagan, *Lawsuits and Litigants*: 23.
14. For example, in the eleventh century, Castilian military leader El Cid fought with the Christian armies as well as with the Muslim rulers of Saragosa and other Muslim armies, to gain control of Valencia. (*Wikipedia*, "El Cid," accessed on March 25, 2016.)
15. See Van Kleffens, *Hispanic Law*: 93-94.
16. See Van Kleffens, *Hispanic Law*: 176-78; Kagan, *Lawsuits and Litigants*: 25.
17. See Vance, *Background*:89-90, 170-172.
18. For a discussion of *Fuero Real* and *Las Siete Partidas*, see Vance, *Background*: 89-1, 93-106; and Van Kleffens, *Hispanic Law*: 153-39.
19. For example, see Case 31 and SANM I #343, in which it is referred to as the laws of Castile compiled by Alfonso X.
20. See Burns, *Las Siete Partidas*.
21. See Van Kleffens, *Hispanic Law*: 167-80.
22. It is also known as *Ordenanzas Reales de Castilla* (Montalvo). (Van Kleffens, *Hispanic Law*: 231.)
23. See Vance, *Background*: 117-118.
24. See Korth and Flusche, "Dowry and Inheritance": 397; Couturier, "Family": 296; Lavrin and Couturier, "Dowries and Wills": 282.
25. A full and a partial copy of this law code was found in the inventory of don Diego de Vargas after his death. Kessell, Hendricks, Dodge, and Miller: *Settling of Accounts*: 240-1, 246-48.
26. For further information on the *Nueva Recopilación* see Cutter, "Administration": 102; Kamen, *Philip of Spain*: 30; Kagan, *Laws and Litigants*: 26; and Vance, "*Background*":121-24.
27. For example, see SANM II #239e; SANM II #473; SANM I # 343; and SANM I #828.
28. See Stuntz, *Hers, His*: 101; St. George Tucker, *Blackstone's Commentaries*, Vol. I: 378, 418-0.
29. See Stuntz, *Hers, His*: 101, 109-2. Stuntz makes the case that nineteenth- and twentieth-century laws of Texas gave more support to women than laws of other states, because of the influence of Spanish law. On this subject, see also Rosen, "Women and Property": 365-67. Van Kleffens suggests that the influence of Spanish laws was felt in the states that were formerly part of Mexico, such as New Mexico, Arizona, California, and Colorado. (Van Kleffens, *Hispanic Law*: 266.) Janet Lecompte writes about the confrontation that occurred after the American conquest between American men and Mexican women and the laws to which they were accustomed. (Lecompte, "Independent Women": 73-5).
30. For further information on this subject, see Korth and Flusche, "Dowry and Inheritance": 396; Rosen, "Women and Property": 365-67; Gauderman, *Quito*: 26-27; Stuntz, *Hers, His*: 88-107. See also Case 12 and SANM II #427.
31. See Twitchell, Ralph Emerson, *Spanish Archives of New Mexico*, Vols. I and II.
32. See Case 12, Case 23, and Case 31; and SANM I #177, SANM II #427, and SANM II #516. See also Couturier, "Family": 296-98, 301; Rosen, "Women and Property": 358–64; Gauderman, *Quito*: 33-40.
33. See Case 31.
34. See Van Kleffens, *Hispanic Law*: 266; Stuntz, *Hers, His*: 138.
35. Spanish Colonial legal wills that include provisions for dowries are SANM I #94, SANM I #161, SANM I #826, and SANM I #841.
36. For dowries see Couturier, "Women and Family": 297; Guaderman, *Quito*: 30-33; Korth and Flusche, "Dowry and Inheritance": 395-408; Lavrin, "Sexuality in Colonial Mexico": 60-61, 261, 334-35; Lavrin and Couturier, "*Dowries and Wills*": 280-304; Rosen, "Women and Property": 358-64; Stuntz, *Hers, His*: 26-27.
37. See Case 16 and SANM I #841, WPA Translation.
38. See Case 12.
39. See Case 31 and SANM I #177, SANM I #343, SANM I #516, SANM I #841, and SANM I #1221, all WPA translations.
40. See Arrom, *Mexico City*: 63-4; Dyer, "Promise of Marriage: 439-55; Lavrin, "Women in Colonial Mexico": 250; Poska, "Elusive Virtue": 142-43; Stamatov, *Family*: 147-53.
41. See Case 17.
42. See Case 28.

43. Lavrin, *Sexuality and Marriage*: 50-1.
44. Arrom, *Women of Mexico City*: 209.
45. See Case 26.
46. For studies on adultery, see Arrom, *Women of Mexico City*: 63, 65, 241-7; Dyer, "Promise of Marriage": 440; Gauderman, *Quito*: 55-3; Lavrin, *Sexuality and Marriage*: 51, 71.
47. See Case 7.
48. See Stuntz, *Hers, His*: 45; Boyer and Spurling, *Colonial Lives*: 7; Arrom, *Women of Mexico City*: 64-65.
49. See Powers, *Crucible*: 128; Boyer and Spurling, *Colonial Lives*: 55; and Case 27.
50. See Case 18.
51. See Case 27.
52. See Case 30.
53. See Gaudeman, *Quito*: 53; Arrom, *Women of Mexico City*: 228-30.
54. See Case 5 and also Case 9, Case 11, Case 13, and Case 26.
55. Lavrin, *Sexuality and Marriage*: 50-51, 70-72.
56. See Case 5.
57. See Arrom, *Women of Mexico City*: 63.
58. See SANM II #498 and West, "Asylum": 151-2.
59. See SANM II #511.
60. See Arrom, *Women of Mexico City*: 64.
61. See Powers, *Crucible*: 136-41.
62. See Case 1.
63. See Case 14.
64. See Case 1.
65. See Case 3, Case 6, and Case 16.
66. See Case 14.
67. On public shaming, see Chuchiak, *Inquisition*: 224, 297.
68. Boyer, "Mala Vida": 253-63; Powers, *Crucible*: 100-01, 194; Lavrin, *Sexuality and Marriage*: 20-21; Twinam, *Public Lives*: 85.
69. Boyer, "Mala Vida": 256.
70. See Case 1, Case 3, Case 5, and Case 8.
71. See Case 6.
72. See SANM I I #187.
73. See Cutter, *Legal Culture*: 41; Cutter, "Administration": 110; and Case 3, Case 5, Case 6, and Case 26.
74. Lavrin, *Sexuality and Marriage*: 28.
75. Powers, *Crucible*: 133-36; Coolidge, "Noble Mistresses": 195-214; Twinam, *Public Lives*: 126-7.
76. See Case 13.
77. See Chávez, *Origins*: 144-45; Brooks, *Captives and Cousins*: 100-02.
78. On the subject of honor, see Burkholder and Johnson, *Colonial Latin America*: 245-47; Dyer, "Promise of Marriage": 445-55; Lavrin, "Women in Colonial Mexico": 247.
79. See Arrom, *Women of Mexico City*: 54.
80. See Case 3.
81. See Case 6.
82. See Case 17.
83. See Case 28.
84. See Powers, *Crucible*: 122-27, 194-95.
85. See SANM II #187.
86. See SANM II #437 and SANM II 439.
87. Much of the material in this section is from publications by Charles Cutter, particularly *Legal Culture*: 105-6, and his "Spanish Borderlands, Civil Law": 414-6, 445-47.
88. See *Wikipedia*, "Due Process Clause, Procedural Due Process," accessed on September 23, 2016; Fielding, "Some Kind of Hearing": 1279-5.
89. Case 25.
90. See Garcia Lopez, *Guía de Protocolos*: 229-61; Sáenz Ramírez, *Los Protocolos*.
91. See Case 5 and Case 17.
92. See Kessell, Hendricks, Dodge, and Miller, *Royal Crown*: 542, 543n1.
93. Cutter, *Legal Culture*: 13, 105-6. For examples of cases that most closely follow these legal procedures see Case 6, Case 17, and Case 19.
94. See Case 5, Case 30, and Case 31.
95. See SANM II #160, and Case 6, Case 8, Case 11, Case 19, and Case 24.
96. See Case 19 and Case 24.
97. See Boyer and Spurling, *Colonial Lives*: 158; and Case 17, Case 23, and Case 26.
98. In Case 14, when Ana María Romero [Villalpando] was threatened with prison, she was actually placed in

the guardhouse. In SANM II #197, not included here, Antonia de Moraga was ordered to be held in the casas reales of Santa Cruz. There is no evidence, however, that she was actually placed there, or even if there was a casas reales in the villa.
99. The material on sanctuaries is drawn from West, "Asylum": 115-1. See also Uribe-Uran, "Church Asylum and the Law":446-472.
100. Ibid., 148, 149n2.
101. See Case 6. See also, Tigges and Salazar, *Spanish Colonial Lives*: 221-34; West, "Asylum": 127.
102. See SANM II #624, which is also described in West, "Asylum": 140-41.
103. See Case 24.
104. Tigges and Salazar, *Spanish Colonial Lives*: 163.
105. See Case 5, Case 17, and Case 28. See also Cutter, *Legal Culture*: 39, 100-01; Ebright, *Advocates for the Oppressed*: 4-11.
106. See Cutter, *Legal Culture*: 101; and SANM II #516.
107. See Case 21, Case 23, and Case 24.
108. See Case 24 and Case 31.
109. For example, see Case 16, Case 23, Case 24 and Case 25; and Tigges and Salazar, *Spanish Colonial Lives*: 491-09, 584-09, 635-44.
110. For example, in Case 27, Nicolás de Aragón's case had previously been heard by the ecclesiastical judge, Santiago de Roybal.
111. Cutter, "Administration": 108-13; Cutter, "Judicial Punishment": 17.
112. See Case 14; Chuchiak, *Inquisition*: 224; Ebright and Hendricks, *Witches*: 232.
113. A French traveler to Latin America commented on this by pointing out that there was "blind protection afforded by the Spanish laws to females in opposition to their husbands." He further noted that when a woman turned to the authorities the judges were ready "to believe everything that an imagination could suggest against her husband." See Socolow, *Women of Colonial Latin America*: 68-69.
114. Cutter, "Judicial Punishment": 124-25. Though the word used is sometimes "cárcel" or "prisión," these words are clarified by a statement from the 1737 interrogatories of Governor Gervasio Cruzat y Góngora's *residentcia*, which states, "…there never has been a jail in this Villa, and that when someone is ordered to be imprisoned [it has been] in the guardhouse where they are better secured." (SANM II #420, roll 7, frame 852 and following.)
115. SANM II #363c; Tigges and Salazar, *Spanish Colonial Lives*: 261-94.
116. Tigges and Salazar, *Spanish Colonial Lives*: 197.
117. Ibid., 404.
118. SANM II #187. See also Cutter, *Legal Culture*, p. 138, for a discussion of capital punishment cases.
119. See Case 27.
120. See Case 24. In the New Mexico cases, the term real amparo was used to mean royal protection. These words also refer to *La Ley de Amparo Real*, a law passed in 1578 giving title to lands granted by the Spanish Crown, but this meaning does not apply here.
121. See Case 10.
122. See SANM II #239a.
123. See Chávez, *New Mexico Roots*: xii; Boyer and Spurling, *Colonial Lives*: 155.
124. See Foucault, Michel. *The History of Sexuality: An Introduction*: 19-1, 61-63; Stamatov, *Family, Kin*: 110-16.
125. See Case 30.
126. See SANM II #463c; Tigges and Salazar, *Spanish Colonial Lives*: 261-4.
127. See Lavrin, "Women in Colonial Mexico": 248; Socolow, *Women of Colonial Latin American*: 114; Lavrin, *Sexuality and Marriage*: 61.
128. See Case 17 and Case 28.
129. Portions of marriage investigations are found in Chávez, *New Mexico Roots*. See, for example, the investigations of José Armijo, p. 125; Ventura Esquibel, p. 488; and Antonio Jorgé, p. 891. The complete records of the investigations are found in the *Diligencias Matrimoniales* microfilm at the New Mexico State Archives, Santa Fe.
130. Antonio Durán y Chávez was the brother of Nicolás Durán y Chávez who appears in Case 8.
131. See Chávez, *Roots*: 306.
132. See Chávez, *Roots*: 488-9; Stamatov, *Family, Kin*: 153. As shown in Case 12, a horse was shown as having a value of fifteen pesos, so two hundred pesos could buy thirteen or fourteen horses and quite a number of cattle or sheep. It would have been considered a goodly amount.
133. See SANM I #430; SANM II #556; Jenkins, "Women of Property": 337-40.
134. See Arrom, *Women of Mexico City*: 209-19; Gaudeman, *Quito*: 49-51; Nizza da Silva, *Brazil*: 313-36; Socolow, *Women of Colonial Latin America*: 68.
135. See Case 7.
136. See Chuchiak, *The Inquisition*: 11-12.

137. For general information on the Spanish Inquisition and the Mexican Tribunal, see Chuchiak, *The Inquisition*; Behar, "*Sexual Witchcraft*;" Greenleaf, "Inquisition in Eighteenth-Century New Mexico;" Lea, *A History of the Inquisition of Spain*; Rawlings, *The Spanish Inquisition*; Riley, *The Inquisition in Colonial Latin America*; Roth, *The Spanish Inquisition*; and Rule, *History of the Inquisition*. On minor heresies and witchcraft, see Chuchiak, *The Inquisition*: 6-7.
137a. Kessell, *Kiva, Cross and Crown*: 165, 184-93.
138. See Case 7, Case 18, and Case 22. See also, Tigges and Salazar, *Spanish Colonial Lives*: 202-14, 240-50, and 320-48.
139. See Case 22.
140. See Case 22 for an example of the refusal of Inquisition officials to accept hearsay evidence.
141. See Chuchiak, *The Inquisition*: 30-33.
142. See Case 18.
143. See Behar, "Sexual Witchcraft": 180; Chuchiak, *The Inquisition*: 83-84; Rawlings, *The Spanish Inquisition*: 2, 28, 30, 92, 102-03.
144. See AGN – Inquisición, Legajo 529: Santa Fe, May 30, 1694, El Paso, September 30, 1693. See also, Tigges and Salazar, *Spanish Colonial Lives*: 202–13.
145. For examples, see Rawlings, *The Spanish Inquisition*: 102-03, 118; and Chuchiak, *The Inquisition*: 107-21.
146. See Case 18 and Case 22.
147. See Case 18.
148. See Chuchiak, *The Inquisition*: 1-2, 218; Boyer, *Bigamists*: 28-32, 231-2; McDougall, "Why Prosecute Bigamy": 11-130.
149. See Ebright, *Advocates*: 122- 3, 288n30; and SANM I #329.
150. For his will, see SANM I #963.
151. See Chávez, *Origins*: 223-24; and Tigges and Salazar, *Spanish Colonial Lives*: 212n9.
152. See Barrett, *Spanish Colonial Settlement*: 131, 142, 201.
153. See Case 13, Case 15, and Case 31. Also, for Rosalia Gárcia de Noriega, see Rock, *Pido y Suplico*: 152.
154. See Case 6 and Case 23.
155. See Ahlborn, "Will of a New Mexico Women": 319-5; Jenkins, "Women of Property": 337- 40.
156. See Jenkins, "Women of Property": 340-3.
157. See Case 1, Case 3, and Case 12.
158. For Ana María Romero [Villalpando], see Case 14 and Case 16; for Catalina de Villalpando, see Case 11 and Case 19.
159. See Case 5 and Case 25.
160. See Case 20; and Tigges and Salazar, *Spanish Colonial Lives*: 61-8.
161. See Case 5, Case 12, Case 17, and Case 30.
162. See Case 5 and Case 17.
163. One of the best sources of information on slavery, ransom, and genízaros is Brooks, *Captives and Cousins*.
164. For a list of twenty-six military campaigns and expeditions, which occurred during the years of 1705 to 1746, see Tigges and Salazar, *Spanish Colonial Lives*: 14.
165. See Case 15 and SANM II #505.
166. The death data, from the New Mexico Mission records, can be found in Tigges and Salazar, *Spanish Colonial Lives*: 29.
167. See Socolow, *Women of Colonial Latin America*: 123, 173. For a discussion of syphilis in the New World, see Downey, *Isabella*: 289-90, 349-50, 431.
168. See Burkholder and Johnson, *Colonial Latin America*: 87; Vollendorf, *Lives of Women*: 181; Boyer, "La Mala Vida": 275.
169. Burkholder and Johnson, *Colonial Latin American*: 234.
170. Chávez, *Origins*; and Case 8.

Documents

1

SISTERS THROW ROCKS AT RIVAL, GOVERNOR THREATENS BANISHMENT
August 17–20, 1697, Source: SANM II #67 and #68

Synopsis and editor's notes: The following documents describe a disagreement between three women from two different New Mexican families who returned to Santa Fe after twelve difficult years in El Paso, having left New Mexico because of the Pueblo Revolt. It is likely they knew each other living in El Paso, or even before that. The women involved were Juana de Argüello, an older widow with eight sons-in-law, and Ana María and Isabel de Herrera, sisters who were younger and unmarried. In the first document, Juana de Argüello complained to the alcalde, Diego Arias de Quiros, that while being with Cristóba Tafoya, an unmarried presidio soldier, in front of the Herrera home, the sisters called her a "bawdry whore" and then hit her on the head with a rock. As a result, Juana claimed, she suffered an affront to her reputation that led to the beating of one of her daughters by her husband (who believed in the slander). In response to the petition, Alcalde Arias de Quiros jailed the two sisters.

In the second document, Juana withdrew her complaint after the sisters agreed to apologize to her and repair her reputation. Juana agreed but on the condition that the sisters be banished and fined twenty-five pesos if they did not comply. The alcalde accepted her request but stated that Cristóbal Tafoya was not to enter or even be outside the Herrera sisters' house.

The suitable-for-marriage Tafoya may be the reason for the behavior of the Herrera sisters. In the document, Juana de Argüello said that he promised to marry one of her own daughters, but due to an impediment of some sort he could not do so. Although the impediment is not explained, it may be that the intended couple was too closely related or that the groom had previously had sex with someone else, both reasons against a marriage. It is known that a year later, in 1698, Cristóbal did marry Isabel Herrera without any impediment mentioned.[1]

In this document, both a *prisíon* and *cárcel* are mentioned, though in eighteenth-century New Mexico prisoners were usually placed in the presidio guardhouse or the alcalde's home. While there may have been a separate jail for civilian prisoners in Santa Fe, it is more likely that in this case the prisíon/cárcel and the guardhouse were one and the same.

That Diego Arias de Quiros, a ranking official in the colony, took the time to investigate a domestic dispute illustrates the importance of keeping peace among the settlers. Subsequent documents indicate that husbands and wives often complained to the alcalde mayor or governor about their spouses (or other persons with whom they lived), neighbors, and relatives. The officials consistently took the time necessary to hear the complaints and hand down decisions that appeased both sides, with the apparent intention of leaving no cause for continuing hostility.

In this legal case, colonists in New Mexico clearly understood that it was the right of men and women, married or unmarried, to petition the alcaldes or governors about their concerns. In the first sentence of her complaint, for instance, Juana states that she appears "in the best and most proper form that I am allowed according to my legal right." This, or a similar phrase, was commonly used by petitioners in addressing the court, both to show their respect and to affirm their legal right to appear. Spanish law allowed women to make such petitions without the permission of their husband or any other person—a legal allowance not found in English law, or in later American law.

In addition, these documents illustrate a pattern in the cases brought forth by women against a spouse or another woman. The complaint would be heard, testimony taken, and a sentence imposed by the alcalde or governor. Then, the woman making the complaint—who, in the end, may have feared the cost of the sentence or the absence of her husband at planting or harvest time—would withdraw the complaint, or, as happened in Juana's case, if the sentence had been pronounced, would ask for a pardon of the accused, to which the governor often agreed. It may be that the shaming in front of the court of the woman's husband or the accused, the apology, and the threat of punishment were enough, or the most that she could expect.

TRANSLATION

SANM II #67

1697
Petition and complaint given by Juana de Argüello[2] against Ana María de Herrera[3] and her sister, Isabel de Herrera[4]

Alcalde Ordinario

[Statement of Juana de Argüello]

I, Juana de Argüello, widow and resident of this Villa of Santa Fe, appear before your majesty in my best and proper form that I am allowed according to my legal right. I say that I am filing a civil and criminal complaint before your majesty against two *mulatta* women, one named Ana María de Herrera and the other one Isabel de Herrera, being as they are living in such a bad manner, as is common public knowledge, and they are the scandal of this villa.

Pulcheria in New Spain in 1763 showing women's costumes. Antonio de Basaras, *Ina Vision del Mexico del Siglo de la Luces, la Codificación de Antonio de Basaras. Origen, Costumes y Estado Presente de Mexicanos y Filipinos, 1763*. Courtesy of the Hispanic Society of America, New York.

It has been brought to the attention of your majesty and it is well-known that Cristóbal de Tafoya[5] tried to marry one of my daughters, who is a widow. However, due to an impediment that was brought forth, they did not marry. Fifteen days ago when I passed by their house, they, the Herrera sisters, threw a rock at me that cracked my skull. Then upon approaching their home to see what the problem was for this behavior they, in front of Cristóbal Tafoya, began insulting me and calling me names saying that I was a bawdry whore[6] and other terrible things. Yesterday afternoon, when Juan de Tafoya[7] and his wife went to buy a small amount of wheat from my son-in-law, Tomás de Bejarano,[8] he [Bejarano], offered a job for Juan Tafoya's brother, Cristóbal. When Juan and I went to tell Cristóbal about it at the place where he was living, the two sisters went to where we were standing. From the edge of the river they began to call me the same names, telling me again that I was a whore, along with other terrible words. One of my sons-in-law being present, he went home and almost killed his wife [Juana's daughter] because of what he had heard. Your majesty knows well enough that I have eight sons-in-law, all of them in good standing, and that no other person has ever called me such names.

Due to all of this, I petition your majesty that you be pleased to have them prove their accusation of me. If they are not punished under the full rigor of justice, my daughters are at a great risk of their lives. All of this I ask to be granted, as I am living alone, a widowed woman with much honor.

Of your majesty I petition and ask with all sincerity that he be pleased to grant what he thinks is the right thing according to justice, and I swear to God and to the sign of the Cross that this my petition is not done in malice, protesting the costs,⁹ and asking for what is necessary, etc.

Juana de Argüello (rubric)

Presentation

At this Villa of Santa Fe, on the 17th of August, 1697, before me Diego Arias de Quiros,¹⁰ *alcalde ordinario* of this villa, was presented with the above contained and upon being reviewed by me I took it as it was presented. According to my legal right I ordered the *alguacil* guarding the jail to go to the house where Ana María de Herrera and her sister live and bring them back as prisoners to this jail. So that this is valid, I signed it along with the scribe of the *cabildo* on this day, etc.

Diego Arias de Quiros (rubric)

SANM II, #68

Petition and complaint of Juana de Argüello against Ana María de Herrera and her sister, Isabel de Herrera.

Alcalde Ordinario

I, Juana de Argüello, resident of the Villa of Santa Fe, appear before your majesty in my best and most proper form according to my legal right. With regard to the complaint that I have presented before your majesty against the Herrera sisters, I say that I am retracting my complaint. This is due to the fact that they have apologized to me in public, stating that are ready to give me back my reputation and the good standing that they wanted to take from me. They also state that they are not and will not get involved with my daughters nor my sons-in-law in any way. If they do not comply with the above stated, [I ask that] they be banished to Villa Nueva de Santa Cruz de la Cañada or to Bernalillo. If at any time they continue to disgrace me I will bring forth charges under the full rigor of justice. Of your honor I ask and petition that you do whatever you think is best, and I swear in due form that this my petition is not done in malice, but for what is necessary, etc.

Juana de Argüello (rubric)

[Auto]

At this Villa of Santa Fe on the 20th of August, 1697, I, Captain Diego Arias de Quiros, alcalde ordinario of this villa, accept the above as it was presented according the legal rights that are due. I order that Ana María de Herrera and her sister, Isabel de Herrera, be released from the jail they are in and appear before me so that I might present them with this petition and with what is provided within it. So that it is valid I signed along with the scribe of the cabildo, etc.

Diego Arias de Quiros (rubric)
before me,
Miguel Tenorio de Alba[11] (rubric)
Scribe for the cabildo

[Retraction and Apology]

Continuing, on the said day, month and year, before me Captain Diego Arias de Quiros, alcalde ordinario of this villa, there appeared before me Juana de Argüello who has retracted the complaint that she has filed against Ana María de Herrera and her sister, Isabel de Herrera. This is under the condition that they retract what they have said about her, Juana de Argüello. They, appearing before me, stated that from this time on, they retract what they stated and ask for her pardon. They also said that from this time on they will not get involved with Juana de Argüuello nor with any person from her home. This they both stated, and so that it is valid, I approved, ordered and signed it with the scribe of the cabildo on this date, etc.

Diego Arias de Quiros (rubric)
before me,
Miguel Tenorio de Alba (rubric)
Scribe for the cabildo

Decree

At this Villa of Santa Fe on the said day, month and year, I, Captain Diego Arias de Quiros, alcalde ordinario of this villa mandate Ana María de Herrera and her sister, Isabel de Herrera, not to admit in their home, or outside of the home, Cristóbal Tafoya, a soldier of this presidio, under any pretext. If they do not obey this order of the royal justice, I will order that they be banished along with a fine of twenty-five pesos[12] to be applied for the public works. All of this will be executed without pardon, and so that it is valid I approved, ordered and signed it along with the scribe of the cabildo, thus done, etc.

Diego Arias de Quiros (rubric)
before me,
Miguel Tenorio de Alba (rubric)
Scribe for the cabildo

TRANSCRIPTION

SANM II #67

1697
Petizion y querella que dio Juana de Arguello contra Ana Maria de Herrera y su hermana Ysabel de Herrera

Señor Alcalde Ordinario

Juana de Arquello vuida y besina de esta Villa de Santa Fee paresco ante Vuestra Majestad en la mas bastante forma que en cuanto a derecho aiga lugar y al mio combenga y digo; que me querello sibil y criminalmente ante Vuestra Majestad de dos mulatas llamada la una Ana Maria de Herrera y la otra Ysabel de Herrera de que siendo como son de tan mal bibir, como es publica bos y fama y ser el escandalo desta Villa.

Que abra flega a notizia de Vuestra Magestad como Xptobal de Tafoia se trato de casarse con una ija mia, de estado buida, y por inpedimento que ubo no se casaron. Presede Señor Alcalde que abra quinse dias que pasando por su casa me arrojaron una piedra y me descalabraron, y subiendo a su casa a desirles que motibo o causa tubieron para ello delante del dicho Xptobal Tafoia y me injuriaron de palabra disiendome en presenzia del el suso dicho que era una puta alcagueta y otras muchas desverguenzas y abiendo ya pasadoles estas desberguenzas, se ofrezio aier tarde que bino en casa de mi yerno Tomas de Bejarano, Juan de Tafoia con su mujer a comprar un poco de trigo y ofresiendole al dicho Juan de Tafoia negozio con su ermano, Xptobal Tafoia lo enbio a llamar de donde nasio que las suso dichas fueron y desde el Rio se pusieron a desirme lo mesmo que llevo referido de como era una alcagueta puta estando uno de mis yernos presente cosa que pudo matar a su mujer por sus malas lenguas y a Vuestra Magestad le consta como a tenido ocho yernos todos hombres de bien y que no a bido quien me aiga dicho otro tanto y asi pido a Vuestra Magestad se sirva de que me lo prueben por que corren mis hijas mucho peligro de las bidas y de no que se castigen con todo rigor de justizia la cual pido se me guarde por mujer sola, buida y onrada =

A Vuestra Magestad pido y suplico con todo rendimiento se sirba de prober lo que mas conbenga en justizia la cual pido y juro por Dios Nuestro Señor y la Señal de la Cruz + que esta mi petizion no es de malizia y protesto costas y en lo nesesario, ut supra.

Juana de Arguello (rubric)

Auto

En esta Villa de Santa Fee en dies y siete dias del mes de Agosto de mil seisientos y nobenta y siete años ante mi el Capitan Diego Arias de Quiros, Alcalde Hordinario desta dicha Villa la presento la contenida, y por mi bista la hube por presentada en cuanto a lugar de derecho y mando al Alguasil portero baia alas casas de la morada de Ana Maria Herrera y de su hermana Ysabel de Herrera y melas traiga presas a esta carsel y para que conste lo firme con el Escribano de Cabildo, fecho ut supra =

    Diego Arias de Quiros (rubric)

SANM II #68

1697

Petizion y querella que dio Juana de Arguello contra Ana Maria de Herrera y su hermana Ysabel de Herrera

Señor Alcalde Ordinario

    Juana de Arguello besina de esta Villa de Santa Fee paresco ante Vuestra Magestad en la mas bastante forma que en cuanto a derecho aiga lugar y al mio convenga y digo que en cuanto ala querella que tengo presentada ante Vuestra Magestad contra las Herreras digo que me bajare dela querella desdisiendose las susos dichas delo que me dijeron en publico y que me debuelban la reputazion y buenos creditos segun y como me quitaron la dicha mi reputazion y que no se metan con mis yjas ni mis yernos por ningun acontestimiento, y de no aserlo como lo llevo referido, salgan luego testeradas para la Villa Nueba o Bernalillo con tal de que en cualquier tiempo que bolbieren a tener algunas desberguenzas le prosigo con todo rigor de justizia; a Vuestra Magestad pido y suplico se sirva de prober lo que mas conbenga y juro en devida forma que esta mi petizion no es de malizia y en lo nezesario, ut supra.

    Juana de Arguello (rubric)

Presentacion

    En esta Villa de Santa Fee en veinte dias del mes de Agosto de mill seis cientos y noventa y siete años ante mi el Capitan Diego Arias de Quiros, Alcalde Ordinario de esta dicha Villa la hube por presentada en cuanto a lugar en derecho y mando a Ana Maria de Herrera y a su hermana Ysabel de Herrera salgan dela prision en que estan y parescan ante mi para hazerles notoria esta petizion y lo proveido en ella para que conste lo firme con el Escribano del Cavildo, fecho ut supra_

    Diego Arias de Quiros (rubric)
    Ante mi
    Miguel Thenorio de Alva (rubric)
    Escribano de Cavildo

Luego yncontinenti en dicho dia, mes y ano ante mi el Capitan Diego Arias de Quiros, Alcalde Ordinario de esta dicha Villa paresieron Juana de Arguello la cual se baja dela querella que tiene dada contra Ana Maria de Herrera y su hermana Ysabel de Herrera con cargo y condision que se desdigan de lo que han dicho ala suso dicha Juana de Arguello las quales ante mi dicho Alcalde Ordinario dijeron que desde luego lo desdisen delo que an dicho y le piden perdon y que a ora ni en ningun tiempo se metteran con la suso dicha ni con persona de su cassa y esto es lo que responden de la una y de la otra parte y para que conste asi lo probey y mande y firme con el escribano de Cavildo, fecho, ut supra.
 Diego Arias de Quiros (rubric)
 Ante mi
 Miguel Tenorio de Alva (rubric)
 Escribano de Cavildo

Auto
 En esta Villa de Santa Fee en dicho dia, mes y ano yo el Capitan Diego Arias de Quiros Alcalde Ordinario de estra dicha Villa mando a Ana Maria de Herrera y a su hermana Ysabel de Herrera que por ningun pretesto consientan ni admitan en su cassa ni fuera de ella a Xptobal Tafoya, soldado de este Presidio con pena que si quebrantaren el mandatto dela Real Justizia desde luego las condeno en pena de destierro y mas en pena de beinte y cinco pesos aplicados para obras publicas todo lo que dicho es se executara ynremisiblemente y para que conste assi lo probey, mande y firme con el Escribano de Cavildo, fecha, ut supra _
 Diego Arias de Quiros (rubric)
 Ante mi
 Miguel Tenoria de Alva (rubric)
 Escribano de Cavildo

Notes

1. See Chávez, *Origins*: 291.
2. Juana de Argüello was the widow of Pedro Martín Serrano de Salazar. He was born in San Luis Potosí, Mexico, in 1671 and died in 1691. As a widow, she was part of the 1692 to 1693 El Paso muster, returning to New Mexico in 1693 with Diego de Vargas to resettle her husband's family's land in northern New Mexico. Known children were Miguel, Antonio, Francisco, Sebastián, María, Juana, and Josefa. Juana was named in a document recording the distribution of tools in 1704; she received three shovels, one axe, one hoe, and one plowshare. (Kessell, Hendricks, and Dodge, *Royal Crown*: 63, 95n110; Kessell, Hendricks, and Dodge, *Boulders*: 1133n7, 1170n91; Kessell, Hendricks, and Dodge, *Disturbances*: 187n106; Christmas, "Santa Fe Tool Distribution of 1704": 21; Chávez, *Origins*: 222-23.)
3. Ana María de Herrera was the daughter of Juan de Herrera and Ana López de Castillo. Juan de Herrera, who died some time before 1680, may have been the person who held the *encomienda* of Santa Clara before the 1680 Pueblo Revolt. Ana María had a *natural* daughter, Antonia López, who married José Trujillo in 1710, as his second wife. By 1715 Trujillo was an alcalde of Santa Cruz, and in July 1716 he signed his name on Inscription Rock. (Kessell, Hendricks, and Dodge, *Boulders*: 956n38.)

4. Isabel de Herrera, sister to Ana María, was also the daughter of Juan de Herrera and Ana López de Castillo. In 1698, a year after this document was written, she married Cristóbal de Tafoya Altamarino. (See below.) When he made out his will in 1718, at Santa Cruz, he listed Juan and Antonio as his legitimate children by Isabel, as well as two natural daughters, Antonia Tafoya Jaramillo and Gertrudis Tafoya Ruiz. (Chávez, *Origins*: 291; Kessell, Hendricks, and Dodge, *Boulders*: 956n38, 956n39, 1134n10, 1170n91.)
5. Cristóbal de Tafoya [Altamirano] was the son of Juan de Tafoya Altamirano and Felipa Taguada de Ulloa. Born in El Real y Minas de Talpujagua, Cristóbal was a soldier in New Mexico by 1695. The following year he was a presidio *alférez* and in June was wounded in the Pueblo Revolt. In 1698 he married Isabel de Herrera. His brothers were Juan and Antonio. (Chávez, *Origins*: 291; Kessell, Hendricks, and Dodge, *Boulders*: 792, 796, 977; Chávez, *Roots*: 1857.)
6. In the Spanish text, the words are "*puta desvergüenzas*," which refers to someone who keeps a house of prostitution.
7. This Juan de Tafoya [Altamirano] was probably the brother of Cristóbal de Tafoya Altamirano, who arrived in New Mexico in 1695. Juan married Josefa Pacheco in 1707, and, after her death, he married María Durán y Chávez in 1708. She was a daughter of the venerable Fernando Durán y Chávez and Lucía Hurtado y Salas. In 1698, Juan is recorded as being a military courier. During the investigation of Diego de Vargas, by then Governor Rodríguez Cubero, Juan de Tafoya claimed that Juan Páez Hurtado tried to kill him to prevent him from delivering information to the viceroy in New Spain. In 1712, Juan was charged with fostering sedition among the Indians. (Kessell, Hendricks, and Dodge, *Boulders*: 462n172, 570n52, 961n74; Kessell, Hendricks, Dodge, and Miller, *Disturbances*: 413, 415, 418.)
8. Tomás de Bejarano was the son of Nicolás de Bejarano and a native of Parral. He married María Martin (Serrano) de Salazar, a daughter of Juana de Argüello and Pedro Martín Serrano de Salazar. Tomás was a soldier and was in New Mexico by 1694. (Kessell, Hendricks, and Dodge, *Boulders*: 203n116, 1133n7, 1141.)
9. This means that she did not wish to pay court costs. These costs could be substantial, including amounts for time spent by the alcalde and other personnel involved in the case, as well for the paper and ink used.
10. Diego Arias de Quiros was from Asturia, Spain. He had arrived in El Paso by at least 1687 and was made presidio captain. In 1694, he was in New Mexico serving as royal alférez (ensign), of Santa Fe. He received a land grant located east of the Governor's Palace and married María Gómez Robledo in 1714. He survived the 1720 attack on the Villasur Expedition and went on to become alcalde mayor and alcalde ordinario of Santa Fe. He was dead by 1746. (Kessell, Hendricks, and Dodge, *Boulders*: 35; Chavez, "Mission Records": 151-152; SANM II #44.)
11. Miguel Tenorio de Alba was a native of New Mexico and one of the first settlers of Santa Cruz. In 1697, he was listed as a blacksmith and from 1697 to 1700 he was the cabildo scribe. In 1700, he gave testimony for Governor Cubero against Diego de Vargas. He and his wife, Agustina Romero, baptized a son, Cayetano, in Santa Cruz in 1711. In 1718, Tenorio de Alba was alcalde for Santa Cruz and the following year he was the alcalde for Taos. He was killed in the Villasur Expedition of 1720. (Kessell, Hendricks, and Dodge, *Boulders*: 570n52; Kessell, Hendricks, Dodge, and Miller, *Disturbance*: 288-91; SANM II #236; NMGS, *Santa Cruz Baptisms*: 1.)
12. At that time, two horses or maybe three thin horses could be bought for thirty pesos. (SANMI #13:57, WPA Translation.)

2

JACINTO SÁNCHEZ GRANTED PERMISSION TO SEARCH FOR A BAR OF LOST SPANISH SILVER
July 17th, 1697, Source: SANM II #69

Synopsis and editor's notes: When settlers moved to New Mexico after the Spanish Reconquest of 1696, they left behind friends, relatives, possessions, and memories. In this document, María de Castro requested permission for her husband to leave the province to collect an inheritance of a bar of silver that she had left behind. In her petition, she asked approval of a power of attorney for her new husband, Jacinto Sánchez [de Iñigo], allowing him to search for the silver. She claimed that the bar, worth 1,100 pesos,[1] was willed to her by her father before her marriage to Jacinto. Because the search necessitated going out of New Mexico to the mines of Sombrerete, in Zacatecas, Mexico, Sánchez had to ask permission from the governor to leave the province.

María stated that upon her father's death the silver bar was left with her uncle (by marriage), Gerónimo de Escobar, and then upon his death and the death of her aunt, Antonia de Castro, the silver went to Captain Joseph Durán de la Peña. María had decided not to collect the silver until she was married, and now wished to do so. She did not have the written will, nor any documentation of the silver having been left with the others. Despite this, her petition was approved by Alcalde Arias de Quiros who allowed Sánchez to leave the province.

What could be more fantastic than a tale of lost or misplaced Spanish silver? It was known that fabulous amounts of silver were discovered in the Sombrerete area in the 1500s, with a second mining boom beginning in the 1640s (and lasting until the early 1700s), and a third mining strike in the 1790s.[2] Unfortunately, no evidence exists that proves Sánchez ever traveled to Sombrerete or that he retrieved any silver. However, being a presidio soldier he may have gone outside the province and to the Sombrerete area as an escort, with no record remaining.

After 1697 when María's request was made, the fortunes of Jacinto and his wife were mixed. Sanchez applied for a land grant near Cochiti Pueblo in 1703, though there is no record that he received it. In 1704, he was part of an escort for Governor Rodríguez Cubero that traveled to Mexico City. A fellow traveler accused him of stealing one of the governor's mules, but Sánchez proved that it was a misunderstanding and that Governor Rodríguez Cubero had in fact given him a mule and horse. It may be that he used this trip to look for his wife's silver. By 1713 Sánchez was the alcalde mayor of Santa Cruz. In 1715, he was again given permission to go outside the province with his son, Francisco. Also that year, a son of Jacinto Sánchez's was stolen by the Apaches, but it is not known if this was Francisco or another child.[3]

This document includes two legal acts. The first is the power of attorney given by María de Castro to her husband, allowing him to search for and collect her property. Under Spanish law, property inherited by a woman was her own, and while her husband could manage the property, the collection of it by him needed to be legally approved. The second legal act is the formal permission allowing Sánchez to leave the province, a requirement for all New Mexican settlers who wished to travel outside the region.

TRANSLATION

Alcalde Ordinario

I, María de Castro,[4] legitimate daughter of Miguel Rodarte[5] and Juana Guerrero,[6] residents of the *reales de minas* of Sombrerete,[7] and a resident of this Villa of Santa Fe, appear before your majesty according to my legal right and in my best and proper form. I say that as a woman, along with my husband, Sergeant Jacinto Sánchez [de Iñigo],[8] who is originally from this kingdom of New Mexico, state that it has been six years that my father Miguel Rodarte passed away. According to his last will and testament, he left for safekeeping a bar of silver of the value of 1,100 pesos in the hands of Gerónimo de Escobar,[9] a native of the Villa of Sombrerete. He was married to Antonia de Castro,[10] my aunt. Being that they have both passed away, the bar of silver is now held by Captain Joseph Durán de la Peña,[11] along with the last will and testament of the same two individuals. He is the executor and keeper of their goods including the bar of silver which is worth 1,100 pesos. This belongs to me since it was left for me by my father, may he be in the glory of God, and which I did not intend to pursue until I got married.

Today, as I have stated above, I find myself married to Sergeant Jacinto Sánchez, and as it being necessary, I give him my full power to collect it. Due to the fact that there is no documentation for this, he is to do everything that he has to do to accomplish this. Because of this I petition of your majesty that he grant me the right to grant it to my husband. As such he, my husband, will have all of the power to accomplish what needs to be done according to what is just, which is what I seek. I swear to the sign of the Cross that this, my petition, is not done in malice, but for what is necessary, etc.

María de Castro (rubric)

Decree

At this Villa of Santa Fe, on the 17th of July, 1697, the above was presented to me by the above stated individual and upon being reviewed by me I took it as it was presented according to every right that I, Captain Diego Arias de Quiros,[12] alcalde ordinario of this said villa have, and as such I grant to [Jacinto Sánchez de Iñigo] the power that the petitioner requests in her petition. So that it is valid, I signed it.

Diego Arias de Quiros (rubric)

TRANSCRIPTION

Señor Alcalde Ordinario

Maria de Castro hija legitima de Miguel Rodarte y Juana Guerrero vezinos del Real y Minas de Sombrerete y residente en esta Villa de Santa Fee en la mejor via y forma que aya lugar en derecho y al mio conbenga ante Vuestra Majestad paresco y digo que como mujer y con junta persona de mi marido el Sargento Jazinto Sanchez originario de este Reino dela Nueba Mexico y haver seis anos que el dicho mi padre Miguel Rodarte murio y dejo en su testamento depositada una barra de platta de un mill y sien pesos en poder de Geronimo de Escobar natural de dicha Villa de Sombrerete y casado con Antonia de Castro mi tia y haviendose muerto los suso dichos para en poder del Capitan Joseph Duran dela Pena los testamentos de los suso dichos como su albasea y tenedor de bienes y tanbien paro en su poder la dicha barra de plata referida de un mil y zien pesos que son mios por havermelos dejado mi padre que sea en gloria con cargo y calidad que no los persibiera hasta ponerme en estado.

Oy como llevo dicho me hallo casada con el dicho Sargento Jazinto Sanchez y por ser presiso de dar mi poder al dicho mi marido para su recaudazion y que por falta de ynstrumento no deje de hazer las deligenzias nesesarias por tanto a Vuestra Majestad pido y suplico de hazerme merzed de que ante Vuestra Majestad pase en poder que le doi al dicho mi marido en que resibire bien y merzed con justizia que pido y juro la Señal de la Santa Cruz esta mi petizion no ser de malicia y en lo nesesario, ut supra =

Maria de Castro (rubric)

Auto

En esta Villa de Santa Fee en dies y siete dias del mes de Julio de mil seisientos y noventa y siete años la presento la contenida y por mi vista la hube por presentada en cuanto a lugar en derecho ante mi el Capitan Diego Arias de Quiros, Alcalde Ordinario de esta dicha Villa y desde luego le doi el poder que la suplicante pide en su petizion y para que conste lo firme.

Diego Arias de Quiros (rubric)

Notes

1. Given that the price of a good horse then ranged from fifteen to twenty pesos, a silver bar worth 1,100 pesos would have been worth the equivalent of fifty-five to seventy horses.
2. See Gerhard, *North Frontier*: 130-32.
3. See SANM II #101; SANM II #160; SANM II #197; SANM II #383a; and Thomas, *Coronado*: 80.

4. María de Castro [Xabalera] came from Sombrerete, the daughter of Miguel de Castro Xabalera (aka Miguel Rodarte) and Juana Guerrero (Herrera). Her family was recruited for the 1695 expedition of Juan Páez Hurtado. She seems to have come with the Bernabé, Catalina, Baltasar, and Cristóbal Rodarte families, some of whom later settled in Santa Cruz. She married Jacinto Sánchez [de Iñigo] in 1696 (see note 8 below). In testimony given in 1713, she calls herself María Rodarte and says she is thirty-six years old, which would make her sixteen years old at the time of this document. (Colligan, *Hurtado*: 33; Kessell, Hendricks, and Dodge, *Royal Crown*: 82n41; Chavez, *Roots*: 299; and Case 6).

5. Miguel Rodarte died in 1691, prior to his family coming to New Mexico. He may have been the second husband of Juana Guerrero (Herrera), or he may have also called himself Miguel de Castro [Xabalera]. (Kessell, Hendricks, and Dodge, *Boulders*: 565n30, 565n33.)

6. Juana Guerrero (Herrera) was the widow of Miguel de Castro [Xabalera]. She was part of the 1695 recruitment for New Mexico settlers; she was listed as being forty years old and a native of Villa de Llerena, Española. She was accompanied by her children, including Bernabé, Catalina, and Baltasar Rodarte, as well as her daughter María de Castro. A man named Cristóbal de Castro, age twenty, is recorded in the marriage records as being the son of Miguel de Castro and Juana Guerrero (Herrera). (Kessell, Hendricks, and Dodge, *Boulders*: 520-22, 565n32-33; Chávez, *Roots*: 299.)

7. The *real de minas* (mining communties) were located in Sombrerete, in the Mexican state of Zacatecas. Villa Llerena was the original name given to the settlement associated with the mines. By the early 1800s the town had a population of 30,000 people and a coin mint. (Gerhard, *North Frontier*: 130-32; and *Wikipedia*, "Villa Llerena" and "Encyclopedia de la Munipias y Delegaciones de Mexico-Estado de Zacatecas," accessed on March 9, 2015.)

8. Jacinto Sánchez [de Iñigo] was a native of New Mexico, born around 1662; he returned to New Mexico in 1693. He married Isabel Telles Girón, and upon her death, he married María (Rodarte) de Castro [Xabalera]. He was part of the muster of refugee colonists in El Paso in 1681, and was a presidio soldier in Santa Fe by 1697, when he was thirty-five years old. In 1703, he applied for a land grant opposite Cochiti Pueblo. By 1713 he was alcalde mayor of Santa Cruz, though for some reason he was not well regarded by Governor Flores Mogollón. Later, he led a small expedition into Moqui country, in 1728, and eventually settled the Río Abajo area of New Mexico. He died in 1734. (Chávez, *Origins*: 280-81; Kessell, Hendricks, and Dodge, *Royal Crown*: 82n41; Kessell, Hendricks, and Dodge, *Boulders*: 565n33; Kessell, Hendricks, Dodge, and Miller, *Disturbances*: 128.)

9. To date, the only information located on Gerónimo de Escobar is what is stated in this document: he was from Sombrerete and was married to Antonia de Castro.

10. Antonia de Castro was the sister of Juana Guerrero (Herrera). Little else is known about her.

11. Joseph Durán de la Peña was the alcalde mayor of Sombrerete in 1693. (Kessell, Hendricks, and Dodge, *Royal Crown*: 355; Case 6.)

12. For information on Diego Arias de Quiros, see Case 1.

3

GOSSIP CREATES DOMESTIC VIOLENCE; JOSEFA SEDAÑO FEARS LOSS OF REPUTATION
August 7–29, 1704, Source: SANM II #102

Synopsis and editor's notes: In 1794, Josefa Sedaño, her husband Nicolás Girón [de Tejeda], and María García traveled to New Mexico with the Farfán Expedition. They almost certainly would have known each other before they arrived. In August 1704, Josefa appeared before the lieutenant governor of New Mexico, Juan Páez Hurtado, petitioning him to act against María García for causing trouble between her and her husband. Josefa stated that he beat her after her close friend, María, claimed that Josefa had entertained men in their home. Josefa said that the accusation was entirely false and that María had made the same accusation against other women. Josefa added that María claimed that her own husband was not at home to help her because he was one of the men being entertained at Josefa's house. Afraid of being killed by her husband, Nicolás Girón, Josefa went to the house of the presidio captain, don Felix Martínez, for protection.

After hearing Josefa's complaint, Lieutenant Governor Páez Hurtado heard the testimony of María García, who said that she did not want to get involved with legal proceedings or to cause a scandal. So, with some reservations, Josefa withdrew her complaint. Páez Hurtado then said that she was free of scandal. He ordered the two women to be friends and stated that they were not to bring the issue before him again, because they would not be heard.

Páez Hurtado had every reason to be touchy about hearing the case. Four months earlier, on April 8, 1704, don Diego de Vargas—governor of New Mexico province and military leader of the 1692 and 1696 Spanish reconquests—died. The colony was left without leadership at a time when famine, sickness, and attacks by hostile Indians seemed likely to make an end of to it. In 1704, the members of the cabildo (the governing body) wrote a desperate letter to the Viceroy of New Spain in which they described their needs and expressed their fear of losing the colony.[1] Although a new governor, Francisco Cuervo y Valdés, had been appointed and assistance was on the way, neither he nor the assistance was in New Mexico when Páez Hurtado was hearing this case.

In this case, as in the first two cases discussed in this book, the full legal proceedings were not followed. No witnesses were called and no procedural comments were made by court officials. This may have been because the case was easily resolved, or perhaps because Juan Páez Hurtado had other matters on his mind.

As in other cases, Josefa's concern was related to the possible loss of her reputation and honor. The words she used to express this are: *credito* (meaning reputation or character), *calumnias* (slanderous words or false charges), *herido discurro* (hurtful words or discussion), *hironear* (offend), and *desonerando* (disgrace). The typical penalty would have been banishment, a common form of punishment in eighteenth-century New Mexico for both men and women, but especially for women. It usually meant sending the guilty party to a respectable home in another place, where the offender would be supervised, taught how to act properly, and, probably, work for the supervisor. The offender was usually banished to a place within the province, although sometimes they were removed to Puebla or even the Philippines.

TRANSLATION

1704
Lieutenant Governor and Captain General

Demand by Josefa [Sedaño][2] given against María [García],[3] wife of Sebastián de Salas[4]

I, Josefa Sedaño, wife of Nicolás Girón [de Tejeda],[5] soldier of this presidio, appear before your majesty[6] in the best form that my legal right allows me. I say that last night, which was the 26th of the present month, being within my own home in the silence of the night there came into the house my husband who said to me, "Do not you know that this is the day that you are to be banished to [Santa Cruz de] La Cañada by the order of your majesty?" Hearing this, I told him that I was not ignoring the order, but that I doubted it was really true because of similar orders.[7] Even if he acted as if he was not concerned, I told him anyway. I told him that the cause of the alleged banishment consisted of the repeated complaints that the wife of Sebastián de Salas gave to your majesty saying that I took the liberty of entertaining others at my home so that her husband could not be of help to her at her home. Upon telling my husband he began to give me a great many blows, and threatened me with being beaten to death. He would have done it if somebody had not passed by and helped me to the house of Captain don Felix Martínez,[8] where I went for fear of my life.

All of this was due to the accusations made by the wife of Sebastián de Salas. Fearing that God and this royal justice will act against my reputation with all of the false charges made against me, notwithstanding the fact that she is my close friend, I say that she does not have a single reason for her hurtful words against me. She has done this against other married women, dishonoring them with her deadly accusations, as all the public well knows. There is hardly anyone in the whole kingdom who is not aware of this.

Thus, this is the complaint, both criminal and civil, that I declare against her, the wife of Sebastián de Salas, and I petition and ask that everything be strongly enforced against her, until I am satisfied that my character has been cleared. All of what I say can be shown by substantial proof that I can provide against the woman so that the proper punishment is given to her. I will provide the needed proof so that I can avoid the immediate danger in which I find myself from my husband who is liable to take my life. I ask that your majesty grant me this favor by making known this complaint through written proceedings. I also ask that, due to all of the false statements that she makes, the person who makes these accusations be required to remain at home in the same way that I am at the present time.⁹

In no manner do I want to permit such a grave accusation be left as it has been in the past by others who have been faced with the same accusation as myself. I am motivated by awareness of the possible scandal and bad acts of the woman. I want to make clear my innocence and lack of guilt. This is so that from now on neither my husband nor anyone else can say that I am dishonored, not now nor at any time This is knowing that the other party has been given notice of all of this, and that the falseness of her damaging complaint is recorded and known by all.

For all of this I petition and ask that your majesty, with all of your greatness, be pleased to rule in my favor for the sake of justice. The above is done under my proper legal right and I swear that it is not done in malice but in what is necessary, etc.

Josefa Sedaño (rubric)

[Response by Captain Juan Páez Hurtado]

Before me, Captain Juan Páez Hurtado, the lieutenant governor and captain general of this kingdom, the above was presented to me by the above. Upon it being seen by me, I took the petition as it was presented according to her legal right, and I ordered that a copy be given to Sebastián de Salas's wife for her to respond to within the time of three days. In the same manner I ordered her not to leave this villa until she gives an answer about the slanderous remarks she made as set forth in the complainant. So that it is valid I signed it along with my secretary of government and war.

Juan Páez Hurtado (rubric)
Lieutenant General

[Response by María García]

I, María García, wife of Sebastián de Salas, soldier of this presidio, appear before your majesty within my proper legal right. I say that having seen, heard and understood the complaint that was given against me as presented by Josefa Sedaño, wife of Nicolás Girón [de Tejeda], and the written proceedings given by your majesty, I herein provide an answer (given at the foot of this document due to the lack of paper)¹⁰ saying that I do not in any way wish to have any legal proceedings with the above-mentioned Josefa Sedaño. This is first of all because she is my close friend, and second, because I wish to end the major scandal caused. For the proof of this, before your honor and through this my written document, I retract everything that I have said and stated against her reputation, with all the strength within my natural power.

Thus I ask pardon with the understanding that with my reply I have the legal right to being the case up in the future if I wish to originate and repeat something else against Josefa. I also wish that this, my response, will serve to give entire satisfaction to Nicolás Girón [de Tejeda], Josefa's husband. This is so that for all time the good reputation of Josefa Sedaño will remain preserved. This is stated with the condition that Nicolás Girón [de Tejeda] has no other reason for protesting against any negative presentation on my part due to the minor assistance of my husband at her home. For all of this I petition and seek that your majesty be well pleased to approve that which he thinks is the most appropriate upon review of my response, and I swear in due form, etc.

    María García (rubric)

[Response by Juan Páez Hurtado]

At this Villa of Santa Fe on the 29th of August, 1704, I, Captain Juan Páez Hurtado, have reviewed María García's response to the complaint given against her presented by Josefa Sedaño. This response she accepts with her entire satisfaction is given, showing that she is content regarding her reputation and she signs it as proof of her response. In attending to this, I say that I will declare and do declare, that Josefa Sedaño is free of the slanderous statements that her comadre, María García, has made. They are to remain on a friendly basis, speaking to each other with all the love of close friends. In addition, I order that they are not to bring up this particular issue [again] because they will not be heard. Also, I order Captain don Felix Martínez to let them know the outcome of these proceedings. He is also to inform Nicolás Girón [de Tejeda] in order that he cannot claim that his wife never informed him. So that it is valid I signed it with my secretary of government and war on this said day.

    Juan Páez Hurtado (rubric)
    Before me
    Alfonso Rael de Aguilar[11] (rubric)
    Secretary of Government and War

TRANSCRIPTION

1704
Villa de Santa Fee
Agosto 27 de 1704
Señor Teniente de Governador y Capitan General
Demanda de Josepha que da por contra Maria mujer de Sebastian de Salas

Josepha Sedaño muger de Nicolas Giron soldado de este Presidio ante Vuestra Magestad paresco en la mejor forma de derecho cual me combenga y digo que ayer noche que se contaron veinte y seis del presente mes estando en mi cassa y en la quietud de ello entro el dicho mi esposo diziendome que si no sabia que salia por oy desterada para La Cañada de orden de Vuestra Magestad aque le respondi que no solamente lo ygnoraba sino es que dudaba cual pudiesse ser la causa de semejante notificazion y aun y se espantaba no sela declarase, a que dijo que la causa hera repetidizimas quexas que la muger de Sebastian de Salas dava a Vuestra Magestad diziendo en ella que de mi casa tomaba la ocassion y divertimiento para no asistir en la suya el dicho su marido y diziendo estas rasones y enpesando a darme muchisimos golpes fue todo uno amenasandome con la muerte que ubiera executado si baliendome de la fuga no ubiese pasado a separarme de la casa del Capitan Dn. Felix Martinez en donde se hallo con manifiesto peligro de la vida.

Ocazionado de la ynpostura de la dicha muger del dicho Sebastian de Salas quien con poco temor de Dios y de la Real Justizia dispone contra mi credito semejante calumnia siendo mis compadres y que con ningun fundamento forma su herrado discurso antes si, a su antojo prebiene las dichas quejas teniendo de costumbre disfamar las mugeres cassadas desonerando con su mordasidad las costumbres de todos como es publico y notorio y que apenas habra una persona en todo el Reyno que caresca desta notizia.

Siendo asi mi querrellos sibil y criminalmente da forma de derecho de dicha muger del suso dicho Sebastian de Salas contra quien pido se prosiga rigorosamente asta darme plena ynformazion de lo con que a mi credito ynpugna pues por lo que ami toca me someto a el castigo que pareciere perteneser a el delito siendo beridica y llena de substancia la ynformasion que puedo yo evadar la dicha muger como siguiendo la pariedad sea en la dicho ejecutado el dicho castigo no probando la calumnia que por lo que mira a el ebidente riesgo en que me hallo de que el dicho mi marido me quita la vida pido a Vuestra Majestad el seguro de ella sirviendose de notificar en su persona auto para dicho efecto y que la dicha muger demandante sea asegurada su persona en casa semejante a la en que yo me hallo en el ynterin que prueba la que con tanta falsedad dipone, pues en ninguna manera quiero permitir quede sin difinir punto de tanta grabedad como lo an dejado otras personas del mesmo estado que yo motibadas del conosimiento del natural escandalozo y mordas dela susa dicha muger y parte contraria tanto para dejar clara mi justizia e ynoziensia cuanto para que en lo adelante ni el dicho mi esposo ni los demas tengan con que hironearme aora ni en tiempo alguno y que del conozimiento de la dicha parte contraria se pase ala realidad de la zertesa y por ella y el conste lo ylexitimo de su quexa tan enperjuicio de mi credito por tanto.

A Vuestra Majestad pido y suplico con todo rendimiento se sirva proveer a mi favor en bista de justizia y yse la dicha que juro en forma de derecho no ser de malicia y en lo nesessario, ut supra.

Josepha Sedaño (rubric)

Ante mi el Capitan Juan Paez Hurtado, Teniente de Governador y Capitan General de este Reyno, la presento la contenida y por mi vista la ube por presentada en quanto a lugar en derecho, y mando, sele de traslado ala muger de Sebastian de Salas, y que responda dentro de tres dias, y asi mismo sele notifique no salga de esta Villa hasta dar satisfazion alas calumnias que dipone contra la quarellante y por que conste la firme con el secretario de governazion y Guerra.

Juan Paez Hurtado (rubric)
Theniente General

Maria Garzia, esposa de Sebastian de Salas, soldado de este Presidio, ante Vuestra Majestad paresco en toda forma de derecho y digo que abiendo visto, oydo y entendido la querella que contra mi da y presento Josepha Sedaño, esposa de Nicolas Giron y el auto de Vuestra Magestad se mi ofrese responder (al pie de ella por causa de no aber papel) que de ninguna manera quiero tener pleyto con la suso dicha Josepha Sedañ, lo uno por ser mi comadre, y lo otro por quitar el mayor escandalo y para prueba de lo dicho ante Vuestra Mersed y por este mi escripto me desdigo de todo quanto ayga hablado y pronunciado contra su credito y llevada de la fuerza de mi natural.

Pido perdon apersibiendo que de esta mi respuesta salga la fuerza y apremio que se me deva aser en caso de querer susistar o reproducir en lo futuro cosa alguna en contra dela susa dicha y quiero que asi mesmo sirva esta mi respuesta de entera satisfazion al dicho Nicolas Giron esposo de la suso dicha para que en todo tiempo quede libre el credito de la dicha Josepha Sedaño protextando el no aber tenido otra causa para mi mala presentacion que la poca asistenzia de mi esposo en su casa y aber tenido la continuazion en la de la suso dicha por todo lo qual a Vuestra Magestad pido y suplico sea servido de proveer lo que estimase por mas conveniente en vista de mi respuesta que juro en forma, ut supra.

Maria Garzia (rubric)

En la Villa de Santa Fee en veinte y nuebe dias del mes de Agosto de mill setecientos y quatro años yo, el Capitan Juan Páez Hurtado, aviendo visto la respuesta dada por Maria Garzia ala querella que contra la suso dicha dio y presento ante mi Josepha Sedaño, y que de ella consta la entera satisfazion que se da para que quede como queda saneado su credito, opinion y firma como consta su respuesta; atento a la qual salbo que devo declarar, como declaro, ala susa dicha Josepha Sedaño por libre de las calumnias que contra ella ubiere publicado la dicha su comadre, Maria Garzia, aquienes se mantengan en buena politica, hablandose con el carino de comadres, y asi mesmo mando alas suso dichas no hablen en este particular, pues no seran oidas; y asi mesmo, ordeno a el Capitan Don Feliz Martinez que les haga notorio este auto y asi pmesmo a Nicolas Giron, para que le conste de la ygnorancia de su esposa, y para que conste lo firme con el secretario de govierno y Guerra en dicho dia =

Juan Paez Hurtado (rubric)
Ante mi

Alphonso Rael de Aguilar (rubric)
Secretario de Governazion y Guerra

Notes

1. See SANM II #114.
2. Josefa Sedaño was born in Querétaro, Mexico, the daughter of Pedro Sedaño and María Correa. She and her husband, Nicolás Girón [de Tejeda], who was from Mexico City, came to New Mexico in 1694 with the Farfán Expedition. In 1722, José de Quintana sold a Santa Fe property "with the consent" of Josefa de Sedaño; that same year, also in Santa Fe, she sold land to Cayetano Lobato and a house to Juan de la Mora Piñeda. (Cháves, *Origins*: 201; SANM I #439; SANM I #508; SANM I #682; Kessell, Hendricks, and Dodge, *Royal Crown*: 324n50; Martinez, "Research Notes": 66-67.
3. The daughter of Nicolás García of Puebla, María García traveled to New Mexico in 1694 with the Farfán Expedition, along with her husband, Sebastián de Salas. At that time, she was twenty-three years of age. (Kessell, Hendricks, and Dodge, *Royal Crown*: 269.)
4. Sebastián de Salas, a native of Seville, was the son of Bernardo de Salas and Josefa de Morales. When Sebastián was twenty-five years old, he came to New Mexico with his wife, María García, on the Farfán Expedition of 1694. Three years later, Salas was a presidio soldier; in 1703, he was the leader of the military squad; and, in 1716, he requested a license from the governor to travel to Nueva Vizscaya. (Chávez, *Origins*: 278; Kessell, Hendricks, Dodge, and Miller, *Disturbances*: 129; Kessell, Hendricks, Dodge, and Miller, *Royal Crown*: 159, 327, n60; SANM II #103.)
5. The son of Tomás de Tejeda and Josefa González de Aragon, Nicolás Girón [de Tejeda] came to New Mexico with his wife, Josefa Sedaño, on the 1694 Farfán Expedition. His parents came from Mexico City and are recorded as living on the street of "rope makers." Both father and son are listed as painters. Nicolás is also listed on the 1704 Santa Fe presidio muster. He participated in the Villasur Expedition of 1720 and is listed among those who died. However, the name "Nicolás Girón" appears as a witness for a baptism in 1733, and it has been suggested that he did return from the expedition and may have been a painter of the Segesser hides. This may be correct, but the sale of property in 1722, as described above, suggests that his wife thought he was dead. (Chávez, "Some Mission Records": 166-67; Kessell, Hendricks, and Dodge, *Royal Crown*: 327; Kessell, Hendricks, and Dodge, *Boulders*: 222; Kessell, Hendricks, and Dodge, *Royal Crown*: 324n50, 330n75.)
6. Juan Páez Hurtado was born in Seville, Spain, in 1663. In 1692, he was in the El Paso presidio as an alférez (ensign) and was *justicia mayor* (local justice) in El Paso in 1693. In 1695, he led a group of settlers to New Mexico. After the death of Governor Vargas in 1704, Páez Hurtado was acting governor until 1705; he served in the same post in 1718 and 1724. He was also lieutenant governor in 1731 and 1736. In 1739, he was the alcalde of Santa Fe. He died on May 5, 1742. (Kessell, Hendricks, and Dodge, *Boulders*: 300, 301n3.)
7. Josefa probably meant that María García, the woman making the accusation against her, had reproached other women for the same thing and these women had not been banished.
8. Felix Martínez [Torrelaguna] was born in Galicia, Spain. He was recruited by Governor don Diego de Vargas to come to New Spain, where he became Vargas's *ayudante* (aide-de-camp) in 1694. Later, Martínez became commander of the El Paso presidio in 1695; captain of the Santa Fe presidio in 1704; and captain-for-life of the Santa Fe presidio (appointed by Viceroy Linares) in 1711. By 1715 he had become the interim governor of the province. Martínez was involved in controversies concerning charges of misuse of government funds and other complaints made by presidio soldiers and his successor Governor Marqués de la Peñuela. The investigations by the viceroy lasted until the mid–1720s. (Chávez, *Origins*: 226; Warner, "Felix Martínez": 31, 45, 56, 61, 90-91.)
9. This language suggests that Josefa had been ordered to stay at home, a kind of "house arrest," and had not been banished outside the community.
10. In the parentheses is a note from the scribe, who tells the reader that María's testimony was placed in small, tightly spaced writing at the bottom of the page (perhaps because he was running out of paper).
11. Alfonso Rael de Aguilar I was a native of Lorca, Spain. By 1692 he was the secretary of government and war and lieutenant-general for Governor Vargas, a position he also held later under Governor Cuervo y Valdés. Rael de Aguilar was also alcalde of Santa Fe; served as legal counsel for the Pueblo Indians; was the *juez commisario* (acting magistrate); and was a sergeant major and then captain of the presidio in Santa Fe. He married Josefa García de Noriega, a daughter of Alfonso García de Noriega and Teresa Barela. He died on April 10, 1735, in Santa Fe and was buried in La Conquistadora Chapel on the Santa Fe Plaza. (Chavez, *Origins*: 263; Kessell and Hendricks, *Force of Arms*: 203n81; Simmons, *Spanish Government*: 86; Cutter, *Protector de Indios*: 47-55.)

4

FAMILY KILLED IN 1696 PUEBLO REVOLT; FEMALE SURVIVORS ASK PERMISSION TO LEAVE THE COLONY
May 25, 1708, Source: SANM II #138

Synopsis and editor's notes: Although the viceroy, the Duke of Albuquerque, sent several missives to New Mexico, they were rarely concerned with individual colonists. However, in 1708, the viceroy belatedly reviewed a petition from two women who had been widowed by the 1696 Pueblo Revolt. They had lost their husbands, as well as children and relatives, and were requesting permission to leave the colony and live in Mexico City. The request had been submitted to the previous viceroy, Condé de Galvé, sometime before 1702, when the Duke of Albuquerque took office. The request appears to have languished for about ten years in Mexico City.

When the viceroy brought the case before his advisory council, he stated that it had already been reviewed by his fiscal officer and others, and he noted the promises made to the colonists and the obligation to remain in the colony after they arrived. In the end, with the support of his advisors, the viceroy granted the two women a license to leave the colony, along with any of their children who were under ten years of age. If they had any boys older than ten, however, they were to remain behind and work at the presidio. The reason given by the viceroy on why he overrode the obligation of the colonists to stay in New Mexico was the sorrowfulness of this particular case.

The original request by the two widows has not been found. Like many of the families in Santa Cruz, they came with the Farfán Expedition in 1694. The two women apparently believed it was their legal right to approach this viceroy with the request to release them from their commitment. Such a request would have taken a certain amount of boldness, desperation, and expense. To date, no record has been found indicating that any members of these two families actually left New Mexico. The case, however, is important, for it is one of the few in which colonists were given permission to permanently leave New Mexico.

TRANSLATION

1708

[Order by the Viceroy]

Don Francisco Fernández de la Cueva,[1] Count of Alburquerque, Marquis of Cuellar, Count of Ledesma and of Huelva, Señor of the Villas of Mimbeltran, La

Codesera, Lanzita Mejores, Pedro Bernardo Aldea Davila, San Esteban Villarejo and of Las Cuevas, Commander of Guadalcanal, a member of the Order of San Fraso and of Ventayan as well as a member of the Order of Alcantara, Gentleman in the Chamber of His Majesty, Viceroy and Lieutenant governor and Captain General of New Mexico and President of the Royal Audience, etc.

Don Juan Fernando de la Cueba y Henriquez, Duque de Alburquerque,
Marquez de Cuellar Condé de Ledesma y de Huelma, Viceroy (1702–1710).
Manuel Rivera, *Los Governantes de Mexico*, 1872:302.

At the general junta,[2] which I called on the 18th of the past month of this year, I saw the petition which was presented by María[3] and Teresa Gómez de Rivera,[4] widows, and former wives of Juan Cortés[5] and of Juan de Atienza,[6] at the time when his most excellent señor, Condé de Galve,[7] was governor of this New Spain. After the families had settled in the provinces of New Mexico,[8] the husbands and the number of children that they had were killed by the Indians of the area who inhumanly tore to pieces Juan Cortés and Juan de Atienza along with two sons and a nephew of María Gómez, leaving them in a blood bath. They also took with them another son that belonged to Teresa.

Don Gaspar de la Serda, Condé de Galvé, Viceroy (1688–1696).
Manuel Rivera, *Los Governantes de Mexico*, 1872: 264.

Due to all of this and all of the sorrow and hurt with which they were left and also due to the extreme poverty and remoteness of the desolate lands, they concluded that they would petition me to grant them, the widows along with the children that both of them have, a license allowing them to come to live in [Mexico City]. In addition to reviewing the petition, I have reviewed the certification of the lieutenant of the secretary of the chamber, noting the obligation that these families made in coming to New Mexico.[9] I have also reviewed the response of the fiscal officer to his majesty, dated the 17th of December of the past year, noting my compliance with the determination of the junta [in allowing them to return to Mexico City].

For the present, I order the Marqués de la Peñuela, governor and captain general of these provinces of New Mexico, that upon being ascertained of the sorrowfulness of the case referred to, allow María and Teresa Gómez, along with children that they have who are less than ten years of age, to leave the area. Any of the sons that they have who are over the age of ten are to be given a job within the presidio where they can serve his majesty and sustain themselves. Mexico, May 25th, 1708.

Duke of Albuquerque (rubric)
At the order of the Duke
Juan Antonio de Morales[10] (rubric)

This is done so that the governor and captain general of the provinces of New Mexico, upon being certain of what is contained in this dispatch, will allow María and Teresa Gómez, along with the children that they have, to leave those provinces, as is stated above.

TRANSCRIPTION

1708

Dn. Francisco Fernandez de la Cueba Enriques, Duque de Alburquerque, Marques de Cuellar, Conde de Ledesma y de Huelva, Señor de las Villas de Mimbeltran, La Codosera, Lanzaita Mejores, Pedro Bernardo Aldea Davila, San Esteban Villarejo y Las Cuebas, Comendador de Guadelcanal, en el Orden de San Fraso y de Bentayan en el de Alcantara, gentile hombre de la Camara de Su Magestad, Su Virrey, y lugar Theniente Governador y Capitan General de esta Nueva España y Presidente de la Real Audienzia de ella, ut supra.

Haviendo visto en la junta general que mande formar en diez y ocho del mes proximo pasado de este año la pretension de Maria y Teresa Gomez de Rivera, viudas, mugeres que fueron de Juan Cortes y Juan de Atienza, que governando esta Nueba Espana el Excellentisimo Señor Conde de Galve, pasaron con las familias pobladoras alas provincias dela Nueba Mexico con dichos sus maridos llevando con sigo copia de hijos que tenian; y haviendo los Yndios de aquella comarca despadazado y muerto inhumanamente a los dichos Juan Cortes y Juan de Atienzia y juntamente a dos hijos y un yerno de la dicha Maria Gomez y desparesiendo otro a la dicha Theresa.

Quedaron los referidos a vista de tan sangriento caso, con que el dolor y sentimiento que pedio que con la suma pobreza y desamparon que tienen en tan remotos y delatadas tierras, concluyendo en suplicarme les consediese lisensia a dichas viudas para que con los hijos que una y otra tienen y les hubieren quedado pasen a vivir a esta cuidad y vistose alo mismo la certificasion del theniente de escribano de camara para saver la obligasion con que estas familias pasaron y lo que el Señor Fiscal de Su Magestad dixo en su respuesta de diez y siete de Diciembre del año pasado conformandome con lo resuelto en dicha junta.

Por el presente ordeno al Marques de la Peñuela, Governador y Capitan General de dichas Provincias del Nuebo Mexico que constandole ser zierto el lastimoso caso que se refiere deje salir de dichas Provincias a las dichas Maria y Theresa Gomez con los hijos que tubieren, no pasando de diez años, y que pasando de esta edad los hijos, procure darles plasas en aquel Presidio donde se mantengan y sirvan a Su Magestad. Mexico y Maio veinte y sinco de mil setezientos y ocho años.

Duque de Alburquerque (rubric)

Por mando del Duque
Juan Antonio de Morales (rubric)

~

Para que el Governador y Capitan General de las Provincias de la Nueva Mexico siendo sierto lo que expresa este despacho deje salir de aquellas Provincias a Maria y Theresa Gomez con los hijos que tubieren en la forma que se expresa.

Notes

1. The Duke of Albuquerque was the Viceroy of New Spain from 1702 to 1711. He was the 10th Duke of Albuquerque; the 8th Duke of Albuquerque was also a viceroy of New Spain.
2. To date, no record has been found of this April 18, 1708, general junta. It may be similar in composition to a 1693 general junta of Condé de Galve that included judges of the royal *audiencia* or high court, alcaldes of the royal criminal chamber of the court, comptrollers of the royal tribunal of accounts, officials of the royal treasury of that tribunal, and the comptroller general of tributes. (Kessell, Hendricks, and Dodge, *Royal Crown*: 226-7.)
3. María Gómez de Rivera was born around 1663 in Puebla. She was the wife of the deceased Juan Cortés and daughter of Juan de Rivera from Los Angeles in New Spain. In the livestock distribution document of 1697, María is noted as a widow with four children. (Chávez, *Origins*: 166; Kessell, Hendricks, and Dodge, *Royal Crown*: 337n117, 339n125; Kessell, Hendricks, and Dodge, *Boulders*: 729.1646.)
4. Teresa Gómez de Rivera was the wife of Juan Fernández de Atienza [Ladron de Guevara] and the daughter of Martín and María de Rivera from Puebla. (Kessell, Hendricks, and Dodge, *Royal Crown*: 323n47.)
5. Juan Cortés, the husband of Maria Gómez de Rivera, was the son of don Fernando Cortés of San Lorenzo in Mexico City. Juan is listed as a cobbler; he and his family came with the Farfán Expedition of 1694 and were original settlers of Santa Cruz. Juan was killed at Nambé during the Pueblo Revolt of 1696, along with his daughter, Josefa, and her husband, José Sánchez. (Kessell, Hendricks, and Dodge, *Royal Crown*: 339n125; Chávez, *Origins*: 166.)
6. Juan [Fernández] de Atienza [Ladron de Guerrera] was the son of Juan Fernández de Avila and Josefa Ladron de Guerrera of Puebla. Known as a maker of filigree, he was the husband of Teresa de Rivera; both of them came to New Mexico with the Farfan Expedition in 1694. He was one of the early settlers of Santa Cruz and still alive in 1695. His wife, Teresa, is listed as living alone with her children in 1697. To date, no record has been found indicating that he was killed in the Pueblo Revolt of 1696, as his wife claims. However, relevant documents state that thirty Spanish people were killed by the Indians during the revolt, without naming them all. He may have been a presidio soldier who was killed in action. (Kessell, Hendricks, and Dodge, *Royal Crown*: 323n47; Kessell, Hendricks, and Dodge, *Boulders*: 644, 1153; Espinosa, *Pueblo Revolt*: 243-45, 261-64.)
7. Condé de Galve was Viceroy of New Spain from 1688 to1696; at that time New Spain included Spanish colonies from Cuba to Mexico to the Philippines. He took action against English pirates and pirates from other countries operating off Acapulco and in the Caribbean, and the French in New Mexico and Coahuila. He was an influential patron of don Diego de Vargas. (Kessell and Hendricks, *Force of Arms*: 33-36; *Wikipedia*, accessed on December 24, 2015; Kagan, *Urban Images*: 160-63.)
8. These people came to New Mexico with the Farfán Expedition of 1694.
9. The decree made by Viceroy Condé de Galve, on April 11, 1693, provided money, sustenance, and transportation for each family, as well as livestock. The decree further stated, "Until they are able to plant and harvest crops for their sustenance in the places they will settle, the governor will aid them, providing everything. They will be made and granted all honors, privileges and favors. Land and sufficient water will be distributed to them." This decree was then certified by the royal and judicial notary. (Kessell, Hendricks, and Dodge, *Royal Crown*: 228-29.)
10. Juan Antonio de Morales appears to have been part of the Duke of Albuquerque's staff, though no information on him has yet been found.

5

SOLDIER AGUSTÍN DE LA PALMA ACCUSED OF RAPE; TAKES SANCTUARY IN THE PARROQUIA
August 11–26, 1711, Source: SANM II #167

Synopsis and editor's notes: In August 1711, Petrona de Carvajal filed a civil and criminal complaint against Agustín Palma before Governor Flores Mogollon. In the complaint, she stated that Palma had raped her ten-year-old daughter, Antonia de Valencia. Petrona said this happened because she was not home, having been banished by the governor. No information was given concerning the reason she was banished or where she was sent. Petrona went on to say that she had left her daughter with another woman, as the governor had suggested, but Palma had forced the woman out of Petrona's house and then raped her daughter. She asked that the governor arrest him and place him in jail.

The alcalde ordinario, Alfonso Rael de Aguilar, ordered that Agustín Palma be imprisoned in the presidio guardhouse with leg irons. However, before the corporal of the guardhouse, Gregorio Ramírez, could do this, Palma took sanctuary in the parish church. Rael de Aguilar then began the investigation by interviewing Antonia. She stated that she was thirteen years old and had been with Palma the previous year when her mother was gone. Agustín Palma, a presidio soldier assigned to Pecos, would bring her and her mother food when he returned. The alcalde then heard the testimony of Palma, who said he had been Petrona's lover and did bring food for the family, but he denied the rape charge. He added that Petrona was just jealous of her daughter. Then José Matheo, a church cantor, testified that Petrona was withdrawing her complaint, but this apparently was not the case and the trial continued.

Palma was given a legal representative, Juan Manuel de Chirinos, who redirected the charge against Palma. He claimed the following: the case should not be heard because it was submitted too late; Petrona filed a charge that was false and due to jealously; and Palma was "lacking any sense," was demented, and not responsible for his actions. Testimony was given by a fellow soldier who stated that it was known throughout the kingdom that Palma was lacking any sense.

The document ends with the legal representative's testimony, with the final pages missing, and the outcome of the investigation unknown. It is known, however, that a person named "Agustín Palma," with the aliases of "Agustín del Rio" and "Toribio," was in New Mexico in 1716, because of a bigamy charge against him. Petrona was not named in the latter as one of Palma's wives.

Little is known about Petrona Carvajal or how she got to New Mexico. She may have found herself in Santa Fe without financial support, perhaps because of abandonment by or death of a husband or family members. With few opportunies available to provide for herself, she may have then looked for help wherever she could find it. In violation of the law (or local morality), she may have found herself giving sexual favors for companionship and in exchange for food. We do not know what happened to her after this court case.

This is one of the few rape cases found in early eighteenth-century New Mexico documents. One other case occurred in 1750, when Margarita García Jurado claimed she was raped, but upon hearing testimony the court acquitted the defendant.[1] As stated in the introduction, the sentence for a convicted rapist was sometimes death, though usually only when the woman raped was a virgin and of high rank. The more common sentence was making the defendant marry the victim, or if that was not possible, provide compensation in the form of a dowry, which enabled her to marry someone else. If she was impoverished, Petrona may have considered the possibility of a dowry for her daughter when bringing the complaint against Palma.

TRANSLATION

Governor and Captain General

[Statement of Petrona de Carvajal]

I, Petrona de Carvajal,[2] resident of this Villa of Santa Fe appear before your honor in my best and proper form in which I find myself according to my right and say that your honor, in the past year, notified me that I had been banished from this villa. But before obeying the order, I came in front of your honor and requested him to care for a young girl [Antonia de Valencia] of the age of ten years whom I would leave behind in the hardships of this world. His honor, with respect to this, nevertheless ordered me to leave, but to leave the girl with some respectable woman.

At the time that I was about to leave, I left the young girl at my home in the care of the wife of Juan de Guido.[3] She was accompanied for a few days by Agustín Palma[4] who without any fear of God, Our Lord, or of the royal justice and incited by the demon, or by his own bad nature (which is most likely the case) instigated a fight with the wife of Juan de Guido, [Isabel de los Reyes Cruz], and forced her out of the home. After this, he found himself alone in the house with my daughter. He then proceeded to tie her hands with a lace[5] and forced himself upon her and had sex with her, telling her that if she said anything he would kill her. All this happened after he had had illicit sex with me, and even though he had fulfilled his sexual appetite with her a few days before. After this occurred, I found out that this was a huge capital offense[6] for which I could possibly be punished for incest and for which he could be punished severely. For all of this I filed a civil and criminal complaint against him. For these circumstances I expect that, because of your honor's piety and Christian zeal, you will take action against him and place him in jail for a lengthy period of time. This is in order to secure his person so that he does not escape and I lose all of the rights that I have as a poor and disabled woman.

All of this I expect to receive from your honor, who I hope will continue the case until it becomes concluded and the said aggressor is punished to the utmost for such a grave crime and for anything else that I can argue. Of your honor I ask and petition in the most humble manner to grant me justice in the manner that I seek, and for that which your honor sees as the most appropriate. I swear to God, Our Lord, and to the Holy Cross that this royal service is not to be done in malice but in what is necessary, etc.

    Petrona de Carvajal (rubric)

Presentation

At this Villa of Santa Fe, headquarters of this kingdom and province of New Mexico, on the 11th day of the month of August, 1711, before me, the admiral don Joseph Chacon Medina Salazar y Villaseñor, knight in the Order of Santiago, Marqués de la Peñuela,[7] governor and captain general of this kingdom and of its provinces and castellan of his forces for his majesty, I took it as it was presented according to its right and reviewed it. In attention to what it represented, and I ordered and did order that these proceedings be turned over to Captain don Alfonso Rael de Aguilar,[8] alcalde ordinario of this villa, so that according to his knowledge he will proceed with it. So that it is valid I approved, ordered and signed it along with me the secretary of government and war, on the said day.

    Marqués de la Peñuela (rubric)
    Before me
    Juan de Ulibarri[9] (rubric)
    Secretary of Government and War

[Remission to Alcalde Ordinario Rael de Aguilar]

One more thing, I, the Marqués, governor and captain general, ordered and do order that the captain don Alfonso Rael de Aguilar, alcalde ordinario of this villa, proceed with all of his authority with the *summaria*[10] regarding the proceedings that were committed giving him full authority and all of my authority so that he will make them final and issue a sentence according to the findings and formalities of the proceedings. So that it is valid I approved and rubricated this before my secretary.

    Peñuela (rubric)
    Ulibarrí (rubric)
    Secretary

Proceedings

In the Villa of Santa Fe on the 12th of August, 1711, I, Captain don Alfonso Rael de Aguilar, alcalde ordinario of this villa, have seen the above proceedings approved by the Marqués de la Peñuela, knight of the Order of Santiago,[11] governor and captain general of this kingdom and provinces of New Mexico and castellan of the forces and presidios for his majesty. Being that he was pleased to commit me to proceed with the review of this case. So as to proceed with it, I mandate and did mandate that an order be issued for the imprisonment of Agustín Palma and that he be brought forth and be placed in protective custody with a pair of shackles at the guardhouse of the royal presidio. So that it is valid I thus approved, ordered and signed it along with the scribe for the cabildo.

 Alfonso Rael de Aguilar (rubric)
 before me
 Cristóbal de Góngora[12] (rubric)
 Scribe for the cabildo

[Indictment and imprisonment]
 Captain don Alfonso Rael de Aguilar, alcalde ordinario of this Villa of Santa Fe, headquarters of the kingdom and provinces of New Mexico for his majesty, etc.

 For now, I order and mandate that the alguacil Miguel Moran, upon seeing this mandate, is to place Agustín Palma into custody and under protection with a pair of shackles in the guardhouse of this royal presidio. So this order is carried out I gave it to the corporal of the guardhouse, Gregorio Ramírez,[13] providing him with the authority in every way for the execution of such, being that he, Agustín Palma, is a soldier of this presidio. He [Ramírez] is given this order because he is aware of the proceedings of this case, and because I have been given full authority by the Marqués de la Peñuela, governor and captain general. I sign this as has been authorized and approved by the order provided and approved on the 11th of the present month of August. So that it is valid, I signed it along with the scribe of the cabildo on this the 12th day of August, 1711.

 Before me
 Cristóbal de Góngora (rubric)
 Scribe for the Cabildo

[Arrest]
 I, Miguel Moran,[14] the first alguacil, in compliance and in obedience to the above mandate of the alcalde ordinario, don Alfonso Rael de Aguilar, came to the guardhouse of this royal presidio which is under the care of Gregorio Ramírez. There, I made known to him this order and upon he having seen it and understanding it, he stated that no one needed to look for Agustín Palma because he had taken refuge[15] in the parish church of this villa. So that it was understood I requested that the scribe, Cristóbal de Góngora, be made aware of this, being that he was present at this time at the guardhouse.

I, Cristóbal de Góngora, scribe for the cabildo, certify in every way that I can and under my proper right, note that this was certain and true as expressed above, and so that it is valid I signed it at this guardhouse of the royal presidio on the 12th of the month of August, 1711.

 Cristóbal de Góngora (rubric)
 Scribe for the Cabildo

Proceedings

 At this Villa of Santa Fe on the 13th of August, 1711, I, Captain Alfonso Rael de Aguilar, alcalde ordinario of this said villa, have seen the response given by the corporal of the guardhouse, Gregorio Ramírez to the order given to him by the alguacil, Miguel Moran, in which he states that the criminal Agustín Palma has found refuge in the Holy Church of this villa. In order to find out if this was true and to see if he was there, I ordered that the Holy Church and the *convento*[16] be searched to find out if the accused was indeed there. To do this permission had to be requested from the Reverend Father Guardian Fray José López Tello,[17] informing him of the order made by his majesty and given to me asking that every effort be given to searching the convento and the Holy Church, and safeguarding the laws and privileges [of sanctuary] that are known, without breaking the laws. So that this is known, I approved, ordered, and signed it along with the assisting scribe for the cabildo.

 Alfonso Rael de Aguilar (rubric)
 Before me
 Cristóbal de Góngora (rubric)
 Scribe for the cabildo

Proceedings of the search

 Continuing, on the said day, month and year, I, Captain Alfonso Rael de Aguilar, alcalde ordinario, in order to carry out these mandates went in the company of the scribe for the cabildo to the convento of Nuestra Padre San Francisco within this villa. There I requested the necessary permission from the Reverend Father Fray José López Tello, guardian of convento, in order to enter and ascertain that which was requested in the above order. Permission was granted by the Reverend, and I proceeded to enter the cloister[18] where I saw that Agustín Palma was being held and in refuge within its sacred part.[19] Knowing that this was certain, I returned and proceeded to continue with the rest of the proceedings that is allowed to me by law. So that it ascertained, I signed it in the presence of the scribe for the cabildo.

 Alfonso Rael de Aguilar (rubric)
 Before me
 Cristóbal de Góngora (rubric)
 Scribe for the cabildo

Proceedings

At the Villa of Santa Fe on the said day, month and year, I, the alcalde ordinario, in order to proceed with the case according to my legal right, I ordered and did order that the complainant Petrona de Carvajal appear before me along with her daughter in order to receive their statement. So that it is valid, I approved, ordered and signed it along with the scribe for the cabildo.

Alfonso Rael de Aguilar (rubric)
Before me
Cristóbal de Góngora (rubric)
Scribe for the cabildo

Declaration of Antonia de Valencia[20]

At this Villa of Santa Fe on the 14th of August, 1711, I, the alcalde ordinario, by virtue of the above proceedings, ordered to appear before me Antonia de Valencia, daughter of Petrona de Carvajal, the complainant. Being present I took her sworn statement, which she made to God, Our Lord and to the sign of the Cross, under her proper right and in which she promised to tell the truth about everything that she knew and what she was asked.

She was asked if she knew Agustín Palma. She stated that she did know him.

She was asked what the reason was that she knew Agustín Palma and for how long. She stated that she has known him for two years.

She was asked if she knew if Agustín Palma had an illicit love affair with her mother, Petrona de Carvajal. She stated that what she knew was that for two years Agustín Palma had an illicit love affair with her mother, Petrona de Carvajal, as she had seen them sleep together. This was her response.

She was asked if Agustín Palma had on any occasion copulated with the said witness. She stated that it has been about one year since her mother had gone to Bernalillo. Agustín Palma had stayed at her home together with this witness and the wife of Juan de Guido, and that on a certain occasion he tied up her arms with a lace [or cord] and covered her mouth so that she would not yell and he took her and ruined her. This was her response.

She was asked for what period in time she had sex with Agustín Palma. She stated that since the time of winter until the time for planting corn. Although he, Agustín Palma, would leave for Pecos, when he returned to this villa he would summon her through the servants of Sebastián González[21] and through the nephew of Juana Domínguez.[22] He would sleep with this witness, copulating with her. Every time Agustín Palma came to see her he would bring her piñole, flour and meat and that they then would all eat together. This was her response.

She stated that everything she has said is the truth according to the sworn statement she has made and that she affirmed and ratified[23] it upon it being read back to her and that she does not have anything to add or delete. She said that she was of the age of thirteen, and so that it is valid, I, the alcalde ordinario signed it along with the present scribe of the cabildo.

 Alfonso Rael de Aguilar (rubric)
 Before me
 Cristóbal de Góngora
 Scribe for the cabildo

Statement of Petrona de Carvajal

 Continuing, I, the alcalde ordinario, in order to proceed with the prosecution of this case, and for further justification of the case made to appear before me Petrona de Carvajal, the complainant. Being present before me, I took her sworn statement which she made to God, Our Lord, and to the sign of the Cross according to her right and under which she promised to tell the truth about everything that she knew and what she was asked.

 She was asked how long it had been since she had had illicit sex with Agustín Palma. She stated that it was for about two years, more or less, this was her answer.

 She was asked when it was that Agustín Palma ruined her daughter. She stated that she does not know when, what she does know is that Agustín Palma told her that he had ruined her, but not to be concerned, that he had done it when she had gone to Bernalillo, and this was her answer.

 She was asked how many times she had copulated with Agustín Palma after she found out that he had ruined her daughter. She stated that she had copulated with Agustín Palma four times, although she does not remember for certain, this was her answer.

 She was asked where and when she found out that her daughter was no longer a virgin. She said that her comadre, Ana María [Almazán],[24] had told her in front of Palma.

 She was asked, after having been told this and being assured of it by Ana María, why she had then committed such a stupid mistake of incest. She stated that because Ana María had told her that they would for certain take her testimony.[25] She said that everything that she has stated is the truth according to the sworn statement she has made and she affirmed and ratified it, saying that she was thirty-six years of age, and did not sign because she did not know how; I, the alcalde ordinario, signed it along with the scribe for the cabildo.

 Alfonso Rael de Aguilar (rubric)
 Before me
 Cristóbal de Góngora (rubric)
 Scribe for the cabildo

Proceedings

At the Villa of Santa Fe on the 14th of August, 1711, I, Captain don Alfonso Rael de Aguilar, alcalde ordinario of this villa, have seen the preceding statements made by Petrona de Carvajal, complainant, and by Antonia de Valencia. According to what they say, I say that the charges are legitimate and that wrongdoing appears to have been committed by Agustín Palma, offender in this case and now under refuge in the Holy Church and convento of this villa. In order to continue in the proper form and according to their rights, I order that the confession of Agustín Palma be taken. However, before this can be done, permission has to be requested and given by the Reverend Father Fray José López Tello, minister and priest of this Holy Parish to his majesty to have him released and freed from the convento and Holy Church so that the above can be accomplished. I thus approved, ordered and signed it along with the scribe for the cabildo.

Alfonso Rael de Aguilar (rubric)
Before me
Cristóbal de Góngora (rubric)
Scribe for the cabildo

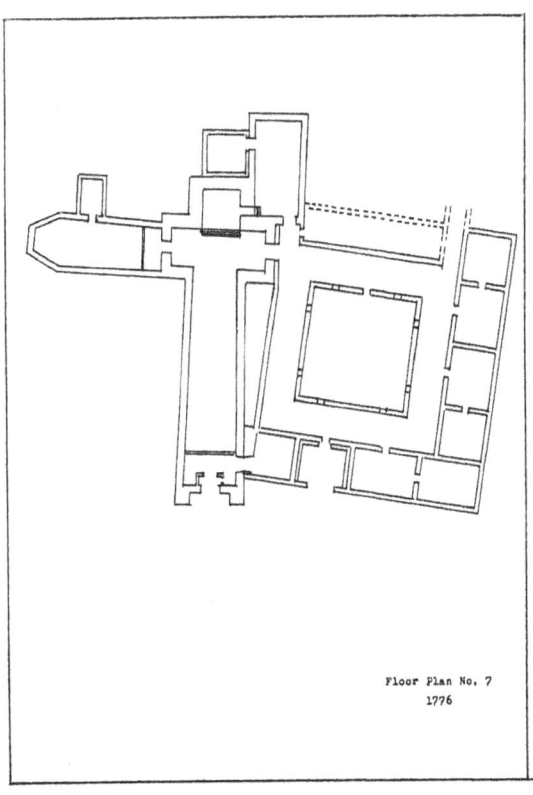

Santa Fe Parroquia and Convento in 1776, based on Domínguez Report of that year. Bruce Ellis, *Bishop Lamy's Santa Fe Cathedral*. 1985:119. Courtesy of the Historical Society of New Mexico and the University of New Mexico Press.

Confession[26] of Agustín Palma, offender

At the Villa of Santa Fe on the 15th of August, 1711, I, Captain don Alfonso Rael de Aguilar, alcalde ordinario of this villa by virtue and in compliance with the above decree, went to the convento of the villa accompanied by the present scribe. There I found the Reverend Father *Predicador*[27] fray José López Tello, curate and minister of the parish of the villa, from whom I requested, in the name of His Majesty to freely give me access to the convento and Holy Church. This is so that I could freely proceed with finding the facts for the said proceedings, always safeguarding the great immunities and privileges of the church, which as alcalde ordinario, I said I would safeguard. Proceeding to the cloister I found within a cell a certain person, from whom I asked for his name, age and what his occupation was, his status, rank and from what place he was a native. This was only after he took a sworn oath, which he made to God, Our Lord and to the sign of the Cross, could he answer, promising to tell the truth about everything that he knew and what he was asked. He then stated that his name was Agustín Palma, that he was forty years of age and that he is a soldier in the royal presidio and castle of this villa, also saying that he is married, Spanish, and that he is a native of this kingdom. This was everything that he stated.

He was asked what reasons he has, and has had, for his having come to seek refuge within this Holy Church and convento. He stated that it was because they wanted to place him in shackles, and not wanting to experience the rigors of justice he had come to stay within this Holy Church. This was his answer.

He was asked why it was that they wanted to place him in shackles. He stated that he had found out that a petition had been presented against him. This was his answer.

He was asked the name of the person who had presented a petition against him was. He stated that it was Petrona de Carvajal, and this was his answer.

He was asked the reason that Petrona de Carvajal had presented such a petition. He stated that he was at the pueblo of Pecos and then came to this villa with the Reverend Father fray Diego Padilla,[28] minister of the pueblo. While he was staying at the home of Petrona for two or three days, she became jealous of her daughter, and it was over this matter that they argued. He told her that she should have a clear conscience, that he did not have any fault in what she was accusing him of, saying that he was not the reason her daughter was no longer a virgin, and that she should not believe anyone. He told her that he was going to return to the pueblo of Pecos, asking her that for the love of God, she should consult with women who were skilled midwives to clear up the issue of whether her daughter was a virgin or not. He stated that he would pay for someone to inspect her, and that he was willing to pay, but that he was leaving for the pueblo of Pecos the following day.

On his return to this villa at a later date from the pueblo of Pecos, he inquired as to whether what he had requested had been done. She answered him, saying that nothing had been done. He then stayed at her home for a number of days, and they once more became argumentative over the same jealousies. Upon his becoming very angry, he then asked her what the problem was, her insisting that he had slept with the daughter and had forced himself upon her. But it was not as she said. He continued saying to her that he had not committed such an offense towards God, and he swore saying it and swearing it for one thousand million times so that he could prove it to her all of this he stated.

He was then asked for how long he had an illicit affair with Petrona de Carvajal. He stated that it lasted for one year, which is what he gave as his answer.

He was then asked to tell the truth and not to deny anything and was asked how many times he copulated with Antonia de Valencia, daughter of Petrona Carvajal. It was understood from the proceedings that he had forced himself upon her, tying up her arms. He stated that this was false, and that they needed to prove it, and that was his answer.

He was then asked if it was true that when he would come from the pueblo of Pecos to this villa he would stop at the home of Sebastián González and would summon Antonia de Valencia, and would then sleep with her having sex with her, and after that he would give her piñole, flour and meat for her to take home. He stated that it was true, that he would have someone summon her and that he would then give her the food to take to her mother, but that everything else that he is asked is false and outrageous and should not be considered, this was his answer.

Although he was asked over and over again the same questions regarding the case, he stated that he had already stated the truth regarding his sworn statement and which he affirmed and ratified upon his confession being read back to him, he said that he did not have anything else to add or delete. He did not sign because he did not know how. I, the alcalde ordinario, and the scribe for the cabildo signed it.

Alfonso Rael de Aguilar (rubric)
Before me
Cristóbal de Góngora (rubric)
Scribe for the cabildo

Statement of José Matheo[29]

At the Villa of Santa Fe on the 16th of August, 1711, I, the alcalde ordinario, state that José Matheo, cantor[30] for the church, appeared before me and the current scribe for the cabildo. He said under oath, which he made to God, Our Lord, and to the Holy Cross, that Agustín Palma had told him that he was very happy because Petrona de Carvajal, the complainant, was once again content with him. This was because at night he [Palma] would leave from the church and sleep with her at her home. Palma told him that she complained about him because her comadre, Ana María, the daughter of Monsonga,[31] had counseled her and had in some way induced her to present a complaint against Agustín Palma. Nevertheless, she was now happy and willing to withdraw her complaint with the understanding that he would sustain them in the same way that he had done before. This witness told [Palma] that he was very happy for him. He, Matheo, then stated that this was what had happened and that it was the truth regarding the sworn statement that he has made, which he affirmed and ratified.

Upon it being read back to him he stated that he did not have anything to add or delete and he is of the age of forty years. He did not sign because he did not know how. I, the Alcalde Ordinario, and the present scribe signed it.

 Alfonso Rael de Aguilar (rubric)
 Before me
 Cristóbal de Góngora (rubric)
 Scribe for the cabildo

Statement of Ana María de Almazán

 At this Villa of Santa Fe on the said day, month and year, I, the alcalde ordinario, upon having seen the above statement and denouncement made by José Matheo, and for further justification of the case, made to appear before me, Ana María de Almazán, resident of this villa. Upon being present I received her sworn statement which she made to God, Our Lord, and to the sign of the Cross, according to her right, and promised to tell the truth about what she knew and what she was asked.

 She was asked if she knew Agustín Palma, Petrona de Carvajal and her daughter, Antonia de Valenzia. She stated that she did know them and this was her answer.

 She was asked if she knows that Agustín Palma had an illicit relation with Petrona de Carvajal, and for how long. She stated that she had not seen them, but what she knows, because it is publically known, is that they were *amancebados*.[32] This was her answer.

 She was asked if she knew that Agustín Palma had ruined Antonia de Valencia. She stated that she knows it, because the wife of Juan Antonio Barrios[33] told her. This was her answer.

 She was asked if she induced Petrona de Carvajal to file a complaint against Agustín Palma. She said that she did not, and that this was the truth of the sworn statement that she has made. This she affirmed and ratified upon her statement being read back to her, and she stated that she does not have anything to add or delete. She gave her age as thirty, and did not sign because she did not know how. I, the alcalde ordinario, along with the scribe for the cabildo signed it.

 Alfonso Rael de Aguilar (rubric)
 Before me
 Cristóbal de Góngora (rubric)
 Scribe for the cabildo

Presentation by Gregorio Ramírez

 At this Villa of Santa Fe on the 20th of August, 1711, there appeared before me, the alcalde ordinario, Gregorio Ramírez, the corporal of the squadron of the guard for this royal presidio, and informed me that the accused Agustín Palma had left the Holy Church and presented himself at the guardhouse. Then I, the alcalde ordinario, gave the order to the corporal of the squadron to hold him prisoner under watchful guard and with a pair of shackles. So that it is valid I signed it along with the scribe for the cabildo, whom I ordered to ascertain that Agustín Palma was found in the guardhouse and to document it within these proceedings.

    Alfonso Rael de Aguilar (rubric)
    Before me
    Cristóbal de Góngora (rubric)
    Scribe for the cabildo

Certification of the imprisonment

    Continuing, I, Cristóbal de Góngora, scribe for the cabildo, in compliance with the order above given by the alcalde ordinario, I proceeded to go to the guardhouse of this presidial castle of the Villa of Santa Fe and within it I found Agustín Palma, who at the time was actually being placed into a pair of shackles and which were then and there being riveted.[34] This I certify and sign on the said day.

    Cristóbal de Góngora (rubric)

Proceedings

    At the Villa of Santa Fe, on the 21st day August, 1711, I, Captain don Alfonso Rael de Aguilar, alcalde ordinario of this villa, having seen the certification given by the present scribe, where he states that he had seen Agustín Palma within the guardhouse, as a prisoner and accused in this case, and for the best justification of it, I ordered and do order that his confession be retaken. And so that it is valid, I signed it along with the current scribe of the cabildo.

    Alfonso Rael de Aguilar (rubric)
    Before me
    Crisóbal de Góngora (rubric)
    Scribe for the cabildo

[Second confession by Agustín Palma]

    At this Villa of Santa Fe on the 21st of August, 1711, I, Captain don Alfonso Rael de Aguilar, alcalde ordinario of this villa, by virtue of the decree approved yesterday, the 20th of the present month, went to the guardhouse in the company of the present scribe. There I found a certain man who is being held prisoner for a certain case and from whom I took his sworn statement which he made to God, Our Lord, and to the sign of the Cross according to his right and under which he promised to tell the truth as to everything that he knew and was asked.

    He was asked to give his name, his age and his occupation, where he was a native of, and what his status was. He said that his name was Agustín Palma, and that he has already given all of this information in his prior confession and statement that he has made and which was taken when he was first brought forth. He also stated that all of this was also done when he was taken from the convento, and that it included his age, status and his occupation. All of this is what he gave as his response.

He was asked if he knew the reason for his imprisonment. He stated that he has already gone through all of this in his prior confession that he made before the alcalde, and which is the reason for his being imprisoned. All of this he ratified once, twice and three times, saying that it was the truth according to the statement he has made. He did not sign because he did not know how. I, alcalde ordinario, signed it in the presence of the scribe for the cabildo.

 Alfonso Rael de Aguilar (rubric)
 before me
 Cristóbal de Góngora
 Scribe for the cabildo

[Legal Representative]

At the Villa of Santa Fe on the 23rd of August, 1711, I, Captain don Alfonso Rael de Aguilar, the judge in this cause, have seen these proceedings and statements which have been made against Agustín Palma, prisoner in this case. In order to receive it as proven and to either prove or disprove that which is contained herein according to these findings, I ordered the scribe for the cabildo to notify some person to act as procurador [legal representative]. This is so this person, on the offender's behalf, will appear before me and will be given copies of the proceedings. He will thus respond to them within the period of three days, giving his counterargument according to what he finds. I thus approved, ordered and signed it along with the present scribe for the cabildo.

 Alfonso Rael de Aguilar (rubric)

Notification

Continuing, I, the present scribe for the cabildo, went to the guardhouse of this villa and there I read and notified Agustín Palma, prisoner, about the above proceedings. He upon having heard and understood them, said he would obey and did obey them. He named as his legal representative Juan Manuel de Chirinos,[35] resident of this villa, to be assigned to defend him, and he will argue in his favor for Agustín Palma, prisoner in this case. So that it is valid I signed it in the presence of the corporal of the squadron, Gregorio Ramírez and Miguel Carrillo,[36] on the said day.

 Cristóbal de Góngora (rubric)
 Scribe for the cabildo

[Power of Attorney][37]

At this Villa of Santa Fe on the 26th of August, 1711, before me Captain Diego Arias de Quiros,[38] alcalde ordinario of this villa acting as presiding judge with two assisting witnesses because there is no public or royal scribe in this kingdom, there appeared before me the accused Agustín Palma, who is a prisoner in the guardhouse of this villa. [Palma] stated that he would give and did give the right of representation to Juan Manuel de Chirinos so that he can appear before the presiding justice, Captain don Alfonso Real de Aguilar, the judge in this case, (and before any other justices of his majesty) that are against this witness in whatever he is being accused of. This is including all of the charges which are being brought against him, and including whatever the proceedings bring up which might result in his favor, along with the petitions and other written materials which may result.

In addition, copies of the proceedings against the said Agustín Palma are to be turned over to [Juan Manuel de Chirinos] so that he can respond to them within the term that is designated. Juan Manuel de Chirinos is to be given every opportunity to come up with all of the judicial proceedings for the defense. This is according to all of the rights allowed and required and necessary for the freedom and general administration which are given as part of the authority of the power of attorney in seeking justice. Chirinos is allowed to set forth in any shape or form whatever is needed by him to perform his work, and is obligated to submit his findings to all of the justices of his majesty for revalidation.[39] So that all of this is valid, I, the alcalde ordinario, signed it along with the witnesses who are present and who were Cristóbal de Góngora and Joseph [Manuel] Giltoméy.[40] Being that the accused does not know how to write, it was signed at his request by one of the said witnesses on the said day.

At the request of Agustín Palma
Cristóbal de Góngora (rubric)
Before me as Presiding Judge
Diego Arias de Quiros (rubric)

Captain don Alfonso Rael de Aguilar, alcalde ordinario of this villa

Presentation of the Procurador]

I, Juan Manuel de Chirinos, resident of this Villa of Santa Fe, [appear] in the name of and under the power of attorney given me by Agustín Palma, prisoner in the guardhouse of this villa for various charges that are brought up against him in the proceedings that appear before the justice of your honor. In order to be allowed to continue with his defense according to his right, your honor is to ensure that all of the proceedings in the matter are turned over to me so that upon reviewing them I can argue and provide everything that can be in favor of Agustín Palma, my client, and which might aid him in safeguarding his rights. For all of this I ask that your mercy be pleased to allow me what I have asked for, for as such I will be granted goodness and mercy under justice, and I swear in due form that this, my petition, is not done in malice. Costs are not allowed, etc.

    Juan Manuel de Chirinos (rubric)

In addition, with all of your solemnity, I present before your honor the power of attorney given to me by Agustín Palma, etc.

    Juan Manuel de Chirinos (rubric)

[Petition Presented to alcalde Alfonso Rael de Aguilar]

    At the Villa of Santa Fe, on the 26th of August, 1711, before me Captain Alfonso Rael de Aguilar, alcalde ordinario, the above stated [legal represenative] presented his petition to me. Upon being reviewed by me I accepted it as it was presented according to all rights and I ordered and did order that this party (give the information that is offered to the current scribe, Cristóbal de Góngora, who is to receive the witnesses according to the necessary rights, and I thus approved, ordered it and signed it)[41] along with the present scribe is to be given the proceedings. I thus approved, ordered and signed it.

    I give the information that is presented before the scribe for the cabildo, Cristóbal de Góngora, who is to ask for the witnesses, and he will do it as necessary. I thus approved, ordered and signed it on this same document.

    Alfonso Rael de Aguilar (rubric)
    before me
    Cristóbal de Góngora (rubric)
    Scribe for the cabildo

Alcalde Ordinario Don Alfonso Rael de Aguilar

I, Juan Manuel de Chirinos, in the name of and with the power of attorney given to me by Agustín Palma, prisoner in the guardhouse of this royal presidio of the Villa of Santa Fe for various charges and other things, appear before your honor in all of the most and proper form that all rights give to my party. I say that on this the 26th of the present month of August I have completed reviewing all of the proceedings that have been brought up against my party within the court of your majesty according to the petition of Petrona de Carvajal. Having gone through them point by point, I find that there is no legal right for having them admitted, because they have not been done within the legal time frame, and as such should not be admitted as they can not serve as a basis for judgement and have no real value or effect.

The individual, [Petrona de Carvajal] states that after having had illicit sex with her, Agustín Palma, having no fear for God, and having fulfilled his sexual appetite with her, violently ruined Antonia de Valencia, her daughter. According to her statement she said that after he had ruined her daughter he, without any fear for God, Our Lord, repeated his actions four times. After the complaint was filed against him, he once more did the same thing [with Petrona], according to her sworn statement. On page five of the said summaria, I can prove that Petrona de Carvajal said she knew for certain that he had ruined her daughter and that he then committed the same offense with Petrona over and over just like he used to do before the complaint was in place.

It can be recognized that it is passion that is involved on her part founded by jealousies without substance, which are held by some unmarried women within this villa (the names of whom I shall now omit). It can be recognized that if all that which she stated was true, there would be no attorney involved.[42] If some days later [after the alleged rape] Petrona de Carvajal, who is or is not a Christian, she would not have persisted in her friendship with my client. Having the illicit sex [with Agustín] proves her charge [of rape] is a false chimera[43] or delusion, which proves that the issue is false. My client also finds little substance in her statement where she speaks about anything to the contrary.

If my client did anything in excess (if it can be proven that he did) it is because he is a man lacking any sense,[44] and is demented, as it is publicly known throughout the kingdom and thus, I shall prove that he is innocent, without a doubt, and with plenty of information. If your honor accepts this, he will understand that my client is not responsible for any crime. Your honor will see this from the reasons that I will place before the open eyes of your honor. Using these reasons, he can judge this case based to the nature of my arguments which prove the false accusations given by Petrona de Carvajal, which shall be null and of no value or affect. All of which I can, I will and I shall do, as is expressed.

Of your honor I ask and request with all respect, that I be allowed to enter this petition in favor of my client, recognizing that everything that has been stated above that has been made against this individual has been made due to the referred circumstances. Your honor upon doing this shall receive the petition with justice which is what I ask. I swear to God, Our Lord, and to the sign of the Cross on behalf of my client, that this my petition, is not done in malice, but what I implore from your honor. I protest costs in whatever is required.

Juan Manuel de Chirinos (rubric)

Presentation
At this Villa of Santa Fe on the 26th of August, 1711, before me, Captain don Alfonso Rael de Aguilar, alcalde ordinario of this villa, the above stated individual presented that which is herein contained. It having been seen by me, I took it as was

presented according to that which is in his right and I ordered and did order that this party give the information that he offers to the scribe Cristóbal de Gngora. Góngora is to receive the witnesses and shall do that which according to the law is required. I thus approved, ordered it and signed it along with the said scribe, on the said day.

(Signatures are missing)

Statement of Juan Antonio Ramos[45]

Continuing, I, the present scribe, in compliance with the decree of above, approved by the alcalde, made to appear before me Juan Manuel de Chirinos, attorney for Agustín Palma, offender in this cause. He presented before me as a witness Juan Antonio Ramos so that he can testify regarding the point which is stated in the above petition by the said attorney. Being present, I took his sworn statement that he made to God, Our Lord, and to the sign of the Cross, according to his right under which he promised to tell the truth in everything that he knew and what he was asked in the following manner. He stated that it is true that he knows that Agustín Palma is a simple man lacking any sense, and that it is known publicly throughout the kingdom. He states that this is the truth regarding the sworn statement that he has made, which he affirmed and ratified. His statement having been read back to him he said that he was twenty-eight years of age, and so that it is valid he signed it before me the present scribe.

  Cristóbal de Góngora (rubric)
  Scribe for the cabildo
  Juan Antonio Ramos (rubric)

Statement

On the said day, month and year, before me the present....

[*Editor's note: The document ends here without the statement and final decision.*]

TRANSCRIPTION

    Señor Governador y Capitan General

  Petrona de Carvajal vezina de esta Villa de Santa Fee paresco ante Vuestra Señoria en la mejor via y forma que aya lugar en derecho qual me conbenga y digo que haviendose servido Vuestra Señoria el ano pasado de mandarme notificar el que yo saliere desterrada de esta dicha Villa antes de el obedesimiento conparesi ante la grandesa de Vuestra Señoria a suplicarle mirara por una nina donzella de edad de dies anos que yo dejava alos contra tiempos del mundo alo qual se sirvio Vuestra

Señoria de mandarme salir luego y que dejara ala dicha mi hija con alguna persona tismorata.

Haviendo obedesido asi puse por execuzion mi viaje dejando en mi casa en la compania dela muger de Juan de Guido quien la acompano unos dias en compania de Agustin Palma que este con poco temor de Dios Nuestro Señor y de la Real Justizia ynsitado de el demonio o de su mal natural (que esto es lo mas sierto) fingio por su conbenencia y apetito un plieto con la dicha muger de Juan de Guido y la echo de mi casa y conseguidolo asi quedandose solo en ella con la dicha mi hija a esta la cojio el suso dicho y amarro con una liga de las manos y con violencia la estrupo y forso amenasandola que si me dezia alguna cosa la havia de matar esto es despues (que hablando con devido respecto) de haver tenido ylisita amistad con migo y haver echo su gusto con migo muchos dias antes por que la nesesidad lo ocasiono de modo que persebere asta que supe era tan depravado y capital delito de castigo por cuya causa me querello sibil y criminalmente de el dicho Agustin Palma por las circumstanzias referidas que espero dela piedad y xptiano zelo de Vuestra Señoria mirara esta causa con vegnidad, haziendo poner al suso dicho luego luego en estrecha prizion para el seguro de su persona por que no se extravie y pierda yo el derecho que me ampara por pobre muger sola y desbalida y por el (word illegible) biolento con la mayor sircumstancia de ynsexto.

Que asi lo espero conseguir de Vuestra Señoria a quien clamo para que siga la causa asta la difinitiba y el dicho agresor sea castigado al tamano de tan grave delicto por tanto y lo demas que alegar puedo, devo y doy por expresado, a Vuestra Señnoria pido y suplico con todo rendimiento se sirva de guardarme justizia dela manera que aqui llevo expresado y lo que a Vuestra Señnoria le paresiere ser mas conbininete y juro a Dios Nuestro Señor y la Santa Cruz no ser de malicia el Real auxilio en Vuestra Señoria ymploro y en lo nesesario, ut supra = entre renglones ynsertos vale = entre renglones adul, no vale, testado adulterio no vale =

Petrona de Carvajal (rubric)

Presentacion

En la villa de Santa Fee, cabesera de este Reyno y Provincia de la Nueba Mexico en onze dias de el mes de Agosto de mill sietecientos y onze años ante el Almirante Dn. Joseph Chacon Medina Salazar y Villa Señor, Cavallero del Orden de Santiago, Marquez dela Penuela, Governador y Capitan General deste Reyno y Sus Provincias y Castellano de Sus Fuerzas y Presidios por Su Magestad y vista por Su Señoria la hubo por presentada en quanto a lugar en derecho y atendiendo a esta representasion mandava y mando se cometan estas dilixencias al Capitan Dn. Alphonso Rael de Aguilar, Alcalde Ordinario de esta Villa para que en su virtud, asi lo execute y para que conste asi lo proveyo, mando y firmo Su Señoria con migo el ynfrascripto Secretario de Governazion y Guerra en dicho dia.

El Marques de la Penuela (rubric)

Ante mi

Juan de Uribarri (rubric)
Secretario de Governazion y Guerra

☞

Otro si mandava y mando dicho Señor Marques, Governador y Capitan General al referido Capitan Dn. Alphonso Rael de Aguilar, Alcalde Ordinario desta dicha Villa prosese en toda forma la sumaria del efecto delas cometidas diligencias, dandoles como le doy plena y toda mi autoridad para que las fonesca y sentensie segun la naturaleza y estado de los autos y para que conste asi lo probeyo y rubrico por ante mi el infraescripto secretario =

Peñuela (rubric)
Ulibarri (rubric)
Secretario

☞

Auto

En la Villa de Santa Fee en doze dias del mes de Agosto de mill setesientos y onse añnos yo el Capitan Dn. Alphonso Rael de Aguilar, Alcalde Ordinario desta dicha Villa haviendo visto el auto de arriva proveydo por el Señor Marquez de la Peñuela, Cavallero del Orden de Santiago, Governador y Capitan General deste Reyno y Provincias de la Nueva Mexico y Castellano de Sus Fuerzas y Presidios por Su Magestad en que por el se sirvio de cometerme el conocimiento de esta causa y para proseguir la mandava y mande se despache mandamiento de prizion contra Agustin Palma y se ponga a buen recaudo con un par de grillos en el Cuerpo de Guardia deste Real Presidio y para que conste asi lo provey, mande y firme con el Scribano de Cabildo =

Alphonso Rael de Aguilar (rubric)
Ante mi
Xptobal de Gongora (rubric)
Scribano de Cabildo

☞

El Capitan Dn. Alphonso Rael de Aguilar, Alcalde Ordinario desta Villa de Santa Fee cavezera del Reyno y Provincias dela Nueba Mexico por Su Magestad, ut supra

Mandamiento

Por el presente ordeno y mando a Miguel Moran mi alguazil que visto este mandamiento ponga preso y a buen recaudo con un par de grillos a Agustin Palma en el Cuerpo de Guardia de este Real Presidio y para su consecuzion le yntime este mi mandamiento al Cavo de la Guardia Gregorio Ramiriz le de todo favor y ayuda para su execuzion por ser soldado de este dicho Presidio dicho Agustin Palma por haverme el conosimiento desta dicha causa y dandome toda y amplia facultad el Señnor Marquez dela Peñnuela, Governador y Capitan General de este dicho firmo como consta de su auto proveydo del dia onze del presente mes de Agosto, y para que conste lo firme con el infrascripto Scribano de Cabildo en doze dias del mes de Agosto de mill setezientos y onze anos =

 Alphonso Rael de Aguilar (rubric)
 Ante mi
 Xptobal de Gongora (rubric)
 Scribano de Cabildo

Yo Miguel Moran primer Alguazil en cumplimiento y obedezimiento del mandamiento de arriba del Señnor Alcalde Ordinario Dn. Alphonso Rael de Aguilar vine al Cuerpo de Guardia deste Real Presidio y de Cavo del Gregorio Ramirez le intime y hise notorio este dicho mandamiento y haviendolo oydo y entendido dijo que no tenian que buscar a el dicho Agustin Palma por que se hallava refuxiado en la yglesia parroquial de esta dicha Villa y para que asi conste pedi a el Señor Scribano Xptobal de Gongora dieze fee de ello por hallarse en la ocazion en dicho Cuerpo de Guardiña =
E yo el dicho Xptobal de Gongora, Scribano de Cabildo, doy fee en quanto puedo y a lugar en derecho ser sierto y verdadero todo lo expresado arriba y para que conste lo firme en este Cuerpo de Guardia deste Real Presidio en doze dias del mes de Agosto de mill sietezientos y onze anos.

 Xptobal de Gongora (rubric)
 Scribano de Cabildo

Auto
En la Villa de Santa Fee en treze dias del mes de Agosto de mill sietecientos y onze años yo el Capitan Dn. Alphonso Rael de Aguilar, Alcalde Ordinario de esta dicha Villa haviendo visto la respuesta que dio el cavo dela Guardia Gregorio Ramirez en el mandamiento que por mi alguazil Miguel Moran le yntimo en que dize hallarze refugiado en la Santa Yglesia de esta dicha Villa Agustin Palma reo en esta causa y para saber la verdad si en dicha yglesia se halla el suso dicho mandava y mande se reconosiese la dicha Santa Yglesia y conbento para se en el se halla el dicho reo, y para ello se pida primero lizencia al Reverendo Padre Guardian Fray Joseph Lopez Tello, yntimandole de parte de Su Magestad y de la mia de libre y franco el dicho convento y Santa Yglesia que sele guardaran todos los fueros y privilegios que son consedidos sin que se haga ningun desafuero y para que asi conste asi lo provey, mande y firme con el infrascripto Scribano de Cabildo =

 Alphonso Rael de Aguilar (rubric)
 Ante mi
 Xptobal de Gongora (rubric)
 Scribano de Cabildo

Diligencia

Luego yncontinente en dicho dia, mes y ano yo el Capitan Dn. Alphonso Rael de Aguilar, Alcalde Ordinario, para la prosecuzion de estas diligencias pase en compania del scribano de cabildo al convento de Nuestro Padre San Francisco de esta dicha Villa y en el pedi la lizencia nesesaria al Reverendo Padre Fray Joseph Lopez Tello, guardian de dicho convento para entrar en el a dar fee en verdadero testimonio de lo que el auto de arriba expresa y consedida por su Reverendo entre adentro y en el claustro vide al dicho Agustin Palma que estaba refugiado en el sagrado y con esta rason y zertesa me bolvi a preseguir en las demas diligencias que el derecho dispone y para que asi conste lo firmo con el presente scribano de cabildo =

Alphonso Rael de Aguilar (rubric)
Ante mi
Xptobal de Gongora (rubric)
Scribano de Cabildo

Auto

En la Villa de Santa Fee en dicho dia, mes y ano yo dicho Alcalde Ordinario para proseguir esta causa segun derecho mandava y mande compareser ante mi y mi jusgado Petrona de Carvajal querellante en esta causa con la dicha su hija para el efecto de resevirle su declaracion y para que conste asi lo provey, mande y firme con el Scribano de Cabildo.

Alphonso Rael de Aguilar (rubric)
Ante mi
Xptobal de Gongora (rubric)
Scribano de Cabildo

Declaracion de Antonia de Valencia

En la Villa de Santa Fee en catorze dias del mes de Agosto de mill setesientos y onze años yo dicho Alcalde Ordinario en virtud del auto de arriva hize parezer ante mi a Antonia Valenzia hija de Petrona de Carvajal querellante la cual estando presente le resevi juramento que lo hizo por Dios Nuestro Señor y una senal de cruz en forma de derecho devajo de cuyo cargo prometio desir verdad en todo lo que supiere y le fuese preguntado

Preguntada si conose a Agustin Palma? Dijo que si lo conose.

Preguntada que por que razon conose al dicho Agustin Palma y quanto tiempo. Dize que lo conose dijo que dos anos a que lo conose

Preguntada si sabe que el dicho Agustin Palma tenia la amistad ylizita con su madre Petrona de Carvajal? Dijo que lo que sabe es que dos anos a tenido el dicho

Agustin Palma la amistad ylizita con la dicha su madre Petrrona de Carvajal y que los bido dormir juntos y esto responde

Preguntada si el dicho Agustin Palma en alguno ocazion tubo con esta declarante copula carnal. Dijo que habra tiempo de un ano que la dicha su madre se fue a Bernalillo y quedo el dicho Agustin Palma en la dicha su casa junto con esta declarante y la muger de Juan de Guido y que en dicha occasion le amarro los brazos con una atadera y le tapo la boca para que no gritara y la echo a perder y esto responde

Preguntada que tiempo tubo la amistad con el dicho Agustin Palma. Dijo que desde el ymbierno asta el tiempo de las siembras de maiz y que aunque se yba a Pecos el dicho Agustin Palma quando benia a esta Villa la embiaba a llamar con los criados de Sebastian Gonzales y con un nieto de Juana Dominguez y dormia con esta declarante teniendo copula carnal y que siempre que benia el dicho Agustin Palma le traya pinole, arina y carne y que comian todos juntos y esto responde

Y que todo lo que tiene dicho es la verdad por el juramento que fecho tiene en que se afirmo y ratifico siendole leydo esta su declaracion que no tiene que anadir ni quitar y que es de edad de trese anos y para que conste lo firme yo dicho Alcalde Ordinario y el presente Scribano de Cabildo

Alphonso Rael de Aguilar (rubric)

Ante mi

Xptobal de Gongora (rubric)

Scribano de Cabildo

Declaracion de Petrona de Carvajal

Yncontinenti yo dicho Alcalde Ordinario para la presecuzion de esta causa y para su mayor justificazion hize pareser a Petrona de Carvajal querellante la qual estando presente le resevi juramento que lo hizo por Dios Nuestro Señnor y una señnal de Cruz en forma de derecho devajo de cuyo cargo prometio dezir verdad en todo lo que supiere y le fuese preguntado

Preguntada que tiempo a que tiene la amistad ylizita con el dicho Agustin Palma? Dijo abra dos anos poco mas o menos y esto responde

Preguntada que tiempo a que el dicho Agustin Palma estrupo ala dicha su hija. Dijo que no sabe quando, que lo que sabe es que el dicho Agustin Palma le dijo a esta declarante que el la havia echado a perder que no se andubiera causando que lo hizo quando esta declarante estava en Bernalillo y esto responde

Preguntada quantas veses tubo esta declarante copula con el dicho Agustin Palma despues que supo que la abia estrupado ala dicha su hija.

Dijo que quatro beses tubo copula con el dicho Agustin Palma aunque siertamente no lo sabe y esto responde

Preguntada que donde probino a tener luz de que la dicha su hija no era donzella.

Dijo que su comadre Ana Maria selo abiso a esta declarante delante del dicho Palma

Preguntada que teniendo esta notizia sierta de la dicha Ana Maria por que cometio tan torpe pecado de ynsexto? Dijo que por que la dicha Ana Maria le dijo a esta declarante que quisas le lebantaban testimonio y que todo lo que tiene dicho es la verdad por el juramento que dicho tiene en que se afirmo y ratifico y que es de edad de treinta y seis anos, no firmo por no saber firmelo yo dicho Alcalde Ordinario con el Scribano de Cabildo.

 Alphonso Rael de Aguilar (rubric)
 Ante mi
 Xristobal de Gongora (rubric)
 Scribano de Cabildo

Auto

En la Villa de Santa Fee en catorze del mes de Agosto de mill sietezientos y onze anos yo el Capitan Dn. Alphonso Rael de Aguilar, Alcalde Ordinario desta dicha Villa, haviendo visto las declaraciones antecedentes fechos por Petrona de Carvajal querellanta y por Antonia Valenzia y lo que por ellas consta los cargos y culpa que por ellas se refiere contra Agustin Palma reo en esta causa y refuxiado en la Santa Yglesia y convento desta dicha Villa y para seguirla en forma y conforme a derecho mandava y mande sele resiva y tome su confesion al dicho Agustin Palma y para ello se preseda primero el requerer al Reverando Padre Fray Joseph Lopez Tello ministro y cura de esta Santa Parroquia de parte de Su Magestad y dela mia de libre y franco del dicho convento y Santa Yglesia para el efecto referido asi lo provey, mande y firme con el Scribano de Cabildo =

 Alphonso Rael de Aguilar (rubric)
 Ante mi
 Xptobal de Gongora (rubric)
 Scribano de Cabildo

Confesion de Agustin Palma

En la Villa de Santa Fee en quinze dias del mes de Agosto de mill setezientos y onze anos yo el Capitan Dn. Alphonso Rael de Aguilar, Alcalde Ordinario desta dicha Villa en virtud y cumplimiento del auto de arriba vine al convento desta dicha Villa en compania del presente scribano y en el alle al Reverendo Padre Predicador Fray Joseph Lopez Tello, cura y ministro dela Parroquia de dicha Villa aquien requeri de parte de Su Magestad y de la mia diese libre y franco el convento y Santa Yglesia para los efectos que con dicho auto se expresan alo qual dijo su Padre que el convento y Santa Yglesia la dava desde luego franca y libre guardandole sus grandes ynmunidades y fueros los cuales dijo el dicho Alcalde Ordinario que los guardaria y pasando al claustro alle en una zelda a un hombre a quien pregunte que como se llama que edad y oficio tiene que estado y calidad y de donde es natural, haviendo presedido primero el juramento que hizo por Dios Nuestro Señor y una Señal de Cruz de vajo de cuyo cargo prometio de dezir verdad en todo lo que supiere y le fuere preguntado y dijo llamarse Agustin Palma, que es de edad de quarenta anos y que es soldado del Real Presidio y Castillo de esta dicha Villa y de estado casado y que es Espanol y que es natural de este dicho Reyno y esto. Rresponde

Preguntado que motives tiene y a tenido para haberse benido a refuxiar a esta Santa Yglesia y convento? Dijo que por que le havian dicho que le querian echar grillos y que por no esperimentar un rigor de justizia se bino a anparar a esta Santa Yglesia y esto responde

Preguntado que por que razon o por que causa le havian de echar los qrillos. Dijo que por que despues supo que habian presentado una petizion contra este confesante y esto responde.

Preguntado que persona fue la que presento la peticion contra el suso dicho. Dijo que Petrona de Carvajal y esto responde.

Preguntado que causa tubo la suso dicha Petrona de Carvajal para que presentara dicha petizion. Dijo que estando este confesante en el Pueblo de los Pecos vino con el Reverendo Padre Fray Diego Padilla, ministro de dicho Pueblo a esta Villa abiendo estado este confesante en la casa de dicha Petrona dos o tres dias esta le pidio selos de su hija y que sobre esta material pleytearon y le dijo este confesante que para descargo de su conciencia no tenia ninguna culpa de lo que sele ynputava ni devia tal cosa y que no se creyera de quantos que ya se bolvia a dicho Pueblo de Pecos y que le pidio por Dios reconosieran mugeres parteras de ciencia y conciencia a la dicha su hija si estaba donzella o no, que lo pagaria por que manana o otro dia no selo cargaran y que bolvio del dicho Pueblo de Pecos a esta Villa y le dijo que si ya havia echo la diligenzia que le havia dicho y que le respondio que que havia de hazer y que se estubo alli muchos dias en la dicha su casa y bolvieron a pleitear sobre los mismos zelos de modo que enfadado este confesante le respondio que ya que, dava y porfiaba en que havia dormido este confesante con la dicha su hija y la havia estrupado que fues e no rabuena pues ella lo dezia, no por que lo deve ni tal ofensa a echo, a Dios Nuestro Señor que lo jura una y mill millones de veses y que pide sele pruebe y esto responde.

Preguntado quanto tiempo tubo la amistad ylizita con la dicha Petrona de Carvajal. Dijo que el tiempo de un ano y esto responde.

Preguntado que diga la verdad y no lo niegue; quantas veses tubo copula carnal con Antonia Valenzia, hija dela dicha Petrona de Carvajal. Pues consta por los autos haverla estrupado por fuerza amarrandole los brazos con una liga? Dijo que es falso y le den la prueba y esto responde.

Preguntado que quando venia del Pueblo de los Pecos a esta dicha Villa paraba en casa de Sevastian Gonzales y embiaba a llamar ala dicha Antonia de Valenzia la qual yba y dormia con ella teniendo acto y copula carnal y despues le dava pinole, arina y carne para que llevara a su casa. Dijo que es verdad, que enbiaba a llamar ala suso dicha y le dava el alimento que se refiere para que llevara a su madre pero que es falso y siniestro lo demas que sele pregunta que ya tiene dicho que no deve tal cosa y esto responde.

Y aunque sele hizieron otras preguntas y repreguntas al caso tocantes, dijo que ya tiene dicho la verdad sobre cargo del juramento que fecho tiene en que se afirmo y ratifico siendole leyda esta su confezion que no tiene que anadir ni quitar no firmo por no saber, firmelo yo dicho Alcalde Ordinario y el presente Scribano de Cabildo =

 Alphonso Rael de Aguilar (rubric)
 Ante mi
 Xptobal de Gongora (rubric)
 Scribano de Cabildo

Declaracion de Jose Matheo

 En la Villa de Santa Fee en diez y seis dias del mes de Agosto de mill setezientos y onze años yo dicho Alcalde Ordinario digo que parecio ante mi y el presente scribano de Cabildo, Joseph Matheo, cantor de la Yglesia y dijo devajo de juramento que hizo por Dios Nuestro Señor y la Santa Cruz como Agustin Palma retraido le dijo como ya estaba contento por que estaba ya contenta Petrona de Carvajal querellante con el que de noche se salia dela Yglesia y que se yba a dormir con la suso dicha a su casa y que esta le dijo que si se havia querellado de el era por que su comadre Ana Maria la hija de la Monsonga selo havia aconsejado y la havia ynduzido para que presentara querella contra el dicho Agustin Palma pero que sin embargo que ella ya estaba contenta y se bajaria de la querella con la condizion de que las mantubiera del mismo modo que lo havia echo antes y que este declarante le dijo que se olgava mucho que esto es lo que paso y declara por verdad so cargo del juramento que fecho tiene en que se afirmo y ratifico y siendole leido este su dicho, dijo no tener que anadir ni quitar y que es de edad de quarenta anos, no firmo por no saber firmelo yo dicho Alcalde Ordinario y el presente Scribano =

 Alphonso Rael de Aguilar (rubric)
 Ante mi
 Xptobal de Gongora (rubric)
 Scribano de Cabildo

Declaracion de Ana Maria Almazan

 En la Villa de Santa Fee en dicho dia mes y ano yo dicho Alcalde Ordinario haviendo visto la declaracion de arriva y denunzasion fecha por Joseph Mateo y para su justificazion hice pareser ante mi a Ana Maria de Almazan vezina de esta Villa ala cual estando presente le resevi su juramento que lo hizo por Dios Nuestro Señnor y una señal de cruz en forma de derecho so cargo delo qual prometio dezir verdad de lo que supiere y le fuere preguntado. Preguntada si conose a Agustin Palma, a Petrona de Carvajal y Antonia de Valenzia, su hija? Dijo que si las conose a las susa dichas y esto responde.

 Preguntada si sabe que el dicho Agustin Palma a tenido la amistad ylizita con la dicha Petrona de Carvajal y que tiempo? Dijo que no los ha visto pero que lo que sabe por que es publico y notorio que estaban amanzebados y esto responde.

Preguntada si sabe que el dicho Agustin Palma estrupo ala dicha Antonia de Valenzia? Dijo que por que selo dijo a esta declarante la muger de Juan Antonio Barrios, y esto responde.

Preguntada si yndujo a dicha Petrona de Carvajal para que se querellara de dicho Agustin Palma? Dijo que no y que esta es la verdad por el juramento que dicho tiene en que se afirmo y ratifico siendole leyda esta su declaracion que no tiene que anadir ni quitar a ello y que es de edad de treinta anos, no firmo por no saver firmelo yo dicho Alcalde Ordinario y el presente Scribano de Cabildo.

Alphonso Rael de Aguilar (rubric)
Ante mi
Xptobal de Gongora (rubric)
Scribano de Cabildo

Presentacion de Gregorio Ramires

En esta Villa de Santa Fee en veinte dias del mes de Agosto de mill sietecientos y onze anos ante mi dicho Alcalde Ordinario parecio Gregorio Ramires, cavo de esquadra dela guardia de este Real Presidio y me dio quenta como Agustin Palma reo en esta causa havia salido dela Santa Yglesia y se presento en el dicho Cuerpo de Guardia con cuya notizia yo dicho Alcalde Ordinario di orden al dicho cavo de esquadra lo tubiese preso y a dicho recaudo con un par de grillos y para que asi conste lo firme con el presente Scribano de Cabildo aquien mande dieze fee si el dicho Agustin Palma se hallava en dicho Cuerpo de Guardia y lo ponga por diligencia en estos autos =

Alphonso Rael de Aguilar (rubric)
Ante mi
Xptobal de Gongora (rubric)
Scribano de Cabildo

Fee de la prision

Luego yncontinenti yo Cristobal de Gongora, Scribano de Cabildo, en cumplimiento del orden de arriva del Señor Alcalde Ordinario fue al Cuerpo de Guardia del Castillo Presidial desta Villa de Santa Fee y en el halle a Agustin Palma que actualmente le estavan poniendo un par de grillos y remachando la chapeta de lo qual doy fee y lo firme en dicho dia =

Xptobal de Gongora (rubric)
Scribano de Cabildo

Auto

En la Villa de Santa Fee en veinte y un dias del mes de Agosto de mill setezientos y onze años yo el Capitan Dn. Alphonso Rael de Aguilar, Alcalde Ordinario desta dicha Villa haviendo visto la fee del presente scribano, a dado de haver visto en el Cuerpo de Guardia a Agustin Palma prezo y reo en esta causa y para le mayor justificacion de ello mandava y mande sele buelba a tomar su confesion y para que asi conste lo firme con el presente scribano del cabildo =

 Alphonso Rael de Aguilar (rubric)
 Ante mi
 Xptobal de Gongora (rubric)
 Scribano de Cabildo

 En la Villa de Santa Fee en veinte y un dias del mes de Agosto de mill seitezientos y onze años yo el Capitan Dn. Alphonso Rael de Aguilar, Alcalde Ordinario de esta dicha Villa en virtud del auto proveydo el dia de ayer veinte del presente mes dela fecha vine al Cuerpo de Guardia en compania del presente scribano y en el alle a un hombre preso por la causa al qual resevi juramento que hizo por Dios Nuestro Señor y una señal de cruz en forma de derecho de bajo de cuya cargo prometio dezir verdad en todo lo que supiere y le fuere preguntado = Preguntado como se llama, que edad y oficio tiene, de donde es natural, de que calidad? Dijo que se llama Agustin Palma, y que ya tiene dicho la confezion y declaracion que hizo y sele tomo quando estava retraydo y declaracion que hizo y sele tomo quando estava traydo en el convento, su edad, calidad y oficio y que esto responde .

 Preguntado, si sabe la causa de su prizion? Dijo que ya tiene dicho en la dicha confezion que ante mi dicho Alcalde hizo y qual es la causa de su prision y que en ella se ratifica una, dos, y tres veses que es la verdad por el juramento que dicho tiene, no firmo por no saber, firmelo yo dicho Alcalde Ordinario y en presencia del Scribano de Cabildo =

 Alphonso Rael de Aguilar (rubric)
 Ante mi
 Xptobal de Gongora (rubric)
 Scribano de Cabildo

 Auto
 En la Villa de Santa Fee en veinte y tres dias del mes de Agosto de mill sietecientos y onze anos yo el Capitan Dn. Alphonso Rael de Aguilar, Jues en la causa haviendo visto estos autos y declaraciones que resultan contra Agustin Palma reo en esta causa y para que se reciva a prueba y le tubiese lo que decir, alegar o provar contra lo contenido en ella por lo que le toca el dicho Agustin Palma mando al ynfraescripto Scribano de Cabildo le notifique hombre procurador para que por si o por el paresca ante mi y en mi jusgado para que sele entreguen los autos y responde dentro del termino opuesto por el derecho que es de tres dias dando los descargos conpetentes que combengan asi

lo provey, mande y firme con el presente Scribano de Cabildo =
    Alphonso Rael de Aguilar (rubric)

Notificazion

    Yncontinenti yo el presente Scribano de Cabildo vine al Cuerpo de Guardia de esta dicha Villa y en el lei y notifique el auto de arriba a Agustin Palma preso en el quien haviendolo oido y entendido dijo que lo obedezia y obedezio nombrando por su procurador a Juan Manuel Chirinos, vezino desta dicha Villa para que lo defienda como constara por su poder que a su favor otorgara el dicho Agustin Palma reo en esta causa y para que conste lo firme estando presente el Cavo de Escuadra Gregorio Ramires y Miguel Carrillo en dicho dia =
    Xptobal de Gongora (rubric)
    Scribano de Cabildo

Poder

    En la Villa de Santa Fee en veinte y seis dias del mes de Agosto de mill setezientos y onze anos ante mi el Capitan Diego Arias de Quiros, Alcalde Ordinario de esta dicha Villa autuando como Juez Receptor con dos testigos de assistensia por no haver Scribano Publico ni Real en este Reyno parecio Agustin Palma, reo, prezo en el Cuerpo de Guardia desta dicha Villa y dijo que dava y dio todo su poder general y especial a Juan Manuel Chirinos para que pueda pareser y paresca ante el jusgado del Capitan Dn. Alphonso Rael de Aguilar, juez en la causa que contra este otorgante esta siguiendo sobre lo que en ella se contiene y ante otras qualesquiera justizias de Su Magestad donde con derecho pueda y deva pedir sobre los cargos que contra el an resultado representando a su favor lo que manifiestan los autos metiendo memorials y peticiones y pidiendo los autos.

    Que sele de traslado delos escriptos que contra el dicho Agustin Palma se hizieron y que responda dentro del termino que sele senalase y que el Señnor Juan de Chirinos pueda hazer todas las diligencias juridicas y extrajudiciales que el derecho le permite para su defensa que para todo le da este poder quanto bastante de derecho se requiere y es nesesario con toda libre franca y general administrazion y con la facultad de poder en juiziar, jurar y substituir con relebazion en forma al cumplimiento de lo que en su virtud hiziere y obrase el dicho Juan de Chirinos obligo su persona y bienes y se someta a todas las justizias de Su Magestad para a su rebalidazion y para que asi conste lo firme yo dicho Alcalde Ordinario y los dichos testigos de casa que lo fueron Xptobal de Gongora y Joseph Gilthomey y por no saber firmar el otorgante lo hizo a su ruego uno de los dichos testigos en dicho dia =
    A ruego de Agustin Palma
    Xptobal de Gongora (rubric)

Ante mi como Juez Receptor
Diego Arias de Quiros (rubric)

Señor Capitan Dn. Alfonso Rael de Aguilar, Alcalde Ordinario desta Villa

Juan Manuel Chirinos besino desta Villa de Santa Fee en nombre y con poder de Agustin Palma preso en el Cuerpo de Guardia desta dicha Villa sobre diferentes cargos que contra el resultan en los autos que ante el jusgado de Vuestra Merced caesen contra el suso dicho Agustin Palma y para poder segir su defensa en derecho se a de zervir Vuestra Merced demandar seme entreguen los autos dela material para que en bista de ellos pueda pedir, alegar y suplicar todo lo que fuere a favor del dicho Agustin Palma de mi parte y fuere conducente ala mallor satisfasion para en guarda de su derecho por tanto a Vuestra Merced pido y suplico se sirva de azer como llevo pedido, que en ello resivire bien y merced con justisia y juro en forma que este escrito era ni hira de mi parte no zer de malicia costas = Ut supra.
Juan Manuel Chirinos (rubric)

Otro si con la solemnidad de Usted ago presentacion ante Vuestra Merced del poder otorgado a mi favor por el dicho Agustin Palma, ut supra.
Juan Manuel Chirinos (rubric)

En la Villa de Santa Fee en veinte y seis dias del mes de Agosto de mill sietezientos y onze anos ante mi el Capitan Dn. Alphonso Rael de Aguilar, Alcalde Ordinario, la presento el contenido y por mi vista la ube por presentada en quanto a lugar en derecho y mandava y mande que a esta parte (de la ynformasion que ofreze ante el presente Scribano Xptobal de Gongora quien recivira los testigos y la ara segun derecho nesesario asi lo provey, mande y firme) con el presente scribano y sele entreguen los autos, asi lo prevey, mande y firme = Le doy ynformazion que ofrese ante el scribano del cabildo Xptobal de Gongora quien remita los testigos y la ara segun es nesesario, asi lo provey, mande y firme en el presente escrito =
Alphonso Rael de Aguilar (rubric)
Ante mi
Xptobal de Gongora (rubric)
Scribano de Cabildo

[*Editor's note:* The information within the parentheses above was crossed out, but has been retained in the transcription.]

Señor Alcalde Ordinario Dn. Alfonso Rael de Aguilar

Juan Manuel Chirinos en nombre y con poder de Agustin Palma, preso en el Cuerpo de Guardia de este Real Presidio dela Villa de Santa Fee sobre diferentes cargos y lo demas, paresco ante Vuestra Merced en la mejor via y forma que a lugar y al derecho de mi parte combenga y digo que abiendo recuedo alla beinte y seis del presente mes de Agosto los autos y causa que contra el dicho mi parte se an echo ante el jusgado de Vuestra Majestad a pedimento de Petrona de Carvajal y reconosidos punto por punto allo no aver lugar en admision por puestos fuera del termino del Real derecho los cuales jusgo por de ningun balor ni efecto.

Pues dise la suso dicha que despues de aver tenido ilisita amistad con ella con poco temor de Dios y llevado de su apetito el dicho mi parte estrupo con biolensia Antonia de Valensia su ija y por la declaracion echa por la dicha Petrona de Carvajal en que dise que despues de aver estrupado el dicho mi parte ala dicha su hija bolbio dicha demandante aver salir ala ofensa contra Dios, Nuestro Sññor, cuatro beses y despues de presentada dicha querella una bes como costa su dicha declaracion que esta a foxas sinco dela dicha sumaria con que pruevo lo contrario con dezir que como su hija dicha Petrona de Carvajal supo con zertidumbre que el dicho parte estrupo ala dicha su hija bolvio a cometer dicha ofensa como lo acostumbraba azer antes de su demanda.

Luego se conose que es passion conosida de la suso dicha fundida en cellos sin sustancia que contra algunos sugetos desta dicha Villa, mugeres casadas (que por aora omito) tenia por que si conociera cer sierto lo que me acomula no ubiera procurador en la amista del dicho mi parte munchos dias despues la dicha Petrona de Carvajal que esta o no es Cristiana pues tubo despues la amista ilisita o esquimera sulla falsa inpostura con que quedo provado por nulo este punto y mas aver allado el dicho mi parte tan poca sustansia en su declaracion pues costa en ella no aver luz ni resquessio para su contra.

A demas que el dicho mi parte costio tal eceso (si es que cele preube) ceria por que es un hombre falto de jussio dementado como es publico como es publico en todo este Reyno, pues probare zer sierto indemasia con plena informazion que si Vuestra Merced es cer cierto la recevira para que por ella reconosca que el dicho mi parte esta acento de cualquiera pena por los motives que pongo ante los beninos ojos de Vuestra Merced para que jusge esta causa segun la naturalesa deste mi alegato pues llevo probado lo contrario de la inpostura falsa, nula y de ningun balor ni efecto puesto por la dicha Petrona de Carvajal, por tanto y lo demas, puedo, devo y aquido; por expresado =

A Vuestra Merced pido y suplico con todo rendimiento se sirva de admitirme esta petision prevellendola a favor del dicho mi parte conosiendo que todo lo que en las declaraciones anteriores se an echo contra el suso dicho es lla sido insierto por sircumstancias referidas que en aserlo Vuestra Merced recivire este vien con justicia que pido y juro a Dios Nuestro Señor y a una senal de cruz en animo de mi parte no ser de malisia este mi escrito el real ausilio en Vuestra Merced imploro, protesto costos y en lo necesario =

Juan Manuel de Chirinos (rubric)

Presentacion

En la Villa de Santa Fee en veinte y siete dias del mes de Agosto de mill sietezientos y onze anos ante mi el Capitan Dn. Alphonso Rael de Aguilar, Alcalde Ordinario desta dicha Villa la presento el contenido y por mi vista la ube por presentada en quanto a lugar en derecho y mandava y mande que esta parte de la ynformazion que ofrese ante el Scribano Xptobal de Gongora quien resivira los testigos y la hara segun derecho nesesario, asi lo provey, mande y firme con el ynfrascripto scribano en dicho dia =

Declaracion de   Juan Antonio Ramos

Yncontinente yo el presente scribano en cumplimiento del auto de arriva proveydo por el Señor Alcalde hize pareser ante mi a Juan Manuel Chirinos, procurador de Agustin Palma, reo en esta causa el qual presento ante mi por testigo a Juan Antonio Ramos para efecto de que declare sobre el punto que sita en la petizion de arriva el dicho procurador el cual estando pdresente le resevi juramento que hizo por Dios Nuestro Señor y una senal de cruz en forma de derecho devajo de cuyo cargo prometio dezir verdad en lo que supiere y le fuese preguntado y siendo al tenor siguiente; dijo que es verdad que conose a dicho Agustin Palma por un hombre simple y falto de juicio que es tan publico que en todo el Reyno se save y que esta es la verdad por el juramento que fecho tiene en que se afirmo y ratifico y leida su declaracion dijo que es de edad de veinte y seis anos y para que conste lo firmo por ante mi el presente scribano.

    Xptobal de Gongora (rubric)
    Scribano de Cabildo
    Juan Antonio Ramos (rubric)

Declaracion

En dicho dia mes y ano ante mi el presente....

[*Editor's note:* The document ends here without a final determination.]

Notes

1. See SANM II #51.
2. Petrona de Carvajal cannot be specifically identified. She may have been part of the family of Juan Antonio Carvajal whose parents, Alonso de Carvajal and Ana Varela, were natives of New Mexico. Or she could have been a relation of Lorenzo de Carvajal and his wife, Sebastiana Frequi, who were living in Bernalillo in 1699. (Cháves, *Origins*: 157, 350.)
3. Juan Guido (possibly Ejido) was born in Guanajuato, Mexico, and married Isabel de los Reyes Cruz in 1696. He came from Zacatecas, Mexico, as a recruit with the Juan Páez Hurtado Expedition in 1696. At that time, he is listed as being from the *lobo* nation, and his wife is listed as being a *coyote*. In documents of this period, the word lobo generally refers to a person with Negro and Indian parents. The term coyote can be defined in a variety of ways, but generally it meant a person who had mestizo and Indian parents. Guido is later shown as living at Santa Cruz with a woman named Antonia. He is probably the person listed as "Juan de Guido y Chirinos" in a 1703 lawsuit. (Chávez, *Origins*: 361; Kessell, Hendricks, and Dodge, *Boulders*: 545-46, 571n53; Chávez, *Roots*: 919; Bustamante, "Matter": 143-45.)
4. In the 1713 Holy Office of the Inquisition bigamy case (Case 18), Agustín Palma is listed as using the aliases of "Agustín del Rio" and "Toribio." In the latter document, he is also described as being a natural, a child of unmarried parents from Casas Grandes, and a soldier at Janos presidio. A 1692 document, which lists fifteen soldiers that were sent from the presidio of San Francisco de Conchos to assist Governor de Vargas, describes an Agustín del Rio as being fully armed with eight horses and one mule. (See Case 18; Kessell and Hendricks, *Force of Arms*: 353.)
5. In the Spanish text, the word used is *liga*, which can also mean garter or cord.
6. In the Spanish text, the words used are "*tan depravado y capital delito*" and refers to incest. Incest was defined as a mortal sin that occurred when a sexual act was committed between a parent and a child (including a stepchild), between brothers and sisters, between an uncle and a niece, and between a married person and an in-law. It could also occur between persons within a kinship range proscribed by the church, including sex between first and second cousins or even third cousins. Sex beween a husband and a sister-in-law would also have been considered incest. In this case, Agustín Palma was not married to Petrona but he had lived with her, so when Petrona had sex with Agustín after he had had sex with her daughter, it could have been considered incest. Incest was grounds for divorce. (Lavrin, *Sexuality and Marriage*: 50, 170-76; Twinam, *Public Lives*: 276, 388.)
7. Admiral Joseph Chacon Medina Salazar y Villaseñor, Marqués de la Peñuela, was governor of of New Mexico from 1707 to 1712. He was responsible for the renovation of San Miguel Chapel in Santa Fe and also for a successful campaign against the Navajo after their raid on Jémez Pueblo. In 1707, when he assumed office, he paid a purchase price for the governorship of four thousand pesos plus one-third of all profits from the office, a standard requirement for governors at that time. (Warner, "Felix Martinez": 35; *New Mexico State Historian*, "Marqués de la Peñuela," accessed on September 17, 2015.)
8. For information on Alfonso Rael de Aguilar, see SANM II #96.
9. Juan de Ulibarrí was born in San Luis Potosí, New Spain. He came to New Mexico with the reconquest, later becoming the alcalde mayor and captain of the El Paso presidio in 1699. By 1702 he was in New Mexico and married to Juana Hurtado. In 1704, he was a captain and second in command at the Santa Fe presidio. By 1709 he was alcalde of Santa Cruz. Juan died in Mexico City in 1716, after being detained by the viceroy. His name dated 1701 are found at the El Morro National Monumnat on Inscription Rock. (NMGS, *Aquí*: 54; Kessell, Hendricks, and Dodge, *Boulders*: 46-47; Chávez, *Origins*: 299.)
10. As described in the introduction, summaria was an overall term for the steps involved in fact finding such as gathering testimony from witnesses, inspection of any injuries, and the arrest and imprisonment of the accused.
11. The prestigious Order of Santiago was a military and religious order established to fight the Moors and protect the pilgrams traveling to Santiago de Compostela. The order was recognized by the Pope in 1175. The knights could live within the religious community and were allowed to marry. After 1230, the headquarters was (and still is) at Ucles in Castile, Spain. (*Encyclopedia Britannica*, "Order of Santiago," accessed on August 22, 2016.)
12. For information on Cristóbal de Góngora, see Case 7.
13. Gregorio Ramírez was the son of José Ramírez and María de Pineda, and a native of Zacatecas, Mexico. He was a presidio soldier in El Paso. He married María Frequi in Santa Fe in 1696, and he died on July 12, 1715. His name appears on a 1697 presidio payroll list. It is not likely that he is the Gregorio Ramírez who deserted in 1693 (unless perhaps he was rehabilitated). (Chávez, *Origins*: 264; Kessell, Hendricks, and Dodge, *Royal Crown*: 546 n22; Kessell, Hendricks, and Dodge, *Boulders*: 1164n40; Kessell, Hendricks, Dodge, and Miller, *Disturbances*: 128; Christmas and Rau, "Una Lista": 199.)

14. Miguel Moran, an alguacil or arresting officer, returned to New Mexico after having been part of the 1692 to 1693 muster at El Paso. In 1697, he was part of the livestock distribution. In 1715, he was one of the "old" assigned to inspect the width of the streets to determine encroachments. He was married to María Celestina de la Cruz. (Kessell, Hendricks, and Dodge, *Royal Crown*: 57; Kessell, Hendricks, and Dodge, *Boulders*: 1140, 1161n14; Chávez, *Origins*: 239; Twitchell, *Old Santa Fe;*55-7.)
15. In the Spanish text, the term for taking refuge is *hallaba refuxiado*; here, it means that Agustín Palma had claimed sanctuary by going inside the church. The more common term for this was "*sanctuario.*"
16. A convento was both a dwelling and an administrative center for the Franciscan friars.
17. Fray José López Tello was a native of Mexico City, who professed his vows as friar in 1702. He arrived in New Mexico in 1707, when he became responsible for the spiritual and educational needs of the Spanish residents in Santa Fe. He became part of a controversy between the governor, the Marqués de la Peñuela, and the Franciscan custos, Juan de Tagle, whereupon it was requested that fray Tello be moved for being too supportive of the governor. However, he was still in New Mexico in 1711, as this document indicates. (Norris, *Year Eighty*: 61-62.)
18. Drawings of the seventeenth-century church show a cloister at the convento. It is not known if this means that the cloister had two stories, with the colonnade around the courtyard, or, more likely, it had one story with a portal. The drawing shows that the cloister had cells, such as described in the document as Agustín Palma's location.
19. In the Spanish text, the word used is "*sagrado,*" meaning a sacred place of refuge or asylum. It appears that persons taking asylum felt the safest in the most sacred, consecrated part of the church. In this case, the cloister seems to have been considered such a place.
20. Antonia de Valencia was thirteen years old in 1711, thus she would have been born about 1698. Except for the information provided in this document, nothing else has been discovered about her. There is one clue: if she took her father's name, her father may have been one of the Santa Fe presidio soldiers named Valencia; for example, Antonio de Valencia, Luis de Valencia, or Antonio Felix Valencia. (Chávez: *Origins*: 397.)
21. Sebastián González [Bas] returned to New Mexico during the reconquest, as a captain. Previously, he lived at Santa Cruz de la Cañada, before the 1689 revolt. In 1683, he was a member of the cabildo in El Paso. Married to Lucía Ortiz, he died on June 11, 1726, at the age of sixty. (Chávez, *Origins*: 189; Kessell and Hendricks, *Force of Arms*: 112n40.)
22. Juana Domínguez was the natural daughter of a pre-revolt family: either Tomé or Antonio Domínguez de Mendoza. In 1692, she and her five daughters were rescued from Indian captivity. She was the third wife of Lorenzo Madrid, a sargento mayor and brother of Roque Madrid. Upon Lorenzo's death, she married Domingo Luján, a presidial soldier. The name of her nephew is not known. It may have been a son of José, or perhaps a nephew of one of her husbands. She had a house and garden located on the Santa Fe Plaza. Her brother was José Domínguez de Mendoza, who died in the Villasur massacre of 1720. (Chávez, *Origins*: 169-70, 216; Kessell, Hendricks, and Dodge, *Boulders*: 1161n12, 1165n7; Hordes, "A History of the Santa Fe Plaza, 1610–1720"; SANM I # 235, WPA translation.)
23. Ratification was a formal part of the Spanish legal procedure in which the person testifiying stated that their written testimony was correct. At times, it constituted a separate section, but here it is part of the testimony. Apparently the scribe, Cristóbal Góngora, could write fast enough so that he could immediately read the document back to her.
24. If Ana María [Almazán] was thirty years old in 1711, she would have been born around 1681. In the livestock distribution document of 1697, she is listed as living alone. She may have been the second wife of Agustín de la Cruz, who furnished adobes for the San Miguel Chapel in 1710. The couple is known to have been in Santa Fe in 1718, when a daughter, María Antonia de la Cruz, was married to Marcos Montoya. (Chávez, *Origins*: 167; Kessell, Hendricks, and Dodge, *Boulders*: 1143.)
25. Petrona did not state why she committed incest, as asked, but instead she volunteers why she said that she had. She appears to have felt that she had to tell the truth, after promising to do so in court before "God and the sign of the Holy Cross."
26. The "*confesión*" is one step of the summaria, as described in the introduction. Note that it includes an explanation and defense, as well as a confession.
27. *Predicador* is a Spanish word for preacher.
28. Fray Diego Padilla was born in Mexico City and professed his vows there in 1680. He was in New Mexico by 1693, and by 1699 he had written a petition regarding the theft of cattle in Tesuque. He was ministering to the missions of Pecos and Galisteo from 1709 to at least 1711. In 1713, he was in Santa Fe. (Kessell, Hendricks, Dodge, and Miller, *Disturbances*: 441n22; Kessell, *Kiva*: 540n14; SANM II #75; SANM II #189.)
29. No information has been located on José Matheo.
30. Cantor is the Spanish word for a church singer or a choir leader. In some specific cases, it refers to a person who sings solo verses or passages to which the choir or congregation responds.
31. In the marriage records of 1727, María Madrid is listed as a mulatta (child of a black parent and a white parent). Records indicate that she was known as "La Monzonga." One of her parents was probably from Monzonga, the name of a small town in Goa region of Mali in West Africa (*Monzonga*, "Populated Place,"

accessed on August 22, 2016; *Mali*, "Map of Mali," accessed on August 22, 2016.) A record dating to 1697 shows that María Madrid was the wife of Cristóbal de la Cruz. María Madrid's daughter, Juana de la Cruz, was also known as "La Mozonga." She was the wife of Juan de Ledesma, a soldier who escaped the 1720 Villasur massacre. It is not clear which of these women was the mother of Ana María [Almazán]. (Kessell, Hendricks, and Dodge, *Boulders*: 1143; Chávez, *Archives*: 156, 162; Chávez, *Origins*: 204.)

32. The Spanish word *amancebados* comes from the verb *amancebar*, which means "to enter into concubinage." In this case, the term meant that they were recognized as a couple, but were not married.
33. Juan Antonio Barrios was a native of Casa Grande and a presidio soldier by 1697. He was married to María González, about whom no information is known. Barrios was with the 1720 Villasur Expedition, but survived the massacre. (Hottz, *Segesser*: 47; Kessell, Hendricks, and Dodge, *Boulders*: 953n20; Kessell, Hendricks, Dodge, and Miller, *Disturbances*: 128.)
34. The Spanish words *"remachando la chapeta"* literally mean "riveting the metal."
35. Juan Manuel de Chirinos was the son of Juan Manuel Martínez de Cervantes and María Antonia Chirinos; apparently he took his mother's last name. He married Catalina de Los Angeles in 1693, and came to New Mexico with the Farfán Expedition in 1694. He settled in Santa Cruz; upon Catalina's death, he married María Guadalupe Navarro. In 1710, he married Juana Montoya. He was in Santa Fe serving as a cabildo scribe between 1718 and 1729. (Chávez, *Origins*: 226-27; Kessell, Hendricks, and Dodge, *Royal Crown*: 36; Kessell, Hendricks, and Dodge, *Boulders*: 644, 670n15, 782.)
36. Miguel Carillo was a native of New Galicia and the son of Agustín Carrillo and Margarita Rodarte. A resident of New Mexico by 1694, he is listed as being a presidio soldier from 1712 to 1719. Both he and his wife, María de Mondragón, were dead by 1727. (Kessell, Hendricks, and Dodge, *Boulders*: 956n50; Christmas and Rau, "Una Lista": 200.)
37. The Spanish word for power of attorney is *poder*. In this case, it seems to apply to the right of representation, rather than a broader right. In other words, Agustín Palma is allowing Chirinos to represent him in matters before the presiding justice.
38. For information on Diego Arias de Quiros, see Case 1 and Case 2.
39. The formal and somewhat difficult language used by Chirinos suggests that it was based on a *guía* (legal handbook).
40. Joseph Manuel Giltoméy was born in the Philippines, the son of don Juan Manuel de Giltoméy, a Spanish official, and Antonia Flores de Valdéz. He was in New Mexico in 1695, living in Santa Cruz. He was left for dead after the 1696 Pueblo Revolt, but survived. He married Isabel de Olivas in 1696. He is included in a presidio muster for April 1704; he was also one of the witnesses at the inventory of Governor Diego de Vargas's possessions, after the governor's death in 1704. In 1715, Giltoméy replaced Cristóbal de Góngora as an adjutant. In 1715, he was given permission to go to El Paso to seek a cure for ailments; he died in 1727. (Chávez, *Origins*: 186, 358; Kessell, Hendricks, and Dodge, *Boulders*: 644, 873; Kessell, Hendricks, Dodge, and Miller, *Settling of Accounts*: 222, 242; Christmas and Rau, "Una Lista": 196.)
41. In the original text, the words within the parentheses were crossed out, but are still visible.
42. Here is a clearer explanation: If everything that Petrona said about the rape was true, then as the mother of Antonia she would not have had sex with Agustín Palma after she returned and found out what had happened. Because Petrona said that she *did* have sex with Palma after the alleged rape, then it proves that the rape did not happen. She was lying and Palma was not guilty and therefore no attorney was needed.
43. The Spanish word *"esquimera"* means "an imaginary creature, a chimera" in English.
44. In the Spanish text, the term is *"falta de jussio dementado."*
45. Juan Antonio Ramos was born in Salveterra, Spain, and then he lived in Sonora, Mexico, in the 1680s. His first wife was Catalina Girón. Sometime after 1697, he married María Mata, the daughter of Miguel Mata and Felipa Duran. In 1699, he is listed as being married to María Canseco (and it is possible these two women might be the same person). In 1697, he petitioned Governor Vargas for additional animals, along with other persons claiming to be from Sombrerete and Zacatecas—all of whom came to New Mexico with the Hurtado Expedition. A presidio soldier by 1714, he was killed while on a campaign in 1715. (Kessell and Hendricks, *Force of Arms*: 119n4; Kessell, Hendricks, and Dodge, *Boulders*: 1168, 1169n69; Kessell, Hendricks, Dodge, and Miller, *Disturbances*: 105; Christmas and Rau, "Una Lista": 503-04; SANM II #239e; Tigges, "Presidial Company": 71-76.)

6

FRANCISCA GÓMEZ DE TORRES ASKS GOVERNOR FOR PROTECTION FROM ABUSIVE HUSBAND
July 13–August 22, 1713   Source: SANM II #196

Synopsis and editor's notes: The Torreses and Lujáns who appear in this case were part of pre-revolt families who returned to New Mexico in 1692 with General Vargas. Many of the others mentioned in this document came with the Farfán Expedition of 1694; they probably all knew each other before arriving in New Mexico. The case begins on July 13, 1713, when María de Torres went to the house of the Santa Cruz alcalde to tell him that her sister, Francisca Gómez de Torres, had been killed by Felix Luján, Francisca's husband. When the alcalde, Jacinto Sánchez [de Iñigo], investigated he found that Francisca was still alive but had badly bruised arms and injuries elsewhere on her body. María de Torres was mistaken about the death of her sister, but it is hardly surprising that she was concerned, for the year before Miguel, Felix's brother, had been found guilty of murdering his wife. Perhaps because of this or another reason, María and Francisca were willing to testify before the alcalde and the governor.

After hearing the accusation, Alcalde Sánchez arrested Luján and took him to his own house, because Santa Cruz did not have a prison. When Sánchez interviewed Francisca, she stated that her husband mistreated her, she was living a *mala vida* (bad life), and she wished to live with her parents. In the meantime, Luján had escaped to take sanctuary in the church at San Ildefonso and then in the church at Santa Clara. Jacinto Sánchez then sent the case to Governor Flores Mogollón in Santa Fe.

In order to discover why Luján was mistreating his wife, Flores Mogollón proceeded to question a variety of people. They all said nearly the same thing: that the couple did not get along and the main problem was that Francisca denied her husband the "conjugal act." Flores Mogollón asked where the rumors had originated about Francisca's refusal to have sex with Luján and her having an affair with her brother-in-law. In her testimony, Francisca repeated that she had had a bad life with Luján and stated that he had punished her and whipped her. Recently, she said, he took her to a field to punish her and she thought that he was going to kill her.

Governor Flores Mogollón determined that the reason Luján beat his wife was jealousy and stated that when Luján came out of sanctuary he would be sentenced to prison. However, sometime later, Francisca approached the governor and said that she forgave Luján and asked that he be pardoned so he could work in his fields, which were being left unattended. She also asked that she and Luján be placed in the home of her parents. Flores Mogollón agreed to this, but stated that Luján first had to come out of sanctuary, which he did.

Governor Flores Mogollón took his time with this case, following the prescribed legal procedures: He stated the *cabeza del proceso* (charge), then ordered the imprisonment of the accused, and asked the alcade to inquire if Luján had any goods that could be embargoed. Each witness stated whether they were related to the plaintiff or the accused and, in most cases, affirmed and ratified their testimony. The governor reviewed Francisca's request for a pardon of Luján, and then he agreed to do so, with the condition that if Luján began to beat her again, he would be given the punishment that he deserved.

TRANSLATION

Jesus, Mary and Joseph
Year of 1713
Villa of Santa Fe, New Mexico

Criminal case presided over by the royal justice against Felix Luján[1] for the bad life[2] he had given to his wife, Francisca [Gómez] de Torres.[3]
Judicial proceeding
Governor and Captain General
Secretary Pinto[4] (rubric)

[Investigation of Complaint]

Sir, today I sent an official notice to your honor stating that yesterday, the 13th of the present month at about seven o'clock in the evening, María de Torres[5] came to my house and informed me that Felix Luján had killed his wife. However, being that I was not at home, this same message was sent to me at the pueblo of San Juan, where I was at the time. I immediately mounted my horse and went to the house and home of Felix Luján. Upon finding him there, I went to seek his wife to see if she was hurt with any possible life threatening injuries, but I found her with only badly bruised arms. I took him as a prisoner until morning when I could examine the cause of these disturbances.

I then took the sworn statement of Francisca [Gómez] de Torres before two witnesses, who were Miguel de Quintana[6] and Joseph de Atienza,[7] the younger, in the following manner. She stated that it was because of her husband that she was mistreated, but it was due to his imagination. She said that if she tried to give him attention he immediately gets mad and if she does not do so, he gets mad anyway. She stated that it had not been even three days past that she had been mistreated, and they were living a life that should not be had by anyone who is married. She would feel better if the royal justice would place her with her parents, so that she would not be mistreated. She stated that it was not the first time that he has left her with her arms bruised; that only a few days before that he had hit her. She stated that she does not want to live with a husband who is so hurtful.

These proceedings being carried out by me, I left him as a prisoner in my home, and I thus came to the determination of submitting them to your honor. However, I found out that he had escaped, and I have not been able to find him nor do I know his whereabouts or where he is in sanctuary. As for his wife I have taken her and placed her in my home for her safety until I receive an order from your honor as to what is to be determined. May Our Lord safeguard your honor for many years. Villa of Santa Cruz, July 14, 1713.

I kiss the hand of your honor
Your most affectionate servant
Jacinto Sánchez [de Iñigo][8] (rubric)

[Charge and imprisonment]

At the Villa of Santa Fe, New Mexico, on the 15th of July, 1713, I don Juan Ignacio Flores Mogollón,[9] governor and captain general of these provinces for his majesty, have seen the note that the alcalde of [Santa Cruz de] La Cañada has written to me dated the 14th of this month. He informed me that María de Torres had gone looking for him on the night of the 13th, to inform him that Felix Luján had killed his wife, Francisca [Gómez] de Torres. Later that same night, the alcalde went to the home of Felix Luján, and finding him there he took him as a prisoner to his own home, where he left him. The alcalde then returned to see if she, Francisca [Gómez] de Torres, had any life-threatening wounds, but found that she had only one badly bruised arm along with some other blows. Upon having asked her what the reason was for what had occurred, she stated before the witnesses, that the alcalde had with him, that without any reason her husband would leave her as she is now. She asked the royal justice, the governor, to separate her from him, placing her with her parents. However, the alcalde, in order to assure her safety took her to his home and his wife. At the time of getting to his home his wife told him that the prisoner, Felix Luján, had escaped.

I order that this written note [of the alcalde] be attached at the cabeza del proceso (head of the proceedings)[10] and that statements be taken from those who were present when Francisca [Gómez] de Torres made her statement. So that in the future this type of a crime is not left without any type of punishment, other witnesses who know about how she has been mistreated should be brought forth and examined, as by this and by the way he, Felix Luján, fled from being a prisoner, the case should be substantiated. Upon his being found, I order that he is to be held a prisoner in order to prove that justice [is done] however it may be. The alcalde mayor is to inquire if Luján has any material goods, and if so, the goods are to be embargoed according to the order that I have given to the alférez Cristóbal de Torres.[11] They are to be turned over to him by the alcalde mayor, who, in the mean time, is to deposit them until this case is determined. I thus approved, ordered and signed it along with my secretary of government and war.

By order of the governor
Don Juan Ignacio

Flores Mogollón (rubric)
before me
Roque de Pinto (rubric)
Secretary of Government and War

Statement of Captain don Alfonso Rael de Aguilar I,[12] fifty-three years of age

At the Villa of Santa Fe, New Mexico on the 16th of July, 1713, I, don Juan Ignacio Flores Mogollón, governor and captain general of these provinces for his majesty, in order to continue with this investigation made to appear before me Captain don Alfonso Rael de Aguilar I, from whom I took his sworn statement which he made to God, Our Lord, and to the sign of the Cross, regarding the charges and to which he promised to tell the truth in whatever he knew and to what he was asked. Upon the heading of the proceedings being read to him, he stated that it was publicly and in other ways well-known that Felix Luján had given his wife, Francisca [Gómez] de Torres, a bad life. He had heard that he would beat her up occasionally without Francisca [Gómez] de Torres having done anything. This [Rael de Aguilar] said is what he knows and is the truth regarding the sworn statement that he has given. He affirmed and ratified it being read back to him and he stated that the generalities of the law[13] do not apply. He stated that he was fifty-three years of age, more or less, and he signed it along with the governor before me, the secretary of government and war.

Don Juan Ignacio
Flores Mogollón (rubric)
Alfonso Rael de Aguilar I (rubric)
By order of the Governor and Captain General
Roque de Pinto (rubric)
Secretary of Government and War

Statement of Miguel de Quintana, thirty-six years of age

At this Villa of Santa Fe, New Mexico, on the 24th of July, 1713, I, the governor and captain general, in order to continue with the investigation of this case, made to appear before me Miguel de Quintana, whom upon being present I received his sworn statement which he made before God, Our Lord, and to the sign of the Cross, and he promised to tell the truth regarding that which he knew and as to what he was asked. Upon having been read the heading of the proceedings he stated that on the 13th of the present month he had gone with the alcalde mayor of [Santa Cruz de] La Cañada as an assisting witness to the home of Felix Luján to take the sworn statement of Francisca [Gómez] de Torres, wife of Felix Luján. This is the same as is written in the letter of the alcalde mayor to me, the governor, and which is at the head of these proceedings. Quintana stated that it has been heard within the last few days that the husband and wife have been fighting, and that the cause of the whole matter was that the wife, Francisca [Gómez] de Torres, denied him the spousal conjugal act. This is what he has heard, but does not remember from whom it was heard. He stated that this was the truth regarding the matter and he affirmed and ratified it upon it being read back to him. He stated that the generalities of the law do not apply to him and that he was thirty-six years of age, more or less. He signed it along with me, the governor, before my secretary of government and war.

One other thing, he stated that he had heard as it was told to him by Domingo Martín[14] that Felix Luján had not done the manly thing for a very long time. He was asked if he knew why this was so, and he stated that he had heard it only publicly, and that Domingo Martín would not say by whom it was stated. He stated that someone else had told him that the problems that Felix Luján had with his wife were because she refused to do the spousal conjugal act with him. The one who told him this was Juan de Atienza[15] in the presence of his brother, Joseph de Atienza. This he stated was what he knew regarding his sworn statement that he has made, etc.

    don Juan Ignacio
    Flores Mogollón (rubric)
    Miguel de Quintana (rubric)
    At the order of the governor
    before me
    Roque de Pinto (rubric)
    Secretary of Government and War

Statement of Joseph de Atienza, the younger, thirty-three years of age

At this said villa on the said day, month and year, I, the governor and captain general, in order to continue with the investigation of this case, made to appear before me Joseph de Atienza, resident of the jurisdiction of [Santa Cruz de] La Cañada, in order to take his sworn statement, to which he promised to tell the truth as to what he knew and what he was asked. After having read to him the opening of the complaint made by the alcalde mayor of La Cañada, he stated that on the 13th of this month the alcalde mayor called on him to go with him as an assisting witness to the home of Felix Luján to take the sworn statement of Francisca [Gómez] de Torres, to examine the injuries that she had received, and to see if her statement is the same as is seen in the alcalde's written document.

He was asked if he knew or has heard what the reason was for her having been mistreated, and if he knows if this has happened in the past. He stated that he did not know that he, Felix, had mistreated her before until he, José, went with the alcalde mayor. At that time, she had some bruises on her left arm and some other ones on a muscle. He said that she had stated that he, Felix, had mistreated her on other occasions. Within two or three days after the last occasion, he had heard Estefania Moreno de Trujillo,[16] the wife of this witness, say that the reason that Felix Luján mistreated his wife was because she denied having a conjugal spousal relation with him and that she did not want to be with him. He stated that this had been told to his wife by the wife of

Jacinto Sánchez [de Iñigo] and that he, José, had also heard it from his brother Juan de Atienza when he was on his way to Santa Fe. This he stated was the truth regarding the sworn statement that he has made and he affirmed and ratified it after his statement was read back to him. He said that the generalities of the law do not apply and stated that he was thirty-two years of age. He signed it along with me, the said governor, before my secretary of government and war.

 Juan Ignacio
 Flores Mogollón (rubric)
 Joseph de Atienza (rubric)
 At the order of the Governor
 before me
 Roque de Pinto (rubric)
 Secretary of Government and War

Statement of Joseph de Atienza Alcalá y Escobar[17.] sixty-four years of age

 Continuing, I, the governor and captain general, in order to proceed with the investigation of this case, made to appear before me Joseph de Atienza Alcalá y Escobar, high marshall of the Holy Office of the Inquisition of this New Spain. From him I received his sworn statement which he made to God, Our Lord and to the sign of the Cross, in which he promised to tell the truth as to what he knew and what he was asked.

 He was asked if he knew Felix Luján and Francisca [Gómez] de Torres, his wife, how long he had known them, and if he knows if he mistreats Francisca de Torres. He stated that he does know them and was present at their marriage, and that it had been about nine years, more or less, when they got married. He does not know if he, Felix, mistreats her, because he has spoken with them very little. He was asked if he knew that on the 13th, María de Torres, the sister of Francisca, had gone to summon the alcalde mayor stating that Felix Luján had killed her sister. He said that he had heard Jacinto Sánchez [de Iñigo], the alcalde mayor, say that María had told him that, and that he had gone with her to the home of Felix Luján where Sánchez took him prisoner. He then took him to his home, where he left him. He then returned to see Francisca [Gómez] de Torres. While there he was told that his prisoner, Felix Luján, had fled. On the following day, being at the home of her father, Cristóbal de Torres, with Francisca [Gómez] de Torres, he saw that one of her arms was badly bruised, and she stated that her husband had done it.

 He was then asked if the reason for all of the problems with the husband and wife were because she would not have a spousal conjugal relation with him. He stated that he did not know and that everything he has stated is the truth regarding the sworn statement that he has made and he affirmed and ratified it after it was read back to him. He said that the generalities of the law do not apply to him, and stated that he was sixty-four years of age and he signed it along with me, the said governor, in front of my secretary of government and war.

don Juan Ignacio
Flores Mogollón (rubric)
At the order of the Governor
before me
Roque de Pinto (rubric)

[Statement of Juan de Atienza, forty-two years of age]

At this said villa on the said day, month and year, I, the governor and captain general, in order to continue with the investigation of this case, made to appear before me Juan de Atienza, resident of the jurisdiction of [Santa Cruz de] La Cañada, from whom I received his sworn statement which he made to God, Our Lord, and to the sign of the Cross, and he swore to tell the truth as to what he knew and was asked. He was asked if he knew Felix Luján and Francisca [Gómez] de Torres, his wife. He stated that he did and that it was nine years, more or less, since they had gotten married. He was asked if he knew that on the 13th of the present month Luján mistreated Francisca quite badly, which obligated her sister, María de Torres, to go and call the justice, saying that she had been killed. He stated that he knew it was certain because the alcalde mayor has told him so on the following day [July 14]. Also he told him that he had taken Felix Luján as a prisoner. He, Felix, had been in refuge at the church of the pueblo of San Ildefonso. Today he knows that he is at that the church of the pueblo of Santa Clara. This he knows because the alcalde mayor told those who were with him on that particular day.

He stated that they had found Francisca [Gómez] de Torres with a bruised arm and other bruises on another muscle, which she did not show them because it was not in a decent place. She had told them that she had complained to another justice about the bad manner in which she was treated, and that she was punished without any reason. Francisca [Gómez] de Torres told this witness that on the eve of the vespers of the day of San Juan, Felix Luján was taking her to the pueblo of San Ildefonso and along the road he made her get totally nude in order to beat her. [Juan] was asked what the reasons were for Felix having given her such a bad life. He stated that he had heard María Rodarte,[18] the wife of Jacinto Sánchez, say that he did it because she, Francisca, would not have a spousal conjugal relation with him. This he says is the truth regarding the sworn statement that he has made and which he affirmed and ratified when it was read back to him. He said that the generalities of the law do not apply and that he was forty-two years of age. He signed it along with me, the governor, before my secretary of government and war.

Juan de Atienza (rubric)
Don Juan Ignacio
Flores Mogollón (rubric)
At the order of the Governor
Before me
Roque de Pinto (rubric)

Statement of Estefania Moreno de Trujillo, thirty-six years of age

    At the Villa of Santa Fe, New Mexico, on the 26th of July, 1713, I, the said governor and captain general, in order to continue with the investigation of this case made to appear before me Estefania Moreno de Trujillo, wife of Joseph de Atienza, whom he mentions in his sworn statement. From her I received her sworn statement which she made to God, Our Lord, and to the sign of the Cross, in which she promised to tell the truth in whatever she knew and what she was asked.

    She was asked if it was true that her husband had been told by the wife of Jacinto Sánchez that all of the problems that were had by Felix Luján and Francisca [Gómez] de Torres came about due to the lack of love with which he treated her and that she denied him a spousal conjugal relation with him. She stated that one morning when she had gone to the home of María Rodarte, the wife of Jacinto Sánchez, the alcalde mayor of [Santa Cruz de] La Cañada, and while they were talking about specific things, María told this witness that she, María Rodarte, was quite miserable because her husband had held Felix Luján as a prisoner, and that he had escaped, and also because [Felix] was so miserable with his wife. Also that María had been told by the prisoner how much he hated his wife and that he had to escape from there. He said that he was miserable with her because she would not have anything to do with him and when he tried to be loveable to her she would not have anything to do with him. This she stated is the truth (and is what she heard María Rodarte say) regarding the sworn statement that she has made and which she affirmed and ratified upon her statement being read back to her. She stated that the generalities of the law did not apply, and said that she was thirty-six years of age. She did not sign because she did not know how; I, the governor, signed it in front of my secretary of government and war.

    don Juan Ignacio
    Flores Mogollón (rubric)
    At the order of the Governor
    before me
    Roque de Pinto (rubric)
    Secretary of Government and War

Statement of María de Castro y Rodarte, thirty-five years of age

    At this Villa of Santa Fe, New Mexico on the 28th of July, 1713, I, the said governor and captain general, in order to continue with the investigation of this case made to appear before me María de Castro y Rodarte, wife of Jacinto Sánchez. She was mentioned in their statements by Joseph de Atienza and by Estefania Moreno de Trujillo. From her I took her sworn statement which she made to God, Our Lord, and to the sign of the Cross, in which she promised to tell the truth as to what she knew and what she was asked.

She was asked if she had told Estefania Moreno de Trujillo, when she was at her home, that Felix Luján had told her that the motive that he had for mistreating his wife was because whenever he, Luján, wanted to get close to his wife and be loveable, she would get mad and would give him any excuse to avoid having a spousal conjugal relation. Luján said that if the royal justice should pay heed to her, they would have to listen to him as well. She stated that when he was being held a prisoner in her home, Felix Luján told her the same thing as asked in the above question and in the same way she told it to Estefania Moreno de Trujillo. She was asked if she knew that Felix Luján mistreated his wife, Francisca [Gómez] de Torres, and had maltreated her on certain occasions. She stated that she did not know anything about it until María de Torres had gone to notify Jacinto Sánchez, the alcalde mayor of the jurisdiction of [Santa Cruz de] La Cañada, telling him that Felix Luján had killed his wife, Francisca [Gómez] de Torres.

This she says is what she knows and is the truth regarding her sworn statement that she has made and which she affirmed and ratified upon it being read back to her. She said that the generalities of the law do not apply and stated that she was thirty-five years of age, more or less. She did not sign because she did not know how. I, the governor, signed it before my secretary of government and war.

Don Juan Ignacio Flores Mogollón (rubric)
At the order of the Governor
before me
Roque de Pinto (rubric)
Secretary of Government and War

Don Juan Ignacio Flores Mogollón, governor and captain general
of these provinces of New Mexico and castellan of his forces and presidios
for the King, Our Lord, etc.

[Order regarding Domingo Martín]

I say that in a statement given by Miguel de Quintana in the proceedings that are being carried out against Felix Luján, he stated that he had heard Domingo Martín talking about the mistreatment that the said Felix Luján gives his wife. Upon being asked about this, Quintana stated that Domingo Martín told him that Felix Luján had not had sex in a very long time. Upon asking Miguel de Quintana why Domingo Martín had told him that, he said that it was commonly known, but that he did not know it for certain. I then proceeded to call Domingo Martín to appear before me so that I could take his sworn statement. This was done by me on the 28th of the present month. However, it has come to my attention that he had suffered some type of a dizzy attack when he was close to the pueblo of Pojoaque and fell from his horse. He had to immediately be taken back to his home due to the accident and because of his advanced age, this making it impossible for him to appear before me.

I order Captain Miguel Tenorio de Alba to proceed to the home of Domingo

Martín to take his sworn statement regarding this matter so that I can ascertain if he did tell this to Miguel de Quintana. I also wish to determine what his motives were for having said what he did, which are bad accusations against the reputation and public opinion of a married woman. I hereby give all of my authority that may be required to Miguel de Quintana for him to bring Domingo Martín to this villa to appear before me. He is to bring him to me in a careful manner as a prisoner, if it is so warranted, and he can seek the necessary assistance from the neighbors in the name of his majesty. For all of this I grant to him the power that is sufficient according to what is granted to me under the reason of my position. I signed it at this Villa of Santa Fe, New Mexico, on the 29th of July, 1713, along with my secretary of government and war.

    Don Juan Ignacio
Flores Mogollón (rubric)
Roque de Pinto (rubric)
Secretary of Government and War

Statement of Domingo Martín, seventy years, more or less

    At Villa Nueva de Santa Cruz on the 29th of July, 1713, I, Captain Miguel Tenorio de Alba,[19] by virtue of the commission that I received on this day from don Juan Ignacio Flores Mogollón, my governor, in order to take the sworn statement from Domingo Martín mentioned by Miguel de Quintana in the proceedings that are being carried out, proceeded to go to the house and dwelling of Domingo Martín. I was accompanied by Roque Jacinto Jaramillo[20] and Tomás de Córdova,[21] witnesses who are to assist me in receiving the statement, which was done in the following manner. Upon being present I took Domingo's sworn statement which he made to God, Our Lord, and to the sign of the Holy Cross, under which he promised to tell the truth according to what he knew and to what he was asked.

    He was asked what it was that he communicated to Miguel de Quintana when they were talking about the bad life that Felix Luján gave to his wife and what the reasons were for him doing this. He stated that Felix had told him, and he had told Miguel de Quintana while they were talking about his wife, that [Martín] was not to be concerned about the mistreatment that he gave his wife, that he had never done anything to her, but that he had not had sex with her. This is what he repeated to Miguel de Quintana, and the reasons for doing so. This witness stated that all of this was commonly known and that he had heard it, but did not mention [it to] anyone specifically. But now that he is obligated to do so under the solemn statement that he is required to make under oath to God, Our Lord, and to the sign of the Holy Cross, he stated that he had heard from Cristóbal de la Cruz Carajuida[22] that the wife of Felix was in a bad state and that this was the reason for Felix to give her a bad life. He stated that Cristóbal de la Cruz [Carajuida] was the one who told him this, and that he, Cruz, had been told this by a servant from the house of Felix, but did not know who the person was who was causing the bad affair, nor had he seen anything. This he said was the truth about what he knows according to the sworn statement that he has made and it having been read back to him, he stated that it was right as it was and as he had declared and has nothing to add or to delete and which he affirmed and ratified according to his sworn statement and said that his age was seventy years more or less and he did not sign it nor did the witnesses. I, the captain, signed it so that it is valid on the said day.

 Miguel Tenorio de Alba (rubric)

Statement of Cristóbal de la Cruz [Carajuida]
 Continuing, on the said day, I, Captain Miguel Tenorio de Alba, in order to take the statement of Cristóbal de la Cruz, I made him appear before me and in the presence of Juan de Dios Martín[23] and Blas Lobato,[24] I took his sworn statement which he made to God, Our Lord, and to the sign of the Holy Cross, under which he swore to tell the truth as to what he was asked.

 He was asked what he had talked about with Domingo Martín regarding the wife of Felix Luján, being that Domingo Martín had mentioned him in his sworn statement. He said that they were talking about the bad life that Felix had given his wife. Domingo Martín told him that a servant from his home had told him that she (the wife of Felix) was having an affair and that was the cause of the problems. He said that he had not seen anything, that he had been told that by an Indian woman, Magdalena Pachané,[25] who today lives at San Ildefonso, and she was the one who told him that the wife of the said Felix was having an affair with Juan Luján, the brother of the said Felix. He stated that this was what he knew regarding his sworn statement which he affirmed and ratified after it was read back to him. He said that it was the way it was as he had so stated and that he does not have anything to add or delete. He said that he was seventy years of age, more or less. He did not sign nor did the witnesses because they did not know how, I, the captain, signed it on the said day.

 Miguel Tenorio de Alba (rubric)

Statement of Magdalena Pachane [Ponachavé]
 On the 31st of July, 1713, I, Captain Miguel Tenorio de Alba, by virtue of the commission given to me by the governor and captain general, made to appear before me Magdalena Ponachavé, Indian of the Tigua nation, who was mentioned by Cristóbal de la Cruz. By de la Cruz interpretating for him, he made her to understand the graveness of her sworn statement. Upon her understanding of that, she swore to God, Our Lord and to the sign of the Holy Cross to tell the truth in what she was asked and as such he took her sworn statement. She promised to tell the truth as to what she knew and what she was asked.

 She was asked what her motive was for having told Cristóbal de la Cruz that the wife of Felix Luján was having an affair with Juan Luján,[26] his brother. She was asked if she had seen [Juan Luján] with her or did someone tell her about it? She stated that for the question that is asked of her, she had told Cristóbal about it, and she had been motivated to do so because she had seen [Juan and Francisca] playing around in the corral. Because of that, she thought so in her heart [that they were having an affair]. This was why she had told Cristóbal, but that she had not told anyone else. She stated that this was the truth and is what she knows regarding her sworn statement that she has made. She affirmed and ratified it after it was read back to her, saying that it was correct and is what she stated and that she has nothing more to add or delete. She stated that she was forty years of age, more or less, and neither her or the witnesses who were present, being Blas Lovato and Juan Alonso de Mondragón,[27] signed because they did not know how. So that it is valid I signed it on the said day.

Miguel Tenorio de Alba (rubric)

[Sentencing of Witness]

At this Villa of Santa Fe, New Mexico, on the 1st of August, 1713, I, don Juan Ignacio Flores Mogollón, governor and captain general of these provinces, after having seen the sworn statements which by virtue of my commission were taken by Miguel Tenorio de Alba, had them added to these proceedings. I have heard the wicked deed that was done by the Indian woman by having spoken badly about Francisca [Gómez] de Torres in having said that she had seen her with her brother-in-law, and thus taking all the good character from the said Francisca [Gómez] de Torres. Thus I order that she be brought to this villa where she is to be left for the period of six months and where she is to be put to work and will be observed.

I also order the alcalde mayor of [Santa Cruz de] La Cañada to proceed to the home of Domingo Martín and notify him that in my name he is to contain himself from here on out by not bringing forth similar issues. This is with the understanding that due to his advanced age I will not punish him at this time like I should for having circulated to others things about the honesty and value of a virtuous woman. The harm he, Domingo Martín, does to himself, being that she is married to his blood nephew. I thus approved, ordered and signed it along with my secretary of government and war.

Don Juan Ignacio
Flores Mogollón (rubric)
by order of the governor
before me
Roque de Pinto (rubric)
Secretary of Government and War

[Statement of Francisca Gómez de Torres]

At this Villa of Santa Fe, New Mexico, on the 2nd of August, 1713, I, the governor and captain general, made appear before me Francisca [Gómez] de Torres, wife of Felix Luján. At my order, she was brought forth before me by her father, Alférez Cristóbal de Torres, at whose home I have placed her. I received her sworn statement which she made before God, Our Lord and to the sign of the Holy Cross, in which she promised to tell the truth after having heard me read to her the paper that was written to me by the alcalde mayor of [Santa Cruz de] La Cañada which is found at the beginning of these proceedings. She said that what she stated before the said alcalde mayor is the truth regarding the bad life that she has had with her husband Felix Luján since they got married, being punished and mistreated by indecent words against her honor and well-being.

She was asked if when he had punished her, she was given the reason for his doing so. She stated that every time that she was punished, it was because he was jealous for any reason because he thought that everyone who came to their home was trying to solicit her. The proof is seen because from the time that they got married she had always lived with her mother-in-law and her sister-in-law, who if it is needed, will come forth and tell the truth. She stated that on the 22nd of June, past, of this year, he whipped her and placed her as they did Christ in her home. Also on the 23rd, the eve of the vespers of the feast day of San Juan, he mounted her on a horse in order to take her to San Ildefonso and upon getting close to the mesa of San Ildefonso he took her through a marshy place to a *cañada* or low valley. Here he made her get down from the horse and made her get naked and he took a rope and the bridle from the horse to whip her, and she asked him why he was doing this.

Church at San Ildefonso Pueblo. Eleanor B. Adams and Fray Angelico Chavez, translators and annotators. *Missions of New Mexico, a Description of New Mexico, 1776.* 1955, 2012:65. Courtesy of Sunstone Press.

He responded telling her that she was a gossiper. She then responded by telling him, "Go ahead and hit me or do not hit me, as I shall give an account of this to the governor." At this time, he contained himself and did not whip her and then he ordered her to get dressed and they continued on their way to San Ildefonso. From that time on she has been in terror thinking that he took her to that cañada so that he could kill her. Even though he had punished her before, he had never taken her to a field and undressed her, for which reason she petitions the royal justice to separate her from him, thinking that he could try and do the same thing on another occasion and kill her.

She said that this was the truth as to what she has declared and is what has happened to her during the time that she has been married. In addition, for over three years till this day he has refused to support her; that not even a pair of shoes has he given her or to her two daughters. She said that God is a witness to the truth to which she refers and she has never given him the slightest reason to suspect her of anything for him to punish her. She did not sign because she did not know how, saying that she was twenty-four years of age, more or less. I, the governor, signed it along with my secretary of government and war.

 Don Juan Ignacio
 Flores Mogollón (rubric)
 at the order of the governor
 before me
 Roque de Pinto (rubric)
 Secretary of Government and War

Decree of Fault and Charges

At this villa on the said day, month and year, I, the governor and captain general, having read the statements found in these proceedings and finding that fault is proved against Felix Luján, upon his being found, he is to be imprisoned and for this purpose I have given this order. I thus approved, ordered and signed it along with my secretary of government and war.

 Don Juan Ignacio
 Flores Mogollón (rubric)
 At the order of the governor
 Before me
 Roque de Pinto (rubric)
 Secretary of Government and War

The following was presented before the governor on the 18th of August, 1713.

I, Francisca Gómez de Torres, resident of this Villa of Santa Fe and wife of Felix Luján, by order of your honor being placed at the home of the Alférez Cristóbal de Torres, my father, appear before your honor in my best and proper form which I have according to my right. I say that having come to this villa at the order of your honor for the mistreatment that my husband has put me through, whom I forgive so that God may forgive me, I petition for the great justice of your honor to be pleased to forgive my husband and release him so that he can go and cultivate his fields. If he desires to live with me I will try and do so with the hopes that we will do whatever God demands from us at this villa, in the home of my father, where I am prompt to do whatever God will order me to do with my husband. For all of this I petition and request with all of the veneration that is due, that your honor will be pleased to do as I ask. This is so that my husband will come to this villa to live with me complying with anything that your honor will agree to for the benefits of justice. I swear in my proper form that this, my request, is not done in malice but only for that which is due to Christians, and in what is necessary, etc.

 Francisca Gómez de Torres (rubric)

[Pardon by Governor]

 Having been reviewed by me, don Juan Ignacio Flores Mogollón, governor and captain general of the kingdom and provinces of New Mexico for his majesty, [I] took [the petition] as it was presented. I have considered the piety with which this party petitions [me] and that she pardons all of the grievances that have been caused by her husband, Felix Luján, and which I am familiar with and which have been proven through these proceedings that I have concluded. Thus I order Captain Jacinto Sánchez, alcalde mayor of Villa Nueva de Santa Cruz and the jurisdiction of La Cañada, that upon being able to find Felix Luján, he will notify him of this, my decree. In this decree, I order that he is to appear before me, and promising to change his ways in life, will come to live with his wife in this villa. Thus I will pardon him for the crimes he has committed in the mistreatment of his wife, and for the escape that he made when he was held prisoner. Hoping that he can be found, and then, upon giving his word, he is to appear before me so that I can sentence him according to the merits of the cause. I thus approved, ordered and signed this along with my secretary of government and war on the 18th of August, 1713.

 This petition is to be returned by the said alcalde mayor upon doing whatever he can in order to fulfill the above decree, etc.

 Don Juan Ignacio
Flores Mogollón (rubric)
at the order of the
Governor and Captain General
before me
Roque de Pinto (rubric)
Secretary of Government and War

 At this pueblo of San Ildefonso on the 21st of August, of this present year of 1713, in compliance and in obedience to the above decree issued by the governor and captain general don Juan Ignacio Flores Mogollón, whom God may guard, Felix Luján having appeared before me. [I], Jacinto Sánchez, alcalde mayor of Villa Nueva de Santa Cruz, and of its jurisdiction, made him read the said decree and order given by the governor. Felix Luján stated that he would obey the said order placed before him in everything that was stated. So that it is valid I, said alcalde mayor, signed it on the said day, month and year along with my assisting witnesses, etc.

 Assisting witness Nicolás Ortiz Ladron de Guevara[28] (rubric)
 Assisting witness Jacinto Sánchez (rubric)

[Pardon of Felix Luján]

 At this Villa of Santa Fe on the 22nd of August, 1713, before me, don Juan Ignacio Flores Mogollón, governor and captain general of this province for his majesty, by virtue of the preceding decree approved by me and cited by the alcalde mayor Jacinto Sánchez, there appeared Felix Luján. For him I pardoned all of the crimes which are contained in the case which I have concluded with the understanding that he amend his life, treating from here on, Francisca [Gómez] de Torres, his wife, with more love and with his promise of having to live in this villa. I then made her appear before me so that they would be in a loveable way together. Having seen that they were together in an amicable way and that they were thankful and sorry for having done what had been done, it was noticed that she was glad to be with him, and those who were present were also happy for them.

 I let him know that if he would begin to hate her again he would be in a bad position, but judging by her reaction I understood her, and I did not punish him as I should have and what he deserved. This is because he had come under a surety out of sanctuary. Telling him to go back would have caused confusion, because if he was outside [the place of sanctuary] I would have had to sentence him according to the merits of the case. So that it is valid I ordered that this petition be added to the proceedings. I thus approved, ordered, and signed it with my secretary of government and war.

 Don Juan Ignacio
 Flores Mogollón (rubric)
 Roque de Pinto (rubric)

TRANSCRIPTION

Jesus, Maria y Joseph
Año de 1713
Villa de Santa Fee de la Nueba Mexico

Causa criminal que de ofizio dela Real Justizia se e seguido contra Pheliz Lujan por la mala vida que le dava a Francisca de Torres, su mujer
Judicial
Señor Governador y Capitan General

Secretario, Pinto (rubric)

Señor Governador y Capitan General

Señor doy notissia a Vuestra Señoria como aller 13 del corriente como alas siete dela noche bino ami cassa Maria de Torres disiendome como Phelix Lujan avia muerto a su mujer y no estando yo en mi cassa seme despacho esta notisia a el Pueblo de San Juan donde me allaba luego me puse a cavallado y paze ala cassa y morada de dicho Phelix Lujan y allandolo presente le aprese para pasar aber si se allava su muger con algunas heridas peligrosas y solo le alle con los brasos acardenalados y siendo esto assi lo deje preso asta que amanesiese y hazer exsamen dela causa de estos disturbios.

Extrajudicialmente recivi juramento a Francisca de Torres en presencia de dos testigos que fueron Miguel de Quintana y Joseph de Atienza, el moso, y resulto el que dixo debaxo de juramento que no fue mas que por antojo de su marido pues vive de tal manera que si le muestra agrado se enoja y sino selo muestra tambien y que no pasar tres dias sin que la deje de maltratar y que viviendo una vida ynmaridable tiene por mayor consuelo el que la Real Justizia la ponga con sus padres para verse libre de semejante tormento y que no es la primera ocassion que la acardenaba pues dias pasados la puso como un sierto azotes y que no quiere vivir con marido tan pessado.

Estas deligencias hize dejandole en mi cassa por preso y biniendo de hazerlas con determinacion de remitirselo a Vuestra Señoria halle averse huido y aviendo hecho deligencias de el nole he podido descubrir ni donde se aya refujiado ami me paresio assertado asegurar a su muger y ponerla en mi cassa hasta ver orden de Vuestra Señoria, y lo que determinara. Nuestro Señor guarde a Vuestra Señoria muchos anos. Villa de Santa Cruz y Julio 14 de mill setezientos y treze años.

Beso la mano de Vuestra Señoria
Su mas afecto servidor
Jasinto Sanchez (rubric)

En la Villa de Santa Fee dela Nueba Mexico en quinze de Julio de mill setezientos y trese años yo Dn. Juan Ygnacio Flores Mogollon, Governador y Capitan General de estas provinzias por Su Magestad haviendo visto el papel que el Alcalde Mayor dela Cañada me escrivio su fecha de catorze de dicho mes en que me da notizia de que Maria de Torres el dia treze en la noche avia ido a buscarle diziendo que Phelix Luxan avia muerto a Francisca de Torres su muger y que luego paso ala casa del suso dicho y allandole en ella le prendio y llevo a su cassa de dicho Alcalde Mayor preso donde lo dexo y bolvio a reconoser si tenia algunas heridas la dicha Francisca de Torres la qual solo reconozio tener unos cardenales en un brazo y otros golpes; y preguntandole el motivo declaro delante de los testigos que llevava que sin ninguna la ponia siempre como son expuesto y que pedia ala Real Justizia la separase de el poniendola con su padre ala qual por asegurarla dicho Alcalde Mayor la llevo asu cassa con su muger quien le dio notisia de juerse juido el preso Feliz Lujan.

Cuyo papel mando se acomule a este auto caveza de proceso y se resivan declaraciones de los que se allaron presentes quando la yso la dicha Francisca de Torres, para que semejante maldad no quede sin castigo se examinen otros testigos que declaren sobre la mala vida que siempre le a dado que con esta y la fuga echa dela carzel sele pueda substanziar la caussa y mando que pudiendo ser avido sea preso que le guardare justizia en lo que la tubiese y el Alcalde Mayor ynquiera si tiene algunos vienes los embargue y en virtud de la orden que di al Alferez Xptobal de Torres sela entregue dicho Alcalde Maior donde estara depositada ynterin que se sustanzia esta causa, asi lo provey, mande y firme con me Secretario de Governazion y Guerra =

Por mando del Señor Governador ante mi
Dn. Juan Ygnacio
Flores Mogollon (rubric)
Roque de Pinto (rubric)
Secretario de Governazion y Guerra

Declaracion del
Capitan don Alfonso
Rael de Aguilar de edad
de 53 años

En la Villa de Santa Fee dela Nueba Mexico en diez y seis dias del mes de Jullio de mill setezientos y treze años yo Dn. Juan Ygnacio Flores Mogollon, Governador y Capitan General de estas provincias por Su Magestad para la averiguasion desta caussa hize parezer ante mi al Capitan Dn. Alphonso Rael de Aguilar a quien rezevi juramento que hizo por Dios Nuestro Senor y la Señal dela Cruz so cargo del qual prometio dezir verdad en lo que supiere y le fuere preguntado; y siendole leido el auto cavesra de prosesso dio y dijo que es notorio publica boz y fama la mala vida que siempre le a dado Pheliz Lujan a Francisca de Torres su muger aquien a oido dezir la aporrea muchas vezes sin que la dicha Francisca de Torres le aya dado motivo y esto es lo que save y la verdad so cargo del juramento que lleva fecho en que se afirmo y ratifico siendole leyda su declaracion que no le tocan los generales dela ley, declaro ser de edad de zinquenta y tres anos poco mas or menos, y lo firmo con migo dicho Governador ante mi Secretario de Governazion   y Guerra =

Dn Juan Ygnacio   Flores Mogollon (rubric)

Alphonso Rael de Aguilar (rubric)
Por mando del Señor
Governador y Capitan General
Roque de Pinto (rubric)
Secretario de Governazion y Guerra

Declaracion de
Miguel de Quintana
de edad de 36 años

En la Villa de Santa Fe dela Nueva Mexico en veinte y quatro dias del mes de Julio de mill setezientos y treze años yo dicho Governador y Capitan General para la averiguazion desta caussa yse psreser ante mi a Miguel de Quintana al qual estando presente le resevi juramento que hizo por Dios Nuestro Señor y la Señal de la Cruz so cargo del qual prometio dezir verdad en lo que supiere y fuere preguntado y siendole leido el auto cavesa de proceso dijo que el dia treze del presente mes fue con el Alcalde Mayor dela Cañada de testigo de asistenzia en cassa de Pheliz Lujan a resevirle su declaracion a Francisca de Torres, mujer de dicho Pheliz Lujan quien declaro lo mismo que contiene la carta que escribio dicho Alcalde Mayor ami dicho Governador; que esta por caveza de estos autos; y que a oido desir que andan de pocos dias a esta parte a pleito marido y muger y que lo ocasionava el negarle dicha Francisca de Torres el debito asu esposo que esto no se aquerda aquien lo oio y que esto es la verdad so cargo del juramento que lleva fecho en que se afirmo y ratifico aviendole leyda esta su declaracion y que no le tocan las generales de la ley, declaro ser de edad de treinta y seis anos poco mas o menos y la firmo con migo dicho Governador ante mi Secretario de Governazion y Guerra.

= Otro si declara que le oyo dezir a Domingo Martin que pues no avia echo el dicho Pheliz Lujan un echo de hombre no avia sido mucho y preguntandole este declarante que por que; le respondio que por las boses que corren y avia dicho Domingo Martin oido dezir que no selas expreso; y que ya se aquerda a quien oio dezir que los pleitos que tenia Feliz Lujan con su muger era por negarle el devito y fue quien selo dixo Juan de Atienza en presenzia de Joseph de Atienza su hermano, y que esto es lo que save so cargo del juramento que lleva fecho; ut supra =

Dn. Juan Ygnazio
Flores Mogollon (rubric)
Miguel de Quintana (rubric)
Por mando del Señor Governador
Ante mi
Roque de Pinto (rubric)
Secretario de Governazion y Guerra

Declaracion de
Joseph de Atienza,
El moso, de
Edad de 33 años

En esta dicha Villa en dicho dia, mes y añno yo dicho Governador y Capitan General para la averiguazion de esta causa hize parezer ante mi a Joseph de Atienza vezino dela jurisdizion de la Canada aquien rezevi juramento que hizo por Dos Nuestro Señor y la Señal de la Cruz so cargo del qual prometio dezir verdad en lo que supiere y fuese preguntado y siendole leido el auto cavesa de parte que esta por cavesa y es del Alcalde Maior dela Cañada; dijo que el dia treze deste mes lo llamo dicho Alcalde Maior para que fuese con el testigo de asistenzia en casa de Feliz Lujan a rezevirle declaracion a Francisca de Torres y reconoser los golpes que tenia y que la dicha declaro lo mismo que dicho papel expressa.

Preguntado si save o a oido dezir por que razon la maltrato y si en otras ocasiones lo a echo; Dijo que el no savia le diesse mala vida asta que fue aquella con el Alcalde Maior que tenia unos cardenales en el brazo ysquierdo y otros que dijo tenia en un muslo y que ella declaro la aporreava en otras ocasiones y que al cavo de dos o tres dias que subzedio lo referido le oio dezir a Estefania Trujillo mujer de este declarante que la mala vida que le dava Pheliz Lujan a su muger era por que le negava el debito y no queria juntarse con el; y que esto selo avia dicho a su mujer la de Jazinto Sanchez y que tanbien lo oyo dezir en el camino biniendo a esta Villa a su hermano Juan de Atienza; y que esto es la verdad so cargo del juramento que lleva fecho en que se afirmo y ratifico siendole leida esta su declaracion que no le tocan las generales de la ley; declaro ser de hedad de treinta y tres anos y lo firmo con migo dicho Governador ante mi Secretario de Governazion y Guerra =

Juan Ygnacio Flores Mogollon (rubric)

Joseph de Atienza (rubric)

Por mando del Senor Governador
Ante mi
Roque de Pinto (rubric)
Secretario de Governazion y Guerra

Declaracion de
Joseph de Atienza
Alcala y Escobar de
Edad de 64 años

Y luego yncontinente yo dicho Governador y Capitan General para la averiguacion de esta caussa hize parecer ante mi a Joseph de Atienza Alcala y Escover, Alguacil Mayor del Santo Oficio dela Ynquisision de esta Nueva España a quien resevi juramento que hiso por Dios Nuestro Señor y la Señal de la Cruz so cargo del qual prometio dezir verdad en lo que supiese y fuere preguntado y siendole si conoze a Phelix Lujan y Francisca de Torres su mujer y quanto tiempo a y si el dicho le da mala vida a Francisca Torres; Dijo que los conose y se allo en su casamiento, y que ya abra nueve anos poco mas o menos que se casaron pero que no save si le da o no mala vida por averlos comunicado mui poco; preguntato si save que el dia treze Maria de Torres hermana dela dicha Francisca avia ydo a llamar al Alcalde Maior disiendole que Pheliz Lujan avia muerto asu mujer; dijo avia oydo a Jazinto Sanchez, Alcalde Maior que la dicha Maria le dio essa notizia y con ella paso dicho Alcalde Maior ala cassa de Feliz Lujan donde lo prendio y lo llevo preso a su casa y dexandolo en ella preso bolvio a reconoser a Francisca de Torres y que oio dezir este declarante se avia juido dela pression dicho Feliz Lujan y que estando oi dia dela fecha ablando con Francisca de Torres en casa de su padre le vido en un brazo encardenal y que le dijo era uno de los que le avia dado su marido.

Preguntado si a oido dezir que la caussa de los disturbios que tenian entre marido y mujer eran por excusarse ella cumplirle el devito; dijo que no tiene notizia y que lo que lleva dicho es la verdad so cargo del juramento que lleva fecho en que se afirmo y ratifico siendole leida esta su declaracion; y que no le tocan las generales dela ley; declaro ser de hedad de sesenta y quatro anos y lo firmo con migo dicho Governador ante mi Secretario de Governazion y Guerra =

Dn. Juan Ygnacio
Flores Mogollon (rubric)
Joseph de Atienza Alcala y Escobar (rubric)
Por mando del Señor Governador
Ante mi
Roque de Pinto (rubric)
Secretario de Governazion y Guerra

[Declaracion de
Juan de Atienza,
Edad de 42 años]

En esta dicha Villa en dicho dia mes y año yo dicho Governador y Capitan General para la averiguazion desta caussa hize parezer ante mi a Juan de Atienza vezino dela jurisdizion dela Canada aquien rezivi juramento que hiso por Dios Nuestro Señor y la Señal dela Cruz so cargo del qual prometio dezir verdad en lo que supiere y fuere preguntado.

Siendole si conose a Pheliz Lujan y Fraancisca de Torres su muger; dijo que si y que a nueve anos poco mas o menos que se casaron. Preguntado si save que el dia treze deste mes la maltrato mucho y obligo a su hermana Maria de Torres a ir a llamar ala justizia diziendole que la avia muerto? Dijo que save ser zierto por averle dicho el Alcalde Maior el dia siguiente y que avia presso al dicho Pheliz Lujan quien estubo efujiado en la Yglesia del Pueblo de San Yldefonso y que oi save se passo ala del Pueblo de Santa Clara y que dicho Alcalde Maior le dijo y los que yvan con el aquel dia.

Como la allaron ala dicha Francisca de Torres con unos cardenales en un brazo y que dijo tener otros en un muslo que no mostro por la dezenzia; y que ella se avia quexado ala justizia dela mala vida que le dava castigandola sin darle motivo; y que dicha Francisca de Torres le dijo a esta declarante que la vispera de San Juan la llevava dicho Phelix Lujan al Pueblo de San Yldefonso y en el camino la desnudo para aporrearla; preguntado si save por que motivo le a dado y da tan mala vida? Dijo que lo que oio dezir a Maria Rodarte, muger de Jazinto Sanchez que Feliz Lujan le avia dicho que el castigarla era por excusarse a cumplirle el devito y que esto es la verdad so cargo del juramento que lleva fecho en que se afirmo y ratifico siendole leyda esta se declaracion

y que no le tocan las generales dela ley; declaro ser de hedad de quarenta y dos anos y lo firmo con migo dicho Governador ante mi Secretario de Governazion y Guerra =
Dn. Juan Ygnacio
Flores Mogollon (rubric)   Juan de Atienza (rubric)
    Por mando del Señor Governador
    Ante mi
    Roque de Pinto (rubric)

Declaracion de
Estefania Moreno de Trujillo
Edad de 36 años

    En la Villa de Santa Fee dela Nueva Mexico en veinte y siete dias del mes de Julio de mil setezientos y treze años yo dicho Governador y Capitan General para la averiguazion desta caussa hize parecer ante mi a Estefania Moreno de Trujillo, mujer de Joseph de Atienza quien la zita en su declaracion, aquien rezevi juramento que hiso por Dios Nuestro Señor y la Señal de la Cruz so cargo del qual prometio dezir verdad en lo que supiese y fuese preguntado.

    Siendole que si es zierto dijo asu marido le avia dicho la mujer de Jazinto Sanchez que el motivo delos disturbios que tenian Phelix Lujan y Francisca de Torres, su mujer, eran nazidos del desamor con que la tratava y negarselo a cumplirle el devito. Dijo que yendo un manana en casa de Maria Rodarte, mujer de Jazinto Sanchez, Alcalde Mayor de la Cañada estando ablando de distintas cosas le dijo la dicha Maria a esta declarante estoi con gran pesadumbre que mi marido tenia preso aqui a Feliz Lujan y se a juido y lo estava por desabrimiento con su mujer y que la dicha Maria avia oydo dezir al preso que como se ofia a su mujer se avia de oir a el y que si desabria con ella por que si llegava azerle algun carino lo despedia con desabrimiento y no le permitia y que esto es la verdad, (y lo que oio dezir ala dicha Maria Rodarte), so cargo del juramento que lleva fecho en que se afirmo y ratifico siendole leida esta su declaracion y que no le tocan las generales dela lei, declaro ser de hedad de treinta y seis anos, no firmo por no saver firmelo yo dicho Governador ante mi Secretario de Governazion y Guerra =
    Dn. Juan Ygnacio
    Flores Mogollon (rubric)
    Por mando del Señor Governador
    Ante mi
    Roque de Pinto (rubric)
    Secretario de Governazion y Guerra

[Declaracion de
Maria de Castro y Rodarte
De edad de 35 años]

En la Villa de Santa Fee dela Nueva Mexico en veinte y ocho dias del mes de Jullio de
mill setezientos y treze años yo dicho Governador y Capitan General para la averiguazion desta caussa hize pareser ante mi a Maria de Castro y Rodarte, mujer de Jasinto Sanchez, aquien zita en su declaracion Joseph de Atienza y Estefania Moreno de Trujillo, aquien rezevi juramento que hizo por Dios Nuestro Señor y la Señal dela Cruz so cargo del qual prometio dezir verdad en lo que supiere y fuese preguntada.

Siendole si le avia dicho a Estefania Moreno estando en su casa que le avia dicho Felix Lujan que el motivo que tenia para darle mala vida a su mujer era el motivo que siempre que dicho Lujan se arrimava a su mujer azerle algun carino se enojava y sele excusava a pagarle el devito y que como se ohia asu mujer tanvien la real justizia le oiria a el; Dixo que estando en su casa preso el dicho Feliz Lujan le dijo a esta declarante lo mismo que la pregunta meziona y dela misma forma selo refirio a Estefania Moreno de Trujillo; Preguntada si save que el dicho Pheliz Lujan le diese mala vida a Francisca de Torres, su mujer y que la ubiesse maltratado en otras ocasiones? Dixo que no avia tenido notizia de cosa alguna asta que Maria de Torres le fue a dar notizia a Jazinto Sanchez, Alcalde Maior dela jurisdizion dela Cañada su marido deziendole avia muerto Pheliz Lujan a Francisca de Torres, su muger.

Que esto save y es la verdad so cargo del juramento que lleva fecho en que se afirmo y ratifico siendole leido esta su declaracion y que no le tocan las generales de la ley, declaro ser de hedad de treinta y sinco anos poco mas of menos, no firmo por no saver firmelo yo dicho Governador ante mi Secretario de Governazion y Guerra =

Dn. Juan Ygnacio Flores Mogollon (rubric)
Por mando del Señor Governador
Ante mi
Roque de Pinto (rubric)
Secretario de Governazion y Guerra

Don Juan Ygnacio Flores Mogollon, Governador y Captian General destas Provincias dela Nueva Mexico y Castellano de Sus Fuerzas y Presidios por el Rey Nuestro Senor, ut supra =

Digo que por quanto en una declaracion que aze Miguel Quintana en unos autos que se siguen contra Pheliz Lujan depone que le oyo dezir a Domingo Martin ablando sobre el maltrato que dicho Pheliz Lujan dava a su mujer respondio al dicho Domingo Martin que pues no avia echo Feliz Lujan un echo de hombre no avia sido mucho y preguntandole Miguel de Quintana que por que le respondio Domingo Martin que por las boses que corren; y avia oido dezir que no selas expreso; y siendo llamado por me el dicho Domingo Martin para tomarle su declaracion sobre este punto biniendo ayer que se contaron veinte y ocho del corriente en obedezimiento de lo mandado, se me a dado notizia le dio un baguido junto al Pueblo de Pujoaque que se cayo del cavallo y fue presiso bolverlo a su casa por el azidente y su mucha edad y que esta le ymposivilita a venir ami presenzia.

Mando al Capitan Miguel Thenorio de Alva pase ala casa de dicho Domingo Martin aquien le reziva juramento so cargo del qual declaro si es zierto aver dicho lo referido a Miguel de Quintana y que motivos tiene para averlo dicho; que son mal asonantes contras el credito y opinion de una muger casada y en caso que niegue aver dicho tal; Doi comision quan bastante sea nesesaria para que requiera a Miguel de Quintana se benga con el a esta Villa ami presenzia trayendolo con cuidado como presso y si fuere nesesario en virtud de este despacho pedira el auxilio que nezesitara alos vezinos en nombre de Su Magestad para todo lo referido le doi el poder bastante segun me es conzedido por razon de mi empleo; y lo firme en esta Villa de Santa Fee dela Nueba Mexico en veynte y nueve de Jullio de mill setezientos y treze =
Con mi Secretario de Governazion y Guerra
Dn. Juan Ygnacio Flores Mogollon (rubric)
Roque de Pinto (rubric)
Secretario de Governazion y Guerra

Declaracion de
Domingo Martin
Edad de 70 años
mas o menos

En la Villa Nueva de Santa Cruz en veinte y nuebe dias del mes de Jullio de este año de mill sietecientos y treze yo el Capitan Miguel Thenorio de Alba en virtud de commission que oi dia dela fecha resevi del Señor Dn. Juan Ygnacio Flores Mogollon, mi governador para efecto de que tomase una declaracion a Domingo Martin sitado de Miguel de Quintana en unas diligencias que dicho queda sigiendo pase ala casa y morada de dicho Domingo Martin acompanado de Roque Jasinto Jaramillo y Thomas de Cordova testigos que lleve para resevir dicha declaracion que fue segun el thenor del orden y estando presente le resevi juramento que iso por Dios Nuestro Señor y la Señal dela Santa Cruz devajo de cuyo cargo prometio dezir verdad en lo que supiere y le fuere preguntado.

Siendo lo que fue lo que le comunica a Miguel de Quintana hablando a serca de la mala vida que le dava Felix Lujan a su muger y que motivos tubo para comunicarselo? Dijo que como havia dicho Felix a su muger combersando con el dicho Miguel de Quintana sobre algunas razones que ubo en esta materia le dijo Usted no se espante ni admire del maltrato que antes no a echo nada, pues no a echo un echo de hombre que dicho Quintana le replico que en que se fundava para desirseme tan cosa a que respondio este declarante que por las boses que corrian y havia oido dezir y que no le mensione sujeto ninguno y que a ora que esta ligado con el solemne juramento a Dios Nuestro Senor y la Señal de la Santa Cruz declara haver savido de Xptobal de la Cruz Carajuida que la dicho muger de Felix ya dicho estava en mal estado que esa era la causa de darle mala vida y que dicho Xptobal dela Cruz asi mismo lo comunico que a el selo avia dicho una criada de casa de dicho Felix pero no savia el sujeto con quien era esta mala amistad ni lo avia visto que esta es la verdad y lo que save por el juramento que fecho tiene y haviendole leido esta su declaracion dijo estar segun y como declaro que no tiene que anadir ni quitar a ella que se afirmo y ratifico en esta su declaracion que es de edad de setenta anos poco mas o menos y no firmo este declarante ni los testigos, firmelo yo dicho Capitan para que conste en dicho dia.

⁂

Declaracion de
Xptobal de la Cruz

 Y luego yncontinenti en dicho dia yo dicho Capitan Miguel Thenorio de Alva haviendo resultado la zitazion de Xptobal de la Cruz (Carajuida) le ise pareser ante mi y en presensia de Juan de Dios Martin y Blas Lobato y le resevi juramento en forma de derecho por Dios Nuestro Señor y la Señal de la Sancta Cruz debajo de cuio cargo prometio dezir verdad en lo que le fuere preguntado

 Preguntado que platica tubo con Domingo Martin a serca de la muger de Felix Lujan que dicho Domingo Martin lo a sitado en su declaracion? Dijo que hablando dela mala vida que dicho Felix le dava a su muger le comunico al dicho Domingo Martin que una criada de su casa le avia dicho que estava en mal estado y esa seria la causa que el dicho declarante no lo savia ni lo avia visto que quien selo comunico era una Yndia Magdalena Ponachave que oi vive en San Yldephonso que esta le dijo que la muger de dicho Felix tenia la mala amistad de Juan Lujan su hermano de dicho Felix que esta es la verdad y lo que save so cargo de su juramento en que se afirmo y ratifico y haviendole leido su declaracion dijo estar segun y como lleva declarado que no tiene que anadir ni quitar que es de edad de setenta anos poco mas o menos y no firmo ni los testigos por no saver frimelo yo dicho Capitan en dicho dia.
 Miguel Thenorio
 de Alva (rubric)

⁂

Declaracion de
Magdalena Pachane

 En treinta y un dias del mes de Jullio del año de mill setecientos y treze anos yo el Capitan Miguel Thenorio de Alva en virtud de comision del Señor Governador y Capitan General hize parecer ante mi a Magdalena Pachane yndia dela nazion Tigua zitada de Xptobal dela Cruz aquien por ynterpretazion del dicho le di a entender la gravedad del juramento y enterada en el lo iso por Dios Nuestro Señor y la Señal de la Santa Cruz debajo de cuio cargo le rezevi juramento y por el prometio de dezir verdad en lo que supiere y le fuere preguntado.

 Siendolo que motivo tubo para haverle dicho el dicho Xptobal de la Cruz que la muger de Felix Lujan estava en mala amistad con Juan Lujan su hermano si la avia visto con ella o se lo havian dicho, diga y declare. Dijo que en lo que sele pregunta haverle dicho a Xptobal de la Cruz es cierto que selo dijo que fue motivada de haverlos

visto en una occasion jugando en el corral a los dos y que asi lo penso en su corazon y selo dijo al dicho Xptobal que no selo a dicho esta declarante a persona ninguna que esta es la verdad y lo que save so cargo del juramento que fecho tiene en que se afirmo y ratifico siendole leida su declaracion que esta segun y como declaro que no tiene que anadir ni quitar que es de edad de quarenta anos poco mas o menos y no firmo ni los testigos por no saver que lo fueron Blas Lovato y Juan Alonso de Mondragon que presentes se allavan y para que conste lo firme en dicho dia.
    Miguel Thenorio
    de Alva (rubric)

En la Villa de Santa Fee dela Nueva Mexico en primer de Agosto de mill setezientos y treze yo Dn. Juan Ygnacio Flores Mogollon, Governador y Capitan General de estas provincias haviendo visto las declaraciones que en virtud de mi comision rezivio Miguel Thenorio de Alva mando se acomulen a estos autos y reconozida la maldad dela Yndia en aver dado por sentado mal proceder en Francisca de Torres por desir averla visto chazear con su cunado quitandole el credito a su honestad y prozeder mando que en fundamento averlo propalado a otros contra el credito dela dicha Francisca de Torres sea traeida a esta Villa donde se deposite por tiempo de seis meses donde le agan travajar y quede advertida para lo Adelante.

    Asi mismo mando al Alclade Maior dela Canada passé ala casa de Domingo Martin y le notifique en mi nombre se contenga en lo adelante en dar credito a semejantes notizias con aperzevimiento, que atendiendo a su mucha edad no lo castigo a ora como correspondia el aver propladolo a otros contra el credito y honestidad de una muger virtuosa en que se quita el suio propio dicho Domingo Martin por estar casado con su sobrino carnal asi lo provey, mande y firme con mi Secretario de Governazion y Guerra =
    Dn. Juan Ygnacio Flores Mogollon (rubric)
    Por mando del Señor
    Governador
    Ante mi
    Roque de Pinto (rubric)
    Secretario de Governazion y Guerra

En la Villa de Santa Fee dela Nueva Mexico en dos dias del mes de Agosto de mill setezientos y treze años yo dicho Governador y Capitan General hize parezer ante mi a Francisca de Torres, muger de Pheliz Lujan que la trajo ami prezensia su padre el Alferez Xptobal de Torres de mi orden en cuia cassa la tengo depositada aquien rezivi juramento que hizo por Dios Nuestro Señor y la Señal dela Cruz so cargo del qual prometio dezir verdad y siendole leido el papel que me escribio el Alcalde Maior dela Cañada que esta por cavesa de estos autos. Dijo ser zierto aver declarado ante dicho

Alcalde Maior lo que en el papel consta dela mala vida que desde que se caso le da su marido Pheliz Lujan castigandola y maltratandola con palabras yndecorosas y mui ajenas asu estado y buen prozeda =

Preguntada si quando la a castigado le a representado por que motivo? Dijo que siempre que la a castigado es pidiendole zelos pensando que quantos llegan a su casa y pasan la solizitan y que prueva real de su prozeder es que desde que se caso asta un ano a esta parte vivio siempre con su suegra y cunada quienes en prueba de su verdad y reconocimiento si nezesario fuese lo podran declarar y que el dia veinte y dos de Junio pasado de este ano la azoto y puso como un Xpto en su cassa y el dia veinte y tres vispera de San Juan la monto a cavallo para llevarla a San Yldephonso llegando zerca de la mesa la metio por una zienega a una cañada donde la yso appear y desnudar en queros cojiendo una reata para darle y despues el freno del cavallo a que esta declarante le dijo que por que la ponia de aquel modo.

Le respondio que por que era habladora y le respondio aque esta declarante le dijo ella pues darme o no darme por que e de dar quenta al Senor Governador y entonses se contubo y no la azoto y la mando bestir y prosigueron su viaje a San Yldephonso y desde entonzes a quedado tan atemorizada pues creyo fixamente que el averla llevado aquella cañada seria para quitarle la vida pues aunque la a castigado siempre nunca avia executado con ella otro tanto de llevarla al campo y desnudarla por cuia rason buelve a pedir ala Real Justizia la tenga separada de el por el rezelo que le asiste no buelva a executar lo mismo en otra occasion y la mate.

Que esto es la verdad delo que lleva declarado y lo que le a pasado en el tiempo que a que es cassada y que demas de tres anos a esta parte en el todo se a negado asistirla que ni un par de zapatos le a dado a ella ni a sus dos hijas y que Dios es testigo dela verdad que refiere y que nunca le a dado el menor motivo de sospecha para que la aiga castigado y no firmo por no saver y que es de edad de veinte y quatro anos poco mas o menos firmelo yo dicho Governador y me Secretario de Governazion y Guerra.

Por mando del
Don. Juan Ygnacio Flores Mogollon (rubric)
Señor Governador
Ante mi
Roque de Pinto (rubric)
Secretario de Governazion y Guerra

Auto de Culpa y cargo

En la dicha Villa en dicho dia, mes y año yo dicho Governador y Capitan General aviendo visto las declaraciones echas en estos autos y que de ellas resulta culpa contra Pheliz Lujan le ago cargo y pudiendo ser avido mando sea preso para cuio efecto tengo dado orden, assi lo provey, mande y firme con mi Secretario de Governazion y Guerra =

Dn. Juan Ygnacio Flores Mogollon (rubric)
Por mando del

Señor Governador
Ante mi
Roque de Pinto (rubric)
Secretario de Governazion y Guerra

En 18 de Agosto de 1713 la presento la contenida ante el Señor Governador =
    Francisca Gomez de Torres, residente en esta Villa de Santa Fee y muger de Felix Lujan y de orden de Vuestra Señoria puesta en cassa del Alferez Xptobal de Torres, mi padre, paresco ante Vuestra Señoria en la mejor forma que aya lugar en derecho y al mio combenga y digo que haviendome venido a esta Villa de orden de Vuestra Señoria por el mal tratimiento que dicho mi esposso me azia lo que le perdono por que Dios me perdone ami y suplico ala gran justificazion de Vuestra Señoria sea servido de aserlo a dicho mi esposso y que salga a cultivar sus simenteras y si quisiere vivir con migo hago las dilixencias de aserlo para que se venga y aga lo que Dios le manda de estar con migo en esta Villa en casa de dicho mi padre donde estoy prompta a hazer lo que Dios me manda con dicho mi esposo por todo qual a Vuestra Señoria pido y suplico en la veneraxion devidas sea muy servido de azer como llevo dicho y que dicho mi esposso venga a esta Villa libre de todo que espone resevir de Vuestra Señoria este veneficio con justicia y juro en devida forma este mi pedimento no ser de malisia si por azer lo que devo a Xptianos y en lo nessesario, ut supra.
    Francisca Gomez de Torres (rubric)

    Y vista por mi Dn. Juan Ygnacio Flores Mogollon, Governador y Capitan General de este Reino y provincias dela Nueva Mexico por Su Magestad; la ube por presentada y considerando la piedad con que esta parte obra en remitir y perdonar todos los agravios que a rezevido de Feliz Lujan su marido que me constan y tengo provado por los autos y caussa que le tengo fulminado, mando al Capitan Jazinto Sanchez, Alcalde Maior dela Villa Nueva de Santa Cruz y jurisdizion dela Cañada pudiendo averlo en parte donde pueda notificarle este mi auto en que le ordeno comparesca en mi prezensia y reduziendose a mudar de vida y biniendose a vivir con su esposa a esta Villa le remitire y perdonare asi el delito cometido en el mal trato dado a su mujer como en el que cometio con la fuga que hizo dela prission donde estava y devajo de este seguro y palabra podra compareser y excusandose azerlo abre de castigarlo conforme a los meritos dela caussa siempre que pueda ser avido assi lo provey mande y firme con mi Secretario de Governazion y Guerra en diez y ocho dias del mes de Agosto de mill setezientos y treze =
    Y esta petizion debolvera dicho Alcalde Maior con la delixencia que hiziere para acomularla a los autos fecho ut supra =
    Dn. Juan Ygnacio Flores Mogollon (rubric)
    Por mando del Señor

Governador y Capitan General
Ante mi
Roque de Pinto (rubric)
Secretario de Governazion y Guerra

En este Pueblo de San Ildefonso en beinte y un dia del mes de Agosto deste presente año de mill setesientos y trese en cumplimiento y obedesimiento del auto de arriva probeido por el Señor Governador y Capitan General Dn. Juan Ygnacio Flores Mogollon a quien Guarde Dios, abiendo paresido ante mi el Sargento Reformado Jazinto Sanchez, Alcalde Maior de la Villa Nueba de Santa Cruz y su jurisdicion Feliz Lujan aquien yse ler dicho auto y ordenasion de dicho Señor Governador dijo dicho Feliz Lujan que le obedesia y ponia dicha ordenasa sobre su cabesa con toda obedensia y para que conste lo firme yo dicho Alcalde Maior autuando como Jues Receptor con dos testigos de mi asistenzia en dicho dia mes y ano, ut supra.
Testigo de asistenzia,
Nicolas Hortiz Ladron de Guevara (rubric)
Testigo de asistenzia
Jazinto Sanchez (rubric)

En la Villa de Santa Fee dela Nueva Mexico en veinte y dos dias del mes de Agosto de mil setezientos y treze años ante mi Dn. Juan Ygnacio Flores Mogollon, Governador y Capitan General de esta Provincia por Su Majestad en virtud del auto antezedente por mi proveido y zitazion hecha por el Alcalde Maior Jazinto Sanchez parecio Feliz Lujan a quien requiere le perdonava de los delitos que constan en la caussa que le tengo fulminado con tal de que enmienda su vida tratando de aqui adelante a su muger Francisca de Torres con mas amor y con la calidad de aver de vivir en esta Villa y la hize parezer ante mi para que quedasen amistados y estandolo; en ygual de estar arrepentido y reconozer la grazia que sele hazia ami vista y la de otros que estavan presents.

La dio a entender amenazandola la tendria donde quisiese y a la respuesta que ella dio comprehendi su renunzia y no le castigue como merezia por aver benido de vajo de seguro y salido de sagrado y hize echar con confusion diziendole se retirase a el por que de cojerlo fuera le a de castigar segun los meritos dela causa y para que conste siempre mando se acomule esta petizion alos autos, asi lo provey, mande y firme con mi Secretario de Governazion y Guerra =
Dn. Juan Ygnazio
Flores Mogollon (rubric)
Roque de Pinto (rubric)
Secretario de Governazion y Guerra

Notes

1. Felix Luján was the brother of Juan Luján [Romero], both of whom were the sons (or perhaps nephews) of Matias Luján and Francisca Romero. The family returned to New Mexico from El Paso to their land held near San Ildefonso, which they owned from before the 1680 Pueblo Revolt. Matias was an alcalde mayor of Picuris and an interpreter. Felix also had another brother, Miguel Luján, and a sister, Juana Luján. In 1712, Miguel was found guilty of murdering his wife, Catalina Valdéz, and was taken to Mexico for punishment, but escaped. The behavior of both men suggests a pattern of family violence. Their sister, Juana Luján, is listed in the marriage investigation records as "impeding" the marriage of Ventura Esquibel, whom she claimed had promised to marry her. Later, Juana gave up her accusation, in return for financial compensation, and she eventually married Francisco Martín. The settlement of her estate, in 1762, indicates that she was a wealthy woman, rich in land, goods, and livestock. (Chávez, *Origins*: 213; Kessell, Hendricks, and Dodge, *Boulders*: 653, 655, 1050; Stamatov, *Family, Kin and Community*: 99-110, 153-185; Ahlborn, "Will of a New Mexican Women": 319-55.)
2. The term *mala vida* (bad life) was commonly used in eighteenth-century New Mexican complaints, lawsuits, petitions for separation or divorce, bigamy cases, and other legal documents. In the broadest terms, it referred to the unhappy life brought about by the abuse of power by one spouse over another, usually by a man over a woman (but sometimes it was the reverse). In particular, it referred to failure to provide financial support, desertion, gambling, overwork, physical and verbal abuse, or adultery. (Bayer, "Mala Vida": 252, 260-80.)
3. Francisca [Gómez] de Torres, a native of New Mexico, was the daughter of Cristóbal de Torres and Angela de Leyba. Cristóbal was a soldier in El Paso in 1698; an alférez in Albuquerque in 1710; and alcalde mayor of Santa Cruz in 1719. He was given a land grant near Chama in 1724. (Chávez, *Origins*: 294; Kessell, Hendricks, and Dodge, *Royal Crown*: 175n31.)
4. Roque de Pinto was frequently listed as Governor Flores Mogollón's secretary of government and war. Apparently, Pinto came to New Mexico at the same time as the governor (and perhaps with him). Pinto was given the rank of captain in December 1714, and then on May 31, 1715, he resigned, stating that he could not fulfill his responsibilities because of serious injuries for which there was no cure. (Christmas and Rau, "Una lista": 195-96.)
5. María de Torres was the sister of Francisca. In 1708, she married Antonio de Salazar, the son of Agustín de Salazar and Felipa de Gamboa. Agustín was a blind interpreter whose father may have been Bartolomé de Salazar, the alcalde of Zuni and Moqui, before the 1680 Pueblo Revolt. Antonio de Salazar asked for lands in Santa Cruz in 1714. (Chávez, *Origins*: 279.)
6. Miguel de Quintana, born in Mexico City, came with the Farfán Expedition in 1694. He was married to Gertrudis Moreno Trujillo, and by 1695 he was in Santa Cruz, where he later died in 1748. He was literate, sometimes signing documents for persons who were not, and was known to be a poet. In 1704, he and nineteen other colonists received permission to go outside the colony, probably to trade. (Chávez, *Origins*: 261; Kessell, Hendricks, and Dodge, *Boulders*: 644, 782; SANM II #103.)
7. Joseph de Atienza [Servillano], the younger, was the brother of Juan de Atienza; both were sons of Joseph de Atienza de Alcalá y Escobar and Gertrudis Sevillano de Mancilla. The family came with the Farfán Expedition of 1694 from Mexico City. Joseph the younger, married Estefania Moreno de Trujillo (see note 16 below). In November 1704, he was one of twenty persons who received a license to leave the colony. (Cháves, *Origins*: 139; Kessell and Hendricks, *Royal Crown*: 320n36; SANM II #103.)
8. For information on Jacinto Sánchez de Iñigo, see Case 2.
9. Don Juan Ignacio Flores Mogollón was from Sevilla, Spain, and previously had been the governor of Nuevo León in New Spain. He was governor of New Mexico from 1712 to 1715. While governor, he attempted to destroy the kivas of the Pueblo Indians, demanded that the Indians remove all their guns, and required them to wear Spanish-style clothing. According to Kessell, Flores Mogollón and the previous governor, Marqués de la Peñuela, were the last New Mexico governors who made such attempts to change Pueblo culture and traditions. (Warner, *Felix Martínez*: 61; Kessell, *Kiva*: 312-9.)
10. The cabeza del proceso was the official statement of a complaint providing the basis for the investigation. It was intended to be found at the head of the proceedings. (Cutter, *Legal Culture*: 114.)
11. Cristóbal de Torres, a native of New Mexico, was married to Angela de Leyba. He was part of the muster in El Paso in 1681. In 1697, he was a soldier in El Paso; in 1698, he was one of the governor's couriers; and, by 1704 he was listed as a sergeant in Bernalillo. In 1710, he was an alférez in Albuquerque and given a land grant near Chama in 1724. (Chávez, *Origins*: 294; Kessell, Hendricks, and Dodge, *Royal Crown*: 175n31; Kessell, Hendricks, Dodge, and Miller, *Accounts*: 222; Kessell, Hendricks, Dodge, and Miller, *Disturbances*: 101, 422.)
12. For information on don Alfonso Rael de Aguilar I, see Case 3.

13. The Spanish phrase *"no le tocan los generales de la ley"* (and variations of it) means that the person testifying is impartial—in other words, not related to the accused and not having any reason to be biased toward the accused. (Rodriguez del Barco, "Repreguntas a los Generales de la Ley"; see also, the introduction to this book.)
14. Domingo Martín [Serrano] was a soldier in El Paso in 1692 and then returned to New Mexico with Diego de Vargas. He was the brother of Luis Martín Serrano II; both were the sons of Luis Martín Serrano I (or possibly Hernan Martín Serrano). As such, Domingo was one of the elders of the Martín Serrano clan. His first wife was Josefa de Herrera. In 1695, he received a land grant from Governor Vargas in Santa Fe. In 1725, he married Juana Bautista Olivas. (Chávez, *Origins*: 222; SANM I #177; Kessell, Hendricks, and Dodge, *Royal Crown*: 60, 92n94; Kessell, Hendricks, and Dodge, *Boulders*: 959n64; Chávez, *Roots*: 222.)
15. Juan de Atienza [Sevillano] (aka de Atienza Alcalá y Escobar) was the son of Joseph de Atienza Alcalá y Escobar and brother of Joseph de Atienza described above. In 1694, he came to New Mexico with his family as part of the Farfán Expedition. His first wife was Juana de Corranza. Juan was the alcalde mayor of Santa Cruz. He was named the official "Protector of the Indians," a position he held from 1713 to 1716 (and was the last appointee in that position). (Cutter, *Protector*: 53-57; Esquibel, "Mexico City": 67; Kessell, Hendricks, Dodge, and Miller, *Settling*: 315.)
16. Estefania Moreno de Trujillo was the wife of Joseph de Atienza and the daughter of Nicolás Moreno Trujillo. They were natives of the Valley of Mexico. (Chávez, *Origins*: 139.)
17. Joseph de Atienza Alcalá y Escobar was the father of Juan and Joseph described above. He came from Toledo, Spain, with the 1694 Farfán Expedition. He stated that he was the high marshall of the Holy Office of the Inquisition and a member of the Third Order of St. Dominic. The latter was a religious lay group started by St. Dominic in 1216, for the study and preaching of the faith. In 1716, Joseph the elder returned to Spain. (Chávez, *Origins*: 139; Kessell, Hendricks, and Dodge, *Royal Crown*: 320n36; Addis and Arnold, *Catholic Dictionary*: 775-76.)
18. For information on María de Castro y Rodarte, see Case 2.
19. Miguel Tenorio de Alba was a native of Zacatecas, Mexico, and one of the first settlers of Santa Cruz. From 1697 to 1700, he was the cabildo scribe. In 1700, he gave testimony for Governor Cubero against Diego de Vargas. He and his wife, Agustina Romero, baptised a son named Cayetano in Santa Cruz in 1711. In 1718, Miguel was alcalde for Santa Cruz and then in 1719 for Taos. He was killed during the Villasur Expedition of 1720. (Kessell, Hendricks, and Dodge, *Boulders*: 570n52; Kessell, Hendricks, Dodge, and Miller, *Disturbances*: 288-91; SANM II #236; NMGS, *New Mexico Baptisms, Santa Cruz*: 1.)
20. Roque Jacinto Jaramillo, a native of Mexico City, traveled to New Mexico with the Farfán Expedition in 1694. His parents were José Jaramillo Negrete, a mason, and María de Sotomayor. By 1711 Roque was living in Santa Cruz. His wife was Petrona de Cardenas, who also came with the 1694 colonists. In 1746, he was given revalidation of a land grant in Río Arriba. (Chávez, *Origins*: 199; SANM I #413.)
21. Tomás de Córdova was the son of Antonio de Córdova and Eugenia de Herrera from Mexico City. In 1683, Antonio was a notary and a presidial soldier in El Paso, where he later died. According to Fray Angelico Chávez, Tomás married Francisca de Torres in Bernalillo in 1716. It is not known if this is the same Francisca de Torres described in this document. (Chávez, *Origins*: 165, 352.)
22. Cristóbal de la Cruz Carajuida is listed in the 1697 livestock distribution document as being married to María Madrid. He may have been part of the large de la Cruz family that came to New Mexico with the Hurtado Expedition in 1695. Chávez suggests that the de la Cruz group may have been a family of Mexican Indians. (Chávez, *Origins*: 167; Kessell, Hendricks, and Dodge, *Royal Crown*: 62, 94n102; Kessell, Hendricks, and Dodge, *Boulders*: 1163n33.)
23. Juan de Dios [Sandoval] Martín was born in Mexico City around 1658 and died on March 12, 1732, in Santa Cruz. He was the brother-in-law of Diego Martín. (Archdiocese of Santa Fe, *Santa Cruz Deaths*: AASF #39, F. 77: 339; SANM I #412; Christmas and Rau, "Una Lista": 198.)
24. Blas Lobato was probably a son of Bartolomé Lobato and Lucía Ana Negrete, who were natives of Zacatecas, Mexico, and part of the Hurtado Expedition in 1695. Blas is listed as a soldier, alive, on June 10, 1715, but was killed later that year. (Christmas and Rau, "Una Lista": 200; Chávez, *Origins*: 206; SANM I #777; SANM II #239a.)
25. Magdalena Pachane (or Ponachavé, as it appears in a document) is described as an Indian, however, the name is Portuguese and is now also found in Brazil. (*Wikipedia*, accessed on December 4, 2013.) It may be that her name was Tiwa and sounded like "Ponachavé" and the scribe thought it sounded like a Portuguese name he had heard, for there were Portuguese traders in New Spain. Or, someone with the name of Pachane gave her the name.
26. Juan Luján [Romero], a brother of Felix, was the son or nephew of Matias Luján and Francisca Romero. Juan married María Trujillo in 1717, with Baltazar Trujillo (probably María's father) as a witness. (Chávez, *Origins*: 213, 297.)

27. Juan Alonso de Mondragón (aka Monroy) was the son of Sebastián Mondragón (or Monroy) and María Bernal, natives of New Mexico. Juan married Sebastiana Trujillo (or Martín) in Santa Cruz in 1715. In both 1713 and 1716, he was involved in the sale of land in Santa Cruz. (Chavez, *Origins*: 233, 375; SANM I #9; SANM I #740.)
28. Nicolás Ortiz II [Niño] Ladron de Guevara was the son Nicolás Ortiz I and Mariana Coronado who came to New Mexico in 1693. In 1697, Nicolás Ortiz II received a citation from Governor Vargas for military valor that stated he was distinguished for action at Black Mesa, Taos, Jémez, and Chimayó. He married Juana Baca in 1702. In 1713, he was a captain of the Santa Fe militia, and by the time of his death, in 1742, he owned many pieces of property in Santa Fe. Four of his children were Francisco, Nicolás III, Toribio, and Ana María. (Chávez, *Origins*: 247-49.)

7

CRISTÓBAL DE GÓNGORA CLAIMS DIVORCE FROM WIFE;
SHE RESISTS
June 4, 1705–May 4, 1712, Source: *Diligencia Matrimonial*,
roll 60, f 369-372

Synopsis and editor's note: Cristóbal de Góngora, age eighteen, came to New Mexico with his family in the Farfán Expedition of 1694. Shortly thereafter, probably about 1697, he married Inez Aspitia, a widow. In 1701, by the time he was twenty-five, he had become the scribe for the Santa Fe cabildo, and in 1708, he was called a "sergeant" when requesting a land grant in Albuquerque west of the Río Grande. Four years later, he was serving as the secretary of government and war for Governor Marqués de la Peñuela. His signature is a grand one—illustrating his literacy and, perhaps, his pride in being able to sign, for many New Mexicans in that period could not sign their names. In 1715, Góngora left Santa Fe for El Paso.

We know very little about Inez de Aspitia, except that she was a native of Mexico City and had come with her husband, Cristóbal de Valverde, and a daughter, Teresa, in the Farfán Expedition of 1694—the same expedition in which Cristóbal de Góngora had traveled. Her husband may have died on the way, or sometime after arriving in New Mexico, for we know that she had remarried by 1697. This document shows that the marriage was a difficult one, with Inez trying to resolve problems and to reconcile with Góngora, beginning in the late 1600s and extending over the following fourteen years. She may have had little financial or other support from her family, or other settlers in New Mexico, and therefore had to look solely to Cristóbal for assistance. It is not known if she accompanied him when he left for El Paso in 1715.

In the following document, which included testimony from 1705 and 1712, Cristóbal de Góngora stated that troubles with his marriage had begun by 1698. When Inez was away from the house, while he was looking for tobacco, he found human bones under a blanket. Suspecting witchcraft, he asked fray Juan Mingues to investigate. When the friar entered the house, to which Inez had returned, he confirmed evidence of witchcraft, and then he ordered Inez to keep his visit a secret. To ensure this, he announced her "excommunicated" and told her that this would only be lifted if she kept his visit and findings a secret. Given the evidence discovered in his house, Gongóra asked for a divorce from his wife. Fray Juan Álvarez granted him a divorce under an interim "extra-judicial license," with the proviso that Gongóra financially supported Inez. Two years later, Fray Joseph de Arranegui reunited the couple, but Góngora later stated that during those years he had not shared her bed. Later, they were separated once again and then rejoined again by a priest.

In 1705, Inez petitioned *Vice-custos* fray Juan de Tagle asking him to explain why Góngora had not lived with her as "a husband" and why she was excommunicated by fray Menchero. Fray Tagle responded to her petition by interviewing Góngora, who told fray Tagle about finding the evidence of witchcraft and also gave him evidence proving that Inez had a lover, Joseph Antonio Romero. Góngora stated that this proved that Inez was an adulteress, further reason for divorce.

No further records relating to Inez's complaint appeared until 1712, when she once again went before fray Tagle, who was by then *comisario* of the Holy Office of the Inquisition. Inez said that she and her husband had been separated for fifteen years, but she did not understand the reasons for it. She complained that Góngora had given her no financial support and that he called her a witch. Fray Tagle then ordered Góngora to give her four *reales* a day and suggested that he knew Góngora had the ability to do so, probably referring to the fact that Góngora was the scribe and secretary to the governor. In response, Góngora stated that fray Álvarez had granted him an extra-judicial divorce that did not require financial support, but even so he had given her clothes and provisions. When asked why he had not been living a "married life" with Inez, he did not answer the question and said he had given that information to the Tribunal of the Holy Office of the Inquisition. To date, no record has been found of a formal denunciation of Inez or an investigation of the case by the Holy Office, although Góngora's testimony suggests that there was one.

In 1715, Góngora left Santa Fe for El Paso;[1] there is no evidence of his return after this date, nor any further information about Inez.

It is important to note that a "divorce" during this period meant something different to the church and residents of New Mexico than it does today. When Góngora and the friars used the word *divorcio*, it referred to what we would call a "legal separation." In this early period, then, divorcio meant the couple did not have to live together, their financial assets could be divided, and neither partner could remarry unless the other one died. For the Roman Catholic Church, marriage was (and continues to be) a sacred sacrament that was not to be dissolved easily.

In another case, of early 1695, Inez Martín asked for a divorce because of her husband's apparent impotence. According to Suzanne Stamatov's translation of the case, Inez complained that "her husband owed her the marital debt and that she remained in the state that she had been when her mother bore her." Remarkably, the ecclesiastical judge in the case prescribed medicines for the husband to take and asked that Inez wait for four months. No evidence has been found indicating how (or if) the marital troubles of Inez were resolved.[2]

TRANSLATION

1705

Presentation of a petition before Reverend Father Juan de Tagle,[3] Vice-custos of this realm and provinces of New Mexico

I, Inez de Aspitia,[4] citizen of this realm and resident of this Villa of Santa Fe, appear before your very Reverend Father in due form as may benefit my cause. I state, kneeling at the feet of your person, that I am married to Cristóbal de Góngora,[5] my legitimate husband. He has not lived a married life with me for one year without having any reason for this on my part or without assisting me by providing support or clothing. Having recognized, Very Reverend Father, that this is against divine and human law, and that Your Very Reverend Person as Your Honorable Ecclesiastical Judge must protect my cause, I request that my husband be called before you and asked what reasons he has for having separated himself from me.

Likewise, I ask with the humility due Your Revered Person, that you ask the Very Reverend Father Guardian fray [Juan] Mingues[6] about his coming to my house fifteen days ago and searching to his satisfaction the house and the clothing that I was wearing, bringing with him Joseph Velásquez,[7] resident of this villa. His Reverend told me that he did so by order of our very Reverend Father Custos fray Juan Álvarez.[8] When he departed, he left him some papers with the order to carry out the said proceeding. He also told me twice that I was excommunicated and that only he himself could absolve me [which he would not do] if I made the proceedings public, but I do not know the cause of the search.

Therefore, my Father, for the love of God, may your Reverend Person examine this case with pious eyes and may you render your assistance so that my reputation may not be tarnished, considering that all the above may be argued in my favor.

I ask and request, for the love of God, that Your Most Reverend Person be pleased to order the aforementioned persons in my petition to appear before you—who are my husband, the Very Reverend Father Guardian, and Joseph Velásquez—and that you may be pleased to act with piety and justice according to the statements of each one. I swear in due form that my petition is not done in malice, but rather to obtain relief of both my reputation, and that my said husband might live a married life with me as God commands, and as necessary, *ut supra*.

Inez de Aspitia (rubric)

[Order]

Having been viewed by His Reverend, he said and ordered Cristóbal de Góngora, spouse of the petitioner, and Joseph Velásquez to appear before His Reverend in order to make a statement and answer any questions they may be asked by His Reverend, and that the Reverend Father Guardian of the villa, his prelate and ecclesiastical judge also duly appear. So provided, His Reverend ordered and signed it in this Villa of Santa Fe, said day, month and year, *ut supra*.

Fray Juan de Tagle (rubric)
Vice-custos Ecclesiastical Judge
Before me
Fray Joseph de Narváez [Valverde][9] (rubric)
Notary

Petition of Cristóbal de Góngora

In this Villa of Santa Fe on the 5th day of the month of June, 1705, the Reverend Father, vice-custos and ecclesiastical judge, Fray Juan de Tagle, ordered Cristóbal de Góngora, soldier of this presidio of this Villa of Santa Fe, and husband of Inez de Aspitia to appear before the Reverend Father, in whose presence I, fray Joseph de Narváez Valverde, act as notary. He took his oath in due form to God Our Lord and the sign of the Cross to state the truth.

In accordance with the petition presented, he was asked to declare the reason or reasons for which he has not lived a married life with his wife. He responded and said that the reason he has for not living with his wife is that while living in the Villa Nueva de Santa Cruz in the year 1698, one day Inez de Aspitia decided to come and spend time in this Villa of Santa Fe, while the declarant stayed to guard the house. While looking for a *puro de tabaco*[10] among the household items of Inez de Aspitia, he found some bones of a dead person in a bundle underneath a bed covering. The bones appeared to be from two arm bones and another smaller one. To relieve his conscience[11] this declarant reported it secretly to the Reverend Father Fray Francisco Álvarez,[12] Guardian Minister of Villa Nueva [de Santa Cruz] at that time. Upon leaving, the Reverend Father told this declarant return the bones to the place where they had been found and to go with him.

In the meantime, Inez de Aspitia was on her way back from the Villa of Santa Fe. The Reverend Father ordered this declarant to notify him as soon as Inez de Aspitia returned so that he could question her about the reasons she had for possessing the referred to items. He also asked this declarant to take witnesses with him who could attest, being Miguel de Quintana,[13] Joseph Velásquez, and Joseph [Manuel] Giltoméy.[14] Later this declarant tried to separate himself by divorce from his wife. To that time, he presented a petition before the Very Reverend Father custos, Fray Juan Álvarez, living in the pueblo of Tesuque, who granted him an extra-judicial license[15] and permission for a divorce based on his petition.

Since that time Cristóbal Góngora has not been in the company of his wife for about two years. He stated that, against his will, the Reverend Guardian fray Joseph de Arranegui, Guardian of the Villa of Santa Fe, brought them together as man and wife and that since then he has lived with her as stated. But it is true that he never slept with her because he had a separate bed, as the aforementioned or other witnesses that might be presented, could declare.

This continued until last year, 1704. While in the Villa of Santa Fe, this declarant went to the house of his father-in-law, Juan de Chávez,[16] who was in the company of Inez de Aspitia. While there he saw Joseph Antonio Romero[17] come to the house and take out his sword to kill them because of the jealousy he felt upon seeing them together. That was the reason for being separated from her a second time. It was because she committed adultery which can be proved so publicly.

Nonetheless, the declarant, having gone this Holy Week to absolve his conscience, confessed to Father fray Salvador López.[18] Having told him the truth of what happened, fray López expressly ordered this declarant not to be disturbed by such a woman because with the same union that had joined them, the church had separated them. With these reasons this declarant absolved his conscience. Knowing that Inez de Aspitia wanted to submit a formal complaint to the governor against this declarant and fearful that she might try to extort something from him, he returned to confess and get the opinion of the Reverend Father Guardian of this Villa of Santa Fe, the Father Preacher fray Juan Mingues. For these reasons the said Father Guardian gave the same order as Father fray Salvador López, who had been advised by this declarant that the same thing was happening that had happened since the year of 1698 until the present.

This is the truth regarding that which he has been asked, which he swears on his soul. He was asked if he had told the Reverend Guardian fray Juan Mingues twice that he had been granted a divorce by the Reverend Guardian Custos fray Juan Álvarez. He said that yes, he had told him as stated above, that he, fray Álvarez, granted it extra-judicially. Asked in accordance with the petition, if he has helped his wife as needed, he said that since he married her, he has helped her except for the two years mentioned above. This present year of 1705, he has helped and aided her as he was able during this time. Finally, this declarant states that he has other reasons to not live married to his said wife which he has declared before the Reverend Father fray Juan de Zabaleta,[19] the current comisario of the Holy Office.

After being heard by the Reverend Father vice-custos and ecclesiastical judge, he ordered this declaration to cease out of respect, veneration, and due deference to such a holy and honorable tribunal. All of the above that had been stated was signed by Cristóbal de Góngora before the Reverend Father vice-custos and ecclesiastical judge who signed it before me, the undersigned notary. Done. *Ut supra*.

    Fray Juan de Tagle (rubric)
    Vice-custos and Ecclesiastical Judge
    Before me
    Fray Joseph de Narváez [Valverde] (rubric)
    Cristóbal de Góngora

Signature of Cristóbal de Góngora. SANM II #160, roll 3, f 721

[Declaration of Fray Juan Mingues]

In this *convento*[20] of the Villa of Santa Fe, on the 5th day of the month of June of 1705, the Reverend Father vice-custos and ecclesiastical judge, fray Juan de Tagle, examined the petition presented by Inez de Aspitia which contains the accusations brought forth by her about the Reverend Father, current minister of this Villa of Santa Fe.

In order to proceed justly, he called the Preacher fray Juan Mingues, against whom the accusations are laid, to appear before him. Binding him with the religious commands that seemed necessary and having ordered me, fray Joseph de Narváez Valverde, to be present as assistant secretary and notary, he asked him the necessary questions to carry it out regarding to the aforementioned petition, to which he responded.

To the first and most important question about the papers and order that Inez claims were left by our Very Reverend Father custos and ecclesiastical judge, fray Juan Álvarez, or the order by the Reverend Father, fray [Juan] Mingues answered that what he said at her house was that he had an order from the Reverend Father custos not to allow them to live together in a bad state, and that the Reverend Father ordered him to cooperate with the governor in keeping it from happening. The reason for going to the house of Inez was because her husband, Cristóbal de Góngora and his Minister asked him to examine it. He said that in there he would find clothing given to her by a man named Romero with whom she had committed adultery, and that by finding it, he would know the reason for his petition for a separation.

The Reverend Father said that while examining the house in the company of Joseph Velásquez, he found a powder and a blanket on top of some corn, but that he does not know who gave it to Inez. Asked why he took Joseph Velásquez with him and not a different person, he said that he did so in order to have a witness of what Romero had given Inez, and that Velásquez also knew of the relationship that the said [woman] had with Romero. He said that he was glad to be in the company of Joseph Velásquez because he did not want to go to the house alone since he had heard of its bad reputation and wanted to keep his good name.

He said that it is true that as Minister he imposed the penalty of excommunication so that she would not talk about what had happened in the house, and so that she would not go around gossiping, telling, adding or removing anything. He imposed this excommunication *ad terrorem*[21] on her so that he might thereby prevent her from talking about it. He declares that Cristóbal de Góngora told him two times that he had been granted a divorce from her by Our Very Reverend Father Custos fray Juan Álvarez. He has nothing more to say, all the above being stated as said before His Reverend Father vice-custos and ecclesiastical judge. He signed it together with His Reverence said day, month and year. *Ut supra*.

Fray Juan de Tagle (rubric)
Vice-custos and Ecclesiastical Judge

By order of His Reverence
as his assistant secretary
Fray Joseph de Narváez [Valverde] (rubric)
Fray Juan Mingues (rubric)

[Ratification of Inez de Aspitia's Testimony, 1705]

In this Villa of Santa Fe on the 6th day of the month of June, 1705, the Reverend Guardian vice-custos and ecclesiastical judge, fray Juan de Tagle, made Inez de Aspitia appear before him, in order that she may declare under oath if the above petition is her own statement as presented by her, and if she ratifies what is contained therein. Thus it was read to her word by word. Having sworn to God and the Cross to state the truth, she said that this petition is hers and not someone else's, and that she has nothing whatsoever to add or remove from it. Because she did not know how to sign, she did not sign. The Reverend Guardian vice-custos and ecclesiastical judge signed it before me, the undersigned notary. Done. *Ut supra.*

Fray Juan de Tagle (rubric)
Vice-custos and Ecclesiastical Judge
Before me
Fray Joseph de Narváez [Valverde] (rubric)
Notary

[Petition of Inez de Aspitia and Final Determination, 1712]

In the Villa of Santa Fe and convento of Saint Francis on the 9th of May, of the current year of 1712, Inez de Aspitia, wife of Cristóbal de Góngora, appeared before the Reverend Father fray Juan de Tagle, comisaro of the Holy Office [of the Inquisition], custos, and ecclesiastical judge ordinario by Apostolic authority. She was asked the cause or reason that she has for not living a married life with her husband, having passed already some years since they have been separated. Thus she has provided a bad example to others and even created a scandal, paying little attention to the precepts of Our Holy Mother Church. She said that her husband knows the reasons that she has for doing so. Five times they have been reunited as God commands, and as many times they have separated without his having provided her reasons for doing so, she being ignorant of the reason for failing to fulfill his primary obligation. During this whole time, he has not given her the value of even one *real* for her support and clothing. Rather he has brought up certain complaints, even saying that she was a witch, thus immediately excusing himself from the obligation to help her or reunite with her, his spouse.

Having heard the above, the Reverend Father determined that Inez de Aspitia be cared for at the house of Captain Sebastián González[22] until a declaration is taken from her spouse. Afterward, the Reverend Father shall carry out what is most appropriate in the service of both majesties.[23] This is that Cristóbal de Góngora be informed that he must support her, setting it at four reales per day for her food, knowing that he has such ability to pay. If he does not fulfill this obligation in this manner, the corresponding punishments shall apply. This being so provided, the Reverend Father ordered and signed it on said day, month and year. *Ut supra*.

 Before me, the undersigned notary.
 Fray Juan de Tagle (rubric)
 Ecclesiastical Judge
 Before me,
 Fray Lucas Arevalo[24] (rubric)
 Apostolic Notary

[Declaration of Cristóbal de Góngora]

 On said day, month and year Cristóbal de Góngora, spouse of the petitioner, appeared before the Reverend Father. Being present he received his oath to God our Lord and the Holy Cross, by he promised to tell the truth in whatever he was asked.

 Asked what is the reason he has for not living a married life with Inez de Aspitia, he stated that the reasons for not living a married life with her, he reserves for the Most Honorable and Holy Tribunal of the Holy Office, and as such he responds.

 Asked how long they have not lived together, this witness stated that it has been fifteen years since the aforementioned have not lived together. This is because he had requested a divorce for just cause from the Reverend Father fray Juan Álvarez, comisario of the Holy Office at that time. Although this witness asked for the divorce in writing, the Reverend Father granted it to him for an interim period, extra-judicially. This is so he could justify the reason for acting against his wife. They had been reunited on one occasion by the Reverend Father fray Joseph de Arranegui,[25] and another time asked by fray Joseph de Narváez [Valverde] to help or in some way support her.

 Being asked why he had not supported her, he stated that it is true he has supported her a few times to see if he might, in this way, keep her under control, giving her enough for a shirt, skirt, cloth, and a shawl. He gave her some provisions on one occasion, and then also provisions three other times. He said that his wife refused to be kept under control in certain houses, such as that of Nicolás Ortiz,[26] Antonio Montoya,[27] and Lorenzo de Madrid,[28] whom he cites as witnesses. He also said that his wife, not wanting to live in submission, has gone to other areas wherever she desired, providing the very reasons for which this witness has not supported her.

 This is what he knows and declares under the oath that he has made, that it is true and that he has nothing to add or remove from this statement. And that he affirms and ratifies it one, two and three times, and he states that he is thirty-six years of age. And he signed it with his Reverend Father before me, the undersigned notary on said day, month and year. *Ut supra*.

 Fray Juan de Tagle (rubric)
 Ecclesiastical Judge

Cristóbal de Góngora
(rubric)
Before me
Fray Lucas Arevalo (rubric)
Apostolic Notary

TRANSCRIPTION

Presentola la contenida ante el reverendo Padre fray Juan de Tagle vise custodio y jues eclesiastico ordinario en quatro de junio de mill setesientos i cinco años

Mui Reverendo Padre Vice Custodio de este reino y provincias de la Nueva Mexico
    Ynes de Aspitia vezina de este reino, y residente en esta villa de Santa Fee, paresco ante Vuestra Paternidad mui Reverenda en la mas combeniente forma que a mi fabor combenga y digo puesta a las plantas de Vuestra Persona que por quanto soi casada con Christobal de Gongora mi marido lexitimo y haber tiempo de un año que no ase vida maridable conmigo sin haber motivo alguno por lo que a mi parte toca sin atender a darme el sustento ni bestuario. Y habiendo reconosido mui Reverendo Padre el ser contra la ley divina y humana y que Vuestra Persona mui Reverenda como Jues Eclesiastico Hordinario deve amparar mi causa, pido y suplico a Vuestra Persona sea llamado el dicho mi marido a su bista y preguntado qual sea la causa de haberse apartado de mi.
    Como asi mesmo a el mui reverendo Padre guardian de esta dicha villa, le suplico con el rendimiento devido a Vuestra Persona Reverenda le pregunte con que horde[n] fue abra cosa de quinse dias a mi casa y la registro a su satisfacion casa y ropa que yo tenia puesta llebando en su compania a Joseph(e) B[e]lasques vezino de esta dicha villa diziendome su reverencia que por horden de nuestro mui reverendo Padre custodio fray Juan Albares lo hasia que quando se fue le habia dexado unos papeles para la execusion, de dicha deligensia y me dixo tambien que estaba descomulgada yo por dos beses y que si lo dibulgaba solo su persona me podia a absolber; y asi Padre mio por amor de dios que Vuestra Persona Reverenda mire esta causa con piadosos ojos y atienda a que no quede mi hopinion deslusida pues no se yo la causa de dicho rejistro por todo lo qual y lo mas que en mi fabor pueda alegar.
    A Vuestra Persona Reverenda pido y suplico por amor de Dios se sirva de que comparescan en su presensia los susodichos en mi peticiones que son el dicho mi marido, el mui reverendo Padre guardian, y Joseph B[e]lasques y segun reconosciere en la narrasion de cada uno hobre con pieda[d] y justizia lo que fuere serbido y juro en devida forma no ser de malisia mi pedimiento, sino por alcansar el alivio asi en mi reputacion como en que mi dicho marido aga vida maridable conmigo como Dios manda y en lo nessesario etcetera
    Ynes de Aspitia (rubric)

Y vista por su reverenda dixo manda comparescan ante su reverenda Christoval de Gongora esposo de la contenida, y Joseph Velasquez, a declarar lo que por su reverenda les fuere preguntado y que en quanto a el compareser el reverendo Padre guardian de la villa obrara como su prela(lo)do i como jues esclesiastico lo mas conveniente asi lo proveyo mando i firmo su reverenda en esta villa de Santa Fe de dicho dia mes i año *ut supra*

    Fray Joan de Tagle (rubric)
    Vice Custodio
    Juez Eclesiastico
    Ante mi, Fray Joseph de Narbaiz (rubric)
    Notario

Petision de Christobal de Gongora

En esta villa de Santa Fe en sinco dias del mes de junio de mill setesientos y sinco años, el reverendo Padre visse custodio y jues eclesiastico fray Juan de Tagle, hizo parescer ante su reverenda a Christoval de Gongora, soldado de este precidio de dicha villa de Santa Fe y esposo dela susodicha Ynes de Aspitia, en cuya presencia estando yo fray Joseph Narbaiz Valverde presente como notario hizo su juramento en toda forma a Dios nuestro Señor i la señal de la cruz de dezir verdad.

Preguntado al tenor dela peticion presentada declarase el motivo o motivos que tenia para no hazer vida maridable con dicha su esposa respondio i dixo: que la causa de no hazer vida con la dicha su muger es que viviendo en la Villa Nueva de Santa Cruz el año de noventa i ocho acaso un dia le dio gana de benirse a pasear a esta villa de Santa Fe ala dicha Ynes de Aspitia y este declarante abiendose quedado en guarda de su casa un dia, yendo a buscar un puro de tobaco entre los trastes de la dicha Ynes de Aspeitia hallo en un enboltorio entre un manto unos guesos de difuncto, que eran al pareser dos canillas de un braso, i otra mas pequeña i que por descargar su consciencia fue este declarante a dar parte debajo de cijilo al reverendo Padre fray Francisco Alvarez ministro guardian que era entonces de aquella Villa Nueva i dicho Padre le dixo a este declarante que en su compañia fuese i bolviera a poner los dichos guesos en el lugar donde los abia hallado.

Interim bolvia la dicha Ynes de Aspitia de esta dicha villa de Santa Fe abiendose ido encargado este declarante por dicho Padre guardian que luego que llegase dicha Ynes de Aspitia le abisara para ir ala execusion de preguntarle los motivos que tenia para lo referido i llebar en su compañia testigos que dieren fe siendo Miguel de Quintana Joseph Belasques i Joseph Giltomei i que luego este declarante trato de apartarse por diborcio de la dicha su muger pues para ello presento peticion ante el muy reverendo Padre custodio fray Juan Alvarez que entonces lo era viviendo en el pueblo de Thezuqui lo qual lisencia y permiso le dio extrajudicialmente por el dicho escrito i que desde entonces estuvo sin la compania de la dicha su muger como dos años, i que contra la voluntad deste declarante los junto como a marido i muger el reverendo guardian fray Joseph de Arranegui siendo guardian de dicha villa de Santa Fe y que desde entonces se junto como dicho es aunque es verdad que jamas durmio con ella porque tenia su cama aparte como lo declarara la susodicha o otros testigos que presentara.

Hasta el año pasado de setesientos i quatro que estando en esta villa de Santa Fe fuera de su casa este declarante abiendo ido a su casa a buscarle Juan de Chaves su padrastro, estando en la compañia de la dicha Ynes de Aspitia bino para la casa Joseph Antonio Romero sacando la espada para querer matar a uno i a otro por celo que le dio de averlos visto dentro de la casa juntos i que la causa fue esta de averse apartado esta segunda ves, por averle echo adulterio que se le provara por ser tan publico, i que no obstante por descargar este declarante su conciencia esta semana santa abiendose ido a confesar con el Padre fray Salvador Lopez i dichole la verdad de lo que pasaba le mando a este declarante expresamente no se acordara de tal muger porque con la misma union que los abia juntado la yglesia asi lo abia apartado a cuyos razones le descargo a este declarante su consciencia i abiendo sabido que la dicha Ynes de Aspitia queria meter peticion de querella contra este declarante ante el señor governador timido de que le hiziese alguna estorcion bolvio a confesarse i a tomar parescer del Padre guardian deste dicha villa de Santa Fe que lo es el Padre predicador fray Juan Mingues por cuya causa le hizo dicho Padre guardian el mismo mandato que el dicho Padre fray Salvador Lopez por averle informado este declarante lo mismo que le pasaba i paso el año de noventa i ocho asta el presente.

Que esta es la verdad en quanto a lo que se le tiene preguntado lo qual jura en su anima i declara i dize sobre la pregunta de que si le dixo por dos veses que tenia diborcio echo por el reverendo Padre custodio fray Juan Alvarez a dicho reverendo Padre guardian fray Juan Mingues, dixo que si se lo dixo como lo tiene dicho arriva que se lo dio extrajudicial y preguntado al tenor de la peticion si a socorrido a su muger con lo nesesario, dixo que desde que se caso, menos los dos años antes mencionados, i este año presente de setesientos i sinco, el demas tiempo le a mandado i socorrido con lo que a podido, y esto responde, y por fin dize este declarante que para no hazer vida con dicha su muger tiene otros motibos que tiene declarados ante el reverendo Padre fray Juan de Sabaleta como comissario que es del santo officio.

Lo qual oido por dicho reverendo Padre visse custodio i juez eclesiastico mando sesase en esta declaracion por el repecto, veneracion, i devido acatamiento a tan santo i recto tribunal, y todo lo que declarado lo firmo dicho declarante Christoval de Gongora ante dicho reverendo Padre visse custodio y juez eclesiastico quien juntamente lo firmo ante mi el infrascripto notario fecho. *Ut supra.*

    Fray Juan de Tagle (rubric)
    Vice Custodio y Jues Ecclesiastico
    Cristobal de Gongora (rubric)
    Ante mi
    Fray Joseph Narbaiz
    Notario

En este convento de la villa de Santa Fee, en sinco dias del mes de junio de mil setecientos i sinco años el reverendo Padre vise custodio y jues eclesiastico fray Juan de Tagle abiendo visto la peticion presentada por Ynes de Aspitia, y en ella la calumnia puesta por la susodicha a el reverendo Padre ministro presente de esta dicha villa de Santa Fee; para proceder en justicia llamo a su presencia a el Padre predicador fray Juan Mingues contra quien es puesta dicha calumnia, i ligandole con los preseptos religiosos que le parecieron nessesarios, mandandome estar presente a mi fray Joseph Narvaiz Valverde, como su procecretario i notario nombrado por su reverencia, al tenor de la peticion supra escripta le hizo las preguntas nesesarias para su descargo, a que respondio.

Dixo: ala primera, i esencial que es que su reverencia muestre los papeles dichos i orden que en la peticion resan aver dicho le dexo nuestro muy reverendo Padre custodio y juez ecclesiastico fray Juan Alvarez, o la orden de su paternidad reverenda para no mostrarlos, que esta glosada su propocicion pues lo que en su casa le dixo fue que tenia orden del reverendo Padre custodio para no consentir el que viviesen en mal estado ningunos i su paternidad le ordeno coperase con el buen celo de el señor governador en evitarlo.

Que la causa de aver ido ala casa dela susodicha fue porque Christoval de Gongora marido de la susodicha le pidio como a su ministro viera i reconociera su casa, i en ella allaria la ropa que le abia dado un hombre que le hacia adulterio llamado Romero para que hallandola conosiera la causa del apartamiento que hacia y dize dicho reverendo Padre que registrando la casa en compañia de Joseph Velasquez hallo sobre un poco de mais una polbora i un[a] manta pero que no sabe quien se la dio y preguntado porque llebo consigo a Joseph Velasquez i no a otro, dixo que porque se lo puso por testigo de lo que tenia la susodicha que le abia dado el dicho Romero; i que sabia tambien el susodicho la amistad que la dicha tenia con dicho Romero, i que se alegro de ir en conpañia del dicho Joseph Velasquez a causa de no ir solo a su casa por aver oido tenía malafama, i mirar por su crédito.

Dixo ser verdad que le impuso como su ministro la pena de excomunion para que no parlase lo que abia pasado en su casa porque no anduviese en platillos contando, añadiendo o quitando nada, lo qual excomunion le impuso *ad terrorem*, para con ella obligarla a que no anduviese en quentos y que declara que el dicho Christoval de Gongora le dixo por dos veses que tenia diborcio echo ante nuestro muy reverendo Padre custodio fray Juan Alvarez quien ce lo dio y que no tiene otra cosa que decir.

Lo qual todo declaro como dicho es ante dicho reverendo Padre visse custodio y juez eclesiastico i lo firmo juntamente con su reverencia dicho dia mes, i año, *ut supra*.

Fray Joan de Tagle (rubric)
Fray Juan Mingues (rubric)
Vice Custodio y Jues Ecclesiastico
Por mandado de su reverence como
su Procecretario

Fray Joseph Narbaiz Valverde (rubric)
Valverde

～

En esta villa de Santa Fe en seis dias del mes de junio de mill setesientos i sinco años el reverendo guardian vissecustodio y jues eclesiastico fray Juan de Tagle hizo paresiere ante si Ynes de Aspitia, para que debaxo de juramento declare si la peticion de arriba es dictada suya i por ella presentada i si en lo que en ella se contiene se ratifica, lo qual se le leyo verbo ad verbum i aviendo jurado a Dios i la cruz de desir la verdad dixo que es esta e no otra la peticion suya i que no tiene que añadir ni quitar en ella cosa alguna, o que se ratifica en lo en ella dicho, i por no saver firmar no firmo firmo dicho reverendo Padre vissecustodio y juez eclesiastico ante mi el infrascripto notario fecho. *Ut supra.*
Fray Joan de Tagle (rubric)
Vise Custodio y Juez Eclesiastico
ante mi
Fray Joseph Narbaiz (rubric)
Notario

～

En la villa de Santa Fe, y convento de San Francisco en nuebe dias del mes de mayo, deste presente año de mill setecientos y doze años parezio ante el reverendo Padre fray Juan de Tagle comisario del santo oficio, custodio y juez eclesiastico ordinario por autoridad apostolica Ynes de Aspectia, esposa de Christobal de Gongora y siendo preguntado qual es la causa o motivo que tiene para no hacer vida maridable con el dicho su esposo haviendo algunos años que se hallan separados dando mal exemplo a los demas y aun provocando a escandalo, hasiendo poco caso de los preceptos de Nuestra Santa Madre Yglesia, dixo: que a dicho su esposo sabe quales son los motibos que tiene para ello, que zinco vezes los an juntado como Dios manda, y tantas se an apartado sin averle dado motivos por hello, ygnorando qual sea la causa de faltar a su primera obligazion; y que en todo este tienpo no le ha devido el balor de un real, para su mantenimiento y bestido antes si a sabido que el dicho Christobal de Gongora su esposo le a levantado algunos testimonios, aun hasta desir le que hera echizera escusandose, en un todo, de asistirle, ni querer juntarse con dicho su esposa.

Aviendo oido este suso dicho determino su paternidad reverenda el que la dicha Ynes de Aspeetia estuviese recogida en casa del capitan Sebastian Gonzales hasta tanto se toma la declaracion al dicho su esposo, y despues ejecutara su paternidad reverenda lo que mas convenga al servizio de anbas magestades notificandole al dicho Christobal de Gongora le asista, y señalandole quatro reales cada dia, para su alimento sabiendo que para hello tiene forma, y de no cunplir lo assi, se le aplicaran las penas que le corresponden, asi lo pro(e)v[e]io mando, y firmo su paternidad reverenda en dicho dia mes y año *ut supra* por ante mi el infraescripto notario.

Fray Joan de Tagle (rubric)
Juez Eclesiastico
Por ante mi
Fray Lucas Arevalo (rubric)
Notario Apostolico

⁂

En dicho dia mes y año parezio ante su paternidad reverenda Christobal de Gongora esposo dela contenida al qual estando presente se le rezibio juramento a Dios nuestro Señor y la santa cruz en forma de derecho so cargo del qual le fue[re] preguntado, y prometio de decir verdad

Preguntado, qual es el motivo que tiene para no hacer vida maridable con la dicha Ynes de Aspetia dixo: que los motibos que tiene para no haser vida con la susodicha, reserva para el mui recto y santo tribunal del santo oficio, y esto responde

Preguntado, quanto tienpo ha que no biven juntos; dixo: este testigo; que a tienpo de quinze años quel susodicho no l(a)[o] haze: por aver pedido divorzio por justos motivos al reverendo Padre fray Juan Albarez comisario del santo oficio que fue entonzes; si vien es; que aunque se lo pidio por escripto este testigo, se lo concedio su paternidad extrajudicialmente *interim* si justificaba la causa, que por este declarante hazia contra la dicha su esposa que aunque los juntaron en una ocasion el reverendo Padre fray Joseph de Arranegui, y en otra el fray Joseph Narbaiz, que fue, por la acudiera en alguna manera la asistiera.

Y siendo preguntado por que no la ha asistido dixo: que es verdad que le a asistido, algunas vezes, por ver si con eso podia tenerla sujeta dandole para la camisa, naguas, paño de [illegible] revozo, y algun vastimento [illegible] se le dio por una vez y el vastimento en tres vezes; y que viendo este testigo que la dicha su mujer reusava a estar en sujezion en algunas casas, como son la de Nicolas Ortiz, Antonio Montoya y Lorenzo de Madrid, aquienes zita por testigos, y que la dicha su esposa, procurando no vibir en sujezion se ha ido a otras partes donde le prevenia su antojo motibos para que este testigo no la alla asistido exactamente y que esto y lo que sabe y declara devaxo del juramento que fecho tiene, que es la verdad; y que no tiene que añadir ni quitar a esta declaracion, en que se afirma y ratifica una, dos, y tres vezes, y que declara ser de edad de treinta y seis años y lo firmo con su paternidad reverenda por ante mi el infraesripto notario en dicho dia mes y año. *Ut supra.*

Fray Joan de Tagle (rubric)
Juez Eclesiastico
Cristobal de Gongora (rubric)
Por ante mi
Fray Lucas Arebalo (rubric)
Notario Apostolico

⁂

This document was translated and transcribed by Aaron Taylor.

Notes

1. See *Diligencia Matrimonia*, 1714 #22.
2. See Stamatov, *Family, Kin, and Community*, 24.
3. Fray Juan de Tagle ministered to San Ildefonso and Santa Clara pueblos from 1701 to 1726. He was vice-custos of the Franciscan friars from 1704 to 1706. (Norris, *Year Eighty*: 24, 50, 63; Kessell, Hendricks, and Dodge, *Royal Crown*: 28n12.)
4. Inez de Aspitia was a native of Mexico City and was married to Cristóbal de Valverde. In the Farfán Expedition recruitment records of 1693, they are listed along with a daughter, Teresa. If this is the same person, Valverde must have died by 1697, because in 1712 Cristóbal de Góngora says that they had been separated for fifteen years (since 1697). The Farfán Expedition records also indicate that in 1693 Cristóbal de Góngora was recruited with his parents and siblings. Perhaps, Inez and Góngora met on the route to Santa Fe, when both were part of the expedition. (Kessell, Hendriks, and Dodge, *Royal Crown*:247; 340n130)
5. Cristóbal de Góngora was the great-grandson of Bartolomé Góngora of Andalusia, Spain, who was the author of several books and a recipient of favor from several viceroys. Born about 1684, Cristóbal was the son of a wax worker from Mexico City who came to New Mexico with his family during the 1694 Farfán Expedition. Cristóbal was a presidio soldier and clerk of the cabildo in Santa Fe and served as a notary from 1701 to 1712. In 1715, he was a notary in El Paso. (Chávez, *Origins*: 188; Kessell, Hendricks, and Dodge, *Boulders*: 671n28; Esquibel, "Residents": 55, 67.)
6. Fray Juan Mingues was born in Mexico City in 1677 and professed his vows in 1694. In 1705, he accompanied Governor Francisco Cuervo y Valdés to New Mexico. According to Juan Candelaria's remembrances, Mingues became the first Franciscan friar for the new Villa of Albuquerque, later resided in the Palace of the Governors in Santa Fe, and served as the presidio chaplain. Fray Mingues died during the Villasur Expedition in 1720. (Norris, *Year Eighty*: 86; NMGS, *Aquí*: 527-30.)
7. Joseph Velásquez (aka Velasco) traveled from Durango, Mexico, with the Farfán Expedition to New Mexico in 1694. He is listed as a carpenter, and his first wife was María de Tapia. Upon the latter's death, he married María Mestas. (Chávez, *Origins*: 31; Kessell, Hendricks, Dodge, *Royal Crown*: 341n132.)
8. Fray Juan Álvarez professed his vows at Mexico City in 1679 and was in New Mexico by at least 1696, when he was a notary in Santa Cruz. From 1700 to 1704, he served at Zia, Santa Ana, and Bernalillo. (Chávez, *Archives*: 8, 20, 241; Norris, *Year Eighty*: 165.)
9. Fray Joseph de Narváez Valverde was a lay brother in New Mexico from 1694 to 1706, during which time he acted as a surgeon, notary, and ecclesiastical secretary. He also appears in Case 18. (Norris, *Year Eighty*: 50; Kessell, Hendricks, Dodge, and Miller, *Disturbances*: 551n51; Chávez, *Roots*: 1371.)
10. The Spanish term *"puro de tobaco"* can be translated as "cigar," but it more likely referred to a little roll of paper filled with finely chopped tobacco.
11. The phrase "to relieve one's conscience" are the words with which a denunciation often begins when made to the Holy Office of the Inquisition. Certain Edicts of Faith asked parishioners to denounce persons who committed sins, such as witchcraft and adultery. See also, Case 22.
12. By 1696 fray Francisco Álvarez was in New Mexico, where he served as a notary in Santa Cruz and as a guardian. By 1700 he was serving in Zia, Santa Ana, and Bernalillo. (Chávez, *Archives*: 8, 241.)
13. Miguel de Quintana was born in 1677 in Mexico City and traveled to New Mexico from Mexico City with the Farfán Expedition in 1694. His was married to Gertrudis de la Santa Trinidad Moreno de Trujillo. He settled in Santa Cruz and lived there until 1748. He was known as a poet and a writer; later, he was denounced for his writing by the Franciscans. His name often appears as a witness in early eighteenth-century New Mexico court documents. (Chávez, *Origins*: 261; Kessell, Hendricks, and Dodge, *Royal Crown*: 336n115.)
14. Joseph Manuel Giltoméy was born in the Philippines, the son of don Juan Manuel de Giltoméy and Antonia Flores de Valdéz. He was in New Mexico in 1695, living in Santa Cruz. Though left for dead, he survived the Pueblo Revolt of 1696. He married Isabel de Olivas in 1696. He was included in a presidio muster in April 1704, and he was one of the witnesses at the inventory of Diego de Vargas, after the governor's death in 1704. In 1715, he was given permission to go to El Paso to seek a cure for his ailments. He died in 1727. (Chávez, *Origins*: 186, 358; Kessell, Hendricks, and Dodge, *Boulders*: 644, 873; Kessell, Hendricks, Dodge, and Miller, *Settling*: 222, 242; Christmas and Rau, "Una Lista": 196.)
15. This "extra-judicial" license for a "divorcio" may have been a temporary measure to allow the couple to be separated until an investigation could be undertaken later. Góngora, however, appears to have considered the separation/divorce to be final.
16. Juan de Chavéz [de Medina] was the natural son of Juana de Medina who came to New Mexico with the Farfán Expedition of 1694. He married Peronila de la Cueva, who was the mother of Cristóbal de Góngora, in 1694. (Kessell, Hendricks, and Dodge, *Royal Crown*: 326n58.)

17. Joseph Antonio Romero was a native of Carmona in Castile, Spain. He came to New Mexico from Zacatecas, Mexico, with the Hurtado Expedition in 1695, and was part of a "false household" created by Juan Páez Hurtado to meet the household requirement of the Spanish Crown for new settlers. By 1697 he was a presidio soldier. (Chávez, *Origins*: 272; Kessell, Hendricks, Dodge, and Miller, *Disturbances*: 362n23, 510; Kessell, Hendricks, and Dodge, *Boulders*: 128. Also, for information on the "false households" see Colligan, *Juan Páez Hurtado Expedition*: 71-118.)
18. Fray Salvador López came to New Mexico by at least 1705, when he served in Santa Ana and Bernalillo. In 1707, he was a notary in Santa Fe; by 1712 he was in Santa Cruz; and by 1715 he was a vice-custos in El Paso. (Chávez, *Archives*: 11, 250.)
19. Fray Juan de Zabaleta was in Socorro in 1693; and, in 1694 and 1699, he served as the comisario of the Holy Office. He also served in Bernalillo from 1702 to 1705. (Chávez *Archives*: 14, 258.)
20. The convento is the place where the Franciscan friars lived and worked.
21. *Ad terrorem* is a Latin phrase meaning "to cause terror or fear."
22. Sebastián González passed muster in El Paso in 1680 and returned to New Mexico with the Spanish Reconquest. He was married to Lucía Ortiz, and he died in 1726. (Chávez, *Origins*: 40, 189.)
23. The words "both majesties" refers to the two crowns of Spain—Castile and Aragon—even though Spain had been united for more than two centuries.
24. Fray Lucas Arevalo arrived in New Spain in 1706, and he served in Taos, San Ildefonso, and Tesuque. He was in Santa Fe by 1709 and was a notary in Albuquerque by 1712. He appears to have left the province by 1719. (Chávez, *Archives*: 9, 243.)
25. Fray Joseph de Arranegui was born in Spain and professed his vows by 1700. He was in Pecos by 1700 and remained there into 1708. He was also in Albuquerque in 1708. (Kessell, *Kiva*: 498; Chávez, *Archives*: 9, 242.)
26. This is most likely Nicolás Ortiz I who traveled from Mexico City with the Farfán Expedition in 1694; he was a contemporary of Antonio Montoya who is mentioned in note 27 below. Ortiz was married to Mariana Coronado Barba. It is possible that the person mentioned in the document is Nicolás Ortiz I's son, Nicolás Bernardo Niño de Ladron Ortiz, who spent most of his life in Santa Fe. (Kessell, Hendricks, and Dodge, *Royal Crown*: 332n80; Patricia Sanchez Rau, email communication to the author, April 26, 2016.)
27. Antonio Montoya was the son of Diego de Montoya and María de Vera. Antonio returned to New Mexico in 1692; he was previously married to María Hurtado in El Paso. By 1703 he was a member of the cabildo. (Kessell, Hendricks, and Dodge, *Royal Crown*: 78n23; Chávez, *Origins*: 235-36, 376-77; SANM II #94a.)
28. Lorenzo de Madrid was born in New Mexico around 1634. He was the brother of Roque Madrid. He was a member of the Santa Fe cabildo in 1677; in El Paso he was a sergeant major; he was again a member of the Santa Fe cabildo in 1694; and he was an alcalde in Santa Cruz in 1696. He was married to Ana Ortiz [Baca], Ana Anaya Almazán, and then Juana Domínguez. (Kessell and Hendricks, *Force of Arms*: 319n5.)

8

BATTERED WOMAN WALKS FROM ATRISCO TO SANTA FE IN FEAR OF HUSBAND AND MOTHER-IN-LAW
October 22, 1714–November 10, 1714 Source: SANM II #213

Synopsis and editor's notes: Both Juana Montaño de Sotomayor and Nicolás de Chávez came from pre-revolt families who returned to New Mexico with the Spanish Reconquest in 1692. Juana was the daughter of Isabel Jorge de Sotomayor and the granddaughter of Antonio Baca, a presidio *sergeanto major*. Nicolás was the son of don Fernando Durán y Chávez, who was the son of a pre-revolt *encomendero*, and doña Lucía Hurtado y Salas, sister of Martín Hurtado, the first alcalde of Albuquerque.

In 1714, Juana had a child by Nicolás, after he had promised to marry her. She then had a second child, by Nicolás or possibly another man, and continued to press Nicolás to marry her. Juana, however, was refused by Nicolás, who said that although he did promise to marry her, he was only a boy at the time and did not know any better. When Juana and her relatives protested, Governor Flores Mogollón imprisoned Nicolás in the Albuquerque garrison guardhouse, where he remained until he finally agreed to marry Juana.[1] The couple then went to live with his mother, doña Lucía, and her unmarried children. By this time, Nicolás's father, don Fernando, was dead.

Juana discovered that married life with Nicolás and residing with his mother and family was not as she had hoped. In a complaint that she later made to Governor Flores Mogollón, Juana said, "Since the marriage, I have been repeated[ly] beaten, called bad names and given little to wear, not even shoes." Perhaps even worse, she said, she was made to work in the kitchen and out in the fields where she had to gather corn like a servant.

In October, when her husband went to a trade fair in San Juan, she visited her sister, Juana Montoya, who had married Pedro de Chávez, one of Nicolás's brothers. But Juana's mother-in-law found her, and then the mother-in-law and two young brothers-in-law dragged her back to their house. When Juana's husband returned, she was again beaten by him. Some days later, when Juana returned to her sister's house, her brother-in-law urged her to go with them when they traveled by *carreta* (cart) to the Río Grande, where they planned to wash their clothes. After arriving there, they would show her the best place to ford the river and get away from her husband and his family

In her later testimony to Governor Flores Mogollón, Juana stated that after being taken to the ford and crossing the river she walked all night, without encountering anyone. When she arrived at a place between Sandia and Bernalillo, she finally rested.

Then, she continued walking until she got to Las Bocas at the mouth of the Santa Fe River at the Río Grande, where she stayed all night. In the morning, she left for Santa Fe, having been given a ride on the mule of a passerby named Cristóbal Martín. In the end, she said, she arrived at the house of another one of her sisters and talked to her brother-in-law, Salvador de Santistevan, an officer with the presidio. She then submitted a complaint to Governor Flores Mogollón, who then heard testimony from several people, including a midwife who had examined Juana's injuries.

The case ended without any testimony given by Nicolás or his mother and no determination was made by the governor. Likely, the families settled the matter out of court. Documents indicate that Juana returned to her husband, and by 1734 she had eleven more children. Later, her husband Nicolás was involved in several court cases. In 1719, for instance, he accused two Albuquerque men of wounding and insulting him.[2] Then, in 1733, he was sued for non-payment of a dowry for Juana's second child (one of the daughters born before the marriage).[3] Finally, in 1744, he was in court over a boundary dispute, perhaps relating to the large properties he owned in the Isleta area.[4]

Juana clearly knew her legal rights. As with many other women who told their stories in these documents, she used the court to try and improve her *mala vida* (bad life). But she had few options. Divorce was rarely accepted and when it was approved it was only a legal separation. Plus, there were scant economic opportunities for women. Without property or an inheritance of her own, Juana chose to return to her husband and his family, which was followed by a long string of pregnancies. The one legal right that she did have was asking for help from the governor and, by making her situation known to all, perhaps finding some support elsewhere. She outlived Nicolás, who died in 1768.[5]

Although the case record is not complete, it appears that Governor Flores Mogollón followed an abbreviated legal procedure. He heard Juana's complaint and identified the charge. Then he asked for testimony and formally placed a criminal charge against Nicolás de Chávez and his mother, Lucía Hurtado y Salas. The governor did not arrest or imprison either one of them (the typical sentence given), perhaps because of Nicolás and Lucía's social position in the colony. As in other cases he heard, Governor Flores Mogollón was supportive of Juana's request for redress. He noted, for instance, that Juana had fled from the husband and mother-in-law placing herself at the mercy of the royal justice in order to be defended, a statement that must have sounded hopeful to the injured Juana Montaño de Sotomayor.

TRANSLATION

Complaint against Nicolás de Chávez

At the Villa of Santa Fe, New Mexico, on the 22nd of October, 1714, before me don Juan Ignacio Flores Mogollón,[6] governor and captain general of these provinces for his majesty, appeared Juana Montaño [de Sotomayor],[7] legitimate wife of Nicolás de Chávez,[8] resident of the Villa of Albuquerque at the place of Atrisco.[9] She appeared before me with all her respect and goodness complaining about the bad treatment that she had received from her husband from the very beginning of the time that they got married. She said that he beat her up repeatedly, called her terrible words, and treated her indecently in the manner of the way he clothed her, not giving her even a pair of shoes. He made her work in the kitchen to serve him, her mother-in-law, and all of his family, and he made her go to gather the corn in the field with her mother-in-law, who likewise has always treated her badly by insulting her.

Women working in a *cocina* in New Spain. Antonio de Basaras, *Una Vision del Mexico del Siglo de la Luces, la Codificación de Antonio de Basaras. Origen, Costumes y Estado Presente de Mexicanos y Filipinos*, 1763. Courtesy of the Hispanic Society of America, New York.

Because of all of this when her husband left to go to a trade fair at the pueblo of San Juan in the area of [Santa Cruz de] La Cañada, she left the home of her mother-in-law, and went to the home of her sister, María Magdalena Montaño [Moreno],[10] wife of Antonio de Chávez.[11] She did this so that her sister, the wife of Antonio de Chávez, could console her about the bad treatment that she received from her mother-in-law,

Lucía Hurtado [y Salas].[12] After her arrival at the home of her sister-in-law, her mother-in-law came to take her back, bringing with her one of her young sons named Pedro along with another young boy, a nephew. She ordered them to carry her out and take her to her house, Lucía Hurtado taking her out of the house herself pulling Juana by the hair. Antonio de Silva[13] was present at the time and can be summoned as proof of this being the truth.

Once she had been returned to the home of her mother-in-law, she was mistreated horribly with unkind words, her mother-in-law telling her that she should lock her up until her husband returned within two weeks. She made her work in the kitchen, hitting her and insulting her. If she had not been defended by her sister-in-law, Isabel de Chávez,[14] she would most likely had been killed, as she was so badly treated that she had to hide behind the skirts of Isabel. When her husband returned, he hit her with a strap for yoking oxen and she had to be defended again by her sister-in-law, Isabel de Chávez, who told him that she was not a slave.[15] She said that after all of this time that she had been whipped and hurt so much, she wanted to leave to get my assistance and tell me [the governor] all about the problem and see if I could do anything about it.

On Saturday, the 20th of the present month in the early afternoon, Juana told her mother-in-law that she was going to go to her sister's home who lived close by, so that she would expurgate[16] her. With her approval, she went to the home of her sister, who was the wife of Antonio de Chávez, her brother-in-law. She found her in the company of Juana Montoya, wife of another brother-in-law, don Pedro de Chávez.[17] Upon seeing her so mistreated she told her, "Comadre, what are you waiting for? It is best if you leave and go to the Villa of Santa Fe. Do you await a blow that will leave you dead?" At that time, they were both going to the river[18] to wash clothes, which was at the time that the sun was setting. Her sister told her to go with them and they would show her the place to ford the river so that she could leave.

Once they showed her the place, she proceeded to cross the river and left on foot by herself and walked all night until she reached a place [near] Sandia and Bernalillo, where she rested. Then she continued to walk by herself without encountering anyone until she arrived at Los Bocas[19] as the sun was setting, where she rested for the night. Early the next morning she left for the Villa of Santa Fe, where she arrived on Monday at about midday. At the entrance close to the ranch known as that of "Tafoya,"[20] she saw a man approaching her riding a white mule. Taking care that it was not her husband, she hid beneath a cedar tree and upon recognizing that it was not him, she went out and talked to the man. He said that his name was Cristóbal [Martín],[21] who asked her where she was coming from, and told her "Señora, get on this mule and I will take you to your home or to wherever it is that you are going." Being that she could not get on the mule due to her being treated so badly, Cristóbal helped her to get on the mule. She then told him to take her to the home of her brother-in-law, the alférez [Salvador de] Santistevan[22] where he left her.

I, the governor, then asked her if she knew where Cristóbal [Martín] lived, and she stated that he was staying at the home of Nicolás Valverde.[23] She then showed me her right arm and I saw that it had a bad bruise that had been hit by a blow, and she told me that she was like that all over her entire body. I then ordered that she be examined by a midwife, who under a sworn statement is to declare the manner in which she finds her. In the meantime, until everything is found and understood, she is to stay at the home of her brother-in-law, the alférez Salvador de Santistevan who is to see to it that she is well cared for until she is healed.

So that it is valid I ordered that this be placed as the heading of the proceeding, and ordered that testimony be taken from the persons that are referred to and who know what occurred. Then I placed a criminal charge against her husband and her mother-in-law, Lucía Hurtado, from whom she had come to place herself at the mercy of the royal justice in order to be defended. She swore to God Our Lord and to the sign of the Cross that everything was the truth as referred, and she did not sign because she said that she did not know how. I, the governor, signed it along with my secretary of government and war on the said day, month and year.

    Don Juan Ignacio
    Flores Mogollón (rubric)
    At the order of the
    Governor and Captain General
    Roque de Pinto [24](rubric)
    Secretary of Government and War

Statement of María Magdalena [Montaño] Moreno

Continuing, on the same day, month and year, before me the governor and captain general, appeared María Magdalena Moreno, midwife, from whom, upon being present I took her sworn statement that she made to God, Our Lord, and to the sign of the Cross, about which she promised to tell the truth as to what she was asked.

Upon doing so, she was asked if she had examined the body of Juana Montaño and if she had noticed anything unusual or any injuries. She stated that upon complying with what had been ordered of her, she examined her entire body and she found her with bruises and blows that appeared to have been made by a whip. She said that what she has stated is the truth regarding the sworn statement that she has made, which she affirmed and ratified and stated that she was of the age of fifty years more or less. She did not sign because she did not know how, and I, the governor, signed it along with my secretary of government and war.

    Flores [Mogollon](rubric)
    By order of the Governor
    Before me
    Roque de Pinto (rubric)
    Secretary of Government and War

Statement of Antonio de Silva

At the Villa of Santa Fe, New Mexico on the 7th of November, 1714, I, the governor and captain general, made to appear before me Antonio de Silva, resident of the villa of Albuquerque, who was named by Juana Montaño [de Sotomayor] in her complaint. He being present, I took his sworn statement which he made to God, Our Lord, and to the sign of the Cross, in which he promised to tell the truth as to whatever he was asked.

He was asked if he was present at the home of María Magdalena Montaño [Moreno], wife of Antonio de Chávez, on the afternoon that Juana Montaño [de Sotomayor] went to the said house, and when her mother-in-law, Lucía Hurtado [y Salas] with one of her sons and a nephew arrived, and when she ordered them to take her, Juana, and carry her to her home. This was when Lucía Hurtado [y Salas] took her out of the house pulling her by her hair.

Silva stated that he found himself at the home of Antonio de Chávez on the day in question, but that it happened in the morning, not in the afternoon. He was present there after Juana Montaño [de Sotomayor] had arrived. He had also found himself earlier in the day at the home of Lucía Hurtado [y Salas], when she saw that she [Juana Montaño de Sotomayor] left her home with Lucía's daughter, Isabel de Chávez. Lucía then said to this witness, "Let us go look for Juana Montaño, as she has fled from the house now that her husband is absent." He, Silva, then left following both of them and they went into the home of María Magdalena. He stated that Lucía's son Perico[25] and her nephew did not go with them, it being that both young boys were already at the home of María Magdalena. Lucía Hurtado [y Salas] then ordered the young boys to take Juana and carry her to her home, being that Juana did not want to leave and kept resisting them. Then Lucía Hurtado [y Salas] grabbed her by the arm, holding her, at which time she ordered the young boys to carry her, which they did. They took her outside for a short distance and from there she left on her own.

He was asked if he knew the reason for Juana Montaño [de Sotomayor] leaving the home of her mother-in-law, and if she went straight to her sister's. He stated that she, Juana Montaño [de Sotomayor], had gone straight to the home of her sister, María Magdalena. Upon getting there she was hesitant to go inside because she saw that her brother-in-law, Pedro, and another young boy were there, but then they made her go into the home. However, he does not know what the reason was for her to leave the house of her mother-in-law.

He was then asked if he knows or has heard that the reason for her leaving was due to the bad life that her husband, Nicolás de Chávez, has given her and or the reason that he has whipped her on various occasions, the last time being a few days before she left her house. He was also asked if he knew or saw that she was hurt or had an injury to her right arm from the whippings that she had received. He stated that he had not heard that her husband had whipped Juana Montaño [de Sotomayor], nor what the motive was for her to leave the home. He said had heard that the injury to the right arm was due to an accident caused by a hot pan[26] that was in the fire.

Silva was then asked if he knew or has heard that on the afternoon that Juana Montaño left for this villa after having left from the home of her mother-in-law, she then went to the home of her sister, María Magdalena Montaño [Moreno]. This was where Juana Montoya, wife of don Pedro de Chávez, was present, and where the two of them, upon seeing the condition she was in after being so badly treated, asked her why she had come to see them. It was when Juana told them that she had permission from her mother-in-law, she having told her that she needed to be purged by her sister. At this time, [María and Juana] both told her that she should leave and go to the Villa [of Santa Fe]a before her husband killed her. They then told her that they were both about to leave for the river to wash their clothes and that she should go with them. They would show her where the crossing to the river was so that she could go across and leave. She then left with them, crossed the river and left for this villa.

He stated that he did not know what the question was that was referred to by all these circumstances, but that the afternoon that Juana Montaño left for this villa, this witness went to the house of Lucía Hurtado. He saw that she was in a carreta in the company of Antonio de Chávez, husband of Maria Magdalena Montaño, the two together.

He then stated that everything that he has said is the truth regarding the sworn statement that he has made which he affirmed and ratified and that he is not affected by the generalities of the law, and stated that he was fifty years of age and he signed it along with me, the governor and my secretary of government and war.

don Juan Ignacio
Flores Mogollón (rubric)
Antonio de Silva (rubric)
Roque de Pinto (rubric)
Secretary of Government and War

Statement of Cristóbal Martín

At this villa on the 10th of November, 1714, I, the governor and captain general, made to appear before me Cristóbal Martín, who is named by Juana Montaño in her complaint. I took his sworn statement which he made to God, Our Lord, and to the sign of the Cross, in which he promised to tell the truth as to what he was asked and as to what he knew.

He was asked if while riding upon a gray mule he encountered Juana Montaño at the *paraje* named El Rancho de Tafoya, and gave her a ride. He stated that this was true. While he was riding on the gray mule looking for a young boy who had gone to the mountains from the Paraje de Tafoya, at about midday he saw Juana Montaño sitting beneath a cedar tree. Upon conversing with her, he asked her where she was coming from and what she was doing there. She answered him saying that she had walked all the way from Albuquerque fleeing from the bad treatment that she was receiving from her husband and that she was seeking protection from a justice.

This witness, seeing that she could not move, he asked her if other than being extremely tired from the trip she was hurt badly by her husband. She showed him one arm, and he noticed that it was all bruised as if she had an injury from a blow. Seeing that she was in this condition this witness then told her, "Señora, climb on this mule and tell me where you want me to take you." She then answered him saying, "Could you take me to the home of the Alférez Santistevan, my brother-in-law?" This witness then got off the mule and he helped her get on it, seeing that she did not have the strength to do it on her own, and then took her to the home of the Alférez Santistevan. Because he was not there at the time he turned her over to the alférez's wife, and that since that time he has not seen her again.

This he says is the truth and is what occurred regarding the sworn statement that he has made and which he affirmed and ratified, saying that he was thirty-five years of age. He did not sign because he did not know how, I, the governor, signed it along with my secretary of government and war.

    Flores Mogollón (rubric)
    By order of
    Governor and Captain General
    Roque de Pinto (rubric)
    Secretary of Government and War

TRANSCRIPTION

Querella contra Nicolas de Chaves

En la Villa de Santa Fee de la Nueva Mexico en veinte y dos dias del mes de Octubre de mill setezientos y catorze años ante mi Dn. Juan Ygnacio Flores Mogollon, Governador y Capitan General destas provinzias por Su Magestad parezio Juana Montaño mujer lexitima de Nicolas de Chaves vezino dela Villa de Alburquerque en el stio de Atrisco y me represento benir ami recurso y amparo por el mal tratamiento que desde la ora que se caso le da su marido azotandola repetidas bezes maltratandola de palabras y tratandola yndezentemente en su bestuario sin averle dado unos zapatos haciendola que sirvuese y travajase en la cozina sirviendole a el y a su suegra y toda su familia ocupandola en que fuese a cojer el mais a la milpa con su suegra quien asi mismo la a maltratado siempre dandole muchos baldones.

Que causada de ellos le presizo aviendo ydo su marido a un resgate al Pueblo de San Juan ala Canada a salido de en casa de su suegra con quien vivia y yrse en casa de Maria Magdalena Montaño su hermana, muger de Antonio de Chavez aque la amparase del mal tratamiento que le dava su suegra Luzia Hurtado; y que luego que llego a dicha casa binieron por ella dicha su suegra quien llevo con sigo a un mozo hijo suyo llamado Pedro y otro muchacho nieto y les mando que la cargasen y llevasen a su casa aviendola sacado arrastrando de los cavellos la dicha Luzia Hurtado y allandose presente Antonio de Silva quien lo podia declarar para prueba de su verdad.

Que aviendola llevado a casa dela dicha su suegra la maltrato mucho de palabras diziendole la avia de enzerrar asta que biniese su marido abia dos semanas en la cozina la azoto y apaleo; que a no entrar a defenderla Ysabel de Chavez su cuñada rezela la ubiera muerto dejandola tan maltratada que no se puede mover pues haviendola apartado su cunada y estando esta declarante en las faldas dela dicha Ysabel bolvio el dicho su marido con una coyunda azotarla y defendiendola la dicha Ysabel de Chaves su cunada le dijo a su marido que si era ereje y que despues en todo este tiempo que a que la azoto a sido el maltrato tanto que deseaba occasion de salirse para benir ami prezenzia a darme notizia a que la anparase y pusiese remedio.

Que el sabado veinte del corriente por la tarde le dijo a su suegra Señora pasare en casa de mi hermana que vive zerca a que me expulgue y que con esta lizensia paso en casa dela dicha que es muger de Antonio de Chaves, su cunado, y que la allo en compania de Juana Montoya mujer de su cunado, Dn. Pedro de Chavez y que estas le dijeron biendola tan maltratada comadre que quieres esperar mejor es que te bayas ala Villa quieres aguardar que te de un golpe que te deje muerta y que entonzes yban las dos al rio a lavar que se yva poniendo el sol; bente con nosotros te ensenaremos el vado por donde puedes pasar y yrte.

Que aviendoselo mostrado paso el rio y se bino sola apie caminando toda la noche; llego entre Bernalillo y Zandia alli descanso y camino sola sin encontrar a nadie y llego el Domingo al ponerse el sol alas Bocas y alli descanso aquella noche y por la madrugada se bino para esta Villa donde llego ayer Lunes a medio dia y que ala entrada junto el rancho que llaman de Tafoya bido benir un hombre en una mula blanca y rezelandose que fuese su marido se escondio de vajo de un sabino y que aviendo reconozido no ser su marido salio y le ablo al dicho hombre que dise llamarse Xptobal que este le pregunto de donde benia y le dijo Señora suba en esta mula la llevare a su casa o a donde ba; y entonzes como no podia subir por lo maltratada que benia la cargo el dicho Xptobal poniendola sobre la mula y le dijo me apeara Usted en casa de mi cuñado el Alferez Santisteban donde la dejo.

Preguntandole yo dicho Governador si supo donde vivia el dicho Xptobal dijo que supo posava en casa de Nicolas Balverde y aviendome mostrado el brazo derecho le bi una erida o golpe en el y diziendome que tenia todo su cuerpo de aquel modo mando que la reconosca una partera quien devajo de juramento declare el modo que la allare y que en el ynterin que se justifica todo lo que a declarado se mantenga en deposito en casa de dicho su cunado Alferez Salvador de Santistevan quien ara se cure con todo cuidado.

Para que conste lo hize poner por deligenzia y mando se rezivan ynformaziones con las personas que refiere de todo lo subzedido y dijo se querellava criminalmente del dicho su marido y su suegra Luzia Hurtado y que para ello avia benido a ponerse al amparo dela real justizia para que la defienda y juro por Dios Nuestro Señor y la Señal de la Cruz ser zierto todo lo referido y no firmo por que dijo no saver firmelo yo dicho Governador con mi Secretario de Governazion y Guerra en dicha dia, mes y año =

Dn. Juan Ygnacio
Flores Mogollon (rubric)
Por mando del Señor
Governador y Capitan General
Roque de Pinto (rubric)
Secretario de Governazion y Guerra

Declaracion de Maria Magdalena Moreno

Y luego incontinenti en dicho dia, mes y año, ante mi dicho Governador y Capitan General parezio Maria Magdalena Moreno partera ala qual estando presente le rezevi juramento que hizo por Dios Nuestro Señor y la Señal dela Cruz so cargo del cual prometio dezir verdad en lo que fuere preguntado y siendolo si le reconosio a Juana Montaño el cuerpo y si tenia notificado en el algunas señales o eridas?

Dijo que cumpliendo con lo por mi mandado le reconozio ala dicha todo el cuerpo y la allo toda llena de cardenales y golpes que le pareze fueron azotes y que lo que lleva declarado es la verdad so cargo del juramento que fecho lleva en que se afirmo y ratifico y que es de edad de zinquenta años poco mas o menos, no firmo por no saver firmelo yo dicho Governador con mi Secretario de Governazion y Guerra =

Don. Juan Ygnacio
Flores Mogollon (rubric)
Por mando del or Governador
Ante mi
Roque de Pinto (rubric)
Secretario de Governazion y Guerra

Declaracion de Antonio de Silva

En la Villa de Santa Fee de la Nueva Mexico en siete dias del mes de Noviembre de mill setezientos y catorze años yo dicho Governador y Capitan General hize parezer ante mi a Antonio de Silva vezino de la Villa de Alburquerque a quien zita en su querella Juana Montaño el qual estando presente le rezevi juramento que hizo por Dios Nuestro Señor y la señal dela cruz so cargo del qual prometio dezir verdad en lo que fuere preguntado y siendolo si se allo presente en casa de Maria Magdalena Montaño, muger de Antonio de Chavez la tarde que Juana Montaño fue a dicha casa y que estando en ella bino su suegra Luzia Hurtado con un hijo suyo y otro nieto y les mando la cargasen y llevasen a su casa y que dicha Luzia Hurtado la saco arrastrando delos cabellos.

Dijo, que se allo en casa de Antonio de Chaves el dia que la pregunta refiere que no fue por la tarde sino por la mañana y que al allarse en dicha casa fue despues que estava en ella Juana Montaño y que este declarante estava aquella manana en casa de Luzia Hurtado que la vido salir con su hija Ysavel de Chaves que le dijeron a este declarante bamos buscando a Juana Montaño mujer de Nicolas que se a salido de casa juida estando su marido ausente, y que este declarante se fue de tras de las dos que entraron en casa de Maria Magdalena donde se entro con ellas y que no yva su hijo Perico ni su nieto por que los tales muchachos estavan en casa de la dicha Maria Magdalena y que les mando la dicha Luzia Hurtado alos dicho muchachos cargasen a Juana Montaño y la llevasen a su casa por que no queria yr y que vido que se resistia a yr con los muchachos la Juana Montaño y su suegra Luzia Hurtado la agarro por el brazo ynstando a que azerla llevar y que entonzes que quando mando a los muchachos la cargasen y que estos la alzaron en peso y la sacaron un corto trecho y luego fue por su pie.

Preguntado si save por que motivo se avia salido de su casa de su suegra la dicha Juana Montaño y si se fue derecho en casa de su hermana? Dijo que derecho avia ydo la dicha Juana Montaño en casa de su hermana Maria Magdalena y que al llegar a ella vido a su cuñado Pedro y el otro muchacho y se rezelo de entrar asta que los muchachos le hizieron que entrara en dicha casa y que no save por que motivo se salio de en casa de su suegra. Preguntado si supo o oyo dezir que el motivo de averse salido era la mala vida que su marido Nicolas de Chaves le dava y el averla azotado en distintas ocaciones que la ultima fue pocos dias antes del que se salio de su casa y si vido o supo que estava lastimada de los azotes pues trahia en el brazo derecho una herida o lastimadura; dijo que no a oido dezir ubiese su marido azotado ala dicha Juana Montaño, ni el motivo por que se salio de su casa y que oio dezir que la lastimadura del brazo casualmente sela dio Juana Montaño con un cazo que estava ala lumbre.

Preguntado si save y oyo dezir que aquella tarde que se salio la dicha Juana Montaño para benir a esta Villa despues de aver buelto en casa de su suegra se bino en casa de su hermana Maria Magdalena Montaño y que estava con la dicha Juana Montoya muger de Dn. Pedro de Chaves y que estas dos viendola llegar tan maltratada le dijeron a que bienes y que ella respondio que benia con lizensia de su suegra que le avia dicho benia a que la espulgase su hermana y que entonzes las dos le dijeron que azes que no te bas ala Villa esperas a que te mate to marido y que entonzes yran azi a el rio las dos a lavar y le dijeron bente con nosotras te ensenaremos el bado para que pases el rio y bete; y que se fue con ellas paso el rio y se vino a esta Villa.

Dijo que no save lo que la pregunta refiere de zircumstanzias pero que la tarde que se bino a esta Villa la dicha Juana Montaño este declarante yva para en casa de Luzia Hurtado y bido que la dicha Juana Montaño yba en una carreta y en su compania Antonio de Chaves marido de la dicha Maria Magdalena Montaño que los dos juntos yban con la carreta y que todo lo que lleva declarado es la verdad so cargo del juramento que fecho lleva en que se afirmo y ratifico y que no le tocan las generales de la ley y dijo ser de hedad de zinquenta años y lo firmo con migo dicho governador y mi secretario de governazion y guerra =

Dn. Juan Ygnacio
Flores Mogollon (rubric)
Antonio de Silva (rubric)
Roque de Pinto (rubric)
Secretario de Governazion y Guerra

Declaracion de Xptobal Martin

En esta dicha Villa en dies dias del mes de Noviembre de mil setezientos y catorxe años yo dicho Governador y Capitan General hize parezer ante mi a Xptobal Martin a quien zita en su declaracion y querella Juana Montaño al qual le rezevi juramento que hizo por Dios Nuestro Señor y la señal dela cruz so cargo del qual prometio dezir verdad en lo que supiere.

Fuere preguntado y siendolo si illendo este declarante en una mula ruzia encontro en el Paraje que llaman El Rancho de Tafoya a Juana Montaño muger de Nicolas de Chaves y si la ablo? Dijo que es zierto yendo este declarante en la mula rezia en busca de un muchacho que avia ydo al monte en el dicho Paraje de Tafoya seria como medio dia bido sentada al pie de un savino ala dicha Juana Montaño a quien este declarante abla preguntandole de donde benia o que hazia alli que le respondio la dicha benia a pie desde Alburquerque huyendo del mal trato que le dava su marido a ampararse dela justizia.

Que este declarante biendo que no se podia mober pues le dijo que demas de el cansansio benia mui aporreada de su marido y le vido un brazo que le mostro la dicha una erida o golpe como cardenal y biendola de aquel modo este declarante le dijo Señora suba en esta mula y digame donde quiere que la lleve y entonses le respondio pues me llevara Usted en casa del Alferez Santistevan mi cunado y que en tonzes este declarante se apeo y la subio en la mula por que ella no podia y la llevo en casa del Alferez Santistevan que por no estar alli entrega a su mujer y que desde entonses no la a buelto aver mas.

Que esto es la verdad y lo que paso so cargo del juramento que fecho tiene en que se afirmo y ratifico y dijo ser de edad de treinta y sinco años, no firmo por no saver, firmelo yo dicho Governador con mi Secretario de Governazion y Guerra =

>Flores (rubric)
>Por mando del Señor
>Governador y Capitan General
>Roque de Pinto (rubric)
>Secretario de Governazion y Guerra

Notes

1. See SANM II #208.
2. See SANM II #299.
3. See SANM I #841.
4. See SANM I # 92; SANM I #184.
5. See Stamatov, *Family, Kin*: 225.
6. For information on Juan Ignacio Flores Mogollón, see Case 6.
7. Juana Montaño de Sotomayor was the daughter of Juan Antonio Montaño de Sotomayor and Isabel Jorge de Vera. Isabel was the granddaughter of Antonio Baca, a pre-revolt settler. She is recorded as owning a house and garden lot on the Santa Fe Plaza, where Juana may have lived as a child. Juan and Isabel returned to New Mexico with Governor Vargas in 1692. Juana's sisters were María Magdalena Montaño [Moreno], who married Antonio Durán y Chávez, and Leonor Montaño, who married Luis Durán y Chávez. (Hordes, "History of the Santa Fe Plaza": 133-39; Chávez, *Origins*: 233-34; NMGS, *Aquí*: 69-70.)
8. Nicolás de Chávez was the sixth child of don Fernando Durán y Chávez and doña Lucía Hurtado y Salas, who returned to New Mexico in 1692. Born in 1686, Nicolás died in Isleta, on May 19, 1768. During his lifetime, he acquired property south of Isleta and was involved in several land disputes in the area. (Chávez, *Origins*: 161-63; SANM II #299; SANM II #465; SANM II #516; and SANM II #841.)
9. See Map 4 in the appendix.
10. María Magdalena Montaño [Moreno] was the sister of Juana Montaño de Sotomayor and married to Antonio Durán y Chávez, a son of don Fernando Durán y Chávez and doña Lucía Hurtado y Salas. María apparently died sometime before 1718, as her husband is listed as "widowed" in a 1718 marriage record. (Chávez, *Origins*: 162-64, 233-34; and Chávez, *Roots*: 305-06.)
11. Antonio de Chávez was the eldest son of don Fernando Durán y Chávez and doña Lucía Hurtado y Salas. His

first wife was María Magdalena Montaño [Moreno], as stated above. In 1718, when marrying for the second time, he requested a dispensation for illicit copulation with a relative of his bride and third-degree consanguinity. The bride, Doña Antonia Baca, is listed as being fifteen years old, her parent's unknown, and very poor. Antonio was granted the dispensation on the condition that he labor one day a week for four months at the parish church, beg alms for the Poor Souls, and donate 1,000 adobes for the church in Albuquerque and for the cemetery in Bernalillo. He was also instructed to make one hundred adobes for the churches in Albuquerque and Bernalillo, including working for one whole week at each place. The document states that these conditions were placed on him so that others would be deterred from similar sinful behavior. (Chávez, *Roots*: 305-06; Chávez, *Origins*: 233-34.)

12. Lucía Hurtado y Salas was the wife of don Fernando Durán y Chávez, of the pre-revolt Durán y Chávez family. Her father was Andrés Hurtado, who was born in Zacatecas, Mexico, and was a military captain in New Mexico in 1664. Lucía's mother was Bernardina de Salas y Orozco and her brother was Martín Hurtado, one of the founders of the Villa of Albuquerque and the city's first alcalde and garrison commander. (Chávez, *Origins*: 49, 133, 197; Kessell, Hendricks, and Dodge, *Boulders*: 1171n106.)

13. Antonio de Silva was the son of Salvador de Silva and Gregoria Ruiz, both of whom journeyed from Querétaro, Mexico, to New Mexico with the Farfán Expedition in 1694. Antonio settled in Santa Cruz, later moving to Bernalillo and then Albuquerque. In the 1698 investigations of Governor Rodríguez Cubero, he testified against don Diego de Vargas. In 1707, he was a soldier living in Albuquerque, and he also served as a notary. He appears to have died by 1732. (Chávez, *Origins*: 288; Kessell, Hendricks, and Dodge, *Royal Crown*: 331n78; Kessell, Hendricks, Dodge, and Miller, *Settling*: 163-64.)

14. Isabel de Chávez was the daughter of don Fernando Durán y Chávez and doña Lucía Hurtado y Salas, and she was the sister of Nicolás and Antonio de Chávez. She was married to Jacinto Paláez, and after his death she married Baltazar de Mata in 1705. (Kessell, Hendricks, and Dodge, *Royal Crown*: 178n41.)

15. In the Spanish text, the word used is *ereje* and the literal translation is "heretic." However, the word probably referred to a non-Christian Indian who had been taken captive and made a servant in the house.

16. In the Spanish text, the word used is *expulgue*, which literally means "purge;" in the 1700s, such a purge was probably done with some kind of folk emetic.

17. Pedro de Chávez was another son of Fernando Durán y Chávez and Lucía Hurtado y Salas. He married Juana Montoya in 1703 and was one of the founders of Albuquerque in 1706. By 1713 he was a militia squadron leader, and in 1716 he participated in the campaign against the Moqui pueblos. He died in 1635. (Chávez, *Origins*: 161; and see the extensive discussion in NMGS, *Aquí*: 182-88.)

18. This river was called Río del Norte, or, as we know it today, the Río Grande.

19. Los Bocas literally means "the mouth" in Spanish and is located where the Santa Fe River empties into the Río Grande. See the Map 3 in the appendix.

20. The specific location of the Tafoya ranch is unknown; it was probably somewhere between La Cieneguilla and Santa Fe. It is likely the land grant referred to in SANM I #961 and SANM I #962.

21. This is probably the Cristóbal Martín who was also known as "Cristóbal Martínez Gallego," a resident in Río Abajo in the 1730s. He was also known as "el Cojo" (the cripple). It is unlikely that he is the Cristóbal Martín of Chimayó, a son of Hernan Martín Serrano II and married to Antonia Moraga (Ebright, Hendricks, and Hughes, *Four Square Leagues*: 61.)

22. Salvador de Santistevan was born about 1679, in Mexico City, to Andre de Santistevan and Juana de la Concepción. He was in Santa Fe by 1695, when he married Polonia Montaño, a sister of Juana, in Santa Fe. In 1697, he is listed in a muster of presidio soldiers. In 1714, he was the alférez of Santa Fe. On a 1723 presidio muster, Salvador was listed as an ayudante (aide-de-camp), with arms and seven horses. According to Fray Angelico Chávez, he owned land on the west bank of the Río Grande across from Santa Cruz. From his testimony, it appears that he also owned land near Santa Fe. (Kessell, Hendricks, and Dodge, *Royal Crown*: 191n163; Christmas, *Military Records*: 49; Chávez, *Origins*: 284.)

23. Nicolás Valverde, a native of Parral, Mexico, was born about 1666. In 1701, he and Salvador de Santistevan requested validation of a land grant in Chama from Governor Rodríguez Cubero. He is listed as working on San Miguel Chapel in Santa Fe in 1710 and as being married in New Mexico in 1716. In 1729, he was a soldier at the presidio. (Chávez, *Origins*: 304; Kessell, Hendricks, Dodge, and Miller, *Disturbances*: 129.)

24. For information on Roque de Pinto, see Case 6.

25. "Perico" ("Little Pedro") was the nickname given to Pedro Gómez de Chávez, the tenth and last child of Fernando Durán y Chávez and Lucía Hurtado y Salas. The name was probably given to differentiate him from his older brother, Pedro de Chávez. Perico lived in Atrisco until 1732, when he sold his inherited lands to Bernabé Baca and to Antonia de Chávez, the widowed second wife of an older brother. He then moved to Río Arriba where, in 1737, he married Petrona Martín [Serrano], a daughter of Francisco Martín Serrano (descendent of a pre-revolt family) and Juana García. Petrona was also a sister of Juana García, the wife of Juan García de la Mora. (Chávez, *Origins*: 161-63, 222.)

26. In the Spanish text, the phrase is *"con un cazo que estava ala lumbre,"* which could also mean a hot ember or poker.

9

COUPLE PUNISHED FOR COHABITATION
July 23–24, 1715, Source: SANM II #227

Synopsis and editor's notes: This short case is included because it shows how the Holy Office of the Inquisition and the secular authority involved themselves with marriage, or in this case, not being married. The authority in this case was Juan García de la Riva. As the Santa Fe alcalde ordinario (examining justice of the Santa Fe Cabildo) and as the *aguacil ordinario* (arresting officer for the Holy Office of the Inquisition in Santa Fe), de la Riva was responsible for apprehending and sentencing persons who committed *pecados* (public sins), as identified by the Franciscan priests, and those who violated the Spanish law. In this case, the sin and illegal act was cohabitation—a man and woman who lived together without being married. The Spanish term for this was *amancebado* and it was considered to be a violation of public morals and a minor heresy by the Holy Office of the Inquisition.

In his dual roles, Juan García de la Riva responded to a notice from a priest and other persons regarding the cohabitation of Francisco Cadena and a single woman. It took several tries for de la Riva to find him, and when he did he put Cadena in jail for only one night. He also fined him goods equivalent to one *marca* (8 ounces of silver). The value of this fine in pesos or trade goods (like hides or corn) is not known. The short case was handled by de la Riva in a casual way, following few of the usual Spanish legal procedures.

The position of the Catholic Church, through the Holy Office of the Inquisition, was that marriage was a sacrament and sexual union of any kind without marriage, such as cohabitation, was a sin and a minor heresy. It was also considered a sin to not report such misconduct. During this period, the public was informed of these sins through the reading of an Edict of Faith (or Anathema) by the priest at Sunday Mass. It has been recorded, for instance, that an Edict of Faith was read in Santa Fe in June 1716, as well as on other occasions before that date. (See the introduction.) Here is an early example of an Edict of Faith on cohabitation that was read in Mexico City in 1576: "Also, you are required by this edict to depose against or denounce any married couples who do not conduct married life living together in harmony; or any other persons who, having not received the sacrament of matrimony, live together in sin as if they were married."[1]

In the Santa Fe case of cohabitation, it is possible that fray Joseph Antonio Guerrero, the minister of the church in the villa, made or at least supported the denunciation against Francisco Cadena.

Research on the regulation of public morals in New Spain have shown that cohabitation was common enough, particularly in a villa like Santa Fe, with a mobile population of one hundred or so soldiers, the governor's personnel, and Camino Real traders. Other than a fine, the punishment for cohabitation was often a requirement that the couple get married, unless, of course, they were married to someone else, as may have been the case in this situation. If marriage was not possible, separating the couple through banishment was an alternative sentence.[2]

As described in the translation below, Cadena was married to Ana de la Cruz, a Tesuque Indian, and then in 1716, he is also listed as being married to Leonor Montaño, a widow. It is not known if he was living with either of these women at the time of the denouncement.

TRANSLATION

[Arrest and Release of Francisco Cadena]

At the Villa of Santa Fe on the 23rd of July, 1715, I, Captain Juan García de la Riva,[3] alcalde ordinario of this villa, have received notice from the priest and other persons that Francisco Cadena,[4] resident of this villa, is cohabitating with a single woman. Having gone on different occasions to bring him in, and he having escaped on various occasions, I was still able to find him and bring him in on a certain day at the hour of the evening prayer. I found him at the small house of Simon de Córdova,[5] where Cadena was *asiendo tiempo* (killing time) before he would go to the house of the said woman. Due to the fact that it is such a public sin, I brought him as a prisoner to the public jail of this villa.

On the following day, the 24the of the said month, I ordered that he be released from jail. I notified him of the sentence for the first offense of cohabitation, and made him pay what amounts to one silver marca.[6] This being the truth of the matter, I signed it on the said day, which is the 24th of the present month of July along with my assisting witnesses.

    Juan García de la Riva (rubric)
    Witnesses
    Lorenzo de Casados[7] (rubric)
    Juan Manuel de Chirinos[8] (rubric)

TRANSCRIPTION

En la Villa de Santa Fee en beinte y tres dias del mes de Jullio de mil zetesientos y quinse añ os yo el Captian Juan Garcia dela Rivas, Alcalde Ordinario de dicho Villa abiendo tenido notissia por los ministros y otras personas que Francisco Cadena besino desta dicha Villa esta amanzebado con una muger soltera y abiendo ydo distintas beses a cogerlo y averse escapade barias beses sin embargo lo cogi el dia dicho zerca dela orasion de la noche en una casita de Simon de Cordova donde estava asiendo tiempo para irse en casa de dicha muger y por zer el pecado tan publico lo traje preso ala carsel publica desta dicha Villa.

Otro dia beinte y quatro de dicho mes lo mande sacar de dicha carsel y le notifique este auto por primer requirimiento de dicho amanzebimiento y le hise pagar lo que importa un marco de plata y por ser berdad lo firme en dicho dia beine y cuatro del presente mes de Jullio con los testigos de mi assistenzia =

    Juan Garcia de la Riva (rubric)
    Testigos
    Lorenzo de Casados (rubric)
    Juan Manuel de Chirinos (rubric)

Notes

1. See Chuchiak, *Inquisition*: 109.
2. For further information on the punishment for cohabitation, see Boyer, *Bigamists*: 28-29; Rawlings, *Spanish Inquisition*: 121; Twinam, *Public Lives*: 87; Lavrin, *Sexuality and Marriage*: 62-67.)
3. Juan García de la Riva was born in Mexico City, the son of don Miguel García de la Riva and doña Micaela Velasco, who came to New Mexico in 1694 with the Farfán Expedition. Juan's father is listed as a weaver from Mexico City. Juan was chosen by Governor Diego de Vargas as the first alcalde of Santa Cruz in 1696, and he was an alcalde ordinario in Santa Fe in 1708, at the age of thirty-one. He was also an alguacil mayor (arresting officer) of the Holy Office of the Inquisition; in New Mexico, the latter was staffed by the Franciscans. (Chávez, *Origins*: 183; Tigges and Salazar, *Colonial Lives*: 205; Esquibel, "Mexico City": 68; SANM I #2.)
4. A native of New Mexico, Francisco Cadena [Hinojos] was the son of Francisco de la Cruz and Antonia de Hinojos. He was in New Mexico by 1710, when he worked on the reconstruction of San Miguel Chapel in Santa Fe. He had married Ana de la Cruz, a Tesuque Indian, but in 1716, he married Leonor Montaño, the widow of Luis de Chávez and a sister of Juana Montaño de Sotomayor (see Case 8). Luis de Chávez was the son of don Fernando Durán y Chávez. According to Fray Angelico Chávez, in 1680 Francisco Cadena was taken captive as a child by the Picuris Indians. He died in 1757, at the age of ninety. (Chávez, *Origins*: 154, 163, 349; Kubler, *San Miguel*: 19.)
5. Simon de Córdova II was the son of Simon de Córdova I and Juana de la Encarnación of Zacatecas, Mexico. In 1714, when he was twenty-five years old, Simon II married María de Guadalupe. He may be the brother of María de Córdova of Santa Cruz, who married Bernardo Romero. (Chávez, *Origins*: 165, 352.)
6. A marca weighed 8 ozs. And was the basic monetary weight of gold or silver bullion at the mints of New Spain, as prescribed by the *Ordenanzas de la Minería*. One estimate is that a peso was worth 1.74 ounces, so the fine could have been a little over four pesos. (Stampa, "Weights and Measures": 17; Kessell, Hendricks, Dodge, and Miller, *Settling of Accounts*: 129.) Why García de la Riva asked for goods worth one silver marca, rather than goods worth a certain amount in pesos, is unknown. It is possible he worked in the mines or for the mint in New Spain and was familiar with the term.
7. Francisco Lorenzo de Casados was born in Cadiz, Spain, and, according to Fray Angelico Chávez, was a *forcado*—a convict punished with forced labor. Casados was in New Mexico by 1694, having traveled with the Farfán Expedition. In 1715, he was a militia captain; he was buried in El Paso in 1729. His son, Francisco Joseph de Casados, a resident of Santa Fe, was married to María de Archibeque, one of the daughters of Juan de Archibeque. (Chávez, *Origins*: 137; Kessell, Hendricks, and Dodge, *Royal Crown*: 341n133; Esquibel, "Mexico City": 69.)
8. For information on Juan Manuel de Chirinos, see Case 5.

10

INHERITANCE OF TWO COWS DEMANDED BY ORPHANED DAUGHTER
1715, Source: SANM II #239c

Synopsis and editor's notes: This document from 1715 is one of several in this book in which a woman used her legal right to petition the governor for help in collecting an inheritance, or, as in this case, a gift probably intended as a dowry. As in many of these requests, the proof of ownership had been lost and the validity of the request was based on the memory of witnesses.

In this case, Catalina de Villalpando asked for assistance in collecting two cows that were given to her by her uncle, Bartolo de Albizu. She was asking the governor for help because she had not heard from her father, Juan de Villalpando, for a number of years and therefore considered herself an orphan who could no longer seek assistance from her father. But, she stated, as an orphan she did come under the category of persons who were to be favored by the king and the governor.

The problem was that her uncle had given the cows to Santa Fe presidio-soldier Alonso García de Noriega so that he could deliver them to Catalina but he never did. Instead, he took the cows to his home and gave Catalina a promissory note stating that he would give her two bulls. Catalina's cows, however, had been bred and instead of two bulls she wanted the cows and their calves, a total of four animals, and she wanted the cows available to be bred again.

This document appears to be only a fragment of a more extensive case, for there is no record of the response from the governor. However, for some reason, this fragment of two folios was filed in the archives of New Mexico, where it remains to this day. It may be that the response from the governor has been lost, or perhaps the case was settled without any action by the governor.

Catalina de Villalpando's name also appears in a document dating to 1719, in which she argues with a neighbor over access to a walkway between their houses.[1] In that case, she states that she is twenty-five or twenty-six years old, which means that she is twenty-one or twenty-two in the case concerning the cows.

In making her plea, Catalina requested that it be favored by the governor because "the governor is the father of this kingdom and as such feels sorry for all the poor people and in particular the orphans." Variations on this phrase appear in other documents of this period, suggesting that the governor's job, and for that matter the king's job, was to help the abandoned and needy. For instance, in Case 12 in this book, a woman refers to the *real auxilio* (royal kindness), and in Case 24, a woman reminds the governor of the *real amparo* (royal protection) for widows and others and stated that the governor represents the "the real life image of the king."

TRANSLATION

1715

Governor and Captain General[2]

I, Catalina de Villalpando,[3] orphan daughter of Juan de Villalpando.[4] As it has been a number of years since we have heard anything from my father, I now consider myself an orphan and appear before your honor, in my best and most proper form according to my legal right. I ask that I may be favored by the royal aid of your honor from which I request assistance regarding two cows that had been given to me by an uncle of mine by the name of Bartolo de Albizu.[5] He sent them to me with Alonso García,[6] a soldier in this royal castle of New Mexico, who went to where my uncle had his home. My uncle faithfully gave them to him so that he would turn them over to me.

To date, Alonso García de Noriega has not turned the cows over to me nor any offspring they would have had, as they were cows that were bred. The time that has elapsed since my uncle sent them to me is three years, and during all of this period he has been stubborn about the whole matter. It has not been possible for me to try to get them from him because he comes up with different excuses. Recently he left me a promissory note stating that he would give me a payment of two bulls, but I would not accept them, as what my uncle had sent to me were two cows that were bred.

For this purpose, sir, I can give you the required information from individuals who were present and saw that the cows were turned over to Alonso García [de Noriega] and taken to his home. Those who were there were Francisco de Tapia[7] and Bernardo Madrid,[8] as they had accompanied [Alonso García de Noriega], as well as Captain Salvador Montoya,[9] who carried the letter from my uncle, but as it was lost, I cannot provide it to your honor. Since the time that the cows were to be sent to me, I have not seen them. At this time, I request of your honor that [Alonso García de Noriega] be punished for this. As such I also request that I be favored by you with what is due to me, as you are the father of this kingdom and as such you feel sorry for all of the poor people and in particular for the orphans.

I swear to God, Our Lord, that this, my request, is not done in malice but is for the sake of justice, and what I ask is for the best, etc.

Catalina de Villalpando (rubric)

TRANSCRIPTION

1715

Señor Governador y Capitan General

Catarina de Villalpando guerfana de Juan de Villalpando pues por tal me tengo pues a añnos que no emos tenido razon del dicho mi padre lla si me contemplo guerfana paresco postrada ante Vuestra Señoria en la mas bastante forma que ayga derecho y a el mio combengo y digo Señor que me llego a favorezer del Real auxilio de Vuestra Señoria me aga justisia que pido a Vuestra Señoria tocante a dos bacas que las quales me las abia enbiado un tio mio llamado Bartolo de Alviso las quales zelas entrego a Alonso Garcia siendo soldado de este Real Castillo dela Nueba Mexico en occasion que fue el dicho Alonso Garcia a tener donde este mi tio tiene su morada de quien se fio para que melas entregara y no me an dado cumplimiento a dichas bacas ni las crias que al pie binieron y las quales crias eran enbras.

El tiempo que a que melas despacho el dicho mi tio abra cosa de tres añnos y en todo este tiempo ze a dado por desentendido y no a sido possible el que me ayga balido el aberzelo requerido siempre si me a dado con entretenidas y por ultimo me dejo un bale de dos toros los quales no azepto por ser embras las que me embiava el dicho mi tio asi las de bientre como las que al pie benian.

Desto Sñor prometo ynformasion con personas legas lla bonador quienes bieron entregar las dichas bacas y las trujo a su casa el dicho Alonso Garcia que esto lo puede declarar Francisco de Tapia y Bernardo Madri que fueron en su compania y el Capitan Salvador Montoya quien llevo la carta del dicho mi tio que por aberse perdido no zela muestro a Vuestra Señoria y pues a este tiempo que me las enbiaron ze me enteren las dichas bacas con las paresiones que Vuestra Señoria fuere serbido de sentensiar por tanto pido a Vuestra Señoria me favoresca pues es padre deste Reyno y ze con duela de todos los pobres e en particular de los guerfanos.

Juro a Dios Nuestro Señor no zer de malisia este mi escripto si justisia que pido y en lo nezesario, ut supra =

Catarina de Villalpando (rubric)

Notes

1. See Case 19.
2. This either refers to Governor Flores Mogollón, who was in office from 1712 to October 1715, or to Felix Martínez, who became governor on October 5, 1715. (Warner: *Felix Martínez*: 92.)
3. Catarina de Villalpando was the daughter of Juan de Villa el Pando (or Villalpando) and Ana María Romero [Villalpando], whose outspoken behavior may have been a model for Catalina. Catalina married Antonio Martín of Embudo. They had at least seven children, one of whom was baptized in Embudo on November 11, 1735. Antonio is mentioned in a 1767 will of Juan Francisco Martín as being owed a stallion and three mares. (Chávez, *Origins*: 312; Chávez, *Roots*: 1718; NMGS, *Santa Cruz Baptisms*: 33; SANM I #600, WPA translation. For Ana María Romero, Catalina's mother, see Case 14 and Case 16.)
4. Juan de Villalpando was a native of Villa de Leon and a presidio soldier. He married Ana María Romero in 1694. In the 1697 livestock distribution document, he is listed along with his wife Ana María Romero and daughter Catalina. Juan and Ana María had seven children in total, including Ambrosio, Pablo, and Juan Rosalío. (Chávez, *Origins*: 312; Kessell, Hendricks, and Dodge, *Boulders*: 1140, 1161n15.)
5. To date, no information has been found on Bartolo de Albizu. Although his last name was spelled in various ways: Alvisu, Albisu, Alviso, he was most likely a part of the pre-revolt Albizu family (See Chávez, *Origins*, 2-3).
6. This may be the Alonso García de Noriega who was a soldier in Juan Páez Hurtado's expedition against the Apaches in 1715. If so, he is listed as a corporal and as fully armed and provided with seven horses. Alonso García's name appears in a marriage investigation of 1707. He had apparently been cohabitating with María

de la Rosa Manzañares (Candelaria), with whom he had two children and who he promised to marry. Felix Candelaria made a complaint, and when Alonso and María were discovered in bed together they were, according to fray Angelico Chávez, married on the spot (and the official church marriage was performed later). (Thomas, *After Coronado*: 88, 90; Kessell, Hendricks, and Dodge, *Boulders*: 1166n60; Chávez, *Roots*: 592.)

7. Francisco de Tapia was the son of Francisco de Tapia and María de Chávez. His family returned to New Mexico with the Spanish Reconquest. In 1697, he married Magdalena Nieto. He was a presidio soldier by at least 1704 and was killed during the 1720 Villasur Expedition. (Chávez, *Origins*: 292, 395; Hottz, *Segesser Hides*: 46.)

8. Bernardo Madrid was the son of Pedro Madrid and Isabel de la Serna, and the grandson of Roque Madrid, who took a leading part in the Spanish Reconquest entrada in 1692 and 1693. Presidio records show that Bernardo replaced Juan Griego on June 16, 1713. Bernardo married Gertrudis Martín of Pojoaque in 1714. He was killed during the 1720 Villasur Expedition. (Chávez, *Origins*: 216; Hottz, *Segesser Hides*: 46; Kessell, Hendricks, and Dodge, *Royal Crown*: 87n65; Christmas and Rau, "Una Lista": 200.)

9. Salvador Montoya was the son of Diego Montoya, and Josefa de Hinojos who came to New Mexico with Diego de Vargas in 1693. Diego Montoya was a Santa Fe cabildo member by 1692. The family later moved to the Río Abajo area. In 1700 Salvador Montoya married Manuela García de la Riva of Bernalillo, a sister of Juan García de la Riva. Like his father before him, Salvador became a member of the Santa Fe cabildo, in 1715. He was also a member of the confraternity of La Conquistadora. He died in 1727. (Chávez, *Origins*: 236; Kessell and Hendricks, *Force of Arms*: 420, 467; Kessell, Hendricks, and Dodge, *Royal Crown*: 549n34; Kessell, Hendricks, and Dodge, *Boulders*: 958n59.)

11

TWO MALE SERVANTS FIGHT OVER WOMAN ON THE OTHER SIDE OF THE SANTA FE RIVER
August 14–19, 1715, Source: SANM II #239b

Synopsis and editor's notes: In the early eighteenth century, Santa Fe was a town with many soldiers and only a few Hispanic women. In this case, the lack of available women led to a competition between two men over one woman, or at least it was perceived as a competition. This, in turn, led to a fight in which all three were involved.

On August 14, 1715, a young woman appeared at the house of the Santa Fe alcalde, Captain Juan García de la Riva, to report a fight in a field on the south side of the Santa Fe River. She said that two men, Juan [López] Grande and Francisco Xavier de Rosa, were fighting each other over her mother, a married woman. Her mother tried to stop the fight by pulling the hair of her lover, Juan Grande, but for her pains she was hit with a stick. The alcalde took both men to the jail, and he ordered the married woman to go home. The document does not give the name of either the mother or the daughter.

In later testimony before the alcalde, Juan Grande said that he had been having an affair with the woman for six years, while her husband was out of the province. He was trying to assist her as much as he could and because of that he did not want other men to go into her home, as he felt he had certain rights. Francisco Xavier de Rosa, on the other hand, said that he was at the woman's house to summon her son to cut some hay for the horse of their master, Captain Felix Martínez. He said that he was not interested in the mother, however, he *was* interested in her daughter.

After hearing the testimony, García de la Riva charged Juan Grande with causing a scandal by living with the woman (cohabitation) and by being in a fight. He separated the couple and ordered Juan Grande to travel with his master, Captain Francisco Ruiz, who had been given permission to leave the colony for other reasons. Likewise, Francisco Xavier de Rosa was admonished for fighting and was additionally ordered to serve his master, Captain Martínez; if he did not comply, Francisco was threatened with additional punishment.

In managing this rather sordid business, Alcalde García de la Riva carried out an abbreviated proceeding by interviewing the two men, but not the woman, her children, or any bystanders. While he could have ordered a fine for cohabitation, as he did in an earlier case, García de la Riva seemed more interested in restoring harmony among the complainants and keeping the peace in Santa Fe.

The document does raise several interesting points. First, the unnamed woman—who had at least two children and a husband who had been gone for six years (and there was no sign of his return)—would have found herself in a precarious position if she didn't have the support of her lover, Juan Grande. With him leaving Santa Fe, she likely would have had to look again to the presidio soldiers (or their servants) to find another protector, who would give her financial support. Second, it appears that there was a jail in Santa Fe at this time, which García de la Riva describes grandly as being in the *sala de audiencia* (courtroom) of the *casa reales* (government buildings) of the *ayuntamiento* (local governing body). His elaborate description is curious and may reflect his time in Mexico City. At that time, the local government body was called the cabildo and the term ayuntamiento was not used in New Mexico as the term for the local government until one hundred years later, after the Mexican revolution. Also, there may have been a sala de audiencia in a wealthier province further south, but in Santa Fe court hearings were more likely to be held in a large, multipurpose room in one of the government buildings.

TRANSLATION

1715

Case against Juan [López] Grande[1] and Francisco Xavier de Rosa[2]

Proceeding

At the Villa of Santa Fe on the 14th of August, 1715, I, Captain Juan García de la Riva,[3] alcalde ordinario of this villa, being at my home at about three o'clock in the afternoon, there appeared before me a young woman who appeared to be very afraid. She informed me that on the other side of the river of this villa Juan Grande and Francisco Xavier de Rosa were fighting and that Juan Grande was also hitting her mother. Upon understanding what she was telling me, I hurriedly went to where it was occurring and found that Juan Grande and Francisco were indeed fighting. I also found that the mother of the young lady had been beaten and had a wound on her head caused by Juan Grande. It was learned from a number of persons who were present that the incident came about due to the woman who was involved with Juan Grande. Because she was a married woman, I ordered her to go to her home.

I took Juan Grande and Francisco as prisoners to the public jail of this villa. In order to prosecute the two that were involved, I ordered that this statement be placed as the heading of these proceedings. I also ordered that Miguel Moran,[4] who is in charge of the jail, secure each one of them. So that this is valid, I signed as acting judge along with the scribe for the cabildo at the Villa of Santa Fe on the said day and year of the date.

    Juan García de la Riva (rubric)
    Juan Manuel de Chirinos[5] (rubric)
    Scribe of the Cabildo

Statement of Francisco Xavier de Rosa

Upon continuing, on the 16th of August, 1715, I, the said alcalde ordinario, went to the casas reales[6] of the ayuntamiento and within the sala de audiencia, made to appear before me the said Francisco Xavier de Rosa, a prisoner within the jail inside of the house of the ayuntamiento, from whom I took his sworn statement according to his right and to God, Our Lord, and the sign of the Holy Cross, and upon having done this he promised to tell the truth as to what he knew and what he was asked.

He was asked why he had a fight with Juan Grande. He said that it was because Juan Grande found him in the home of the woman and then became disturbed and told him to go outside with him. Having walked a short distance, close to the home of Pedro de Segura,[7] Juan Grande told him that they had a matter to settle. After saying this, [Juan Grande] attempted to strike him with a thick stick. This was his answer.

He was asked if it is true that he had an illicit affair with this woman and if that was the reason for Juan Grande beginning the fight. He stated that he has not had an illicit affair with the woman and that the love he has is for the daughter. This was his answer.

He was asked why on the day of the fight he went to the home of woman. He said that it was true that he went there. The reason was to summon a son of the woman to cut hay for a horse of Captain don Felix Martínez,[8] his master and that of the woman's son. At the same time Juan López Grande arrived and he spoke to him as he stated above.

Having been asked other questions, he stated that he did not know anything else other than the sworn statement that he has made and which he affirmed and ratified. Upon his sworn statement being read back to him, he said that it was as is, that he has nothing to add or delete, and that he is twenty-three or twenty-four years of age, more or less. He did not sign because he did not know how. I, the alcalde, signed it along with my assisting witnesses on the said day.

Juan García de la Riva (rubric)
Assisting witness
Antonio Durán de Armijo[9] (rubric)
Assisting witness
Juan Manuel de Chirinos (rubric)

Statement of Juan López Grande

Continuing on the said day and being in court within the hall of the ayuntamiento inside the casas reales of the cabildo, I made to appear before me Juan López Grande. At my order, he is also a prisoner within the jail in the house of the cabildo for a dispute or fight that he had with Francisco Xavier de Rosa, likewise a prisoner, due to a fight over a married woman. Being in my presence, I took his sworn statement that he made to God, Our Lord, and to the sign of the Holy Cross, as to what he knew and what he was asked, and having done so, he promised to tell the truth.

He was asked why on a certain occasion when he found Francisco Xavier de Rosa at the home of the above mentioned woman, he took Francisco out to fight with him, and why it mattered that [Francisco] was at the home. He stated that it was true that he had an affair with the above woman and that was the reason for having taken Francisco out to fight with him. This was his answer.

He was asked how it was that he had an affair with her and that she would allow Francisco to enter her home. He stated that it was true that he did not want Francisco to enter the home of the woman, even though up until now he had not done anything to her other than being friendly. The woman has two children who have been with her all along including the times that her husband has been out of the province. It was because of the children that he would try to help her as much as he could, and that it was understood that as long as he was doing this that he did not want any other man to go into her home. This was his answer.

He was asked for how long of a period had he been seeing the woman. He said that the truth of the matter was that it had been over six years since he has known her, and that this was the truth about what he has stated.

He was asked how it was that the fight occurred on the other side of the river of this villa and how it was that the woman was there so that he could inflict such a bad wound on her head. He stated that she had gone after them when he took the servant Francisco Xavier out to fight with him. Upon beginning to fight with Francisco, having hit him five or six blows with a thick stick, the woman arrived throwing rocks at him, Juan Grande, and she grabbed him by the hair. When this was happening he told her to get away and pushed her, but the woman continued to grab his hair. It was at this time that he hit her with the stick that he had in his hand. He said that the woman was at the fault of the whole matter because she was the one who allowed Francisco Xavier de Rosa to enter her home where he, Juan Grande, had certain rights. He had heard from certain other individuals that he, Francisco, was involved with her and that she had certain entertainments with him. Since he had heard this about them, he had been spying on them until on this certain day when he found Francisco at her home, he beat them both. This he said was the truth in the sworn statement that he has made and does not know anything else.

He was asked if he would affirm and ratify what he has said, and he said that he would. His declaration being read back to him he said that he had nothing to add or delete and that he was forty years of age. He did not sign because he did not know how. I, the alcalde, signed it along with my assisting witnesses on the 16th of August, 1715, acting as presiding judge.

    Juan García de la Riva (rubric)
Assisting witness
    Antonio Durán de Armijo (rubric)
Assisting witness
    Juan Manuel de Chirinos (rubric)

At this Villa of Santa Fe on the 19th of August, 1715, I, Captain Juan García de la Rivas, alcalde ordinario of the said villa, having reviewed the two statements in the summaria[10] which are found against the two guilty and confessed offenders, and in particular Juan López Grande. He is the one found to be the most guilty and is charged with the public scandal of cohabitating with a married woman for more than six years. As such I find and condemn Juan López Grande to go serve his master, Captain Francisco Ruiz,[11] to whom he owes his pay. He is to make the trip outside the province with him, and the trip will serve as his banishment under the penalty of being amancebados, as is well-known by everyone, and for having wounded the woman on her head. The banishment is also for the fight with Francisco, being that he had no proof against him for anything as he claims in his sworn statement.

As for Francisco, the only thing I can find against him for which I can condemn and do condemn him, is for having been involved in the fight with Juan [López] Grande over the accusation made by Grande. Thus I order him to go serve his master, Captain don Felix Martínez, who is to see to it that he does not break this sentence that I have given him according to the legal authority that I have.

For all this I ordered the official to bring both of them before me, and I made the sentence known to them, to which they stated that they would obey and did obey the order. They did not sign because they did not know how, I, the alcalde, signed it along with my assisting witnesses on the said day, etc.

Juan García de la Riva (rubric)
Witness
Antonio Durán de Armijo (rubric)
Witness
Juan Manuel de Chirinos (rubric)

TRANSCRIPTION

Causa contra Juan Lopez y Francisco de Rosas

Auto

En la Villa de Santa Fee en catorze dias del mes de Agosto del ano de setezientos y quinse yo el Capitan Juan Garcia de la Rivas, Alcalde Ordinario de dicha Villa estando en mi casa oras al parezer de las tres de la tarde entro una muchacha mui asustada y me dijo que en la otra banda de esta dicha Villa estava peleando Juan Grande y Francisco Xaviel de Rosas y que a su madre la estavan aporreando el dicho Juan Grande y luego que yo dicho Alcalde oyi y entendi lo que la muchacha me dijo sali a toda deligensia y a los dichos Juan Grande y Francisco cogi en la pendensia y alle ala muger que la dicha muchacha me dijo zer su madre ala cual abia aporreado y descalabrado el dicho Juan Grande y abiendo entendido por algunas personas que ze allaron en dicho pleito fue causado por dicha muger y por ser casada la mande fuese a su casa.

A los dichos Juan Grande y Francisco traxe presos ala carsel publica de esta Villa y para poder prozeder contra los dichos mando este auto le zirva de cavesa de proseso y que Miguel Moran minister porteco de la carcel azegurarse a cada uno de porsi delos suso dichos y para que conste lo firme como Jues Receptor con el Escribano de Cavildo en dicha Villa de Santa Fee dia y ano dela fecha =

    Juan Garcia de la Riva (rubric)
    Juan Manuel de Chirinos (rubric)
    Escribano de Cavildo

Declaracion de Francisco Xabiel

    Y luego incontinente en dies y seis de Agosto del mil zetesientos y quinse anos yo dicho Alcalde Ordinario pase alas casa del Alluntamiento y en su sala de audiensia yse pareser ante mi a Francisco Xabiel de Rosas preso en la carcel de dichas casas Reales de Alluntamiento a quien rezevi juramento en forma de derecho por Dios Nuestro Senor y la zenal dela Santa Cruz y abiendolo echo prometio dezir verdad en lo que supiere y le fuere preguntado

    1 - Preguntado que por que tubo pleyto con Juan Grande? Dijo que por que el dicho Juan Grande lo allo en casa de una muger y que entonses ze altero y le dijo a este declarante bengase con migo y a poco andar junto ala casa de Pedro de Zegura le dijo el dicho Juan Grande tenemos un negocio que ajustar y disiendole esto le fue descargando con un garrote a este declarante y esto responde

    2 - Preguntado que si es berdad tiene amistad con la dicha muger ynlisita por culla causa el dicho Juan Grande reino con el ? Dijo que no tiene amistad inlisita con la dicha muger que la amistad que tiene con ella este es su ija y esto responde

    3 - Preguntado que este dia de la pendensia a que fue este declarante ala casa de dicha muger, diga y declare ? Dijo que es berdad que fue a llamar un hijo de la dicha mujer para que fuera a cortar sacate para el caballo del Capitan Dn. Felix Martinez amo deste declarante y del dicho muchacho cuando llego el dicho Juan Grande y le dijo lo que dicho tiene arriva y abiendole echo otras preguntas y repreguntas dijo no saber mas so cargo del juramento en que se afirmo y ratifico y abiendole leido esta su declaracion dijo que asi era y que no tenia que anadir ni quitar y que es de edad de beinte y tres anos o beinte y cuatro anos poco mas o menos y no firmo por no saber firmelo yo dicho Alcalde con los infraescriptos testigos de mi asistensia en dicho dia =

    Juan Garcia dela Rivas (rubric)
    Testigo assistenzia
    Antonio Duran de Armijo (rubric)
    Testigo de asistenzia
    Juan Manuel Chirinos (rubric)

Declaracion de Juan Grande

    Y luego incontinente en dicho dia, estando en juisio en la sala dicha de audiensia delas casas Reales de Cavildo yse pareser asi mesmo a Juan Lopez Grande preso por mi orden en la carsel de dichas casas de Cavildo por un pleito o pendensia que tubo con Francisco Xabiel de Rosas asi mesmo preso el cual pleito fue por una muger casada y abiendolo tenido en mi presenzia le resevi juramento en forma de derecho por Dios Nuestro Senor y la Santa Cruz delo que supiese y fuere preguntado y abeindolo echo prometio el desir verdad.

 1 - Preguntado que por que occasion cuando allo a Francisco Xabiel de Rosas en casa de la muger de ariva referida saco al dicho Francisco a rrenir que que le iva en que el dicho estubiese en la casa? Dijo que era berdad abia tenido su amistad de dicha muger y que por eso abia sacado al dicho Francisco a rrenir, y esto responde.

 2 - Preguntado que como dise abia tenido su amistad que esta abia tenido la que por que defendia el que el dicho Francisco entrara en la casa de dicha muger? Dijo que es verdad que no queria que entrase en la casa de dicho muger el dicho Francisco por que aunque al presente no tenia con la muger cosa alguna mas que una buena amistad y asi mismo tenia en dicha muger dos hijos los quales a bido en la dicha todo el tiempo que su marido estava en la tierra fuera y que por dichos sus hijos le asistia en lo que podia y que le tenia dicho que supuesto que este declarante los sustentava que no queria entraze otro ombre alguno en la casa, y esto responde.

 3 - Preguntado que que tanto tiempo a que esta en mal estado con la dicha muger? Dijo que es berdad que a mas de zeis anos que la comunica y que es berdad lo que lla va dich

Preguntado que como abiendo sido la pendensia en la otra banda del rio desta Villa se avia aparesido la dicha muger alli para que el la descalabrara tan mal? Dijo que quando el saco al moso Francisco Xabiel para pelear entonses salio la dicha tras los dos y contra este declarante y que abiendose agarado con el dicho Francisco que fue cuando le dio sinco o seis palos al dicho Francisco entonses llego la dicha muger tirandole de pedradas y agarro a este declarante de los cavellos y el bisto ze agarrado de ella le dijo quiteze alla y aun la arrenpujo y biendo este que la dicha muger presestia en agararlo de los cavellos entonses le dio con un garrotillo que tralla en la mano y que de todo tenia la culpa la muger por que le avia amonestado que no consintieze en la casa al dicho Francisco de Rosas por que el tenia sierta ziensia que se avian enredado llasi mismo selo abian dicho diferentes personas a este declarante y que no se andubiera moliendo por la dicha pues tenia entretenimiento con el dicho Francisco y que desde que este declarante tiene estas malisias y notias como dicho tiene le dieron desde entonses los andubo espiando asta este dia que allo al dicho Francisco en la casa que fue cuando los aporreo y que esta es la berdad so cargo de el juramento que fecho tiene y que no sabe otra cosa.

Preguntado que si se afirma y ratifica en lo que a dicho? Dijo que si se afirma y ratifica en lo que a dicho y abiendole leido su declaracion dijo no tenia que anadir ni quitar y es de edad de cuarenta anos y no firmo por no saber firmelo yo dicho Alcalde con los testigos de mi asistensia en dies y seis dias del mes de Agosto de mill zetesientos y quinze anos, y como Jues Receptor.

 Juan Garcia dela Riva (rubric)
 Jues Receptor

Testigo de asistensia
Antonio Duran de Armijo (rubric)
Juan Manuel Chirinos (rubric)

En esta Villa de Santa Fee en dies y nuebe dias del mes de Agosto del ano de mill setesientos y quinze anos yo el Capitan Juan Garcia dela Rivas, Alcalde Ordinario de dicho Villa abiendo bisto las dos declaraciones desta sumaria en que estan reos combictos y confesos en especial Juan Lopez Grande quien se alla mas cargado con el publico escandalo de amansebado mas de seis anos con la muger casada por quien los referidos vivieron con grande escandalo desta republica fallo que devo condenar y condeno a Juan Lopez Grande a que balla a servir al Capitan Francisco Ruis, su amo, y a quien deve su dinero y que aga el biaje con su dicho amo ala tierra fuera y que dicho viaje le zirva de destierro en pena de dicho amenzevamiento como de aber tenido como dicho es publicamente y aber descalabrado a dicha muger lla si mesmo el dicho Francisco por no aber tenido probansa en su contra sobre lo qual dicho Juan Grande le calunia en su declaracion pues no es suficiente que el dicho Juan Grande diga estava metido con dicha muger dicho Francisco solo si fallo que lo devo condenar y condeno por aber almitido el desafio que le iso el dicho Juan Grande para rrenir con escandalo que lo ubo Grande aquien asi mesmo mando balla a zerbir al Capitan Dn. Felix Martinez su amo quien lo suxetara y que no quebranten esta pena inpuesta que se prozedera contra el trasgrezor a ella con todo rigor de derecho.

Para todo lo qual mande al ministro los traxese en mi presensia aquienes yze notorio esta sentenzia y en su cumplimiento dixeron que lo obedesian y obedesieron y no firmaron por no saber firmelo yo dicho Alcalde con los testigos de mi asistensia en dicho dia ut supra =

Juan Garcia dela Riba (rubric)
Jues Receptor
Testigo
Antonio Duran de Armijo (rubric)
Testigo
Juan Manuel Chirinos (rubric)

Notes

1. Juan López Grande appears to have been a native of Guadalajara, Mexico, who was in New Mexico by 1705, but little else is known about him. (Chávez, *Origins*: 208; Chávez, *Roots*: 918-20.)
2. If, as the document states, Francisco Xavier de Rosa was twenty-four or twenty-five years old in 1715, then he was born in 1692 or 1693. This means that he could be the son of Francisco [González] de la Rosa from Huejotzingo, near Puebla, Mexico, who came to New Mexico with the Farfán Expedition in 1694. This de la Rosa listed himself as a tailor. If this attribution is correct, then his mother would have been Antonia de la Cerda (or Serna) and his grandfather was don Antonio de la Rosa. (Chávez, *Origins*: 113, 191; Kessell, Hendricks, and Dodge, *Royal Crown*: 261, 293.)
3. For information on Juan García de la Riva, see Case 9.
4. For information on Miguel Moran, see Case 5.

5. For information on Juan Manuel de Chirinos, see Case 5.
6. The term casas reales refers to government offices that were originally located on three sides of the Santa Fe Plaza. At the time of this document, they were certainly located on the north side of the plaza, at the current location of the Palace of the Governors (and possibly elsewhere). (Snow, "Plazas of Santa Fe, New Mexico, 1610-1776": 40-61.)
7. Pedro de Segura was a soldier included in the 1697 Santa Fe presidio muster and in the 1704 muster at Bernalillo. He was a native of Cusiguriachi near, Zacatecas, Mexico. His was married to Simona Bonifacia de la Resa, with whom he had two sons, Cayetano and Tomás. He was killed in the 1720 Villasur massacre. (Kessell, Hendricks, Dodge, and Miller, *Disturbances*: 191n154; Hottz, *Segesser*: 46; Chávez, *Roots*: 1803.)
8. For information on Felix Martínez, see Case 3.
9. Antonio Durán de Armijo I was born in Zacatecas, the son of José de Armijo and Catalina Durán. The Durán de Armijo family came to New Mexico with the Farfán Expedition of 1694. In the records of the expedition, he is described as a *mestizo*. In 1695, Antonio married María Quiros in Santa Fe. He was known as a notary, a *curandero* (healer), and as a master barber—meaning someone with medical experience, but not a surgeon. Also, use of the word "master" suggests that he was considered a teacher. Antonio also acted as a legal representative in several lawsuits, and by 1716 he was a master sergeant at the Santa Fe presidio. He died in 1753, at the age of eighty. (Kessell, Hendricks, and Dodge, *Boulders*: 514, 563n27; Jenkins, "Taos": 97; Cutter, *Legal Culture*: 115.)
10. The "summaria" was an initial stage in the judicial process that amounted to a fact-finding inquiry carried out by the magistrate or presiding judge and in this case the alcalde. This is a rare instance when the word summaria is used by the presiding judge. The term was also used in Case 11 and Case 25. (Cutter, *Legal Culture*: 113-17.)
11. Francisco Ruiz could be the son of Juan Ruiz Cordero and María Carrillo Terrazas, both of whom came to New Mexico with the Farfán Expedition of 1694. In 1722, Juan claimed he was a retired adjutant (or military aide). In his will, Juan left his military equipment to his son, Francisco Xavier. The amount and kind of goods named in Juan's will suggest that he was a trader in Chihuahua and El Paso. (Chávez, *Origins*: 279; Christmas and Rau, "Una Lista": 199; SANM I #1206, WPA translation.)

12

PRESIDIO SOLDIER KILLED IN ACTION; WIFE REQUESTS MONEY FROM PRESIDIO INSURANCE FUND
October 22, 1715–November 5, 1716, Source: SANM II #239e

ynopsis and editor's notes: In this document, María Canseco, recent widow of the deceased soldier Juan Antonio Ramos, assumed her legal right by going before Governor Flores Mogollón to ask for a license allowing her to leave Santa Fe. She did so because don Antonio Valverde, lieutenant governor of the El Paso presidio, agreed to give her work at the presidio or at his hacienda. In preparation for leaving, she also asked the governor to calculate the money owed to others by her deceased husband and the amount from the presidio insurance fund owed to her as her husband's widow. The presidio captain, Felix Martínez, calculated Ramos's assets, which included: the value of his military equipment, the ten pesos each soldier received from the presidio insurance fund, and his unpaid salary. Debts included money owed to other soldiers, some of which were probably from gambling, money owed to the governor and Captain Martínez, and payment to the priest for funeral services.

When the calculation was completed, the inheritance was worth some 567 pesos. Under Spanish law, the wife inherited half the amount and any children half. Therefore, María Conseco and her daughter, María Manuela Ramos, should have received about 283 and one-half pesos each.[1] Originally, María Conseco agreed to place her daughter's half of the money in trust with Lieutenant Governor Juan Páez Hurtado, to be used later as a dowry. He would hold the money in trust until María Manuela was of legal age (twenty-five). The inheritance would then be paid to her in "goods of the land." To accomplish this, María Conseco granted power of attorney to Juan Páez Hurtado and gave up her right as her daughter's guardian. For his part, Hurtado was required to post a surety as a guarantee.

After agreeing to give Páez Hurtado the guardianship, María Conseco changed her mind and sent the governor a petition asking that the entire inheritance be given in *dinero* (cash) to her and her daughter, because they were so poor. The governor approved her petition and prepared a written document for María Canseco's signature. The presiding judge and alcalde ordinario, Captain Francisco Lorenzo de Casados, was careful to point out that when the earlier power of attorney with Páez Hurtado was cancelled María Canseco had therefore renounced the Spanish laws that protected the inheritance and dowries of women from persons wishing to take unfair advantage. He was referring to the Roman *Senatus Consultum Velleianum* and the laws of Justinian's Code that protected the inheritance and dowry rights of women, which had been incorporated into Spanish law.[2]

It is not known why María Canseco changed her mind. Perhaps she believed that 283 pesos were not enough for her daughter and her to live on until she began work in El Paso. It is also possible that she did not believe that the money held in trust would remain there until her daughter reached the age of twenty-five, especially if the mother and daughter, and possibly Juan Páez Hurtado, were no longer living in Santa Fe. María may have felt that cash in hand was better than goods held in trust for many years. Whatever the reason, Governor Flores Mogollón complied with her request.

One has to wonder if María Conseco ever received the money, for it was not due to be paid until the next presidio payroll came up from Chihuahua or Mexico City. Because the soldiers were not always paid on a regular basis, and sometimes with shoddy goods instead of cash, it is possible that she would have had to wait a long time before she received what was due to her.

There is an incomplete background story to María Canseco and Juan Antonio Ramos. In 1705, Governor Cuervo y Valdés banished both of them from Santa Fe, stipulating that they must be gone within twenty-four hours. They were sent to the Villa of Santa Cruz for four years. The governor stated that the banishment was "for reasons I will omit for now and will reserve for myself" and added that the couple were "unworthy of living in the community." The punishment for noncompliance of his order was fierce: two hundred lashes and four years of banishment to Zuni, with no possibility of a pardon. It is not known what crime Canseco and Ramos committed for which they were banished.[3]

María Conseco's inheritance case differs from many others in this book in that it was not an investigation or trial. Nevertheless, some of the standard legal procedures were followed, including the written documentation of each step of the process and the *remisión* (transfer) of the written procedures from one official to another. The power of attorney transferring the disposition of the daughter's inheritance from the mother to Juan Páez Hurtado was carefully written out, as was the surety that Páez Hurtado was required to provide and the cancellation of the power of attorney.

Leaving aside the drama of a husband's death and the widow's attempt to ensure a stable financial future for herself and her daughter, the document is of great value because it provides a price list for a soldier's possessions in early eighteenth-century New Mexico (or at least the value of these possessions as determined by Captain Felix Martínez).

TRANSLATION

1715

Villa of Santa Fe, New Mexico

Petition presented by María Canseco,[4] widow of the Juan Antonio Ramos,[5] so that the account held by the deceased with this presidio can be adjusted in the amount of 283 pesos and seven reales, in favor of [María] Manuela Ramos,[6] minor daughter of the deceased Antonio Ramos, and of María Canseco.

At this Villa of Santa Fe, New Mexico the 22nd of October, 1715, the following was presented to the governor and captain general

[Petition of María Canseco]

I, María Canseco, widow in this kingdom of New Mexico of Juan Antonio Ramos, former soldier of this royal castle, appear prostrated at the feet of your honor in my best and most proper form which my legal right allows me, and I say, sir, that my work has increased considerably ever since the death of my husband.[7] Not having anyone to turn to but God, I am requesting the assistance through the royal kindness of your honor, which I hope will be favorable for what I ask in this petition. I hope that you will be kind enough to grant me permission to go to El Paso del Rio del Norte in order to assist the general don Antonio Valverde,[8] who is most kind in giving me a job, which will give me relief from things that I have to do.[9] All of this I ask and petition from your honor, seeking that you will grant to me the license to leave. I thus await [the license] from the powerful hand of your honor. I thus swear before God and the Holy Cross that my petition is not done in malice, but in what is necessary.
María Canseco (rubric)

Equestrian Soldiers of New Spain. Antonio de Basaras, in *A Vision del Mexico del Siglo de la Luces, la Codificación de Antonio de Basaras. Origen, Costumes y Estado Presente de Mexicanos y Filipinos, 1763*. Courtesy of the Hispanic Society of America, New York.

Another thing, I ask and petition of your honor that you be pleased to do me the favor of calcuting the amount so that I may be aware of what I am due so that it is paid to me. Also, I ask the same for what my deceased husband might owe, so that the amount might be paid. I am willing to pay them with whatever is owed to me according to Captain don Felix [Martínez].[10] Also I ask that I might get paid by those who owe to me, who are the following: Pedro Martín,[11] fifteen pesos, and the servant of Captain don Felix,[12] fourteen pesos. This is all I expect from your honor, which is all for good.

Decree

Upon reviewing the petition, I, don Juan Ignacio Flores Mogollón,[13] governor and captain general of this kingdom and province of New Mexico and castellan of his forces and presidios, accept it as it was presented and grant the license which this party seeks in order to go to the presidio of El Paso. I also order captain don Felix Martínez, who is the one in charge of things at this presidio, to calculate the accounts of the soldier Juan Antonio Ramos, deceased who was part of the presidio. Don Felix Martínez is to be assisted by the general Juan Páez Hurtado,[14] whose name is to be listed at the end of this decree. They are to annotate the entire account, calculating the salary up until the time that Ramos died. In addition, his weapons are to be valuated along with the horses that were left by the deceased as is known by the captain. In addition, he, don Martínez, is to add the ten pesos that are given by soldiers, one to the other as is agreed upon according to their written agreement and promise which this presidio has overseen.[15]

The account is to be charged according to what is owed and adjusted accordingly with me for half of the salary for this year, and was up until the 16th of June. In addition, the account is to be charged with the expenses that have been made by the captain with his funeral and burial, as well as what he had given the widow for provisions. After having seen what is left after the liquidation of everything it is to be paid to the widow, who is to receive a receipt for her assurance. I also order that the Pedro Martín and the servant of the aforementioned captain [Martinez] who is named herein appear before me in order to ascertain if they owe what is stated. General Juan Páez Hurtado shall make this decree known to the captain. I thus commission him as required so that he might appear at the time of the liquidation of the accounts, which he shall bring forth to me signed as it is ordered at the foot of this document so that it is valid forever.

I thus approved, ordered and signed it along with my secretary of government and war at this Villa of Santa Fe, New Mexico, on the 22nd of October, 1715.

don Juan Ignacio
Flores Mogollón (rubric)
At the order of the governor and captain general
Roque de Pinto[16] (rubric)
Secretary of Government and War

[Order to Captain Felix Martínez]

At this Villa of Santa Fe on the 26th of October, 1715, in compliance with the above decree, I informed the captain don Felix Martínez, who upon understanding the contents of the above, he stated that he would obey and execute it as is ordered, and so that it is valid he signed it on the said day, etc, along with the captain.

Juan Páez Hurtado (rubric)
Felix Martínez (rubric)

Statement of what is to be owed to the widow María Conseco, as follows:
First of all for five horses, at 15 pesos each, 75 pesos
For a riding saddle, 25 pesos
For an old gun case, 2 pesos
For a bridle, 5 pesos
For some disassembled spurs and boots, 6 pesos
For some small pillows, 3 pesos
For some powder pouches, 4 pesos
For an old hide, 25 pesos
For an old spade, 6 pesos
For an old shoulder belt, 3 pesos
For a leather shield, 4 pesos
For a jacket, 4 pesos

Total: 162 pesos

In addition, there are from the 10 pesos given by the agreement of the ninety-nine Soldiers, 990 pesos

Also, there should be for two months and five days from June 16th up to August 21st, the day that he died, 77. 4 pesos

Everything added together amounts to: 1,229.4 pesos

What the widow owes is as follows:
First of all she owes the governor 353.4 pesos
She owes Nicolás de Apodaca[17] 80 pesos for a debt, 80 pesos
She also owes 140 pesos that were paid to the Padre Antonio Camargo[18] for the burial and novena[19] services, 140 pesos
She also owes for the deceased Ramírez[20] 10 pesos
She also owes 78 pesos for an advance provided by Captain Felix [Martínez] as is recorded in his books, 78 pesos

Everything together totals 661.4 ½ pesos

Therefore, subtracting 661.4 ½,[21] there remains for the said widow 567 pesos and seven and one-half *tominos*,[22] for which I shall issue a promissory note in order to pay her when the presidio payroll arrives. So that it is valid, I signed it at this Villa of Santa Fe on the 27th of October, 1715.
    Juan Páez Hurtado (rubric)
    Felix Martínez (rubric)

[Provision for daughter]
    At the Villa of Santa Fe, New Mexico, on the 29th of October, 1715, I, don Juan Ignacio Flores Mogollón, governor and captain general of this kingdom and province of New Mexico for his majesty, have reviewed the above account and the reasons for owing to the said widow the amount of 567 pesos and seven and one-half tominos. I was then informed that Juan Antonio Ramos, deceased, left a minor daughter named [María] Manuela Ramos. Thus, I order that the captain don Felix Martínez prepare two promissory notes, in equal amounts, for the 567 pesos and seven and one-half reales, one to give to the widow and another one to be made out in favor of the said minor. They shall submit these notes to me to deposit with a person of total trustworthiness, who shall be the general don Juan Páez Hurtado. I order him to appear before me and obligate himself in every respect to hold the said amount in deposit until the said minor becomes of age, or if for some other reason at my order or that of another competent judge shall order to do otherwise. I thus approved, ordered and signed it with my secretary of government and war.
    don Juan Ignacio
    Flores Mogollón (rubric)
    Before me
    Roque de Pinto (rubric)
    Secretary of Government and War

Bond held in favor of [María] Manuela Ramos, minor daughter of Juan Antonio Ramos
    At this Villa of Santa Fe, New Mexico, on the 31st[23] of October, 1715, before me Governor and Captain General by virtue of that which was ordered by me, there appeared before me General don Juan Páez Hurtado, resident of this villa and alcalde ordinario of the same. He stated that by virtue of what was ordered of him, it is true that he had received an invoice signed by Captain don Felix Martínez for the quantity of 283 pesos, seven and one-half reales, which was the amount that was owed to and belonged through inheritance to [María] Manuela Ramos, minor daughter of Juan Antonio Ramos, deceased. This amount he received on her behalf as guardian of

[María] Manuela Ramos, and is to hold for her through a power of attorney until she comes of age, or until he is ordered to turn over to her by a competent judge. At such time what she is to be given is to be in horses, or cattle, or goods from within the kingdom. Juan Páez Hurtado is to be obligated personally in goods that he has.[24]

In doing so, he renounces the laws, *fueros*,[25] and rights within his favor, and in general that of any right which gives power to any judge or justices of his majesty, and in particular to the governor and captain general who is, or will be, of this kingdom, so that he has the power accordingly to a determination already handed down and to something already judged.[26] As such I, the governor and captain general, faithfully say that I know the grantor with whom I signed it before my secretary of government and war, and I order that he inform María Canseco, widow of the said Juan Antonio Ramos and mother of the minor of this proceeding, so that she is aware of what transpired and was done at this said Villa of Santa Fe on the said day, month and year. Amended, in thirty, valid.

    don Juan Ignacio
    Flores Mogollón (rubric)
    Juan Páez Hurtado (rubric)
    Before me
    Roque de Pinto (rubric)
    Secretary of Government and War

Bond in favor of [María] Manuela Ramos minor daughter of Juan Antonio Ramos, resident of Santa Fe, November, 1716,

This document was copied on this day of this date as is indicated within these proceedings, to which I certify and sign.

    Francisco Lorenzo de Casados[27] (rubric)

Villa of Santa Fe, October 30, 1716
Governor and Captain General don Felix Martínez

[Request by María Canseco]

I, María Canseco, widow of Juan Antonio Ramos, deceased, soldier of this presidio of this Villa of Santa Fe, appear before your honor and ask, for the dinero that remained under the power of your honor as valuator and is being held by the lieutenant Juan Páez Hurtado, through the decision of your honor. Seeing that my daughter, María Manuela [Ramos], as well as myself, are in dire need, I, seek that your honor will concede to this, my petition, and swear that this is not done in malice, but in what is necessary, etc.

    María Canseco (rubric)

[Presentation]

The above was presented to me, Captain don Felix Martínez, governor and captain general of this kingdom, and I ordered that a copy be given to General Juan Páez Hurtado so that he can respond to it within the term of the law, and so that it is valid I signed it on the said day.

Felix Martínez (rubric)

Governor and Captain General

[Response by Juan Páez Hurtado]

I, General Juan Páez Hurtado, lieutenant general of this kingdom, in fulfillment of the decree of your honor of the 30th of October regarding the petition presented by María Canseco, mother of María [Manuela] Antonia [sic] Ramos, legitimate daughter of Juan Antonio Ramos, after having reviewed its content say that I am ready to turn over the number of pesos as so stated in the written notice approved by me in her favor. This includes the cancellation of the written bond, which is to be attached to these proceedings. The alcalde ordinario is to provide a sworn oath that he had turned over the amount to his satisfaction, with the receipt being signed by a witness presented by the petitioner. Of your honor I petition that after I have attended to what is required, he be pleased to relieve me of the obligation in which I find myself. I thus swear this is done according to form and for what is necessary, etc.

Juan Páez Hurtado (rubric)

[Order for cancellation of bond]

At the Villa of Santa Fe on the 3rd day of the month of November, 1716, before me don Felix Martínez, governor and captain general of this kingdom and provinces of New Mexico, the above was presented by he to which it referred. Upon finding that the party is ready and willing to turn over the quantity that is under his power and is holding as guardian of María Manuela [Ramos], minor, I order that once the said quantity is turned over before a competent judge, an oath of cancellation of the written bond be given so that this party is removed from it, and so that it is valid I signed it along with my secretary of government and war.

Felix Martínez (rubric)
Before me
Miguel Tenorio de Alba (rubric)
Secretary of Government and War

Cancellation of the bond made by General Juan Páez Hurtado

    At the Villa of Santa Fe, New Mexico, on the 5th of November, 1716, before me Captain Francisco Lorenzo de Casados, alcalde ordinario of this villa acting as presiding judge along with my presiding witnesses due to the lack of a public and royal scribe, appeared before me María Canseco, widow of Juan Antonio Ramos, mother of María Manuela Ramos, who I certify that I know. I state that upon her having presented a written document before the governor and captain general of this kingdom on the 30th of October of the current year, in which she requested that because she was in dire need, as was her daughter, they be given the amount of pesos that are stated in the written [bond] that was made by the general don Juan Páez Hurtado, who at that time was ordered to be given a written copy. To this request he answered that he would be willing and ready to turn over the quantity of 283 pesos and seven and one-half reales that he has under his care as guardian of the María Manuela [Ramos], minor, with the understanding that the written agreement of obligation be cancelled. Upon this being done, he then stated that he had turned over the said quantity of the stated 283 and seven and one-half reales to María Canseco in goods that are current in the area.

    To this she stated that she had been paid to her satisfaction, and that from this time forward, she is owed nothing by the general, as is so stated in the written agreement. The agreement is to be torn and cancelled, leaving without any value nor in any manner valid. It is herein totally cancelled and forever thus to remain with respect to the renouncement of the laws in her favor and to those of *Justiniano aucilio de vellano senatus consultos*[28] which speaks in favor of the women and states that they are not to be taken advantage of now nor at any time, nor can she accuse me of anything. With this understanding, I ordered it to be done. She did not sign because she did not know how. The sargento major, don Alfonso Rael de Aguilar,[29] signed for her at her request, along with me the alcalde ordinario, and my assisting witnesses, Maestro de Campo Thomas Olguín,[30] Ayudante don Joseph [Manuel] Giltoméy[31] and Antonio de Salazar,[32] who were all present and residents of this villa.

    At the request of María Canseco
    Alfonso Rael de Aguilar (rubric)
    Before me as presiding judge
    Francisco Lorenzo de Casados (rubric)
    Assisting witness
    Pedro Enriquez de Rivera[33] (rubric)
Assisting witness
Dimas Girón[34] (rubric)

TRANSCRIPTION

Villa de Santa Fee de la Nueba Mexico,
Año de 1715

Petizion de Maria Canseco buida de Juan Antonio Ramos para que sele ajusten las quentas que dicho difunto tubo en este Presidio y obligazion de 283 pesos y siete reales, que el General Dn. Juan Páez Hurtado hizo a favor de Manuela Ramos hijo menor de Juan Antonio Ramos difunto y Maria Canseco

En esta Villa de Santa Fee de la Nueva Mexico, en 22 de Octubre de 1715, la presento la contenida ante el Señor Governador y Capitan General

Señor Governador y Capitan General

Maria Canseco buida en este Reino dela Nueba Mexico de Juan Antonio Ramos, soldado que fue deste Real Castillo paresco postrada alos pies de Vuestra Señoria en la mas bastante forma y derecho que me combenga y digo Señor que son mis trabajos mui cresidos que estoi pasando despues que mi esposo murio y no tener aquien bolver mis ojos despues de Dios y avia que me llego a favorezer de el Real Ausilio de la grandesa de Vuestra Señoria la cual espero me sera balida en este mi pedimento que ago en esta mi petision me aga ondero de consederme lizensia para salir al Passo de el Rio del Norte asestir con mi trabajo al General Dn. Antonio Balverde quien ze conzuela de mis trabajos donde tendre Alivio y descanso y asi pido y suplico a Vuestra Señoria me favoresca en conzederme dicha lizencia que asi le aguardo de la poderosa mano de Vuestra Señoria y juro a Dios y ala Santa Cruz no ser de malizia esta mi petizion y en lo nezesario.
Maria Canzeco (rubric)

Otro, si pido y suplico a Vuestra Señoria se me aga favor de azer de que ze me ajusten las cuentas para saver lo que seme deve y se me page y lo que mi difunto deviere lo pagare ala persona o personas a quienes les ubiere devido pues estoi pronta a satisfazer las detas de lo que ze me pagase y diere el Capitan Dn. Felix asi mesmo page lo que me deven que son los siguientes, Pedro Martin, quinze pesos, el criado de el Capitan Dn. Felix catorze pesos, no mas espero de Vuestra Señoria el bien por entero.

Auto
Y vista por mi Dn. Juan Ygnacio Flores Mogollon, Governador y Capitan

General deste Reino y Provincias dela Nueba Mexico y Castellano de Sus Fuerzas y Presidios por Su Magestad la ube por presentada y conzedo la lizensia que pide esta parte para yr al Presidio del Paso y mando al Capitan Dn. Felix Martinez como quien corre con los avios del Presidio ajusta las cuentas del soldado Juan Antonio Ramos, difunto, mando que fue desta parte y que sea con asistenzia del General Juan Paez Hurtado poniendo al pie deste auto la quenta aumandole el sueldo asta el dia que fallezio y juntamente, en lo que se abaluaron las armas y cavallos que dejo dicho difunto y persivio dicho Capitan y asi mismo avonandole los dies pesos de cada soldado en que se heredan.

Unos a otros en virtud de la escriptura y compromiso que tiene fecho este presidio y cargandole lo que quedo deviendo en la quenta que sele ajusto dela que tubo con migo en que sele avono la mitad del sueldo deste año, que fue asta diez y seis de Junio y asi mismo cargandole todos los gastos que dicho Capitan ubiere fecho en su funeral y entierro como en lo que ubiere dado ala biuda para sus alimientos, y reconozido lo que queda liquido selo pa gue a dicha buida de quien cobrara resivo para su resguardo; y asi mismo mando conparescan en mi prezencia Pedro Martin y el criado de dicho Capitan menzionado en este escripto para que declaren si es zierto deven a esta parte lo que pide y dicho General Juan Paez Hurtado ara notorio este auto a dicho Capitan y le doi la comision que se requiere para que se alle por mi ala liquidazion de dichas quentas las quales me trahira firmadas como esta mandado al pie deste escripto por que en todo tiempo conste asi lo provei, mande y firme con mi Secretario de Governazion y Guerra en esta Villa de Santa Fee dela Nueba Mexico en veinte y dos de Octubre de mill setezientos y quinze años =

Dn. Juan Ygnacio Flores Mogollon (rubric)
Por mando del Señor Governador y Capitan General
Roque de Pintto (rubric)
Secretario de Governazion y Guerra

En esta Villa de Santa Fee en beinte y seis dias del de Octubre de mill setesientos y quinse años en cumplimiento del auto de ariba lo hize notorio a el Capitan Dn. Feliz Martinez quien enterado de su contexto dixo le obedeze y que lo executara como sele ordena y por que conste lo firme en dicho dia ut supra con el dicho Capitan.

Juan Paez Hurtado (rubric)
Felix Martinez (rubric)

Memoria de lo que a de aver la viuda Maria Canseco, que es como sigue.

Primeramente por sinco cavallos, (a 15 pesos), 75 pesos
Por una silla gineta, 25 pesos
Por una funda vieja, 2 pesos
Por un freno, 5 pesos
Por unas espuelas desharmanadas y botines, 6 pesos

Por unos coginillos, 3 pesos
Por unas bolsas de polvora, 4 pesos
Por una cuera vieja, 25 pesos
Por una espada vieja, 6 pesos
Por una tahali, 3 pesos
Por una adarga, 4 pesos
Por una chamarra, 4 pesos

[Todo]: 162 pesos

Mas a de aver de los dies pesos del compromiso de los nobenta y nuebe soldados, 990 pesos

Mas a de aver de dos meses y sinco dias desde 16 de Junio hasta 21 de Agosto que murio, 77.4

Que juntas las partidas hasen, 1,229.4

Lo que deve la vuida es lo siguiente:
    Primeramente, deve al Señor Governador, 353.4

    Mas deve a Nicolas de Apodaca ochenta pesos de un vale, 80 pesos

    Mas deve ciento y quarenta pesos que se pagaron a el Padre Antonio Camargo del entierro y nobenario, 140

    Mas deve dies pesos a el difunto Ramirez, 10

    Mas deve setenta y ocho pesos que le a suplido el Capitan Feliz como consta de su libro, 78

    Cuyas partidas amontan, 661.

Por manera que rebajados seis cientos sesenta y uno y quatro reales y medio sele sestan a dicha vuida quinientas sesenta y siete pesos siete tomines y medio, delos quales le dare vale para pagarselos luego que llegue el abio del Presidio, y por que conste lo firme en esta Villa de Santa Fee en beinte y siete dias del mes de Octubre de mill setecientos y quinse
    Juan Paes Hurtado (rubric)
    Phelix Martinez (rubric)

En la Villa de Santa Fee dela Nueva Mexico en veinte y nueve dias del mes de Octubre de mill setezientos y quinze años, yo Dn. Juan Ygnacio Flores Mogollon, Governador y Capitan General de este Reino y Provincias dela Nueva Mexico por Su Magestad haviendo visto la quenta antezedente y que por ella consta deversele ala dicha viuda quinientos y sesenta y siete pesos siete reales y medio y constandome que el dicho Juan Antonio Ramos difunto dejo una hija menor llamada Manuela Ramos, mando que el dicho Capitan Dn. Feliz Martinez aga dos vales por yguales partes delos dichos quinientos y sesenta y siete pesos y siete reales y medio, el uno que entregara ala biuda y otro que ara a favor dela dicha menor que me remitira para depositarlo en persona de toda seguridad que es el General Dn. Juan Paez Hurtado aquien mando conparesca ante mi y haga obligazion en toda forma de tener la dicha cantidad en deposito asta que la dicha menor tome estado; o que otra cosa por mi o por otro juez competente le sea mandado, asi lo provey, mande y firme con mi Secretaria de Governazion y Guerra =

 Dn. Juan Ygnacio Flores Mogollon (rubric)
 Ante mi
 Roque de Pintto (rubric)
 Secretario de Governazion y Guerra

Obligazion a favor de Manuela Ramos menor hija de Juan Antonio Ramos

 En esta Villa de Santa Fee dela Nueva Mexico en treinta y uno de Octubre de mill setezientos y quinze años ante mi dicho Governador y Capitan General en virtud delo por mi mandado parezio presente el General Dn. Juan Paez Hurtado vezino desta Villa y Alcalde Ordinario en ella y dijo que en virtud de lo por mi mandado es verdad que tiene rezevido un vale firmado del Capitan Dn. Felix Martinez de cantidad de dosientos y ochenta y tres pesos siete reales y medio los mismos que le tocaron y pertenezieron de herenzia a Manuela Ramos, hija menor de Juan Antonio Ramos difunto; los quales rezive en si por tutela dela dicha Manuela Ramos los quales tendra en su poder asta que la dicha tome estado; o que le sea mandados entregar por Juez Competente y que la dicha entrega la a de azer en cavallos, o bacas o generos de este Reino y que a ello se obliga con su persona y vienes avidos.

 Por aver y renunzio las leyes, fueros y derecho de su favor y la general del derecho en forma dando poder a qualesquiera juezes y justizias de Su Magestad y en expezial al Señor Governador y Capitan General que es o fuere deste Reino para que a ello le aprime como por sentenzia pasada en autoridad de cosa jusgada y yo dicho Governador y Capitan General doi fee conosco al otorgante con quien lo firme ante mi Secretario de Governazion y Guerra aquien mando de testimonio de esta obligazion a Maria Canseco viuda del dicho Juan Antonio Ramos y madre dela dicha menor para que le conste que es fecho en esta dicha Villa de Santa Fee en dicho dia mes y año dicho = enmendado = en treinta = vale =

 Dn. Juan Ygnacio Flores Mogollon (rubric)
 Juan Paez Hurtado (rubric)
 Ante mi

Roque de Pinto (rubric)
Secretario de Governazion y Guerra

⁓

[*Note in margin*]
Obligazion a favor de Manuela Ramos
menor hija de Juan Antonio Ramos vezina
de Santa Fee, Noviembre de 1716 años
Ante mi el Capitan Francisco Lorenzo
de Casados se transelo esta escriptura oy
dia dela fecha como constan con estos
autos, doy fee y lo firme.
Francisco Lorenzo de
Casados (rubric)

Villa de Santa Fee y Octobre 30 de 1716
Señor Governador y Capitan General

Dn. Felis Martines
  Yo Maria Canseco buida de Juan Antonio Ramos, difunto, soldado de este Presidio de esta Villa de Santa Fe paresco ante Vuestra Señoria pidiendo Señor el dinero que quedo en poder de Vuestra Señoria el evaluador para en el Señor Teniente Juan Paez Hurtado en portuno a Vuestra Señoria por ber a mi hija Maria Manuela de Ramos y llo con bastante nesesidad y espero en el patrosinio de Vuestra Señoria me otorgara este mi pedimento y juro no ser de malisia y en lo nesesario, ut supra.
  Maria Canseco (rubric)

⁓

[*Note in margin*]
Por presentada ante mi el Capitan Dn.
Phelix Martinez Gobernador y Capitan
General deste Reyno y mando sele de traslado
al General Juan Paez Hurtado y que responda
dentro del termino de la lei y por que conste lo
irme en dicho dia.
Phelix Martinez (rubric)

Señor Governador y Capitan General
  El General Juan Paez Hurtado, Theniente General de este Reyno en cumplimiento del decreto de Vuestra Señoria del dia treinta de Octubre ala peticion presentada por Maria Canseco, madre de Maria Antonia Ramos, hija legitima de Juan Antonio Ramos, y aviendo visto su contexto digo que estoy pronto a enterar la cantidad de

pesos que resa la escriptura otorgada por mi a su favor, con tal que se chansele la escriptura y a ella se acomule en estas diligencias, y que con el Alcalde Ordinario de fee de aver enterado la cantidad a su satisfazion firmando el resivo un testigo por la suplicante por todo lo qual a Vuestra Señoria suplico que atendiendo ala nesesidad que representa se sirva de exonerarme de la obligazion en que estoy, asi lo juro en forma y en lo nesesario, ut supra.

Juan Paez Hurtado (rubric)

En la Villa de Santa Fee en tres dias del mes de Noviembre de mill setezientos y diez y seis años ante mi Dn. Pheliz Martinez, Governador y Capitan General deste Reyno y Provinzias dela Nueba Mexico, la presento el contenido en ella y en atenzion a estar esta parte lleno y prompto a entregar, y ultimar la cantidad despues que en su poder parar de la tutela de Maria Manuela la menor, como su tutador en cuya atenzion mando que entregada la dicha cantidad ante Juez Competente que de fee se chanzele la escridptura de obligazion por donde conste quedar esta parte ebadido de ella y para que conste lo firme con mi Secretario de Governazion y Guerra =

Phelix Martinez (rubric)
Ante mi
Miguel Thenorio de Alba (rubric)
Secretario de Governazion y Guerra

[*Note in margin*]
Chanzelazion dela
escriptura de obligazion
que hizo el General
Juan Paez Hurtado

En la Villa de Santa Fee dela Nueva Mexico en sinco dias del mes de Noviembre de mill setecientos y dies y seis años ante mi el Capitan Francisco Lorenzo Casados, Alcalde Ordinario desta dicha Villa autuando ante mi como Juez Receptor a falta de escribano publico y rreal con los testigos ynfraescriptos de mi asistenzia parecio Maria Canseco viuda de Juan Antonio Ramos madre de Maria Manuela Ramos a quien doi fee que conosco y dijo que aviendo presentado escrito ante el Señor Governador y Capitan General deste Reyno el dia treinta de Octubre de este presente año suplicando que por hallarse con bastante nezesidad la suso dicha como su hija fueze servido sele entregase la cantidad de pesos que se espresan en la escriptura de obligazion que a favor de dicha su hija hizo el General Dn. Juan Paez Hurtado a quien mando dicho Señor sele diese traslado y respondio a el que se hallava prometio a entregar y ulitmar la cantidad de docientos y ochenta y tres pesos siete reales y medio que en su poder paran como curador dela dicha Maria Manuela, menor, con la calidad que se chanzele dicha escriptura de obligazion lo qual poniendolo por execucion doi fee entrego la referida cantidad delos dichos docientos ochenta y tres pesos y siete reales y medio ala dicha Maria Canseco en generos corrientes dela tierra .

De que confeza la suso dicha ser la dicha paga a su satisfaccion de que quedo pagada y que a ora ni en ningun tiempo le pedida al dicho General cosa alguna dela cantidad que en dicha escriptura expreza la qual la da por rota y chanzelada, dandola por de ningun efecto ni valor ni que pueda en manera alguna hazerla y que siempre le zera sierto y seguro todo lo espresado sobre que renuncia las leies de su favor y delas delos emperadores Justiniano aucilio de bellano senataz consultos que ablan en favor delas mugeres de que no se baldra de ellas a ora ni en ningun tiempo de que fue acuzada por mi la suso dicha y asi lo otorgo y no firmo por no saver, firmelo a su ruego el Sargento Maior Dn. Alphonso Rael de Aguilar con migo dicho Alcalde Ordinario y los testigos de mi asistencia siendo los ynstrumentales el Maestro de Campo Thomas Olguin, el Ayudante Dn. Joseph Giltomey y Antonio de Zalazar presentes y vesinos de esta dicha Villa =

 A ruego de Maria Canseco
 Alphonso Rael de Aguilar (rubric)
 Ante mi como Juez Receptor
 Francisco Lorenso
 de Casados (rubric)
 Testigo de asistensia
 Pedro Enriques de Rivera (rubric)
 Testigo de asistensia
 Dimas Giron (rubric)

Notes

1. If a horse was valued at fifteen pesos, as indicated in Martínez's calculation, the inheritance of 568 pesos would have been worth thirty-eight or thirty-nine horses.
2. These laws are further discussed in the introduction of this book. In this and other documents, *Velleianum* is spelled in a variety of ways such as *Vellano* or *Veleyano*.
3. See SANM II #115.
4. María Canseco became Juan Antonio Ramos's wife in 1699. She may have been the "María de los Reyes Canseco" who was recruited as part of the 1695 Hurtado Expedition, or perhaps the daughter of this María. Juan Antonio Ramos was killed in 1715, and in that same year, María petitioned the governor for payment from the presidio soldiers' insurance fund. (Kessell, Hendricks, and Dodge, *Boulders*: 503-03, 559n17, 1169n74.)
5. Juan Antonio Ramos was born in Salveterra, Spain, and may have lived in Sonora, Mexico, in the 1680s. His first wife was Catalina Girón. After her death (and sometime after 1697), he married María Mata, the daughter of Miguel Mata and Felipa Durán. In 1699, he married again, to a María Canseco, though it is possible these two Marías were the same person. In 1697, Juan was one of several persons petitioning Governor Vargas for additional livestock. All the petitioners claimed to be from Sombrerete and Zacatecas, Mexico, and came to New Mexico with the 1695 Hurtado Expedition. Juan was a presidio soldier by 1714 and killed during a campaign in 1715. (Kessell and Hendricks, *Force of Arms*: 119n64; Kessell, Hendricks, and Dodge, *Boulders*: 1168n69; Kessell, Hendricks, Dodge, and Miller, *Disturbances*: 105; Christmas and Rau, "Una Lista": 199; Tigges, "Presidial Company": 71-76.)
6. To date, no information other than what appears in this document has been found on María Manuela Ramos.
7. In the Spanish text, the word used for work is "*trabajos*" and it is unclear whether it referred to a job or to the many things she had to do on her own without a husband to help her.
8. Antonio Valverde [de Cosio], originally from Santander, Spain, came to New Mexico with don Diego de

Vargas in 1693 and served as "captain for life" of the El Paso presidio; later, he served as the alcalde mayor of the area. From 1717 to 1722, he was lieutenant governor and then governor of New Mexico. When he died in 1728, he was the owner of a large farming, livestock, and winegrowing operation near El Paso. (Kessell, Hendricks, Dodge, and Miller, *Accounts*: 258.)

9. There is no record of what kind of "work" this was, but it could have been a job as a washerwoman or cook at the El Paso presidio. Or, Antonio Valverde [de Cosio], who had ranching interests in the area, may have had need for a worker such as María Canseco.
10. For information on Felix Martínez, see Case 3.
11. To date, no information has been located on Pedro Martín. It is likely that he was part of the Martín Serrano family. (Kessell, Hendricks, and Dodge, *Boulders*: 1133n7.)
12. In the document in Case 11, a Francisco Xavier de Rosa was named as the servant of Captain Martínez, but it is not known if this is the same person as in this document.
13. For information on Juan Ignacio Flores Mogollón, see Case 6.
14. For information on Juan Páez Hurtado, see Case 3.
15. SANM II #239a refers to a petition made by the presidio soldiers establishing an insurance fund for families of presidio soldiers killed in action. It required each soldier to contribute one peso to the fund.
16. For information on Roque de Pinto, see Case 6.
17. To date, no information has been found on Nicolás de Apodaca. He may have been related to the pre-revolt Apodaca family that returned to New Mexico after the Spanish Reconquest. (Chávez, *Origins*: 126-27.)
18. Padre Antonio Camargo was a native of Santander, Spain, who professed his vows in Mexico City in 1697 and arrived in New Mexico in 1699. He served in Tesuque, Bernalillo, San Felipe, Nambé, and San Ildefonso. He was custos of the province from 1709 to 1717. (Kessell, Hendricks, Dodge, and Miller, *Disturbances*: 443n130; Chávez, *Origins*: 244; Norris, *Year Eighty*: 84-85.)
19. A novena refers to prayers and services for the dead made for nine consecutive days.
20. This is likely Gregorio Ramírez who was killed in 1715. He was born in Zacatecas, Mexico, and was a soldier at El Paso. He came to New Mexico in 1696, and he was on the 1697 list of the Santa Fe presidio soldiers. (Kessell, Hendricks, and Dodge, *Royal Crown*: 546n22; Kessell, Hendricks, and Dodge, *Boulders*: 1164n40; Kessell, Hendricks, Dodge, and Miller, *Disturbances*: 128; Chávez, *Origins*: 264.)
21. A "real" was 1/8 of a peso.
22. The exact value of a "*tomino*" (or "*tomín*") at that time is uncertain. However, it is referred to as the lowest value of Spanish money. Certainly it is less than a "real." It was also a term then used for a small measure of weight for gold and silver. For silver, the tomín was equal to .019 ounces. (Stampa, "Weights and Measures": 17.)
23. Amended from "twenty" by the scribe.
24. In other words, he pledges his own goods as a guarantee that the inheritance will be held for María Manuela Ramos.
25. The word *fueros* could mean statutes, military privileges, compilations of the law, or judicial power concerning a particular group or rank of persons.
26. This language means that the power of attorney signed by Juan Páez Hurtado overrides any other right given to him as an official or any determination made by a judge or by the governor of New Mexico. It may be the standard language in a power-of-attorney agreement for this period.
27. See Case 9.
28. Since the money provided for María Manuela Ramos would have constituted a dowry, Francisco Lorenzo Casados was alluding to the Spanish laws written to ensure that a dowry provided economic protection and security for a woman upon her marriage. These laws can be traced back to the Romans and were codified in the 539 Code of Justinian. This code was included in the teachings of the jurists at Bologna, Italy, in the 1100s, and was included in *Las Siete Partidas* laws compiled by Alfonso X of Castile, Spain. To use this specific language in this document, Rael de Aguilar must have had some formal legal training or worked with someone who did. (Nunez, *La Dote*: 27-31; Van Kleffens, *Hispanic Law*: 174-75, 182-84.)
29. For information on Alfonso Rael de Aguilar, see Case 3 and the introduction.
30. Thomas [López] Olguín (aka Holguin) was the son of Captain Juan López Olguín II, a native of New Mexico who returned from El Paso by 1697. Juan's name is carved on Inscription Rock in El Morro, New Mexico. Thomas was a campaign captain at the Santa Fe presidio by at least 1706, and by 1707 he was an ayudante (aide-de-camp). He owned land along the Río Grande near Tomé/Fuenclara. (Chávez, *Origins*: 169-70; Kessell, Hendricks, Dodge, and Miller, *Disturbances*: 99, 100, 285; Barrett, *Spanish Colonial Settlement Landscapes*: 145-55, 212; Chávez, "Mission Records": 160-61; Scholes, Simmons, and Esquibel, *Domínguez de Mendoza*: 414n211.)
31. Joseph Manuel Giltoméy was in New Mexico, living in Santa Cruz, by at least 1695. Born in the Philippines, he was the son of Juan Manuel de Giltoméy and Antonia Flores de Valdéz. Juan Manuel was probably a Spanish official. Joseph survived the Pueblo Revolt of 1696, though he had been left for dead. He married Isabel de Olivas in 1696; was included in a presidio muster in April 1704; and was one of the witnesses at the inventory of the possessions of don Diego de Vargas after the governor's death in 1704. In 1715, Joseph Man-

uel Giltoméy replaced Cristóbal de Góngora as an adjutant after Góngora left for El Paso. That same year, Giltoméy was given permission to go to El Paso to seek a cure for his ailments. He died in 1727. (Chávez, *Origins*: 186, 358; Kessell, Hendricks, and Dodge, *Boulders*: 644, 873; Kessell, Hendricks, Dodge, and Miller, *Settling*: 222, 242; Christmas and Rau, "Una Lista": 196.)

32. Antonio de Salazar was the son of Agustín de Salazar and Felipa Gamboa. Agustín was a pre-revolt settler, later known as the blind interpreter for General Diego de Vargas. Antonio is listed as being married to María de Torres, the daughter of Diego Torres, in Santa Fe, in 1708. In 1714, Antonio withdrew from the presidio and was replaced by Vicente de Armijo. Salazar is listed in a claim for a land grant west of the Río del Norte, which had been made to his grandfather, Alonso Martín Barba. (Christmas and Rau, "Una List": 198; Chávez, *Origins*: 279.)

33. To date, no information has been found on Pedro Enriquez de Rivera.

34. Dimas Girón was the son of Tomás Girón de Tejeda and Josefa Muñiz de Castro of Mexico City; all three came to New Mexico with the 1694 Farfán Expedition. In the 1693 muster for the expedition, Tomás is listed as a painter. He later worked on the restoration of San Miguel Chapel in Santa Fe. Dimas Girón was a soldier with Juan Páez Hurtado's 1715 campaign against the Apaches. In 1719, he was replaced at the presidio by Joseph Trujillo. Dimas was married to María Domínguez. His will was written in 1736, and he died shortly thereafter. (Kessell, Hendricks, and Dodge, *Boulders*: 644, 670n2, 1152; Christmas and Rau, "Una Lista": 198; Thomas, *After Coronado*: 87; Chávez, *Origins*: 200.)

13

MISTRESS OF DECEASED GOVERNOR CUERVO Y VALDÉS SEARCHES FOR PROMISED FINANCIAL GUARANTEE OF 10,000 PESOS
January 14–16, 1716, Source: SANM II #265

Synopsis and editor's notes: Doña Micaela de Velasco—in an effort to assist her daughter, doña María Francisca García de la Riva, an unmarried mother of two children—traveled from Mexico City to Santa Fe looking for a financial agreement from the father of her daughter's children, who was the former governor of New Mexico, Francisco Cuervo y Valdés. Doña Micaela was the wife of don Miguel García de Riva, a silk weaver from Mexico City who came to Santa Fe with his family as part of the 1694 Farfán-Velasco Expedition. After Velasco left the group, General Diego de Vargas made García de Riva the militia captain. By 1713 he had died, and his wife and some of his children had returned to Mexico City.

In 1716, doña Micaela de Velasco petitioned the Santa Fe cabildo asking for a letter that had been written from Governor Cuervo y Valdés to her daughter, doña María Francisca García de la Riva. Doña Micaela stated that after Governor Cuervo y Valdés's wife died, while he and his family were in Santa Fe, he asked to marry doña Micaela's daughter, doña María Francisca. However, Cuervo y Valdés told her that he could not do so at that time because he needed special permission from the king. Instead, he signed a note stating if they did not marry he would give her 10,000 pesos for seducing her (acknowledging the fact that doña María Francisca was a virgin). The agreement was made in writing before Sargent Major Alfonso Rael de Aguilar, with a copy given to doña María Francisca.

In 1707, when Cuervo y Valdés's term of office in New Mexico expired, he and María Francisca left New Mexico for Mexico City, where doña María Francisca had two illegitimate children. Unfortunately, Cuervo y Valdés died in 1714, without marrying doña María Francisca, and by that time the written agreement for the 10,000 pesos had been lost or stolen. In his will, Cuervo y Valdés did recognize the children as his and gave them both his name: Francisco Antonio Cuervo, age seven, and Ana María Cuervo, age one. The will made no provision for them or for doña María Francisca, but it did include a section referring to a memorial about "a secret thing." Cuervo y Valdés stated, "[T]he content is secret and relates to the unburdening of my conscience. . . . [T]he executors will take from my estate what will be required to see the complete fulfillment of my wish."[1] It is not known if this related to his illegitimate children.

Doña María Francisca then made a claim on the legitimate heirs, but without success. So, in 1716, her mother, doña Micaela de Velasco, decided to take things into her own hands and went to New Mexico to request that the cabildo records be searched for Cuervo y Valdés's agreement. A search was conducted but no such document was found. Testimony was given by Governor Felix Martínez and several cabildo officials confirming that they had seen the written agreement and had witnessed Cuervo y Valdés's signature. Alfonso Rael de Aguilar pointed out that in 1707 copies of documents were not kept in the cabildo archives as they should have been and were instead given to the persons for whom they were written. At this point the document ends.

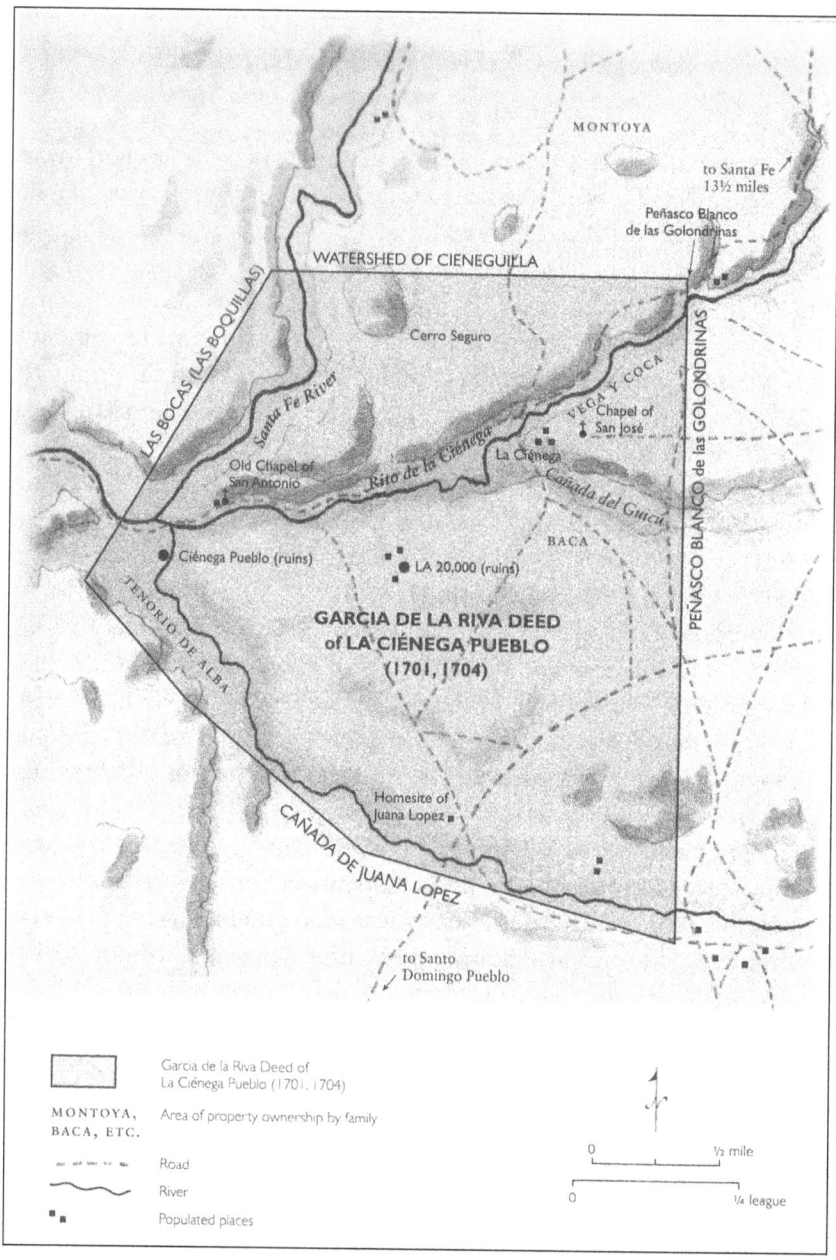

Plan of García de la Riva Property at La Ciénega, 1601–1704. Malcolm Ebright, *Advocates of the Oppressed, Hispanos, Indians, Genízaros and Their Land in New Mexico*, University of New Mexico Press, 2014:121. Courtesy of Malcolm Ebright.

In his will, Cuervo y Valdés referred to his two illegitimate children as *hijos naturales* and in so doing he gave them a certain status. This topic is discussed by Grace Coolidge in her study of mistresses in Spanish society, in which she explains how the Spanish provided for different categories of illegitimate children.[2] The most prestigious status was that of hijos naturales, when children were born to parents of a high rank who were not married (but there was no legal impediment to marriage). Therefore, because Cuervo y Valdés stated in his will that he had conceived the children after becoming a widower, and he had called the two illegitimate children naturales, doña María Francisca's children would fit into this category. If Cuervo y Valdés and doña María Francisca had subsequently married, then the two children would have become legitimate. However, with Cuervo y Valdés's death and no marriage, there was no clear provision for the support of doña María Francisca or her children.

It is not known whether Cuervo y Valdés ever intended to marry doña María Francisca, but his claim that he needed a special license to do so was true. A similar case occurred in 1775, when doña María del Carmen López Nieto of Bolivia and don Ramón de Rivera became lovers and had a child together. Because he was a high level officer in the Spanish bureaucracy and she was of high rank but a colonist, he needed a dispensation from Madrid to marry her. She became pregnant before that happened and died in childbirth, though her daughter lived. In 1795, twenty years later, don Rivera wrote to doña María's sister and recognized the child as his, stating: "I recognize her as my natural daughter born of your sister doña María del Carmen, who is in heaven and whom I would have married, as you know, if the royal permission had arrived to do it. But as God chose to carry her away, I was not able to put into practice my desires after I obtained the necessary license and my transfer to Lima."[3]

TRANSLATION

1716

Testimony regarding the proceedings that were carried out regarding a written petition by doña María Francisca [García] de la Riva.[4]

Governor and Captain General

[I], doña Micaela de Velasco[5] widow of Captain Miguel García de la Riva,[6] resident of the City of Mexico, former resident of this Villa of Santa Fe, appear before your honor in the best form possible that is allowed to me according to my legal right. I state I am found in this villa due to the fact that I have come to visit my children all the way from the city of Mexico. [Also] I have received two letters from my legitimate daughter, doña María Francisca [García] de la Riva, in which she informs me that she has pending litigation in Santa Fe with the heirs of General don Francisco Cuervo y Valdés,[7] now deceased, in regard to 10,000 pesos which was agreed to through a promissory note to her. It was done before the sergeant major don Alfonso Rael de Aguilar,[8] the alcalde ordinario of this villa. This was when I, along with my daughter, lived [in Santa Fe], during which time the general don Francisco Cuervo was governor of this kingdom and when he turned over the original note to my daughter.

I then left the kingdom of New Mexico with all of my family for the city of Mexico by virtue of the permission that was given to me by his most excellent viceroy who was at the time, the duke of Alburquerque.[9] After having made my residence within the city of Mexico, the general don Francisco Cuervo solicited with all of his kindness and loveable words and love which he had for my daughter giving her the note in order to seduce her, which so happened. He gave her the written letter with much caution, and it so happened that he somehow got it back and he never returned it to my daughter. So that she is able to establish the truth of this matter, I petition your honor to search through the archives of the government and war as well as those of the cabildo in order to see where this letter can be found. This is so that if it is found I can obtain a copy or testimony showing that it exists. If it is not found, sergeant major don Alfonso [Rael] de Aguilar can give his sworn statement, under penalty of the law, whether it is true that such a letter was executed before him and what the contents were, stating precisely the reasons were for having made the letter. He can do this as one who was confided in as the secretary of government and war under don Francisco Cuervo.

All of this being presented, I request that your honor fulfill it for me. I petition for this with all of my regard, asking that you will be well served to do as I request, all of which is done according to justice. I swear that it is not done in malice, protesting the costs, but only for that which is necessary, etc. Doña Micaela de Velasco.

Presentation

At the Villa of Santa Fe, New Mexico, on the 14th of January, 1716, before me, I, the captain don Felix Martínez,[10] governor and captain general of this kingdom and provinces of New Mexico and castellan of his forces and presidios for his majesty, accepted it as it was presented by doña Micaela de Velasco.

Decree

Upon having been reviewed by me, I took the petition as it was presented according to her legal right. Having considered it according to what it was worth, I ordered my secretary of government and war and the scribe of the cabildo to search their archives very carefully. Upon them finding the instrument they shall give her what she requests with a certification. Upon not finding it, they shall certify that it was not found. I order the sergeant major don Alfonso Rael de Aguilar and don Joseph Manuel Giltoméy[11] to appear before me, the governor, and state whatever it is they know regarding the statement that the petitioner makes. So that it is valid, I thus approved, ordered and signed this along with my secretary of government and war on the said day.

Felix Martínez
Before me, Miguel Tenorio de Alba[12]
Secretary of Government and War

Certification of Captain Miguel Tenorio de Alba, Secretary of Government and War
Continuing, I, the secretary of government and war, in fulfillment of the above decree demanded by the captain don Felix Martínez, governor and captain general of this kingdom of New Mexico, have searched through all of papers that are contained in the archives in my care for this government, and I did not find within them the instrument that doña Micaela de Velasco seeks. As such I certified it as being the truth, which I certify according to my right, and which I signed on the 14th of January, 1716.

Miguel Tenorio de Alba,
Secretary of Government and War
Certification of Juan Manuel de Chirinos[13]
Scribe for the cabildo

Continuing, I, the scribe for the cabildo, in fulfillment of the decree ordered by don Felix Martínez, governor and captain general of this kingdom of New Mexico, have searched through the papers and inventory of the archives of the cabildo and did not find within them nor in the inventories the instrument that doña Micaela de Velasco requests. So that this is valid, I certified it as being the truth and as such it stands according to my right and I signed it on the 14th of January, 1716.

Juan Manuel de Chirinos
Scribe for the Cabildo

Decree and statement of Sargento Mayor don Alfonso Rael de Aguilar
At this Villa of Santa Fe, New Mexico, on the 15th of January, 1716, I, Captain Felix Martínez, being that I am in perpetuity appointed governor and captain general of this presidio castle of this Villa of Santa Fe of the kingdom and province of New Mexico and castellan of his forces and presidios for his majesty, by virtue of this decree I made to appear before me the sergeant major don Alfonso Rael de Aguilar. From him, upon being present, I took his sworn statement which he made to God, Our Lord, and to a sign of the Cross, under which he promised to tell the truth about everything that he knew and what he was asked.

Upon reading the document presented by doña Micaela de Velasco and being familiar with what was presented in its contents, Rael de Aguilar, stated that in the past year of 1707, he found himself as the alcalde ordinario of this villa and secretary of government and war under the governor don Francisco Cuervo y Valdés, who was governor and captain general of this kingdom at that time. It was confided to Rael de Aguilar in his capacity [as secretary], that a note for 10,000 pesos was given by the governor to doña María Francisca García de la Riva. The note obligated him to pay this to her or to someone empowered by her, for his having had an illicit affair with her having given his word of promising to marry her at the time of the affair. At this time, she was found to be intact and a virgin, which he took from her. In such a condition he should have married her, and thus he promised to give to her the sum of 10,000 pesos for which he gave her the promissory note. He authorized it and signed it before me as the alcalde ordinario, as has been stated, with all of the clauses being enforceable and validated obligating him to do so according to the said written document. This agreement he was supposed to fulfill. He could not marry her at that time because he had the duty of being the governor and captain general and royal official of the royal treasury of the city of Guadalajara. Because of this, he was required to obtain proper permission or a license to marry from the king, our lord. Thus, being that he had the affair with her, he was obligated to pay her the specific quantity of the 10,000 pesos, as was set forth in writing.

Those who were present at the time were the governor, the sergeant major, don Juan de Uribarrí, and the ayudante don Joseph Manuel Giltoméy, who can also give their statements regarding this matter and who know this because they saw the general don Francisco Cuervo y Valdés gave the original to doña María Francisca. She then had a natural son named don Francisco Antonio Xavier y Cuervo[14] whom he recognized as such. This was public knowledge within this villa and throughout the kingdom.

In the past it had been the custom that all of the original documents that were written and authenticated were turned over to the person to whom they were made. This is the reason for nothing being found in this case. All of this was continued in this manner until the year of 1713, when things were changed at the request of Joseph Manuel Giltoméy, scribe for the cabildo, and at the insistence of the general don Juan Ignacio Flores Mogollón, who was the then governor and captain general of this kingdom. He had seen that there were numerous documents [in the archives] that were not authorized and very few originals, among none of which could you find any civil or criminal complaints.

In order to preserve these documents, the governor Flores Mogollón issued an order for all of the residents of the kingdom to appear before the illustrious cabildo of the villa with their deeds and documents involving their land grants. This was so that they would be filed and their ownership would be recognized and so that they could be made available and well-known. The alcaldes were not to return the original documents that they witnessed, but merely informing them that the originals were to remain with the illustrious cabildo.

This order was then given to all of the jurisdictions, insisting that all of them were to heed the order so that they could observe and execute it. It was from that year of 1713 until the present that this order has been observed, and it has been with great care that the original documents are not given back to anyone. All of what has been done is hereby affirmed and ratified after it was read back to him. He stated that he was fifty-seven years of age, and he signed it along with me, the governor and captain general, and with my secretary of government and war.

    Felix Martínez
    Alfonso Rael de Aguilar
    Before me, Miguel Tenorio de Alba,
    Secretary of Government and War

Decree and statement of don Joseph Manuel Giltoméy

    At the Villa of Santa Fe on the said day, month and year, I the said governor and captain general, have heard the statement that has been given by the sergeant major don Alfonso Rael de Aguilar, who said in his sworn statement that when the written note was made by the general don Francisco Cuervo y Valdés and given to doña María Francisca García de la Riva. In order to ascertain this fact, I made to appear before me the ayudante don Joseph Manuel Giltoméy. Upon his being present I took his sworn statement which he made to God, Our Lord, and the sign of the Holy Cross, under which he promised to tell the truth as to what he knew and what he was asked.

    After having read to him the written note that was presented by doña Micaela de Velasco and the said statement given by the sergeant major, he stated that it was true that he was present at the time that the written statement was presented by doña María Francisca. She was a virgin for which reason the governor was obligated to marry her and or to give her a promissory note in the amount of 10,000 pesos in the case that he did not marry her. This was because there had been a specific order issued by his majesty which was to be carried out if this happened. Also, because [doña Micaela de Velasco] stated that doña María Francisca had given birth to a natural son whose name was don Francisco Antonio Xavier [y Cuervo].

    The reason that she took the original note was because it was the custom in this kingdom not to leave any written testimony [in the archives], something that was done until the year of 1713. This was the year that he became the scribe of the cabildo, which was in existence in this kingdom at the time under his majesty. The cabildo members were elected for one year at a time, for which reason no special care was given to the archives by those who have held the position. The above matter was known by him, Giltoméy because of the fact that he had served within the household of General don Francisco Cuervo since the time that he had become governor until he left this kingdom. Giltoméy also knew that sergeant major don Juan de Uribarrí, as a confident of the general, was aware of the matter, and as such has been named as a witness regarding the written note.

    He said that everything that he has stated is the truth. He affirmed and ratified it after his written statement was read back to him and said that he was of the age of fifty-one years, more or less. He signed it along with me, the governor and captain general, and my secretary of government and war.

    Felix Martínez
    Joseph Manuel Giltoméy

Before me, Miguel Tenorio de Alba
Secretary of Government and War

[Clarification]
All of this concurs with the original, from which I, Captain Miguel Tenorio de Alba, secretary of government and war ordered this to be copied and is done word by word and corrected accordingly. It is certified that it corresponds with its original which was ordered to be done by doña Micaela de Velasco and was given to her with this written testimony remaining in my power. Those who were witnesses to it being done correctly and accurately were the ayudante don Joseph Manuel Giltoméy, Pedro Enriquez de Rivera[15] and the royal alférez Ramón García Jurado.[16] So that it is valid, I signed it at this Villa of Santa Fe on the 16th of January, 1716, being done on six pages of common paper because sealed paper does not exist in these parts.

In testimony to the truth I thus sign it and place my accustomed to rubric.
Miguel Tenorio de Alba (rubric)
Secretary of Government and War

TRANSCRIPTION

Testimonio de las diligencias que se hisieron sobre una escriptura de Da. Maria Francisca de la Ribas, En 6 foxas.

Señor Governador y Capitan General = Da. Micaela de Velasco viuda del Capitan Miguel Garsia dela Rivas vezina dela Cuidad de Mexico residente en esta Villa de Santa Fee, paresco ante Vuestra Señoria en la mejor forma que el derecho me consede y digo, que allandome en esta dicha Villa por aver venido aver a mis hijos desde dicha Cuidad de Mexico e resivido dos cartas de Doña Maria Francisca dela Rivas mi hija lexitima en que me da la notisia tiene pleyto pendiente en dicha Cuidad con los herederos del General Dn. Francisco Cuerbo y Valdes, ya difunto, sobre diez mill pesos de que le hizo escriptura a fabor dela dicha mi hija la qual paso ante el Sargento Mayor Dn. Alfonso Rael de Aguilar, Alcalde Ordinario desta dicha Villa, viviendo yo, y la dicha mi hija en ella y governando este Reyno dicho General Dn. Francisco Cuerbo quien sela entrego orixinal ala dicha mi hija.

Aviendo salido yo con la dicha mi hija y toda mi familia de este Reyno dela Nueva Mexico para la Cuidad de Mexico en virtud de lisensia que para ello me consedio el Excellentisimo Señor Virrey que fue Duque de Alburquerque, y aviendo tenido mi residensia en dicha Cuidad de Mexico dicho General Dn. Francisco Cuerbo solicito con grandes ynstansias y con palabras carinosas y amorosas el que le deve hisiese la dicha mi hija dicha escriptura para verla y aserse bastante capas de su contenido para ultimarle lo que en ella se expressava y tenia hecha obligasion lo qual consiguio con dicha mi hija entregandole dicha escriptura obrando con cautela pues la dicha escriptura nunca sela volvio ala dicha mi hija y para que la suso dicha pueda justificar la verdad de este hecho se a de servir Vuestra Señoria de que se rexistren los archibos asi el de gobernazion y guerra como el de cavildo para el reconocimiento de poder ver en qual de ellos para el testimonio de dicha escriptura, y allado que sea seme de un tanto autorisado de manera que aga fee y de no allarlo que el Sargento Mayor Dn. Alphonso Rael de Aguilar jure y declare devajo de juramento sobre pena de el si es verdad que la dicha escriptura passo ante el suso dicho que clausulas se contenian y que como confidente y Secretario de Govierno y Guerra de dicho Dn. Francisco Cuerbo/ Le comunicara presisamente los motivos que hubo para azerla por todo lo qual y lo mas que aze ami fabor a Vuestra Señoria pido y suplico con todo rendimiento sea muy servido de mandar hazer como llevo pedido que es de justisia y juro en forma no es de malisia protexto costas y en lo nessesario ut supra = Doña Micaela de Velasco =

Presentacion

En la Villa de Santa Fee dela Nueba Mexico en catorze dias del mes de Henero de mill setecientos diez y seis años ante mi el Capitan Dn. Felix Martinez, Governador y Capitan General deste Reino y Provincias dela Nueba Mexico y Castellano de Sus Fuerzas y Presidios por Su Magestad la presento la contenida =

Auto

Y por mi vista la hube por presentada en quanto a lugar en derecho y en atension alo justo de su pedimento mando ami Secretario de Gobernazion y Guerra y a el Escribano de Cavildo rexistren sus archibos con cuydado y de allar en ellos el ynstrumento que la suplicante refiere le de un tanto autorisado en manera que aga fee y de no allarlo asi lo zertifiquen y mando al Sargento Maior Dn. Alfonso Rael de Aguilar y a Dn. Joseph Manuel Gilthomey conparescan ante mi dicho Governador a declarar lo que supieren sobre el punto que la suplicante pide y para que conste asi lo probey, mande y firme con mi Secretario de Governazion y Guerra en dicho dia = Felix Martinez = ante mi Miguel Tenorio de Alva, Secretario de Governazion y Guerra.

 Zertificazion del Capitan
 Miguel Tenorio de Alva, Secretario
 de Governazion y Guerra

Y luego yncontinenti yo dicho Secretario de Governazion y Guerra en cumplimiento del auto de ariva proveydo por el ñ Capitan Dn. Felix Martinez, Governador y Capitan General deste Reyno dela Nueva Mexico rexistre todos los papeles que constan en el archivo de mi cargo de esta governazion y no ay en el el ynstrumento que Doña Micaela de Velasco solisita desi lo zertifico en testimonio de verdad y que haga fee quanta aya lugar en derecho y lo firme en catorze dias del mes de Henero de mill setecientos y dies y seis años =

    Miguel Tenorio de Alva,
    Secretario de Governazion y Guerra
    Zertificazion de
    Juan Manuel Chirinos
    Secretario de Cavildo

    Y luego yncontinenti yo dicho Escribano de Cavildo en cumplimiento del auto probeydo por el Señor Dn. Felix Martinez, Governador y Capitan General deste Reyno dela Nueba Mexico, rexistre los papeles e imbentario del Archibo de Cavildo y no ay en el ni en dicho ynbentario el ynstrumento que Doñna Micaela de Velasco pide para que assi conste lo zertifico en testimonio de verdad y que aga fee en lugar y en derecho y lo firme en catorze dias del mes de Henero de mill setecientos y diez y seis años = Juan Manuel Chirinos, Escribano de Cavildo =

Auto y declaracion del Sargento Mallor Dn. Alfonso Rael de Aguilar
    En la Villa de Santa Fe dela Nueba Mexico en quinze dias del mes de Henero de mill setecientos y diez y seis años yo el Capitan Dn. Felix Martinez que lo soy Vitalicio de este Castillo Presidial de dicha Villa de Santa Fee, Governador y Capitan General deste Reyno y Provincia dela Nueva Mexico y Castellano de Sus Fuerzas y Presidios por Su Magestad en virtud del auto de susso dicho por mi probeydo hize parezer ante mi al Sargento Maior Dn. Alfonso Rael de Aguilar al qual estando presente le rezevi juramento que hizo por Dios Nuestro Señor y una Señal de Cruz devajo de cuyo cargo prometio de dezir verdad en todo lo que supiere y le fuere preguntado.
    Aviendole leydo el escrito presentada Micaela de Velasco asiendose capaz de su contenido dixo que por el año passado de setecientos y siete allandose de Alcalde Ordinario desta dicha Villa y Secretario de Governazion y Guerra del Governador Dn. Francisco Cuerbo y Valdez, Governador y Capitan General que entonses era deste dicho Reyno le confirio a este declarante como le era presiso aser una escriptura de diez mill pesos a a fabor de Da. Maria Francisca Garzia de la Rivas obligandose por ella a pagar sela ala suso dicha o aquien su poder tubiere por razon de que avia tenido amistad ylisita de vajo de palabra de cassamiento que le avia dado quando la ubo por averla conosida yntacta y virgen cuyo estrupo hizo de bajo de dicha calidad y palabra de cassamiento que le avia dado quando la ubo de que se avia de cassar con la suso dicha y de no azerlo la dotava en la dicha cantidad de dichos diez mill pesos cuya escriptura le hizo, zelebro y otorgo y la firmo dicho Dn. Francisco Cuerbo ante este declarante como Alcalde Ordinario como ba espresado poniendo todas las clausulas

fuerzas y zircumstancias que la material requeria para su mayor validasion obligandose como se obligo por dicha escriptura a cassarse con la suso dicha y que no lo podia azer ni executar en aquel tiempo a caussa de allarse con los empleos de Governador y Capitan General y official Real de la Real Caxa dela Cuidad de Guadalaxara y que para ello era menester lisensia del Rey Nuestro Señor y que con tanto que la conseguia se obligava a pagar por dicha escriptura la referida cantidad de dichos diez mill pesos a cuya selebrasion.

Se allaron presentes el Governador y Sargento Maior Dn. Juan de Uribarri y el Ayudante Dn. Joseph Manuel Gilthomey quienes pueden declarar sobre esta material y que save por que lo vio que la dicha escriptura sela entrego dicho General Dn. Francisco Cuerbo, orexinal ala dicha Doña Maria Francisca en quien tubo un hijo natural llamado Dn. Francisco Antonio Xabier y Cuerbo, y que asi lo conosio por tal y esto era muy publico en esta Villa y en todo el Reyno.

Que no quedo testimonio en el Archibo por que la entrego orixinal el dicho Dn. Francisco Cuerbo como a sido costumbre en este Reyno, que las escripturas que se an hecho y otorgado se an entregado orixinales poniendo que de pedimento de la parte se entregen asi y no queda testimonio poniendo fee de ello al pie de dichas escripturas como asi lo hizo este declarante en la referida, y que esto sea acostumbrado como lleva dicho asta el año de mill setezientos y treze que por pedimiento de Joseph Manuel Gilthomey, Escribano de Cavildo en que representa al General Dn. Juan Ygnacio Flores Mogollon, Governador y Capitan General que fue deste dicho Reyno que aviendo reconosido el archivo que estaba a su cargo delos papeles avia visto que estavan muchos sin autorisar y pocas escripturas orixinales, ningunos testimonios de que se podian orixinar muchos pleytos y discordias.

Para obiarlos se sirviese dicho Señor despedir su mandamiento para que todos los vezinos deste Reyno comparesieren ante el Ylustrissimo Cavildo desta dicha Villa con los titulos y mersedes de sus tierras y demas ynstrumentos para que los reconoscan y se tome la razon dellos y que los Alcalde Mayores no entrieguen los ynstrumentos que ante si otorgaron orixinales alas partes sino testimonios reminiendo dichos orixinales a dicho Yllustrisimo Cavildo.

Cuyo mandamiento expidio a todas la jurisdiciones, y se yntimo alos vezinos de esta Villa para que assi se observase y executase y desde dicho tiempo del año de treze asta el presente se a puesto gran cuydado en no entregar las escripturas orixinales y que todo lo que lleva fecho en que se afirmo y ratifico siendole leyda esta su declaracion y que es de edad de cinquenta y siete añnos y lo firmo con migo dicho Governador y Capitan General y mi Secretario de Governazion y Guerra = Felix Martinez = Alfonso Rael de Aguilar = Ante mi Miguel Tenorio de Alva; Secretario de Governazion y Guerra =

Auto y declaracion de Dn. Joseph Manuel Gilthomey

En la Villa de Santa Fee en dicho dia, mes y año yo dicho Governador y Capitan General en virtud de la zitacion que haze en su declaracion el Sargento Maior Dn.

Alfonso Rael de Aguilar de que se allo presente al tiempo y quando se otorgo la escriptura que a su fabor hiso el General Dn. Francisco Cuerbo y Valdez a Doña Maria Francisca Garcia de la Rivas y para sindicar la verdad de este hecho hize parezer ante mi al dicho Ayudante Dn. Joseph Manuel Gilthomey al qual estando presente le resevi juramento que hizo por Dios Nuestro Señor y la Señal dela Santa Cruz devajo de cuyo cargo prometio de dezir verdad en lo que supiere y le fuere preguntado.

Aviendole leydo el escrito presentado por Doña Micaela de Velasco y dicha zitasion hecha por el dicho Sargento Maior dixo que es verdad que este declarante se allo presente al otorgamiento de dicha escriptura y que en ella confiessa dicho General Dn. Francisco Cuerbo aver afido a dicha Doña Maria Francisca virgen por que se obligo a cassarse con ella y asi mismo en dotarla en diez mill pesos en casso de no cassarse por ser presiso lisensia expresa de Su Magestad para executar y asi mismo declaro en dicha escriptura que un hijo que la dicha Doña Maria Francisca avia parido lo reconosia por su hijo natural que se llamava Dn. Francisco Antonio Xabier.

Que el aver llevado la escriptura orixinal fue por ser costumbre en este Reyno no dejar testimonio ni razon los que las asian el año de mill setecientos y treze que este declarante entro de escribano de Cavildo por averlo en este Reyno por Su Magestad y elexirse dicho empleo cada año y asi no an tenido este cuydado los que lo an exersido, y el saverlo este declarante todo lo que estava dicho es por aver servido en cassa de dicho General Dn. Francisco Cuerbo desde que entro por governador asta que se fue de este Reyno y lo mismo save el Sargento Mayor Dn. Juan de Urribarri como confidente de dicho General y que este declarante esta puesto por testigo en dicha escriptura y todo lo que lleva dicho es la verdad so cargo del juramento que tiene hecho en que se afirmo y ratifico siendole leyda esta su declaracion y que es de edad de sinquenta y un años poco mas o menos y lo firmo con migo dicho Governador y Capitan General y mi Secretario de Governazion y Guerra = Felix Martinez = Joseph Manuel Gilthomey = Ante mi: Miguel Tenorio de Alva = Secretario de Governazion y Guerra =

Concuerda con su original de donde yo el Capitan Miguel Tenorio de Alva, Secretario de Governazion y Guerra hize sacar y trasuntar ala letra ba cierta y verdadero correxido y consertado y corresponde con su original que a pedimento de Doña Micaela de VelascoP sele entregue quedando este testimonio en mi poder y fueron testigos alo ver correxir y consertar el Ayudante Dn. Joseph Manuel Gilthomey y Pedro Enriquez de Rivera y el Alferez Real Ramon Garcia Jurado y para que conste lo firme en esta Villa de Santa Fee en diez y seis dias del mes de Henero de mill setecientos y diez y seis años en seis ojas de papel comun por que el sellado no corre en estas partes =

En testimonio de verdad hago mi firma y rubrica acostumbrada =
Miguel Tenorio de Alba (rubric)
Secretario de Governazion y Guerra

Notes

1. See Hendricks, "Last Years": 3. There is,evidence that before his death Cuervo made provision for the son, Francisco Antonio Xavier. When the son was six, he was granted a position *en futura* in the royal treasury at Zacatecas. In 1735, the viceroy recognized him as a member of a noble family and granted him "quasi possession" of nobility for him and his heirs. (Flager, "From Asturias to New Mexico: don Francisoc Cuervo y Valdes":258.
2. See Coolidge, "Vile and Abject": 200-01.
3. Twinam, "Honor, Sexuality and Illegitimacy": 67-69; quoted from *Archivo general de la nación Charcas* 560, o. 15 (1795).
4. Doña María Francisca García de la Riva was the daughter of Captain Miguel García de la Riva and doña Micaela de Velasco, both from Mexico City. As stated above, she had two "natural" children by Governor Francisco Cuervo y Valdés, named Francisco Antonio Xavier Cuervo and Ana María Cuervo, both born after Cuervo's wife died. (Hendricks, "Last Years": 3.)
5. Doña Micaela de Velasco was the wife of don Miguel García de la Riva. A deed of 1707 indicates that she bought land from Sebastián Rodríguez in Santa Fe "on the other side of the river." In 1707, she sold a house and lot in Santa Fe; the house was located on the Santa Fe Plaza and consisted of a hall and two rooms with some space for a garden. It appears to have been traded for land located elsewhere. (SANM I #1028, WPA translation; SANM I #411, WPA translation.)
6. Don Miguel García de la Riva was a silk weaver and a native of Mexico City, who married doña Micaela de Velasco in 1671. He and his family came with the Farfán-Velasco Expedition of 1694; he was made the militia captain of the expedition by don Diego de Vargas in place of Cristóbal de Velasco. Fray Farfán praised García de la Riva for keeping many of the members of the expedition from deserting. In New Mexico, García de la Riva purchased the land surrounding the ancient pueblo of Ciénega. The land passed to his son Juan and then a part of it went to a granddaughter through Miguel García de la Riva's daughter, Teodora, the wife of General Juan Páez Hurtado. Juan García de la Riva married a daughter of Alfonso Rael de Aguilar. Miguel died sometime before 1713. (Kessell, Hendricks, and Dodge, *Royal Crown*: 293, 318n31; Kessell, Hendricks, and Dodge, *Boulders*: 102-03, 284-85, 368; Kessell, Hendricks, Dodge, and Miller, *Settling of Accounts*: 220; SANM I #411, WPA translation; Ebright, "Advocates": 119-24.)
7. Francisco Cuervo y Valdés was appointed the interim governor of New Mexico upon the death of don Diego de Vargas. He entered Santa Fe in 1705, founded the new Villa of Albuquerque in 1706, and, according to him, re-founded the Villa of Santa Cruz, which had been partly abandoned after the 1696 Pueblo Revolt. In 1707, he was succeeded as governor by the Marqués de la Peñuela. (Kessell, *Kiva*: 303, 310.)
8. For information on Alfonso Rael de Aguilar, see Case 3. Note that his daughter was Feliciana Rael de Aguilar, who was married to Juan García de la Riva.
9. For information on the Duke of Albuquerque, see Case 4.
10. For information on Felix Martínez, see Case 3.
11. For information on Joseph Manuel Giltoméy, see Case 12.
12. For information on Miguel Tenorio de Alba, see SANM II #96.
13. For information on Juan Manuel de Chirinos, see Case 5.
14. For information on Francisco Antonio Xavier y Cuervo, see Hendricks, "Last Years": 3.
15. To date, no information has been located on Pedro Enriquez de Rivera. The name is similar to that of fray Payo de Rivera Enriquez, the archbishop of Mexico City from 1669 to 1680 and the Viceroy of New Spain from 1673 to 1680, though no specific connection between the two are known. There was also a don Manuel Enriquez in Taos around 1720, though again no connection is known. Lastly, it is possible this may be the same person as (or a relation of) Miguel Enriquez, who was the secretary of government and war for acting governor Juan Páez Hurtado from 1715 to 1716. (Kessell, Hendricks, and Dodge, *Royal Crown*: 314n3; Chávez, *Origins*: 354; SANM I #240.)
16. Ramón García Jurado's parents were José García Jurado and María Rodríguez de Alba who came from Puebla, Mexico, with the Farfán Expedition in 1694. José García Jurado held many positions in New Mexico, including procurador general (legal agent) for the Santa Fe cabildo, and alguacil mayor. Ramón García Jurado married Antonia de Espindola, originally from Zacatecas, Mexico, in 1697, and upon her death married Bernardina Hurtado, daughter of the first alcalde of Albuquerque, Martín Hurtado. Ramón was alférez real during the campaign against the Moqui pueblos in 1716. When he served as alcalde for the Bernalillo area in 1732, he was accused of mistreating the Indians and was banished to Zuni Pueblo for two years. In a document dated 1744, he called himself the procurador general for Albuquerque. (Chávez, *Origins*: 183-84; Cutter, *Protector*: 46-75; Cutter, *Legal Culture*: 101; Kessell, Hendricks, and Dodge, *Boulders*: 111n2, 218, 11-75.)

14

ANA MARÍA ROMERO [VILLALPANDO] SPREADS SCANDAL; SENTENCED TO HUMILIATING PUNISHMENT
January 20, 1716, Source: SANM II #267

Synopsis and editor's note: On January 20, 1716, Ana María Romero [Villalpando] was banished from Santa Fe to Albuquerque for two years for making slanderous remarks about another married woman. In one instance, Ana María told the woman (who is not identified in the document) in front of her husband that she was a whore. Ana María did so, she explained, because the other woman accused her of being an adulteress. So, she stated, if she was one then the other woman was one, too. The scribe for the case made an editorial comment by dryly noting that this was enough reason for a fight.

The argument between the two women was resolved by mutual apologies but the husband of the other (unidentified) woman did not know this and brought a complaint against Ana María before the alcalde ordinario, Juan García de la Riva. The husband was later informed about the apologies by a soldier from El Paso—called a "good Christian"—who heard about it from his wife. The document does not give the names of either person.

Upon receiving the complaint, García de la Riva directed the scribe to go to Ana María's house and tell her that she was banished to Albuquerque for two years, and if she did not agree with the sentence, or decided to retaliate, she would be forced to a ride on a horse around the Santa Fe Plaza naked from the waist up and with a gag in her mouth. Not surprisingly, Ana María agreed to leave, although it is unclear whether she actually ever went to Albuquerque. As will be seen in Case 16, she was involved in yet another legal matter in Santa Fe only seven months later.

What reason did Juan García de la Riva have for threatening Ana María with being gagged and stripped and sent for a ride around the plaza during the frigid month of January? It may have been because García de la Riva was *alguacil mayor* (high sheriff) of the Holy Office of the Inquisition for the New Mexico jurisdiction. As such, he would have been aware of the Inquisition's instructions for punishing women who made slanderous remarks and behaved in an unseemly way. Additionally, García de la Riva was the alcalde ordinario—an official with local sheriff's duties—of the Santa Fe cabildo.

Shedding further light on this document are two Inquisition cases that occurred nearly one hundred and eighty years earlier involving two women who were punished by public shaming. In the first, a case dating to 1536, a denunciation was made against María de Armenta of Mexico City for "superstition acts" and "sorcery." She stated she was originally from the Canary Islands, where she had learned "spells" from a black woman. In addition to confessing to sorcery, she confessed that she had had carnal relations with two brothers, though she did not know they were related at the time. Her punishment was to wear a pointed "*coza*"[1] (hat), be stripped naked, and stand on the steps of the church while her sins were announced for all to hear.

The second case, dating to 1538, also occurred in Mexico City and involved a woman named María de Sotomayer, originally from Toledo, Spain, who was condemned for bigamy. When she left Spain for Mexico her husband was alive, but upon arriving in Mexico City she learned that he had died. So, she married another man. It turned out, however, that her first husband was still alive. Because of her apparent bigamy, the Inquisition sentenced her to be stripped from the waist up and be paraded before the congregation barefoot (and holding a candle), after which she was to hear the penitential mass on the subject of matrimony. She was also supposed to lose half of her possessions and be placed on a ship for Spain, where she would be joined by her first husband. Ignoring all of this, she traveled to Peru and then returned to Mexico City, where she was arrested again. This time, all her goods were confiscated and she was sent back to Spain. As the inventory of her goods indicated, she was a woman of some wealth.

TRANSLATION

1716

Banishment proceedings against Ana María Romero [Villalpando]

[Sentence]

At the Villa of Santa Fe, on the 20th of January, 1716, I, Captain Juan García de la Riva,[2] High Sheriff of the Holy Office and the alcalde ordinario of this villa, attending to the greater service of God, peace, and tranquility, at this time I order and did order that Ana María Romero [Villalpando][3] be banished from this villa to that of Albuquerque for the period of two years leaving within the time period of twenty-four hours. This is with the understanding that upon her making her appearance before being sent there, she is ordered to be paraded through the plaza and public streets of this villa. This is for being *atrevimiento* [bold and shameless][4] enough to tell a married woman that she was a whore in front of her husband. It is also for Ana María saying if she was accused of cohabitating with someone, so was she, the other woman, cohabitating with so and so,[5] which was a matter for bringing about an argument.[6] All of this has caused both parties to make legal complaints one against the other, resulting in having the minister of justice of this royal office[7] summoned to come forth. He has taken the matter in hand so that it will end with good results.

The matter was brought forth and attended to because the married man had noticed some peculiar things after Ana María Romero told his wife in front of him that which is presented above. Ana María Romero has likewise told me, the alcalde, that after these complaints were brought forth she and the married woman made up and became friends again without the married man knowing anything about it, which he discovered only by accident. His wife revealed that [and] at this time he has allowed her back into his home because there was nothing to the accusations. All of this was described to him by a *Santo Cristo*[8] from knowledge that he had heard from his wife. This individual was a soldier from El Paso, who happened to be around on a number of occasions and knew the substance of this matter.

For all of this, I order the scribe of the cabildo, Juan Manuel de Chirinos,[9] to proceed to the home of Ana María Romero to notify her of this decree. If she is opposed to the order and retaliates, he is to bring her back as a prisoner to the public jail of this villa where he is to place her under security and then she is to be paraded nude to the waist on a horse with a gag in the mouth. Matters similar to this (to which I have referred above), have to be dealt with in this manner.

The scribe shall show with a note at the bottom of the page as part of these proceedings that he has complied with the order and is to assure that the above person has left [on her banishment]. So that all of this is valid I signed it along with the said scribe of the cabildo on the said day, month and year, etc.

Juan García de la Riva (rubric)
Before me
Juan Manuel de Chirinos (rubric)
Scribe of the Cabildo

[Remission of sentence to Ana María Romero Villalpando]

Continuing, I, the scribe of the cabildo, went to the home of Ana María Romero [Villalpando], where I notified her of the above decree which was handed down by the alcalde. She said that she would obey and did obey the sentence stated above. She did not sign because she did not know how. I, the said scribe of the cabildo, signed it at the Villa of Santa Fe on the 20th of January, 1716. Present was the minister of justice, Miguel Moran.[10]

Juan Manuel de Chirinos (rubric)
Scribe of the Cabildo

TRANSCRIPTION

1716

Auto de destierro contra Ana Maria Romero

En la Villa de Santa Fee en beinte dias del mes de Henero de mill zetesientos y dies y seis años yo el Capitan Juan Garcia de las Rivas, Alguacil Mallor del Santo Oficio y Alcalde Ordinario de esta dicha Villa, atendiendo al maior zervicio de Dios, pas y quietud por el presente ordeno y mando Ana Maria Romero desterada desta dicha Villa ala de Alburquerque por dos años dentro beinte y cuatro oras con aperzebimiento que en lo entrando asiendo la manden pasear por la plaza y calles publicas de esta dicha Villa por mordas y aber tenido atrebimiento de dezirle a una muger casada que era una puta en presenzia de su marido y que si ella estava amanzebada que tambien ella lo estaba con fulano y fulano materia tan peliagada y donde zea segido el que anden los dichos casados al pleito y a parte uno de otro pues an sido menester la justisia de su Real Oficio ayga metido la mano en que se conpongan.

Aun apenas se an podido ajustar por razon que da el dicho hombre casado de que algo le a bisto a su muger pues le dijo delante del lo que ba referido y asi mesmo aberme dicho a mi dicho Alcalde que despues de este pleyto que tubieron ysieron las amistades la dicha muger casada y esta sin saberlo el hombre casado y que esta sele atraslusido por muy sierto le a conzentido en su casa a su muger no se que maldad y que esto descubrio por un Santo Cristo de pla que tiene su muger el cual conosio claramente ser de un soldado de El Paso por aberselo bisto diferentes veses por todo lo cual mando al Escribano de Cavildo Juan Manuel Chirinos pase ala casa y morada dela dicha Ana Maria Romero y la notifique este mi auto y si se pusiere en algunas mallorias mela traera presa ala carzel publica desta Villa donde la pondra a buen recaudo que semejanate maldad mereze executando en ella lo que arriva llevo referido de pazearla desnuda asta la sintura y sobre un caballo con la dicha mordasa en la boca.

El dicho Escribano pondra al pie deste auto su obedesimiento y dara fe de aber salido la dicha y para que asi conste lo firme con dicho Escribano de Cavildo en dicho mes y ano, ut supra.

Juan Garcia de la Riva (rubric)
Ante mi
Juan Manuel Chirinos (rubric)
Escribano de Cavildo

Y luego incontinente yo dicho Escribano de Cavildo pase ala casa y morada de Ana Maria Romero aquien notifique el auto de arriba probeydo por el Señor Alcalde llo oido que fui dela susa dicha dijo que lo obedesia y obedezio y no firmo por no saber firmelo yo dicho Escribano de Cavildo en la Villa de Santa Fee en beinte dias del mes de Henero de mill zetesientos y dies y seis años todo lo cual passo, presente Miguel Moran ministro de justicia.

Juan Manuel Chirinos (rubric)
Escribano de Cavildo

Notes

1. The Spanish word *coza* is literally a "silly hat." The word derives from *coroza*—a dunce or fool's hat—the tall pointed hat used by the Holy Office of the Inquisition as punishment and a symbol of shame. (The six-

teenth-century cases are as referred to in Chuchiak, *Inquisition*: 22227, 295, 297, 418.)

2. For information on Juan García de la Riva, see Case 11.
3. Ana María Romero [Villalpando] was the daughter of Alonso Cadmos Romero and María Tapia. Upon the death of Alonso Romero, María Tapia married Mateo Trujillo and one of their daughters was Juana Trujillo (see Case 16). Ana María was married to Juan de Villalpando, a presidio soldier who had died by 1718. A cabildo inventory of 1715 indicates that Ana María Romero owned land in Santa Fe in 1703. She had a daughter named Catalina de Villalpando. (SANM I #1136; SANM II #239c; Kessell, Hendricks, and Dodge, *Boulders*: 561n22, 1161n15; Kessell, Hendricks, and Dodge, *Royal Crown*: 83n43.)
4. The Spanish word atrevimiento has a variety of meanings, including bold, daring, insolent, rude, and shameless.
5. In the Spanish text, the term for "so and so" is *fulano y fulano*.
6. Ana María Romero appears to be answering an accusation of cohabitation by the other woman, which, because she is married, would be adultery. In response, Ana María tells this other woman that if she is guilty of this, so then is the other woman (with a man she does not name).
7. In Spanish, the full title is *ministro la justicia de su real oficio*, a grand title for someone who appears to be an agent of the alcalde ordinario and who acted as an officer of justice or as sheriff. The person in this position was Miguel Moran (see Case 5).
8. The term Santa Cristo—or "Good Christian"—may simply have meant that the man was known as a respectable fellow. However, it could also have meant that he was a "Christianized Indian," as Luisa Elisa Alcalá explains in her discussion of colonial Indians in New Spain. (See Alcalá, *Contested Visions in the Spanish Colonial World*: 231-35.)
9. For information on Juan Manuel de Chirinos, see Case 9.
10. For information on Miguel Moran, see Case 5.

15

NEW MEXICAN RANCHERS LUCÍA HURTADO Y SALAS AND LUIS GARCÍA DE NORIEGA END COURT CASE WITH EMBRACE; COW RECOVERED
March 8, 1716, Source: SANM II #269

Synopsis and editor's notes: In this short document, Captain Luis García de Noriega, one of the first founders of Albuquerque and an influential property owner, accused doña Lucía Hurtado y Salas, widow of the venerable don Fernando Durán y Chávez II, of stealing a cow. He made the complaint after observing that a cow in her herd had similar coloring to those in his herd and was double branded. Lucía then sued him for making a false accusation. On March 8, 1716, Luis García de Noriega, doña Lucía Hurtado y Salas, and her two sons, Antonio and Nicolás de Chávez, all appeared in court before Alcalde Antonio Gutiérrez for what appeared to be the final meeting. After some discussion, the two parties both withdrew their complaints and the meeting ended peacefully with doña Lucía Hurtado y Salas and Captain Luis García de Noriega embracing each other. All four persons witnessed the agreement.

Luis García de Noriega's comment that the cow in question had two brands does not suggest malfeasance on Lucía Hurtado y Salas's part. In early 1700s New Mexico, when livestock was sold the existing registered brand, called the *fierro*, was covered with a second registered brand, called the *venta*. Then, the animal was marked with the new owner's brand. The multiple marks on an animal made it difficult to read the most current owner's brand.

Luis García de Noriega may have enjoyed getting doña Lucía Hurtado y Salas's attention by accusing her of stealing one of his cows, but for Alcalde Antonio Gutiérrez it must have been a challenge trying to get these two people to come to terms. Most residents of the Río Abajo area would have recognized them as being influential and prosperous settlers. As mentioned above, doña Lucía Hurtado y Salas was the widow of don Fernando Durán y Chávez II, the son of a pre-revolt encomendero and heir to family land in New Mexico. Having fled New Mexico in 1680 during the Pueblo Revolt, he and his family returned to New Mexico with the Spanish Reconquest and were granted land at Atrisco, part of the old Atrisco estancia. Don Fernando II became an alcalde and captain in the Bernalillo area. Doña Lucía was the sister of Martín Hurtado—a founder of Albuquerque and the city's first alcalde and squadron leader. Based on other documents, such as Case 8, we know that Lucía Hurtado y Salas was outspoken, used to getting her own way, and certain to put up a fight against a slight to her reputation.

Luis García de Noriega, besides being a wealthy landowner, had served as an alcalde of Albuquerque. His family was in New Mexico by at least 1636 (his father was the pre-revolt settler, Alonso García de Noriega II). Luis had a large estate with land called "San Antonio" in Albuquerque; when he died, an inventory of his estate was valued at 6,108 pesos (after all debts were settled). A document relating to an inheritance lawsuit by the daughter of his first wife is found in see Case 31.

TRANSLATION

At this Villa of San Felipe de Albuquerque, on the 8th of March, 1716, there appeared before me, the captain Antonio Gutiérrez[1], alcalde mayor and war captain of this villa, doña Lucía Hurtado [y Salas],[2] don Antonio de Chávez[3], and don Nicolás de Chávez,[4] sons of doña Lucía, along with the Captain Luis García [de Noriega].[5] They have litigation pending and have appeared before certain personages, both secular and ecclesiastical, in order to arrive at peace and quiet agreeable to her. Being that two of these individuals agreed to make peace, doña Lucía and Captain Luis, asked to be pardoned and they embraced each other.

Captain Luis García de Noriega stated that the cause of the whole complaint was that he had been missing a cow of the same color that he had seen at the home of doña Isabel de Chávez,[6] which he consequently claimed belonged to him. But later on he found out that he was wrong and apologized, and was able to restore his reputation, honor and fame before the said lady, Lucía Hurtado, and her sons. Upon Captain Luis García doing this, doña Lucía Hurtado retracted her complaint. Captain Luis García stated that the reason for him making his claim was because the brands that the cow had was similar to the brands on a cow that he had from Bisuayn.[7] But on looking more closely the two brands on the cow's hide were distinct from the ones he had on the cattle he had from Bisuayn.

So that this is valid, the two complainants signed it, along with me and my assisting witnesses, who were Captain Juan González [Bas],[8] the Alférez Pedro López,[9] Antonio de Silva,[10] and Sebastián Canseco.[11]

At the request of Captain Luis García [de Noriega],
Antonio de Silva (rubric)
At the request of doña Lucía Hurtado [y Salas],
Antonio de Ulibarrí[12] (rubric)
Antonio de Chávez (rubric)
At the request of don Nicolás de Chávez,
Antonio de Silva (rubric)

Upon reviewing the agreement decided by the parties, I submitted the proceedings to your honor, the lieutenant general of this kingdom, don Juan Páez Hurtado, and so that it is valid I signed it as presiding judge along with my assisting witnesses on the said day, month and year, etc.

    Assisting witness
    Antonio de Silva (rubric)
    Assisting witness
    Juan González Bas (rubric)
    Before me as presiding judge, which I certify,
    Antonio Gutiérrez (rubric)

TRANSCRIPTION

En esta Villa de San Phelipe de Alburquerque en ocho dias del mes de Marzo de mill setesientos y dies y seis años comparesieron ante mi el Capitan Antonio Gutierrez Alcalde Mayor y Capitan Aguerra de esta dicha Villa y su jurisdizion Dna. Luzia Hurtado y Dn. Antonio de Chavez, Dn. Nicolas de Chavez, hijos de dicha Dña. Luzia, y el Capitan Luis Garcia quienes tienen pleitos pendiente por averse ante puesto personas eclesiasticas y seculares ala composion de buena paz y quietud areglandose a ella unas y otras personas quienes hizieron amistad pidiendose perdon y dandose los brazos.

Dixo el dicho Capitan Luis Garzia que la causa de averle faltado una baca del mismo color del quero que vido en casa de Dna. Ysabel de Chavez tuvo motivo para dexir era su baca por lo que haviendose enganado se desdize y restituya su reputazion onra y fama a dicha Señnora y sus hijos y aviendolo echo assi dicho Capitan Luis Garcia se baxo Dna. Luzia Hurtado dela querella por que dize el dicho Capitan Luis Garcia que el hierro que tenia la baca que le falto era el de Bisuayn y en este quero que vido tiene dos hierros distintos del de Bisuayn.

Para que asi conste lo firmaron con migo los dichos pleiteantes y los testigos de mi asistensia que lo fueron el Capitan Juan Gonzales, el Alferez Pedro Lopes, Antonio de Silva y Sevastian Canseco.

    A ruego del Capitan Luis Garcia
    Antonio de Silva (rubric)
    A ruego de Dna. Luzia Hurtado
    Antonio de Uribarrí (rubric)
    Antonio de Chabes (rubric)
    A ruego de Dn. Nicolas de Chabes
    Antonio de Silva (rubric)

Y por mi vista dicha composision delas partes hago remission a Vuestra Señoria Theniente General deste Reino Dn. Juan Paes Hurtado de dichos autos y para que asi

conste lo firme como Jues Receptor con los testigos de mi asistensia en dicho dia,mes y año, ut supra =
    Testigo de asistenzia
     Antonio de Silva (rubric)
    Testigo de asistenzia
    Juan Gonzales Bas (rubric)
    Ante mi como Jues Receptor de que doy fee
    Antonio Gutierrez (rubric)

Notes

1. Antonio Gutiérrez was the son of Felipe Gutiérrez and Isabel de Salazar, pre-revolt settlers in New Mexico. In 1702, Antonio married Gregoria Góngora; four years later, he became one of the first founders of Albuquerque. In 1716, he was granted lands between the Río Puerco and the Río Grande, in an area called Sitio de Gutiérrez. In 1729, when he was forty-seven years old, he was killed by an Apache arrow. (Chávez, *Origins*: 194; Alexander, *Cottonwoods*: 8; NMGS, *Aquí*: 277.)
2. For information on Lucía Hurtado y Salas, see Case 8.
3. For information on Antonio de Chávez, see Case 8.
4. For information on Nicolás de Chávez, see Case 8.
5. Luis García [de Noriega] married Josefa Xavier y Baca in 1703. They had only one child, Rosalia, who married Salvador Martínez. His second wife was Barbara García Jurado. An ancestor, Alonso García de Noriega I, was in New Mexico by 1636. Luis García [de Noriega] was listed in the military muster at Bernalillo in 1704. Sometime after that, he and his two brothers received the San Antonio land grant near Albuquerque from Governor de la Peñuela. After Luis's death in 1746, his will was contested in several lengthy probate cases (see Case 31). (Kessell, Hendricks, Dodge, and Miller, *Settling of Accounts*: 222; Chávez, *Origins*: 161; NMGS, *Aquí*: 185, 277, 291, 403, 405, 425, 462, 465-66; and SANM I #87, SANM I #178, SANM I 199, all WPA translations.)
6. Isabel de Chávez was a daughter of doña Lucía Hurtado y Salas. For more information on Isabel, see Case 8.
7. Bisuayn (or Bisuain) appears to be the name of the person from whom Luis García [de Noriega] bought cattle. The name is not a common one in New Mexico, but an internet search (on October 5, 2015) shows a José Bisuain living in Chihuahua, Mexico. Regarding the double branding, see Tigges, "Santa Fe Brand Registration": 122.
8. Juan González Bas II was the son of Juan González Bas I and Nicolasa Zaldivar Jorge. Juan returned to New Mexico with his family, settling in Bernalillo and Albuquerque. He was captain of the Albuquerque squadron by 1710, alcalde mayor of Albuquerque in 1712, and served in many administrative positions, including lieutenant governor. His wife was María López del Castillo. He had a son name Juan, with whom he is sometimes confused. (Barrett, *Conquest*: 176; Chávez, *Origins*: 189; Kessell, Hendricks, and Dodge, *Boulders*: 1173n109.)
9. Pedro López is probably the "Pedro López Gallardo" who was a presidio soldier and originally from Querétaro, Mexico. He was the son of Pedro López and Antonia Gallardo. In 1694, he married Sebastiana Martín. (Kessell, Hendricks, and Dodge, *Boulders*: 1161n17; Tigges, "The Santa Fe Presidial Company": 71.)
10. For information on Antonio de Silva, see Case 8.
11. Sebastián Canseco probably came to New Mexico as part of the Juan Páez Hurtado Expedition in 1695. He is listed as a "coyote" and as a native of the mining community of Sombrerete, Zacatecas, Mexico. He married María Gutiérrez (or García) in 1697; the couple was among the first settlers of Santa Cruz, and they were in Santa Fe for the cattle distribution of 1697. This also may be the same person who sold land in Pojoaque in 1703 and was on trial for a robbery in 1697. (Kessell, Hendricks, and Dodge, *Boulders*: 494, 557n10, 559n17, 1148; Colligan, *Hurtado*: 34-35; SANM I #928.)
12. For information on Antonio de Ulibarrí, see SANM II #205.

16

PEDRO MONTES VIGIL ACCUSES ANA MARÍA ROMERO OF GOSSIP, AND FATHER-IN-LAW OF RENEGING ON MARRIAGE PORTION
August 11–18, 1716, Source: SANM II #273

Synopsis and editor's notes: In August 1716, Ana María Romero [Villalpando],[1] perhaps not banished to Albuquerque after all (see Case 14), was once again involved in a complaint before the alcalde ordinario. The case began when Pedro Montes Vigil[2] petitioned the alcalde with a counter-complaint to the one that Ana María allegedly made against him. He said that Ana María, in support of her stepsister, Juana Trujillo[3] (Pedro's wife), had complained to Alcalde Ordinario Juan García de la Riva that Pedro was mistreating Juana. Pedro stated that Ana María had hidden his wife from him, when Juana stayed with Ana María for protection. He added that he did not mistreat his wife, even when she made excuses for not wanting to have sex with him, as Ana María claimed. According to Pedro, all the things Ana María said were lies.

Ana María responded that she only went to the alcalde to complain about Pedro coming to her house and verbally abusing her and her daughter. In addition, she said her stepsister did not stay with her, but rather at the home of Miguel Moran, the jailer, and it was Captain Pedro Luján who took Juana from Moran's to her home. She further stated that she had nothing to do with his wife leaving him, nor with any of his other concerns with Mateo Trujillo, Juana's father and Ana María's stepfather.

At this point, Pedro Montes Vigil backed down from his complaint about Ana María and no more was heard about it. His petition to the alcalde now claimed that Mateo Trujillo, his father-in-law, owed him his "marriage portion"—probably meaning his wife's dowry. Pedro explained that he was to have received three rooms in a house that Mateo Trujillo built, but this had not happened. Mateo Trujillo, who owned several Santa Fe properties, responded by saying that when Pedro Vigil married his daughter, he did agree to give him three rooms. Pedro, however, wanted some land on the south side of the river, to which Mateo Trujillo agreed and gave him a deed for it. But then, after about two years, Pedro sold the land (with the consent of his wife) to General Juan Páez Hurtado. Mateo Trujillo further said that he had several sons and if he gave more to Pedro Montes Vigil, there would be less for them and they would be out on the street with nothing. Disgusted with it all, Mateo Trujillo concluded by stating that Pedro Montes Vigil should stop annoying him with frivolous demands.

The document ended at this point with no further action taken. Documents relating to the rest of the case may have been lost or, more likely, Pedro Montes Vigil withdrew his complaint, sensing that he would not win his case.

That Pedro Montes Vigil said he sold the property with the consent of his wife suggests that this marriage portion was, in fact, his wife's dowry. Under Spanish law the dowry belonged to the wife and while the husband could manage it, the property could only be sold with the wife's approval.

Mateo Trujillo's statement that he gave Pedro Montes Vigil three rooms in a house reflects the concept of land ownership in eighteenth-century New Mexico. Typically, land with or without structures could be bought, sold, or gifted as parcels as we do now. In addition, the ownership of portions of houses could also be transferred without the adjacent land. In some ways this is similar to present-day condominium arrangements in which a series of attached housing units can be separately sold. In 1700s New Mexico, and probably elsewhere in New Spain, the owner could divide a house into portions and then sell or gift only a single piece.

This case is one of the few in which we hear mention of an early eighteenth-century Spanish woman working outside the home. In her testimony to the alcalde, Ana María says that she was working at the house of Salvador de Montoya when Pedro Vigil went to her house with his complaint. She may have been a cook or a housekeeper.

In handling this case, assigned to him by alcalde Juan García de la Riva, Captain Francisco Lorenzo de Casados conscientiously follows legal procedures. He heard testimony from both sides, managed to sidestep the conflicting claims of Ana María Romero [Villalpando] and Pedro Montes Vigil, and he made certain that each side had a copy of the testimony and had three days in which to make a response. He did not have witnesses ratify or affirm the testimony, but maybe he felt it was not necessary.

TRANSLATION

1716

Alcalde Ordinario

[Petition by Juan García de la Riva]

The captain Juan García de la Riva[4] petitions the captain Lorenzo de Casados,[5] alcalde ordinario, to continue with these proceedings, being that he is about leave on a trip to Moqui and thus cannot proceed with them. So that this is valid, I rubricated it at this villa on the 11th of August, 1716.

rubric of [Juan] García de la Riva

I, Pedro Vigil, resident of this kingdom appear before your majesty in my best possible form that I am allowed according to my legal right and say that being that it has come to my attention that Ana María, the wife of Villalpando,[6] has filed a complaint against me. The complaint says that I went to her home and maltreated my wife

[Juana Trujillo] and scolded her over the fact that she always was excusing herself when I desired to have sex with her. This is not as your majesty has been informed. In order to prove this, your majesty should make her appear before him and accordingly should take her statement concerning this matter, and if I am wrong he will punish me accordingly. If there is no proof of what she states, she should be punished, as the law dictates, for making accusations against me. As far as I am concerned all of the above is false and is the reason that I am making the complaint against Ana María as well as for having hidden my wife. Because of all of this, I petition of your majesty and ask that he do as I have asked which is for the sake of justice. I swear to God, Our Lord and to the sign of the Holy Cross that my petition is not done for malice but for what is necessary, etc.

 Pedro Vigil (rubric)

At the Villa of Santa Fe on the 11th of August, 1716, I, Captain Francisco Lorenzo de Casados, the alcalde ordinario, have seen the request from Captain Juan García de la Riva [that I review this case] because he is occupied preparing for the journey that he is about to partake on to the province of Moqui[7] with the governor and captain general of this kingdom of New Mexico. I agree to do it, and take complaint as it was presented by the petitioner. I gave a copy of the entire thing to Ana María who is to respond to it according to the satisfaction of Pedro Vigil. So that it is valid I signed it acting as Presiding Judge along with my assisting witnesses on the said day, month and year.

 Francisco Lorenzo de Casados (rubric)
 Assisting Witness
 Juan Manuel de Chirinos[8] (rubric)
 Assisting Witness
 Joseph Manuel Giltoméy[9] (rubric)

Alcalde Ordinario

[Statement of Ana María Romero Villalpando]

I, Ana María Romero, resident of this Villa of Santa Fe appear before your majesty in the best possible form that I have and which I am allowed. In response to the order of your majesty and to the petition that Pedro Vigil, my brother-in-law, presented before the captain Juan García [de la Riva], alcalde ordinario of this villa, and based on what was presented in it by Pedro Vigil, I file a complaint against him. I do not deny that I went to see the royal justice in order to see what it was that Pedro Vigil is claiming against me, and I am ready to see to it that he does not blame me for anything. I am ready to see to it that he, Pedro Vigil, does not accuse me of any wrongdoing, and am willing to comply with whatever is demanded of me. If he owes anything to my stepfather, Mateo Trujillo,[10] he can comply with whatever it is without getting me involved.

While I was working at the home of the *regidor* Salvador de Montoya,[11] Pedro Vigil went to my home and abused me and my daughter in what he said and did. This is the reason that I went to see the justice so that the alcalde can summon Pedro Vigil so that he does not get involved with me. As for what he says in his written complaint, I say that he is not right in saying that I hid his wife. Pedro Luján[12] can say when he and Miguel Moran[13] returned the wife of Pedro Vigil, being that Captain Pedro Luján brought her back from the road that goes to [Santa Cruz de] La Cañada where she had stayed at the home of Miguel Moran. She should be brought forth so that she can state if I said anything to her about leaving or hiding from her husband.

For all of this I ask and petition of your majesty to be well pleased to do as I have requested, from which I shall be well served and receive mercy with justice and so that Pedro Vigil will leave me alone and not cause me any harm. I swear in due form and in what is necessary, etc.

Ana María Romero (rubric)

[Copy given to Pedro Vigil]

At the Villa of Santa Fe, New Mexico, on the 12th of August, 1716, before me, Captain Francisco Lorenzo de Casados, alcalde ordinario of this villa, the petition was presented by the herein stated within it. Being seen by me, I took as it was presented and ordered Ana María Romero bring forth the witnesses which she offers and that a copy be given to Pedro Vigil. I thus approved it and signed it along with my assisting witnesses.

Francisco Lorenzo de Casados (rubric)
Witness
Juan Manuel Chirinos (rubric)
Witness
Joseph Manuel Giltoméy (rubric)

[Petition of PedroVigil]

Villa of Santa Fe, August 11, 1716

I, Pedro Vigil, resident of this kingdom appear before your majesty in the best form that my legal right allows me. I say that when I was married to Juana Trujillo, daughter of Mateo Trujillo, he promised to give me part of the house that he has constructed in this villa which part was three rooms,[14] and this has not yet been done. I have been demanding him to do this for quite a while, but it not being done, I petitioned your majesty to demand that this be done. I admit that I was given a piece of land which I sold to the general Juan Páez Hurtado.[15] My father-in-law states that he has satisfied his commitment, saying that instead of giving me a part of the house he gave me the lands. Because of this I petition your majesty that you do as I ask and that I receive for the goodness, mercy and justice that which I seek and swear that this is not done in malice, but for what is necessary, etc.

 Pedro Vigil (rubric)

[Petition received]
 At this Villa of Santa Fe, a province of New Mexico, on the 11th day of the month of August, before me, Captain Francisco Lorenzo de Casados, alcalde ordinario of this villa, the above petition was presented to me by the above stated. Having been seen by me, I took it as it was presented. I order that as soon as Mateo Trujillo returns to this villa he be given a copy of it and upon him receiving it, he is to respond to it within the period of three days. I thus approved, ordered and signed it, acting as presiding judge along with my assisting witnesses due to the lack of a public or royal scribe, there not being one in this kingdom, on the said day, month and year.

 Francisco Lorenzo de Casados (rubric)
 Assisting witness
 Antonio Durán de Armijo (rubric)
 Assisting witness
 Joseph Manuel Giltoméy (rubric)

Alcalde Ordinario

[Statement of Mateo Trujillo]
 I, Mateo Trujillo, a resident of this Kingdom and a resident of the Villa of Santa Fe, appear before your majesty in my best possible form that my legal right allows me. I say that with the veneration that I owe, I am responding to the complaint that Pedro Vigil, my son-in-law, has filed against me. He says that when he married my daughter, Juana Trujillo, I had agreed to give to him three rooms within the house that I have in this villa. I do not deny that this was so, but within a few days he asked me if I could possibly give him a piece of land that is outside of this villa so that he could build his home and live there without bothering anyone. I then asked him if he would be content with that. He told me that he would.
 Then, Pedro Vigil and I went to the site that I had outside of this villa on the other side of the river, and I showed him what I had there. I then gave to him not only enough land to build a house, but also enough for a garden and to plant other things. He was satisfied with that. There not having been made any kind of a document for the three rooms, we agreed that he would take the piece of land instead of the three rooms, and I gave him a deed for the land. Then about two years hence, with the consent of his wife, he sold the piece of land to the general don Juan Páez Hurtado, being that I had given it to him.
 Now, he wants to have rights to the house and be an heir for the rest of his life.

During the final days of my life, there is no way that I will leave my sons without any inheritance, not having anything left that they can share in equal parts because Pedro Vigil took more then what he should have and rightfully belongs to me. He sold the piece of land, and now he wants to leave my sons out in the street without anything.

Therefore, I ask and implore that your Majesty be willing to admit this, my petition, and order my son-in-law, Pedro Vigil, not to be annoying me with frivolous demands nor to be prejudicial toward me in whatever he claims, being that he has no right whatsoever to do so. I gave to him what I rightfully owed him and he sold it. For all of this I ask for justice and swear in due form that this is not done in malice, but for what is necessary, etc.

 Mateo Trujillo (rubric)

[Petition presented to Pedro Vigil]

 At the Villa of Santa Fe, New Mexico, on the 18th of August, 1716, before me, Captain Francisco Lorenzo de Casados, alcalde ordinario, this petition was taken with the herein contained within it. Having been seen by me, I took it as it was presented and ordered Pedro Vigil to respond to it within the time requested and to give his side of what has been presented. I thus approved, ordered and signed it along with my assisting witnesses, on the said day.

 Francisco Lorenzo de Casados (rubric)
 Assisting witness
 Joseph Manuel Giltoméy (rubric)

[*Editor's note:* The document ends without further action.]

TRANSCRIPTION

1716

[*Note in margin*]
El Capitan Juan Garcia dela Rivas suplica
al Capitan Francisco Lorenzo de Casados, Alcalde
Ordinario siga estas deligencias que yo coro el biaxe
prosimo a Moqui no puedo y para que conste lo rubrique
en esta Villa en onze de Agosto de mill setezientos y dies
y seis años.
[rubric of Garcia de la Rivas]

Señor Alcalde Ordinario

Pedro Vijil vesino de este Reino ante Vuestra Magestad paresco en la mayor forma que me conste de el derecho y digo que haviendo tenido notorio de que ante Vuestra Magestad se a querellado Ana Maria la muger de Villalpando de que fui a su casa y maltrate a mi muger y la apremie sobre que se escusava a pedir lo que yo demando no siendo como Vuestra Majestad es ynformado pues para prueba de esto se a de servir hazer conparesca mi muger y con apremio sele reziva juramento de esta ympostura quedando me prueba me castigara con la pena correspondiente y de no aver prueba se castigara que contra mi a delatado como le corresponde con la pena del talion pues conosco ser siniestro todo lo depuesto por que me querello de la dicha Ana Maria asi por esto como por haver escondido a mi muger.

Por todo lo qual a Vuestra Magestad pido y suplico se sirva hazer como llevo pedido que es de justizia y juro a Dios Nuestro Señor y la Señal de la Santa Cruz este escrito no ser de malisia y en lo nesesario, ut supra =

Pedro Vijil (rubric)

En la Villa de Santa Fee en onze dias del mes de Agosto de mill setecientos y diez y seis años yo el Capitan Francisco Lorenzo de Casados, Alcalde Ordinario aviendo visto la suplica que el Capitan Juan Garsia dela Rivas ase desta petision por que se alla ocupado en aviante para la jornada que esta para executar ala Provinsia de Moqui con el Señor Governador y Capitan General deste Reino dela Nueva Mexico la admito y doy por presentada por el suplicante y por mi vista le doy traslado de ella a Ana Maria quien responda y de entera satisfasion ala parte de Pedro Vijil en lo que demanda y para que conste lo firme autuando ante mi como Jues Receptor con los ynfraescriptos testigos de mi asistenzia en dicho dia, mes y año =

Francisco Lorenzo de Casados (rubric)
Testigo de asistenzia
Juan Manuel Chirinos (rubric)
Testigo de asistenzia
Joseph Manuel Gilthomey (rubric)

Señor Alcalde Ordinario

Ana Maria Romero vezina dela Villa de Santa Fee paresco ante Vuestra Magestad en la major forma que aya lugar y al mio combenga y digo respondiendo al mandato de Vuestra Magestad y ala petision que Pedro Vijil mi cunado hermano presento ante el Capitan Juan Garsia, Alcalde Ordinario desta dicha Villa y por lo expresado en ella hize remission y cometio a Vuestra Magestad en que dize Pedro de Vijil yo me querello del extrajudicialmente siendo asi que no niego que fui a ver ala Real Justisia para que consubiessen de que me perjudicase dicho Pedro Vijil pues yo estoy prebenido no me meta en cossa y executando lo que se me tiene mandado no es dar querella sino prebenir el que se consubiesse dicho Pedro Vijil quien si tiene prestos con mi padre Mateo Truxillo puede aserla sin meterme a mi en nada

 Pues estando yo en cassa del Rexidor Salvador de Montoya travajando dicho Pedro Vijil fue ami cassa y nos maltrato de palabra y obra ami hija por lo que me presiso ver ala justicia para que connebiesen a dicho Pedro Vijil y no se metiesse con migo y en quanto alo que el suso dicho tiene dicho en su escripto digo que no propone bien en dezir yo le oculto a su muger pues puede dezir Pedro Lujan desde donde volvio a su muger del dicho Pedro Vijil y Miguel Moran que por ver dela dicha su muger se que estubo con dicho Miguel Moran y que la revolvio del camino dela Cañada dicho Capitan Pedro Lujan y que sea la suso dicha llamada para que declare si yo le e dicho nada de que se oculte o esconda del dicho su marido.

 Por todo lo qual a Vuestra Majestad pido y suplico sea muy servido de aser como llevo representado de que reziviere bien y merzed con justizia y que dicho Pedro Vijil me dexe y no me ande hasiendo perjuicio, juro en forma y en lo nesesario, ut supra =

 Ana Maria Romero (rubric)

     ~

 En la Villa de Santa Fee de la Nueba Mexico en doze dias del mes de Agosto de mill setecientos y diez y seis años ante mi el Capitan Francisco Lorenzo de Casados, Alcalde Ordinario de esta dicha Villa se presento esta petision por la contenida en ella = Y por mi vista la hube por presentada y mando a dicha Ana Maria Romero traiga los testigos que ofrese y sele de traslado de ella a Pedro Vijil asi lo probey y firme con los ynfraescriptos testigos de mi asistenzia =

 Francisco Lorenzo de Casados (rubric)
 Testigo
 Juan Manuel Chirinos (rubric)
 Joseph Manuel Gilthomey (rubric)

     ~

Petisiones de Pedro Vijil, Mateo Truxillo y Ana Maria Romero
Villa de Santa Fee y Agosto 11 de 1716 años

 Pedro Vijil vezino de este Reino paresco ante Vuestra Magestad en la mejor forma que el derecho me conzede y digo que haviendo casado con Juana Truxillo hija de mi Señor Matheo Truxillo me dio dela casa que tiene en esta Villa fabricada tres quartos y no haviendo havido occasion para aclarar esto a muchos dias que selo ando requiriendo paresca ser de mandarlo y no aviendolo compuesto me presisa la fuerza ahazerlo para que Vuestra Magestad le mande comparezca a dar cumplimiento adbirtiendo que unicamente he rezevido un pedazo de tierra que vendi al General Juan Paez y jusgo que con el quiere haver dado me satisfazion dicho mi suegro de dicha casa que esta se repartara como dichas tierras y me mandara dar satisfazion de ymporte.

Por tanto a Vuestra Magestad pido y suplico haga como llevo pedido en que reziviere bien, merzed y justizia, esto pido a Vuestra Magestad y juro este escrito en toda forma no ser de malicia y en lo nesesario, ut supra.

Pedro Vijil (rubric)

En la Villa de Santa Fee, Provincias dela Nueva Mexico en onze dias del mes de Agosto ante mi el Capitan Francisco Lorenso de Casados, Alcalde Ordinario de ella se presento esta petizion por el contenido en ella y vista por mi dicho Alcalde Ordinario la admiti y hube por presentada y mando que luego que venga a esta Villa Mateo Truxillo sele de traslado de ella y aviendola resevido desde dia responda en el termino de tres dias, asi lo probey, mande y firme actuando ante mi como Jues Receptor con los ynfraescriptos testigos de mi asistenzia a falta de Escribano Pueblco ni Real que no lo ay en este Reyno = En dicho dia, mes y año =

Francisco Lorenzo de Casados (rubric)
Testigo de asistenzia
Antonio Duran de Armijo (rubric)
Testigo de asistenzia
Joseph Manuel Gilthomey (rubric)

Alcalde ordinario

Mateo Truxillo vezino deste Reino y residente en esta Villa de Santa Fee paresco ante Vuestra Magestad en la mejor forma que aya lugar en derecho y al mio conbenga y digo con la veneracion que devo respondiendo ala demanda que Pedro Vijil mi yerno me pone de que al tiempo y quando se caso con mi hija Juana Truxillo le avia senalado en la cassa que tengo en esta dicha Villa tres cuartos no lo niego que fue asi pero de alli a pocos dias me dixese que si yo tenia gusto de que le diese fuera de esta dicha Villa un pedaso d tierra para azer en el cassa y vivir con mas desembaraso fuera del concurso alo que le pregunte que si in eso se contentava; me dixo que si y luego fuimos.

El dicho Pedro Vijil y yo al sitio que yo tenia fuera desta dicha Villa ala otra vanda del Rio y le ensene lo que alli tenia y le di no tan solamente para que fabricase cassa sino para que hiziesse guerta y sembrase y aviendose contentado con ella y no haviendose hecho escripto por los dichos tres quartos en esa conformidad me largo los dichos tres quartos por dicho pedaso de tierra de que le entregue escriptura y con ella vendio dicho pedaso de tierra al Señor Theniente General Dn. Juan Paes Hurtado amas de dos años poco mas o menos que como suyo que selo avia dado a su muger con su consentimiento pudo aserlo.

Ora quiere tener derecho a la casa y eredarme en vida no es rason ni cabe que yo dexe a otros hijos que tengo sin que tengan en que albergarse que el fin de mis dias puede pretender derecho y este viniendo a monton para que se partan por yguales partes y no querer dicho Pedro Vijil llevarse mas partes delo que es mio y quedar mejorado aviendo vendido el pedaso de tierras y que se queden los dichos mis hijos en la calle por todo lo qual a Vuestra Majestad pido y suplico sea muy servido de admitir esta mi petision y mandar a dicho Pedro Vijil mi yerno no ande ynquietandome con demandas fribolas ni me aga perjuicio pues en lo que pretende no tiene derecho ninguno pues le senale lo que le podia perteneser y lo vendio, pido justisia y juro en forma no ser de malicia y en lo nesesario, ut supra.

 Mateo Truxillo (rubric)

 En la Villa de Santa Fee dela Nueba Mexico en dies y ocho dias del mes de Agosto de mill setecientos y dies y seis años ante mi el Capitan Francisco Lorenzo de Casados, Alcalde Ordinario de ella se presento esta peticion por el contenido en ella que vista por mi la hube por presentada y mando a Pedro Vijil reponda en el termino presentario y de la ynformacion plena de lo que dize asi lo probey, mande y firme con los testigos ynfraescriptos de mi asistenzia en dicho dia.

 Francisco Lorenzo de Casados (rubric)
 Testigo de asistenzia
 Joseph Manuel Gilthomey (rubric)

Notes

1. For further information on Ana María Romero [Villalpando], see Case 14.
2. Pedro Montes Vigil was born in Zacatecas, Mexico, sometime between 1683 and 1687, to Francisco Montes Vigil and María Jiménez de Ancizo. Pedro came to New Mexico in 1695, and by 1710 he was employed in the reconstruction of San Miguel Chapel in Santa Fe. At that time, he was also a collector of alms (along with Bernardino Sena). By 1724 he owned property in Santa Fe and by 1732 in Embudo. (Chávez, *Origins*: 311-12; Kessell, Hendricks, and Dodge, *Boulders*: 508, 561n22; Kubler, *San Miguel*: 225-6; SANM I #1034; SANM I #1038.)
3. Juana Trujillo was the daughter of Mateo Trujillo and María de Tapia. María de Tapia was also the mother of Ana María Romero [Villalpando]. (Kessell, Hendricks, and Dodge, *Boulders*: 508, 561n22.)
4. For more information on Juan García de la Riva, see Case 9.
5. For more information on Francisco Lorenzo de Casados, see Case 9.
6. For information on Juan de Villalpando, see Case 10.
7. In 1716, Governor Martínez, accompanied by Franciscan friars, organized a campaign to subdue the Moquis (or the Hopi as we know them today). The Moquis, as they had earlier, rejected the efforts of the Spanish and the friars. (Norris, *Eighty*: 84.)
8. For information on Juan Manuel de Chirinos, see Case 9.
9. For information on Joseph Manuel Giltoméy, see Case 5.
10. Mateo Trujillo was born in New Mexico about 1650. His wife, María de Tapia, was the widow of Alonso Romero. Mateo Trujillo was part of the El Paso muster of 1693; the following year, he received a land grant near Santa Clara Pueblo. He was thought to have been killed in the Pueblo Revolt of 1696, but later he arrived in Santa Fe alive. In 1703 and 1722, he bought property in Santa Fe. (Kessell, Hendricks, and Dodge, *Royal Crown*: 45, 83n43; Kessell, Hendricks, and Dodge, *Boulders*: 561n21-22; Kessell, Hendricks, Dodge, and Miller, *Disturbances*: 189 n141; Chávez, *Origins*: 298, 397.)
11. Salvador de Montoya was a *regidor* (councilman) in Santa Fe. (See Case 10.)
12. Born in New Mexico about 1669, Pedro Luján was the son of Captain Juan Luis Luján and Isabel López. In 1691, in El Paso, he married Francisca Martín de Salazar, the daughter of Captain Pedro Martín and Juana

de Argüello. Pedro Luján returned to New Mexico as a soldier with General Vargas. In 1715, he was listed as campaign captain in an expedition against the Apaches. In a 1718 council of war, Pedro is referred to as a captain "who has served his majesty in this kingdom for forty years." (Chávez, *Origins*: 212, 369-70; Thomas, *Coronado*: 90-103; Chávez, *Roots*: 1011.)
13. For information on Miguel Moran, see Case 5.
14. This was probably her dowry or "marriage portion."
15. For information on Juan Páez Hurtado, see Case 3.

17

FATHER DEMANDS MARRIAGE OF PRESIDIO SOLDIER TO SEDUCED PREGNANT DAUGHTER
August 11, 1716–November 6, 1716, Source: SANM II #274

Synopsis and editor's notes: Margarita Brito, with a young child and no husband, may not have had the nerve (or standing) to approach the governor with a complaint about seduction and a breach of promise for marriage by Antonio de Abeytia. However, her father, Juan de León Brito, did. In August 1716, Juan de León Brito, a long time resident of Santa Fe, approached Governor Felix Martínez claiming that Antonio de Abeytia promised marriage to his daughter, made her pregnant, and then refused to marry her. Brito asked the governor to order Abeytia to appear before him so that the case could be heard. Martínez then imprisoned Abeytia in the presidio guardhouse and asked him to choose a *procurador* (legal representative), as was allowed for soldiers and other New Mexico residents. Abeytia chose Antonio Durán de Armijo who was not an *abogado* (trained attorney) but rather a presidio "barber" (or medic) with some knowledge of the law. Abeytia then made a formal request that the governor give Durán de Armijo power of attorney to represent him. The request is full of legal words and phrases that appear to have been borrowed from a version of *Protocolos de Instrumentos Publicos*, or a similar guide used for writing legal documents in the eighteenth century.

Durán de Armijo probably understood that his job was to clear Abeytia of any wrongdoing and get him out of the guardhouse. In order to do so, Durán de Armijo claimed that it could not be shown that Antonio de Abeytia was the father of Margarita Brito's child. Instead, he suggested that the child's father was Cristóbal Lucero de Godoy, a soldier from El Paso presidio, who was in Santa Fe at the relevant time and was known to have had sexual relations with Margarita Brito by her own admission. Durán de Armijo added that Margarita was known as a *"mujer mundane"*—in other words, she was "well-known" among the men in Santa Fe. Durán de Armijo pointed out that just because Antonio de Abeytia had sex with Margarita it did not mean that he was the father of her child; and, besides, Abeytia had already asked the daughter of Nicolás Ortiz to marry him (though in the end she did not). Therefore, Durán de Armijo argued, Abeytia did not have to keep the promise of marriage even though he admitted to having made it. Durán de Armijo finished his defense by announcing that he was going to file a civil and criminal complaint against Juan de León Brito and Margarita Brito for making a false claim.

Juan de León Brito responded by stating that Durán de Armijo was lying and added that just because Abeytia had asked someone else to marry him did not mean that he did not make Margarita pregnant. Brito then asked Governor Martínez to call more witnesses, including his daughter. Margarita appeared and swore "by God as her witness" that Abeytia was the father of her child. She further explained that she had told him so during the previous December, when she heard that Abeytia had proposed marriage to the daughter of Nicolás Ortiz. Testimony was heard from three presidio soldiers, one of whom stated that Abeytia told him he had seduced Margarita Brito and promised to marry her but was not sure he would go through with it.

Unfortunately, the document ends with the soldiers's testimonies. Most likely, some financial agreement was reached between the parties outside of court. Antonio de Abeytia never did wed Margarita as promised; he ended up marrying Rosalia Luján. To date, no further information has been discovered about Margarita Brito or her child.

This seduction and breach of promise case illustrates the importance given in early eighteenth-century New Mexico to promises of marriage or betrothal. Studies of the period indicate that the *"palabra de casamiente"* (a promise to marry) in many western European countries was considered tantamount to marriage and violation of it was grounds for a lawsuit. This was especially the case when the promise was accompanied by a written document, a gift, and/or sexual contact. This situation existed despite the fact that in the mid-1500s the Council of Trent confirmed that a marriage was legal only when it was presided over by a priest.

A common solution to a breach of promise case, especially when pregnancy was involved, was marriage. In Margarita Brito's case, however, it could not be proven that Abeytia was the father of her child or that he was her only lover, and, therefore, the judge could not order Abeytia to marry her. Another remedy for a breach of promise was a monetary fine that could be used by the woman as a dowry with which to attract a husband. It is not known if this happened in Margarita Brito's case.

For another breach of promise situation, see Case 28 in this book. In that instance, it was a man who made the breach of promise complaint. His request to marry had been accepted, gifts were given, and he said there had been a sexual union, but the bride decided to become betrothed to someone else. The procurador, Isidro Sánchez, presented an over-the-top defense for his client but to no effect.

The association of Margarita Brito with presidio soldiers of Santa Fe and El Paso is partly explained by a 1720 document (see Case 20). In the latter case, witnesses mentioned that soldiers and citizens spent time gambling at Juan de León Brito's house, which was located near the Santa Fe Plaza. Isidro Sánchez was also involved in this case. (See Map 3)

In regard to legal matters, the proceedings for the Brito case were unusually formal. This may have been because the complaint was made against a presidio soldier and Governor Martínez presided. More witnesses were called than was typical; each procedure, including transmittal of documents and actions of the governor's staff, were noted; and responses were required within three days. In addition, all testimony was affirmed and ratified and copies of all the testimony were sent to the parties involved. However, there was no final determination or sentencing in the case, probably because it was settled out of court with possible compensation for Margarita Brito or her father.

TRANSLATION

1716

Complaint by Juan de León Brito due to his daughter being deflowered

Governor and Captain General

[Complaint by Juan de León Brito]

I, Juan de León Brito,[1] resident of this Villa of Santa Fe, appear before your honor in my best and proper form according to my legal right and say that I am filing a complaint against Antonio de Abeytia,[2] soldier of this royal castle in as much as he has acted as a scoundrel by taking the virginity of one of my daughters by telling her that he would marry her. As a result, my daughter said that she became pregnant, and upon a request from Abeytia my wife made certain that she was indeed pregnant which as it turned out, she was. As such, having given his promise, he owes it to his honor[3] to marry her.

Upon my coming here from [Santa Cruz de la] Cañada, my wife informed me of what had happened. As I am the father to the girl I took it upon myself to see Antonio de Abeytia. He denied owing her marriage saying to me that he owes her nothing. This is even though he told Domingo Valdéz[4] that he had promised to marry her according to his promise. Because of all of this, I ask that justice prevail, saying that I am a poor man, and you, your honor, are as father of this whole kingdom. Because your honor is God fearing,[5] God who is the consul that guides me, I ask that Antonio de Abeytia appear before your honor so that he can state and declare that which he told my wife. Because of all of this, I ask and petition of your honor that you be pleased to do me justice, it being that Antonio de Abeytia does not want to marry my daughter, and it being left up to you to do something so that he does not get away with the trick that he has done, and so that he is obliged to do something reasonable. I swear to God, Our Lord, that this my petition is not done in malice, but for the sake of justice, which is what I ask of your honor, and for what is necessary, etc.

Juan de León Brito (rubric)

[Imprisonment of Antonio de Abeytia]

At this Villa of Santa Fe on the 11th day of August, 1716, before me don Felix Martínez,[6] captain for life of this royal presidio, governor and captain general of this kingdom and provinces of New Mexico and castellan of his forces for his majesty, I took this petition as it was presented. Upon my reviewing it according to every legal right, I ordered the sergeant of the company of this presidial castle to place Antonio de Abeytia, a soldier in his company, in prison within the royal guardhouse. He is to name a legal representative to defend him. This legal representative is to be given a copy of this document, and respond to it within the period of three days. I thus approve, order and sign this along with my secretary of government and war, on the said day.

Before me,
Miguel Tenorio de Alba[7] (rubric)
Secretary of Government and War

[Power of attorney for legal representative]

At this Villa of Santa Fe, headquarters of this kingdom and provinces of New Mexico, on the 12th of August, 1716, before me, Captain Francisco Lorenzo de Casados,[8] alcalde ordinario of this villa, acting as presiding judge, along with my assisting witnesses being that there is no public scribe anywhere in this kingdom nor for many leagues, there appeared before me Antonio de Abeytia, soldier in this presidial castle of this Villa of Santa Fe.

In the presence of the witnesses, Sergeant Juan de la Mora Piñeda,[9] Manuel Tenorio [de Alba],[10] and the corporal of the squadron, Juan Luján,[11] all being present before Antonio de Abeytia, whom they all knew, they stated that he gave all of his power of attorney[12] as is required and needed, to the sergeant of militia, Antonio Durán de Armijo.[13] This is so that in his name and as a legal representative Antonio Durán de Armijo will defend him against the written complaint issued against him by Juan de León Brito, resident of this villa. He will defend Abeytia before the governor and captain general of this kingdom, who ordered him to be held prisoner in the royal guardhouse.

Because the proceedings for his defense have not been prepared, his being a prisoner, he gives a special authority to Sergeant Antonio Durán de Armijo to defend him in whatever is necessary in all civil and criminal proceedings that are at hand or that may arise in the future with anyone, and as such he is to be defended. In order for him to do this and argue and defend all of the accusations made against Abeytia, Durán de Armijo is given the authority to appear for him for anything. [This is so that he may appear before the governor and captain general of this realm and before all His Majesty's royal justices, hearing and tribunals, wherein he may lawfully make petitions, requsitions, protests, citations, pleadings, requests, objections, and present documents, witnesses, informations and other papers and notes which may be necessary; so that he request and receive documents from whomever they may belong to and from the opposing party; so that he receive and acknowledge oaths taken, and so that in the ecclesiastical tribunal he may prepare and submit unlimited disclosures that may be read and demanded and to whomever it may be agreeable; so that he may take testimony regarding that which may be found to be in his favor, object to judges, scribes, and other administrative officials, and swear on oath these objections; and so that he may follow or desist from them as he so wishes; so that he may hear interlocutory and definitive autos and judgements and may consent to those favorable and object to those which are adverse; and so that he may appeal and follow them as is required in all instances until their final determination and sentencing.

For all of this and anything else which may be pertinent, I, Antonio de Abeytia, give and authorize this power freely, for the general administration and faculty to arrive at justice, swearing and holding on to, and revoking the titles and naming others to replace them anew, all of this which I may remove according to my right.][14] Thus I authorize and sign this along with the alcalde ordinario and the assisting witnesses as mentioned above and on the present common paper because the sealed type is not available in these parts.

    Francisco Lorenzo de Casados
    Antonio de Abeytia
    Assisting witness
    Joseph Manuel Giltoméy[15]
    Assisting witness
    Juan Manuel de Chirinos[16]

[Copy of original testimony]

The above [language] agrees with the original from which I, Captain Francisco Lorenzo de Casados, alcalde ordinario of this Villa of Santa Fe, was ordered to make a copy to the letter as requested by Antonio de Abeytia in order to hand over a literal copy of this testimony to Sergeant Antonio Durán de Armijo. This was done properly and true and corresponds with its original which is held in the palace archives under my charge. Those witnesses who saw that this was done correctly were: Sergeant Juan de la Mora Piñeda, the corporal of the squadron, Juan Luján, and Manuel Tenorio [de Alba]. So that it is valid it was signed before me as presiding judge with my assisting witnesses, being that there is no public or royal scribe in this kingdom.

Done at this Villa of Santa Fe on the 12th of August, 1716, on two folios of common paper because the sealed paper is not available in this Kingdom.

In testimony of the truth I sign and rubricate this as I usually do.

    Francisco Lorenzo de Casados (rubric)
    Assisting witness
    Joseph Manuel Giltoméy (rubric)
    Assisting witness
    Juan Manuel Chirinos (rubric)

Governor and Captain General

[Request for legal representative]

    I, the sergeant of the militia, Antonio Durán [de Armijo], appear before your honor in the best manner that my legal right allows me and say that I have been named to defend Antonio de Abyetia, soldier of this royal presidio[17] of Nuestra Señora de Los Remedios y La Exaltacion de la Santa Cruz. Abyetia is found as a prisoner in the royal guardhouse at the order of your honor because of a complaint by Juan de León Brito. I have been given all of the necessary authority [for a legal representative] that I may need, for which reason I petition and ask your honor with all the due veneration that is owed and can be proven. I swear on behalf of this party that this request is not done in malice, but for what is necessary. The costs are being protested.

    Antonio Durán de Armijo (rubric)

Presentation

    At this Villa of Santa Fe on the 11th day of the month of August, 1716, before me, Felix Martínez, captain for life as I am for this royal presidio, governor and captain general of this kingdom and province of New Mexico and castellan of his forces, this document having been reviewed by me, I took it as it was presented according to their legal rights. As such I thus admit it for use and for the purpose of its use by the defense. So that it is valid I signed it along with my secretary of government and war, on the said day.

    Felix Martínez (rubric)
    Miguel Tenorio de Alba (rubric)
    Secretary of Government and War

Governor and Captain General

    I, the Sergeant of militia, Antonio Durán de Armijo, on behalf of Antonio de Abeytia, soldier of this royal presidio of Nuestra Señora de Los Remedios y La Exaltacion de la Santa Cruz, appear before your honor in my best and proper form that I am granted according to my legal right. I say that my party finds himself a prisoner within the royal guardhouse at the order of your honor because of a complaint filed by Juan de León Brito, who has spoken badly about him saying that he deflowered his daughter [Margarita]. He, Abeytia, denies that he did it, saying that the one who deflowered her was Cristóbal Lucero [de Godoy],[18] a soldier of the presidio of El Paso.

    He states that a daughter, Petrona Paula [Lucero][19] of Cristóbal Lucero, says that once while working at the home of Juan de León Brito, the daughter of Brito told her how [Petrona's] father had done that to her, mistreating her. On a second trip to Santa Fe, Lucero caught her, Margarita, with Juan Telles,[20] also a soldier with the presidio of El Paso. Speaking with all of the due respect that is owed to your honor, Telles said that Lucero hit her on her buttocks. He, Lucero, then told her, Margarita, in front of the soldier Ramón de Medina,[21] Agustín Luján,[22] a resident of this Villa of Santa Fe, and a daughter of Cristóbal Lucero, Petrona Paula, that regarding Margarita's state of pregnancy, which she says she had, he, Lucero, could not be totally convinced that it was his as others have been with her, as is publicly known. This is according to what has been told to my party Abeytia, and which needs to be confirmed.

Also, in regard to her saying that my party gave her his promise to marry her, how can it be so as it is only according to what her mother says, being as he, Abeytia, had already asked another woman to marry him. Also, my party says that he has heard it said that she is a well-known[23] woman, and this was told to the mother and she was not ignorant of it. How can Margarita say she is a person in love, which is something that she told my party and which could be true, when he answered her mother saying that he did not owe her daughter his honor [because she could be pregnant by someone else].[24]

For this reason, I am filing a civil and criminal complaint against Juan de León and his daughter so that your honor as judge can examine separately the father and daughter who made false claims against Abeytia, take as compensation the goods that they possess, so that they are personally punished. This is so they do not bring up testimony for which there is no sure evidence. If my party owes such a thing, he is willing to pay for it as a law-abiding person but this does not apply if my party is not the wrongdoer in all this.

For all of this I ask and petition of your honor with all of the veneration owed [to him], that he be pleased to administer justice to me, and that he will order that the witnesses be examined. Until proof is given, I object to arguing any further, and I swear on the behalf of my party that I ask only for that which is most appropriate according to justice and in what is necessary, etc.

Antonio Durán de Armijo (rubric)

Presentation

At the Villa of Santa Fe on the 12th of August, 1716, before me don Felix Martínez, being that I am captain for life of this royal presidio, governor and captain general of this kingdom and provinces of New Mexico and castellan of his forces for his majesty, being presented by the above stated and reviewed by me, I accepted it as it was presented according to his right. I order that a copy be given to the other party, who is to respond to it within the period of three days. So that it is valid I signed it with my secretary of government and war on the said day.

Felix Martínez (rubric)
Before me,
Miguel Tenorio de Alba (rubric)
Secretary of Government and War

Governor and Captain General

[Statement by Juan de León Brito]

I, Juan de León Brito, resident of this Villa of Santa Fe, appear before your honor in my best and proper form according to my legal right and I say that regarding the petition that the sergeant Antonio Durán de Armijo filed with your honor arguing in favor of the legal right of Antonio de Abeytia, soldier in this royal castle of New Mexico, I respond that what he states against my daughter are falsities. It is a certainty that Antonio de Abeytia is the one who deflowered her and no other person, and she is ready to swear to say that it was him and no other person without it bothering her conscience, or sending her soul to hell. According to the defendant, he states that my daughter told Petrona Paula [Lucero] that her father had deflowered her. But that is incorrect, as that is not what Petrona Paula states, but she merely states that she did not say such a thing concerning the matter.

Therefore, your honor, you should be pleased to call upon the subjects who are mentioned in the petition presented by the sergeant Antonio Durán de Armijo who say that they saw when my daughter was spanked on the buttocks and also call upon my daughter, who has not been induced by her mother or by any other person. When he, Abeytia states that it could not possibly be him, as he had already promised to marry another woman, this can be very easily argued, particularly if it happened before my daughter was deflowered. In addition, sir, your honor could confirm it and mete out justice. I swear to God and to the Holy Cross that this, my document, is not done in malice, but for what is necessary, etc.

Juan de León Brito (rubric)

Presentation

At this Villa of Santa Fe on the 10th of October, 1716, before me, Captain don Felix Martínez, as I am for life of this royal presidio, governor and captain general of this kingdom and castellan of his forces for his majesty, upon being reviewed by me I took it as it was presented according to their rights. I order that a copy be given to Sergeant Antonio Durán de Armijo and that he respond to it within three days. So that it is valid I signed it along with my secretary of government and war.

Felix Martínez (rubric)
Before me,
Miguel Tenorio de Alba (rubric)
Secretary of Government and War

Governor and Captain General

[Presentation by Antonio Durán de Armijo for Antonio de Abeytia]

I, the Sergeant of militia, Antonio Durán de Armijo, on behalf and with the power of representation for Antonio de Abeytia, who is wrongly acused by Juan de

León Brito, before your honor I appear in my best and proper form that I am allowed by right. I say that in regard to that which Juan de León states in favor of Margarita[25] his daughter, I say that whatever statement she makes and is ready to swear to above, where she says that she would not go to hell,[26] we cannot go solely by that. We have to consider that which is stated by my party.

For this reason, I petition the grandness of your honor that you not only be pleased to question the persons that I have named in my first document, but I also request that your honor call forth María Domínguez,[27] with the permission of her mother, who is Juana, the Sacristan.[28] Your honor will see what transpired at the time of the incident when Margarita was in the process of hauling water with Cristóbal Lucero. From having examined Petrona Paula, your honor has learned when she was deflowered. Concerning the charge that has been made that she was not seduced then, your honor will be satisfied without asking for the punishment that was suggested [for Abeytia].

For all of this I ask and petition your honor with the due respect to be pleased to examine the witnesses for the proof that I have given. I swear in proper form on behalf of my party that this, my document, is not done in malice but only to accomplish justice, all of which I request out of the goodness of Your Honor, protesting the costs, and what is necessary, etc.

Antonio Durán de Armijo (rubric)

Presentation

At this Villa of Santa Fe, on the 22nd of October, 1716, before me, Captain don Felix Martínez, that I am for life of this royal presidio of the villa, governor and captain general of this kingdom and castellan of his forces for his majesty, the above mentioned presented it to me, and upon my review I accepted it as it was presented according to his right. I ordered that this case be presented to be proven. For this reason, my secretary of government and war is to summon testimony from the parties. I thus approved it and signed it with my secretary on the said day.

Felix Martínez (rubric)
Before me,
Miguel Tenorio de Alba (rubric)
Secretary of Government and War

Notification

At this Villa of Santa Fe on the said day, month and year, I, the present secretary of government and war, in compliance with the order above given, made it known to the parties who all stated that they would comply as ordered, and so that it is valid I signed it.

Miguel Tenorio de Alba (rubric)
Secretary of Government and War

Statement of Margarita Brito

At this Villa of Santa Fe on the 3rd of November, 1716, in compliance with that which was ordered by me, there appeared before me Margarita Brito, legitimate daughter of Juan de León Brito and María Granillo,[29] complainants in this case. From whom upon her being present I took her sworn statement according to her legal right and for which she promised to tell the truth in whatever it was that I asked her.

She was asked if it was true that Antonio de Abeytia, soldier of this presidio, owed her his honor and if it was with the promise to marry her or because she was promised to be given something. She stated that it is true that he owes her his honor, and that she gave in to him because of his promise to marry her. This declarant knew that Antonio de Abeytia's mother did not want him to marry her, would not give in to him, but then he told her that even if his mother did not want him to marry her, he would. Thus believing him she gave in. From this union she had with Antonio de Abeytia she became pregnant. She swears, with God being her witness, that the daughter that she gave birth to is the daughter of Antonio de Abeytia, and that he has been aware of this since she told him so in the month of December past, when he asked for the hand in marriage of the daughter of Captain Nicolás Ortiz. This she gave as her answer.

She was asked if she had any witnesses who knew what happened between her and Antonio de Abeytia. She stated that Domingo Valdéz, known as "El Tata," told her that Antonio de Abeytia had told him how he had taken her with his promise of marrying her and that he should get married to her, this was her answer.

She was asked if before she had the illicit relation or thereafter she has made love with any other person, and she was told to answer what she knows regarding this question. She stated that she has not known any other man, nor does she owe anything to anyone. She stated that she has only known one man, Antonio de Abeytia, and that she has not lived with anyone, nor has been in any way forced by her parents. She asks only to restore her honor, and for him to comply with his promise that he has given to her. She said that this is the truth regarding the sworn statement that she has made, which she affirmed and ratified upon her statement being read back to her. She said that it was as she had declared it and does not have anything to add or delete and that she is twenty years of age, more or less. She did not sign because she did not know how. I, the governor and captain general, signed it along with my secretary of government and war on the said day.

Felix Martínez (rubric)
Before me,
Miguel Tenorio de Alba (rubric)
Secretary of Government and War

Statement of Domingo Valdéz

At the Villa of Santa Fe, on the 4th of November, 1716, I, the said governor and captain general in prosecution of these proceedings, made appear before me Domingo Valdéz, cited by Margarita Brito, from whom upon being present I received his sworn statement according to his legal right to which he promised to tell the truth as to what he knew and was asked.

He was asked what it was that he told Margarita Brito about what Antonio de Abeytia, prisoner in this case, told him. He stated that when they were talking [Antonio de Abeytia] told him how he had an illicit affair with Margarita Brito, and that he was not certain if things would work out with them, and that if it did not work out with her, it would not work out, this is what he answered.

He was asked if he knew or has heard anyone say that Margarita had an affair with anyone else prior to the one with Abeytia. He was told to state what he knew. He said that he had not heard or seen anything about what he was asked, and that this was the truth regarding the sworn statement that he has made. This he affirmed and ratified upon his statement being read back to him, and he said that he had nothing to add or delete, saying that he was twenty years of age, more or less. He did not sign because he did not know how. I, the governor, signed it along with my secretary of government and war on the said day.

Felix Martínez (rubric)
Before me,
Miguel Tenorio de Alba (rubric)
Secretary of Government and War

Statement of Ramón de Medina

At this Villa of Santa Fe on the 6th of November, 1716, I, Captain don Felix Martínez, governor and captain general of this kingdom and provinces of New Mexico, continuing with the prosecution of these proceedings made to appear before me Ramón de Medina, soldier of this presidio. He was presented as a witness for Antonio de Abeytia in order that he offer proof for the accused party. Upon being present I received his sworn statement which he made before God and to the sign of the Holy Cross, and he promised to tell the truth as to what he was asked and what he knew.

He was asked if he knew Margarita Brito and if he knew that Antonio de Abeytia, likewise a soldier, took her when she was a virgin, and if Abeytia had given her his promise to marry her, or has heard that anyone said that. He stated that he does know Margarita Brito and Antonio de Abeytia, and that on a certain night while guarding the horse herd along with Antonio de Abeytia, Abeytia told him that he would give anything to be able to go to the villa. He asked him why that was, and Abeytia told him that because he was jealous of Juan Telles, a soldier from El Paso. On this same occasion he told [Ramón de Medina] how he, [Abeytia], had taken Margarita Brito's virginity. Also, on another occasion, Petrona Paula, daughter of Juan Antonio Barrios,[30] told the master barber, Antonio Durán [de Armijo], that while working together with

Margarita Brito, she told [Petrona Paula Lucero] that once he had ruined her and though she had his child, he could care less about her. Also on another occasion when Cristóbal Lucero arrived from El Paso, he said that he had hit [Margarita] because he found her with Juan Telles. This, he said, was what he heard Petrona Paula say, as well as Agustín Luján, being that [Luján] was with this witness at the time.

This, he says, is what he knows according to his sworn statement that he has made and which he affirmed and ratified after his statement was read back to him, and said that he did not have anything to add or subtract. He stated that the *generales*[31] do not apply and also stated that he was twenty-two years of age, more or less. He did not sign because he did not know how. I, the said governor and captain general, signed it along with my secretary of government and war.

    Felix Martínez (rubric)
    Before me,
    Miguel Tenorio de Alba (rubric)
    Secretary of Government and War

Statement of Agustín Luján

    Continuing, on the said day, month and year, I, the governor and captain general, made to appear before me Agustín Luján, cited by Ramón de Medina, from whom upon being present I received his sworn statement which he made in due form before God, Our Lord, and the sign of the Holy Cross, in which he promised to tell the truth as to what he knew and was asked.

He was asked if he knew Margarita Brito, daughter of Juan de León [Brito] and Antonio de Abeytia, soldier of this presidio, and if he knows or has heard that Antonio de Abeytia took the said Margarita's virginity with the promise to marry her. He said that he knows both of the individuals who are mentioned, but does not know if he took her as a virgin, or if he gave her his promise of marriage. He said that he only had heard from Petrona Paula, daughter of Cristóbal Lucero, who was brought up by Juan Antonio Barrios, that on a certain occasion Margarita Brito told Petrona Paula that after her father, [Cristóbal] Lucero, had taken her virginity but that he did not care about her. Also, on another occasion that Cristóbal Lucero had hit [Margarita] because he was jealous after finding her with Juan Telles.

This he said is the truth and what he knows regarding his sworn statement that he has given. After his sworn statement was read back to him he stated that he did not have anything to add or delete from it and that it is certain and as stated. He further stated that the generalities do not apply and that he is fifty years of age, more or less. He did not sign because he did not know how. I, the governor and captain general, signed it along with my secretary of government and war on the said day.

    Felix Martínez (rubric)
    Before me,
    Miguel Tenorio de Alba (rubric)
    Secretary of Government and War

[*Editor's note:* The document ends without a final determination.]

TRANSCRIPTION

1716

Demanda puesta por Juan de Leon Brito Por haver estuprado a una hija suya
consta de catorze foxas

Señor Governador y Capitan General
  Juan de Leon Brito besino de esta Villa de Santa Fee paresco ante Vuestra Señoria en la mas bastante forma que ayga lugar y el mio conbengo y digo Señor que me querello de Antonio de Abeytia, soldado deste Real Castillo por quanto a obrado picaramente con aber desflorado a una hija mia con socapa de que se havia de casar con la dicha mi hija con palabra que le dio y la dicha mi hija sela dio causa de que la tenga embarasada y aviendole mi esposa echo el requerimiento al dicho Antonio de Avieta dize y responde que si es verdad que le deve su onrra y le tiene dada palabra de casamiento.
  Aviendo yo benido de La Cañada me yso savidor la dicha mi esposa y como padre que soi de la muchacha me ocasiono a ber al dicho Antonio de Aveitia quien a mi me lo a negado diziendo que no deve tal cosa cuando ze lo tiene comunicado a Domingo Baldes que el se casaua con la dicha mi hija por deverle su onrra y asi Señor pido justisia a Vuestra Señoria que soy un pobre pues es Vuestra Señoria padre de todo este Reyno y es Vuestra Señoria muy temoroso de Dios que es el Consuelo que me asiste y que el dicho Antonio de Aveitia comparesca ante Vuestra Señoria para que diga y declare lo que a la dicha mi esposa le dijo, por tanto pido y suplico a Vuestra Señoria sea muy servido de azerme justisia y de no quererse casar el dicho Antonio de Avietia la dote pues del todo no ze a de quedar con su picardia pues es muy puesto en rason = y juro a Dios Nuestro Señor no zer de malisia esta mi petizion si justisia que pido a Vuestra Señoria y en lo nesesario ut supra .
  Juan de Leon Brito (rubric)

  En la Villa de Santa Fee en onze dias del mes de Agosto de el año de mill setesientos y dies y seis años ante mi el Capitan Dn. Phelix Martinez que lo soi Vitalicio deste Real Presidio, Governador y Capitan General deste Reyno y Provincias dela Nueva Mexico y Castellano de Sus Fuerzas por Su Magestad la presentada el contenido y por mi vista la ube por presentada en quanto a lugar en derecho y mando a el Sarxento dela Compañia deste Castillo Presidial ponga preso en el Real Cuerpo de Guardia a Antonio de Bectia soldado de su compania a quien mando nombre procurador que lo defienda y al que nombrare sele de traslado de este escrito y que responda dentro del termino de tres dias asi lo provey, mande y firme con mi Secretario de Governazion y Guerra en dicho dia =

    Phelix Martinez (rubric)
    Ante mi
    Miguel Thenorio de Alva (rubric)
    Secretario de Governazion y Guerra

En La Villa de Santa Fee cavesera de este Reyno y Provinsias de la Nueva Mexico en doze dias del mes de Agosto de mill setecientos y diez y seis años ante mi el Capitan Francisco Lorenzo de Casados, Alcalde Ordinario de esta dicha Villa actuando ante mi como Jues Receptor y con los ynfraescriptos testigos de mi asistensia por no aver en este Reino escribano publico ni real ni en muchas leguas parecio Antonio de Beytia soldado de este Castillo Presidial en dicha Villa de Santa Fee.

En presencia de los testigos el Sargento Juan de la Mora Pineda, Manuel Tenorio y el Cavo de Esquadra Juan Lujan, que presentes se allaron en cuya presencia dixo dicho Antonio de Beytia aquien lo conosco que dava todo su poder cumplido qual bastante se requiere y es nesesario al Sargento de Milisias Antonio Duran de Armijo para que en su nombre y representado su misma persona le defienda en una querella que contra el suso dicho Antonio de Beytia tiene puesta Juan de Leon Brito vezino de esta dicha Villa por escripto ante el Señor Governador y Capitan General de este Reyno quien le mando poner preso en el Real Cuerpo de Guardia.

Por no poder haser las dilixensias de su defensa por estar preso le da a dicho Sargento Antonio Duran de Armijo este poder espesial para que pueda en todos sus pleitos con toda facultad defender sus causas y negocios siviles y criminals que al presente tiene y en adelante sele recresieren con quales quiera personas assi demandando como defendiendo y para que pueda seguir y alegar los meritos que el otorgante tiene para lo qual pueda parezer y paresca azer el Señor Governador y Capitan General de este Reyno y todas las Reales Justicias de su Majestad, audiensias y jusgados donde con derecho deva y en ellos haga pedimientos, requerimentos, protextas, zitaciones, alegaciones, contradiciones, presente ecritos, testigos, pruebas, ynformaciones y los demas papeles y recaudos que fueran nesesarios que pida y saque de cuyo poder estubieren, y los de contrario presentados que vea jurar y reconoser y en el jusgado ecclesiastico saque sensuras, ynfinem revelaciones que haga leer, intimar donde, y a quien combenga y saque testimonio delo que se revelare en su virtud, recuse jueses, escribanos y otros ministros y jure en su animas las tales recusasiones y las siga o se desista de ellas como le paresiere oyga autos y sentensias ynterlocutorias y difinitivas las faborables consienta y de las en contrario apele y suplique siga el grado por todas ynstancias y sentensias asta su final determinazion que para todo lo dicho y lo demas anexso y pertenesiente le da y otorga este poder con libre y general administrazion y facultad de en juicier, jurar y sostenir, revocar los titulos y nombrar otros de nuebo a todo lo qual releva segun derecho. Assi lo otorgo y firmo con migo dicho Alcalde

Ordinario y los ynfraescriptos testigos de mi asistenzia delos ariva mencionados y en el presente papel comun por que el sellado no corre en estas partes.

 Francisco Lorenzo de Casados
 Antonio de Beytia
 testigo de assistencia
 Joseph Manuel Gilthomey
 testigo de asistencia
 Juan Manuel Chirinos

     ☞

 Concuerda con su orixinal de donde yo el Capitan Francisco Lorenzo de Casados, Alcalde Oridinario de esta Villa de Santa Fee hize sacar ala letra a pedimento de Antonio de Beytia para entregar este testimonio al Sargento Antonio Duran de Armijo, ba cierto y verdadero y corresponde con su orixinal que queda en el archibo de mi cargo y fueron testigos al ver sacar correxir y consertar; el Sargento Juan dela Mora Pineda, el Cavo de Esquadra Juan Lujan y Manuel Tenorio y para que conste lo firme actuando ante mi como Juez Receptor por no aver escribano publico ni Real en este Reino y con los ynfraescriptos testigos de mi assistenzia fecho en esta dicha Villa de Santa Fee en doze dias del mes de Agosto de mil setecientos y diez y seis años y en dos fojas de papel comun por que el sellado no corre en este Reyno = En testimonio de verdad hago mi firma y rubrica acostumbrada.

 Francisco Lorenzo de Casados (rubric)
 Testigo de assistenzia
 Joseph Manuel Gilthomey (rubric)
 Testigo de assistenzia
 Juan Manuel Chirinos (rubric)

     ☞

    Señor Governador y Capitan General

 El Sargento de Milicia Antonio Duran de Armijo ante Vuestra Señoria parece en la mejor forma que el derecho le conzede y dice se a nombrado por su defensor Antonio de Beitia soldado de este Real Presidio de Nuestra Señora de Los Remedios y la Exaltacion de la Santa Cruz, preso en el Real Cuerpo de Guardia por orden de Vuestra Señoria por querella de Juan de Leon Brito con el poder adjunto por todo lo cual a Vuestra Señoria pide y suplica con la beneracion debida se sirba de probeer lo que mas conbenga y jura en anima de su parte este su pedimento no ser de malicia y en lo nesesario, costas protesto

 Antonio Duran de Armijo (rubric)

     ☞

Presentacion

En la Villa de Santa Fee en doze dias del mes de Agosto del año de mill setecientos y dies y seis ante mi el Capitan Dn. Phelix Martinez que lo soi Vitalicio de este Real Presidio, Governador y Capitan General deste Reino y Provinzias de la Nueba Mexico y Castellano de Sus Fuerzas y por mi vista la hube por presentada en quanto a lugar en derecho y desde luego lo admito al uso y exercicio de defensor y para que conste lo firme con mi Secretario de Governazion y Guerra, en dicho dia.

Phelix Martinez (rubric)
Miguel Thenorio de Alba (rubric)
Secretario de Governazion y Guerra

Señor Governador y Capitan General

El Sargento de Milicia Antonio Duran de Armino en nombre y con poder de Antonio de Beitia soldado deste Real Presido de Nuestra Señora de los Remedios y La Exaltacion de la Santa Cruz, ante Vuestra Señoria parece en la major forma que el derecho le concede y dice que allandose preso su parte de orden de Vuestra Señoria en el Real Cuerpo de Guardia por querella de Juan de Leon Brito diciendo y ablando con terminos decorosos lebantandole desfloro a su hija siendo asi que quien la perdio fue Xptobal Luzero, soldado del Presidio del Paso.

Que dice una hija del dicho que estando labrando en la casa de Juan del Leon le comunico la hija de Juan de Leon como su padre la abia perdido y abia obrado mal con ella y que al Segundo biaje la cojio con Juan Telles tambien soldado del Presidio del Pasoy ablando con el debido respecto que se debe ala grandessa de Vuestra Señoria dice le espoleo las nalgas y le dijo delante del soldado Ramon de Medina y Agustin Lujan bezino desta Villa de Santa Fee y se llama la dicha hija de Xptobal Luzero, Petrona Paula que asi es su nombre tocante al embarazo que dice tiene como puede afirmarse a decir es suio a donde an entrado otros segun se a dicho en lo public segun selo an comunicado a mi parte y esto no se puede afirmar.

Lo otro que dice mi parte le dio palabra de casamiento como puede ser que es el dicho de su madre si el tenga otra muger pedida para mi esposa por otra parte si dice mi parte la comunico como muger mundana y la correspondio y que su madre no lo ingnoraba que que puede decir ciendo parte apacionada que tocante al requerimiento que a mi parte hizo es berdad pero que le respondio no debia tal honrra a su hija y asi me querello sibil y criminalmente de Juan de Leon por aberme llegado al credito y de su hija para que Vuestra Señoria como juez los ponga independientes a padre y hija que me afiansen la calumnia con los bienes que tubieren y sus personas sean oprimadas para que no lebanten testimonios que asi no ai honrra segura que si debiera tal cosa mi parte con pagar conforme es la persona ajustada pero no cabe no ciendo mi parte el malechor por todo lo cual

A Vuestra Señoria pido y suplico con la benerasion devida se sirba de administrarme justicia y mande Vuestra Señoria que a su tenor se examinen los testigos que

dada la probansa protesto alegar mas en forma y juro en anima de mi parte pedir lo que mas conbenga es justicia y en lo nesesario ut supra =
 Antonio Duran de Armijo (rubric)

Presentacion
 En la Villa de Santa Fee en doze dias del mes de Agosto del año de mill setesientos y dies y seis ante mi el Capitan Dn. Phelix Martinez que lo soi vitalicio de este Real Presidio, Governador y Capitan General de este Reino y Provincias de la Nueba Mexico y Castellano de Sus Fuerzas por Su Magestad la present el contenido.
 Por mi vista la hube por presentada en quanto a lugar en derecho y mando sele de traslado ala parte y que responda dentro de tres dias y para que conste lo firme con mi Secretario de Governazion y Guerra en dicho dia =
 Phelix Martinez (rubric)
 Ante mi
 Miguel Thenorio de Alva (rubric)
 Secretario de Governazion y Guerra

Señor Governador y Capitan General
 Juan de Leon Brito bezino de esta Villa de Santa Fee paresco ante Vuestra Señoria en la mas bastante forma que ayga luger en derecho y al mio conbenga y digo que respondo ala petizion que el Sargento Antonio Duran de Armijo metio ante Vuestra Señoria alegando en el derecho de Antonio de Aveitia soldado deste Real Castillo de la Nueba Mexico alo qual digo que son calumnias las que ponen a mi hija pues esta sierta en que el dicho Antonio de Aveitia es el que la perdio y no otra persona pues se alla mui sufiziente en jurar como el fue sin encargar su consienzia ni enfernal su alma pues dize su defensor que mi hija selo comunico a Petrona Paula que su padre la avia perdido no dise tal cosa la dicha Petrona Paula que lo que dize es no aver dicho cosa en esta materia.
 Asi Señor Vuestra Señoria zer muy servido de mandar llamar a los suxetos que resan en la petizion del dicho Sargento Antonio Duran de Armijo pues dise paso delante de ellos cuando la espolearon y la dicha mi hija no a sido indusita de su madre ni de otra persona tambien dise que como podia ser pues tenia pedida a otra muger para su esposa es cosa mui fasil de aberiguar; si fue antes que perdiera ala dicha mi hija al demas Señor que Nuestra Señoria esa sera la rason y la justisia al que estubiese y juro a Dios y ala Santa Cruz no ser de malisia este mi escripto y en lo nezesario ut supra.
 Juan de Leon Brito (rubric)

Presentacion

En la Villa de Santa Fee en dies dias del mes de Octubre de mill setezientos y dies y seis años ante mi el Capitan Dn. Phelix Martinez que lo soi Vitalicio de este Real Presdio, Governador y Capitan General de este Reino y Castellano de Sus Fuerzas por Su Magestad.

Auto

Por mi vista la ube por presentada en quanto a lugar en derecho y mando sele de traslado al Sargento Antonio Duran de Armijo y que responda dentro de tres dias y para que conste lo firme con mi Secretario de Governazion y Guerra

Phelix Martinez (rubric)
Ante mi
Miguel Thenorio de Alba (rubric)
Secretario de Governazion y Guerra

Señor Governador y Capitan General

El Sargento de Milicia Antonio Duran de Armijo en nombre y con poder de Antonio de Beitia calumniado por querella de Juan de Leon Brito ante Vuestra Señoria parece en la mejor forma que el derecho le conzede y dice que tocante a lo que responde dicho Juan de Leon a fabor de Margarita su hija digo que lo que puede decir ella que se atreba a jurar eso y mucho mas aunque quedo mas infernada que lo que esta que no emos de estar solo a su dicho que el testimonio lo que falzamente dispone de mi parte.

Asi suplico ala grandeza de Vuestra Señoria se sirba no solo de examinar las personas que tengo dichas en mi primer escrito y juntamente mande Vuestra Señoria llamar a Maria Dominguez con licensia de su madre que es Juana la sacristana y bera Vuestra Señoria lo que le susedio en tiempo del fracaso bajando por agua con Xptobal Luzero y de ai conosera Vuestra Señoria el tiempo que a que largo su flor tocante a aber examinado a Petrona Paula i so mal que eso queda a largo del Juez que dise no fue inducida satisfacion sin pedir la acusacion manifiesta por todo lo cual.

A Vuestra Señoria pido y suplico con la beneracion de vida se sirba de examinar los testigos para la prueba de lo que tengo representado que juro en devida forma en anima de mi parte este mi escrito no ser de malicia si por alcansar justicia y esta imploro en el patrocinio de Vuestra Señoria costas protesto y en lo nesesario, ut supra
Antonio Duran de Armijo (rubric)

Presentacion

En la Villa de Santa Fee en veinte y dos dias del mes de Octubre del año de mill setecientos y dies y sies ante me el Capitan Dn. Phelix Martinez que lo soi Vitalicio del

Real Presidio de dicha Villa, Governador y Capitan General deste Reino y Castellano de Sus Fuerzas por Su Magestad. La presento el contenido y por mi vista la hube por presentada en quanto a lugar en derecho y mando se reziva esta causa a prueba y para ello mi Secretario de Governazion y Guerra sitara a las partes, asi lo provei y firme con dicho mi Secretario dicho dia =
    Phelix Martinez (rubric)
    Ante mi
    Miguel Thenorio de Alba (rubric)
    Secretario de Gobernazion y Guerra

Notificazion
    En esta Villa de Santa Fee en dicho dia, mes y año, yo el presente Secretario de Governazion y Guerra en cumplimiento del auto de arriba lo hize notorio alas partes quienes dixeron lo executaran como seles ordena y para que conste lo firme
    Miguel Thenorio de Alba (rubric)
    Secretario de Governazion y Guerra

Declaracion de Margarita Brito
    En esta Villa de Santa Fee en tres dias del mes de Noviembre de mill setesientos dies y seis años en cumplimiento delo por mi mandado parecio en mi presencia Margarita Brito hija lexitima de Juan de Leon Brito y de Maria Granillo querellante en esta causa ala qual estando presente le resivi juramento en forma de derecho so cargo del qual prometio dezir verdad en lo que por mi le fuere preguntado.
    Preguntada si es verdad que Antonio de Bectia soldado de este Presidio le deve su honrra y si fue con palabra de casamiento o por dadivas que le ofrecio; Dixo que es verdad le deve su honor y que se entrego a el con palabra que le dio de casamiento y que requiriendole esta declarante y resistiendose a no dejarse gozar reselosa de que la madre de dicho Antonio de Bectia no lo dejase casar con esta declarante le respondio que aunque su madre no quisiese el si queria y se casaria con ella y en esta suposision la gozo y que de este ayuntamiento que tubo con dicho Antonio de Bectia quedo preñada y que pone a Dios por testigo de no tener una nina que pario mas padre que dicho Antonio de Bectia quien la comunico desde el mes de Diziembre proximo pasado hasta que pidio ala hija del Capitan Nicolas Ortiz para casarse con ella y esto responde.
    Preguntada si tiene algunos testigos que sepan lo que paso entre ella y dicho Antonio de Bectia diga lo que save; Dixo que a Domingo Valdes llamado el Tata le dixo a esta declarante que Antonio de Bectia le avia dicho como la havia gosado con palabra de casamiento y que se havia de casar con ella y esto responde.
    Preguntada si antes que tubiese la communicazion ylisita o despues a tenido amores con otra persona, diga lo que hubiere en este particular; Dijo que no a conosido mas hombre ni deve tal cosa a ninguno sino solo con dicho Antonio de Bectia y

que no a sido amenazada, ni forzada de sus padres sino por restuarar su honor y que le cumpla la palabra que le tiene dada.

Que esta es la verdad so cargo del juramento que fecho tiene en que se afirmo y ratifico siendole leida su declaracion y dijo estar como lleva declarado que no tiene que anadir ni quitar que es de edad de veinte año poco mas o menos, no firmo por no saver firmelo yo dicho Governador y Capitan General con mi Secretario de Governazion y Guerra en dicho dia =

Phelix Martinez (rubric)
Ante mi
Miguel Thenorio de Alba (rubric)
Secretario de Governazion y Guerra

Declaracion de Domingo Valdes

En la Villa de Santa Fee en quatro dias del mes de Nobiembre de mill setecientos y dies y seis años yo dicho Governador y Capitan General en prosecucion de estas diligencias hize parezer ante mi a Domingo Valdes sitado por Margarita Brito, al qual estando presente le resivi juramento en forma de derecho so cargo del qual prometio dezir verdad en lo que supiere y le fuere preguntado.

Preguntado que fue lo que le dijo a Margarita Brito haverle dicho Antonio de Bectia reo en esta causa; Dijo que Antonio de Bectia hablando con este declarante le dijo como tenia amistad ylisita con la dicha Margarita Brito, y que como ella obraria bien con el seria otra cosa y que si no obraba bien obreria el mal con ella y esto responde.

Preguntado save o a oido dezir a algunas personas que la dicha Margarita aya tenido antes que con Antonio de Bectia, o despues alguna mala amistad, diga lo que save; Dijo que ni lo a oido ni visto nada delo que sele pregunta, y esta es la verdad so cargo del juramento que fecho tiene en que se afirmo y ratifico siendole leida su declaracion que no tiene que anadir ni quitar que es de edad de veinte años poco mas o menos, no firmo por no saver, firmelo yo dicho Governador con mi Secretario de Governazion y Guerra dicho dia =

Phelix Martinez (rubric)
Ante mi
Miguel Thenorio de Alba (rubric)
Secretario de Governazion y Guerra

Declaracion de Ramon de Medina

En la Villa de Santa Fee en seis dias del mes de Noviembre del año de mill setesientos y dies y seis, yo el Capitan Dn. Phelix Martinez, Governador y Capitan General deste Reyno y Provinzias dela Nueva Mexico en prosecusion de estas diligencias hize parezer ante mi a Ramon de Medina, soldado de este Presidio a el qual presento por testigo para la prueba que ofrese la parte de Antonio de Bectia al qual estando presente le resevi juramento que iso por Dios Nuestro Señnor y la Señal de la Santa Cruz so cargo del qual prometio dezir verdad en lo que supiere y le fuere preguntado.

    Preguntado si conose a Margarita Brito y si save que Antonio de Bectia asi mesmo soldado la goso siendo donzella y si le a dado palabra de casamiento, o lo a oido dezir a alguno; Dixo que conose a Margarita Brito y a Antonio de Bectia y que estando este declarante una noche en la cavallada le dixo el dicho Antonio de Bectia que diera qualquiera cosa por poder venir ala Villa; y preguntadole el por que le respondio que por que tenia zelos de Juan Tellos soldado de El Paso; y en esta occasion le dixo a este declarante como el dicho Bectia havia gosado de su virginidad de Margarita Brito; y asi mesmo en otra occasion oyo que le desia al maestro barber, Antonio Duran, Petrona Paula hija de Juan Antonio Barrios, estando labrando con la dicha Margarita Brito le dixo esta a Petrona Paula mira gran picaro a andado tu padre pues despues que me hecho a perder no ase caso de mi.

    Que en otra occasion que vino de El Paso a esta Villa Xptobal Luzero padre de dicha Petrona Paula la espoleo por que la cojio con Juan Tellez; y que esto lo oio este declarante a la dicha Petrona Paula y lo mismo le oyo Agustin Luxan por estar junto con este declarante en la occasion.

    Que esto es lo que sabe y la verdad so cargo del juramento que fecho tiene en que se afirma y ratifica siendole leida su declaracion que no tiene que añadir ni que quitar y que no le tocan las generals que es de edad de veinte y dos años poco mas o menos, no firmo por no saver firmelo yo dicho Governador y Capitan General con mi Secretario de Governazion y Guerra =

    Phelix Martinez (rubric)
    Ante mi
    Miguel Thenorio de Alba (rubric)

Declaracion de Agustin Luxan

    Y luego yncontinenti en dicho dia mes y año yo dicho Governador y Capitan General hize parezer ante mi a Agustin Luxan sitado por Ramon Medina a el qual estando presente le resevi juramento que iso en forma de derecho por Dios Nuestro Señor y la Señal de la Santa Cruz so cargo del qual prometio dezir verdad en lo que supiere y le fuere preguntado.

    Preguntado si conose a Margarita Brito hija de Juan de Leon y a Antonio de Bectia soldado de este Presidio, y si save o a oido dezir que dicho Antonio de Bectia gozo donzella a la dicha Margarita con palabra de casamiento; Dixo que conose a los dos que sele pregunta y que no save si la gozo donzella, o le dio palabra de casamiento; y que solo oyo dezir a Petrona Paula hija de Xptobal Luzero a quien a criado Juan Antonio Barrios que en una occasion le avia dicho Margarita Brito a Petrona Paula que despues que su padre le avia quitado su virginidad no asia causo de ella; y que en otra ocasion dicho Xptobal Luzero la havia espoleado de zelos de haverla cojido con Juan Tellez.

Que esta es la verdad y lo que save so cargo del juramento que fecho tiene siendole leida su declaracion que no tiene que añadir ni quitar a ella que esta segun y como declare que no le tocan las generales que es de edad de sinquenta años poco mas o menos y no firmo por no saver firmelo dicho Governador y Capitan General con mi Secretario de Gobernazion y Guerra en dicho dia =
    Phelix Martinez (rubric)
    Ante mi
    Miguel Thenorio de Alba (rubric)
    Secretario de Governazion y Guerra

[*Editor's note:* The document ends without a final determination.]

Notes

1. Juan de León Brito was the son of Juan Brito and Ursula Durán. He married Sebastiana Madrid in El Paso in 1692, and upon her death he married María de los Reyes Granillo in 1694. In the marriage record, he is listed as a Mexican Indian and "*poblador*" (first settler). There is additional evidence that he was either a Tlascalan Indian or an Indian from one of the Mexican tribes favored by the Spanish. He was likely prosperous and devout, for in 1710 he donated 1,000 adobes for the rebuilding of San Miguel Chapel in Santa Fe. When he donated land in 1713, he was listed as living in the Barrio de Analco neighborhood of Santa Fe, on the south side of the river, adjacent to the road to Pecos, and thus near the Santa Fe Plaza and San Miguel Chapel. He was a member of the Conquistadora Confraternity and, in addition to Margarita, he had four daughters and three sons. In a 1728 request for a Santa Fe land grant reaffirmation, he claimed that his land had been given to his father by Governor Vargas. He died on October 14, 1752. (Chávez, *Origins*: 149, 339; Burkholder, "Authority": 231; SANM I #85; SANM I #165, WPA translations; Kubler, *San Miguel*: 23; Twitchell, *Spanish Archives of New Mexico*, Vol. II: 36-39; Ebright, "Advocates": 55-57, 305 n96.)
2. Antonio de Abeytia was the son of Diego de Vectia [Abeytia], a native of Durango, Mexico, and probably Catalina Leal. He was an alférez or standard bearer for the militia at Santa Cruz in 1735. He was married to Rosalia Luján, the daughter of José Luján. In 1765, he was a captain at Santa Cruz. (Chávez, *Origins*: 119.)
3. In the Spanish text, the phrase is "*le dev su honrai*" and literally means "owed it to his honor." In this context, a more accurate translation would be: "it was his duty to honor his promise." This phrase is used several times in this document by Juan de León Brito and by Antonio de Abeytia and his legal representative. For further information on seduction, honor, and marriage, see Lavrin, *Sexuality and Marriage in Colonial Latin America*: 64-65; Waldron, "The Sinner and the Bishop": 161, 174; and Socolow, "Acceptable Parties": 226.
4. Domingo "El Tata" Valdéz was the son of José Luis Valdéz, a native of Oviedo, Spain, and María Medina de Cobrera. "Tata" is a term used by small children when referring to a parent. It could also refer to a timid person. Domingo was married to Ana María Marquez. He was a presidio soldier in 1716; three years later, he was twenty-three years old and living in Santa Fe; and, in 1720, he sold his house. (SANM I #171; SANM I #1043; Chávez, *Origins*: 301; Christmas and Rau, "Una Lista": 197.)
5. In the Spanish text, the phrase is "*muy temoroso de Dios*" and literally means "greatly afraid of God."
6. For information on Felix Martínez, see Case 3.
7. Miguel Tenorio de Alba was from Zacatecas, Mexico, and traveled to New Mexico with the Hurtado Expedition of 1695. He was one of the first settlers of Santa Cruz and is listed as being a blacksmith in 1697. He was also a cabildo scribe and a secretary of government and war. He and his wife, Agustina Romero, were in Santa Cruz in 1711, when they baptized a son, Cayetano. In 1715, Miguel was a presidio campaign captain; three years later, he was alcalde and war captain for Santa Cruz; and, in 1719, he was alcalde and war captain for Taos Pueblo. He was killed while serving in the 1720 Villasur Expedition. (Kessell, Hendricks, and Dodge, *Boulders*: 570n52; SANM II #236; NMGS, *Santa Cruz*: 1; Christmas and Rau, "Una Lista": 196.)
8. For information on Francisco Lorenzo de Casados, see Case 12.
9. Juan de la Mora Piñeda was a native of Sombrerete, Mexico, and was in New Mexico by 1695. He is listed as a presidio soldier in 1697 and 1712. In 1708, he was married to Clara de Chávez, a natural daughter of don Fernando Durán y Chávez. Juan was alcalde mayor of Taos between 1715 and 1729, and he had a son named Juan de la Mora. (Chávez, *Origins*: 161, 258; Kessell, Hendricks, Dodge, and Miller, *Disturbances*: 128; Tigges, "Presidial Company": 75.)
10. Manuel Tenorio de Alba [aka Manuel López] was the son of Alfonso López and Luisa Gómez de Arellano.

He was married to Francisca de la Vega y Coca, daughter of Captain Miguel de la Vega y Coca and María Montoya. Manuel was captain and alcalde at Pecos from 1725 to about 1738. (Chávez, *Origins*: 293; Chávez, *Roots*: 1721n5; Kessell, *Kiva*: 505; Colligan, *Hurtado*: 54.)

11. Juan Luján is likely the corporal who was the son of Juan Domingo Luján and Juana Domínguez of Santa Fe. He married María Martín Serrano in 1698; in 1715, he was a soldier in the campaign against the Apache; and when his mother died in 1717, he was the executor for her will. (Chávez, *Origins*: 212; Kessell, Hendricks, and Dodge, *Boulders*: 1074.)
12. In Spanish, the term is *"poder cumplido"* and means the complete power of attorney.
13. Antonio Durán de Armijo was born in Zacatecas, Mexico, and traveled to New Mexico in 1695 with the Hurtado Expedition. In Zacatecas, he was known as a notary and a "master barber"—a person with some medical experience capable of teaching others. He was a sergeant at the Santa Fe presidio by 1716. He and his wife, María de Quiros, had at least three children. He died in 1753, when he was about eighty years old. (Chávez, *Origins*: 136-37; Jenkins, "Taos": 97; Colligan, *Hurtado*: 40-41.)
14. The words in brackets were probably taken directly from a Spanish legal manual on the duties and privileges of legal representatives. The translator of this section, Aaron Taylor, found similar language in a 1783 document that includes a lengthy list of all the things that a legal representative was allowed to do. (See Ramirez, *Los Protocolos de la Villa de Nuestra Señora Santa Anna de Camargo*: 85-86.) A similar legal manual, *Guia de Protocolos de Instrumentos Publicos del Siglo XVIII*, includes an example of *"poder amplio complido"* under the heading of "Poder Especial." (See Lopez, *Guia de Protocolos*: 264-66).
15. For information on Jospeh Manuel Giltoméy, see Case 5.
16. For information on Juan Manuel de Chirinos, see Case 5.
17. This is incorrect. At that time, Santa Cruz had a garrison from the Santa Fe presidio, but was not a presidio itself.
18. Cristóbal Lucero de Godoy appears to have been a son of Nicolás Lucero de Godoy and a brother of Miguel Lucero de Godoy. He was born in 1683 and was a presidio soldier in 1710. (Kessell, Hendricks, and Dodge, *Boulders*: 954n220.)
19. To date, nothing more is known about Petrona Paula [Lucero] than what appears in this case. (See also note 30 below.)
20. Juan Telles [Girón] is probably a brother of Captain José Telles Girón, who is named in the El Paso muster of 1692. (Kessell, Hendricks, and Dodge, *Royal Crown*: 39.)
21. Ramón de Medina was born in Zacatecas, Mexico, the son of Diego de Medina, a Santa Fe presidal soldier, and María Telles Jirón. His first wife was Juana Rodríguez and the second was Valentina Montes de Oca. In a 1712 deed record, he is mentioned as selling land in Santa Fe. He is also listed in the 1710 to 1712 Santa Fe presidio muster. He died during the Villasur massacre of 1720. (SANM II #940; Christmas and Rau, "Una Lista": 200; Christmas, *Military Records*: 46; Chávez, *Origins*: 228; Tigges, "Presidial Soldiers": 74.)
22. Agustín de Luján was born about 1666 in New Mexico. He was included in the El Paso garrison muster of 1681 and was a Santa Fe presidio soldier by 1697. In 1701, he married María Luisa [Perea] Maese, sister-in-law of Alcalde Martín Hurtado. (Chávez, *Origins*: 213; Kessell, Hendricks, and Dodge, *Royal Crown*: 83; Kessell, Hendricks, Dodge, and Miller, *Disturbances*: 127.)
23. The Spanish term "mujer mundane" was the term for a common prostitute.
24. In this difficult paragraph, Antonio Durán de Armijo seems to be saying that while Margarita Brito may have been in love with Antonio de Abeytia that does not mean that he made her pregnant, especially since it appears that she "knew" other men. At the end of the paragraph, Durán de Armijo states that even if the two were pledged, this does not prove that his client was the wrongdoer.
25. Margarita Brito is listed along with her parents, Juan de León Brito and María Granillo, and sister, María, in the livestock distribution document of 1697. She is also named, along with her four sisters and a brother, in a 1713 donation deed. (Kessell, Hendricks, and Dodge, *Boulders*: 1163n28; SANM II #165, WPA translation.)
26. In most documents, witnesses were sworn in using the phrase "before God our Lord and the sign of the Holy Cross." In this case, the sense is that if she swears this and tells the truth then she will not go to hell.
27. María Domínguez may have been the woman who married Tomás Girón de Tejeda in Santa Fe, where they lived as late as 1718. Alternatively, she may have been the mother of Juan Luján (described in note 11 above). (Kessell, Hendricks, and Dodge, *Boulders*: 670n20.)
28. "Juana, the Sacristan" was likely Juana Domínguez, a sister of José Domínguez de Mendoza and a natural daughter of Tomé Domínguez de Mendoza II, a wealthy pre-revolt settler. A sacristan is a custodian of sacred vessels, vestments, and other sacred objects.
29. María [de los Reyes] Granillo was a wife of Juan de León Brito by 1694. She was raised in the household of Luis Granillo, the lieutenant governor under Governor Vargas in 1697. She died at age eighty in 1732. (Kessell, Hendricks, and Dodge, *Boulders*: 1163n28; Kessell, Hendricks, Dodge, and Miller, *Disturbances*: 127.)
30. For information on Juan Antonio Barrios, see Case 5. Petrona Paula [Lucero] was brought up by Barrios.
31. The Spanish word generales, part of the more formal phrase "*las generals de la ley*," refers to the special interests or relationship a person testifying might have for the accused. The purpose was to identify the degree of partiality included in the testimony. (*Wikipedia*, "Generales de la Leyes," accessed on July 18, 2016.)

18

BIGAMY CASE HEARD BY INQUISITION TRIBUNAL AGAINST AGUSTÍN DE LA PALMA; SEVERE PUNISHMENT IMPOSED
September 7–December 28, 1717, Source: AGN Inq Leg. 553 Exp. 53, Df #52 and #53

Synopsis and editor's notes: When discussed in Case 5, Agustín de la Palma, a soldier from the Janos presidio and later Santa Fe, was being accused of having raped the daughter of Petrona de Carvajal.[1] There is no evidence that he was found guilty of that crime. However, in 1717, after a lengthy investigation by the Holy Office of the Inquisition, he did confess to bigamy—considered a heinous crime by the Inquisition.

The charge, as shown below in the first document, states that Agustín de la Palma had at least two aliases: Agustín del Rio and Toribio and was first married to María de Espejo. Later, he married an Indian named Lucía, but she left him and he had a relationship with another woman, whose name is not given.

After an eight-month-long investigation, the inquisitors prepared a second document that indicates that Agustín de la Palma confessed to everything, including a previous charge of bigamy that had originally been dropped for lack of proof. The witnesses to his confession were two captains of the Santa Fe presidio. In the document, de la Palma renounced all forms of heresy (bigamy being only a minor heresy); stated that he would guard the Holy Faith and give obedience to the Pope; and agreed that all persons who acted against the Faith deserved condemnation. He went on to say that he submitted to this correction and would abjure his crime before a cross and with his hands on the Holy gospels and the missal open.

The second document stated that Agustín de la Palma's confession was made before the Santa Fe church congregation and an additional record, not included here, also stated that most of the congregation was in attendance.[2] This was in accordance with the Holy Office of the Inquisition's instructions for an "abjuration" that demands the confessant appear before the congregation "standing uncovered and guarded."[3]

These two documents comprise the end of what would have been a lengthy process. The case would have begun with a denouncement by either a church official or a member of the parish, followed by a preliminary investigation including the gathering of information by the tribunal inquisitors. The inquisitors kept the nature of the investigation secret from the denounced person and any witnesses. Upon it being determined that an act of heresy had occurred, the Holy Office officials imprisoned the accused and sequestered his goods, which were used to pay for the costs of the trial and prison.

Although the inquisitors were usually convinced of the prisoner's guilt at the time of the arrest, they did not make a final condemnation without a trial and a full confession. The belief was that only a confession—sometimes called the "queen of all proofs"—was true evidence of guilt. Torture, or "torment" as it was called, could be used to solicit a confession, though by the 1700s Spanish Inquisition rules prohibited any torture that caused death, permanent injury, or shed blood. According to a 1970s study of 50,000 Inquisition trial records from Spain, dating from 1540 to 1700, most of the accused had confessed before torture occurred and torture was rarely used in cases of minor heresy such as bigamy.[3]

Because the record of Agustín de la Palma's trial has not been located, the circumstances that brought about his confession are unknown. However, as the existing documents relating to his case indicate, when prisoners confessed and showed penitence they were then required to make a formal abjuration of their heresy and the inquisitors handed down a penance.[4] The procedure and language for the sentence and the confession came from Holy Office *cartillas* (manuals), parts of which have been found in a copy of the *Orden Processor* (Order of Proceedings). The latter provides the technical information and direction by which the Holy Office was to carry out its business.[5]

Seal of the Mexican Tribunal of the Spanish Inquisition. John Kessell, *Kiva, Cross and Crown,* University of New Mexico Press, 1979:172. Courtesy John Kessell.

TRANSLATION 1

1717

Presented in the Holy Office of Mexico on the 7th day of the month of September of 1717 to the Inquisitors Señores Cienfuego[6] and [illegible]

I, the Inquisitor Fiscal of the Holy Office,[7] have seen the proceedings remitted by the Comisario fray Juan de Tagle [8] of New Mexico with his letter of April 16th of this year about and because of what was sent by dispatch and order of March 2nd of last year. I am ordering and entrusting that the case against the person of Agustín del Rio,[9] alias de la Palma, alias Toribio, be sent to the comisario as is requested in my letter of the 13th of March in conformity with what was provided in it.

I state that from the proceedings, hearings and charges made against him and given to the accused after he was imprisoned, it is of record and appears that two marriages were contracted by him in bad faith, as I stated in more detail later in my document. This the prisoner confessed in the hearing on the charges made against him. While the first wife, María de Espejo,[10] was living he married a second time to the Indian Lucía[11] at the mission of Guazapares.[12] He had such cunning and craftiness that these two people [whom he mentions elsewhere] who knew each other, swore before Father Antonio Gómez[13] of the Company of Jesus that the first wife had died and that he was a widower.

Being ashamed of his second wife, he left her, taking up with another woman, being in her company and taking her to various places under the pretext that she was his legitimate wife. Even in the proceedings against him the prisoner attempted to moderate these accusations. Wishing to excuse himself, he confessed his fault in tears of repentance in some ways changing the details of the circumstances. Finally, he confessed fully and entirely to all, as it was related in the proceedings. He also revealed that he had earlier been imprisoned in that kingdom[14] by order of the Holy Office for the same offense, but he denied the accusation at that time. He had the slyness to get himself released from prison because it was not clearly proven that the wife lived.

For all that I ask and beseech Your Honor that in consideration of the obstacles that one is given, as the comisario points out in his letter, and the additional confusion that may occur, please see fit to render in writing a definitive ruling. With the assistance of the ordinario and advisor, see to it that he is condemned in the kingdom to the pain and abjuration of two hundred lashes and five years of penal servitude.

The comisario should be informed of the instruction necessary so that it can be carried out on the person of the prisoner in that kingdom. The sentence is to be executed in the plaza of one of the fortified presidios in the way it was in previous years by Carlos de Solis,[15] mulatto, who lived in the Castillo de la Concepción on the Río de San Juan.[16] This is so that the prisoner may be properly punished as he deserves for his broken and wanton life and as demanded by his particular crime with the punishment serving as an example to warn others and to satisfy divine justice. I expect that this shall be done quickly and to good effect.

I ask this for justice, presented without malice. If another petition is necessary I will expedite this as necessary.

September 6, 1717. Don Francisco Antonio de Palacio de Hoyo[17]

TRANSLATION 2

1717

[Agustín de la] Palma, taking the oath

I, Agustín del Rio, alias de la Palma, alias Toribio, native of Casas Grandes near the presidio of Janos, am here present before you Señor Reverend Father Tagle as Comisario (whom you are) of the Holy Office of the Inquisition of this New Spain in this villa and royal presidio of Santa Fe of New Mexico and its jurisdiction.

Being present and having made the sign of the Cross and the most Holy Gospels that I touched with my very own hands in recognition of the true Catholic and apostolic faith, I denounce all forms of heresy that rises against the Holy Catholic Faith and the gospel of our Redeemer and Savior Jesus Christ and against the Holy Apostolic See and the Roman Church, especially that in the Tribunal of the Holy Office before which I stand accused and suspected. I swear and promise to hold and guard always that Holy Faith held and guarded and taught by the Holy Mother Church and that I will always be obedient to our Holy Father the Pope and those who succeed him canonically in the Holy Apostolic seat and in what they determine, and I confess that all those who are against this Holy Catholic faith deserve condemnation.

I promise never to be joined with them and to do what I can to reveal their heresies when I know of them to whichever Señor Inquisitor I find to examine them or to a prelate of the Holy Mother Church wherever I may be. I swear and promise to receive with humility and patience the penance given me or which will be given with all my strength and ability and will complete it in all and for all neither being nor coming against it. I consent and am satisfied that if at any time (may God not permit it) I being in or come into the aforementioned actions against anyone or take part in them and if it is viewed as impenitence in me, I will submit to the correction and severity of the sacred canons so that in me as a person who has recanted, if I have broken the law, the censures and punishments will be executed as decreed.

With my abjuration I pray the present notary will testify as to those present so that they are recorded as witnesses the Captain don Francisco Lorenzo de Casados[18] and the Captain Juan de Archibeque,[19] and the Reverend Father Comisario of the Holy Office, fray Juan de Tagle, who signed for me because I, Agustín de la Palma, did not know how.

Today, Tuesday the 28th of December of the year 1717.

Passed before me
Fray Juan de Tagle (Rubric)
Comisario of the Holy Office
Fray Joseph Narváez Valverde[20] (rubric)
Notary of the Holy Office

I swear the testimony is true that on Tuesday 28th of December of the present year of 1717, the following persons were present: Predicador fray Juan de Mingues[21] having removed his vestments after celebrating Mass, the Deacon Father fray Gerónimo de Liñan[22] and the Subdeacon, the Father Preacher fray Juan del Pino,[23] and the secular witnesses the Captain Francisco Lorenzo de Casados and the Captain Juan de Archibeque. On his knees was Agustín de la Palma, alias del Rio, alias Toribio, in the presence of Reverend Father Predicador fray Juan de Tagle, Comisario of the Holy Office as he is in the kingdom of New Mexico in the Parish Church of this Villa of Santa Fe. De la Palma was before a cross with his hands on the Holy Gospels, and the missal open, where he abjured his crime, according to the order of the [illegible] Tribunal of the Inquisition.

He, Agustín de la Palma, did not sign for not knowing how. The Reverend Father Comisario signed for him along with me, the fray Joseph Narváez Valverde, notary as the above confirms. In testimony of truth I signed in the Villa of Santa Fe on 28th day of the month of December in the year of 1717.
Fray Joseph Narváez Valverde (Rubric)
Notary of the Holy Office

TRANSCRIPTION 1

Presentado en este santo oficio de Mexico
En siete días del mes de Marzo de Septiembre Mil setecientos dies y siete años
al Señores Inquisidores Cienfuego [illegible]

El Inquisidor fiscal de este Santo Oficio a visto las diligencias que el Comisario del nuebo Mexico Fray Juan de Tagle remite con su carta de 16 de Abril de este año, sobre y en razon de lo que por despacho y orden del Vuesta Señoria de 26 y 28 de Marzo del año pasado ce le ordenó y cargó en la causa contra la persona de Agustin del Rio, alias de la Palma, alias Toribio que fueren y se remiteran a dicho comisarios en conformidad de lo pedido por mi escrito del 13 de dicho mes de Marzo y lo del proveydo:

Y digo que por dicha diligencias, audiencias y cargos dadas y hechas al Reo después de haver le preso consta y parece ser ciertos los dos matrimonios que contraxo segun y como mas largamente expresé en dicho me escrito y este Reo lo confeso en dichas audiencias y cargoes que en ella se le hicieran haver los contrahido con mala fe, y casa(n)dose segunda bez con la India Lucia en las Missiones del (Guazapares) estando viva la primera llamada Maria de Espero, teniendo arte y mania paraque los dos conocidos quel (sic)_jurassen y dixesen ante el Padre Antonio Gomes de la Compañia de Jesús que parese fue el que hizo oficio de Párroco en el segundo Matrimonio que era suia y como habia muerto su primera mujer.

Después de Verquenza para largando a dicha India Lucia malla a mitarse con otra trayendola en su compañía llevandola por varias partes con el pretexto de que era su legitima muger; y aun pues este Reo en dichas audiencias y Cargos que en ellas le hizo el comisario arreglándose a los siette que Informa del acusación se le Remittieron para este fin, confesó su delito donde muestra lagrimas de arrepentimiento fue no solo queriendo disculparse en algun modo y apoderle perjuandose y variando en algunas circunstancias hasta que llena y enteramente le confesó y como entodo havia sido como en auto de todo, Vino tambien después que ya en otra ocasion havia estado preso en aquel Reyno de orden de la santa oficio sobre el mismo delito, negandole por entonces, y theniendo maña para dexar sui effecto aquella prision y librarse de ella por no estar entonces concluyamente provado este delito, ni la supervivencia de la primera muger como se halla de aser

Por todo lo qual al Vuestra Señoria pido y suplico que en atención a la larga distancia y mas embarazos que se dexan entender y insinúa el comisario en la referida carta se sirva de rotar esta causa en definitiva y con asistencia del ordinario y consultores condenado a este Reo en la pena ordinaria y abjuración de len doscientos azotes y cinco años de presidio, mandando se execute en su persona y que se lo meta a dicho comisario la Instrucción necesaria para que en aquel reyno se le execute todo y que quede puesto en vivo de sus presidios en plaza desgastador al modo que en años pasados se mando executar y executo con Carlos de Solis, mulato, que residía en el Castillo de la Concepción del Rio de San Juan que así quedara este Reo castigado como merece y lo demanda su maleficado delito, rotta y estragada vida, y ejemplificado escarmentados otros y en lo dalle satisfecha la divina justicia, cuios desagravios tan inmediatamente corten porquenta del General aquien sobrevido pido justicia y dire en forma de Derecho no hacerlo de malicia y deba mas formal Petición me conviene la epacena y en lo necesario ecetera Septiembre 6 de 1717

Don Francisco Antonio de Palacio y del Hoyo (rubric)

TRANSCRIPTION 2

1717

Juración

Yo Agustín del Río, alias de la Palma, alias Toribio, natural de casas grandes Junto el Presidio de Janos, que aquí estoí presente ante Vuestro Padre Predicador Comisario (que es) del Santo Officio del Inquisición de esta Nueba España en esta Villa y Real Presidio de Santa Fe del Nuevo Mexico y su jurisdicción.

Que aquí estoi presente puesta ante mi esta señal de la Cruz y los sacrosantos evangelicos que con mis manos corporales toco reconociendo la verdadera Católica y Apostolica fe, abjuro de delito le Anathematiso a toda especie de herejia que se levante contra la Santa Fe Católica y Ley Evangelica de Nuestro Redentor y Salvador Jesu Cristo y contra la Santa Sede Apostolica Iglesia Romana, especialmente aquella de que yo en el Tribunal del Santo Officio he sido acusado y estoy levemente sospechoso y juro y prometo de tener y guardar siempre aquella Santa fe que tiene guarda y enseña la Santa Madre Iglesia i que sere siempre obediente a nuestro señor el Papa y a sus subiesores que canónicamente subsediesen en la Santa Silla Apostolica y a sus determinaciones: y confieso que todos aquellos que contra nuestra Santa Fe Católica viniesen son dignos de condenación

Yo prometo de nunca me juntos con ellos y que en quanto en mi fuere los persequire las herejias que de ellos supiere los rebelare a cualquiera Señor Ynquisitador de la herejica probedad y Prelade de la Santa Madre Iglesia de donde quiera que me hallare; y Juro y prometo que resivire humillamente i con paciencia la penitencia que me ha sido o que fuese impuesta con todas mis fuersas y poder i la cumplire en todo i por todo sin ir ni benir contra ello y quiero y consiento y me complase y que si yo en algun tiempo (lo que Dios no permita) fuese o biniese contra las cosas susodichas o contra qual quiera cosa o parte de ello se havido y benido por impenitente, y me someto a la correcion y le severidad de los sacros Canones para que en mi como persona que abjura de delito sean ejecutadas las censuras y penas en ellos contenidas y consiento que aquellos me sean dadas y las haya de se [Illegible] quando quiera que algo se me provare haver quebrantado lo susodicho por mi abjurado y ruego al presente Notario que me lo de por testimonio, y a los presentes que de ello sean testigos estando atras ello por testigos el Capitan Don Francisco Lorenzo Casado y el Capitan Juan de Archibec presente el Reverendo Padre Comisario del Santo Officio Fray Juan de Tagle quien lo firmo por no saber firmar yo dicho Agustin le la Palma oi Martes veintiocho del mes de Diziembe de mill setecientos diez y siete años

    Fray Juan de Tagle (Rubric)
    Comisario del Santo Officio
    Paso ante mí
    Fray Joseph Narváez Valverde
    Notario del Santo Officio

Doy fe i verdadero testimonio como del dia Martes que se contara veintiocho del mes de diciembre del presente año de mill setecientos i diecisiete, estando presente Padre Predicador Fray Juan Mingues de vestido, acabado de cantar Missa, i de Diacono Padre Fray Jerónimo de Liñan, y Subdiacono el Padre Predicador Fray Juan del Pino, los testigos seculares el Capitan Don Francisco Lorenzo Casado y el Capitan Juan de Archibec, ancado de rodillas Agustin de la Palma, alias del Rio, alias Toribio, en presencia del Reverendo Padre Predicador Fray Juan de Tagle Comisario del Santo Officio lo es de este Reyno de la Nueva Mexico en la Iglesia Parochial de esta Villa de Santa Fe presente una Cruz y puestas las manos sobre los Santos Evangelicos, abierto el Misal, hizo la Abjurasion; deleto segun el orden del [illegible] Tribunal de la Inquisition.

La qual por no saber firmar dicho Agustin de la Palma la firmo el Reverendo Padre Comisario, y juntamente yo el Fray Jospeh Narbaiz Valerde, Notario como de arriba consta. En testimonio de verdad lo firme in dicha Villa de Santa fe en beintiocho dias del mes de diciembre de [mil] setecientos i diecisiete años.

Fray Joseph Narvaiz y Valverde, Notario (Rubric)

This document was transcribed and translated by Dorothy Mazon and Rick Hendricks.

Notes

1. See Case 5.
2. See Greenleaf, "Inquisition": 210; Rule, *History of the Inquisition*: 359.
3. See Rawlings, *Spanish Inquisition*: 12-13.
4. For Spanish Inquisition procedures, see Boyer, *Lives of the Bigamists*; Chuchiak, *Inquisition in New Spain*: 43-8; 218-19; Greenleaf, "Inquisition": 29-59; and Rawlings, *Spanish Inquisition*: 115-34. For language from manuals or examples of charges and confessions, see: Chuchiak, *Inquisition in New Spain*: 264-65; Roth, *Spanish Inquisition*: 277-83; and Rule, *History of the Inquisition*: 353-55. The latter is an especially useful source; for instance, the same language used in Agustín de la Palma's abjuration is found in the examples on page 359.
5. Chuchiak, *Inquisition in New Spain*: 43-48, 218-19; Roth, *Spanish Inquisition*: 277-83.
6. To date, no information has been found on Inquisitor Cienfuego.
7. The "Inquisitor Fiscal of the Holy Office" is the prosecuting attorney. (Chuchiak, *Inquisition in New Spain*: 15.)
8. Comisario was the title given to the head of the local commission of the Spanish Holy Office of the Inquisition. In New Mexico, the Franciscans were the representatives of the Inquisition. The local comisario was responsible for proclaiming the edicts of faith, making visitations to their districts, and for receiving denunciations and testimonies about suspected heresies. (See Chuchiak, *Inquisition in New Spain*: 25.) Fray Juan de Tagle was a comisario of the Holy Office and a custos (head) of the Franciscan Custodia, of which New Mexico was a part. He also ministered to San Ildefonso Pueblo for twenty-five years (from 1701 to 1726) and in Santa Fe.
9. Presumably, this is the same Agustín de la Palma who is discussed in Case 5.
10. To date, no information has been found on María de Espejo.
11. To date, no information has been found on an Indian woman named Lucía.
12. Guazapares was a Mexican mining town; it is located about equidistant between the city of Chihuahua and the Gulf of California.
13. To date, no information has been found on Father Antonio Gómez.
14. In the confession document, Agustín de la Palma says he is from Casas Grandes near the presidio of Janos. The latter was located in what is now known as the state of Chihuahua, Mexico.
15. To date, no information has been found on Carlos de Solís.
16. The Castillo de la Concepcíon is a fortress in Nicaragua near the border with Costa Rica. It was completed in 1675 on the site of a former fortress as defense against pirates, although it was burned in 1685 by pirate William Dampier. The ruins are in the initial stage of approval as a UNESCO World Heritage site. (*Wikipedia*, "Castillo de la concepcín," accessed on February 19, 2016; Peary, "The River of San Juan de Nicaragua": 57-86.)
17. To date, no information has been found on Francisco Antonio de Palacio de Hoyo.
18. For information on Francisco Lorenzo de Casados, see Case 9.
19. Juan de Archibeque was born in Bayonne, France, in 1671, as Jean l'Archeveque. He accompanied the La Salle Expedition to the Mississippi in 1684, but fled after the murder of the expedition's leader. Juan and another survivor of the expedition, Jacques Grolet (later Gurulé), lived with Indians for two years and eventually encountered Spanish troops. Juan and Jacques were then sent to the mines in San Luis Potosí and then to Spain, returning in 1693. Juan de Archibeque was in New Mexico by 1694, having come with the Farfán Expedition. He married Antonia Gutiérrez in 1694, and upon her death married doña Manuela de Roybal, daughter of don Santiago Roybal, captain and high sheriff of the Holy Office of the Inquisition. In 1720, he was killed on the Villasur Expedition (Kessell, Hendricks, and Dodge, *Royal Crown*: 341n135; Esquibel, "Residents": 68; Chávez, "Some Mission Records": 159).
20. Fray Joseph Narváez Valverde was a lay brother in New Mexico from 1694 to 1706. His duties included acting

as a surgeon, notary, and ecclesiastical secretary. (Norris, *Year Eighty*: 50; Kessell, Hendricks, Dodge, and Miller, *Disturbances*: 551n51.)

21. For information on Fray Juan de Mingues, see Case 17.
22. Fray Gerónimo de Liñan was in New Mexico from 1711 to 1719, but he had to leave after being accused of solicitation in the confessional. He served in several places, including Albuquerque, Galisteo, Pecos, Laguna, and Picuris. He was also a notary at Santa Cruz. (Chávez, *Archives*: 10, 250; Norris, *Year Eighty*: 170.)
23. Fray Juan del Pino was a native of Puebla. He professed his vows at San Francisco de Mexico in 1706. In 1745, he was relieved from the post of vice-custos for health reasons. (Norris, *Year Eighty*: 172; Chávez, *Archives*: 162.)

19

PRICKLY PEAR CACTUS CAUSE OF ALTERCATION BETWEEN SANTA FE NEIGHBORS
April 17–May 10, 1719, Source: SANM II #296

Synopsis and editor's notes: This confrontation began in Santa Fe when an Indian servant woman was sent to tell the alcalde that Manuel, the fourteen-year-old son of Joseph Domínguez, was hit on the head with a rock by Catalina de Villalpando and was bleeding. When the alcalde arrived at the Domínguez house, he asked María de Castaneda, a local curandera (healer), to look at the wound. She declared it was not dangerous, but gave it a stitch. When Alcalde Francisco Joseph Bueno de Bohorques y Corcuera interviewed Manuel Domínguez and Catalina de Villapando, he was told that Manuel had been planting *nogales* (prickley pear cactus) in a space between the Domínguez and Villalpando houses to prevent people from using it as a passageway. When a young girl and young boy began using the pathway anyway and uprooted the cactus, Manuel told the young girl to stop but she refused. He began hitting her on her feet with a stick and then shoved the small boy against the fence. Then, the girl's older sister, Catalina de Villalpando, came out to the pathway and also started to uproot the cactus. Manuel told her to stop and called her a "bad name." Catalina then threw a rock at him, hitting him on the head, and he threw a rock at her, hitting her on the back.

After hearing this, the alcalde then had Catalina taken to the home of Ventura de Esquivel and asked more questions of both her and Manuel. Upon hearing their descriptions of the fight, he ordered Catalina to be released and both of them to behave themselves in the future. He said there would be no punishment because the charges were minor and there had been no formal complaint.

Even in such a minor case the alcalde followed the standard legal procedures of the period. He formally listed the charge, inspected the site, and had the injury examined by a healer. After that, he took written testimony from the accuser, the accused, and the woman who looked at the wound. Some days later, he examined the wound as well, to make sure it was healed, gave both participants a warning, and ordered the older woman, Catalina, to pay the court costs. The latter was probably to cover the time spent by the alcalde, witnesses, and healer, as well as the cost of the paper and ink used to record the case. Perhaps the alcalde took such care with the case because he was inexperienced and wished to handle every aspect expertly and correctly. Or, perhaps he wanted to impress his uncle: research on the alcalde's background suggests he was a nephew of Governor Valverde. In any event, this case is a good example of Spanish law at work in the daily lives of eighteenth-century New Mexicans.

The Indian servant woman who reported the case may have been a *"rescate"*—a ransomed Indian who had been purchased from nomadic Indians at a trade fair. Such a person would have been placed with a Spanish family to work for them as a servant and to learn Spanish ways. In theory, the rescates would have been released when they reached adulthood and then would find a place among the *genízaro* communities, like Abiquiu or Belén, which included detribalized Indians. In some cases, rescates remained with the family as a servant. As the alcalde indicates in his comment below, in this case the Indian servant appears to have been an Apache.

TRANSLATION

1719

[Legal proceeding initiated]

In this Villa of Santa Fe, headquarters of this kingdom of New Mexico, on the 17th of the present month of this year of 1719, at about two o'clock in the afternoon, there appeared before me, Captain don Francisco Joseph Bueno [de Bohorques y] Corcuera,[1] the alcalde mayor of this villa, an Indian woman who appeared to be an Apache. She stated that she was from the home of the adjutant Joseph Domínguez, and said that she was sent by her master to call upon me and ask that I go to see a young man who was the son of Joseph Domínguez.[2] He had fainted from a blow to the head and would not be attended to until I went to see him. As such I placed this request as a legal proceeding at the head of the case. I certified it as the presiding judge along with my assisting witnesses due to the lack of a public or royal scribe, there not being one in this kingdom, as well as on plain paper, there not being any of the sealed variety within these parts, to which I certify.

Before me as presiding judge
don Francisco Joseph Bueno de Bohorques y Corcuera (rubric)
Assisting witness
Juan Manuel Chirinos[3] (rubric)
Assisting witness
Juan de Paz Bustillos[4] (rubric)

Continuing, I proceeded to the said home accompanied by the witnesses where I saw a young person of about the age of fourteen, whose face was soaked with blood. Upon recognizing him and seeing from where the blood was flowing, I saw that it was from an injury upon his head which was about three to four fingers long above the forehead, quite large, requiring three to four stitches. But there not being a surgeon or barber who could assist him, I ordered that they look for someone who could aid him in the best manner possible and who could know if his skull was fractured. Later

I would return to take his sworn statement being that it was not possible to do it at the time.

So that this is valid I placed it as a legal proceeding under the jurisdiction of the royal justice under which I acted as presiding judge along with my assisting witnesses, to which I certify.

Before me as presiding judge
don Francisco Joseph Bueno de Bohorques y Corcuera (rubric)
Assisting witness
Juan Manuel Chirinos (rubric)
Assisting witness
Juan de Paz Bustillos (rubric)

Continuing, I, the alcalde mayor, accompanied by the witnesses, proceeded to the house of the adjutante Joseph Domínguez, where the injured person was, to take his sworn statement. From this I could determine the reason and extent of the injury, by whom he was treated, and in what way I could proceed against the aggressor. Being at his home, I, the alcalde mayor, made to appear before me the individual who had taken care of the patient's injury so that under a sworn statement she could declare its extent. So that it is valid I placed this as a proceeding acting as the presiding judge along with my assisting witnesses, to which I certify and I signed it.

don Francisco Joseph Bueno de Bohorques y Corcuera (rubric)
Assisting witness
Juan de Paz Bustillos (rubric)
Assisting witness
Juan Manuel Chirinos (rubric)

[Statement of María de Castaneda[5]]

Continuing on the said day, month and year, at the said home, María de Castaneda appeared before me, the alcalde mayor, from whom I took her sworn statement that she made to God, Our Lord, and to the sign of the most Holy Cross. Under her proper legal right she stated that she would tell the truth as to what she knew and could understand about the injury that she had cared for [Manuel Domínguez].[6]

She stated that it was true that she had cared for the injury to his head. She said that she knew from experiences with others that she had helped heal that there was no risk from it. She was asked if the skull was fractured. She stated that it was not. She was asked if stitches were required. She stated that it was true that it should have required two, but that she had made only one because, among other things, it was not deep enough. She said that this was the truth and that she was satisfied with it and she felt it was sufficient according to what she knew. She stated that she was forty years of age, more or less, and did not sign because she did not know how. I, the alcalde mayor, signed along with my assisting witnesses who acted along with me, the presiding judge, to which I certify.

    don Francisco Jospeh Bueno de Bohorques y Corcuera (rubric)
Assisting witness
Juan de Paz Bustillos (rubric)
Assisting witness
Juan Manuel Chirinos (rubric)

[Statement of Manuel Domínguez]

    Continuing, on the said day, month and year, I, the alcalde mayor, being present at his home and having in my presence Manuel Domínguez, I took his sworn statement which he made to God and to the Holy Cross, to tell the truth as to what he knew and what he was asked.

    He was asked if it was true that his name is Manuel Domínguez and if he was fourteen or fifteen years of age, more or less. He was asked how he had gotten the injury on his on the head. He stated that he was within the entry area that his father, the adjutant Joseph Domínguez, and he were planting some prickly pear cactus as his father had ordered him to do. This was to block a pathway that was being used through there. He told a young daughter[7] of Ana María [Romero Villalpando],[8] who is known as "la Panda," not to be going through there, that it was not a public pathway. She answered him by telling him that she could if she wished. In addition, he said that the young girl was uprooting the cactus that he had already planted. When the young girl saw him headed to where she was, she went to her home to call her sister, Catalina,[9] who then came out to continue to uproot the cactus. At this time Manuel returned to defend the plants that he had told the young girl not to uproot. But she had already uprooted them and thrown them away. He then retrieved them to replant them and told Catalina not to be doing that. Catalina spoke back to him with some other remark and at the same time she picked up a rock and threw it at him, which was the way that he got the injury on his head. Then, as he was going back to his home, Catalina threw another rock at him but it did not quite reach him.

    Manuel was then asked if he had anything else to say about what had happened to him with Catalina, or if he had given her any other reason for her doing what she did. He stated that there was nothing else, and that this was the truth as shown in the sworn statement that he has made. He did not sign because he did not know how. I signed it along with my assisting witnesses acting as presiding judge, to which I certify.

    don Francisco Jospeh Bueno de Bohorques y Corcuera (rubric)
Assisting witness
Juan de Paz Bustillos (rubric)
Assisting witness
Juan Manuel Chirinos (rubric)

[Catalina taken to the home of Ventura de Esquivel]

Continuing, on the said day, I, the alcalde mayor, upon seeing the above statement and the proceedings that were carried out by [Juan] Joseph de Archuleta,[10] minister of justice,[11] he was ordered to bring forth Catalina. Being in my presence, I charged her with what the case had revealed against her. She did not deny that she hit Manuel Domínguez on the head with a rock which resulted in an injury. There not being a jail for women in this villa, I ordered the said minister to take her and place her at the home of Ventura de Esquivel,[12] a soldier of this royal presidio.

Under my authority and that of the king, Our Lord, I ordered him to hold her with all due care until I decided otherwise. I thus designated this as an official proceeding being that it was executed by [Juan Joseph Archuleta] before me as presiding judge along with my assisting witnesses, to which I certify.

don Francisco Joseph Bueno (rubric)
Assisting witness
Juan de Paz Bustillos (rubric)
Assisting witness
Juan Manuel Chirinos (rubric)

[Proceedings]

On the 18th of the present month and year, I, the alcalde mayor, reviewed these proceedings that were made by me and for the determination of this criminal case which I followed in my capacity as Justice. I then proceded to take the statement of Catalina and all of the others who were cited as witnesses due to the fact that the injured person did not cite anyone. So that it is valid, I designated it as an official proceeding that is before me, acting as I do as presiding judge along with my assisting witnesses. To this I certify and I signed it.

don Francisco Jospeh Bueno de Bohorques y Corcuera (rubric)
Assisting witness
Juan de Paz Bustillos (rubric)
Assisting witness
Juan Manuel Chirinos (rubric)

[Statement of Catalina Villalpando]

Continuing on the said day, month and year, I, the alcalde mayor, ordered the minister Juan Joseph de Archuleta to bring forth before me Catalina. Upon being brought forth and in my presence under oath which she made to God, Our Lord, and to the sign of the most Holy Cross, she promised to tell the truth as to what she knew and what she was asked.

She stated that it was the truth that she is the right person and that her name is Catalina de Villalpando. She said that she lives in a house that is contiguous one house with another, there not being anything in between except a fence of branches, and a pathway to walk through. She further said that she ordered her younger sister to go and look for a sieve in the neighborhood. It happened that Manuel Domínguez was there with a cedar stick in his hand and upon seeing the young girl going through the pathway he told her not to go there, that it was not a public walk through. Being that the young girl continued to go through he hit her with the stick on her feet and he grabbed by the arm a little boy that had gone with her and threw him against the fence. Upon the youngsters going inside crying, the defendant [Catalina] came out of the home asking him why he had hit the little girl and boy. He told her that he had hit them because, "They were Apaches dogs like you," telling her that it was not a through road that everyone could cross. She then told him to take the cactus and plant them somewhere else. He answered her telling her that he was not going to do it. She then proceeded to pull them out.

While she was pulling them out he went and hit her with the stick that he had and he told her that she was a whore. At this she picked up a rock which she immediately found close by and threw it at him. At this time, she saw that he was soaked with blood, being that she had hit him on the head and injured him. Then Manuel picked up another rock and threw it at her, hitting her in the ribs, being that she had turned her back to him. Turning around to see him, she saw that he had gone into his home. Thus she left him and proceeded to go into her own home.

She was asked if anything else had happened other than what she had stated and if there was anyone else who was present at the time. She said that nothing else happened other than what she had said in her sworn statement, and that there was no one around who had seen them being that they were alone. She said that her age was twenty-five or twenty-six and did not sign because she did not know how. I signed it along with my assisting witnesses who acted along with me as presiding judge, to which I certify.

    don Francisco Jospeh Bueno (rubric)
Assisting witness
Juan de Paz Bustillos (rubric)
Assisting witness
Juan Manuel Chirinos (rubric)

[Determination]

At this villa on the 10th of May of the present year, I, the alcalde mayor, was told by Manuel Domínguez, that he is healed of his injury. I made him appear before me and my witnesses. Having seen him and the wound that he had, I saw that he was healed from it, seeing that the flesh had healed and that he had nothing but the scar. I then asked him if it bothered him to sleep or for anything else or if he had pain in the area. He stated that he did not. For that reason, I felt assured about the whole issue, to which I certify. So that it is thus valid I placed it as a proceeding acting as presiding judge with my assisting witnesses who signed it along with me.

    Assisting witness
Juan Manuel Chirinos (rubric)
Assisting wit ess
Juan de Paz Bustillos (rubric)
don Francisco Bueno (rubric)

[Decree]

Continuing at this villa after being seen by me, the alcalde mayor, due to the minor charges that have been made against Catalina de Villalpando, I gave her freedom and released her from being held where she was. I cautioned her as I did Manuel Domínguez, telling them that in the future they are to contain themselves and if for any reason or other I came to know that they had any type of dissention, they would be punished as being disobedient to a royal justice. Because there was no complaint against Catalina as an aggressor, for now I only ordered her to pay the expenses of the proceedings. Thus I notified them, their being in my presence. I acted as presiding judge with my assisting witnesses due to the lack of a public or royal scribe, there not being one in this kingdom, and on common paper because the sealed type is not found in these parts, to which I certify and sign.

    Assisting witness
Juan Manuel Chirinos (rubric)
Assisting witness
Juan de Paz Bustillos (rubric)
Assisting witness
don Francisco Bueno (rubric)

[Notification]

On the said day, month and year, I, the alcalde mayor, informed the above stated about the decree personally, their being before me. They having heard it and fully understanding it stated that they will obey and would obey. They did not sign because they did not know how. I, the alcalde mayor, signed it along with my assisting witnesses, acting as presiding judge due to the lack of a public or royal scribe, which there is none in this kingdom, to which I certify.

    Assisting witness
Juan Manuel Chirinos (rubric)
Assisting witness
Juan de Paz Bustillos (rubric)

This came before me as presiding judge
   don Francisco Joseph Bueno de Bohorques y Corcuera (rubric)

TRANSCRIPTION

En esta Villa de Santa Fee cabesera de este Reyno dela Nueba Mexico en dies y siete dias del presente mes de este año de mill setesientos y diesinuebe, como alas dos dela tarde ante mi el Capitan Dn. Francisco Joseph Bueno y Corcuera, Alcalde Mallor de dicha Villa paresio una Yndia al parecer Apacha y dijo era de en casa del Alludante Joseph Dominguez y que su ama la enbiava a que me llamara para que biera a un moso mansebo hijo del dicho Joseph Dominguez que estava desmallado de una partidura en la cabesa y que no lo abian curado asta que yo lo biera; y asi lo puse por delixencia y cabesa de causa anutuando ante mi como Jues Receptor con los testigos ynfraescriptos de mi asistensia por falta de escribano publica ni real que no lo ay en este Reyno y en el presente papel comun por que el sellado no corre en estas partes, de que doy fee.
   Ante mi como Jues Receptor
   Dn. Francisco Joseph Bueno de Bohorques y Corcuera (rubric)
   Testigo de asistenzia
   Juan Manuel Chirinos (rubric)
   Testigo de asistenzia
   Juan de Paz Bustillos (rubric)

Y luego yncontinente pase a dicha casa acompanados de dichos testigos a donde bide a un moso como de edad de catorse a quinse anos banado en sangre la cara a quien abiendo reconosido y bisto de que prosedia le bide una herida en la cabesa como cosa de tres a quatro dedos mas ariva dela frente algo larga que nesesitaria de dos o tres puntos y que no abiendo aqui sirujano ni barber que la pudiera reconoser mande en dicha que buscaran quien lo curaba lo mejor que pudiera y reconosieran si tenia el casco lastimado mientras yo bolvia a tomarle la declaracion por que entonses no estaba para ello. Y para que asi conste lo puse por dilixencia de oficio dela Real Justicia actuando ante mi como Jues Receptor con los testigos ynfraescriptos de mi asistenzia de que doy fee y lo firme.
   Ante mi como Jues Receptor
   Dn. Francisco Joseph Bueno de Bohorques y Corcuera (rubric)
   Testigo de asistenzia
   Juan Manuel Chirinos (rubric)
   Testigo de asistenzia
   Juan de Paz Bustillos (rubric)

Y luego yncontinente yo dicho Alcalde Mallor acompanado de dichos testigos pase ala casa del dicho Alludante Joseph Dominguez donde estava dicho herido a tomarle su declaracion y por ella aberiguar la causa por que zela abian dado la dicha herida y saber la calidad de ella de quien lo curo para con mas justificazion poder proseder ala abiriguasion contra el agresor y estando en dicha casa yo dicho Alcalde Mallor yse pareser ante mi ala persona que abia curado la erida de dicho pasiente para que debajo de juramento declarada la calidad de ella, y para que asi conste lo puse por dilixensia actuando ante mi como Jues Receptor con dos testigos ynfraescriptos de mi asistenzia de que doy fee y lo firme.

Ante mi como Jues Receptor
Dn. Francisco Joseph Bueno de Bohorques y Corcuera (rubric)
Testigo de asistenzia
Juan Manuel Chirinos (rubric)
Testigo de asistenzia
Juan de Paz Bustillos (rubric)

Yncontinente en dicho dia en dicha casa paresio presente ante mi dicho Alcalde Maior Maria de Castaneda a quien debajo de juramento que hiso a Dios Nuestro Señor y ala Señal de la Santissima Cruz en forma de derecho de desir berdad en lo que supiera en su saber y entender dela herida que abia curado al dicho Manuel; dijo que era berdad que le abia curado de una herida que tiene en la cabesa en que reconosio por la esperencia que tiene de otras que a curado que no es de riesgo; y preguntada si tenia partido el casco; dijo que no; y preguntadole si abia abido menester puntos; dijo que era berdad que abia menester dos pero que no le dio mas de uno por que no estaba profunda por lo de mas y que esto es la berdad y lo que siente para descargo de su consiencia so cargo del juramento que tiene fecho y que es de hedad de cuarenta años poco mas o menos y que no firmo por que no saber, firmelo yo dicho Alcalde Mallor con los testigos ynfraescriptos de mi asistenzia autuando ante mi como Jues Receptor de que doi fee.

Ante mi como Jues Receptor
Dn. Francisco Joseph Bueno de Bohorques y Corcuera (rubric)
Testigo de asistenzia
Juan Manuel Chirinos (rubric)
Testigo de asistenzia
Juan de Paz Bustillos (rubric)

Y luego yncontinentemente en dicho dia, yo dicho Alcalde Mallor estando en dicha casa y teniendo presente al dicho Manuel Dominguez le resivi declaracion que yso de bajo de juramento a Dios Nuestro Señor y ala Santa Cruz de desir berdad en lo que supiera y le fuera preguntado.

Yy preguntadole si es berdad que se llama Manuel Dominguez y que hera de edad de catorze a quinse años poco mas o menos. Preguntadole de que le abia prosedido la herida que tiene en la cabesa. Dijo que estando en el gabal que tiene senbrado su padre el Alludante Joseph Dominguez poniendo unos nopales espinosos que su padre le abia mandado poner para enbarasar el que no ubiese paso por alli salio una muchachita hija de Ana Maria que llllaman "la panda" ala qual le dijo no pases por ay que ese no es camino y ella le dijo que si queria pasar y que tembien estava la dicha muchachita desenterando los nopales y que asi que lo bido ir para alla se fue a su casa llamando a su hermana Cathalina la qual bino y se puso a desenterar los nopales y que dicho Manuel bolvio a querer defender que no los desenterada lla las abia desenteradas y tiradolas y que por qual las cojio para bolberlas a enterar le dio un enbion la dicha Cathalina aquien el le corespondio con otro y que entonses ella also una piedra y le tiro con la qual le ronpio la cabesa y que biniendo el para su casa le tiro otra la dicha Cathalina aunque no le alcanso.

Y preguntadole al dicho declarante que otra cosa le abia pasado con la dicha o si le abia dado mas motivo del que lleva dicha; dijo que no y que esta es la berdad so cargo del juramento que tiene fecho y que no firma por que no sabe, firmelo yo con los testigos ynfraescriptos de mi asistenzia autuando como Jues Receptor de que doy fee.

    Dn. Francisco Joseph Bueno (rubric)
Testigo de asistenzia
Juan Manuel Chirinos (rubric)
Testigo de asistenzia
Juan de Paz Bustillos (rubric)

En dicho dia luego yncontinentemente yo dicho Alcalde Mallor mande en bista dela declaracion de ariva y las dilixensias por mi echas en estos autos a Juan Joseph de Archuleta ministro de justicia que fuese a traer presa ala dicha Cathalina ala qual estando en mi presensia le yse el cargo delo que en esta causa resulta conta ella y no abiendose negado a que es berdad que le dio con una pierda de que result la herida del dicho Manuel Dominguez en la cavesa y no abiendo en esta Villa carsel para mugeres le mande a dicho ministro la llevara y pusiera en deposito en casa de Bentura de Esquibel soldado de este Real Presidio y le requiriera de mi parte y del Rey Nuestro Señor la tubiese con todo cuidado en el interin que yo disponia otra cosa, y asi lo pongo por delixencia por aberlo executado asi dicho ministro autuando ante mi como Jues Receptor con los testigos de mi asistenzia de que doi fee =

    Dn. Francisco Joseph Bueno(rubric)
Testigo de asistenzia
Juan Manuel Chirinos (rubric)
Testigo de asistenzia
Juan de Paz Bustillos (rubric)

En el dia dies y ocho del presente mes y año yo dicho Alcalde Mallor en bista de las dilixensias por mi echas para la justificasion de esta causa criminal que sigo de oficio de Justicia pase a tomar declaracion ala dicha Cathalina y alos demas que sitan aberse allado presentes por quanto el herido no sita a nadie y para que asi conste lo pongo por delixensia en este auto autuando ante mi como Jues Receptor con los testigos ynfraescriptos de mi assistenzia de que doy fee y lo firme.

Dn. Francisco Joseph Bueno (rubric)
Testigo de asistenzia
Juan Manuel Chirinos (rubric)
Testigo de asistenzia
Juan de Paz Bustillos (rubric)

Y luego yncontinente en dicho dia yo dicho Alcalde Mallor mando al Ministro Juan Joseph de Archuleta que truxese a mi presencia a dicha Cathalina ala qual aviendo la traido y estando presente de bajo de juramento que yso a Dios Nuestro Señor y ala Señal de la Santissima Cruz de desir berdad en lo que supiera y le fuera preguntado.

Le resevi su declaracion por lo qual dijo que es berdad que es ella misma y que se llama Cathalina de Villalpando y que por bivir alli contigua una casa con otra que no ay mas que una serca de ramas de por medio y estar echo bedera de camino por alli enbio a una muchachita Hermana sulla a que buscara un zedaso en la vezindad estava alli Manuel Dominguez con un palo de sabino en la mano y que entonses biendo salir a dicha muchacha por dicha bedera le dijo no pases por ay que no es eze camino el dicho Manuel y que por fiando la muchachita a querer pasar le dio en los pies con el palo que tenia en la mano y a otro muchachito que llebava con sigo lo tiro de un braso a dentro dela zerca y que abiendo entrado los muchachos llorando salio dicha declarante y le dijo por que les das alos muchachos. Respondio son otros perros Apaches como tu, no es ese camino por donde todos crusan. Ella le dijo quita esas espinas y ponlas en otra parte y que respondio el que no queria que.

Entonses la declarante fue a quitarlas y que estando las quitando le dio con el palo un palo y le dijo que era una puta alo qual la dicha declarante also una piedra que allo a mano y de que bes le tiro con ella con la qual lo bido banado en sangre por que sin embargo de que le dio en la cabesa y lo descalabro el dicho Manuel also otra y le tiro con ella ala declarante y le dio en las costillas por aber buelto la espalda para yrse a su casa que sin embargo bolvio la cara para el y abiendo bisto que se metia en su casa lo dejo y se metio en la sulla dicha declarante =

Y preguntadole si abia pasado otra cosa mas delo que lleva declarado o quien se avia allado presente; dijo que no paso mas delo que lleva dicho so cargo del juramento que tiene fecho y que no ubo nadie que los biera por que estaban solos y que es de hedad de beinte y cinco a beinte y seis años y que no firma por no saber firmelo yo con los testigos ynfraescriptos de mi asistenzia autuando ante mi como Jues Receptor de que doy fee.

 Dn. Francisco Joseph Bueno (rubric)
 Testigo de asistenzia
 Juan Manuel Chirinos (rubric)
 Testigo de asistenzia
 Juan de Paz Bustillos (rubric)

 En dicha Villa yo dicho Alcalde Mallor en dies dias del mes de Mallo del presente año abiendo sabido por Manuel Dominguez contenido en esta causa se allaba bueno de su erida lo yse pareser ante mi y dichos testigos aquien estando presente y abiendo reconosido y biendole la herida reconosi lla esta sano del todo por aber unido la carne y no tener ya mas que la señal de ella y abiendole preguntado al dicho se le inpedia para dormir o para algo o zentia algun dolor en aquella parte dijo que no por lo qual reconosi estar azegurado ya de ella de que doy fee y para que asi conste lo puse por dilixencia autuando ante mi como Juez Receptor con los testigos ynfraescriptos de mi asistenzia que lo firmaron con migo.

 Testigo de asistenzia
 Juan Manuel Chirinos (rubric)
 Testigo de asistenzia
 Juan de Paz Bustillos (rubric)
 Dn. Francisco Joseph Bueno (rubric)

 Y luego yncontinente en dicha Villa bisto por mi dicho Alcalde Mallor el estado de esta causa del poco cargo que de ella resulta contra la dicha Catalina de Villalpando la ube de dar por libre y suelta del deposito en que se allava amonestandole como lo yse asi a ella como el dicho Manuel Dominguez en que en lo de adelante ze contubiesen y que por ningun pretexto ni occasion ninguna supiese yo que abian tenido dissension ninguna por que zerian castigados como ynobedientes ala Real Justizia; y por quanto no abido querella de parte contra la dicha Cathalina por agresora por aora solo le condeno en que pagese las costas de lo autuado y asi se lo notifique estando presentes autuando ante mi como Jues Receptor con los testigos ynfraescriptos de mi asistenzia por falta de escribano publico ni real que no lo ay en este Reyno y en el presente papel comun por que el sellado no corre en estas partes de que doy fee y lo firme.

 Testigo de asistenzia
 Juan Manuel Chirinos (rubric)
 Testigo de asistenzia
 Juan de Paz Bustillos (rubric)
 Dn. Francisco Joseph Bueno (rubric)

En dicha Villa en dicho dia, mes y año yo dicho Alcalde Mallor notifique el auto de ariva alos dichos en su persona estando presentes los quales abiendolo oydo y entendido dixeron que lo obedesian y obedesieron y que no firmaban por que no savian firmelo yo dicho Alcalde Mallor con los testigos ynfraescriptos de mi asistenzia y lo puse por diligensia autuando ante mi como Jues Receptor a falta de Escribano Publico ni Real que no lo ay en este Reyno, de que doi fee.

Testigo de asistenzia
Juan Manuel Chirinos (rubric)
Testigo de asistenzia
Juan de Paz Bustillos (rubric)
Paso ante mi como Jues Receptor
Dn. Francisco Joseph Bueno de Bohorques y Corcuera (rubric)

Notes

1. Francisco Joseph Bueno de Bohorques y Corcuera is listed in the 1714 Santa Fe presidio records as a corporal; that same year, he asked for permission to leave New Mexico to look for a cure for an injury he received when his horse kicked him in the leg. By 1718 he was an alcalde of Santa Fe. He also served as an aide to Governor Valverde and Governor Bustamante and probably came to New Mexico with Valverde. In 1934, historian Fernando Ocaranza states that Francisco Joseph Bueno was the nephew of Governor Valverde. (Christmas and Rau, "Una Lista": 197; SANM I #170; SANM II #317a; Ocaranza, *Establecimientos*: 134-36.)
2. The Joseph Domínguez in this document could be "José Domínguez de Mendoza," a natural son of either Tomé Domínguez de Mendoza II or Antonio Domínguez de Mendoza and Ana Velasco of Río Abajo. José was an adjutant of Governor Vargas in 1696 and later married Geronima Varela de Perea; they had two children, María and Manuel. In 1704, Joseph Domínguez is listed as being a lieutenant of the presidio cavalry; later, he was appointed a captain. In 1720, he was killed during the Villasur Expedition. (Chávez, *Origins*: 169-70; Chávez, "Mission Records": 156, 160-61; Kessell, Hendricks, Dodge, and Miller, *Disturbances*: 99, 100, 285; Barrett, *Spanish Colonial Settlement Landscapes*: 145-55.)
3. For information on Juan Manuel de Chirinos, see Case 5.
4. Juan de Paz Bustillos was born in Mexico City about 1650 and married María Antonia de Alanis in 1692. He may also be the "Juan de Bustos" who came to New Mexico with the Farfán Expedition in 1694. Bustos appears in the 1697 livestock distribution document, with a daughter Josefa. By 1699 he owned land in Santa Cruz. (Kessell, Hendricks, and Dodge, *Royal Crown*: 340n128, 341n134; Kessell, Hendricks, and Dodge, *Boulders*: 1152.)
5. María de Castaneda is listed as being in New Mexico in 1697, with a daughter also named María. In the same year, she testified that she came with the Hurtado Expedition in 1695, as "María de San Nicolás," a single woman. (Kessell, Hendricks, and Dodge, *Boulders*: 566n37, 1147.)
6. In 1723, a Manuel Domínguez is listed as being married to María, the daughter of Cristóbal Martín and Antonia Moraga of Chimayó, but it is not known if this is the same person. If Manuel Domínguez was fourteen or fifteen years old in 1719, then he would have been eighteen or nineteen years old in 1723, old enough for marriage. (Kessell, Hendricks, and Dodge, *Boulders*: 960n71; Chávez, *Origins*: 168.)
7. This may be the Josefa Villalpando who married Antonio Sandoval of Santa Cruz in 1722. (Chávez, *Origins*: 400.)
8 For information on Ana María Romero Villalpando, see Case 14.
9. For information on Catalina de Villapando, see Case 10.
10. [Juan] Joseph de Archuleta was the son of Agustín Archuleta and María Roma. He was part of the 1692 to 1693 El Paso muster. He came to New Mexico with don Diego de Vargas sometime in 1692 or 1693 and married María de la Cruz in 1713. (Kessell, Hendricks, and Dodge, *Royal Crown*: 96n115.)
11. This probably means that [Juan] Joseph de Archuleta was the arresting officer, a kind of sheriff.

12. Ventura [Buenaventura] de Esquivel was the son of Antonio de Caraña and María de Esquivel. When he asked to marry Rosa Bernardina Lucero de Godoy in 1702, Juana Luján made a written protest saying that he had promised to marry her and that her son was Esquivel's. Ventura de Esquivel denied this and the wedding with Rosa took place. In 1734, he petitioned for land from Governor Gervasio Cruzat y Góngora, but his request was denied. (Chávez, *Origins*: 173, 355; Chávez, *Roots*: 488-90; SANM II #259.)

20

ISIDRO SÁNCHEZ CONFESSES TO ROBBING PRESIDIO STOREHOUSE, LIEUTENANT-GOVERNOR VILLASUR INVESTIGATES
March 25–April 3, 1720, Source: SANM II #307

Synopsis and editor's notes: The name of the irrepressible Isidro Sánchez[1] appears several times in early eighteenth-century Spanish Colonial documents. In each case, his testimony, and sometimes his behavior, border on the outrageous. He was also literate; in fact, the elaborate signature and rubric he used in the documents rivals that of some governors.

In later years, he frequently served as a witness for court cases. He may have had some legal training, for he wrote petitions for clients and represented them in court, at least until 1745 when the governor ordered him to stop representing complainants.

Sánchez's name first appears in this Santa Fe document of 1719, when he was twenty-one years old. Apparently, he did not have a job or any other visible means of support, and he gambled frequently but not very successfully. In late March, not long before Lieutenant-General don Pedro de Villasur left Santa Fe in mid-June for his ill-fated expedition to the north, Sánchez, some soldiers, and a few local men were gambling at Juan de León Brito's house when some of them became suspicious about the origin of textiles, shoes, chocolate, and other goods that Isidro gambled with. When asked about the goods, Sánchez replied that his mother had sent him some money with which he purchased the goods, but his fellow gamblers did not believe him. After an official complaint was filed, Lieutenant-Governor Villasur had Sánchez arrested and placed in leg irons in the presidio barracks.

When he was brought forward to give testimony before Lieutenant-Governor Villasur, Sánchez admitted to stealing from the Palace of the Governors' storehouse. He explained that the "devil led him" to enter the second story of the presidio storehouse at night to steal some goods and then hide them. Having been successful, he went back the following night and stole some more goods that he hid nearby. This testimonial document is especially valuable to historians because of Sánchez's description of the palace's architecture (when he explains his method for getting in and out of a balcony window) and the fabrics he stole.

Unfortunately, pages are missing from both the beginning and end of the manuscript and the complete record of the case does not exist, so it is not known what sentence Lieutenant-Governor Villasur imposed for Isidro's larceny. We do know that at that time Sánchez was not yet a soldier and was not a part of the Villasur Expedition. Sometime between 1720 and 1731, however, he became a member of the Albuquerque squadron and at some point he threatened his sergeant with an arquebus (an early type of firearm). For the latter, he was expelled from the military. Later, as can be seen in Case 28 in this book, Sánchez tried his hand at being a legal representative.

As the present document indicates, the procedures for a military trial were similar to those of non-military trials in eighteenth-century New Mexico. A charge was made and testimony was given by witnesses before Lieutenant-Governor Villasur and his secretary, though no assisting witnesses signed the document as they would have in civilian cases. As was typical, the accused, Sánchez, was imprisoned and then ordered to give a statement before the lieutenant-governor. Villasur, who found discrepancies in Sánchez's testimony, asked him to clarify his answers. Sánchez was complying with this request when this document ends abruptly.

This was not the first time that a presidio building in Santa Fe had been robbed. A document dating to 1694, for instance, indicates that when Agustín Sáez lived with his wife in the second story of a warehouse containing supplies for presidio soldiers, he had entered the storehouse through a trap door and stole some soap and chiles. This information came to light when Sáez was giving testimony when on trial for adultery. He was convicted for stealing the soap and chiles, as well as for the theft of coconuts decorated with silver, caramel candies, and other goods from the residence of Governor Vargas.[2] In 1764, the presidio storehouse was robbed once again, this time by two brothers, Manuel and Pedro Moya, along with their mother as an accessory.[3]

After an investigation of the Villasur massacre, questions were asked about why don Pedro de Villasur was in Santa Fe in March of 1720, when the headquarters for the lieutenant-governor at that time was in El Paso. Also, he was questioned about why he was in charge of the 1720 expedition instead of New Mexico governor Antonio de Valverde Cossio. Valverde explained, in a 1726 hearing before Brigadier don Pedro de Rivera, that because he had duplicate orders and obligations to serve Viceroy Marqués de Valero he had turned his command over to Villasur. When arguments were made during the hearing that Villasur was inexperienced, Valverde countered by stating that the Spaniard Villasur had been an ensign and captain at the El Paso presidio, alcalde mayor and captain of war for a province in Nueva Vizscaya, and he had served as the alcalde mayor for the fort and mines of Cusihuiriachi and Chihuahua in Mexico.[4]

Although no Spanish Colonial women are featured in this case, the document was included here because some of the cloth that Isidro Sánchez stole from the presidio storehouse may have been purchased by Santa Fe officials with an eye toward selling it to women in the province (as well as to presidio personnel) and for trade with the Indians. The document is also included because it has a description of the Palace of the Governors, it is a delight to read, and it may be one of the last documents in which Lieutenant-Governor Villasur appears before he leaves on his disastrous expedition to the north.

TRANSLATION

[Testimony of Francisco Rendón][5]

In the Villa of Santa Fe on the said day and month and year, I, the Lieutenant-General Villasur, for the prosecution of this case, made appear before me Francisco Rendón, soldier of this presidial fortress. Being present, I received the oath that he made by God our Lord and the sign of the Cross, under which he promised to tell the truth in whatever he might know and be asked. Thus he said that][6] he won from Sánchez a new shirt. Likewise, he knows and saw Isidro Sánchez gamble a *vara*[7] of *diez y ocheno*[8] cloth. He has heard it said that Juan de Medina[9] won from him another shirt of the above-mentioned cloth.

Also, he heard that in the [Barrio de] Analco,[10] in the house of Juan de León [Brito],[11] Sánchez had gambled, and lost ten pairs of shoes and a vara of *bretaña*,[12] and that Juan de León took them. He knows this because Isidro Sánchez also did this with him, who exchanged three varas of bretaña [that he won] for other articles of clothing. This witness Rendón asked Sánchez where the above-mentioned articles came from, insisting on being told because Sánchez was a vagabond. Sánchez responded that it came from a payment that his mother had sent of 1,000 pesos.

This is what he knows, and it is true under the oath that he has made, which he affirmed and ratified, having been read this, his declaration. He said he is of the age of forty-two years, and he signed it with me, the secretary of government and war.

Don Pedro de Villasur (rubric)
Francisco Rendón (rubric)
Before me
Miguel Tenorio de Alba[13]
Secretary of Government and War

Testimony of Juan Cayetano Lobato[14]

In the Villa of Santa Fe on the said day and month and year, I, the lieutenant general, for the prosecution of this case, made appear before me [Juan] Cayetano Lobato, soldier of this presidial fortress. Being present, I received the oath that he made by God our Lord and the sign of the Cross, under which he promised to tell the truth in whatever he might know and be asked.

In accordance with the preliminary order for a hearing, he said it is true that Isidro Sánchez gave this witness a new shirt, and likewise he gave him three varas of *escarleta*[15] so that he could order a doublet to be made. And having asked him where all this came from, he said that I, the lieutenant general, had given it to him. Although he had heard it said that Isidro Sánchez has gambled, this witness has neither seen [the gambling], nor has it been done in front of him. He knows that Isidro Sánchez has no profession from which he could have gotten all the aforementioned. This is what he knows to be true under the oath that he has made. He affirmed and ratified it, having been read this, his declaration. He states to be of the age of twenty-four years. He did not sign because he does not know how. I, the lieutenant general, signed it with the secretary of government and war.

Don Pedro de Villasur (rubric)

Before me
Miguel Tenorio de Alba
Secretary of Government and War (rubric)

Order for imprisonment[16]

In the Villa of Santa Fe on the said day, month, and year, I, the lieutenant general don Pedro de Villasur, having followed this case and procedures recorded herein with the proceedings, bring a charge against Isidro Sánchez. In order to proceed against him and to know the truth, I order that Isidro Sánchez be held and put in safekeeping in the barracks of the presidial fortress with a pair of shackles. I order this imprisonment to be carried out by the ayudante don Joseph Manuel Giltoméy,[17] as the corporal of the guard, without permitting or allowing him to speak with anyone until his statement is received. Thus I approved, ordered, and signed it with my secretary of government and war.

Don Pedro de Villasur (rubric)
Before me
Miguel Tenorio de Alba
Secretary of Government and War (rubric)

Decree

In the Villa of Santa Fe on the 25th day of the month of March, 1720, I, General don Pedro de Villasur, the lieutenant governor and captain general of this realm, by virtue of the above order signed by me ordered ayudante don Joseph Giltoméy, as corporal of the guard of this presidial fortress, to hold Isidro Sánchez as prisoner with a pair of shackles, which he carried out promptly. In order to proceed against the aforementioned and to continue this case lawfully, I order that a statement be received and that appropriate justice be served accordingly. Thus I approved, ordered and signed it with my secretary of government and war.

Don Pedro de Villasur (rubric)
Before me
Miguel Tenorio de Alba
Secretary of Government and War (rubric)

Statement of Isidro Sánchez

In the Villa of Santa Fe on the 25th day of the month of March, 1720, I, the general Don Pedro de Villasur, lieutenant of the governor and captain general of this said realm, for the prosecution of this case and by virtue of the order on the reverse [of this document] approved by me, made a prisoner in this case appear before me.

He being present, I received his oath that he made by God our Lord and the sign of the Cross, under which he promised to tell that truth in whatever he may know or be asked.

Asked his name, age, profession, and where he was originally from, he said that his name is Isidro Sánchez, that he is twenty-one years of age, that he has no profession, and that he is a native of Zacatecas. Asked if he knows the reason for his imprisonment, he said that he does not know. Asked if he has gambled with Vicente de Armijo[18] and what *género* [fabric][19] he gambled with and when, he said that it is true that he gambled with Vicente de Armijo about fifteen days ago, and that he won from this confessant three varas of *bayeta*,[20] two varas of bretaña, two pairs of small shoes, two pounds of chocolate, and a new, unworn shirt of bretaña. This is his response. Asked if he has gambled with Alfonso Rael de Aguilar,[21] and what types of fabrics were gambled. He said that he gambled and lost the two mentioned shirts, a belt knife, a *zinidorrito*,[22] a *sala* [outer skirt or petticoat] of about two varas in length, and some women's shoes. Having said that there was no more to answer, he was asked again how he could negate the truth when the deposition record shows that he had gambled other articles of clothing. He said that it is true that he gambled three-quarters [of a vara] of cloth from Querétaro, and a white doublet of *nanquín*[23] that he had won from Vicente de Armijo, and this is his response.

Collegio de Propagando Fide. Querétaro was the location of the Collegio de Propaganda Fide, a college for teaching Franciscan missionaries. Fray Zephyrin Engelhardt, *The Franciscans in Arizona*, Holy Childhood Indian School, Harbor Springs, Michigan, 1899:39.

Asked about how many of the mentioned items he had gambled, he said in the same manner he had gambled and lost to Juan de Medina a new shirt of bretaña, and two pairs of small shoes. Some of this had been won from him, and the others he gave in exchange for a load of wood and two varas of bretaña. This is his response. Asked what dealings or exchanges he had with Francisco Rendón, soldier of this fortress, he said that he had given to Francisco Rendón three varas of bretaña for a hat that he, Rendón, had given him and some stockings. Likewise, he admits to having gambled in the Barrio de Analco in the house of Juan de León [Brito], for a vara of bretaña and some small shoes. He also admits to having in his house three varas of escarleta, and that he gave a shirt to Cayetano Lobato for which he gambled. He also has in his home two varas of bretaña.

Being asked where all these items came from, he said that last summer, passing through the plaza, this confessant saw the balcony of the palace half open, and being deceived by the devil, an evil thought came to him of climbing up to the balcony. To do this he first entered the guardhouse and he spoke with the soldier that was on guard (who was Luis Ortiz[24]), from whom he asked for the stub of a candle. Heading out again, having said farewell to the guard, he returned again about midnight without being recognized by the post and he climbed up to the balcony of the palace, using a ladder to get to a small window nearby.

Entering through the open window of said balcony, he lit the candle (this being the candle stub already mentioned) with a fire striker, stone, tinder, and straw that he had brought prepared. He went down the stairs that led to the store, familiarizing himself with what was contained therein, and he took several fabrics [the name of which] he does not recall. Then, bundling them up in a *campeche*[25] and taking advantage of the door that opened to the street, he left through it carrying these fabrics. He carried them down the street looking for a place to hide them. Passing by the house of don Felix Martínez,[26] he heard the footsteps of someone following him from behind. To hide himself, he pushed himself up against the door, and he found that it was open. So he hid there the goods that he was carrying in order to retrieve them the following night so that he could go and bury them in some other location. The next day in the morning a young girl of the district having found the door to the Palace open and realizing that some fabrics were missing, an investigation was made by the presidio soldiers.

Having discovered the cloth on top of the counter, the store being empty of people on this same occasion about dinnertime, he entered again through the balcony that he found open and he came down at dark. Being in the store committing the theft, he sensed that they were coming in from the house to close the balcony. Therefore, he rested. About midnight he came and opened the door to the balcony that was shut with a latch, and with a rope he lowered the two bundles that he had made. He put one behind the *vigas* that were in the plaza, and the other he went to bury behind the hacienda made while don Juan Ignacio Flores [Mogollón][27] was governor. Afterward, he returned for the bundle that was by the vigas, but realizing that the moon had appeared and was waning, he left it so as not to be noticed.

The bundle was discovered in the morning when it happened that some boys were playing ball and it landed among the vigas. Going to where the bundle was located, the boys came upon it and notified the guards. He was asked for what reason he had placed the [one] bundle under the vigas, but took the other one to hide it so far away, when he could have taken them together. He responded that the one he had taken to hide was heavier and larger than the one he had left, and that he had planned on coming back for it. In all this that he has admitted he states that he was alone and not accompanied by anyone, nor pressured by anything except his own evil nature. From the bundle that he buried came the goods that he lost gambling and wasted as he has said and confessed. This is the truth by God under the oath that he has made. Having been read this, his statement, he affirmed it and ratified it and signed it with me, the lieutenant general with the undersigned secretary of government and war.

    Pedro de Villasur (rubric)
    Isidro Sánchez
    Before me
    Miguel Tenorio de Alba (rubric)
    Secretary of Government and War

Signatures of don Pedro Villasur, Isidro Sanchez, and Miguel Tenorio de Alba. SANM II #307, roll.5, f. 1012.

Auto

In the Villa of Santa Fe, on the 3rd day of the month of April, 1720, I, General don Pedro de Villasur, lieutenant governor and captain general of this realm and the provinces of New Mexico, for his majesty, state that the sergeant major don Alfonso Rael de Aguilar notified me of how he had discussed with the ayudante don Joseph Giltoméy the difficulty of he, Isidro Sánchez, being able to climb up to the balcony without having anyone to help. They decided to investigate and taking one of the bars from the window they found that with little effort they were able to remove it from the frame. With this being the case and being informed to this fact, I, the lieutenant general, went in person to authenticate this fact. While carrying this out, I found the mentioned bar had been taken out from where it was. I realized that the theft, or thefts, had been committed using the [opened] space, and that this empty space had subsequently been closed up within the frame. As for the said bar, I ordered it removed in order to install a new bar and make other necessary repairs.[28]

Because Isidro Sánchez has failed [to tell] the truth in his statement that he made before me on the 27th day of the previous month of March, in which he committed perjury regarding that which he was charged, he shall he give a deposition and state the reasons that he had not truthfully answered in his statement. Thus I order that the defendant and prisoner Isidro Sánchez appear before me in this case, and that he make a second statement, and that he tell the truth about whatever he may be asked. This includes how on many occasions he has entered in to the shop by said window and what persons accompanied him, because it cannot be believed that alone he could have done such thefts without someone helping him climb up or keeping guard while he was inside the store. His testimony is also to include what fabrics he took from there, where he took them to be hid so that they would not be discovered, and those that were given to me by Vicente de Armijo that are in my possession.

Thus I approved, ordered and signed it with my secretary of government and war.

Don Pedro de Villasur (rubric)
Before me
Miguel Tenorio de Alba
Secretary of Government and War (rubric)

Second statement by Isidro Sánchez

In the Villa of Santa Fe on said day, month and year I, the lieutenant general, by virtue of the document above approved by me, ordered Isidro Sánchez, defendant in this case, to appear before me. Being present I took the oath that he made by God our Lord and the sign of the Cross, under which he promised to state the truth in whatever he may be asked.

Having done this according to the mentioned document, he said that it is true that having realized that the way [to enter the store] was to be found through the balcony, he prepared a *belduque*.[29] Having it notched and sharpened, which he himself did, he cut one of the bars of the little window that is on the back side of the store. He did this because the window was somewhat high up. He put four adobe bricks on the floor and waited for midnight. The guard was enjoying himself playing a guitar, and having managed to remove the bar, he entered the store and lit a light. Once inside he took various fabrics and came out again, putting the said bar carefully back in place so that it would not fall out suspiciously. He removed the adobes that he had put there, and while he was committing the malicious act.

[*Editor's note:* The document ends here; the last pages are missing.]

TRANSCRIPTION

[Testimony of Francisco Rendón[30]]

.... gano al referido una camisa nueva y asimismo save y lo vido jugo el dicho Ysidro Sanchez una bara de paño diez y ocheno y que a oydo dezir que Juan de Medina le gano otra camissa de las referidas

Como que tamvien en el barrio de Analco en cassa de Juan de Leon havia jugado rifado y perdido diez pares de zapatos y una bara de bretaña y que esta la saco el dicho Juan de Leon y que save por que le passo al mismo testigo que el dicho Ysidro Sanchez le hizo camvio por otras prendas tres baras de bretaña; y que le pregunto este testigo de donde le benia lo referido haziendole fuerza viendole hecho bagamundo le respondio que hera de una libranza que su madre le havia enviado de mill pesos.

Que esto es lo que save y la verdad por el juramento que tiene fecho en que se afirmo y ratifico siendole leyda esta su declaracion, y es de hedad de quarenta y dos años y lo firmo conmigo y el secretario de governacion y guerra

Don Pedro de Villasur (rubric)
Francisco Rendon (rubric)
Ante mi
Miguel Thenorio de Alva
Secretario de governacion y guerra

Testimonio Juan Cayetano Lobato

En la villa de Santa Fee en dicho dia mes y año yo el dicho theniente general para la prosecuzion de esta causa hize parezer, ante mi a Cayetano Lobato soldado deste castillo

presidial al qual estando pressente le rezevi juramento que hizo por Dios nuestro Señor y una señal de cruz debajo de cuyo cargo prometio de dezir verdad en lo que supiere y le fuere preguntado y haviendolo sido al thenor del auto cabeza del prozesso dijo; que es verdad que el dicho Ysidro Sanchez, le dio a este testigo una camisa nueva dada y asi mismo le dio tres baras de escarlata para que le mandara hazer una armilla, y que preguntadole de donde le benia todo esto, dijo que yo, dicho theniente general se lo havia dado: que aunque a oydo dezir que el dicho Ysidro Sanchez a jugado, este testigo no lo a visto ni delante de el, lo a hecho que save que el dicho Ysidro Sanchez, no tiene ofizio de donde le benga que todo lo rreferido, es lo que le consta y la verdad por el juramento que fecho tiene en que se afirmo y ratifico, siendole leyda esta su declaracion y dijo ser de hedad de veynte y quatro años y no firmo por no saver firmelo yo dicho theniente general con el secretario de governacion y guerra =

Don Pedro de Villasur (rubric)
Ante mi
Miguel Thenorio de Alva (rubric)
Secretario de governacion y guerra

Auto de prission

En la villa de Santa Fee en dicho dia mes y año yo dicho theniente general don Pedro de Villasur, haviendo seguido esta causa y deligenzias y que por ella consta y la sumaria, el cargo que resulta contra Ysidro Sanchez, y para prozeder contra el, y saver la verdad; mando que el dicho Ysidro Sanchez sea preso y puesto a buen recaudo, en el cuerpo de guardia de este castillo presidial, con un par de grillos cuya prission mando [execute] al ayudante don Joseph Manuel de Jilthomey, sin que permita ni consienta como cavo de la guardia hable con persona alguna hasta que se le rreziva su confession: asi lo provey mande y firme con mi secretario de governacion y guerra = entre renglones = execute = vale =

Don Pedro de Villasur
Ante mi
Miguel Thenorio de Alva
Secretario de governacion y guerra (rubric)

Auto

En la villa de Santa Fee en veynte y zinco dias del mes de marzo de mill setezientos y veynte años yo el general don Pedro de Villasur thenyente de governador y capitan general de este dicho reyno em virtud, del auto de arriva por mi proveydo en que le di orden al ayudante don

Joseph de Jilthomey como cavo de la guardia de este castillo presidial pusiesse presso a Ysidro Sanchez con un par de grillos lo qual executo puntualmente; y para prozeder contra el susso dicho y seguir esta caussa segun derecho mando que se le reziva su confesion y segun ella determinar en justizia lo que comviniere asi lo provey mande y firme con mi secretario de governacion y guerra =

Confesion de Ysidro Sanchez

En la villa de Santa Fee en veynte y zinco dias del mes de marzo de mill setezientos y veynte años yo el general don Pedro de Villasur thenyente de governador y capitan general de este dicho reyno para la prosecuzion de esta caussa y em virtud del auto de la buelta por mi proveydo hize pareser ante mi a un hombre preso por esta caussa al qual estando presente le rezevi juramento que hizo por Dios nuestro Señor y una señal de cruz debajo de cuyo cargo prometio de dezir verdad en lo que supiere y le fuere preguntado

Preguntado como se llama que hedad y ofizio tiene y de donde es, natural dijo que se llama Ysidro Sanchez que es de hedad de veynte y un años y que no tiene ofizio ninguno y que es natural de la Ciudad de Zacatecas Preguntado que si save la caussa de prission dijo que no la save Preguntado que si a jugado con Vizente de Armijo y que generos le jugo y en que ocassion dijo que es verdad que jugo con Vizente de Armijo abra quinze dias y que le gano a este confesante tres baras de bayeta, dos baras de bretaña dos pares de zapatillos = dos libras de chocolate; y una camissa; nueva sin estrenar, de bretaña; y responde Preguntado que si a jugado con Alonsso Rael de Aguilar y que generos fueron los que jugo dijo que le jugo y perdio dos camissas de las referidas: un cuchillo de zinta un zinidorrito, de saya (saya) como de cosas de dos baras = unos zapatillos de muger; y haviendo dicho que no mas le fue repreguntado como niega la verdad quando consta de las deposiziones haverle jugado otras prendas, y dijo que es verdad que le jugo tres quartas de paño querentano y una armilla blanca de lanquin que esta se la havia ganado a Vizente de Armijo y responde.

Preguntado que con quantas mas de las referidas a jugado dijo que asimismo a jugado y perdido [con Juan de Medina] una camissa nueva de bretaña dos pares de zapatillas los unos le gano y los otros le dio por una carga de leña: y dos baras de bretaña; y responde Preguntado que cambalache o camvio tubo con Francisco Rendon soldado de este presidio dijo haverle dado al dicho Francisco Rendon tres baras de bretaña, por un sombrero que le dio y unas medias; y asimismo confiessa haber jugado en el barrio de Analco en cassa de Juan de Leon, una bara de bretaña y unos zapatillos: como tamvien confiessa tener en su cassa tres baras de escarlata y le dio una camissa de las referidas a Cayetano Lobato lo qual, jugo; y que tiene asimismo en su cassa dos baras de bretaña.

Y siendo preguntado de donde le benian estos vienes dijo, que avra este berano pasado; viniendo este confesante por la plaza, vido el balcon de palazio avierto que engañado del demonio le vino el mal pensamyento de suvir por el balcon y que para ello entro primero a la guardia, y estubo platicando con el soldado que estava de guardia que hera Luis Ortiz a quien le pidio un cavo de bela, y bolviendosse a salir despidiendose de la dicha posta a cossa de media noche, vino otra vez y sin reconozer, la posta se suvio al balcon de palazio sirviendole de escalon, una ventanilla que esta ynmediata y entrando por la bentana que estava avierta de dicho balcon enzendio luz, que fue el cavo de candelas ya dicho, con eslavon piedra, yesca y una pajuela que para ello llevaba prevenida bajo las escaleras que haze[n] para la tienda haziendose capaz de lo que en ella avia, cojio distintos generos que no se acuerda de ellos y embueltos en un campeche, o campeches usando la ocassion de la puerta, de la calle se salio por ella, y estos generos, los cargo y bajando por toda la calle abajo buscando a donde esconderlos al pasar por las cassas de don Feliz Martinez sintio passos de uno que yba, tras de el, y por recatarsse, se arrimo a la puerta de la tienda de dicha cassa, y la hallo que estava avierta con que con esta ocassion oculto alli, los vienes que llevaba, y sacarlos la noche siguiente; para irlos a enterrar a otra parte.

Que otro dia por la mañana haviendose, hallado la puerta de la tienda de palazio avierta y echandose menos algunos generos, se hizo la deligenzia y por una muchacha de la vecindad.

Se descubrio estar la puerta entre avierta de la cassa de don Pheliz Martinez. y haver visto enzima del mostrador ropa, estando la tienda bazia; y que con esta misma ocassion, en otra que se ofrezio, como a las oras de zenar, bolvio a entrar por el balcon que hallo avierto y bajo a escuras, y estando en la tienda, haziendo el robo sintio que dela cassa vinieron azerrar, el balcon con que asi que se sosego como ora de media noche vino y abrio la puerta del balcon que estava zerrada con una aldavita, y con una soga descolgo, dos emboltones, que llebava echos, que detras delas vigas que estava en la plaza, pusso el uno, y el otro: fue, y lo enterro detras dela hazienda que hizo siendo governador don Juan Ygnazio Flores y despues bolvio por el que estava en las vigas, y que reconoziendo que havia apuntado la luna que estava de menguante lo dejo estar por no ser sentido.

Que de la guardia vieron el bulto y este se descubrio por la mañana por la ocasion de que jugando unos muchachos a la pelota se les metio dentro de dichas vigas y yendo a dar adonde estava el emboltorio dichos muchachos dieron con el, y avissaron Preguntado que que motivo tubo para meter debajo de las vigas el emboltorio y llevarsse el otro a esconder tan lejos pues los pudiera haver llebado juntos a que respondio, que el que havia llevado a esconder hera el mas pesado y mayor y que por esto lo havia dejado para despues benia por el que a todo esto que lleva confessado se hallo solo que no fue acompañado de ninguno, ni ynsistido sino de su mal natural, que de este emboltorio que lleva dicho que enterro; son los vienes que a gastado jugado y desperdiziado, que esto que lleva dicho y confesado es la verdad segun Dios por el juramento que tiene fecho en que siendole leyda esta su confesion se afirmo y ratifico y la firmo conmigo dicho thenyente general con el ynfraescripto secretario de governacion y guerra = entre renglones = con Juan de Medina = vale =

Don Pedro de Villasur (rubric)
Ysidro Sanchez
Ante mi
Miguel Thenorio de Alva
Secretario de governacion y guerra (rubric)

Auto

En la villa de Santa Fe, en tres dias de el mes, de abril de mill setezientos y veynte años yo el general don Pedro de Villasur theniente de governador y capitan general, de este reyno y provinzias de la Nueva Mexico, por su magestad digo que haviendome, dado la notizia elsargento mayor don Alphonsso Rael de Aguilar como estando discurriendo con el ayudante don Joseph de Jilthomey. la dificultad que havia para poder subir al bal[c]on sin que hubiesse perssona que ayudasse a ello; en que los dichos hizieron la experienzia y agarrando las verjas de una bentana hallaron que a poca deligenzia la sacaron de el marco: con cuya razon y notizia yo dicho theniente general fui em perssona y dar fee de ello lo qual pusse por execuzion hallando la referida verja quitada por donde se reconozio que por el hueco de ella se havia hecho el rovo o rovos como tamvien haver aserrado el marco de dicha ventana y la dicha berja la qual mande luego se quitasse para ponerle nueva berja y los demas reparos combenientes.

Por que el dicho Ysidro Sanchez en el todo a faltado a la verdad en la confession que tiene fecha ante mi el dia veynte y siete del passado mes de marzo. en que se halla perjuro sobre que le hago cargo, y para que de, su descargo y los motivos que tubo para estar negativo en la dicha su confession mando sea, comparezido ante mi el dicho Ysidro Sanchez reo y presso por esta caussa y haga segunda confession y en ella diga la verdad, y sea preguntado. que en quantas ocasiones. a entrado ala tienda por la dicha ventana; que perssonas le acompañaron porque no es de creer que solo pudiera hazer dichos rovos sin que tubiesse persona que le ayudasse, asi para poder subir como para su seguro quando estava dentro de dicha tienda: y los generos que de ella saco. adonde los llebava que se los guardasse para que no pudieran ser, descubiertas: y los que me consta aver dado Vizente de Armijo, que paran en mi poder.

Asi lo provey mande y firme con mi secretario de governacion y guerra =
Don Pedro de Villasur (rubric)
Ante mi
Miguel Thenorio de Alva
Secretario de governacion y guerra (rubric)

Segunda confesion de Ysidro Sanchez

En la villa de Santa Fee en dicho dia mes y año yo, dicho theniente general, en virtud del auto de susso por mi proveydo, hize parezer ante mi a Ysidro Sanchez reo en esta caussa al qual estando pressente le rezevi juramento que hiço por Dios nuestro Señor y la señal de la cruz, debajo de cuyo cargo prometio de dezir verdad, en lo que supiere y le fuere preguntado.

Haviendolo sido al thenor. del referido auto dijo; que es verdad, que haviendo visto el remedio que se havia puesto enel balcon previno un cuchillo belduque y haziendolo sierra que el mismo lo afilo, y corto una de las berjas de la bentanilla
que cae ala trastienda que esto lo hizo por estar algo alta dicha ventana pusso para poder hazer quatro adoves enel suelo buscando la ora de media noche. y que la guardia estubiera con una guitarra divertida, y que haviendo ejecutado el azerrar la verja entro y sacando luz. alla dentro saco diferentes generos y buelto a salir, pusso la dicha verja con todo disimulo porque no se cayera en malizia y quito los adoves que havia puesto: y que mientras estubo en la faena de

[*Editor's note:* The document ends with the last pages missing.]

This document translated and transcribed by Aaron Taylor

Notes

1. Isidro Sánchez—whose full name is Isidro Sánchez Bañares y Tagle—was a native of Zacatecas, Mexico, born in about 1699 or 1700. His parents were don Alfonso Sánchez Bañales and doña María Flores Liscano. In 1725, he married Teresa Varela Jaramillo, and by 1731 he was a soldier in the Albuquerque squadron, but was expelled from the presidio for lack of respect shown to an officer. By 1764 his name was recorded as "don Isidro Sánchez Bañales de Tagle." He died in 1770. (Chávez, *Origins*: 281; SANM II #306; SANM II #363c; Tigges, *Colonial Lives*: 261-94; Chávez, *Roots*: 158, 1699.)
2. See Hordes, "History of the Santa Fe Plaza": 139; SANM II #79.

3. See SANM II #624; West, "Asylum": 140-41.
4. See Jones, *Pueblo Warriors*: 100-02; Thomas, *After Coronado*: 222-23.
5. Francisco Rendón was living in Santa Fe by 1711; he bought and sold land in the villa, with at least some of it located on the south side of the river. He was not part of the Villasur Expedition of 1720. In 1721, he was as an interpreter on the campaign against the Moqui. He married Petrona López, and upon her death he married Catarina Maese in 1727. Catarina died in 1751 and Francisco died in 1757. (Chávez, Thomas, *Moment* 156; Chávez, *Origins*: 265.)
6. The language within the brackets does not appear in the document, the first page having been lost. The language is reconstructed from a typical introduction to testimony as shown later in the document.
7. A vara is a standard of linear measure equaling about thirty-three inches.
8. "Diez y ocheno" is a type of cloth that has a warp consisting of 1,800 threads, the warp being the longitudinal threads (or width) of the fabric. (Real Academia Española, *Dictionario de la Lengua Española de la Real Academia Española*, "Dieziocheno," accessed on October 11, 2015.)
9. Juan [Lorenzo] de Medina of Mexico City and his wife, Antonia Sedaño of Querétaro, came to New Mexico with the Farfán Expedition in 1694. His second wife was Juana Anaya Almazán. Juan died in 1731. (Kessell, Hendricks, and Dodge, *Boulders*: 330n75; Kessell, Hendricks, and Dodge, *Royal Crown*: 1066n8, 1175n26.)
10. The Barrio de Analco was located on the south side of the Santa Fe River. Juan de León Brito's house was located near the road to Pecos. (See Case 17.)
11. For information on Juan de León Brito, see Case 17.
12. The Spanish word bretaña refers to a fine linen fabric made in Brittany that was available in Spain by at least the 1400s (and probably earlier). (*Diccionario de Comercio Medieval*, "Bretaña," accessed on October 11, 2015.) "Fine wide linen" was also listed as a trade item in the 1743 will of merchant Vicente de Armijo. (See SANM I #26, WPA translation.) In 1749, Chihuahua merchant don Joseph de Aramburu asked Governor Tomás Vélez Cachupín to help him collect payment from a New Mexico merchant for varas of cloth, one of which was described as "fine cloth from Brittany." (See SANM II #506.)
13. For information on Miguel Tenorio de Alba, see Case 1 and Case 2.
14. Juan Cayetano Lobato was the son of Bartolomé Lobato and Lucía Ana Negrete. Juan was a soldier by 1695 and in 1716 he married Lucía Chirinos. (Chavez, *Origins*: 206.)
15. The Spanish word escarleta refers to a fine and expensive woolen fabric that was often dyed with kermes—a dye made from the dried female bodies of a scale insect called Kermes ilices, which was produced in many colors, but the most common was an intense crimson red. Because of this, the word "scarlet" came to refer to the color red. By the early 1600s the Dutch began using cochineal—a red dye made from the dried bodies of female cochineal insects—to create an even brighter red. (Maricahl, "The Cochineal Commodity Chain": 54-56; Scott, *Fashion*: 119; Roquero, "*Crimson to Scarlet*": 94-97.)
16. This would be similar to an arrest warrant or remand, ordering Isidro Sánchez to be held for questioning.
17. For information on Joseph Manuel Giltoméy, see Case 5.
18. Because Vicente de Armijo is named here, it is possible that the complete document included testimony from him. Vicente came with his parents, José de Armijo and Catalina Durán, from Zacatecas to New Mexico in 1695. In 1703, Vicente was granted a parcel of land south of the river in Santa Fe by don Diego de Vargas. Vicente had three sons, all named Salvador. His 1743 will indicates that he was a merchant; included are items such as wall tapestries made of skins, knives and awls, buffalo hides and other skins, and three brass mortars. His will also states that he owed Juan Vigil for five varas of "fine wide linen." (Chavez, *Origins*: 137-38; and SANM I #26, SANM I #367, SANM I #1136, all WPA translations.)
19. In this case, the Spanish word género refers to "*tela o tejido*" which means fabric or textiles. (Real Academia Española, *Dictionario de la Lengua Española de la Real Academia Española*, "Género," accessed on October 11, 2015.)
20. In current usage, the Spanish word bayeta refers to a type of loosely woven, absorbent cotton cloth used for dishcloths or cleaning. In the eighteenth century, it referred to a wool or cotton felt (or a flannel-like fabric) used for trade; bayeta was often used for personal blankets or saddle blankets. The word probably comes from the French "*baies*." (*Wikipedia*, "Bayeta," accessed on August 27, 2016; Padilla and Anderson, *Red*: 46, 151, 244.)
21. For information on Alfonso Rael de Aguilar, see Case 13. It is possible that the missing pages of the original document included testimony given by him
22. The word "zinidorrito" is derived from a Nahuatl word; in Spanish, the word is "*ceñador*." It can mean a loincloth, a narrow piece of cloth, or a belt. (Campbell, *Pipil Language of El Salvador*: 425.)
23. In the original text this appears as "*lanquín*," but it was probably an error by the scribe and the intended word was likely *nanquín*. The English word is "nankeen"—a cloth made from cotton, often of a yellowish color, originally made in Nanjing, China. In the 1700s, Nanjing was (and still is) an industrial center that exported textiles. (Real Academia Española, *Dictionario de la Lengua Española de la Real Academia Española*, "Nanquín," accessed on October 11, 2015; *Wikipedia*, "Nanquín," accessed on October 12, 2015.)
24. Born in Mexico City, Luis Ortiz came to New Mexico in 1604, when he was six years old, with his parents Nicolás Ortiz and doña Mariana Coronado. The Ortiz family was one of the first settlers of Santa Cruz. Luis

is listed as being a presidio soldier by 1712. (Chávez, *Origins*: 382, 247.)
25. The Spanish word campeche refers to a fabric, usually cotton, in the color of violet, dark blue, or black; the dye for this fabric was created from the logwood tree that grows in the Bay of Campeche, Yucatán Peninsula. (Cámara, "Logwood": 324-29.)
26. For information on Felix Martínez, see Case 3. A 1738 inspection of the house of former interim governor Felix Martínez indicates that it had eleven rooms, two hallways, 105 carved vigas, and 212 corbels. (See SANM I #521, WPA translation.)
27. For information on Juan Ignazio Flores Mogollón, see Case 6.
28. The meaning here is unclear, but it appears that what Lieutenant-General Villasur and Alfonso Rael de Aguilar saw was a window frame with bars and not glass.
29. A belduque is a short, pointed sword or knife.
30. This incomplete testimony is from Francisco Rendón.

21

MOTHER ACCUSES DAUGHTER AND SON-IN-LAW OF ONGOING AFFAIR
October 26-November 3, 1728, Source: SANM II #354a

Synopsis and editor's notes: The indomitable Antonia de Moraga was one of the eighteenth-century New Mexican women who took advantage of the laws allowing women to own and administer property and to submit lawsuits and claims to the governors in defense of those properties. For Antonia, this included land in Santa Fe ciénaga and on the hill above the plaza as well as land in northern New Mexico. (See Map 3.) In 1728, at the age of seventy, with a husband who was blind, Antonia found herself with an additional problem: a daughter who was out of control.[1] Although she probably thought she would never do such a thing, she approached the alcalde and asked for help with her wayward daughter and rascally son-in-law.

In her complaint, brought before Alcalde Francisco Montes Vigil, Antonia claimed that her son-in-law, Antonio de Torres, married to her daughter Gertrudis Martín, was having an affair with another one of her daughters, Juana Martín. When giving evidence of the affair, she explained that she saw the couple in the bedroom together at night and she believed that Juana's four illegitimate children looked just like Antonio. Antonia further stated that Juana had been beaten up twice for her behavior, but she had not stopped. Additionally, Antonia had complained to a previous alcalde, but nothing came of it.

After receiving the complaint, Alcalde Francisco Montes Vigil put Antonio de Torres in jail in Santa Cruz and placed Juana Martín in the home of a Chimayó resident. He took testimony from some of Antonia's children, a niece, a son-in-law, the wife and mother of Antonio, an Apache servant, and finally the errant couple, Antonio and Juana Martín. Most of the witnesses knew about the affair and some had heard about the beatings. Antonio de Torres stated that he did sleep in a room with Juana and an Indian woman, but he was not having an affair with Juana. The testimony given by Juana suggests that she may have been mentally handicapped in some way, for her comments appear unfocused and confused. She did state that she was beaten twice by members of her family. At first, she denied having an affair with Antonio; then, she admitted that it had been going on for three years. Initially, she said that she did not know who the father was of her four children; then, she admitted to knowing the father of one. She had also complained openly, to a family member two years earlier, about Antonio de Torres always making her pregnant, thus admitting to the affair.

In the end, Alcalde Francisco Montes Vigil gathered up all of the written testimony and submitted it to Governor Juan Domingo de Bustamante. That was the last anyone heard of the business. Of Juana and her children, no further information has been found; she is not listed in marriage records of the period. It may be that some arrangement was made with Antonio de Torres, but no evidence has been found confirming this.

The whole business suggests that Antonia de Moraga was trying to use the legal system (as she had done so successfully in the past) to deal with Juana Martín and her four illegitimate children, all of whom were disturbing the peace and order of her household. Physical punishment had not deterred Juana, so Antonia made a second attempt at disciplining her daughter by submitting a complaint to the alcalde. In terms of the law, Alcalde Francisco Montes Vigil followed formal legal procedures in addressing Antonia's complaint about Antonio de Torres.

Although Antonia did not mention adultery specifically, and in fact she appeared to be more concerned about her daughter's illegitimate children, an affair by a married man with his unmarried sister-in-law certainly made him an adulterer. At the very least, it was cohabitation or, more forthrightly, fornication. All were actionable offenses under Spanish law. This may explain why Alcalde Montes Vigil took such care with the case. He had each witness return to affirm and ratify their testimony, not just state it as part of their statement. He structured the testimony of witnesses by asking them a series of similar questions. He considered sequestering the goods of Antonio de Torres, as provided under Spanish law, but did not do so because he stated that Antonio appeared to have nothing worth sequestering. Finally, he made a formal statement concerning the transer of documents to the governor. It would be interesting to know what the governor had thought of the situation!

TRANSLATION

1718

Proceedings and accusation of Antonia de Moraga[2]

At the Villa of Santa Cruz on the 26th of October, 1728, there appeared before me, Captain Francisco Montes Vigil,[3] alcalde mayor and war captain of this villa and its jurisdiction, acting as presiding judge with two assisting witnesses, Antonia de Moraga, wife of Cristóbal Martín,[4] residents of this jurisdiction at the *puesto* of Chimayó.

She stated that she has been notified by her two daughters, Gertrudis Martín,[5] wife of Antonio de Torres,[6] and the other one, Juana Martín,[7] that Antonio Torres was a wicked person and had been having an illicit affair with Juana Martín, his sister-in-law. The evidence was that he had children from both of them, four with his wife, and four others with his sister-in-law. It can be easily seen in their stature, color and other bodily signs, and he does not deny it. She said that having been notified by her two daughters of this terrible thing, she was forced to bring this complaint regarding these excesses before me, although during the time of Captain Cristóbal de Torres[8] she had brought forth the complaint, but it was denied.

In order to ascertain all of this, she, Antonia, was asked if she had noticed anything unusual happening between the two in-laws, Juana and Antonio. She stated that she had seen them playing around in her house, combing each other's hair, and holding hands, but she ignored them. In addition to these actions and suspicions, she, Antonia, got up one night and because she did not have a candle, lit some corn leaves. Then she went into a room where Antonio de Torres, her daughter Juana, and an Apache woman named María[9] were sleeping. She saw that near the top of the bed, near where Antonio was laying, were some white petticoats[10] that belonged to her daughter, Juana. On the following day, she took her daughter and hung[11] her, and whipped her, asking her why she had given her petticoats to her brother-in-law. She said that her daughter told her that she had loaned them to him.

She was then asked if she had seen them together in bed on the night that she entered the room with the burning corn leaves when the wife, Gertrudis was downstream at [Santa Cruz de] La Cañada.[12] She declared that she had not. She was asked if she had spoken with anyone else about this issue. She declared that she had not. She said she only knew that her granddaughter, María de la Encarnación,[13] had told her grandmother, Francisca [Maese][14] (known as La Abuelita), what Maria's father, Cristobal Martin[15] the younger and the son of the complainant, had said. Cristóbal said that when Juana was very ill, she told him to get this nasty pig, Antonio Torres, out of there, that he was only making her have children. This Juana had stated two years earlier.

Everything that this complainant is bringing forth about Antonio Torres she has argued about and brought forth before. Her husband, Cristóbal Martín I, has only told her that he likes his son-in-law, and not to be arguing with him, [and] saying that he was lazy and was controlled by the devil. But she has ignored him. In addition to all of this, her son, Simon Martín,[16] who may be in God's hands, hung Juana, and as a brother he beat her up so badly that she was left breathless. This happened at the home of the complainant. Antonia had been told by her daughter, Gertrudis, that she, Juana, is jealous of her sister.

All of what she has stated is the truth and what she knows and says according to her conscience, which was the reason for the complaint and sworn statement that she has made. Having been read to her word by word, she stated that it was well written and that she does not have anything to add or delete. She ratified it, saying that she was seventy years of age, more or less, and did not sign because she did not know how. I, the alcalde mayor, acting as presiding judge signed it along with my assisting witnesses on the said day, month and year, etc.

Decree of imprisonment and placement

Continuing, on the same day, month and year, I, the alcalde mayor and war captain, upon seeing the above complaint made by Antonia de Moraga, and the results of what occurred, according to my obligation, discharge of my conscience, and for holding the office of royal justice, I placed in prison Antonio de Torres. Juana Martín I placed into the home of Antonio Bernal,[19] but I did not embargo the goods of the accused because there were none. So that it is valid I signed it along with my assisting witnesses on the said day, month and year.

    Francisco Montes Vigil (rubric)
Assisting witness
    Joseph de Atienza y Alcalá[17] (rubric)
Assisting witness
    Miguel de Quintana[18] (rubric)

Statement of María de la Encarnación

On the said day, month and year, I, the alcalde mayor in order to continue with the prosecution of these proceedings, made appear before me María de la Encarnación, granddaughter and cited by Antonia de Moraga, from whom I received her sworn statement which she made to God, Our Lord, and to the sign of the Holy Cross, under which she promised to tell the truth as to what she knew and was asked.

She was asked if she knew that Francisca [Maese], who is known as La Abuelita, had told her father that Antonio de Torres had an illicit affair with her aunt, Juana Martín. She said that she had, that Francisca had told her father and that she had heard her say it. She was asked what else she had heard. She said that she did not hear anything else because she left to go for water. She was asked if there was anyone else present when she heard this. She stated that there was no one else and that she does not know anything else regarding the sworn statement that she has made and which she ratified. She was asked what her age was, but she did not know. According to her features, she must be about twelve or thirteen years of age. She did not sign because she did not know how. I, the alcalde mayor, signed it along with my assisting witnesses on the said day, etc.

    Francisco Montes Vigil (rubric)
Presiding Judge
Assisting witness
    Joseph de Atienza y Alcalá (rubric)
Assisting witness
    Miguel de Quintana (rubric)

Statement of Cristóbal Martín [the younger]

On the said day, month and year, I, the alcalde mayor made appear before me Cristóbal Martín, the younger, cited by María de la Encarnación, his daughter, from whom I received his sworn statement which he made before God and the Holy Cross under which he promised to tell the truth as to what he knew and what he was asked.

He was asked if Francisca [Maese], the one who is known as La Abuelita, told him that Antonio de Torres had an illicit affair with Juana Martín, his, Cristóbal's, sister. He stated that she had, and that in order to punish this bad deed, his mother, who is Antonia de Moraga, had gone to inform the justice. He said that he had been told this in front of his daughter María de la Encarnación. This is what he knows and is the truth regarding the sworn statement that he has made, which he ratified and said that he was fifty years of age, more or less. He did not sign because he did not know how. Upon it being read back to him, he said that it was good as stated and that he does not have anything to add or delete. So that it is valid I, the alcalde mayor, signed it along with the said assisting witnesses on the said day, etc.

Francisco Montes Vigil (rubric)
Presiding Judge
Assisting witness
Joseph de Atienza y Alcalá (rubric)
Assisting witness
Miguel de Quintana (rubric)

Statement of María, Apache

On the 27th of October, 1728, I, the alcalde mayor, made to appear before me the Apache Indian, María, who was cited by Antonia de Moraga and from whom I received her statement, being that she was not allowed to give a sworn statement, as follows.[20] She was asked if while sleeping in a room where Antonio Torres and Juana Martín were, she saw when Antonia de Moraga went into the room with some burning leaves. She said that she slept heavily and did not see her. She did see when they punished Juana on the following day. She asked Juana why her mother had punished her and she stated that because they had found her with Antonio Torres. This she says is what she knows and nothing else. So that it is valid, I, the alcalde mayor, signed it along with my assisting witnesses on the said day, month and year.

Francisco Montes Vigil (rubric)
Presiding Judge
Assisting witness
Joseph de Atienza y Alcalá (rubric)
Assisting witness
Miguel de Quintana (rubric)

Statement of Francisca Maese

On the said day, month and year, I, the alcalde mayor and war captain, made to appear before me Francisca Maese, the one who is known as La Abuelita, and who is cited by Cristóbal Martín, from whom I took her sworn statement which she made to God and to the sign of the Holy Cross, under which she promised to tell the truth as to what she knew and what she was asked.

She was asked if she told Cristóbal Martín that her son Antonio Torres, had an illicit relation with Juana Martín, his sister-in-law. She stated that she did tell him in the presence of María de la Encarnación who is cited above. She was asked if she likewise told her that Antonia de Moraga had gone to report it to the justice so that the wrongdoing could be punished. She stated that she did tell her. She was asked how it was that she knew that her son had an affair with Juana Martín, the sister-in-law. She said that upon going to see her daughter-in-law, Gertrudis Martín, at the home of Antonia de Moraga, she had heard Antonia telling this to her two daughters, Gertrudis and Juana Martín, and that she also thought it was strange that Antonio Torres was at the home of Antonia.

She stated that upon hearing this being said she did not enter the home because she was embarrassed, and turned around and left. Later she was told about it by Cristóbal Martín, telling her about it as her son-in-law, being that he was married to a young lady, Juliana Maese, who was raised by her. He told her all of this so that they would punish Antonio Torres at that place and get him out of the home before it was reported to the justice. She added that Cristóbal Martin, the elder, had just recently returned to the kingdom and as such was not aware of any of these things.

She stated that this was the truth about what she knows, and nothing else, according to the sworn statement that she has made, which she ratified and upon her sworn statement being read back to her, she stated that it was properly written and that she did not have anything to add or to delete, saying that she was fifty-one years of age. She did not sign because she did not know how. I, alcalde mayor, signed it along with my assisting witnesses on the said day.

Francisco Montes Vigil (rubric)
Presiding Judge
Assisting witness
Joseph de Atienza [y Alcalá] (rubric)
Assisting witness
Miguel de Quintana (rubric)

Statement of Gertrudis Martín

On the said day, month and year, I, the alcalde mayor and war captain, made to appear before me Gertrudis Martín, the daughter of Antonia de Moraga, and wife of Antonio Torres, from whom I took her sworn statement which she made to God and to the sign of the Cross, under which she promised to tell the truth as to what she knew and what she was asked.

She was asked if she had complained to her mother because she was jealous of her sister Juana Martín. She stated that this was false because she had not complained about any such thing. She was asked if she knew that her mother had punished her sister, Juana. She stated that she had, and that her mother had told her that it was because she was shameless. She was asked if she knew that her brother Simon Martín, had punished her sister Juana Martín, and for what reason. She said that she knew nothing. She was asked if she had been approached by any other judge regarding this matter. She said that although she had gone to see Captain Cristóbal de Torres, it was because she did not want to be with her mother-in-law, and that she had not seen any reason to assume that her husband had any illicit relations with her sister.

This she said was the truth and is what she knows regarding the sworn statement that she has made, which she ratified upon it being read back to her, saying that it was correctly written. She said that she has nothing to add or delete and that she is twenty-five years of age, and did not sign because she did not know how. I, the alcalde mayor, signed it along with my assisting witnesses on the said day.

Francisco Montes Vigil (rubric)
Presiding Judge
Assisting witness
Joseph de Atienza [y Alcalá] (rubric)
Assisting witness
Miguel de Quintana (rubric)

Statement of Juana Martín

On the said day, month and year, I, the alcalde mayor made to appear before me Juana Martín who is being held at my order at the home of Antonio Bernal. Upon finding her present before me I took her sworn statement which she made to God and to the sign of the Cross under which she promised to tell the truth about what she knew and what she was asked.

She was asked what her reasons were for her to complain to her mother about Antonio Torres, her brother-in-law, telling her mother that he was worthless and that he had an illicit affair with her. She said that this was not so, that she has not told her mother anything. She was asked why she was so playful with Antonio Torres, playing with his hair and holding hands which her mother saw. She said that this was false.

She was asked that if on a certain night, while being in a room with Antonio de Torres and an Indian named María, her mother entered the room with some burning corn leaves [and] she found near the head of Antonio Torres the white petticoat of this witness. She stated that this was true. She was asked if her mother had scolded her for finding her white petticoats where they were. She said that she has scolded her and that she, Juana, told her that Antonio de Torres had asked her to lend them to him. She was asked if it was because of this that her mother punished her the following day. She stated that she did not punish her. She was asked if the Indian, María, had asked her why her mother had whipped her. Was it because she caught you with Antonio Torres? She said that was not true. She was asked if when she was very ill, she told her mother to get this filthy pig out of here, as all he does is make me bear children. She stated that this was false, that she did not say such a thing. She was asked why her brother Simon

Martín, whom God may save, hung her in the storage room and beat her up so badly that she was left breathless. She stated that it was not so.

She was asked how many children she had, and whose they were. She said that she had two sons, but does not know who the father is. She was asked if she had an illicit affair with Antonio Torres, her brother-in-law. She stated that she had, that it had been going on for three years. She was asked if she had any children with Antonio Torres. She said that she had not. She was asked if she did not have another two children. She was asked to whom the two children that she confesses as having belonged. She said that she did not know whose they were. Out of necessity for the need of some petticoats and a blouse, she had an affair with a servant from Río Arriba, but that she does not know him, nor does she know his name.

All of this she says is the truth and what she knows according to the sworn statement that she has made and which she ratified. She was asked what her age was, but she could not give an answer. She appears to be about forty, more or less, according to her features. Upon her statement being read back to her, she said that it was properly written and that she does not have anything to add or delete. She did not sign because she does not know how, I, the alcalde mayor, signed it along with my assisting witnesses on the said day, etc.

Francisco Montes Vigil (rubric)
Presiding Judge
Assisting witness
Joseph de Atienza y Alcalá (rubric)
Assisting witness
Miguel de Quintana (rubric)

Confession of Antonio Torres

Continuing, on the said day, month and year, I, the alcalde mayor, made to appear before me Antonio de Torres, held as a prisoner at my order, and from whom I received his sworn statement which he made to God, Our Lord and to the sign of the Cross under which he promised to tell the truth as to what he knew and what he was asked.

He was asked if he knew why he was being held prisoner. He answered and stated that he knows it only by hearsay, but not according to his actions. He was asked what the hearsay reasons are that he is held as a prisoner. He answered that it is because his mother-in-law, Antonia de Moraga, accused him of cohabitation with her daughter, Juana. This was his answer. He was asked if he was cohabitating with the said Juana. He stated that he was not.

He was asked if one night when he was sleeping in a room where Juana Martín and an Apache Indian named María were, Antonia de Moraga entered the room with some burning corn leaves. He stated that it is true that she entered the room. He was asked if he knew why she entered. He stated that he did not know. He was asked if he was awake when she entered. He stated that he was not. He was asked how it was that he had seen her. He stated that Antonia de Moraga had so stated in these proceedings. He was asked that if when [Antonia de] Moraga entered he had the petticoats belonging to Juana Martín in the bed. He stated that he did, that he had them at the head of the bed. He was asked if the petticoats were white or some other color. He stated that he did not know which ones they were. He was asked if Antonia de Moraga asked him why he had them at the head of the bed. He stated that she did not tell him anything, nor did he know if she told Juana anything, because he was asleep. He was asked who the persons who were sleeping in the room were. He stated that there was an Indian woman named María, Juana Martín and himself.

He was asked if he knows if Juana Martín has any children. He stated that he did not know, but that he has heard Antonia de Moraga say that she has children, but does not know how many. He was asked if he knows that Antonia de Moraga has punished Juana at any time and for what reason. He stated that he did not know nor that her brother Simon Martín, whom God may have with him, had done so. He was asked why Captain Cristóbal de Torres quarreled with him. He said that because his wife had gone to complain that she did not want to stay with his mother. He was asked if his wife was in the room when Antonia de Moraga entered the room. He stated that she was not.

He further stated that this was the truth and is what he knows regarding the testimony that he has made which he ratified. Upon his statement being read back to him he stated that it was correctly written, that he did not have anything to add or to delete, and that he was of the age of twenty-five. He did not sign because he did not know how. I, the alcalde mayor, signed it along with my assisting witnesses on the said day, etc.

Francisco Montes Vigil (rubric)
Presiding Judge
Assisting witness
Joseph de Atienza y Alcalá (rubric)
Assisting witness
Miguel de Quintana (rubric)

Statement of Dionisio Cortés[21]

On the 29th of October, 1728, I, the alcalde mayor and war captain, for the best disposition of these proceedings made appear before me Dionisio Cortés, son-in-law of Antonia de Moraga. From him I took his sworn statement which he made to God and to the Holy Cross, under which he promised to tell the truth as to what he knew and what he was asked.

He was asked if he knows or has heard it said that Antonio Torres has had an illicit affair with Juana Martín, sister-in-law of this witness. He stated that he did not know. He was asked if Antonia de Moraga has punished Juana, and for what reason. He said that he did not know. He was asked if he knew that Simon Martín, may he be with God, had given Juana a beating that left her unable to talk. He stated that he had, but he did not know the reason for it, that he only heard the voices outside. He heard Antonia de Moraga telling Simon that because he had already gotten involved [by beating Juana], he should get rid of the pig Torres because she could not stand him any longer. In addition, she said that he should get back the petticoats and blouse. He was asked what Simon had said to her. Dionisio responded that Simon said nothing, that he mounted his horse and left. He was asked if he knows how many children Juana has. He said that there were four, and that they are all alive. He was asked how long it had been since Simon had given her a beating. He stated that it had been over one and one-half years.

This is what he knows and is the truth regarding the sworn statement that he has made, which he ratified. Upon his statement being read back to him word by word, he said that it was well written and that he did not have anything to add or delete, and that he is thirty-six years of age, more or less. Because he said that he did not know how to write, I, the alcalde mayor, signed it with my assisting witnesses on the said day.

Francisco Montes Vigil (rubric)
Presiding Judge
Assisting witness
Joseph de Atienza y Alcalá (rubric)
Assisting witness
Miguel de Quintana (rubric)

Statement of María Martín[22]

On the said day, month and year, I, the alcalde mayor and war captain, made to appear before me María Martín, daughter of Antonia de Moraga, from whom I received her sworn statement which she made to God and to the Holy Cross, under which she promised to tell the truth as to what she knew and what she was asked.

She was asked if she knew that her sisters Gertrudis and Juana Martín complained to their mother about Antonio Torres or why it was that he stated that he did not know about it. She was also asked if she knew that her mother had punished her sister, Juana Martín, and for what reason. She stated that her mother did punish her but does not know the reason. She was asked if she knew that her brother, Simon Martín, gave her, Juana, a beating that left her breathless and what the reason was. She stated that she heard the Inditos[23] from her mother's house say that Juana had been given a beating because of all of the children to whom she had given birth. She stated that this occurred about one year ago. She was asked if she knew who they were. She said that she did not know, but that she knows that there are three sons.

She stated that this was the truth about what she knows about the sworn statement that she has given, and which she ratified. Upon her statement being read back to her, she stated that it was correct according to the way that she had stated and that she has nothing to add or delete, and is thirty years of age, more or less. She did not sign because she did not know how, I, the alcalde mayor, signed it along with my assisting witnesses on the said day, etc.

Francisco Montes Vigil (rubric)
Presiding judge
Assisting witness
Joseph de Atienza y Alcalá (rubric)
Assisting witness
Miguel de Quintana (rubric)

Ratification of María de la Encarnación
On the said day, month and year, I, the alcalde mayor and war captain, made to appear before me María de la Encarnación to whom her statement was read. She stated that it was correct as it was and according to the way she made it and that she does not have anything to add or to delete and which she ratified and affirmed according to her sworn statement that she has made. She did not sign because she did not know how. I, the alcalde mayor, signed along with my assisting witnesses on the said day, month and year.

Francisco Montes Vigil (rubric)
Presiding Judge
Assisting witness
Joseph de Atienza y Alcalá (rubric)
Assisting witness
Miguel de Quintana (rubric)

[*Editor's note*: Formal ratifications were also prepared for Francisca Maese, Gertrudis Martín, Dionisio Cortés, María Martín, and María the Apache using the exact same language. They are not translated here, but can be found in the Spanish transcription below.]

Submission of Proceedings
At the Villa of Santa Cruz on the 3rd of November, 1728, I, Captain Francisco Montes Vigil, alcalde mayor and war captain of this villa and of its jurisdiction, have concluded this case totally with all of its proceedings and statements which are found within it. I submit it along with all of the pleadings to your honor so that according to all of its merits will determine according to what he will be pleased to do, and so that it is valid, I sign it acting as presiding judge with my assisting witnesses on the said day, month and year, etc.

Francisco Montes Vigil (rubric)
Presiding Judge
Assisting witness
Joseph de Atienza y Alcalá (rubric)
Assisting witness
Miguel de Quintana (rubric)

[*Editor's note:* The document ends with no sentence from the governor.]

TRANSCRIPTION

1728

Auto y delata de Antonia de Moraga

En la Villa de Santa Cruz en veinte y seis dias del mes de Octubre de mill setesientos y veinte y ocho años yo el Capitan Francisco Montes Vigil, Alcalde Mayor y Capitan Aguerra desta dicha Villa y su jurisdicion actuando como Jues Receptor con dos testigos de mi assistencia a causa de aber paresido ante mi Antonia de Moraga muger de Xptobal Martin, vezinos desta jurisdicion en el Puesto de Chimayo, diziendo que por quanto a tenido notisia de sus dos hijas llamadas la una Gertrudes Martin mujer de Antonio Torres y la otra Juana Martin de que el dicho Antonio Torres era un malbado y tenia amistad ylisita con la dicha Juana Martin, su cunada, teniendo la ebidencia de tener hijos en una y otra en su muger quatro y en su cunado otros quatro, y que le haze fuerza el ver que en los rostros, colores y señales del cuerpo no desdisen y que teniendo notisia como dicho lleba de sus dos hijas desta maldad tubo por combeniente delatar ante mi estos excesos y aunque en tiempo del Capitan Xptobal de Torres dio cuenta la dicha Getrudes, solo sabe que lo rino.

Y para mas seguro sele pregunto si fuera de esto a visto algunas acciones en los dos cunados, y dijo que los a visto estar retosando en su casa tizandoles los cabellos, el a ella y dandole de punetas y que los a renido; y que debajo de estas acciones y sospechos se levanto la delatante una noche, y por no aver candela ensendio unas ojas de mais y entro en un aposento donde estaban durmiendo el dicho Antonio de Torres, la dicha su hija Juana, y una Yndia Apacha llamada Maria, y que vido que en la cama del dicho Antonio estaban por cabesera las naguas blancas dela dicha su hija Juana y que otro dia por la mañana cojio a su hija Juana y la colgo y la azoto disiendole que para que avia dado las naguas a su cunado, a que le respondio que selas avia prestado.

Preguntada si no vido alos dos cunados estar juntos en la cama? Dijo que no y que esta noche que entro con las ojas, estaba la mujer del dicho Antonio Torres en La Cañada avajo; preguntada si a cominicado estas materias con otras personas? Dijo que no que solo sabia que su nieta le avia dicho que Francisca la que llaman la aguelita, la madre del contenido selo avia dicho a su padre Xptobal Martin, el moso, hijo dela delatante, y que solo si declara que estando la dicha su hija Juana mui mala le dijo echen de aqui este cochino que me esta haziendo hijos; y que esto le dijo a ora dos años.

Que devajo de lo que tiene declarado a tenido boses y a pleiteado con el dicho Antonio Torres y que su esposo le a dicho a esta declarante que quiera a su yerno y que no se pleite con el y que esta declarante no le a dicho la causa, y que solo le a dicho que es un floxo endemoneado, y que asi mismo su hijo Simon Martin que Dios aya, colgo ala dicha Juana como hermano y sobre esta materia le dio una buelta que la dejo sin habla en casa dela declarante, y que su hija Gertrudes le a dicho que tiene selos de su hermana Juana Martin.

    Que esta es la verdad y lo que sabe y declara para descargo de su consienzia para cullo efecto sele rezivio juramento que lo hiso por Dios Nuestro Señor y la Señal dela Cruz devajo de cullo cargo tiene echo esta su delatacion que leida de verbo ad verbum dijo estar bien ecripta y que no tiene que anadir ni quitar y en ella se ratifico y dijo ser de edad de setenta años poco mas o menos y no firmo por que dijo no saber firmela yo dicho Alcalde Mayor actuando como Juez Rezeptor con los testigos de mi asistenzia en dicho dia, mes y año, ut supra=

    Francisco Montes Vijil (rubric)
    Jues Receptor
    De asistenzia
    Joseph de Atienzia y Alcala (rubric)
    De asistenzia
    Miguel de Quintana (rubric)

Auto de prizion y deposito

    Y luego yncontinente en dicho dia, mes y año yo dicho Alcalde Mayor y Capitan Aguerra en vista de la delatacion de arriba echa por Antonia de Moraga y lo que de ella resulta en cumplimiento de mi obligazion descargo de mi consienzia y officio dela Real Justizia puse en prision a Antonio de Torres y ala dicha Juana Martin de deposito en casa de Antonio Bernal, y no paze a embargo de bienes por no tenerlos y para que conte lo firme con los ynfraescriptos testigos de mi asistenzia en dicho dia mes y año.

    Francisco Montes Vijil (rubric)
    Jues Receptor
    De asistenzia
    Joseph de Atienzia y Alcala (rubric)
    De asistenzia
    Miguel de Quintana (rubric)

Declaracion de   Maria de la Encarnasion

    En dicho dia mes y año yo dicho Alcalde Mayor para la prosecuzion destas deligencias hize parezer ante mi a Maria dela Encarnacion, nieta y sitada de Antonia de Moraga a quien rezevi juramento que lo hizo por Dios Nuestro Señor y la Santa Cruz devajo de cullo cargo prometio dezir verdad en lo que supiera y le fuere preguntado.

    Siendole si sabe que Francisca la que llaman la aguelita le avia dicho a su padre desta declarante que Antonio de Torres tenia Amistad ylisita con su tia, Juana Martin? Dijo que si que la dicha Francisca selo dijo a su padre y que selo oyo dezir. Preguntada que otra cosa oyo? Dijo que no oyo otra cosa por que luego se fue por agua; y preguntada si avia otra persona delante cuando oyo esto? Dijo que no, y que no sabe otra cosa que esta es la verdad so cargo del juramento que fecho tiene en que se ratifico; y preguntada de sue dad, no supo dar razon, segun su aspect, tendra de doze a treze años y no firmo por no saber, firmelo yo dicho Alcalde Maior con los ynfraescriptos testigos de mi asistenzia en dicho dia, ut supra

 Francisco Montes Vijil (rubric)
Jues Receptor
De asistenzia
Joseph de Atienzia y Alcala (rubric)
De asistenzia
Miguel de Quintana (rubric)

Declaracion de Xptobal Martin

 En dicho dia mes y año yo dicho Alcalde Mayor hize parser ante mi a Xptobal Martin, el moso, zitado por Maria de la Encarnacion su hija a quein le resevi juramento que lo hizo por Dios y la Santa Cruz debajo de cullo cargo prometio dezir verdad en lo que supiera y le fuera preguntado.

 Siendolo si Francisca la que llaman la Aguelita le dijo que Antonio de Torres tenia Amistad ylisita con Juana Martin, su Hermana, dixo que si y que para que se castigara esta maldad avia benido a dar quenta a la justizia su madre deste declarante que es Antonia de Moraga, y que esto selo dijo delante de su hija Maria de la Encarnacion y que esto es lo que sabe, y la verdad so cargo del juramento que fecho tiene en que se ratifico y dijo ser de edad de sincuenta años poco mas o menos y no firmo por que dixo no saver, y leida esta su declaracion dijo que esta segun y como y que no tiene que anadir ni que quitar y para que conste la firme yo dicho Alcalde Maior con los ynfraescriptos testigos de mi asistenzia en dicho dia, ut supra

 Francisco Montes Vijil (rubric)
Jues Receptor
De asistenzia
Joseph de Atienzia y Alcala (rubric)
De asistenzia
Miguel de Quintana (rubric)

Dicho de Maria, Apacha

 En veinte y siete dias del mes de Octubre de mill setezientos y veinte y ocho años yo dicho Alcalde Mayor hize parezer ante mi a Maria, Yndia Apacha, zitada de Antonia de Moraga a quien rezevi su dicho por no hallarla capaz de juramento en la forma siguiente: si estando durmiendo en un aposento donde estava durmiendo Antonio Torres y Juana Martin vido que Antonia de Moraga entro una noche con unas ojas ensendidas a dicho aposento; dijo que ella durmia mucho y que no la vido y que si la vido azotar otro dia a su hija Juana, y que le pregunto esta declarante a dicha Juana que por que la avia azotado su madre que quisas la avia cogido con Antonio Torres, y que esto sabe y no otra cossa, y para que conste lo firme yo dicho Alcalde Mayor con los ynfraesciptos testigos de mi asistensia en dicho dia, mes y aóo _

    Francisco Montes Vijil (rubric)
Jues Receptor
De asistenzia
Joseph de Atienzia y Alcala (rubric)
De asistenzia
Miguel de Quintana (rubric)

Declaracion de Francisca Maese
    En dicho dia, mes y año yo dicho Alcalde Mayor y Capitan Aguerra hize parezer ante mi a Francisca Maese la que llaman la Aguelita zitada de Xptobal Martin, a quien le rezevi juramento que lo hizo por Dios Nuestro Señor y la Señal dela Cruz devajo de cullo cargo prometio dezir verdad en lo que supiera y le fuera preguntado.
    Siendole si le dijo a Xptobal Martin que Antonio Torres hijo desa declarante tenia ylisita amiztad con Juana Martin, su cunada; dijo que si selo dijo en presencia de Maria de la Encarnacion arriba zitada; preguntada que si le dijo asi mismo que Antonia de Moraga avia benido a dar parte ala justisia para que se castigase esta maldad; dijo que si selo dijo; preguntada que como o de donde sabe que su hijo tiene amistad con Juana Martin, cunada; dijo que llendo a ver a su nuera Gertrudes Martin en casa de la Moraga.
    Oyo a dicha Moraga que selo estava disiendo a sus dos hijas Getrudes y Juana Martin y que ya sele hazia escrupulo que estubiera el dicho Antonio Torres en casa de dicha Moraga y que ollendo esta declarante estas vozes no entro ala casa de verguenza, y que se bolbio. Entonses selo dijo a Xptobal Martin, y que selo dijo como yerno pore star casado con una nina que crio esta declarante, y que selo dijo con fin de que lo castigasen alla y lo echasen de la casa antes de dar parte ala justizia, q que le respondio que el dicho Xptobal Martin era resien llegado a este Reino y el no sabia estas cosas.
    Que esta es la verdad y lo que sabe y no otra cosa de vajo del juramento que fecho tiene en que se ratifico y leida esta su declaracion dijo estar bien escrita que no tiene que anadir ni quitar y dijo ser de edad de sinquenta y un años y no firmo por no sabe, firmelo yo dicho Alcalde Mayor con los dichos testigos de mi asistenzia en dicho dia.
    Francisco Montes Vijil (rubric)
Jues Receptor
De asistenzia
Joseph de Atienzia y Alcala (rubric)
De asistenzia
Miguel de Quintana (rubric)

Declaracion de Gertrudes Martin

En dicho dia, mes y año yo dicho Alcalde Mayor y Capitan Aguerra hize parecer ante mi a Getrudes Martin, hija de Antonia de Moraga, y esposa de Antonio Torres a quien resevi juramento que lo hizo por Dios y la Señal dela Cruz de vajo de cullo cargo prometio dezir verdad en lo que supiere y le fuere preguntado.

Siendole si se a quejado a su madre Antonia de Moraga a causa de tener selos de su hermana Juana Martin? Dijo que es falzo que no se a quejado de tal cosa; preguntada si sabe que su madre a castigado a su hermana, Juana; Dijo que la a visto castigar y que su madre le a dicho que por desvergonsada; preguntada si sabe que su hermano Simon Martin castigo a su hermana Juana Martin, y sobre que motibo; Dijo que no supo nada; Preguntada que si se a quejado a otro Jues sobre esta materia? Dijo que aunque vido al Capitan Xptobal Torres, fue por que no queria estar con su sugura, y que no a visto accion por donde presume que su marido aya tenido ylisita amistad con su Hermana.

Que esta es la verdad y lo que sabe de vajo del juramento que fecho tiene en que se ratifico y leida esta su declaracion dijo estar bien escripta y que no tiene que anadir ni quitar que es de edad de veinte y sinco años y no firmo por no saber firmela yo dicho Alcalde Mayor con los testigos de mi asistenzia en dicho dia.

Francisco Montes Vijil (rubric)
Jues Receptor
De asistenzia
Joseph de Atienzia y Alcala (rubric)
De asistenzia
Miguel de Quintana (rubric)

Declaracion de Juana Martin

En dicho dia, mes y año yo dicho Alcalde Mayor hize parezer ante mi a Juana Martin depositada de mi orden en casa de Antonio Bernal y estando presente le resevi juramento que lo hizo por Dios y la Señal dela Cruz de vajo de cullo cargo prometio desir verdad en lo que supiera y le fuera preguntado.

Siendole, que motibos tubo para quejarse a su madre de Antonio Torres, su cunado disiendole que era un malbado y que tenia ylisita amistad con esta declarante; Dijo que es falso que no le a dicho nada; Preguntada por que estando retozando con el dicho Antonio Torres tirandole los cabellos y dandole punetes los bido su madre; Dijo que es falzo; Preguntada si una noche estando en un aposento esta declarante y Antonio de Torres, y una Yndia llamada Maria entro su madre con unas hojas de mais ensendidas y hallo que en la cabesera del dicho Antonio Torres estaban las naguas blancas desta declarante; Dijo que es verdad; Preguntada si la rino su made por allar asi las naguas blancas; Dijo que si la rino y que esta declarante le dijo que selas avia pedido prestadas el dicho Antonio de Torres; Preguntada, si sobre esta accion otro dia la castigo su madre; Dijo que no la castigo; Preguntada si la dicha Yndia Maria le pregunto por que te azoto tu madre, quisas te cogio con Antonio Torres; Dijo que es falso; Preguntada si estando mui mala le dijo a su madre que echen de aqui este cochino que me esta asiendo hijos; Respondio que es falso que no dijo tal; Preguntada por que su hermano Simon Martin, que Dios aya la colgo en la dispensa y le dio una buelta que la dejo sin abla; Dijo que es falso.

Preguntada quantos hijos tiene y cullos son; Dijo que tiene dos hijos pero que no sabe cullos son; Preguntada si a tenido amistad con Antonio Torres su cunado; Dijo que si, que tres años ha que tiene ylisita amistad con el; Preguntada si a tenido hijos con el dicho Antonio Torres; Dijo que no; Preguntada si no tiene otros dos hijos; Dijo que no; Preguntada cullos son los dos hijos que confiesa tener; Dijo que no sabe cullos son y que por nesesidad de unas naguas y una camisa tubo amistad con un criado del Rio Arriba pero que no lo conose, ni sabe como se llama.

Que esta es la verdad y lo que sabe devajo del juramento que fecho tiene en que se ratifico y preguntada que edad tiene no supo dar rason, segun su aspecto tendra quarenta años poco mas o menos, y leida esta su declaracion dijo estar bien escripta y que no tiene que anadir ni quitar y no firmo por no saber, firmela yo dicho Alcalde Mayor con los ynfraescriptos de mi asistenzia, en dicho dia, ut supra.

Francisco Montes Vijil (rubric)
Jues Receptor
De asistenzia
Joseph de Atienzia y Alcala (rubric)
De asistenzia
Miguel de Quintana (rubric)

Confecion de Antonio Torres

Luego yncontinente en dicho dia, mes y año yo dicho Alcalde Maior hize parezer ante mi a Antonio de Torres preso de mi orden a quien rezevi juramento que lo hizo por Dios Nuestro Señor y la Señal de la Cruz de vajo de cullo cargo prometio dezir verdad en lo que supiera y le fuere preguntado.

Siendole si sabe por que esta preso; Respondio y dijo que por cuentos lo sabe, pero de su motibo no lo sabe; Preguntado quales son los cuentos por que sabe esta preso; Respondio que por que le a lebantado su suegra Antonia de Moraga que esta con su hija Juana amansebada y esto responde; Preguntado si esta amansebado con dicha Juana, dijo que no; Preguntado si estando durmiendo una noche en un aposento donde estava Juana Martin y una Yndia Apacha llamada Maria entro la dicha Antonia de Moraga con unas ojas de mais ensendidas; Dijo que es verdad que entro; Preguntado si sabe a que entro; Dijo que no lo sabe; Preguntado si estaba dispierto cuando entro; Dijo que no; Preguntado que como la vido; Dijo que la dicha Antonia de Moraga selo dijo a ora en este pleito; Preguntado si cuando entro la dicha Moraga tenia unas naguas de Juana Martin en su cama; Dijo que si las tenia en su cabesera; Preguntado si eran las naguas blancas o otras; Dijo que no sabe quales eran; Preguntado si le dijo Antonia de Moraga que por que tenia las naguas en la cabesera; Dijo que no le dijo nada, ni ala dicha Juana le dijo nada por que estaba dormido este declarante; Preguntado que personas estaban durmiendo en dicho aposento; Dijo que una Yndia llamada Maria, Juana Martin, y este declarante.

Preguntado si sabe que la dicha Juana Martin tenga algunos hijos; Dijo que no lo sabe, pero que le a oido desir a Antonia de Moraga que tiene hijos, pero que no sabe quantos; Preguntado si sabe que Antonia de Moraga aya castigado ala dicha Juana alguna ves, y por que; Dijo que no lo sabe, ni su hermano Simon Martin, que Dios aya; Preguntado por que en una ocasion lo rino el Capitan Xptobal Torres; Dijo que por que su mujer sele fue a quejar de que no queria estar con su madre deste declarante; Preguntado si su esposa estaba en dicho aposento cuando entro la dicha Antonia de Moraga; Dijo que no.

Que esta es la verdad y lo que sabe de vajo del juramento que fecho tiene en que se ratifico y leida esta su declaracion dijo que esta bien escrita y que no tenia que anadir ni quitar, es de edad de veinte y sinco años y no firmo por no saber firmelo yo dicho Alcalde Maior con los testigos de mi asistensia en dicho dia ut supra =

Francisco Montes Vijil (rubric)
Jues Receptor
De asistenzia
Joseph de Atienzia y Alcala (rubric)
De asistenzia
Miguel de Quintana (rubric)

Declaracion de Leonicio Cortes

En veinte y nuebe dias del mes de Octubre de mil setecientos y veinte y ocho años yo dicho Alcalde Mayor y Capitan Aguerra a mayor abandamiento destas deligencias hize parezer ante mi a Leonicio Cortez yerno de Antonia de Moraga a quien resevi juramento por Dios y la Santa Cruz de vajo de cullo cargo prometio dezir verdad en lo que supiere y le fuere preguntado.

Siendole si sabe o a oido dezir que Antonio Torres aya tenido ylisita amistad con Juana Martin cunada deste declarante; Dijo que no; Preguntado si sabe que Antonia de Moraga aiga castigado a la dicha Juana, y por que causa; Dijo que no lo sabe; Preguntado si sabe que Simon Martin, que Dios aya, le dio una buelta ala dicha Juana que la dejo sin abla; Dijo que si, y que no sabe por que, que solo ollo las voses alla fuera y que en ellas apersibio que la dicha Antonia de Moraga le dijo al dicho Simon ya que te que te has metido en esto quitame de aqui este cochino que ya no lo puedo sufrir y a demas que ya que te as metido en eso naguas y camissa le avias de dar;

Preguntado que respondio el dicho Simon; Dijo que nada, que se subio a caballo y se fue; Preguntado si sabe quantos hijos tiene la dicha Juana; Dijo que quatro y que todos estan vivos; Preguntado que tiempo abra que el dicho Simon le dio esta buelta; Dijo que abra mas de año y medio.

Que esto es lo que sabe y la verdad so cargo del juramento que fecho tiene en que se ratifico y leida esta su declaracion de verbo, ad verbum dijo estar bien escripta y que no tiene que anadir ni quitar, es de edad de treinta y seis años poco mas o menos y no firmo por que dijo no saber firmelo yo dicho Alcalde Maior con los ynfraescriptos testigos de mi asistencia en dicho dia

    Francisco Montes Vijil (rubric)
    Jues Receptor
    De asistenzia
    Joseph de Atienzia y Alcala (rubric)
    De asistenzia
    Miguel de Quintana (rubric)

Declaracion de Maria Martin

En dicho dia, mes y año yo dicho Alcalde Mayor y Capitan Aguerra hize parser ante mi a Maria Martin hija de Antonia de Moraga a quien resevi juramento que lo hizo por Dios, y la Santa Cruz devajo de cullo cargo

Siendole si sabe que sus hermanas Gertrudes y Juana Martin se allan quejado a su madre de Antonio Torres o por que dijo que no lo sabe; Preguntada si sabe que su dicha madre aya castigado a su hermana Juana Martin y por que causa; Dijo que sabe que la a castigado pero no sabe por que; Preguntada si sabe que su hermano Simon Martin le dio una buelta ala dicha Juana que la dejo sin abla y por que causa; Dijo que oyo dezir a los Ynditos de casa de su madre que sela avia dado por los muchachos que pario y que esto abra tiempo de un año; Preguntada si sabe cullos sean los paridos; Dijo que no lo sabe, que solo sabe que tiene tres hijos.

Que esto es la verdad y lo que sabe devajo del juramento que fecho tiene en que se ratifico y leida esta su declaracion dijo es segun y como la tiene echa y que no tiene que anadir ni quitar y es de edad de treinta años poco mas o menos y no firmo por no saver firmelo yo dicho Alcalde Mayor con los ynfraescriptos testigos de mi assistenzia en dicho dia ut supra.

    Francisco Montes Vijil (rubric)
    Jues Receptor
    De asistenzia
    Joseph de Atienzia y Alcala (rubric)
    De asistenzia
    Miguel de Quintana (rubric)

Ratificazion de Antonia de Moraga

Y luego yncontinente en dicho dia, mes y año, yo dicho Alcalde Mayor y Capitan Aguerra aviendo rezevido las declaraciones arriva expresadas para la prosecucion destas diligencias y ponerlas en el grado que se requieren, hize parezer ante mi a Antonia de Moraga a quien sele leyo su declaracion de verbo adverbum, y leida y entendida dijo esta segun y como la tiene echa, y que no tiene que anadir ni quitar, y en ella se ratifico y afirmo de vajo del juramento que fecho tiene, y no firmo por no saver, firmela yo dicho Alcalde Mayor con los ynfraescriptos testigos de mi assistenzia en dicho dia ut supra.

 Francisco Montes Vijil (rubric)
 Jues Receptor
 De asistenzia
 Joseph de Atienzia y Alcala (rubric)
 De asistenzia
 Miguel de Quintana (rubric)

Ratificacion de Maria de la Encarnacion

 En dicho dia, mes y año yo dicho Alcalde Mayor y Capitan Aguerra hize parezer ante mi a Maria de la Encarnacion a quien leida su declaracion dijo esta segun y como la yso y que no tiene que anadir ni quitar y en ella se afirmo y ratifico de vajo del juramento que fecho tiene, y no firmo por no saver, firmela yo dicho Alcalde Mayor con dichos testigos de mi assistenzia en dicho dia, mes y año.

 Francisco Montes Vijil (rubric)
 Jues Receptor
 De asistenzia
 Joseph de Atienzia y Alcala (rubric)
 De asistenzia
 Miguel de Quintana (rubric)

Ratificazion de Francisca Maese

 En dicho dia, mes y año yo dicho Alcalde Mayor hize parezer ante mi a Francisca Maese, la que llaman La Aguelita, a quien lei su declaracion y sida y entendida dijo que esta segun y como la tiene echa y que no tiene que anadir ni quitar y en ella se afirmo y ratifico de vajo del juramento que fecho tiene y no firmo por no saver, firmela yo dicho Alcalde Mayor con los dichos testigos de mi assistenzia en dicho dia, mes y año.

 Francisco Montes Vijil (rubric)
 Jues Receptor
 De asistenzia
 Joseph de Atienzia y Alcala (rubric)
 De asistenzia
 Miguel de Quintana (rubric)

Ratificazion de Gertrudes Martin

 En dicho dia, mes y año yo dicho Alcalde Maior hize parecer ante mi a Getrudes

Martin, muger de Antonio de Torres a quien lei su declaracion que oida y entendida dijo estar segun y como la tiene echa, y que no tiene que anadir ni quitar y en ella se afirmo y ratifico de vajo del juramento que fecho tiene y no firmo por no saber, firmela yo dicho Alcalde Mayor con los ynfraescriptos testigos de mi assistenzia en dicho dia, ut supra.

 Francisco Montes Vijil (rubric)
 Jues Receptor
 De asistenzia
 Joseph de Atienzia y Alcala (rubric)
 De asistenzia
 Miguel de Quintana (rubric)

Ratificazion de Leonicio Cortes

 En esta dicha Villa Nueva de Santa Cruz en treinta dias del mes de Octubre de mill setesientos y veinte ocho año yo dicho Alcalde Maior y Capitan Aguerra hize pareser ante mi a Leonisio Cortes a quien leida su declaracion de verbo adverbum dijo esta segun y como la tiene echa y que no tiene que anadir ni quitar y que en ella se afirma y ratifica de vajo de juramento que fecho tiene y no firmo por no saber, firmela yo dicho Alcalde Mayor con los ynfraescriptos testigos de mi asistenzia en dicho dia, mes y año.

 Francisco Montes Vijil (rubric)
 Jues Receptor
 De asistenzia
 Joseph de Atienzia y Alcala (rubric)
 De asistenzia
 Miguel de Quintana (rubric)

Ratificazion de Maria Martin

 En dicho dia, mes y año yo dicho Alcalde Maior y Capitan Aguerra hize parecer ante mi a Maria Martin, a quien lei su declaracion de verbo adverbum, quien aviendola oydo y entendido dijo estar bien escrita que la conose por suya y que no tiene que anadir ni quitar y en ella se afirmo y ratifico devajo del juramento que fecho tiene y no firmo por no saber firmela yo dicho Alcalde Mayor con los ynfraescriptos testigos de mi assistenzia en dicho dia, mes y año.

 Francisco Montes Vijil (rubric)
 Jues Receptor
 De asistenzia
 Joseph de Atienzia y Alcala (rubric)
 De asistenzia
 Miguel de Quintana (rubric)

Ratificazion de Maria Apacha

En dos dias del mes de Nobiembre de mil setesientos y veinte y ocho años yo dicho Alcalde Mayor hize parezer ante mi a Maria, Yndia Apacha, y dandole a entender su dicho se ratifico en el y para que conste lo firme con los ynfraescriptos testigos de mi assistenzia en dicho dia____

Francisco Montes Vijil (rubric)
Jues Receptor
De asistenzia
Joseph de Atienzia y Alcala (rubric)
De asistenzia
Miguel de Quintana (rubric)

Auto de Remizion

En La Villa Nueva de Santa Cruz en tres dias del mes de Nobiembre de mil setesientos y veinte y ocho año yo el Capitan Francisco Montes Vijil, Alcalde Mayor y Capitan Aguerra de esta y su jurisdizion, aviendo concluido esta causa en sustancia de sus declaraciones y deligencias que en ella se contienen hago remision de ella y los trasgresores para que Su Señoria segun el merito de ella, determine lo que fuere servido y para que conste lo firme actuando como Jues Receptor con los ynfraescriptos testigos de mi asistenzia en dicho dia, mes y año fecho ut supra.

Francisco Montes Vijil (rubric)
Jues Receptor
De asistenzia
Joseph de Atienzia y Alcala (rubric)
De asistenzia
Miguel de Quintana (rubric)

[*Editor's note*: The document ends with no sentence from the governor.]

Notes

1. For further information on Antonia de Moraga and property ownership, see Jenkins, "New Mexico Women of Property": 340-45; SANM I #491; SANM I #501; and SANM II #197.
2. Antonia de Moraga was probably the granddaughter of Diego de Moraga and Juana Bernal and the great-granddaughter of Juan Griego. Her parents were Juan de Moraga and María Montaño. They were part of the El Paso muster of 1692 and 1693 and returned to New Mexico with the Spanish Reconquest. Antonia married Cristóbal Martín Serrano I and together they had the following children: Cristóbal II, Simon, Diego, Miguel, Josefa, Antonio de Jesus, and Juan Luis. In addition, they had Gertrudis who married Antonio de Torres; María who married Manuel Antonio Domínguez; and Juana and Francisco. In 1697 Antonia received a grant near the Santa Fe Ciénaga and land above the plaza reclaiming what had belonged to her pre-revolt ancestors. After a lawsuit in which her ownership was confirmed, she sold the land (Chávez, *Origins*: 224,

239, 372-73; Kessell, Hendricks, and Dodge, *Royal* Crown: 79n28; Kessell, Hendricks, and Dodge, *Boulders*: 960n71, 1139; Ellis, "La Garita":6.)

3. Francisco Montes Vigil originally came from Zacatecas, Mexico. In 1696, he worked with Juan Páez Hurtado in recruiting settlers for New Mexico. In 1710, Francisco was given a land grant after Alameda Pueblo in Río Abajo was abandoned by the Tewa Indians. He later sold it to Juan González Bas. Presidio records show that Francisco was promoted to lieutenant in 1713, but he requested a discharge in 1715, due to serious injuries. However, in a muster of June 18, 1723, he is listed as a soldier with weapons and seven horses. In 1732, his son, Manuel Vigil, also a soldier, stated that his father had left him a piece of land in Santa Cruz de la Cañada including a large room with a patio. Another son, Pedro, is described in Case 16. (Kessell, Hendricks, and Dodge, *Boulders*: 561n22; Kessell, Hendricks, Dodge, and Miller, *Disturbances*: 222-228, 299n1; Christmas and Rau, "Una Lista": 195; Christmas, *Military Records*: 49; SANM I #302; SANM I #1220.)

4. As stated in note 2 above, Cristóbal Martín Serrano I had returned to New Mexico by 1693. His father was Hernán Martín Serrano II and his mother was Hernán's third wife, Josefa de la Asencíon. He died in Santa Cruz in 1736. (Chávez, *Origins*: 73, 324; Kessell, Hendricks, and Dodge, *Boulders*: 960n71; SANM II #390.)

5. Gertrudis Martín was the daughter of Antonia de Moraga and Cristóbal Martín I. According to this document, she was married to Antonio de Torres. She died intestate in 1763, in Santa Cruz. (See SANM I #559.)

6. According to this document, Antonio de Torres was the son of Francisca Maese. His father's name, however, is unknown. (Chávez, *Origins*: 295.)

7. Juana Martín was a daughter of Antonia de Moraga and Cristóbal Martín I. There is no indication that she married. She may be the woman who brought a criminal charge in 1744 against Joseph de Armijo, who she complained was threating her. (See Case 26.)

8. Cristóbal de Torres II was a native of New Mexico. In 1698, he was a soldier in El Paso, and in 1710, he stated that he was forty-four or forty-five years old. His wife was Angela de Leyba. Their children were Diego, Francisca, María (who married Diego Martín), and Margarita. Cristóbal de Torres II was also the recipient of a land grant near Chama in 1724 and made his will out in 1727. He does not appear to have been related to Antonio de Torres. (Chávez, *Origins*: 294.)

9. To date, no additional information has been found on an Apache woman named María.

10. In the Spanish text, the words used are "*las naguas blancas*," which means "white petticoats."

11. In the Spanish text, the verb used is "*colgar*," which means "to hang," but it may also have meant that she was tied to a post or something similar.

12. In asking this question, the alcalde seemed to be looking for evidence that Juana and Antonio were having sexual relations with each other. In other documents, the question has been phrased as: "Were they together in bed as man and wife?" (See, for instance, Case 27.)

13. María de la Encarnación was the daughter of Cristóbal Martín Serrano II, by his second wife Juliana Maese. (Chávez, *Origins*: 373.)

14. Francisca (known as "La Abuelita") was the grandmother of María de la Encarnación and the mother of Juliana Maese, the second wife of Cristóbal Martín Serrano II.

15. Cristóbal Martín Serrano II was married to María Montoya in 1698; upon her death, he married Juliana Maese. According to this document, in 1728 he was about fifty years old. (Chávez, *Origins*: 373.)

16. As this document states, Simon Martín was "in God's hands" (dead) by the time this was written. In 1705, he is listed as being a soldier and married to "Petronila" or "Petrona Domínguez," the widow of the soldier Bartolomé de Trujillo. (Kessell, Hendricks, and Dodge, *Royal Crown*: 82n36.)

17. More often referred to as "Joseph de Atienza, "Joseph de Atienza y Alcalá" also appears in Case 6.

18. For information on Miguel de Quintana, see Case 6.

19. Antonio Bernal was a citizen of Santa Cruz in 1702. He may have been related to the Francisco Bernal who was listed in the El Paso muster of 1691. Antonio's daughters, Gertrudis and Polonia, were born in 1713 and 1715 respectively. (Chávez, *Origins*: 12, 347; Kessell, Hendricks, Dodge, and Miller, *Settling of Accounts*: 161.)

20. At that time, nomadic Indians (such as the Apaches) and minors were allowed to give testimony but could not swear to it. Apparently, it was believed that Indians and children would not understand the obligations of making a sworn statement, which was made "before God, Our Lord, and the sign of the Holy Cross." (Tigges and Salazar, *Spanish Colonial Lives*: 651.)

21. Dionisio Cortés [del Castillo] was a son of José Cortés del Castillo from Puebla, Mexico, and of María Caravajal from Querétaro, Mexico, both of whom came to New Mexico with the Farfán Expedition, in1694. Upon the death of José Cortés in 1703, María married Antonio Martín Serrano who appears to have been a brother of Cristóbal Martín Serrano I and therefore an uncle of Josefa Martín (who was married to Dionisio Cortés in 1718). (Chávez, *Origins*: 266, 222, 353, 372.)

22. María Martín was the wife of Manuel Antonio Domínguez. She may have been the María Martín whose will was recorded in 1768. (Chávez, *Origins*: 225; SANM I #587.)

23. The *inditos* may be the children of Maria, the Apache servant, or they could have been part of a "rescate trade" made at one the trade fairs.

22

BIGAMY CASE DROPPED WHEN MURDER OF WIFE DISCOVERED
January 10, 1725–July 7, 1736, Source: AGN Leg. 849. Vol. 83c, 832, 862, 872, f52-73

Synopsis and editor's notes: When Juan García de la Mora arrived in New Mexico in the early1730s, he traveled to Ojo Caliente, one of the northern-most villages. In October 1733, he married Josefa Martín, a member of the large Martín Serrano family of pre-revolt settlers who had returned to New Mexico. At the time of his marriage, de la Mora stated that he was from the archbishopric of Toledo within the kingdom of Castile, Spain, that he did not have a wife, and he knew of no impediment to being married.

In April 1734, about six months later, Diego de Ugarte, a merchant from Mexico City staying in Santa Fe, approached fray José Antonio Guerrero, the comisario of the Holy Office of the Inquisition for New Mexico, stating that to "clear his conscience" he wished to report that Juan García de la Mora married for a second time while his first wife was still living. Fray Guerrero told Ugarte to keep this a secret and not to tell anyone. Urgarte's testimony was written down and noted by fray Guerrero as "hearsay" and without actual proof.

Then, three other people, all of whom wished to unburden their consciences, voluntarily approached the comisario to tell him they had also heard that Juan García de la Mora had been married a second time while his first wife was living. None of them, however, had any proof to support their testimony. Upon the request of the comisario, they named persons who were also aware of this information. When interviewing the witnesses, who did not come forth voluntarily, fray Guerrero used the standard investigative procedures of the period. First, he asked the witnesses if they had heard anything said against the Holy Faith, but without telling them the reason for his asking. When most of the witnesses answered that they did not know anything, fray Guerrero replied that they had, in fact, been a witness to information about Juan García de la Mora and he demanded that they divulge what they knew. When they complied with his request, with some being more cooperative than others, they were told to keep their interviews a secret. Most of the men interviewed were merchants from Santa Fe; many of them admitted to hearing a rumor about de la Mora's conduct when in El Paso or Chihuahua the previous February.

Because none of the persons interviewed had anything other than hearsay information to share, the officials of the Holy Office in Mexico City looked for witnesses among the Franciscans. The only friar to come forward was fray Juan Miguel Menchero, who had traveled with Juan García de la Mora from El Paso to northern New Mexico when they first arrived in New Spain. Fray Menchero stated that de la

Mora told him that he had been married but that he was a widower, and fray Menchero had heard nothing else to the contrary. This testimony, however, was also noted down as hearsay.

Still searching for definitive information on the death of Juan García de la Mora's first wife, the Holy Office in Mexico City sent a letter to Spain requesting information from the Council of the Holy Office in Toledo. In May 1736, officials appointed by the council went to Pozuelo de Calatrava,[1] the hometown of de la Mora located in Castile (south of Toledo). There the officials found the February 1725 marriage record for Juan García de la Mora and María de Hornero. The inquisitors interviewed witnesses to the wedding, who stated that they remembered attending the event and also recalled what happened after that, for it was all public knowledge. They explained that after a few months of marriage, de la Mora suspected that his wife had a lover. After taking letters from his wife that proved her adultery, de la Mora followed his wife to her mother's house where she had run for safety and stabbed her. Seven or eight days later she died from her wounds.

Juan García de la Mora then left Pozuelo de Calatrava for Seville, and, according to a letter written to his mother, departed for Havana, Cuba, in the company of a gunpowder merchant.[2] From there, he went to Mexico City, El Paso, and then to the northern region of New Mexico.

After gathering what information they could, Holy Office of the Inquisition officials prepared a secret report, under the seal of the Holy Office, in the Chamber of the Secret Office of the Inquisition, in Toledo on June 16, 1736. A duplicate copy was sent to the tribunal in Mexico City. The only information found in this "secret report" was a note saying that the officials in El Paso did not do a good job of certifying the witnesses. It also said they should do better next time, but that it didn't matter in this instance because de la Mora had not committed bigamy. The officials made no mention of the murder of de la Mora's wife.

De la Mora became a successful merchant and Camino Real trader, traveling between Santa Cruz and Albuquerque to Chihuahua and Mexico City. In 1735, at the time of the investigation by the Holy Office of the Inquisition, he was involved in a dispute with Diego Torres about illegal trading with the Comanches.[3] It is not known if de la Mora was aware of the bigamy investigation, though given the number of witnesses interviewed (and despite of the pledges of secrecy) someone surely told him. In 1752, we find de la Mora just returned from Chihuahua and involved in a lawsuit with another trader regarding trading with the Zunis.[4]

Travel to El Paso and Chihuahua was not uncommon at that time. For instance, this document indicates that of the nine witnesses interviewed by fray Guerrero, five said they heard about de la Mora's two marriages while in El Paso and one heard about it when he was in Chihuahua. Other documents prove that merchant caravans, probably accompanied by a military escort, had been making the thirty-day trip to El Paso and the forty-day trip to Chihuahua since at least 1724.[4a]

The fact that four witnesses came forward of their own accord to denounce Juan García de la Mora shows the success of the Franciscans' methods used to collect denunciations from parishioners on matters such as bigamy. On a designated Sunday, at Mass, or at the time of some religious festival, an Edict of Faith, sometimes called the "Edict of Anathema," would be read by one of the Franciscans as part of the Mass. Records indicate that an edict was read in El Paso in 1693 and 1694 and in Santa Fe in 1716 and 1734, and there were likely many more such edict readings.[5] As shown here, when making a denunciation a person began with the words: "I wish to clear my conscience" and then followed with the specific denunciation. The comisario then asked about other persons who might have witnessed or heard about the heretical behavior, all of which, as indicated in this case, was kept secret.

This document consists of testimonies, reports, and transmittals about the case compiled by Inquisition officials arranged in an order that was not chronological. For clarity, the material has been rearranged in a chronological fashion in the translation, so the activity of the inquisitors can be more easily followed. The transcription of the Spanish text, however, contains the material in its original order.

TRANSLATION

1734

Villa of Santa Fe in New Mexico

The Inquisitor Fiscal[6] of this Holy Office of Mexico City to don Juan García de la Mora, Spaniard, citizen of the Villa of Santa Fe in New Mexico. On suspicion of being married twice; his first wife died before he married the second one.

[*Editor's note*: The following testimony was gathered from witnesses in 1734. It provided the basis for the further investigation of bigamy.]

Diego de Ugarte,[7] hearsay [about words spoken by] don José Terrus[8]

In the Villa of Santa Fe, capital of the kingdom of New Mexico, on the 7th of the month of April of this year, 1734, at nine in the morning before the Reverend Father [Guerrero], comisario of the Holy Office of this kingdom, there appeared without being called and who swore to tell the truth, a man who said his name was Diego Ugarte, unmarried, a native of Mexico City, and a resident in this villa.

To clear his conscience, he states and makes the denunciation that on a day he does not remember, he was talking about marriages with don José Terrus who said that there was a person in the kingdom on whom having married must weigh. Antonio Durán de Armijo[9] responded that he was present and that he should shut up. Diego de Ugarte asked don José Terrus what case he was talking about. Don José advised him that it was don Juan García de la Mora, and that for this presumption he had no proof. A few days ago, meeting with Juan de Abeytia,[10] he, Ugarte, said that yes it had been revealed that don Juan García de la Mora was married in Spain. Terrus responded he had heard this said and that a priest in El Paso had written to this kingdom a letter about the matter. Speaking with the general, don Juan Páez Hurtado, about the same matter, the general said that the late Reverend Father fray Simón [Díaz] de Acosta[11] had told him that don Juan García de la Mora was married in Spain. He also said that Juan de Abeytia told him that don Juan García de la Mora communicated this to fray Simón that he was married in Spain. Later he, Ugarte, saw him marry Josefa Martín[12] in this kingdom.

This is the truth by the oath he swore. Having been read to him, he said it was written correctly and that he did not say so out of hatred or ill will. He promised to keep the secret[13] and signed it with the Reverend Father Comisario before me, the undersigned notary.

    Fray José Antonio Guerrero (rubric)
    Comisario of the Holy Office
    Diego de Ugarte (rubric)
    Done before me
    José Yrigoyen[14] (rubric)
    Notary of the Holy Office

Francisco Mascareñas,[15] hearsay from Juan de Abeytia, Antonio Durán de Armijo

In the Villa of Santa Fe, capital of the kingdom of New Mexico, on the 8th day of the month of April of the present year, 1734, at seven in the morning, before the Reverend Father Comisario of the Holy Office of this kingdom, there appeared a man without being called. Being sworn in legal form that he would tell the truth, he said his name was Francisco Mascareñas, soldier of this presidio of the Villa of Santa Fe, married, thirty years old.

For the unburdening of his conscience, he says and makes the denunciation that in the month of March, when he was on guard duty on a day he does not remember, he heard it said by Juan de Abeytia that don Juan García de la Mora, who married Josefa Martín in this kingdom, was previously married in Spain. Abeytia had been in the house of Antonio Durán de Armijo, notary[16] of the Archdiocese, and he heard the notary say to don José Terrus, a Catalan, that he was going to make his report and that if he wanted to Terrus could make other useless reports[17] like the one about don Juan García de la Mora. This he heard from Juan de Abeytia of the [illegible] of don José Abeytia and of Antonio de Armenta.[18]

This is the truth by the oath he made. Having been read to him, he said it was written correctly and that he does not say this out of hatred or ill will. He promised to keep the secret and it was signed for him because he did not know how by the Reverend Father Comisario before me, the undersigned notary.

    Fray José Antonio Guerrero (rubric)
    Comisario of the Holy Office
    Executed before me
    José Yrigoyen (rubric)
    Notary of the Holy Office

Vicente de Armijo,[19] hearsay from Juan Fernández de la Pedrera[20]

In the Villa of Santa Fe, capital the kingdom of New Mexico, on the 8th day of the month of April of the present year, 1734, at around four in the afternoon before the Reverend Father Comisario of the Holy Office of this kingdom, there appeared without being called and swearing in legal form to tell the truth, was a man who said his name was Vicente de Armijo, married, forty-two years old, and a merchant.

To unburden his conscience, he said and made the accusation that in the month of December on a day he cannot remember, at around eight at night, in the Plazuela of the Company in Chihuahua,[21] he heard Juan Fernández de la Pedrera say that Juan García de la Mora, who married Josefa Martín in this kingdom, was married elsewhere. He said this [illegible] and this is the truth by the oath he swore. Having been read to him, he said it was written correctly, that he is a citizen of this villa, that he does not say it out of hatred or ill will, and that he promised to keep the secret. Because he did not know how to sign, the Reverend Father Comisario signed it before me, the undersigned notary.

Fray José Antonio Guerrero (rubric)
Comisario of the Holy Office
Executed before me
José Yrigoyen (rubric)
Notary of the Holy Office

José Terrus, hearsay from Fray José López Tello, from El Paso [del Río del] Norte, minister of doctrine.[22]

In the Villa of Santa Fe, capital of the kingdom of New Mexico, on the 5th day of the month of November of the present year, 1734, at about two in the afternoon, before the Reverend Father Comisario of the Holy Office of this kingdom, there appeared having been summoned and swearing in legal form that he would tell the truth, a man who said his name was José Terrus, native of Cataluña, Diocese of Vique, Spain,[23] citizen of the Villa of Santa Fe, married, and thirty-one years old.

Asked whether he knows or presumes why he has been summoned, he said he neither knew nor presumed [illegible] that in this Holy Office there is information [illegible]. Asked whether he knows or has heard that someone has said or done anything that might be or appears to be against Our Holy Catholic faith, the evangelical law that Our Holy Catholic Roman Church preaches and teaches or against the upright and free exercise of the Holy Office, he said that he had not heard anything said. He was then told that in this Holy Office there is information that when he was in a certain place, a certain person said to him that there was a man in the kingdom who after being married in Spain had married in this kingdom. He said that one day when he was with the Reverend Father fray José López Tello, minister and preacher of El Paso del Río del Norte, when the Reverend Father was talking to him, he said "Reverend Father, don Juan García de la Mora got married." The Reverend Father responded, "This cannot be because he [illegible] was married in Spain." Some people whom he cannot remember or on what day or days they said it, told him this.

This is the truth by the oath he swore. Having been read to him, he said it was written correctly, and he does not say this out of hatred or ill will. He promised to keep the secret and signed it with the Reverend Father Commisaro and the undersigned notary.

    Fray José Antonio Guerrero (rubric)
    Comisario of the Holy Office
    José Terrus (rubric)
    Executed before me
    José Yrigoyen (rubric)
    Notary of the Holy Office

Juan Montes Vigil[24] hearsay from Juan Fernández

In this Villa of Santa Fe, capital of the kingdom of New Mexico, on the 5th day of the month of November of the present year, 1734, at 2:30 in the afternoon, before the Reverend Father Comisario of the Holy Office of this kingdom, there appeared, having been summoned, and swore in legal form that he would tell the truth a man who said his name was Juan Montes Vigil, native of Zacatecas, citizen of the Villa of Santa Fe, trader and merchant, married, age forty-four.

Asked whether he knew or presumed why he had been summoned, he said he neither knew nor presumed. Asked whether he knows or has heard said anything that was or appears to be against Our Holy Faith, the evangelical law that Our Mother Apostolic Roman Church preaches and teaches, he said that he neither knows nor remembers. He was told that in this Holy Office there is information that when he was at a certain place, it was said in his presence that in this kingdom, there was a man who after marrying in Spain had married in this kingdom. He said that when he was in El Paso del Río del Norte around the month of February, on a date he does not remember in the present year of [17]34, Juan Fernández said that Father fray José [López] Tello, minister of El Paso del Río del Norte, had told him that he had heard that Juan García de la Mora was married in Spain and later married in New Mexico and that Vicente de Armijo had heard this.

This is the truth by the oath he swore. Having been read to him, he said that it was written correctly and that he does not say this out of hatred or ill will. He promised to keep the secret. Because he did not know how to sign his name, the reverend father signed it before me, the undersigned notary.

    José Antonio Guerrero (rubric)
    Comisario of the Holy Office
    Executed before me
    José Yrigoyen (rubric)
    Notary of the Holy Office

Juan Páez Hurtado,[25] Lieutenant of New Mexico, hearsay from don José Terrus and don José Orcasitas[26]

In the royal Villa of Santa Fe, capital of the kingdom of New Mexico, on the 5th day of the month of November of the present year, 1734, at about 2:30 in the afternoon, there appeared before me, the Reverend Father Comisario of the Holy Office of this kingdom, having been summoned and swore in legal form to tell the truth, a man who said his name was Juan Páez Hurtado, native of the Villa of Villafranca de los Palacios,[27] lieutenant general of this kingdom, citizen of the Villa of Santa Fe, married, age seventy-two.

Asked whether he knows or presumes why he has been summoned, he said that he neither knows nor presumes why he has been summoned. Asked whether he knows or has heard said anything that appears to be against Our Holy Faith, the evangelical law that Our Mother Apostolic Roman Church preaches and teaches, he said that he does not know anything. He was told that in this Holy Office there is information that in a certain place on a certain day it was said in his presence that a certain man who married in this kingdom was married in Spain. He says that he heard don José Terrus and don José Orcasitas, citizens of El Paso, say that when Father fray José [López] Tello heard of the marriage of Juan García de la Mora, he was greatly amazed because the Reverend Father said that he was married in Spain. Everyone who came from El Paso told him so, but he had heard various people say that before coming to this kingdom, he had killed his wife.

This is the truth by the oath he swore. Having been read to him, he said it was written correctly and that he did not say this out of hatred or ill will. He promised to keep the secret and signed it with the Reverend Father Comisario before me, the undersigned notary.

Fray José Antonio Guerrero (rubric)
Comisario of the Holy Office
Juan Páez Hurtado (rubric)
Executed before me
José Yrigoyen (rubric)
Notary of the Holy Office

Antonio Durán de Armijo, [illegible]

In this Villa of Santa Fe, capital of the kingdom of New Mexico, on the 6th day of the month of November of the present year, 1734, before the Reverend Father the Comisario of this Holy Office, at around nine in the morning, there appeared, having been summoned, and swearing in legal form to tell the truth, a man who said his name was Antonio Durán de Armijo, barber and notary of office of the ecclesiastical judge, native of Nuestra Señora de los Zacatecas, citizen of the Villa of Santa Fe, about sixty-three years old.

Asked whether he knew or presumed why he had been summoned, he said he neither knew nor presumed why he had been summoned. Asked whether he knew that someone had said or done anything that was or appeared to be against Our Holy Catholic faith, which Our Holy Mother Catholic Apostolic Roman Church preaches and teaches, or against the upright and free exercise of the Holy Office, he said no. He was told that in this Holy Office there is information that at a certain time in a certain place, in his presence a certain man said that there was a man in the kingdom on whom marrying had to weigh, and he responded that he should be quiet, that this was a case for the [Holy] Inquisition.

He said that he remembered that he heard it said but that he did not remember by whom, or where, or in the presence of whom, and that he had married. It was a fact that in the kingdom Juan García de la Mora married a woman whose name he did not remember. He heard it said that this had been said in El Paso del Río del Norte. He was told that in this Holy Office there is information that when he was in his house carrying out some prenuptial investigations, the prospective groom [Juan García de la Mora] asked him why he wanted to do more worthless investigations like what's-his-name?[28] He said that he did not remember but that if he remembered at some time, he would say so, but he is certain for now that he has not said such a thing. This is the truth by the oath he swore. Having read it to him and been heard, he said that it is written correctly and that he does not say this out of hatred or ill will. He promised to keep the secret and signed it with the Reverend Father Comisario before me, the undersigned notary.

Fray José Antonio Guerrero (rubric)
Comisario of the Holy Office
Antonio Durán de Armijo (rubric)
Executed before me
José Yrigoyen (rubric)
Notary of the Holy Office

José Orcasitas, hearsay from fray José López Tello, minister of doctrine of El Paso del [Río del] Norte.

In this Villa of Santa Fe, capital of the kingdom of New Mexico, on the 2nd day of the month of August, 1735, at nine in the morning, there appeared, having been summoned and sworn in legal form to tell the truth, was a man who said his name was José Orcasitas, traveling merchant, unmarried, age about twenty-four.

Asked whether he knows or presumes why he has been summoned, he said he neither knows nor presumes. Asked whether he knows or has heard that someone has said or done anything that might or appears to be against Our Holy Catholic faith, the evangelical law that Our Holy Catholic Roman Church preaches and teaches, or against the upright and free exercise of the Holy Office, he said that he had not heard anything. He was told that in this Holy Office there is information that on a certain day in a certain place, he said in front of some people that a certain person who married in this kingdom was married in Spain.

He said that this is true he said that in a place but before whom he does not remember. He said that in El Paso del Río del Norte he heard the Reverend Father fray José López Tello say "I do not know how don Juan García de la Mora married." From the minister himself, [he heard] that he is married in Spain. He does not remember before who this was. He said this and that it is the truth by the oath he swore.

Having read it to him, he said it was written correctly and that he does not say this out of hatred or ill will. He promised to keep the secret and signed it with the Reverend Father Comisario before me, the undersigned notary.

    Fray José Antonio Guerrero (rubric)
    Comisario of the Holy Office
    José Orcasitas (rubric)
    Executed before me
    José Yrigoyen (rubric)
    Notary of the Holy Office

Antonio de Armenta

In the Villa of Santa Fe on the 2nd day of the month of August of 1734, before the Reverend Father Comisario of the Holy Office, there appeared without being called and swearing in legal form that he would tell the truth, a man who said his name was Antonio de Armenta, soldier and squad leader of the royal presidio of the Villa of Santa Fe, thirty-four years of age.

Asked whether he knew or presumed why he had been called, he said he neither knew nor presumed why. Asked whether he knew that someone had said or done anything that was or appeared to be against Our Holy Catholic faith, which Our Holy Mother Catholic Apostolic Roman Church preaches and teaches, or against the upright and free exercise of the Holy Office, he said that he neither knew nor had heard it said. He was told that in this Holy Office there is information that in a certain place, on a certain day, it was said in his presence that a man who was married in Spain had married in this kingdom. He, Armenta, responded that he heard it said and did not remember by whom, nor the place, nor before whom it was said that don Juan García de la Mora who was married in his land had married in this kingdom, that this is the truth by the oath he swore.

Having been read to him, he said it was written correctly and that he did not say it out of hatred or ill will. He promised to keep the secret and signed it with the Reverend Father Comisario before me, the undersigned notary.

    Fray José Antonio Guerrero (rubric)
    Comisario of the Holy Office
    Antonio de Armenta (rubric)
    Executed before me
    José Yrigoyen (rubric)
    Notary of the Holy Office

[*Editor's note:* In October, 1733, Fray José Antonio Guerrero sent the following two documents to the Holy Office in Mexico City as evidence of the marriage of Juan García de la Mora and Josefa Martín.]

Bachiller don José de Bustamante, vicar and the ecclesiastical judge of New Mexico so that he may be aware of don Juan García de la Mora and Josefa Martín.

Bachiller don José de Bustamante, vicar and ecclesiastical judge of this kingdom, its jurisdiction and district, appear before the Most Excellent Doctor José Benito Crespo,[29] member of the Order of Santiago, by the grace of God and of the Holy Apostolic See, Bishop of this bishopric, member of the Council of His Majesty, My lord.

By the present document, the Most Reverend Father Preacher, retired, fray Juan [Sánchez] de la Cruz,[30] minister of the Pueblo de San Juan de la Soledad del Río Arriba, will minister on three feast days, *Inter Misarum Solemnia*,[31] as is set forth by the Holy Council to don Juan García de la Mora, Spaniard, (widower of doña María de Hornero[32]), native of the Villa of Pozuelo de Almagro[33] in the kingdom of Castile, archbishopric of Toledo, legitimate son of don Juan García de la Mora,[34] deceased, and of doña Manuela González,[35] citizen of the villa. This is for the marriage he wants to contract with Josefa Martín, Spaniard, citizen of Río Arriba, legitimate daughter of Marcial Martín and doña Lugarda de Medina, Spaniards, citizens of that place.

There being no impediment whatsoever (if one should arise, send it to me), I married and veiled them according to the order of Our Holy Mother Church, and he will record it in the book in his charge.

Done in this Villa of Santa Fe on the 14th day of the month of October, 1733.

Bachiller José de Bustamante (rubric)
By order of vicar and ecclesiastical judge
Antonio Durán de Armijo (rubric)
Public Notary

Certification of the marriage entry of don Juan García de la Mora, widower of doña María de Ornelas, and Josefa Martín.

I, fray José Antonio Guerrero, Comisario of the Holy Office in this kingdom of New Mexico, certify that on the 11th day of November, 1733, in the chapel of Nuestra Señora de la Soledad del Río Arriba, which belongs to the mission of San Juan, with the permission of the Reverend Father fray Juan [Sánchez] de la Cruz, minister of that district, I married and veiled don Juan García de la Mora and Josefa Martín, legitimate daughter of Marcial Martín and Lugarda de Medina. The witnesses were Alférez don

[Juan] José Moreno³⁶ and doña Juana Roybal.³⁷ Present were the parish priest and many others.

So that it may be of record, I signed it on August 3, 1735.

Fray José Antonio Guerrero (rubric)

[*Editor's note*: The testimony above ends the 1734 investigation of witnesses and the material sent by fray José Antonio Guerrero to the Holy Office in Mexico City. The following documents include a transmittal letter of August 1735 that was also sent to the Holy Office by fray Guerrero].

Most Illustrious Sir

I am sending to Your Excellency two denunciations. The one with the letter "A" contains the accusation of bigamy. The one with the letter "B" is a denunciation about irreverent behavior, the holy sacrament of baptism, concubinage and others³⁸ that are not in condition to send to Your Excellency. May God make you prosper and live many years for the glory, exaltation and defense of our Holy Faith, Villa of Santa Fe, August 2, 1735.

At the feet of Your Excellency
Your humble son,
fray José Antonio Guerrero³⁹ (rubric)

[*Note in margin*]
Advise this
Comisario of receipt and
alert him that confirmations⁴³
of the testimonies are lacking.

Received in the Holy Office of the Inquisition of Mexico City on the 19th day of the month of November, 1735.
Inquisitors [Pedro] Navarro [de Isla],⁴⁰ [Pedro Anselmo Sánchez de] Tagle,⁴¹ [Diego Mangado y] Clavijo.⁴² [rubrics]

Although now there is no need for obtaining a confirmation, or anything else in the marriage of don Manuel⁴⁴ García de la Mora, in similar cases and in others of substance, testimony sent must always be confirmed by honest persons, if they are available, in accord with what is ordered in the printed instruction for Comisarios. This is because when witnesses give evidence without it being confirmed, one is obligated to return their statements or copies of them for said confirmations, which is inconvenient over such long distances.

Our time is taken up with making the copies and in doing what the council orders about the other accusation of making friends in order to hide concubinage,⁴⁵ which is not a matter for the Holy Office; rather it is the Ecclesiastical Judge who must hear it. Summon Fathers [Juan Miguel] Menchero[46] and [Diego] Trujillo,[47] who can provide information about the marriage in Spain. (rubric)

[*Note in margin*]
On December 1, 1735
Comisario [fray Guerrero] wrote
this as ordered in the
decree on the reverse. (rubric)

[*Note in margin*]
On said day, [Yrigoyen] wrote
to the Comisario [fray Guerrero]
in El Paso del Río del Norte for him
to question Father [José López]
Tello[48] about what is stated. (rubric)

Those who were to carry out the examination are Juan Fernández, don José de Bustamente,[49] and Juan de Abeytia. They are absent from the kingdom, and I do not know where the Reverend Father fray Tello is in the jurisdiction of El Paso del Río del Norte whose Comisario is the Reverend Father fray Andrés Varo.[50] The Reverend Father fray Simón Díaz de Acosta died in the convent of El Paso. In proof thereof, I signed it in the Villa of Santa Fe on the 3rd of the month of August, 1735.
    José Yrigoyen (rubric)
    Notary of the Holy Office

[*Editor's note*: As requested by the Holy Office officials, the following item was testimony given by fray Juan Miguel Menchero about Juan García de la Mora.]

[*Note in margin*]
Declaration of the
Reverend Father
fray Juan [Miguel] Menchero,
don Juan García de la Mora

In the Holy Office of the Inquisition of Mexico City on the 5th day of the month of December, 1735, in the morning session, the Inquisitor, Licenciado don Pedro Anselmo Sánchez de Tagle, summoned to enter a priest of the Order of Saint Francis. When he was present, his oath was received, which he swore in *verbo sacerdotis tacto pectore*,[51] under which he promised to tell the truth about everything he knew and was asked. He said that his name was fray Juan Miguel Menchero, Examiner[52] of this Holy

Office and of this Province of the Holy Gospel, more than forty years of age.

Asked whether he knows or presumes why he has been summoned to this Holy Office, he said he had some basis for suspecting that he could have been called about don Juan García de la Mora, said to be a native of the Villa of Almagro in the kingdoms of Spain, Archbishopric of Toledo. This is because about two years earlier, fray José Ortiz de Velasco,[53] Custodian of New Mexico, wrote him asking about don Juan García de la Mora who intended to wed in that kingdom, and asking whether he knew if he was married or not.

To this he responded, in essence, what he will now say. In the year thirty, being ready to make a trip to that kingdom of New Mexico, de la Mora arrived and asked him for assistance. Menchero surmised that he was a fellow countryman because he said he was a native of the Villa of Almagro. Having heard the declarant's surname, he supposed that he was also from that place because most of his relatives lived here. For that reason, he took de la Mora with him to New Mexico and sought to live as a Christian. At the same time, he was able to hear and heard that he was a widower in Spain because he had killed his wife. Neither in the time he was with him, which would be about a year and a half, nor later, did he learn anything certain to the contrary. All he had heard since was that he had remarried in the kingdom of New Mexico.

Now he added that the first time that de la Mora sought him out for assistance, he did not say his surname was Mora but another, different one that he cannot remember. But later, after very few days, he discovered for himself the correct name and surnames and that because of them he appears to have been and is in the places of his subsequent residences since he has not heard any other variation.

Asked whether he knows another person or other persons who might provide information about don Juan García de la Mora, especially whether he is a widower or married in Spain. He said that he does not know of anyone. He did hear him say that he had come from Spain to Havana in the company of a gunpowder contractor[54] and from there to here he came with another comrade, but he does not know the name and whereabouts of either of the two, nor of a person from the Villa of Almagro who might provide useful information about the undersigned. This is what he can say to the questions they have asked him and the truth by the oath he has sworn. With that, he was ordered to leave the hearing, and before [he did so] he signed his testimony.

Fray Juan Miguel Menchero (rubric)
Executed before me
Don José Carrillo y Biezma[55] secretary (rubric)

[*Editor's note*: The following paragraphs include a transmittal letter and the findings of the investigation by the Council of the Holy Office in Toledo.]

From Licenciado don Pedro Navarro de Ysla (rubric)
To the Reverend Father fray José Antonio Guerrero, Comisario of this office in the Villa of Santa Fe in the kingdom of New Mexico.

With this letter on four written pages, I am sending you the proceedings carried out at the order of the Council of the Inquisition of Toledo to substantiate the marriage contracted in the Villa of Pozuelo de Calatrava by don Juan García de Mora and doña María de Hornero, which you have requested in your letter of 9th December of 1735, so that putting these papers with the others of this case you can examine, take note, and deliver justice. May God keep you. Madrid, July 7, 1736.

To the Apostolic Inquisitors of the Holy Office of the Inquisition of the Council of the Inquisition Mexico City, Andrés Cabrejas (rubric), Gabriel Bermúdez (rubric), Fray Juan Raspeña (rubric), Mexico City.

I, don Pedro Vélez de Escalante[56] secretary of the secret of this Holy Office of the Inquisition of Toledo, certify, that with the letter from the members of the Council of the Holy Office of the 30th of April 1736, received the letter that the Tribunal of Mexico City wrote to your excellency so that the investigation into the marriage that don Juan García de la Mora, native of Pozuelo de Almagro, and doña María de Hornero would be carried out. This was whether it was true that he killed his wife and if the marriage was legally acceptable, as well as when the burial entry was written for doña María. Whatever resulted from this investigation was to be sent in duplicate to the councilmen.

In fulfillment thereof, on the 5th of May of said year, a commission in legal form was given to ministers who were satisfactory to the Tribunal. Having gone to the Villa of Pozuelo de Calatrava, they made an authentic copy of the betrothal entry of don Juan García de la Mora and doña María de Hornero, which is the following:

Betrothal and Veiling Entry
In the parish church of this Villa of Pozuelo de Calatrava on the 10th day of the month of January, 1725, I, Licenciado fray don Juan Martínez Cobo[57] of the habit of Calatrava, rector and *cura propio*[58] of this villa, solemnly betrothed them by which they made a valid sacrament and marriage.

Afterward I gave the nuptial blessings, according to the Roman Ritual and what Our Holy Mother Church commands, to Juan García de la Mora, son of Juan García de la Mora and Manuela González, his wife, and to María Hornero, daughter of Simón de Hornero and Juliana de Ledesma, all citizens and natives of this villa. This had been preceded by the three reading of the banns that the Holy Council of Trent and the synods of this archbishopric order done at the time of the offering of the High Mass on three consecutive feast days. These were, first, the *infra octave*[59] Sunday of the Birth of the Lord; second; the Day of the Circumcision; and third, Epiphany. From these no impediment arose that might prevent the marriage. Likewise, this was preceded by the dispatch from the vicar of Cuidad Real. The witnesses were: Miguel de Hornero,[60]

Lucas García de la Puente,[61] and Pedro López Merino.[62] The godparents were Andrés Delgado de Herrera[63] and Catalina Seguido,[64] his wife. All were citizens of this villa. So that it may be of record, I signed it.

Licenciado fray don Juan Martínez Cobo

The ministers certify that the entry is correctly written and faithfully copied and composed.

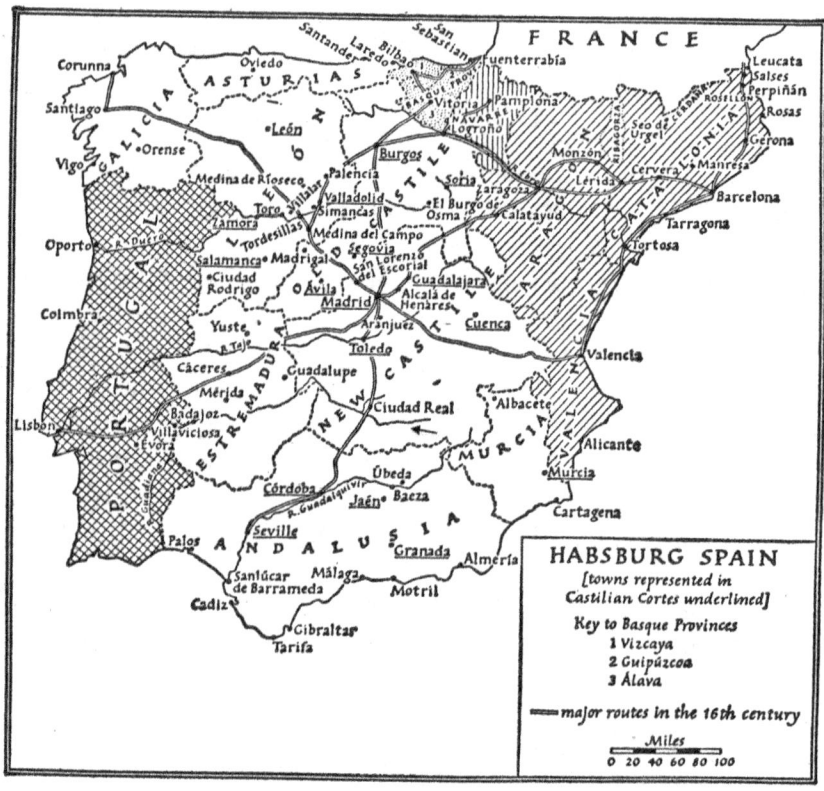

Map of Hapsburg Spain showing the locations of Toledo and Cuidad Real. J. H. Elliott, *Imperial Spain 1469-1716*. New American Library, 1963:16

[Examination of witnesses]

Going on later to examine the attesting witnesses who were at the betrothal and veiling, they all stated that they remember having attended the marriage that Juan García de la Mora and María de Hornero contracted. They also said that it is public knowledge in that villa that after a few months of marriage, it was said that Juan García de la Mora was jealous regarding his wife María de Hornero. Having found some papers written by the person he suspected, he tried forcibly to take them from her to read the content of them, and in effect, he did take them. While he was reading them, María de Hornero sought refuge in her mother's house. Later, Juan García de la

Mora entered the house and finding his wife in bed, he stabbed her. After about seven or eight days, María de Hornero died from the stab wounds.

Immediately after Juan García de la Mora did what has been stated to his wife, he left the Villa del Pozuelo. They found out he went to Seville whence he left for the kingdoms of the Indies. From there Juan García de la Mora wrote his mother, and the witnesses know this because they have read several letters, two of them dated in Havana, which are the last they saw. They read them four years ago and have not had any more news of him.

All of the witnesses responded essentially what has been related. After three days passed, they affirmed before honest, religious persons all they had said and declared without altering or adding anything at all.

Later, the ministers went on to prepare a transcript of the burial entry of María de Hornero, whose contents, to the letter, are as follows:

Burial Entry

María de Hornero, former wife of Juan García de la Mora, citizens of this Villa of Pozuelo de Calatrava, died there on the 11th day of the month of May 1725. She received the Holy Sacraments and made a will by means of a power of attorney, which she gave to Juliana de León,[65] widow of Simón de Hornero, and mother of the deceased. By means of this power of attorney, I, [Licenciado], direct what is customary for the ordered obligatory bequests, and name for her heir, Juliana de León, her mother, and as executors, me, the prior, and José Granados,[66] her brother-in-law, husband of Josefa de Hornero,[67] her sister. The aforesaid Juliana de León, exercising power of attorney, ordered that fifty-five low masses be said for her soul and intention, and a mass with the body present. Those powers of attorney were executed before Juan Martínez de Agustín,[68] the public scribe and scribe for the town council of this villa, together with the clauses of the will that María de Hornero executed on the 7th day of May of said year. She was buried in the parish church in the tomb of her ancestors on the 12th day of said month. I paid what was customary. So that it may be of record, I signed it.

Licenciado fray don Juan Martínez Cobo.[69]

The ministers certified that the entry they prepared was well and faithfully copied and in accord with the original.

[Proceedings, Transmittal]

It is also of record from the depositions of the witnesses and the secret report that the ministers made that Juan García de la Mora is from a very honorable family and that during the time he lived in the Villa of Pozuelo, he comported himself like an upright man with good relationships with those with whom he dealt and communicated. For this he was liked by all the distinguished people of that villa, for which reason today they regret the misfortune that befell him with his wife, which was why he left.

All this is of record at greater length. It appears that these proceedings are to remain in the Chamber of this Secret Office.

By the proceedings of this tribunal of the 12th of the present month and year, I again order that certification be sent in duplicate to the members of the Council in obedience to what was ordered by their letter of the 30th of April of this year. In fulfillment whereof so that it may be of record, I provide the present document sealed with the seal of the Holy Office and signed by my hand in the chamber of the secret office of the Inquisition of Toledo on the 26th of June 1736.

Don Pedro Vélez de Escalante (rubric)

[Note in Margin]
Decree of the Council
In the Council on the first of
July, 1736, Councilmen,
[Andrés] Cabrejas,[70]
[Gabriel] Bermúdez,
[Luis de] Velasco,
[Antonio Gerónimo de] Mier,
and [Juan] Raspeña.

[Transmittal]
Send the authorized copy in duplicate to the tribunal from which it originates. It is followed by the rubric of the *relator*,[71] Doctor Losano. This certified copy and decree agree with their originals what for now remain in the secretariat in my charge to which I refer of which I certify and sign.

Don Sebastián Ramos y Ruiz (rubric)

[Transmittal]
With this letter I am sending you on four pages of text of the proceedings carried out by order of the Council of the Inquisition of Toledo, to substantiate the marriage contracted in the Villa of Pozuelo de Calatrava by don Juan García de Mora and doña María de Hornero, which was requested in your letter of 2nd December of this past year, so that with these papers and the others about this case you will examine, vote, and render justice. My God keep you. Madrid, 7th July 1736.

Licenciado Luis de Velasco (rubric)
Gabriel Bermúdez (rubric)
Licenciado don Antonio Gerónimo de Mier (rubric)

[*Editor's note:* Nothing more is included in this document about an acquittal for Juan García de la Mora for bigamy or about the murder of his wife. The document ends with a 1737 letter from fray José Antonio Guerrero answering the earlier December 1735 Holy Office complaint about the lack of confirmations by witnesses. (See above.) In June 1736, fray Guerrero responded and attached another version of the earlier letter as follows.

[*Note in Margin*]
Received in this Holy
Office of Mexico City
on the eighth of January,
1737. Inquisitors Navarro,
Tagle, and Clavijo.

Most Illustrious Sir:

On the 15th of May of the present year, I received Your Most Illustrious Sir's letter, which I send enclosed. [See the following document.] Having seen it, I am informed of the confirmations that are to be made in cases of substance. I shall keep very much in mind in the future what is expressed in the instruction at numbers nineteen and twenty, confessing as I do confess my lack of awareness. At the feet of Your Most Illustrious Sir with the submission I owe, I remain asking the Lord Our Highness to augment and preserve Your Most Illustrious Person for the defense of Our Faith. San Francisco de Nambé, New Mexico. June 25, 1736.

At the feet of your Illustrious Person, your humble and known servant and chaplain,
Fray José Antonio Guerrero (rubric)

[*Editor's note:* The following is a second copy of December 1, 1735 letter from the Holy Office.]

In this Tribunal, the letter from our Comisario of 3rd August 1735 past was received with the proceedings that accompanied it against don Juan García de la Mora, for suspicion that he was married twice. Upon examination, our Comisario is advised that they lack confirmations of the deposed witnesses. Even though for now there is no need to make these confirmations or do anything else about the marriage carried out by [de la] Mora,[72] our Comisario is advised that in similar cases, it is always necessary to send the witnesses confirmed, before honorable persons, in accord with what it ordered in the printed instruction for Comisarios, at numbers nineteen and twenty of the instruction. The witnesses are not authenticated if they do not come with a confirmation. With this defect of the confirmations, the Tribunal is obligated to return their statements or copies of them so that the confirmations can be carried out. This is very inconvenient over such long distances and takes up the time in making the copies and delays the time of returning them.

With respect to the other accusation about making compadres [friends],[73] which came with the ones cited, and in doing what the Council orders about whether or not it should hear it, regarding the concubinage alone, it does not involve the

Holy Office, but it does involve the Ecclesiastical Judge who must hear it.

May God keep our Comisario, and so forth. Inquisition of Mexico City, 1st December 1735.

    Licenciado don Pedro Anselmo Sánchez de Tagle (rubric)
    Licenciado don Diego Mangado y Clavijo (rubric)
    By order of the Holy Office
    Don José Carrillo y Biezma, Secretary

TRANSCRIPTION

Villa de Santa Fe en el Nuebo Mexico Año de 1734

El señor Inquisidor fiscal deste santo officio de Mexico a Don Juan Garcia de la Mora. Gachupin, Vecino de la Villa de Santa fee en el Nuevo Mexico. Por sospechas de dos vezes vezes casado murió. Su primera Muger ante decasare la segunda.

[*Note in margin*]
[Recivida en el Santo
Oficio de la Inqquisicion
de Mexico en diez y
nueve días del mes de
Noviembre de mill
setecientos y treinta y cinco
años señores Inquisidores
Navarro, Tagle y
Clavijo (rubric)

Y que aunque, ahora no hay necesidad de hazerse dicha ratificacion, ni otra cosa Alguna en el casamiento de Don Manuel Garcia de la Mora, en causas Semejantes, y en otras de substancia, Siempre ha de remitir los testigos ratificados, ante Personas honestas si las hubiere en conformidad de lo que ordena en la ynstruzion ympreza de comisarios, Porque haciendo fee los testigos Sin estar ratificados, Se obliga con la falta de ratificacion, a debolver Sus declaraciones o copias de ellas para dichas ratificaciones, lo que tiene inconveniente en tan largas distancias;

Abisele a este Comissario del Recibo, y Se le advierta faltan las ratificaciones de los testigos

Remito a Vuestra Illustrisima dos denuncias la que tiene la letra A- contiene denuncia de: duplici matrimonio. La de la letra B- una presentacion de haber hecho yreberencia y simular con el Santo Sacramento del Bautismo torpes apetitos otros que ay no están en estado de remitirlas a Vuestra Illustrisima a quien dios Nuestro Señor Prospere y dilate por muchos añps para lustre exaltación y defense de Nuestra Santa Fee, villa de Santa Fe 2 agusto de 1735 años.

A los pies de Vuestra Illustrisima
su himilde hijo.
Fray Joseph Anttonio Guerrero (rubric)

※

Y nos ocupa el tiempo para Sacar dichas copias y en orden a lo del consejo de el otra de encompadrar, para tapar, el amancebamiento no toca eso al Santo Oficio, sino es al Juez eclesiastico, que deba conocer = Y Citese Al Padre Menchero, y a Trujillo, que pueden dar razon, de dicho matrimonio, de España (rubric)

※

En 1º de Diziembre de 1735 años Se le escribio a este comisario como Se manda en el decreto de la Buelta (rubric)

En dicho dia Se escribio al comisario del Paso de el Rio del Norte para que esaminase al padre Tello sobre lo que es citado (rubric)

※

[*Note in margin*]
Diego de Ugarte
de oidas de Don
Joseph Terrus

En la Villa de Santa Fee capital el Reyno de la Nueba Mexico en siete dias del Mes de Abril de este presente año de Mill setecientos treinta y quatro a las Nuebe de la Mañana ante el Reverendo Padre Comisario del Santo Officio de este dicho Reyno, parecio Sin Ser llamado Y juro en fee que dira Verdad Un hombre que dixo llamarse Diego Ugarte Soltero Natural de la Cuidad de Mexico y residente en esta dicha Villa el cual por descargo de Su conciencia dice y denuncia que estando Un dia que no Se acuerda Con Don Joseph Terrus hablando aserca de Casamientos dixo que Uno estaba en el Reyno que le avia de pesar averse Cassado, y respondio Antonio Duran de Armijo que presente que estaba que Callara, y que el dicho Diego de Ugarte dixo a dicho Don Joseph Terrus que era el Casso de que se habla y que Se le previno que era
Don Juan Garcia de la Mora, y que para esta presumpcion no tubo indicio y

que a pocos dias Concurriendo Con Juan de Abeytia, dixo que Si rrugia, ser cassado dicho Don Juan Garcia de la Mora En españa y respondio que havia Oido decir y que Un religioso del Passo havia escrito a este Reyno una carta acerca de la materia. y hablando Con el General Don Juan Paes aserca de lo mismo dixo decho General de que el Reverendo Padre Fray Simon de Acosta difunto dixo que era Cassado en España dicho Don Juan Garcia de la Mora y que Juan de Abeytia le dixo que dicho Don Juan Garcia de la Mora Communico Con dicho Padre Fray Simon que era cassado En españa y que despues lo Vio Cassado en este Reyno Con Josepha Martin, y esta es la Verdad por el fecho juramento y siendole leido dixo estar bien escrito que no lo dice por odio ni Mala Voluntad prometio el Secreto y lo firmo Con dicho Reverendo Padre Comissario ante mi el Infrascripto Nottario.

 fray Joseph Anttonio Guerrero (rubric)
 Comissario de el Santo Officio
 Diego de Ugartte (rubric)
 Passo ante mi
 Joseph Yrigoyen (rubric)
 Nottario del Santo Officio

[*Note in margin*]
Francisco Mascareñas
de oidas de Juan de
Abeytia Antonio Duran
de Armijo

 En la Villa de Santa Fee capital el Reyno de la Nueba Mexico en ocho dias del mes de Abril de el presente año de mill setecientos treinta y cuatro a las siete de la mañana ante el Reverendo Padre Comisario del Santo Officio de este Reyno, parecio sin ser llamado y juro en forma que dira verdad Un hombre que dixo llamarse Francisco Mascareñas soldado de este Presidio de la Villa de Santa Fee Cassado de edad de treinta anos el cual por descargo de su conciencia dice y denuncia que estando por el mes de Marzo En el cuerpo de Guardia Un dia que no Se acuerda oio decir a Juan de Abeytia que Don Juan Garcia de la Mora que casso en este Reyno con Josepha Martin, era Cassado en España, que dicho Abeytia avia estado en cassa de Anttonio Duran de Armijo Notario del Vicario foraneo, y que dixo dicho Notario a Don Joseph terrus Catalan que iba a hacer Sus informaciones que Si queria hacer otras informaciones nulas como las que abia hecho Don Juan Garcia de la Mora, y que esto lo oyo a Juan de Abeytia de las [illegible] te de Don Joseph Abeytia y de Antonio Armenta y que esta es la Verdad por el fecho Juramento y Siendole leido dixo estar bien escrito que no lo dice por odio ni mala Voluntad prometio el Secreto y lo firmo por el por no Saber dicho Reverendo Padre Comisario ante mi el infrascripto Notario.

 fray Joseph Antonio Guerrero (rubric)
 Comisario del Santo Officio

Passo ante mi
Joseph Yrigoen (rubric)
Notario del Santo Officioo

⁓

[*Note in margin*]
Vicente de Armijo de oídas de
Juan Fernandez de la Pedrera

En la Villa de Santa fee capital el Reyno de la Nueba Mexico en Ocho dias del mes de Abril de el presente año de mil Setecientos treinta y cuatro Como a las quatro de la tarde ante ante el Reverendo Padre Comisario del Santo Officio de este Reyno parecio Sin Ser llamado, y juro en forma que dira Verdad Un hombre que dixo llamarse Vicente de Armijo Cassado, de edad de Sinquenta y dos años tratante el qual por descargo de su Consiencia dice y denuncia que por el mes de Disiembre en dia que no se acuerda Como a las ocho de la Noche en la plasuela de la Compañia de Chiguagua Oyo decir a Juan Fernandez de la Pedrera que Juan Garcia de la Mora que casso en este Reyno Con Josepha Martin era Cassado en otra parte y El lo dixo que lo [...] y esta es la Verdad por el fecho juramento y siendole leido dixo estar bien escrito que es Vencio de esta Villa que no lo dice por odio ni mala Voluntad prometio el Secreto y por no Saber firmar lo firmo dicho Reverendo Padre Comissario ante mi el Infrascripto Nottario

fray Joseph Anttonio Guerrero (rubric)
Comissario de el Santo Officio
Passo ante mi
Joseph Yrigoyen (rubric)
Nottario del Santo Officio

⁓

[*Note in margin*]
Joseph Terrus
de oídas de fray Joseph Lopez
Tello ministro doctinero
del paso del Norte

En la Villa de Santa Fee Capital del Reyno de la Nueba Mexico en Sinco dias del mes de Noviembre de este presente año de Mil setesientos treinta y quatro años Como a las dos de la tarde ante el Reverendo Padre Comisario del Santo Officio de este reyno parecio siendo llamado y juro en forma que dira Verdad, Un hombre que dijo llamarse Joseph Terrus, Natural de Cataluña del obispado de Vique, Vecino de dicha Villa de Santa Fe, Cassado, de treinta y Un años de edad y preguntado si sabe o presume para que a ssido llamado dijo que no lo sabe ni lo presume ... que en este Santo Officio ai informacion Preguntado si Sabe o ha oido decir que alguna persona halla dicho o hecho alguna Cossa que sea O paresca ser contra Nuestra Santa fe Catholica, Ley Evangelica que Predica y enseña nuestra Santa Iglesia Catholica Romana o contra el recto y libre ejercicio del Santo Officio dijo que no ha oido decir cossa. [illegible] que en este Santo Officio hai informacion de que estando en sierto logar le dixo sierto sujeto que ... en el Reyno cassado que algun dia[illegible] averse Cassado y dice que se ha cassado que estando Un dia con el Reverendo Padre fray Joseph Lopez Tello Ministro Predicador del passo del Rio del Norte hablando le dixo Padre Reverendo Se casso don Juan Garcia de la Mora y le respondio el Padre Reverendo no puede ser porque el propio [...] que estaba Cassado en España que esto le ha dicho algunas personas que no se acuerda a quienes ni el lugar ni el dia o dias que lo ha dicho y esta es la Verdad por el fecho juramento y siendole leido dixo estar bien escrito que no lo dice por Odio ni Mala Voluntad prometio el Secreto y lo firmo con dicho Reverendo Padro Comissario ante mi el infrascripto Nottario.

 Joseph Antonio Guerrero (rubric)
 Comisario del Santo Officio
 Joseph Terrus (rubric)
 Passo ante mi
 Joseph Yrigoyen (rubric)
 Nottario del Santo Officio

[Note in margin:]
Juan Montes Vigil
de oídas de fray
Juan Fernandes

En esta Villa de Santa Fee Capital del Reyno de la Nueba Mexico en Sinco dias del Mes de Noviembre de este presente año de Mill Sete Sientos y treinta y quatro A las dos y media de la tarde ante el Reverendo Padre Comisario del Santo Officio de este dicho Reyno, paresio Siendo llamado, y Juro en forma que dira Verdad Un hombre que dixo llamarse Juan Montes Vigil Natural de Zacatecas Vesino de dicha Villa de Santa Fee tratante y contratante Cassado de Edad de quarenta y quatro años y preguntado Si sabe o presume, para que ha ssido llamado, dixo que no sabe ni lo presume. Y preguntado si Sabe o ha oido decir que alguna persona halla hecho o dicho alguna Cossa que sea O paresca ser contra Nuestra Santa fe, Ley Evangelica que Predica y enseña nuestra Santa Iglesia Catholica Romana y contra el recto y libre ejercicio del Santo Officio dijo que no ha oido ni se acuerda, fuele dicho que en este Santo Officio ai informacion de que estando en sierta parte se dixo en su presencia que en este Reyno avia Un sujeto que despues de [illegible] Cassado en españa Casso en dicho reyno Y dice que estando en el Passo del Rio del Norte por el mes de febrero Un dia que no se acuerda de este presente año de treinta y quatro dixo Juan fernandes que el Padre fray Joseph tello Ministro del Passo del Rio del Norte le havia dicho que Juan Garcia de la Mora le oyo que era cassado en España y despues Casso en la Nueba Mexico que lo oyo Bisente Armijo y que esta es la verdad por el fecho juramento y Siendo le leido dixo estar bien escrita que no lo dice por odio, ni mala Voluntad prometio el secreto y por no saber firmar lo firmo dicho Reverendo Padre ante mi el infraescripto Notario.

 Joseph Antonio Guerrero (rubric)
 Comisario del Santo Officio
 Passo ante mi
 Joseph Yrigoyen (rubric)
 Nottario del Santo Officio

[*Note in margin*]
Juan Paez
Hurtado de Mendoza teniente
de nuevo Mexico de oidas
de Don Joseph terrus y Don
Joseph Orcasitas.

 En la Villa de Santa Fe capital del reyno de la Nueba Mexico en Sinco dias del mes de Noviembre de este presente año de Mill setecientos y treinta y quatro a las dos y media de la tarde poco mas ante el Reverendo Padre Comisario del Santo Officio de este dicho Reyno parecio siendo llamado, y juro en forma que dira Verdad Un hombre que dixo llamarse Don Juan Paes hurtado Natural de la Villa de Villafranca de los Palacios teniente General de este dicho Reyno Vecino de la Villa de Santa fee Cassado de edad de Setenta y dos años y preguntado Si sabe O presume para que a ssido llamado dixo que no sabe ni presume para que *h*a ssido llamado y preguntado Si sabe o *h*a oido decir alguna cossa que sea o paresca ser contra Nuestra Santa fe, ley evangelica, que predica y enseña nuestra Madre Iglesia Apostolica Romana, dixo: que no sabe fuele dicho que en este Santo Officio *h*ai informacion de que en sierto lugar sierto dia se dixo en su presencia que sierto sujeto que casso en este reyno era cassado en españa y dice que oyo decir a Don Joseph Terrus y a Don Joseph Orcasitas Vesino del Passo que quando supo el Padre fray

Joseph Tello el cassamiento del Don Juan Garcia de la Mora Hizo Grandes admiraciones para que dixo dicho Reverendo Padre que era cassado en España, y que todos los que Vinieron del Paso lo dixeron, pero que Oyo decir a barios que antes de entrar en este Reyno *h*avia Matado a su muger y esta es la Verdad por el fecho juramento y siendole leido dixo estar bien escrito, y que no lo dice por odio ni mala Voluntad: prometio el secreto, y lo firmo con dicho Reverendo Padre Comisario ante mi el infracripto Nottario.

 Fray Joseph Antonio Guerrero (rubric)
 Comisario del Santo Officio
 Juan Paez Hurtado (rubric)
 Passo ante mi

Joseph Yrigoyen (rubric)
Nottario del Santo Officio

En esta Villa de Santa fee capital del Reyno de la Nueba Mexico en Seis dias del mes de Noviembre de este presente año de Mill setecientos y treinta y quatro ante el Reverendo Padre.

[*Note in margin*]
Antonio
Duran De Armijo
[*Translators note* The rest of the line is illegible. Like the other persons interviewed, Armijo probably said that he knew nothing.]

Comisario deste Santo Officio como a las nuebe de la mañana parecio siendo llamado Y juro en forma que dira Verdad un hombre que dijo llamarse Antonio Duran de Armijo, Barbero y Nottario de la Judicatura eclesiastica Natural de Nuestra Señora de los Zacatecas, Vecino de la Villa de Santa fee de edad de Sesenta y tres años poco mas o menos, y preguntado si sabe o presume para que a ssido llamado? dice que no lo sabe ni lo presume, y preguntado si sabe que alguna persona aya dicho, O hecho alguna cossa que sea, o que paresca ser contra Nuestra Santa fee, ley Evangelica, que predica y enseña Nuestra Santa Madre Iglesia Catholica Romana, o contra el recto y libre exercicio del Santo Officio? Dijo que no. Fuele dicho que en este Santo Officio *h*ai informacion de que en sierto tiempo en sierto lugar en su presencia, Sierto hombre dixo que Uno estaba en el Reyno que Se avia de pesar el casarse, y que le respondio que callara que era Casso de inquisicion y dice que se acuerda que oyo decir y no se acuerda a quien ni en que lugar ni ante quienes y que se aVia cassado y de facto se casso en el Reyno Juan Garcia de la Mora con Una Muger que no se acuerda Su nombre y que esto oyo decir que se *h*abia dicho en el Passo del Rio de el Norte. Fuele dicho que en este Santo Officio *h*ai informacion de que estando en su cassa haciendo Siertas dilegencias matrimoniales le dixo a el pretendiente (dicho Antonio Duran de Armijo) que quieres hacer otras informaciones nullas como fulano [?] y dijo que no se acuerda que si se acordara en algún tiempo lo dira; pero que esta sierto por ahora que no *h*a dicho tal. y que esta es la Verdad por el fecho juramento y siendo le leido y oido dixo estar bien escrito que no lo dice por odio ni mala Voluntad. Prometio el secreto y lo firmo con dicho Reverendo Padre Comisario ante mi el infrascripto Nottario.

Fray Joseph Antonio Guerrero (rubric)
Comisario del Santo Officio
Antonio Duran de Armijo (rubric)
Passo ante mi
Joseph Yrigoyen (rubric)
Nottario del Santo Officio

[*Note in margin*]
Joseph Orcasitas a oidos de
Joseph lopez tello
ministro no [illegible
el paso del Norte

    En esta Villa de Santa fee capital del Reyno de la Nueba Mexico en dos dias del mes Agosto de Mill Setezientos y treinta y Sinco años por la mañana a las Nuebe parecio siendo llamado y jura en forma dira Verdad Un hombre que dixo llamarse Joseph Orcasitas Mercader Viandante soltero de edad de Veinte y cuatro años poco mas o menos el qual preguntado Si sabe o presume para que a ssido llamado dixo que no lo sabe ni lo presume, y preguntado Si sabe o a oydo decir alguna cossa que sea o paresca ser contra Nuestra Santa fee Catolica ley Evangelica que predica y enSeña Nuestra Santa Madre Iglesia Catolica Romana, O contra el recto, y libre Exersisio del Santo Officio dixo que no sabe, ni a oido decir Cossa. fuele dicho que En este Santo Officio *hai* informacion de que Sierto dia en Sierto lugar dixo delante algunas personas que Sierto Sujeto que Casso en este Reyno era Cassado en españa, y dice que es Verdad que Ofresiendose hablar en Una parte que no se acuerda, ni ante quienes dixo que en el passo del Rio del Norte Oyo decir a el Reverendo Padre Fray Joseph Lopes Tello yo no se como Se Casso Don Juan Garcia de la Mora por que el propio Ministro que es casado en españa que no se acuerda delante de quienes Se dixo esto y esta es la Verdad por el juramento fecho y siendole leydo dixo estar bien escrito que no lo dice por Odio ni mala Voluntad prometio el Secreto y lo firmo con dicho Reverendo Padre Comisario ante mi el infrascripto Nottario.
    Fray Joseph Antonio Guerrero (rubric)
    Comisario del Santo Officio
    Joseph Orcasitas (rubric)
    Passo ante mi
    Joseph Yrigoyen (rubric)
    Nottario del Santo Officio

    En la Villa de Santa fee en dos dias del Mes de Agosto

Antonio de Armenta
    En de Mill setecientos trienta y quarto años ante el Reverendo Padre Comisario del Santo Officio parrecio sin ser llamado y Juro en forma que dira Verdad Un hombre que dixo llamarse Antonio Armenta Soldado y Cabo de esquadra del Presidio de la Villa de Santa fee de edad de treinta y quatro años el que Juro en forma que dira Verdad y preguntado Si sabe O presume para que *ha* ssido llamado dixo que no save, ni

lo presume y preguntado Si sabe que alguna persona *h*aya dicho o hecho alguna cossa, que sea o paresca ser Contra Nuestra Santa fe Catolica que predica y enseña Nuestro Santa Madre Iglesia Catolica Apostolica Romana, O contra el recto y libre exersisio del Santo Officio dice que no sabe ni *h*a oido decir fuele dicho que en este Santo officio *h*ai informacion que en Sierto lugar, Sierto dia se dixo En su presencia que Un hombre que era Cassado en españa se *h*aVia cassado en este reyno, y responde que lo oyo de decir y no se acuerda a quien, ni el lugar, ni delante de quienes que Don Juan Garcia de la Mora que era Cassado En su tierra se *h*abia Cassado En este Reyno que es esta la Verdad por el juramento fecho, y Siendole leido dixo estar bien escrito, que no lo dice por Odio, ni Mala Voluntad prometio el Secreto y lo firmo Con dicho Reverendo Padre Comisario ante mi el infraescripto Notario.

    Fray Joseph Antonio Guerrero (rubric)
    Comisario del Santo Officio
    Antonio armenta (rubric)
    Passo ante mi
    Joseph Yrigoyen (rubric)
    Nottario del Santo Officio

Digo yo y Certifico como Nottario que Soy del Muy Santo tribunal de la Ynquisicion

Que los Señores que habian de examinar, que Son Juan Fernandes Don Joseph Bustamente y Juan De Abeytia Se hallan ausentes del Reyno pero no se donde El Reverendo Padre Tello esta en la Jurisdiccion del Paso del Rio del Norte Cuyo Comissario es el Reverendo Padre fray Andres Varo: el Reverendo Padre fray Simon Dias de Acosta murio en el convento de dicho Passo, y en fe de ello lo firme en la Villa De Santa Fee En tres dias del Mes de Agosto de Mil Setsientos y trienta y Sinco anos.
    Joseph Yrigoyen (rubric)
    Nottario del Santo Officio

El juez eclesiastico del Nuebo Mexico para que lo sepa Don Juan Garcia de la Mora y Josepha Martin] El Señor Bachiller Don Joseph de Bustamante Vicario y Juez eclesiastico deste Reyno su Jurisdicion y Distrito por el Yllustisimo señor Doctor Jose Benito Crespo del Orden de Santiago por la gracia de Dios y de la Santa Sede Apostolica obispo deste dicho Obispado del Consejo de su Majestad y mi señor.

Por el presente el Reverendisimo Padre Predicador Jubilado fray Juan de la Cruz Ministro del Pueblo de San Juan de la Soledad del Rio arriva aminestara en tres dias festivas Inter Misarum Solemnia según lo despuesto por el Santo Conzelio a Don Juan Garcia de la Mora, español (viudo de Doña Maria de hornero) Natural de la Villa del Pozuelo de Almagro en los Reynos de Castilla Arzobispado de Toledo Hijo legitimo de Don Juan Garcia de la Mora ya difunto y de Doña Manuela Gonzalez vezina de dicha

Villa para el Matrimonio que quiere Contraer con Josepha Martin española Vezina del rio arriva Hija legitima de Marcial Martin y de Doña Leogarda de Medina españoles vezinos de dicho puesto y no resultando ympedimento alguno (que si resultase me lo remitira) Los Caseé y Veleé segun Orden de Nuestra Santa Madre Iglesia y lo azentara en el libro de su cargo. Dado en esta Villa de Santa Fee en Catorze dias del mes de octubre de mil setecientos y treinta y tres años =
    Bachiller Joseph Bustamante (rubric)
    Por mandado del Señor Vicario y Juez Eclesiastico
    Antonio Duran de Armijo (rubric)
    Notario Publico

[*Note in margin*]
Zertificazion
de la partida del Casamiento
de Don Juan Garcia de la
Mora Viudo de Doña
Maria de Ornlas con Josepha Martin

    Certifico yo Fray Joseph Antonio Guerrero Comisario del Santo Officio en este reino de la Nueba Mexico que el dia onze de Noviembre del año de Mill setecientos y treinta y tres en la capilla de Nuestra Señora de la Soledad de el rio arriba perteneciente a la Mision de San Juan Con licencia del Reverendo Padre Fray Juan de la Cruz Ministro de aquel partido casse y vele a Don Juan Garcia de la Mora con Josepha Martin hija legitima de Marcial Martin y de Lugarda de Medina y fueron testigos el Alferez Don Joseph Moreno y doña Juana Roibal presente el párroco y otros muchos y para que conste lo firme en tres de Agoto de mil setesientos y treinta y sinco años.
    fray Joseph Anttonio
    Guerra (rubric)

[*Note in margin*]
Declaracion
del Reverendo Padre frayJ
Juan Menchero Don Juan
Garcia de la Mora

En el santo ofizio de la Ynquisicion de Mexico en cinco dias del mes de Diziembre de mill setezientos y treinta y zinco años estando en la Audiencia de la mañana el señor Ynquisidor

    Licenciao don Pedro Anselmo Sanches de Tagle, mando entrar en ella a un religioso del orden de San Francisco que viene llamado de qual siendo presente le ha rezivido juramento que hizo In verbo sazerdotis Tacto pecctore so cargo que del qual prometio de dezir verdad de todo lo que supiere y le fuere preguntado y Dixo llamarse fray Juan Miguel Menchero, calificador deste Santo officio, y desta probincia del Santo evangelio; de êdad, de mas de quarenta años.

Preguntado; Si sabe presume ô sospecha; â la causa para que ha sido llamado â este Santo Officio Dixo que tiene algun fundamento Para sospechar, puede hâbersele llamado Sobre Don Juan Garcia de la Mora Natural que dize Ser de la Villa de Almagro en los Reinos de españa Arzobispado, de Toledo, Respectto de que habra Cosa de dos años que fray Joseph ôrtis de Belasco Custodio de la Nueba Mexico le escribio preguntandole, que Don Juan Garzia de la Mora pretendia casarse, en âquel Reino.

Que Si sabia del dicho Si era casado ô no, A que respondio, ên substanzia lo que ahora dira, y ês, que êl año de Treinta, estando Para hazer biaje para dicho Reino, llego el dicho Mora, â pedirle combeniencia, Suponiendo, el Ser Paisano por deziar que era, Natural de dicha Villa de Almagro, y que habiendo ôido el âpellido del declarante, Supuso tambien el Ser de dicho Paraje por vivir âlli los mas de sus parientes, en que cuya âtension lo lleba consigo, y Procuro vibiese Como, Christhiano, y Por lo mismo Pudo, oier, y oio de el, Ser biudo en España, A causa decâber, êl mismo Muerto â su Muger, sin que en el tiempo que le âcompaño (que Seria Como año y medio) ni despues âca Sepa cosa fixa en conTrario, Si solo hâ oido decir, se bolbio â casar en dicho Reino.

Ya que âhora añade, que la primera vez que êl susodicho le busco, para dicho efecto de Comveniencia, no le dixo Ser su apellido ê de mora, sino ôtro diferente de que no hâze Memoria; Pero si de que despues y a mui pocos dias, el mismo descubrio, êl Propio Nombre, y apellidos, que arriba, le deja dados, y por los quales le pareze â sido y es, en los Parajes de su residencia, posteriores, Sin que âya entendido âlguna ôtra variación.

Preguntado Si sabe de Alguna ôtra ô ôtras personas, que puedan dar razon de dicho Don Juan Garcia de la Mora, y especialmente, de si ês viudo, ô casado ên España dixo que no puede dar razon de ninguna; Porque âunque oyo decir que desde españa a la [H]abana abia benido en compañia de un asentista de Polbos, y desde alla âqui, vino con ôtro camarada de ninguno de los dos sabe el Nombre y paradero; Como ni tampoco, de Sujeto de dicha villa de Almagro que pueda dar razon âpreciable Sobre lo susodicho.

Y que esto es lo que puede decir, a las preguntas que se le an hecho, y la verdad So cargo del Juramento que tiene fecho con lo qual fue mandado salir de la audiencia, y Anttes lo firmo.

Fray Juan Miguel Menchero (rubric)
Passo ante me
Don Joseph Carrillo
y Biezma secretario (rubric)

En 9 de Diciembre de 1735 años se Escribio a los señores del Consexo para la Justificacion del 1º matrimonio la qual se Registro en el libro correspondiente

[*Note in margin*]
Recibido
en este Santo Officio de
Mexico en ocho de enero de mil setesientos
y treinta y siete años
Senores Ynquisidores.
Nabarro, Tagle y Clavijo]

El dia 15 de mayo de este presente año resevi la de Vuestra Señoria Ilustrisima que remito adjunta, y en su bista quedo adbertido para las Ratificaciones que se ofrecieren en causas de substancia Y tendra muy presente para lo de adelante lo que expresa ynstrucion, a los numeros 19 y 20 Confesando como confieso mi inabertencia Y pesto a los pies de Vuestra Señoria lustrisima con el rendimiento que devo, quedo pidiendo al señor Nuestra Alteza por el augmento y conservacion de Vuestra Señoria Ilustrisima para defensa de Nuestra fee. San Francisco de Nambe, de la Nueba Mexico y Junio 25 de 1736.
Ilustrisimo Señor
A los pies de Vuestra Senoria Ilustrisima su humilde y reconocido Criado y Capellan
Fray Joseph Antonio
Guerrero (rubric)

Ên êste tribunal Se recibiô la de Nuestro Comisario de 3 de agosto Prosimo pasado con las diligenzias que la Acompañaban contra Don Juan grazia de la Mora, Por Sospechas, de Ser el Susodicho Dos vezes Casado; Y en su bista, Se le advierte, A nuestro Comisario faltan, las ratificaciones, de los testigos que deponen; Y que âunque por Ahora, No *h*ay Nezesidad, de hazerse dichas Ratificaciones, Ni otra Cosa Alguna ên el Casamiento êjecutado por dicho Mora, Se le prebiene â dicho Nuestro Comisario,que en causas Semexantes, y en otras de Sustancia Siempre *h*â de remitir los testigos Ratificados, Ante personas *h*ônestas, en conformidad, de lo que ôrdena la instruccion, impresa, de comsarios, â los números 19 y 20 de dicha ystruzion,
Por que No *h*azen feê, los testigos, Si no vienen Ratificados, y Con esta falta, de tales Ratifica ciones, ôbliga Al Tribunal,*h*á de volver, Susdeclaraciones (o) Copias de ellas, para que Se executten dichas ratificaciones, lo que ês mui de ynconbeniente, en tan largas distancias y Se ôcupa el tiempo en sacar dichas opias, y demora de tiempo de debolberlas; y Por lo que Mira a la otra denuncia, que bino con las Citadas y en orden a lo de el consejo de si debia ô no encompadrar, Para Sola por el amancebamiento, No toca al Santo Officio, y si al juez êclesiastico, quien debe conocer, de ello, dios guarde â nuestro Comisario et cetera Ynquiscion de Mexico y Diciembre 1º de 1735 años.

Licenciado Don Pedro Anselmo Sanchez de Tagle (rubric)
Licenciado Don Diego Mangado Y Clavijo (rubric)
Por mandado del Santo Officio
Don Joseph Carrillo y Biezma, Secretario

[*Note in margin*]
Licenciado
Don Pedro Navarro de
Ysla (rubric)

Al reverendo padre
fray Joseph Antonio
Guerrero, Comisario
de este oficio en la Villa
de Santa feê en el Reino
del Nuebo Mexico

Con esta y en 4 fojas se os remiten las diligencias executadas de orden de el Consejo en la nquisicion de Toledo para la Justificacion de el matrimonio contraydo en la Villa de le Pocuelo de Calatraba, por Don Juan Garcia de Mora, con Doña Maria de [H]ornero, que habeis Su Señoria pedido con vuestra carta de 9 de Diciembre de el año proximo pasado, para que juntos estos papeles, con los demas de esta Causa la beais noteis y hagáis Justicia Dios os Guarde Madrid y Jullio 7 de 1736.

A los Inquisidores Apostolicos De el Santo Oficio de la Inquisicion Del Consejo de la Inquisicion Mexico, Andres Cabrejas (rubric), Gabriel Bermudez (rubric), Fray Juan Raspeña (rubric). Mexico

Don Pedro Velez de Escalante secretario del Secreto de este Santo oficio de la Ynquisicion de Toledo Certifico, que con carta de los señores del consejo de la Santa Inquisicion de Treynta de Abril de mil setecientos y treynta y seis, se Recivio de la que el tribunal de Mexico escribio
a Su Alteza para que se hiziese abriguacion del Matrimonio que contrajo Don Juan Garcia de la Mora, natural de Pozuelo de Almagro con Doña Maria de ornero, y si fue cierto que el susodicho mato a la Referida su Muger y que Justifique dicho Matrimonio como asimismo si hubiese allecido dicha Doña Maria se conpulse la partida de entierro, y de lo que Resultase Remita testimonio por duplicado a dichos Señores.
Y su cumplimiento, en cinco de Mayo de dicho año se dio comision en forma, a Ministros de
la Satifacion del tribunal, los que *haviendo* pasado a la Villa del Pozuelo de

Calatraba, conpulsaon la partida de desposorio del dicho Don Juan Garcia de la Mora con dicha Doña Maria de Hornero que es la siguiente.

Partida de Desposorio y Velasiones.
En la Parroquial de esta Villa del Pozuelo de Calatraba en diez dias de el Mes de Henero de mil setecientos y Veynte y cinco años Yo el licenciado fray Don Juan Martinez cobo del *h*avito de Calatraba, Rector, y Cura propio de dicha Villa, desposé solemnemente, que hizieron Valido Sacramento, y Matrimonio, y luego di las Vendiciones nunciales segun el Ritual Romano, y manda Nuestra Santa Madre Yglesia â Juan Garcia de la Mora, hijo de Juan Garcia de la Mora, y Manuela Gonzales su mujer, y Maria Hornero hija de Simon de Hornero, y Juliana de Ledesma, todos Vecinos, y naturales de esta Villa, âviendo precedido las tres amonestaciones que para este efecto, manda el Santo Concilio de trento y senodales de este Arzobispado a el tiempo del ofertorio de la Misa mayor en tres dias de fiesta continuos, que fueron la Dominica infraoctava de la Natividad del Señor, segunda el dia de la Circumcision, y la tercera dia de la Epifania, de las quales no Resulto inpedimento, que embarazase dicho Matrimonio y asimismo precedio despacho de el Señor Vicario de Cuidad r fueron testigos Miguel de Hornero, Lucas Garcia de la Puente, y Pedro Lopez Merino, y Padrinos Andres Delgado de Herrera, y Cathalina seguido su Muger todos Vecinos de esta dicha Villa y para que conste lo firme
Licenciado fray Don Juan Martinez Cobo.

Y certifican los Ministros, estar bien, y fielmente sacada y conpulsada la dicha partida y pasando despues a examinar a los testigos instrumentales que se *h*allaron a dicho desposorio y relaciones, declaron todos, se aquerdan de *h*aver asistido al Matrimonio que contrajo el dicho Juan Garcia dela Mora con Maria de Hornero, y que es publico en aquella Villa, que a pocos Messes de assados se dijo que dicho Juan Garcia de la Mora tenia celos de su Muger dicha Maria de Hornero, y que â Viendola allado Unos papeles escritos por el sugeto de quien el sospechava, *h*izo fuerza para quitarselos, y ver el contenido de ellos, y con efecto se los quito y mientras los leya dicha Maria de Hornero se Refugio a la Cassa de su Madre, y despues el dicho Juan Garcia de la Mora se entro en la dicha Cassa, y *h*allando a su Muger en la Cama la dio de puñaladas, y como a los seis u ocho dias murio de ellas la Referida Maria de Hornero, Y inmediatamente que dicho Juan Garcia de la Mora executo con su Muger queda expresado, se ausento de la dicha Villa del Pozuelo, y supieron se fue a Sevilla desde donde se paso a los Reynos de las Yndias, y desde alli escrivia dicho Juan Garcia de la Mora a su Madre, y lo saven los testigos por aver leydo Varias Cartas, y dos de ellas, con fecha desde la [H]abana que es la Ultima que vieron y leyeron abra quatro años sin que despues ayan tenido mas noticia del contestando en lo sustancial de lo Referido todos los testigos, los que pasados tres dias se Ratificaron ante *h*onestas,

Religiosas Personas en todo lo que tenian dicho, y declarado sin alterar ni añadir cosa alguna. Y despues dichos Ministros pasaron â Conpulsar la partida de entierro de la dicha
Maria de Hornero cuio tenor a la letra es el que se sigue.

⁓

Partida de Entierro

Maria de Hornero, Muger que fue de Juan Garcia de la Mora vecinos de esta Villa de Pozuelo de Calatraba, murio en ella el dia onze de Mayo de mil setecientos y veynte y sinco años, Recivio los Santos Sacramentos, y hizo testamento en Virtud de poder, que dio la Referida a Juliana de leon viuda de Simon de Hornero y su Madre de dicha difunta, y esta en Virtud de dicho podere mando a las mandas forzosas lo acostumbrado, y para su Heredera a la dicha Juliana de leon su Madre y albacea a mi el Prior, y a Joseph Granados su Cuñado marido de Josepha de Hornero su Hermana y la Referida Juliana de leon en fuerza de dicho poder mando se digan por su alma, y Yntencion cincuenta y cinco Missas Rezadas, y Misa de cuerpo presente, los quales dichos poderes se Otorgaron ante Juan Martinez de Agustin Escrivano publico, y del Ayuntamiento de esta Villa adjunto con las Clausulas de el testamento, que otorgo la dicha Maria de Hornero del dia siete de Mayo de dicho Mes y año se enterro en la Parroquial, en sepoltura de su Abolorio el dia dose de dicho Mes pago lo acostumbrado, y para que conste lo firme.

Licenciado fray Don Juan Martinez Cobo =

La qual dicha partida certifican los Ministros que la compulsaron estar bien y fielmente sacada, y concordar con la original.

⁓

[Proceedings, transmittal]

Asimismo consta de las Deposiciones de los Testigos, y del Ynforme secreto que hicieron dichos Ministros que el dicho Juan Garcia de la Mora es de familia muy onrrada, y que el tiempo que vivio en dicha Villa de Pozuelo procedio como Hombre de bien, y buena correspondencia con quien trataba, y comunicaba, por lo que fue querido de todos las personas de estimacion de aquella Villa, por lo que oy estan sintiendo le sucediese la desgracia con su Muger que fue la causa de ausentarse. Como todo mas largamente consta, y pareze de dichos autos que quedare en la Camara de Este secreto. Y por auto de este Tribunal de doze de este presente mes, y año, remando que de ello se remita certificacion por duplicado a los Señores de el Consejo en bedecimiento de lo mandado por su Carta de treynta de Abril de este año, en cuio cumplimiento para que de ello conste doy la presente sellada con el sello de el Santo Officio y firmada de mi mano en la Camara del secreto de la Inquisicion de Toledo en veynte y seis de Junio de Mil setecientos y treynta y seis años.

Don Pedro Velez de Escalante (rubric)

[*Note in margin:*]
Decreto de el Consejo
En el Consejo a primero de
Jullio de 1736, señores
Cabrejas, Bermudez,
Velasco, Mier, Raspeña

Que se remita el Testimonio por duplicado â el Tribunal donde dimana = siguiese la rubric de el Relator, Doctor Losano. Concuerda este Testimonio, y Decreto de el Consejo con sus originales que por a*h*ora quedan en la secretaria a mi cargo a que me Remito y de que Zertifico, firrmo =
 Don Sevastian Ramos
 y Ruiz (rubric)

[*Note in margin*:
Recibido
Don Pedro Velez
de Escalante secretario
del secreto de este santo
oficio de la Ynquisicion de Toledo

 Certifico, que con carta de los señores del con sejo de la Santa General Ynquisicion de Treynta de Abril de mil setecientos y treynta y seis Recivio copia de la Carta que el tribunal de Mexico escribio a Su Alteza para que se hiciese abrigacio del Matrimonio que contrajo Don Juan Garcia de la Mora, natural de Pozuelo de Almagro con Doña Maria de Ornero, y si fuse cierto que el susodicho mato a su Muger y que Justifique dicho Matrimonio como asimismo si hubiese fallecido dicha Doña Maria, se conpulse la partida de entierro, y que de lo que Resultase, se
 Remita testimonio por duplicado a dichos Señores. y su cumplimiento, en cinco de Mayo del dicho año se dio Comision, en forma, a Ministros de la satifacion del Tribunal, los que aviendo pasado a la Villa del Pozuelo de Calatraba, conpulsaron la partida de Desposorio del dicho Don Juan Garcia de la Mora con dicha Doña Maria de Ornero, que es la siguiente

 Partida de Velsiones En la Parroquial de esta Villa del Posuelo de Calatraba en diez dias de mes de Henero de mil setecientos y Veynte y cinco años, Yo el licenciado fray Don Juan Martinez Cobo del avito de Calatraba, Rector, y Cura propio de dicha

Villa, desposé solemnemente por palabras de presente, que hizieron Valido Sacramento y Matrimonio, y luego di las vendiciones nunciales segun el Ritual Romano, y manda Nuestra Santa Madre Yglesia, a Juan Garcia de Mora, hijo de Juan Garcia de Mora y Manuela Gonzales su Muger y Maria de Hornero hija de Simon de Ornero y Juliana de Ledesma, todos Vecinos y naturales de esta Villa, aviendo precedido las tres amonestaciones que para este efecto, manda el Santo Concilio de trento y senodales de este Arzobispado al tiempo del ofertorio de la Misa mayor entre dias de fiesta continuos Con esta se os remiten en quatro fojas utiles las diligencias ejecutadas de orden del Consejo en la Ynquisicion de Toledo, para la Justificacion del matrimonio contrahido en la Villa de Pozuelo de Calatrava por Don Juan Garcia de Mora, con Doña Maria de Ornero, que haveis Señores pedido con vuestra carta de 2 de Diciembre del año proximo pasado, para que juntos estos papeles con los demas de esta causa la veais, voteis y hagais Justicia Dios os guarde de Madrid y Julio 7 de 1736

    Licenciado Luis de Velasco (rubric)
    Gabriel Bermudes (rubric)
    Licenciado Don Antonio Geronimo de Mier (rubric)

This document was translated and transcribed by Dorothy Mazon and Rick Hendricks.

Notes

1. Pozuelo de Calatrava is a town of about 2,000 people located in the District of La Mancha, Spain. It was named for a castle called Calatrava La Nueva built in 1217 as a military and religious institution. Pozuelo literally means "puddle" or "little pond." (*Wikipedia,* "Pozuelo de Calatrava, August 4, 2015).
2. The Spanish Crown had a monopoly on gunpowder, so the merchant mentioned was probably one of the royal contractors.
3. See Tigges and Salazar, *Spanish Colonial Lives*: 368-401.
4. Ibid., 491-509.
4a. See Thomas, *After Coronado*: 241; and Moorhead, *Royal Road*: 46-49.
5. See Tigges and Salazar, *Spanish Colonial Lives*: 201-13.
6. "Fiscal" is the name given to the prosecutor, a kind of public attorney.
7. To date, little has been found about Diego de Ugarte, except that he was a witness in Santa Cruz for a land grant case of Juan Páez Hurtado in 1735. The last name is Basque in origin. (SANM I #320; *Wikipedia*, "Diego de Ugarte," accessed on March 1, 2016.)
8. Don José Terrus stated in his will of 1745 that he married doña Antonia Páez Hurtado, daughter of Juan Páez Hurtado and doña Teodora García de la Riva. His name appears frequently as a witness for various deeds and wills in the Spanish Colonial documents of the mid-eighteenth century. When he died, his wife was the primary executor of his estate, which included a ranch given to him by Juan Páez Hurtado. (See SANM I # 38, SANM I #72, SANM I #103, and SANM I #966, all WPA translations.)
9. For information on Antonio Durán de Armijo, see Case 11.
10. Juan de Abeytia could be the son of Antonio de Abeytia, who was named Juan de Jesús. If so, his grandparents were Diego de Vectia [Abeytia] and Catalina Leal, both of whom came to New Mexico from Zacatecas in 1695. (Chávez, *Origins*: 119.)
11. Fray Simón Díaz de Acosta was the secretary for fray Andrés Varo in El Paso in 1729. (Chávez, *Archdiocese*: 160.)
12. Josefa Martín was the daughter of Marcial Martín and doña Lugarda de Medina. Marcial was the elder son of Sebastián Martín Serrano, a pre-revolt settler, and was executor of his father's will. Marcial was still living in Santa Cruz in 1763. (Chávez, *Origins*: 223-24; SANM I #164, WPA translation.)
13. In the Spanish text, it is called "*el secreto*"—it was a fundamental concept in the operations of the Holy Office

of the Inquisition. Testimony given to the Inquisition was considered similar to the information given in the confessional: it was not to be shared with others.
14. Fray José Yrigoyen came to New Mexico sometime between 1719 and 1725. He was known as being fluent in the several Tano Indian languages. In 1744 and 1745, he accompanied fray Delgado on expeditions to the villages of the Hopis and Navajos. In 1750, perhaps because of local controversies, he was removed from his post in Albuquerque. In 1760, Governor Tomás Vélez Cachupín reported that Yrigoyen was sixty-three years old. Yrigoyen, and the other persons named in these documents as notaries, were most likely "ecclesiastical" notaries, not the secular notaries who were called "*escribanos*" and who had different licensing qualifications. (Rick Hendricks, in interview with author, June 29, 2015; McKnight, "Laws Without Lawyers": 52-53; Norris, *Year Eighty*: 92, 99, 105-06, 126, 140; Tigges and Salazar, *Spanish Colonia Lives*: 483-90.)
15. Francisco Mascareñas was the son of José Mascareñas and María de Acosta who came to New Mexico from Mexico City in 1694. José was a *calderero* (coppersmith or tinker), who originally lived in Santa Cruz and then in Santa Fe. In 1716, Francisco married Antonia López of Santa Cruz. In 1737, he was involved in a lawsuit over a tract of land in Santa Fe. (Chávez, *Origins*: 227-28, 375; SANM II #1256.)
16. Antonio Durán de Armijo is described as "notary of the Archdiocese," which could refer to either an "ecclesiastical" notary or a licensed escribano. It probably meant that he was a respected and literate person.
17. By referring to the testimony as "useless reports" he probably meant that it was all gossip and hearsay and therefore not acceptable as a denunciation.
18. Antonio de Armenta was born about 1700, the son of Salvador Manuel de Armenta and María Lujan (or Maese). He was a soldier at the Santa Fe presidio and a survivor of the 1720 Villasur massacre. He was married to Juana Abeytia, a sister of Juan de Abeytia and a widow of José Antonio Fernández, who was killed at the Villasur massacre. Antonio de Armenta died in 1779, at the age of seventy-five. (Chávez, *Origins*: 343; Chávez, Thomas, *Moments*: 156, 165, 305.)
19. For information on Vicente de Armijo, see Case 20.
20. Juan Fernández de la Pedrera is probably the "Juan Fernández de Pedrera II" whose father of the same name came from Galicia, Spain, and married María Jurado de García of Albuquerque in 1695. Upon her death, his father married María Peláez, the daughter of Jacinto Peláez, a grantee of the La Majada land grant near Cochiti. Juan Fernández II was one of the heirs to that grant. Juan II's second wife was Luisa Tenorio de Alba. Juan II's sister, María Francisca, somehow acquired the Hacienda de Alamo and eventually sold it to José Riaño Tagle. (Ebright, "Advocates": 128-29, 326n45; Ebright, Hendricks, and Hughes, *Four Square Leagues*: 178-89, 383n40; Chávez, *Origins*: 174-75.)
21. This refers to the "Plazuela del Colegio de la Compania de Jesus," a small plaza of the Jesuits. It can still be found in Chihuahua, Mexico, today. (Rick Hendricks, interview with author, June 29, 2016.)
22. In the Spanish text, this is called "*ministero doctrinero*" and means that he was a minister to an Indian pueblo in El Paso. He taught the Catholic doctrine (or catechism) to the pueblo Indians.
23. The diocese of Vic is located in Catalonia, Spain, in the ecclesiastical province of Tarragonia. (*Wikipedia*, "Diocese of Vic," accessed on February 19, 2016.)
24. For information on Juan Montes Vigil, see Case 21.
25. For information on Juan Páez Hurtado, see Case 3.
26. José Orcasitas (or Horcasitas) was the alcalde of Santa Cruz in 1732. The similarly named José Sobrado Horacasitas is listed as the lieutenant alcalde of El Paso in 1765, but this may not be the same person. (Chávez, *Origins*: 381; Ebright, "Advocates": 358n24.)
27. Villafranca de los Palacios—known today as Los Palacios y Villafranca—is a city located in the province of Seville, Spain. (*Wikipedia*, "Los Palacios y Villafranca," accessed on March 4, 2016.)
28. In the Spanish text, this appears as "*fulan de tal*." In addition to "whats-his-name," it means "such and such" or "so and so." (*Barron's Spanish English Dictionary*: 217.)
29. José Benito Crespo was the Bishop of Durango, Mexico, from 1734 to 1737. He expanded the episcopal authority of the archdiocese into New Mexico, challenging the authority of the Franciscan friars. He made a visitation in 1730, though his authority was disputed by fray Andrés Varo. (Kessell, *Kiva*: 325-28.)
30. Fray Juan Sánchez de la Cruz came to New Mexico sometime around 1715 to 1719, and he left in 1749. He was custos for New Mexico in the 1720s. In 1726, he made a complaint against governors Valverde and Bustamante. (Brown, *Pueblo Indians*: 48-49; Norris, *Year Eighty*: 92, 109; Chávez, *Archdiocese*: 158-59.)
31. The Latin phrase *inter Misarum Solemnia* can be translated as "during the Holy Rites of Mass." (Arnold, *Oxford Handbook*: 238.)
32. María de Hornero was the deceased first wife of Juan García de la Mora. Like so many of the witnesses and officials from Spain, we know her only from this document.
33. Pozuelo de Almagro appears to be an alternative name for Pozuela de Calatrava in Spain, which is mentioned in this document as the home of Juan García de la Mora. Pozuelo de Calatrava was at one time a dependency of Almagro, which is now a separate town. (*Wikipedia*, "Pozuelo de Almagro," accessed on March 4, 2016.)
34. To date, no further information has been found on Juan García de la Mora, the accused husband of María de Hornero.
35. To date, no further information has been found on Manuela González.

36. [Juan] José Moreno's will of 1756 states that he was born in Seville, Spain. He later married Juana Roybal, daughter of don Ignacio de Roybal and Francisca Gómez. In 1737, he was alférez and sergeant of the presidio. From 1744 to 1748, he was an alcalde at Pecos. Between 1748 and 1750 he was the collector of church tithes for the Bishop of Durango in Mexico. (See SANM I #533, WPA translation; Kessell, *Kiva*: 537.)
37. Juana Roybal was the wife of [Juan] José Moreno and the daughter of Ignacio de Roybal who came from Galicia, Spain. Ignacio de Roybal was an alcalde of the San Ildefonso jurisdiction and the chief constable of the Holy Office of the Inquisition in New Mexico. He was also a notary. (Kessell, Hendricks, and Dodge, *Boulders*: 952n1; SANM I #305; Chávez, *Origins*: 542n5.)
38. This apparently refers to other denunciations not related to the charge against Juan García de la Mora.
39. Fray José Antonio Guerrero was a *criollo* born in New Spain of Spanish parents. He took his vows in 1692 and arrived in New Mexico in 1699. He was both a comisario and custos in New Mexico, until 1743. (Norris, *Year Eighty*: 45-46, 51, 67, 90m109; Chávez, *Archives*: 10.)
40. Don Pedro Navarro de Isla was a licenciado with the Tribunal of the Holy Office in Mexico City. His name and the other two licenciados mentioned in this document were inscribed on a plaque in the Tribunal offices. It was described in 1820, after the Holy Office of the Inquisition was abolished: "During The Pontificate Of Clement XII: With Philip IV Reigning As King Of Spain: And The Inquisitors General Successively Their Excellencies Lords Don Juan De Camargo, Bishop Of Pamplona, And Don Andres Orbe Y Larrategui, Archbishop Of Valencia: Actual Inquisitors Of New Spain Their Lords Licenciado Don Pedro De Navarro De Isla, Don Pedro Anselmo Sanchez De Tagle, and Don Diego Mangado Y Clavijo. This Work Began On December 5, 1732, And It Ended On The Same Month In 1736 To The Honor And Glory Of God And The Treasurer Don Augustin Antonio Astrullos Y Collantes." (Chuchiak, *Inquisition in New Spain*: 130.)
41. Pedro Anselmo Sánchez de Tagle was a licenciado with the Tribunal of the Holy Office in Mexico City.
42. Diego Mangado y Clavijo was a licenciado with the Tribunal of the Holy Office in Mexico City.
43. At that time, it was required that the written testimony be witnessed and signed by "honorable persons," and each person testifying was to ratify or confirm what they had said after reading the document or it was read to them. Because none of the testimony in these documents was confirmed, it could not be used. The same complaint about lack of ratification is found at the end of this document.
44. This seems to be an error by the scribe, since the person being investigated was Juan García de la Mora.
45. This seems to indicate that if Juan García de la Mora could not prove that he was unmarried when he wed Juana Martín then it means they were living in "amancebamiento" (or cohabitating). The official states that concubinage was not a matter for the Inquisition, but rather a matter for the ecclesiastical judge. The latter was a lay religious person of the diocese under the Bishop of Durango.
46. Fray Juan Miguel Menchero was a long serving missionary in New Mexico. He was born in Castile, Spain, and professed his vows in 1714. Members of his family were merchants from Mexico City. He was in New Mexico by 1729, when he carried out an inspection. He headed a successful mission to Navajo lands in 1746 and a second mission to the Gilas in 1748. The well-known "Menchero map" was prepared as a result of his travels. (Norris, *Year Eighty*: 190-93, 99, 100n107, 177; Wheat, *Mapping*: 84.)
47. Fray [Diego] Trujillo was a scholar at the university in Mexico City in 1679 and the 1680. Later, he became the minister provincial of the Custody of New Mexico. (Norris, *Year Eighty*: 497-98.)
48. Assigned to Santa Fe, Fray José López Tello arrived in New Mexico in 1707. Custos Tagle attempted to remove him from office, claiming that he was negligent in his duties. While in the center of controversy, fray Tello remained in Santa Fe. In 1715, he replaced Tagle as custos; the following year, he was in El Paso and no longer held that position. (Chávez, *Archdiocese*: 17, 27, 202, 250; Norris, *Year Eighty*: 61-62, 65-66.)
49. Bachiller don José de Bustamante was the son, nephew, or brother of Governor Bustamante, who held office from 1722 to 1731. José was not a Franciscan friar, rather he was a member of the secular clergy appointed by the Bishop of Durango as vicar in Santa Fe, in 1736. It was a controversial appointment opposed by the Franciscans. He also served as a priest in Santa Cruz, San Ildefonso, and Nambé. His work in New Mexico seems to have ended sometime after 1736. (Chávez, *Origins*: 151; Chávez, *Archdiocese*: 4, 32, 189, 258.)
50. Fray Andrés Varo was born about 1683; his service in New Mexico ended about 1774, when he was eighty-five. He was custos in 1730 and again in 1749, when he opposed the expansion of the Bishop of Durango outside El Paso. He was also comisario for the Holy Office of the Inquisition. He founded the missions at la Junta de los Rios in 1729. In 1747, he made one of the first in-depth reports on the Franciscan mission in New Mexico. (Norris, *Year Eighty*: 76-78, 117-19, 121-22, 126-27, 179n20; Chávez, *Archdiocese*: 160, 257.)
51. The Latin phrase *"verbo sacerdotis tacto pectore"* means that the priest was swearing with his hand touching his chest or placed over his heart. (Richman, *California*: 207; Gunn, *Early American Writing*: 65.)
52. An examiner, called a *"calificador"* in the Spanish text, was appointed by the Holy Office to examine books and writings; the position was sometimes defined as a spy.
53. Fray José Ortiz de Velasco was a minister in the Philippines before being appointed custos in El Paso (after he recovered from an illness). In 1734, he inspected the northern frontier with the intention of reforming the missionaries. (Chávez, *Diocese*: 160, 279; Norris, *Year Eighty*: 101.)
54. At that period, the sale of gunpowder was a monopoly of the Spanish Crown, who contracted with various agents to sell it. The agents were chosen based on financial bids.

55. José Carrillo y Biezma was the secretary of the Holy Office of the Inquisition in Mexico City, as stated in this document. To date, no additional information on him has been discovered.
56. Pedro Vélez de Escalante was probably the archivist in charge of sorting through the documents and putting them in order in the council's archive. To date, no additional information on him has been found.
57. To date, no additional information has been found on fray Juan Martínez Cobo.
58. The term "cura propio" means a priest who held the parish in his own name. (Robins, *Priest-Indian Conflict*: 262.)
59. The Latin term "*infra octave*" refers to the Sunday following Christmas Day.
60. To date, no additional information has been found on Miguel de Hornero.
61. To date, no additional information has been found on Lucas García de la Puente.
62. To date, no additional information has been found on Pedro López Merino.
63. To date, no additional information has been found on Andrés Delgado de Herrera.
64. To date, no additional information has been found on Catalina Seguido.
65. To date, all that is known about Juliana de León is that she was from Pozuelo de Calatrava, Spain.
66. To date, all that is known about José Granados is that he was from Pozuelo de Calatrava, Spain.
67. To date, all that is known about Josefa de Hornero is that she was from Pozuelo de Calatrava, Spain.
68. Juan Martínez de Agustín was probably responsible for preparing the written report from information gathered by the other Franciscans from the Holy Office in Toledo, Spain.
69. Licenciado fray don Juan Martínez Cobo was the rector of Pozuelo de Calatrava.
70. These people were members of the Council of Toledo for the Holy Office of the Inquisition. To date, no additional information has been found on them.
71. The literal translation of the Spanish word "relator" is "one who writes a report," so it probably referred to a kind of scribe. (Simpson, *Cassell's Latin Dictionary*: 511.)
72. Because evidence was provided that proved he was a widower when he married a second time, the charge of bigamy was dropped.
73. This probably refers to Juan García de la Mora and how he would have been carrying on "concubinage" with Josefa Martín, if he had not been a widower when he married the second time.

23

JUANA DE ANAYA ALMAZÁN CLAIMS LA CIENEGUILLA INHERITANCE
July 14–November 7, 1733, Source: SANM II #386

ynopsis and editor's notes: Juana de Anaya de Almazán's[1] father was Sergeant Major Francisco Anaya de Almazán II, a pre-revolt period alcalde of the Tano pueblos. His father and Juana's grandfather, Francisco de Anaya Almazán I, was a seventeenth-century encomendero who held an *encomienda* grant in the puesto or *sitio* (site) of La Cieneguilla (that was later sold).

During the 1680 Pueblo Revolt, when Francisco de Anaya Almazán II was assisting in the defense of Santa Fe, his entire family was killed. Francisco subsequently survived and made his way to to El Paso with other refugees. While there, he was a member of General Diego de Vargas's staff. When he returned to New Mexico in 1692, Francisco was rewarded with a land grant near the old encomienda in the La Cieneguilla area. He did not receive as much as he requested, however, for most of the land in the area had been reserved by General Vargas for the presidio horse herd. Also, after returning to New Mexico, Francisco de Anaya Almazán II married his third wife, Felipa Sedillo Rico de Rojas, with whom he had three children: Salvador, Juana, and Joaquín. After Franciscos's death in 1714, his widow married Francisco González. When González was out of the kingdom, Juana and Joaquín sold the family land grant to Andrés Montoya. Both Felipa and Salvador de Anaya Almazán, the oldest son, died sometime in 1732 or early 1733.

In this document, Juana de Anaya Almazán petitioned Governor Gervasio Cruzat y Góngora for the 555 pesos that was owed for her father's estate, which she claimed that she and her brother never received. In making her complaint, Juana carefully prepared evidence supporting her claim and collected (and probably briefed) four witnesses to testify in her favor. Juana's argument was that Francisco González held the money in trust for Joaquín and herself, and he had given a paper (or receipt) to Ventura de Esquivel, the brother-law of Salvador, stating that González held the 555 pesos, which they did not receive. She added that she had not received the family home either, which she said her mother had promised her.

The governor assigned the case to Santa Fe alcalde Antonio de Ulibarrí, who interviewed witnesses about the paper that Juana claimed had been given to Ventura de Esquivel. Ventura said that he was not given the paper regarding the 555 pesos but he did recall seeing several certified documents among Salvador de Anaya Almazán's papers. He said that the paper about the trust money was given to Salvador's daughter, María Antonia de Anaya Almazán, and she was supposed to have given it to her aunt, Juana. (Salvador was not a part of the 555 pesos inheritance, for he had already received his inheritance before he died.) When interviewed, María Antonia stated that she was given a certified document, but she did not know what it said.

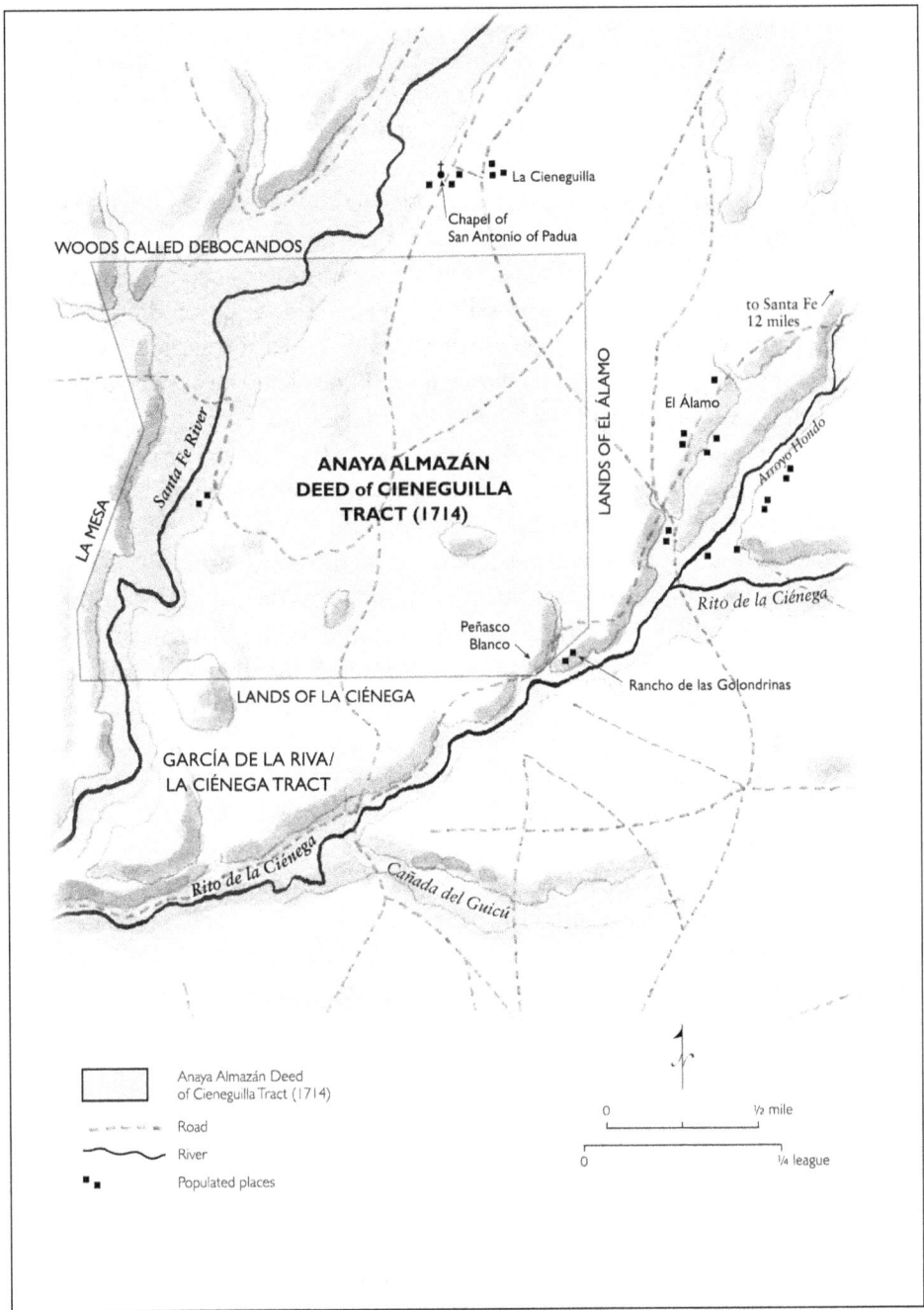

Plan of Anaya Almazán Property at Cieneguilla, 1714. Malcolm Ebright, in *Advocates of the Oppressed*: 136, 2014. Courtesy of Malcolm Ebright.

When Francisco González was interviewed, he had a different story. He accused Juana, María Antonia, and Ventura de Esquivel of lying. He said that 555 pesos were never given to him or held by him and Juana and Joaquín had sold the family land to Andrés Montoya when Francisco was out of the country. Francisco said he objected to the sale, but his wife told him to withdraw any objections. Francisco then urged the governor to look in the archives of the casa reales for the deed of sale for the land and also told him to talk to Andrés Montoya, the purchaser.

In her response, Juana said that Francisco loaned her goods worth seventy pesos, which she claimed he would not have done unless he expected her to pay him back from the 555 pesos. Again, she asked about her portion of the house promised as part of her inheritance. The alcalde then interviewed Rosa Lucero de Godoy, the widow of the deceased Salvador, who said that Ventura de Esquivel did give María Antonia a paper, but she did not know what it said. When the alcalde interviewed Juana's brother, Joaquín de Anaya Almazán, a presidio soldier, he answered carefully and supported his sister, agreeing that they were owed the 555 pesos. But, he added, he did not want the money. At that point, Francisco González, who was probably running out of patience, stated that there was no such document as Juana and her associates were claiming and they made the whole thing up.

Finally, Alcalde Ulibarrí asked Andrés Montoya for the bill of sale for his purchase of the land from Juana and Joaquín. Montoya retrieved the document from the cabildo archives that showed that the land was sold to him by Juana and Joaquín for 125 pesos and that at the time of the sale they stated that they were satisfied and content. The case was then sent to Governor Cruzat y Góngora who said that because the parties had come to an agreement he considered the matter resolved, though he did not state what the substance of the agreement was. Likely, because of the testimony given by Andrés Montoya and the evidence of the bill of sale the matter of the 555 pesos was dropped.

The matter of the house inheritance may have been addressed in the agreement. The January 1733 inventory of goods for Juana's mother, Felipa Sedillo Rico de Rojas, included the ownership of a five-room house. When Juana wrote her will three years later, she left a five-room house to her six unmarried children and a tract of land (in the front and back) to go with it. Could this be the same house that Juana claimed and she did in fact inherit? Was this part of the unstated agreement? If so, Juana's petition to the governor to provide for her family was at least partly successful.

In regard to Spanish law, this is another example of a woman being allowed to submit a petition to the governor to argue for her rights, even though in this case she may have been somewhat misguided about what was legally hers. It is clear that under Spanish law she was able to inherit land, sell that land, and write a will all in her own name. This could not have happened under English or American law where women did not have a separate legal identity. It is also interesting to note that in his testimony Francisco González said that his wife, Felipa Sedillo Rico de Rojas, was the keeper of his accounts and everything else, a clear sign of his recognition of her abilities.

Alcalde Ulibarrí's handing of the legal procedures in this document are not elaborate, but he did ensure that all testimony was affirmed and ratified by the persons testifying, copies were given to opposing parties, and the remisson of proceedings between the governor and alcalde was noted.

Andrés Montoya's bill of sale is still a part of the Spanish Colonial archives, number SANM I #497, and was translated in 1876 by David Miller when it was reviewed and approved by the Surveyor General's Office. Attached to this bill of sale are Governor Diego de Vargas's 1693 grant of the La Cieneguilla tract to Francisco Anaya Almazán II and the 1714 revalidation by Governor Flores Mogollón. The grant was for one *fanega* of "corn-planting" land, land for the raising of two hundred sheep, and land for horses of service and oxen. In regard to the placement and retrieval of the deed in the archives, Alfonso Rael de Aguilar, who strongly supported filing documents in the cabildo archive in 1716, would have been proud.[2]

TRANSLATION

Proceedings brought forth and demanded by Juana de Anaya [Almazán], resident of this Villa of Santa Fe, against Francisco González,[3] her stepfather, over her legitimate share of the *los bienes* (goods) that were left by her parents.

[Petition by Juana de Anaya Almazán]
Juana de Anaya Almazán, resident of this Villa of Santa Fe, legitimate daughter of Sergeant Major Francisco de Anaya Almazán[4] and of Felipa [Sedillo Rico] de Rojas,[5] both deceased, appear before the grandness of your majesty in my best and most proper form according to the right that I am given. I say, that after the death of my father, my mother married Francisco González. The goods legitimately left by my father were given to Francisco González from Salvador de Anaya,[6] my brother, also deceased. This was according to a document from the royal justice that my brother had no authority to sign. The sale amount consisted of 555 pesos. This is the amount that we, my other brother, Joaquín, and I were to be given because we were the minor children.[7]

Because this document was apparently lost when in the power of Ventura de Esquivel,[8] I decided to inquire to see if the amount was correct, seeking as I do of your honor only what I am due. This is amount is 272 pesos and four reales, subtracting sixty-nine pesos that Francisco González has given to me as part of what I am legitimately owed. Of that which is due, I ask that your honor order that it be given to me immediately along with the part of the house which belonged to my parents. For all of this I ask and petition of your honor that he order that I be given that which I have requested and which I shall receive kindly and with mercy according to justice. I swear in my best and proper form that this, my written petition, is not done in malice but only for what is necessary, etc.

Juana de Anaya Almazán (rubric)

[Petition accepted by the governor]

At this Villa of Santa Fe on the 14th of the month of July, 1733, after being reviewed by me, I, Colonel don Gervasio Cruzat y Góngora,[9] governor and captain general of this kingdom of New Mexico, took the petition as it was presented according to her legal right with attention given to that which is requested in the document as due to the demandant. In the case that there are no written documents, she is to swear to what is contained in this petition. As such I approved, ordered and signed it with my assisting witnesses due to the lack of a public or royal scribe of which there is none in this kingdom.

Don Gervasio Cruzat y Góngora (rubric)
Gaspar Bitton[10] (rubric)
Juan Antonio de Unanue[11] (rubric)

Statement of Ventura de Esquivel

At this Villa of Santa Fe, on the 15th of July, 1733, before me, Captain Antonio de Ulibarrí,[12] alcalde mayor and war captain of this villa, appeared Ventura de Esquivel, resident of this villa, whom I state that I know. Being present I read to him the petition that was presented by Juana de Anaya Almazán before the superior government of Colonel don Gervasio Cruzat y Góngora, governor and captain general of this kingdom for his majesty, and which was seen by the governor. Thus, I accepted that which was presented.

I also questioned Ventura de Esquivel about the paper, and he gave as his response that he had no such juridical[13] document. He did, however, declare under oath and the sign of the Holy Cross that because of the death of Salvador de Anaya, his former son-in-law, he did find among some certified documents a paper that was authorized by Antonio Montoya, the former alcalde ordinario of the cabildo of this villa at that time. He recognized this document because it had been read on several occasions. By this he knows that Salvador de Anaya Almazán had given to Francisco González, his stepfather, the amount of 555 pesos [from the sale of the property]. This is the amount that was legitimately held for Joaquín de Anaya Almazán[14] and Juana de Anaya Almazán, because they were minors.

This is what the document stated which was was held and secured by Salvador de Anaya Almazán because he had been appointed executor of the estate of Sergeant Major Francisco de Anaya Almazán, his father. This is so that at no time could the minor children file charges against him. This instrument Ventura de Esquivel gave to María Antonia de Anaya Almazán,[15] the legitimate daughter of Salvador de Anaya Almazán. It is said that the document was lost after it had been given to her by Ventura de Esquivel. She was to have given it to Juana de Anaya, her aunt. It is known by this witness that Salvador did not have any right to any amount because he had already received his legitimate share at the time of the death of his father.

This he stated is the truth regarding the sworn statement that he has signed.

Upon his statement being read back to him he affirmed and ratified it, and stated that he was of the age of forty-nine years, adding that the generalities[16] of the law did not apply to him. So that it is valid for all time he signed it along with me, the alcalde mayor, acting as presiding judge along with my assisting witnesses, due to the lack of a public or royal scribe there not being one in this Kingdom, which I certify.

    Antonio de Ulibarrí (rubric)
    Ventura de Esquivel (rubric)
    Witness
    Juan Manuel de Chirinos[17] (rubric)
    Witness
    Joseph Trujillo[18] (rubric)

[Proceeding]

At this Villa of Santa Fe on the 16th of July, 1733, after the above written petition was reviewed by me, Colonel don Gervacio Cruzat y Góngora, governor and captain general of this kingdom of New Mexico, I should order and did order that María Antonia de Anaya Almazán appear before the captain Antonio de Ulibarrí, alcalde mayor of this villa, and to state in juridical form regarding the documents that are concerned. The alcalde mayor is to follow the proceedings initiated by Juana de Anaya Almazán until they are placed in the state of sentencing. I thus approved, ordered and signed it along with my assisting witnesses due to the lack of a public or royal scribe there not being one in this kingdom.

    don Gervasio Cruzat y Góngora (rubric)
    Gaspar Bitton (rubric)
    Juan Antonio de Unanue (rubric)

Statement of María Antonia de Anaya Almazán

At this Villa of Santa Fe, headquarters of this kingdom of New Mexico on the 17th of July, 1733, before me Antonio de Ulibarrí, alcalde mayor and war captain of this villa there appeared María Antonia de Anaya Almazán resident of this said villa who I swear that I know. Upon her being present I took her sworn statement which she made before God, and to the sign of the Holy Cross, under which she promised to tell the truth as to what she knew.

Her statement was along the same lines as the one given by Ventura de Esquivel who says that he had turned over to this witness a paper authorized by Antonio Montoya, who was alcalde ordinario. She stated that she did not receive such a paper, but that what she did receive was a certification from her father. This she says is the truth according to the sworn statement that she has made and which she certifies and ratifies. She did not sign because she did not know how, stating that she was twenty-five years of age. I, the alcalde mayor, signed it acting as presiding judge along with my assisting witnesses due to the lack of a public or royal scribe, there not being one in this kingdom, to which I certify.

    Antonio de Ulibarrí (rubric)
Witness
Juan Manuel Chirinos (rubric)
Witness
Felipe Tamaris[19] (rubric)

Copy remitted to Francisco González

    At the Villa of Santa Fe on the 17th of July, 1733, before me, Antonio de Ulibarrí, alcalde mayor and war captain of this said villa, say that I herein give a copy of the petition presented by Juana de Anaya Almazán to Francisco González so that he can respond to it within the time of three days. I thus approved, ordered and signed it, acting as presiding judge along with my assisting witnesses due to the lack of a public or royal scribe, there not being one in this kingdom, to which I certify.

    Antonio de Ulibarrí (rubric)
Witness
Juan Manuel Chirinos (rubric)
Witness
Felipe Tamaris (rubric)

Alcalde Mayor and War Captain Antonio de Ulibarrí

Petition of Francisco González

    I, Francisco González, resident and settler of this Villa of Santa Fe, appear before your majesty in my best and most proper form according to my legal right. I say that your majesty was pleased to give me a copy of a document that was presented to him on the 14th of the present month of July by Juana de Anaya Almazán. Upon it being reviewed by me and in full understanding of the contents, it appears to me that Juana de Anaya is lacking in the truth in her demand against me, because that amount [the 555 pesos] was never given to me, and I can prove very clearly what I am saying as follows.

    When Salvador de Anaya was left as executor, it was well-known that the goods left by his father, Sergeant Major Francisco de Anaya, fell into his hands. The suggestion that Ventura de Esquivel made, that he knew for certain what I gave to Salvador [the receipt for the 555 pesos], based on the certification papers that he said he acquired from the sergeant major, was totally false. This can be clearly seen by the sworn statement of María Antonia de Anaya, who swore that she did not receive such a paper, but only received a certification from her father. It can be seen that María Antonia, being the daughter of Salvador de Anaya and blood niece of Juana de Anaya, would rather do more for her relatives than for me.

It is not valid, and cannot be valid, that Ventura de Esquivel gave a paper to María Antonia for her to give it to Juana de Anaya, because it would have been much easier for Ventura de Esquivel to give it to Juana, or to her brother Joaquín. It is also false to say that it was authorized by Antonio Montoya,[20] who was the alcalde mayor at that time. Given, but not conceded to, that if that would have been the case and it was true, it would be available in the cabildo archives [which it is not]. Due to this, and to anything else to be argued by me, [I have shown] the total falsety of the demand, and why it should be done away with.

Of your majesty I ask and petition with your full mercy that I be absolved from the issue because it is by its nature unacceptable. Upon you doing this I shall feel good and merciful according to justice. I swear in due form that this, my written document is not done in malice, but only as to what is necessary, etc.

    Francisco González (rubric)

Copy remitted to Juana de Anaya Almazán

    At the Villa of Santa Fe on the 18th of the month of July, 1733, before me Antonio de Ulibarrí, alcalde mayor and war captain of this villa, Francisco González presented his petition in response to the one presented by Juana de Anaya Almazán. As such I order that a copy be given to Juana de Anaya so that upon her review she can respond to it within the time period of three days. I thus approve, order and sign it along with my assisting witnesses due to the lack of a public or royal scribe, which there is none in this kingdom.

    Antonio de Ulibarrí (rubric)
    Witness
    Felipe Tamaris (rubric)
    Witness
    Juan Manuel Chirinos (rubric)

[Response given by Juana de Anaya Almazán]

    I, Juana de Anaya Almazán, resident of this Villa of Santa Fe, for the most favorable appeal, appear before your majesty. In response to the written document presented by Francisco González and to satisfy what is needed, I say that he is convinced by his own testimony and bad speech and in danger of his conscience, the danger being even now so ominous and foreboding, [to which I argue] as follows.

    First of all, in the statement that Ventura de Esquivel has made and expressed so clearly and openly with all specificity regarding Salvador de Anaya, his son-in-law, shows that Salvador turned over to Francisco González the quantity of 555 pesos. González then gave him a receipt with the understanding and promise that he would turn over the amount that was owed to me and to my brother. This was to be done through the alcalde ordinario Antonio Montoya, under whose authority it was to have been completed and finalized. By doing this, the receipt should have been sufficient and complete enough so that Francisco González would have turned over and executed the amount that was owed to me. Ventura de Esquivel is a witness to all that that was to be carried out in fear of God, Our Lord. He is well thought of throughout the kingdom for all of his good deeds which have until now been well received and performed.

Secondly, why is it that Francisco González omits and is silent about the seventy-one pesos that he has given to me on different occasions supplying me with food, wood, and knives bought at trade fairs, telling me that I should be the only one to remember what he has done, and which is known only by me?[21] Also left in silence is the matter of the part of the house that also belongs to me under my legitimate right as is well-known. This has never been brought up and is maliciously left unmentioned. This I bring up due to justice. It is something that I bring up before Ventura de Esquivel gives his ratification of his statement. This is so that it is not left unmentioned before everything is settled and nothing is done due to the lack of the referred to receipt and before the amount owed is ordered to be paid.

So that no circumstance is lacking, Ventura de Esquivel should state who the person or persons are who knew about what occurred, saw the written document, knew anything about it, or were present when the whole thing occurred at the time when he turned over the receipt to María Antonia de Anaya Almazán. Upon being cited by Ventura de Esquivel, your majesty should be well satisfied to take their statement or statements for this or for anything else that I can argue or should be brought forth.

Of your majesty I ask and petition that you will be well served to order as I request, that Ventura de Esquivel in his ratification that he makes, declare with full specificity, the names of the persons that I have stated who are all knowledgeable about the whole matter and will say if they saw the document. This is so that everything is done juridically and so that no proceedings are left omitted and or are not fully defined, all of which is to be done for the sake of justice. I swear in due form that this is not done in malice, but is done for the sake of justice, which is what I ask and is what is needed, etc.

Juana de Anaya Almazán (rubric)

Statement of Ventura de Esquivel

At the Villa of Santa Fe on the 21st of July, 1733, before me Antonio de Ulibarrí, alcalde mayor of this villa, Juana de Anaya Almazán presented a petition in response to that which was given by Francisco González. In this petition she asks that Ventura de Esquivel ratify the sworn statement that he had made on the 15th of the current month. She also asks that he state who the person or persons were who were present when Ventura de Esquivel turned over a paper to María Antonia de Anaya Almazán, asking those persons if they saw him turn over the document to her, or not. Upon Ventura de Esquivel being present, I took his sworn statement, which he made to God, Our Lord, and to the sign of the Holy Cross, under which he promised to tell the truth as to what he knew. Then the upon the second petition of Juana de Anaya being read to him and upon understanding what he was asked, he stated that what he has stated is true and certain and is nothing but the truth and which he ratifies.

As for the the person or persons who were present when he, Ventura de Esquivel, turned over the juridical document authorized by Antonio Montoya, alcalde ordinario, to María Antonia de Anaya Almazán, they were the following: Rosa Lucero [de Godoy],[22] wife of Ventura de Esquivel, and María Francisca de Esquivel,[23] daughter of Ventura. They can swear and state that they saw him turn over the document and explain what it was about. The witness also stated that Catalina Maese[24] said that Joaquín de Anaya told her that he remembers that Francisco González received the goods and that his sister was happy with it, as she had received them from Salvador de Anaya , her brother, now deceased. As for the sworn statements that his wife, Rosa Lucero , and his daughter are to make, he grants them permission to do so.[25]

He stated that this was the truth regarding everything that he has declared, and upon it being read back to him, he ratified and affirmed it, once, twice and three times, saying that he was forty-nine years of age, and that the generalities do not apply to him. He signed it along with me and my assisting witnesses due to the lack of a public or royal scribe, there not being one in this kingdom, to which I certify.

Antonio de Ulibarrí (rubric)
Ventura de Esquivel (rubric)
Felipe Tamaris (rubric)
Juan Manuel Chirinos (rubric)

[Statement of Rosa Lucero de Godoy]

At the Villa of Santa Fe on the 22nd of July, 1733, I, Antonio de Ulibarrí, alcalde mayor and war captain of this villa, went in person to the home and dwelling of Ventura de Esquivel. In his ratification he declares and cites as a witness his wife, Rosa Lucero, and grants her permission to testify and state how it was that she saw and knew about Ventura de Esquivel turning over a document. This is the document that stated that Salvador de Anaya had given to Francisco González the quantity of 555 pesos and that the document was acquired by María Antonia de Anaya Almazán.

Rosa Lucero, wife of Ventura de Esquivel, and resident of this villa being before me, I proceeded to receive her sworn statement, which she made before God, Our Lord, and to the sign of the Holy Cross, under which she promised to tell the truth as to what she knew and what she was asked. She was asked if she knew or saw if Ventura de Esquivel, her husband, gave some sort of document to María Antonia de Anaya Almazán. She stated that she did see him do it, and she heard him read it on one or two occasions. Because of that she knows that Salvador de Anaya had given to Francisco González the sum of 555 pesos that belonged to Joaquín de Anaya and to Juana de Anaya. Upon his finishing reading the document she saw him, Ventura de Esquivel, her husband, hand it over to María Antonia de Anaya so that she could give it to Juana de Anaya, her aunt.

This, she says is what she saw and knows according to her sworn statement that she has given and which upon it being read back to her she affirmed and ratified it, saying that she was forty-seven years of age, adding that the generalities of the law do not apply to her. She did not sign because she stated that she did not know how. I, the alcalde mayor, signed it along with my assisting witnesses due to the lack of a royal or public scribe, there not being one in this kingdom, which I certify.

 Antonio de Ulibarrí (rubric)
 Juan Manuel Chirinos (rubric)
 Felipe Tamaris (rubric)

Statement of María Francisca de Esquivel

 At the Villa of Santa Fe on the said day, month and year, before me, Antonio de Ulibarrí, alcalde mayor and war captain of this villa, there appeared María Francisca de Esquivel, whom I know, resident of this villa and widow of Salvador de Anaya, who was cited by Ventura de Esquivel, her father. Being before me I took her sworn statement that she made before God, Our Lord, and to the sign of the Cross, under which she promised to tell the truth as to what she knew and what she was asked.

 She was asked if she knew or saw a document that showed that Francisco González had received the legitimate amount that was due to Joaquín de Anaya and to Juana de Anaya. She responded by saying that she had seen it and had heard it having been read by her deceased husband and her father. Within it was stated the amount that the deceased had given to Francisco González which was the amount of 555 pesos. This was the amount that was legitimately due to Joaquín de Anaya and to Juana de Anaya. She also said that the document was read by Ventura de Esquivel, and then it was turned over to María Antonia in the presence of María Francisca de Esquivel so that she would give it to Juana de Anaya, for whom it was intended. She also said that the document was written on one half of a page of paper.

 This she says is the truth regarding the sworn statement that she has made. Upon her sworn statement being read back to her she affirmed and ratified it, saying that she was of the age of thirty years and that the generalities of the law did not apply to her. She did not sign because she said that she did not know how. I, the alcalde mayor, signed it along with my assisting witnesses due to the lack of a public or royal scribe in this kingdom, to which I certify.

 Antonio de Ulibarrí (rubric)
 Juan Manuel Chirinos (rubric)
 Felipe Tamaris (rubric)

Statement of Joaquín de Anaya

 At the Villa of Santa Fe on the 12th[26] of August, 1733, before me, Antonio de Ulibarrí, alcalde mayor and war captain of this villa, appeared Joaquín de Anaya, soldier of this royal presidio whom I know. Upon being before me I took his sworn statement which he made to God, Our Lord, and to the sign of the Cross and under which he promised to tell the truth as to what he knew and was asked, being that he was cited in the sworn statement that was made by Ventura de Esquivel.

He was asked if he knew and was aware that his stepfather, Francisco González, acquired the sum of 555 pesos that legitimately belonged to Joaquín and to his sister. He answered that it was true that it is owed to them, being that he was told by the other Francisco González[27] on two different occasions. He owes them the sum of 555, this being the amount that was paid for the Puesto de la Cieneguilla which was sold by Joaquín de Anaya and Juana de Anaya, his sister, when Francisco González was out of the country. When he returned from outside the country, Francisco wanted to get the sale voided. This witness says it was due to the respect for his mother that he did not. She told Francisco González to leave it sold and to distribute the 555 pesos, or as much as was left.

This witness then told Francisco González that when he paid it to his sister, that he, Joaquín, did not want to take anything for his part, now or ever. If he, Francisco, did not have enough to pay her, he, Joaquín, would help him, being that his sister kept asking Francisco González for her share on a daily basis. This is even though the amount that was received for the Puesto de la Cieneguilla was to be divided among the brother and sister, Joaquín and Juana. Joaquín further said that he did not know or did not remember how much was paid for the said puesto.

This he said was the truth regarding the sworn statement that he has made and which he affirmed and ratified, adding that even if he Francisco González is his stepfather, he cannot lie about anything. He said that he was thirty-three years of age, but did not sign because he said that he did not know how. I, the alcalde mayor, acting as presiding judge, signed it along with my assisting witnesses due to the lack of a public or royal scribe, which there is none in this kingdom, to which I certify.

Antonio de Ulibarrí (rubric)
Juan Manuel Chirinos (rubric)
Felipe Tamaris (rubric)

[Copy remitted to Francisco González]

At the Villa of Santa Fe on the said day, month and year, having received the sworn statement of Joaquín de Anaya, I mandated and ordered that a copy of it be given to Francisco González so that he can respond to it within the time limit of three days. I thus approved, ordered and signed it along with my assisting witnesses acting as presiding judge due the lack of a public or royal scribe, which there is none in this kingdom.

Antonio de Ulibarrí (rubric)
Juan Manuel Chirinos (rubric)
Felipe de Tamaris (rubric)

Alcalde Mayor and War Captain

[Statement of Francisco González]

 I, Francisco González, resident of this Villa of Santa Fe, appear before your majesty in my best and most proper form that my right allows me and say that your majesty was pleased to order that I be given a copy of that which is stated by Joaquín de Anaya in his sworn statement. This states that I told him on two different occasions that I owed them the sum of 555 pesos which resulted from the sale of the Sitio de la Cieneguilla, which they sold during my absence, against my will. Joaquín said that he does not remember what was paid for it. But he does remember that what was received was divided amongst himself and his sister, Juana de Anaya, who in her deliberations makes no mention of such a receipt.

 She remembers only what she wants to remember about what I had given them. The one who gave it to them was their mother, as she was the keeper of my accounts and of everything else that I might acquire. Of anything else that Juana might say, she is the one who was clearly hiding something, such as half the value of the Sitio de la Cieneguilla. She is likely hiding other things that I do not know, things that her mother might have given to her without my knowing it.

 I cannot believe or admire the good conscience of Juana de Anaya or her pointing out what she has received. So that it might come to an understanding of what she has received for the said sitio, your majesty might be better served to order Captain Andrés Montoya[28] to show the bill of sale. This is so that the evidence will show how much she should have been given and what she received.

 I insist that within this, my written statement, I have never agreed to such an obligation nor have I been given any such document. It cannot be proven through the ratification made by Ventura de Esquivel nor by the statement given by his wife or daughter, who by nature can be challenged, for it is not incredible that they can lie for their husband and father. It is incredible that after the elapse of so much time they, neither one nor the other, can remember the amount that they supposed was contained in the document that was supposedly lost. The last will and testament [of Francisco Anaya de Almazán], along with the inventory of goods, should still exist, as not everything can be lost.

 In addition to my sworn statement that I have made, I state that there is no such document, nor was it ever made before Antonio Montoya. This is because those who were alcaldes at that time and the ones who assisted with the inventory of goods were Antonio Aguilera de Ysasi[29] and Joseph Rodríguez,[30] and the scribe was Cristóbal de Góngora.[31] For these reasons, what was purported to be in the documents and the little of information given by Ventura de Esquivel, his wife and daughter, do not provide enough proof, or even semi-proof. As such everything that is sought by Juana de Anaya is an impostor, invented by her natural good character.[32] For this reason, anything else which is in my favor I can and ought to argue, as I did above. As such, I ask of your

majesty that you be pleased, upon reviewing my petition, that you determine and do according to what you think is justifiable, and I swear that this is done in due form and in what is necessary, etc.
    Francisco González (rubric)

[Examination of the sale of La Cieneguilla]
    At the Villa of Santa Fe, on the 26th of August, 1733, I, Captain Antonio de Ulibarrí, alcalde mayor of this said villa, say that I personally went to the Puesto de la Cieneguilla to examine the royal sale that was made to Captain Andrés Montoya by Joaquín de Anaya [Almazán] and Juana de Anaya [Almazán] before Captain Juan García de la Riva, alcalde ordinario of the cabildo of this villa. It is found that the Sitio de la Cieneguilla was sold by Joaquín de Anaya and Juana de Anaya for the sum of 120 pesos as they, Joaquín de Anaya and Juana de Anaya, stated in the document that they received from Captain Andrés Montoya, and they were content and satisfied.
    So that it is forever valid I signed it on the said day, month and year.
    Antonio de Ulibarrí (rubric)

[Remission to the governor]
    At the Villa of Santa Fe on the said day, month and year, having concluded these proceedings at the order of Colonel don Gervasio Cruzat y Góngora, governor and captain general of this kingdom for his majesty, I submit the proceeding to the governor so that upon his review he will determine what is just, which as usual is done for the best. I thus decreed, ordered and signed along with my assisting witnesses due to the lack of a public or royal scribe, which there is none in this Kingdom.
    Antonio de Ulibarrí (rubric)
    Juan Manuel de Chirinos (rubric)
    Felipe Tamaris (rubric)

[Determination]
    At the Villa of Santa Fe on the 7th of November, 1733, I, Colonel don Gervasio Cruzat y Góngora, governor and captain general of this kingdom of New Mexico for his majesty, should say and did say that due to the fact that the parties who litigate this cause have agreed and settled issues before me, I should order and do order that it be left as was agreed taking note of this and including them in these proceedings.[33] I thus approve, order and sign it along with my assisting witnesses due to the lack of a public or royal scribe, which there is none in this kingdom.
    don Gervasio Cruzat y Góngora (rubric)
    Gaspar Bitton (rubric)
    Juan Antonio de Unanue (rubric)

TRANSCRIPTION

Causa seguida y demandada por Juana de Anaya vesina de esta Villa de Santa Fee contra Francisco Gonzales su adastro sobre la legitima que dise le toca de los bienes que dejaron sus padres

Señor Governador y Capitan General

    Juana de Anaya Almasan, vesina de esta Villa de Santa Fee, hija legitima de el Sargento Mayor Francisco de Anaya Almasan y de Phelipa de Rojas ya difuntos paresco ante la grandesda de Vuestra Señoria en la major forma que el derecho me consede y digo; que despues del fayesimiento de el dicho mi padre caso La dicha mi madre con Francisco Gonzales y por que la lejitima de los bienes que dejo el dicho mi Padre los apersibio el dicho Francisco Gonzales los que entego Salvador de Analla Almazan, mi hermano, tambien ya difunto, como constaba de un ynstrumento que el dicho mi hermano no tenia autorisado dela Real Justizia, cuya cantidad eran quinientos sinquenta y sinco pesos, los quales nos tocaban ami y a otro hermano, que eramos los menores.
    Por que dicho ynstrumento se perdio en poder de Ventura de Esquibel, jure y declare si es sierta dicha cantidad, pidiendo como pido a Vuestra Señoria solo lo que ami me pertenee que son dosientos setenta y dos pesos y quatro reales, rebajando sesenta y nuebe pesos que me tiene dados el dicho Francisco Gonzales a quenta de mi legitima, y de lo restante se a de servir Vuestra Señoria mandar que efectivamente me entere dicha cantidad como tambien la parte de la casa que era de los dichos mis padres; por todo lo qual a Vuestra Señoria pido y suplico sea mui servido de mandar seme entere lo que llebo dicho que en ello reciviere bien y merced con justicia que pido y juro en toda forma no ser de malicia este mi escripto y en lo nesesario, ut supra =
    Juana de Anaya (rubric)

    En la Villa de Santa Fee en quatorse dias del mes de Julio de mil setesientos y treinta y tres años vista por mi el Coronel Dn. Gervasio Cruzat y Gongora, Governador y Capitan General de este Reyno dela Nueva Mexico la ube por presentada en lo que a lugar en derecho y en atension a lo que se espresa en este escripto devia mandar y mande compareca Ventura Esquibel ante la Real Justicia y escriva los instrumentos que pertenesen a lo que pide por la parte demandante y en caso que no aya instrumentos jure y declare sobre el contenido de esta petision; asi lo provey y mande y firme con los testigos de mi asistensia a falta de Ecribano Publico y Real que no lo ay en este Reyno =
    Dn. Gervasio Cruzat y Gongora (rubric)

Gaspar Bitton (rubric)
Juan Antonio de Unanue (rubric)

☙

Declaracion de Ventura de Esquibel

En la Villa de Santa Fee en quinze dias del mes de Julio de mill setezientos y treinta y tres años ante mi el Capitan Antonio de Uribarri, Alcalde Maior y Capitan Aguerra desta dicha Villa paresio Ventura de Esquibel vezino de dicha Villa a quien doy fee conosco y estndo presente le lei la petision presentada por Juana de Anaya Almasan ante el Superior Gobierno del Sññor Coronel Dn. Gervasio Cruzat y Gongora, Governador y Capitan General deste Reino por Su Magestad y vista por dicho Señor decreto lo que.

Tambien le notifique al dicho Ventura de Esquibel y dio por repuesta que no ay en poder sullo ynstrumento alguno juridico. Solo si declara de bajo de juramento y la Señal de la Santa Cruz que por muerte de Salvador de Anaya Almasan su llerno que fue que entre unas zertificaciones que el dicho su yerno tenia ayo un papel autorisado de Antonio Montoya Alcalde Ordinario que era en aquel tiempo del Cabildo desta Villa y que le costa por aberlo leydo distintas beses y que en el resave el aber entregado el dicho Salvador de Anaya Almasan a Francisco Gonzales su padrastro la cantidad de quinientos sinquenta y sinco pesos que es la parte dela ligitima que por menor de edad les benia de derecho a Juachin de Anaya Almasan y a Juana de Anaya Almasan.

Que dicho ynstrumento resave el seguro que Salvador de Anaya Almasan tenia por haver quedado por albasea del Sargento Maior Francisco de Anaya Almasan, su padre, para que en ningun tiempo los dichos menores le isiesen el cargo y que dicho ynstrumento selo entrego el dicho Ventura de Esquibel a Maria Antonia de Anaya Almasan hija legitima del dicho Salvador de Anaya Almasan en poder de quien dizen se perdio haviendo selo dado el dicho Ventura de Esquibel para que diese a Juana de Anaya su tia y que le consta a este declarante que su llerno no tenia parte en dicha cantidad por haber resevido en el fallesimiento de su padre la lejitima que le tocava.

Que esta es la berdad so cargo del juramento que fecho tiene en que siendole leyda esta su declaracion se afirmo y ratifico y que es de edad de cuarenta y nueve años y que no le toca en las generales y para que en todo tiempo conste lo firmo con migo dicho Alcalde Maior actuando ante mi como Juez Receptor y los testigos de mi asistenzia a falta de Escribano Publico y Real que no lo ay en este Reino, doy fee =

Antonio de Uribarri (rubric)
Ventura de Esquibel (rubric)
Testigo
Juan Manuel Quiniones (rubric)
Testigo
Joseph Trujillo (rubric)

☙

En la Villa de Santa Fee en dies y seis dias del mes de Julio de mill setezientos treinta y tres años vista la sobre escripta de petision por mi el Coronel Dn. Gervacio Cruzat y Gongora, Governador y Capitan General de este Reyno de la Nueva Mexico devia mandar y mande que Maria Antonia de Anaya y Almasan comparesca ante mi el Capitan Antonio de Uribarri, Alcalde Mayor de esta dicha Villa y declare en forma juridical sobre los instrumentos que se espresan y siga dicho Alcalde Mayor las diligensias que competen ala demanda puesta por Juana de Anaya de Almasan hasta ponerla en estado de sentensia. Asi lo probey, mande y firme con los testigos de mi asistensia a falta de Escribano Publico y Real que no lo ay en este Reino =

 Dn. Gervasio Cruzat y Gongora (rubric)
 Gaspar Bitton (rubric)
 Juan Antonio de Unanue (rubric)

Declaracion de Maria Antonia Anaya Almasan

En la Villa de Santa Fee cabesera deste Reino de la Nueva Mexico en diez y siete dias del mes de Julio de mill setezientos y treinta y tres años ante mi Antonio de Uribarri, Alcalde Maior y Capitan Aguerra de esta dicha Villa paresio Maria Antonia Anaya Almasan vesina desta dicha Villa aquien doy fee conosco y estando presente le resevi juramento que iso por Dios Nuestro Señor y la Señal de la Santa Cruz debajo de cuio cargo prometio de desir berdad en lo supiere y le fuere preguntado y siendolo al tenor de la declaracion hecha por Ventura de Esquibel el qual dize haberle entregado a esta declarante un papel autorisado de Antonio Montoya siendo Alcalde Ordinario y respondio la dicha Maria Antonia que no a resevido tal papel que lo que si declara aber resevido es una zertificacion de su padre y que esta es la berdad por el juramento que fecho tiene en que se afirmo y ratifico, no firmo por no saver y que es de edad de veinte y zinco años firmelo yo dicho Alcalde Maior actuando como Juez Receptor con los testigos ynfraescriptos de mi asistenzia a falta de Escribano Publico y Real que no lo ay en este Reino, doy fee =

 Antonio de Uribarri (rubric)
 Testigo
 Juan Manuel Chirinos (rubric)
 Testigo
 Felipe Tamaris (rubric)

Traslado a Francisco Gonzales

En la Villa de Santa Fee, en diez y ziete dias del mes de Julio de mill setezientos y treinta y tres años ante mi Antonio de Uribarri, Alcalde Maior y Capitan Aguerra de esta dicha Villa digo que doi traslado dela petision presentada por Juana de Anaya Almasan a Francisco Gonzales para que responda dentro del termino de tres dias asi lo provey, mande y firme actuando ante mi como Juez Receptor con los testigos ynfraescriptos de mi asistenzia a falta de Escribano Publico y Real que no lo ay en este Reino; doy fee =

    Antonio de Uribarri (rubric)
    Testigo
    Juan Manuel Chirinos (rubric)
    Testigo
    Felipe Tamaris (rubric)

Petizion de Francisco Gonzales
    Señor Alcalde Maior y Capitan Aguerra Antonio de Uribarri
    Francisco Gonzales vezino y poblador de esta Villa de Santa Fee ante Vuestra Magestad paresco en la mas bastante forma que en derecho aya lugar y digo que Vuestra Magestad fue servido de darme traslado de un escrito que en catorze del corriente mes de Julio presento Juana de Anaya contra mi y delas declaraciones de Ventura de Esquibel hecha en quinse de dicho mes y la de Maria Antonia Anaya Almazan, que vistas unas y otras y enterado de su contenido seme ofreze dezir que Juana de Anaya falta ala verdad en la demanda puesta contra mi, por no haber entrado en mi poder tal cantidad, y se prueba claramente ser como digo.
    Pues quedando Salvador de Anaya por alvasea se biene en conozimiento entrasen en su poder los vienes de el Sargento Mayor Francico de Anaya, su padre, y el suponer Ventura de Esquibel que entre las sertaficaciones de dicho Sargento Maior vido un seguro que yo di a dicho Salvador es totalmente falso como se conbense de tal por la declaracion de Maria Antonia de Anaya. Que totalmente jura no haber resebido tal papel y que lo que resibio fue una zertificazion de su padre, y siendo la dicha Maria Antonia hija de Salvador de Anaya, y sobrina carnal de Juana de Anaya so viene a los ojos que habia de azer mas por sus parientes que por mi.
    Ni vale ni puede valer dezir Ventura de Esquibel sele dio a Maria Antonia para que selo diese a su tia Juana de Anaya siendole mas facil a dicho Ventura de Esquibel el darselo a la dicha Juana, o a su hermano Joaquin, todo lo qual es siniestro como dezir estaba autorizado de Antonio Montoya, Alcalde Ordinario, en aquel tiempo, que dado, y no consedido, que tal ubiera subsedido, constara en el Archibo de Cabildo; por lo qual y lo mas que alegar puedo, para desbaneser siniestra demanda =
    A Vuestra Magestad pido y suplico con todo rendimiento sea servido de darme por absuelto dela instancia por ser de su naturaleza despreciable que en hazerlo asi resiviere bien y merced con justicia, juro en forma este mi escrito no ser malicioso y en lo nesesario, ut supra =
    Francisco Gonzales (rubric)
    Traslado a Juana de Anaya Almasan

En la Villa de Santa Fee en diez y ocho dias del mems de Jullio de mill setesientos y treinta y tres años ante mi Antonio de Uribarri Alcalde Maior y Capitan

Aguerra de esta dicha Villa presento Francisco Gonzales esta petision en respuesta de la presentada por Juana de Anaya Almasan y devia de mandar y mando se de traslado a la dicha Juana de Anaya para que en vista responda en el termino de tres dias, asi lo provei, mande y firme con los testigos ynfraescriptos de mi asistenzia a falta de Escribano Publico ni Real que no lo ay en este Reino =

 Antonio de Uribarri (rubric)
Testigo
Felipe Tamaris (rubric)
Testigo
Juan Manuel Chirinos (rubric)

        ◦

 Juana de Anaya Almasan, vesina de esta Villa de Santa Fee por el recurso mas favorable paresco ante Vuestra Magestad y en respuesta de el escripto presentado por Francisco Gonzales su tenor prosupuesto y y en lo nesesario satisfaciendo digo que esta conbensido por el dicho su escripto que mal le yse oramente y en daño de su consiensia asi tan ya ominosa ni patiba, por lo general y siguiente.

 Lo primero por que consta en la declaracion que tiene fecha Ventura de Esquibel expresa clara y abiertamente con toda yndibiduasion como Salvador de Anaya, su yerno le entrego la cantidad de quinientos sinquenta y sinco pesos al dicho Francisco Gonzales de que le otorgo resivo con obligasion que en toda forma hizo entregar la parte que ami y ami hermano nos tocaba la qual parese ante el Alcalde Ordinario Antonio Montoya, a cuya declaracion se debe estar y parar para que sea bastante y sufisiente para que sele mande al dicho Francisco Gonzales entriegue luego y executibamente la cantidad que ami me toca y pertenese pues es testigo el dicho Ventura de Esquibel de toda ebsesion y temoroso de Dios Nuestro Señor y bien opinado en todo el Reyno por sus buenos y loables operasiones sin que asta a ora la va ya enpenado.

 Lo segundo por que como el dicho Francisco Gonzales omite y para en silencio setenta y un pesos que me tiene entregados en distintas ocasione asi en bastimento y lena, cuchillos de rescate adbirtiendome siempre que yo lo fuera apuntando lo qual le yse y consta por la memoria que tengo en mi poder, y de la misma forma para en silencio la parte de la casa que ami me pertenese con lejitimo derecho con que es bisto estar en el todo conbensido como dicho es; lo qual abasilado ymajinado malisiosamente por no aser la dicha paga y para que con mayor justisia me di ante que el dicho Ventura de Esquibel se ratifique en la dicha su declaracion para que en su bista se determine este negocio pues como dicho es que es bastante y suficiente pues a falta de el referido ynstrumento, obligasion y resibo sele mande aser la dicha paga.

 Para que no falte ninguna sircumstancia que el dicho Ventura de Esquibel declare la persona o personas que bieron dicho ynstrumento y fueron sabidores de el y si se allaron presents alguna o algunas al tiempo y quando le entrego el dicho resibo y obligasion a Maria Antonia de Anaya Almasan; y sitadas que sean por el dicho Ventura de Esquibel se a de servir Vuestra Majestad de reservirles su declaracion o declaraciones por todo lo qual y lo demas que alegar puedo y debo.

A Vuestra Magestad pido y suplico sea mui servido de mandar aser como llebo pedido y que el dicho Ventura de Esquibel en la ratificasion que ysiere declare con toda distinsion las personas como dicho llebo que son sabidores de este negocio, y si el dicho ynstrumento lo bieron y que todo conste juridicamente y no se omita diligensia alguna para que con mayor seguridad se difina pues todo es de justicia y juro en forma no ser de malisia sino es por alcansar justicia que pido y en lo nesesario, ut supra.

Juana de Anaya Almasan (rubric)

En la Villa de Santa Fee en veinte y un dias del mes de Jullio de mill setezientos y treinta y tres años ante mi Antonio de Uribarri, Alcalde Mayor desta dicha Villa presento Juana de Anaia Almasan una petision en respuesta de la presentada por Francisco Gonzales y en ella dise que pide se ratifique Ventura Esquibel de la declaracion que tiene hecha el dia quinze del corriente y que jure y declare la persona o personas que se allaron presentes quando dicho Ventura de Esquibel le entrego un instrumento a Maria Antonia de Anaia Almasan si lo vieron entregar o no, y estando presente el dicho Ventura de Esquibel le resevi juramento que yso por Dios Nuestro Señor y la Señal de Cruz debajo de cuyo cargo prometio de desir berdad en lo que supiere y siendo leida la segunda petision presentada por la dicha Juana de Anaia y enterada de su contesto dijo que lo que tiene declarado es lo cierto y berdadero y que siempre esta sierto en ello como berdad en que se ratifica y que en lo que.

A la persona o personas que se ayaron presents quando el dicho Ventura de Esquibel entrego el ynstrumento juridico autorisado de Antonio Montoia Alcalde Ordinario ala dicha Maria Antonia de Anaia Almasan se allaron presentes Rosa Lucero, muger de dicho Ventura de Esquibel y Maria Francisca de Esquibel hija del dicho que estas pueden jurar y declarar como bieron haber entregado el dicho ynstrumento y aberles dicho las circumstancias del y tambien dize este declarante que Cathalina Maese dize que le dijo Juachin de Anaia que se acuerda que Francisco Gonzales resivio dichos vienes y que su hermana pide bien por aberlos resevido de Salvador de Anaia su hermano, ya difunto, y para la declaracion y juramento que a de azer la dicha Rosa Lucero, su muger, ye hija, les consede lizensia.

Que esta es la berdad de todo lo que lleva dicho en que siendole leida esta su ratificazion se afirmo y ratifico por primera, segunda y terzera bes y que es de edad de quarenta y nueve años y que no les tocan las generales y lo firmo con migo y los testigos de mi asistensia a falta de Escribano Publico y Real que no lo ay en este Reino, doi fee

Antonio de Uribarri (rubric)
Felipe Tamariz (rubric)
Ventura de Esquibel (rubric)
Juan Manuel Chirinos (rubric)

En la Villa de Santa Fee en veinte y dos dias del mes de Julio de mill setezientos y treinta y tres años yo Antonio de Uribarri, Alcalde Maior y Capitan Aguerra de dicha Villa pase en persona ala casa y morada de Ventura de Esquibel quien en su ratificazion declara y sita por testigo a su muger Rosa Lucero a quien le permite lizensia para que jure y declare como bido y sabe aberle entregado el dicho Ventura de Esquibel un instrumento en que constava haber entregado Salvador de Anaia a Francisco Gonzales en que resava la cantidad de quinientos y sinquenta y sinco pesos y que dicho ynstrumento lo apersivio Maria Antonia de Anaia Almasan y estando presente ante mi dicho Alcalde Maior.

Rosa Lucero muger de Ventura de Esquibel y vezina de esta dicha Villa le resevi juramento que iso por Dios Nuestro Señor y la Señal de la Santa Cruz debajo de cuio cargo prometio de desir verdad en lo que supiere y le fuere preguntado y siendole si save o bido si Ventura de Esquibel su marido le dio a Maria Antonia de Anaia Almasan algun papel; a esto responde que si lo bido y lo ollo leer que lo ollo en una o dos ocasiones leer y que resave en el como le avia entregado Salvador de Anaia a Francisco Gonzales la cantidad de quientos sinquenta y sinco pesos que les pertenesia a Juachin de Anaia y a Juana de Anaia y que acabado de leer lo vido que Ventura de Esquibel su marido selo entrego en mano propia a Maria Antonia de Anaia para que selo entregase ala dicha Juana de Anaia, su tia.

Que esto es lo que vido y save por el juramento que fecho tiene en que siendole leida su declaracion se afirmo y ratifico y que es de hedad de quarenta y siete años y que no le tocan las generales de la ley. No firmo por que dijo no saber, firmelo yo dicho Alcalde Mayor con los testigos de mi asistenzia a falta de Escribano Publico y Real que no lo ay en este Reino = doy fee

Antonio de Uribarri (rubric)
Juan Manuel Chirinos (rubric)
Felipe Tamariz (rubric)

En la Villa de Santa Fee en dicho dia, mes y año, ante mi Antonio de Uribarri, Alcalde Maior y Capitan Aguerra de dicha Villa paresio Maria Francisca de Esquibel, vezina de dicha Villa y viuda de Salvador de Anaia a quien sita en su ratificacion Ventura de Esquibel, padre dela dicha a quien doi fee conosco y estando presente le resevi juramento que iso por Dios Nuestro Señor y la Señal de Cruz debajo de cuyo cargo prometio de desir verdad en lo que supiere y le fuere preguntado.

Siendole si save o bido un ynstrumento en que constava aber resevido Francisco Gonzales la legitima que les pertenese a Juachin de Anaia y a Juana de Anaia; a esto responde que lo vio y lo ollo leer muchas beses al difunto su marido y a su padre y que ollo que en el resave aberle entregado el dicho difunto a Francisco Gonzales la cantidad de quinientos y sincuenta y sinco pesos que les pertenesian de ligitima a Juachin de Anaia y a Juana de Anaia y que dicho ynstrumento acabandolo de leer el dicho Ventura de Esquibel selo entrego a Maria Antonia en presenzia dela dicha Maria Francisca de Esquibel para que selo entregase a Juana de Anaia a quien le tocaba y que dicho ynstrumento hera en un medio pliego. Que esta es la verdad so cargo del juramento que fecho tiene en que siendole leida esta su declaracion se afirmo y ratifico y que es de edad edad de treinta años y que no le toca en las generales de la ley; no firmo por que dijo no saber, firmelo yo dicho Alcalde Maior con los testigos de mi asistenzia a falta de Escribano Publico ni Real en este Reyno, doy fee.

 Antonio de Uribarri (rubric)
 Juan Manuel Chirinos (rubric)
 Felipe Tamariz (rubric)

En la Villa de Santa Fee en doze dias del mes de Agosto de mill setezientos y treinta y tres años ante mi Antonio de Uribarri, Alcalde Maior y Capitan Aguerra desta dicha Villa paresio Joaquin de Ania soldado deste Real Presidio aquien doi fee conosco y estando presente le resevi juramento que iso por Dios Nuestro Señor y la Señal de la Cruz de bajo de cuio cargo prometio de desir berdad en lo que supiere y le fuere preguntado como sitado en la declaracion hecha por Ventura de Esquibel.

Preguntado si save y le costa que Francisco Gonsales su padrastro que fue, si persivio la cantidad de quinientos sinquenta y sinco pesos que de legitima les tocava al dicho Juachin y su hermana; a esto responde que es berdad que selos deve por aberselo dicho el otro Francisco Gonsales en dos ocasiones que les era deudor de los quinientos sinquenta y sinco pesos a los dichos dos menores entrando en esta cantidad el Puesto de la Cieneguilla la qual bendieron entre el dicho Juachin de Anaia y Juana de Anaia su hermana estando ausente el dicho Francisco Gonsales y quando vino de afuera quiso quitarla y dar por nula la benta. Y dise este declarante que por respecto de su madre le dijo al dicho Francisco Gonsales que la dejara bendida que se le escalfaria a cada uno de la parte de los quinientos sinquenta y sinco pesos.

Que este declarante le dijo al dicho Francisco Gonsales pagase ala dicha su hermana, que la suia no sela cobrava a ora ni nunca y que sino tenia con que pagar que el le alludaria a pagar por occasion de andarle cobrando la dicha su hermana al dicho Francisco Gonsales cada dia y que la cantidad que dieron por el Puesto de la Cieneguilla se partieron entre los dos hermanos Juachin y Juana y que no save este declarante ni se acuerda la cantidad que dieron por dicho sitio.

Que esta es la berdad so cargo del juramento que fecho tiene en que se afirmo y ratifico y que aunque es su padrastro no puede faltar ala berdad, y que es de edad de treinta y tres años, no firmo por que dijo no saber firmelo yo dicho Alcalde Maior actuando como Juez Rezeptor con los testigos ynfraescriptos de mi asistenzia a falta de Escribano Publico y Real que no lo ai en este Reyno, doi fee =

 Antonio de Uribarri (rubric)
 Juan Manuel Chirinos (rubric)
 Felipe Tamaris (rubric)

En la Villa de Santa Fee en dicho dia, mes y año, aviendo resevidole su jurmento a Juachin de Anaia devia demander y mande se de traslado a Francisco Gonzales para que responda dentro del termino de tres dias, asi lo provei, mande y firme con los testigos de mi asistenzia actuando por resetoria a falta de Escribano Publico y Real que nolo ay en este Reyno =

    Antonio de Uribarri (rubric)
    Juan Manuel Chirinos (rubric)
    Felipe de Tamaris (rubric)

    Señor Alcalde Mayor y Capitan Aguerra

Francisco Gonzales, vezino de esta Villa de Santa Fee paresco ante Vuestra Majestad en la mas bastante forma que en derecho aya lugar y el mio conbenga y digo que Vuestra Majestad fue servido de mandar seme diese traslado delo que depone Joaquin de Anaya en su declaracion de que en dos ocasiones le dixe yo le sera deudor dela cantidad de quinientos cinquenta y cinco pesos yncluyendo en dicha cantidad el Sitio de la Cieneguilla, y que la bendieron en mi auciencia, contra mi boluntad, y que no se acuerdo lo que dieron por ella, y que lo que le dieron lo partio con su hermana Juana de Anaya,, quien en sus escriptos no haze mencion de tal resibo.

Solo se acuerda (delo que supone) averle yo dado, que quien selo daria fue su madre como dueno que hera de mi sueldo y delo demas que yo adquiria, y seria mas delo que confieza, pues quien ocultaba, una cosa tan clara como la mitad de el valor del Sitio de la Cieneguilla, mas bien ocultaria lo que sin saberlo, yo, le daba su madre.

No puedo dexar de admirar la buena conciencia de dicha Juana de Anaya de yr azentando lo que resebia, y para benir en conocimiento delo que tiene resevido de dicho sitio se a de serbir Vuestra Magestad de mandar al Capitan Andres Montoya muestre la escriptura de benta, para por ella sacar lo que a quenta de lo que le pertenesia a resibido.

Ynsistiendo en este mi escripto lo que en mis antesedentes, de no haver hecho yo tal obligazion ni aber dado ynstrumento; ni menos lo prueba la ratificazion de Ventura de Esquibel con el dicho de su esposa y hija que por su naturaleza estan tachados, pues no es creible desmintiesen a su esposo y padre y es marabilla que a el cabo de tanto tiempo se acuerdan una y otra dela cantidad que suponen constaba en dicho ynstrumento que aunque este se ubiera perdido; quedaria el testamento y enbentario de vienes, que no todos se abian de perder.

Ademas de jurar como juro, en toda forma, no aber tal ynstrumento, ni ser hecho, ante Antonio Montoya pues quienes, en aquel año eran Alcaldes y asistieron a el ynbentario, fueron Antonio Aguilera Ysasi y Joseph Rodriguez, y escribano Xptobal de Gongora por cuyas razones, y lo supuesto delos escritos, y la ninguna ynformazion dada con Ventura de Esquibel y su muger y hija, que no solo no haze plena probanza, pero ni semi plena, por ser todo lo pedido, por Juana de Anaya una imposture, inventada de su buen natural por todo lo qual, y lo mas que alegar puedo y debo que

a mi fabor aga, y doy por espresado; a Vuestra Magestad pido y suplico sea servido de en bista de mi pedimento hazer y determinar, lo que hallare ser de justizia, juro este escrito en forma, y en lo nesesario, ut supra =
Francisco Gonzales (rubric)

En la Villa de Santa Fee en veinte y seis dias del mes de Agosto de mil setezientos treinta y tres años, yo el Capitan Antonio de Uribarri, Alcalde Maior desta dicha Villa digo que pase personalmente al Puesto de Cieneguilla a reconoser la benta Real que a fabor del Capitan Andres Montoia otorgaron Juachin de Anaia y Juana de Anaia ante el Capitan Juan Garcia de la Riva, Alcalde Ordinario que era del Cavildo de esta dicha Villa y costa en dicha escriptura aber bendido el dicho Sitio de La Cieneguilla Juachin de Anaia y Juana de Anaia por la cantidad de ziento y veinte pesos que confiesan en dicha escriptura aber resebido el dicho Juachin y Juana de Anaia de mano de dicho Capitan Andres Montoya de que se dieron por contentos y satisfechos y para que en todo tiempo conste lo firme en dicho dia mes y añno
    Antonio de Uribarri (rubric)

En la Villa de Santa Fee en dicho dia mes y añno estando concluidas estas diligencias que por orden del Señor Coronel Dn. Gervasio Cruzat y Gongora, Governador y Capitan General deste Reino por Su Magestad he seguido delas quales ago remision a dicho Señor para que en su vista determine lo que ayare de justizia que zera como siempre lo major, asi lo decrete, mande y firme con los testigos ynfraescriptos de mi asistenzia a falta de Escribano Publico ni Real que no lo ai en este Reino =
    Antonio de Uribarri (rubric)
    Juan Manuel Chirinos (rubric)
    Felipe Tamaris (rubric)

En la Villa de Santa Fee en siete dias del mes de Noviembre de mil sietesientos treinta y tres años yo el Coronel Dn. Gervasio Cruzat y Gongora, Governador y Capitan General de este Reyno dela Nueba Mexico por Su Magestad devia desir y dige que por quanto las partes que letigan esta causa se han combenido y compuesto ante mi devia mandar y mande se este alo combenido tomando testimonio de ello y se inserte en estos autos. Asi lo provey, mande y firme con los testigos de mi asistensia a falta de Escribano Publico y Real que no lo ay en este Reyno =
    Dn. Gervasio Cruzat y Gongora (rubric)
    Gaspar Bitton (rubric)
    Juan Antonio de Unanue (rubric)

Notes

1. Juana de Anaya Almazán was married three times. Her first husband was Lucas Montaño, whom she married sometime prior to 1710, with whom she had a daughter, María Geronima. The second marriage was in 1726 to Juan Lorenzo de Medina of Mexico City, with whom she had three children: Juan Francisco, María Antonia, and Margarita Antonia. Medina died in 1731. Her third husband was Lucas Miguel Moya. An inventory of Juana's mother's estate was filed in the archives in 1736. Juana wrote her own will in 1736. (Chávez, *Origins*: 124; Kessell, Hendricks, and Dodge, *Royal Crown*: 330n75; SANM I #1224 and SANM I #1226, WPA translations.)
2. For information on Alfonso Rael de Aguilar, see Case 13. For information on the Anaya Almazán grant see Ebright, "Oppressed": 134-36. For general information on the La Cieneguilla area see Post, *La Cieneguilla*, and Snow, *Guici*.
3. In a 1694 document, he is recorded as being a mestizo and a native of Parral, Mexico. He came to New Mexico with his cousins, Baltazar Rodarte and Teresa de Jesús, who were probably the children of Juana Guerrero and Miguel Rodarte. (Kessell, Hendricks, and Dodge, *Boulders*: 490-92, 557n7.)
4. Francisco de Anaya Almazán II was born in New Mexico in 1633. Before the 1680 Pueblo Revolt, he served as alcalde of Taos Pueblo. He participated in the defense of Santa Fe in 1680 and joined Antonio de Otermín's reconquest attempt in 1681. Francisco's third wife was Felipa Sedillo Rico de Rojas. He returned to Santa Fe in 1693, as a sergeant major, with don Diego de Vargas. He died sometime between 1713 and 1716. (Kessell and Hendricks, *Force of Arms*: 239n3.)
5. Felipa Sedillo Rico de Rojas was the wife of Francisco de Anaya Almazán. Upon the death of Francisco, she married Francisco González. Her children were Juana de Anaya Almazán, Salvador de Anaya Almazán, and Joaquín de Anaya Almazán. (Kessell, Hendricks, and Dodge, *Boulders*: 959n64; SANM I #1224, WPA translation.)
6. Salvador de Anaya Almazán's parents were Francisco de Anaya Almazán and Felipa Sedillo Rico de Rojas. He had a sister, Juana, and brother, Joaquín. He married Magdalena de Espinola. Their daughter, María Antonia de Anaya Almazán, married Salvador Dios Blea in 1724. Salvador's second wife was María Francisca Esquivel. Salvador was a presidio soldier in 1704; he was dead by 1733. (Chávez, *Origins*: 125; Kessell, Hendricks, Dodge, and Miller, *Accounts*: 222.)
7. The sense here is that Francisco González acted as a trustee for the money, which Juana and Joaquín were to be given when they came of age.
8. Ventura (Buenaventura) de Esquivel may have been a child of Juan Antonio de Esquivel and María de San Nicolás, both of whom came to New Mexico from Mexico City sometime in 1693 or 1694 with the Farfán Expedition. However, in 1702, when Ventura married Rosa Lucero de Godoy, he said his parents were Antonio de Caraña and María de Esquivel. Ventura and Rosa's daughter, María Francisca de Esquivel, married Salvador de Anaya Almazán. Ventura was a servant and a brother to Antonio de Esquivel. (Chávez, *Origins*: 125, 173, 355.)
9. Gervasio Cruzat y Góngora was a native of Pamplona, Spain. His father was the Marquis of Góngora, and his grandfather, Fausto Cruzat y Góngora, was governor and captain general of the Philippines. Gervasio Cruzat y Góngora was a colonel in the Spanish army, and in 1731, he was sent to New Mexico to succeed Juan Domingo de Bustamante as governor. In 1735, he was replaced by Henrique de Olavidé y Micheleña. Gervasio was considered by some to be strict and conservative in his rulings. (Ebright and Hendricks, *Witches*: 28, 278, 279n7; *Wikipedia*, "Gervasio Cruzat y Góngora," accessed on May 5, 2015).
10. In New Mexico by 1728, Gaspar Bitton (or Viton) was married to María Diega Garduño. His name appears as a witness in many New Mexico court documents of the early eighteenth century. He had at least one son, José Gabriel Garduño (or Viton). (Chávez, *Origins*: 313.)
11. Juan Antonio de Unanue's name appears frequently as a witness in court documents of this period. The name is sometimes spelled "Vranes or Nuanes." To date, no other information has been found out about him. It has been speculated that he was related to the better known Felipe Jacogo de Unanue, a presidio military captain in the 1740s. (Twitchell, *Spanish Archives*, Vol. 1: 8, 2, 101-09, 153-54; Rau, "Unanue to Nuanes": 17.)
12. Antonio de Ulibarrí was born in San Luis Potosí, New Spain. In 1699 he became the alcalde mayor and captain of the El Paso presidio. By 1702 he was married to Juana Hurtado and by 1709 he was alcalde of Santa Cruz. His second wife was Francisca de Misquia. Because of charges made against him by certain New Mexican settlers, he was taken to Mexico City, where he died in 1716. (NMGS, *Aquí*: 54; Kessell, Hendricks, and Dodge, *Boulders*: 46-47.)
13. A juridical document is one that is certified as being done according to law.
14. Joaquín de Anaya Almazán was born in 1697, the son of Francisco de Anaya Almazán and his third wife Felipa Sedillo Rico de Rojas. Joaquín passed the Santa Fe presidio muster of March 29, 1723. He married Margarita de Ortega in 1716. Upon her death, he married Josefa Martín in 1719. (Chávez, *Origins*: 125;

Christmas and Rau, "Una Lista": 52; Barrett, *Spanish Colonial Settlement Landscapes*: 106, 199; Christmas and Rau, *La Cienega*: 12.)
15. Born in 1703, María Antonia de Anaya Almazán was the daughter of Salvador de Anaya Almazán and Magdalena de Espiñola. Her father's second wife was María Francisca de Esquivel. María Antonia married Salvador Dias Blea in 1724. (Chávez, *Origins*: 125.)
16. The word "generalities" referred to any restrictions placed on a witness if they were related to (or had some other connection to) one of the participants in the case.
17. For information on Juan Manuel de Chirinos, see Case 5.
18. Captain Joseph Trujillo was the son of Cristóbal Trujillo and María de Manzanares, who were pre-revolt settlers in New Mexico. Joseph was a presidio soldier and one of the eight soldiers assigned to the Santa Cruz garrison in 1701. Sometime around 1701, he was granted land near San Ildefonso and Santa Cruz; the lands were later validated in 1713. In 1706, Joseph was appointed temporary alcalde at Pecos, while Juan de Ulibarrí was on a campaign. Joseph was an alcalde of Santa Cruz in 1715, and his name appears on Inscription Rock at the El Morro National Monument, New Mexico. (Kessell, Hendricks, Dodge, and Miller, *Disturbances*: 128; Kessell, *Kiva*: 505; Chávez, *Origins*: 297; SANM I #72; SANM I #1136.)
19. A native of Valle de San Bartolomé, Mexico, Felipe Tamaris was the son of Isabel Gutiérrez and Francisco Tamaris. His father, Francisco, was a soldier who was killed by Alfonso Real de Aguilar in a quarrel in 1715. Felipe was also a soldier and one of the few survivors of the Villasur Expedition of 1720. In 1707, he married Magalena Baca, with whom he had two children: Rosa Teresa and Pedro. (Chávez, *Origins*: 292, 394; Kessell, Hendricks, and Dodge, *Disturbances*: 188n9.)
20. [Juan] Antonio [Sotomayor] Montoya was part of the 1692 to 1693 muster at the El Paso presidio, where he originally arrived as a convict. He was born in Mexico City and his family arrived in New Mexico in 1677. In 1693, Antonio arrived in New Mexico and by 1703 he was a cabildo member. Two of his daughters married members of the Durán y Chávez family. He also had a son named Andrés Montoya. (Kessell, Hendricks, and Dodge, *Royal Crown*: 78n23; Chávez, *Origins*: 199, 234; SANM II #94a.)
21. She may have described this assistance as a way of proving her case, suggesting that Francisco saw this as a partial payment of the 555 pesos he owed her.
22. Rosa Lucero de Godoy was the wife of Ventura (Buenaventura) Esquivel. Her parents were Antonio Lucero de Godoy and Antonia Varela de Perea (or Losada). Her father served at the El Paso presidio around 1690. In 1693, her family returned to New Mexico, where her father served as the captain at the Santa Fe presidio; in 1703, he was a member of the cabildo. He died in 1716. The family had land holdings in both Santa Fe and Taos. (Kessell and Hendricks, *Force of Arms*: 487n61; Kessell, Hendricks, and Dodge, *Boulders*: 1167n29; SANM II #53; SANM II #95a; Barrett, *Settlement*: 101-92, 199, 210.)
23. María Francisca de Esquivel was the daughter of Rosa Lucero de Godoy and Ventura de Esquivel, and a granddaughter of Juan Antonio Esquivel and María de St. Nicolás. She was twelve years old when her family traveled from Mexico City to New Mexico with the Farfán Expedition of 1693 to 1694. María Francisca married Salvador Anaya de Almazán. (Chávez, *Origins*: 171; Kessell, Hendricks, and Dodge, *Royal Crown*: 337n19.)
24. Catalina Maese was the granddaughter of Alonso (López) Maese and Catalina Montaño, who fled New Mexcio in 1680. Alonso passed a military muster in El Paso in 1681. Catalina's parents were Miguel Maese and María Varela (or María Perea de Losado) who returned to New Mexico in 1693. Miguel was killed later by Apaches returning from El Paso. Catalina married Juan Antonio Domínguez, and then she married Francisco Rendón in 1727. (Chávez, *Origins*: 217, 371.)
25. Ventura de Esquivel seems to have given his wife, Rosa Lucero de Godoy, and his daughter, María Francisca de Esquivel, permission to testify even though women could legally testify without any such permission.
26. The date, August 12, seems to be out of chronological order. It may be that the testimony was taken earlier and inserted, or perhaps the scribe made an error and it was meant to be the "22nd" of August.
27. He seems to be referring to a different Francisco González than the one featured in this case. There are several men listed with this same name during this time period.
28. Andrés Montoya was the son of Captain Antonio Montoya and María Hurtado. His parents returned to New Mexico with don Diego de Vargas and reclaimed some of their property in Santa Fe. From 1731 to 1732, Andrés was an alcalde mayor of the three northern Queres Pueblos. He married Antonia Lucero de Godoy, and later he married María Sisneros. He died in 1740. This may be the same Montoya who donated "sixteen beams" for San Miguel Chapel in Santa Fe. (Chávez, *Origins*: 235-36; Kubler, *San Miguel*: 23.)
29. Captain Antonio Aguilera de Ysasi was a native of Mexico City who traveled to New Mexico in 1694 with the Farfán Expedition. He was a member of the Santa Fe cabildo by 1697. He also served as *alguacil mayor* (chief constable) from at least 1703 to 1705. (Kessell, Hendricks, and Dodge, *Royal Crown*: 324n52; SANM II #137b; Esquibel, "Residents": 68.)
30. This Joseph Rodríguez may be the Joseph Rodríguez who came to New Mexico from Segovia, Spain. If so, he and his wife, María de Samano, joined the Farfan Expedition of 1693 to 1694. Later, he married María López Conejo, and by 1696 he was living in Santa Cruz. (Chávez, *Origins*: 268-69; Kessell, Hendricks, and Dodge, *Royal Crown*: 328n65.)

31. For information on Cristóbal de Góngora, see Case 5.
32. This is probably a sarcastic remark.
33. This language suggests that the case was settled out of court and with no transcript of what was included in the agreement.

24

FIGHT BETWEEN CHIMAYÓ COUSINS RESULTS IN HEAD INJURY; MOTHER COMPLAINS
September 10-October 23, 1733, Source: SANM II #390

Synposis and editor's notes: When Nicolás Martín hit his cousin, Mateo Martín, in the head with a rock Mateo's mother, Josefa de la Asención, appeared before the lieutenant alcalde, Pedro Sánchez de Iñigo, with a complaint about the assault on her son. While she was there, she also complained about how Nicolás's father had insulted her. Josefa was then the third wife of the long-lived Hernán Martín Serrano, who was born in 1606 and was an encomendero before the 1680 Pueblo Revolt. He returned to New Mexico with General Diego de Vargas and served as a captain and an interpreter. Hernán was Mateo Martín's father and the brother of Luis Martín Serrano, the great-grandfather of Nicolás Martín. Nicolás's parents were Francisco Martín Serrano and Juana García de los Rios. These relationships made Mateo and Nicolás cousins.

The large Martín Serrano family had returned to their lands in Chimayó, New Mexico, in 1692, with the Spanish Reconquest. A 1705 military muster listed nine male adult members of the Martín Serrano family in the Santa Cruz jurisdiction, in which Chimayó was located.[1]

In line with proper Spanish legal procedure, Pedro Sánchez de Iñigo asked Francisco Xavier Romero, a surgeon, to inspect the head injury, fearing that it had penetrated or concussed the skull. Sánchez de Iñigo then took testimony from witnesses, who explained the background of the altercation: When Mateo met Nicolás on the road, Mateo complained about the damage that Nicolás's horse had done to his cornfield. Nicolás said he was a liar and Mateo responded by saying he was a dog. They began to fight but were separated by another cousin, Diego Martín Moraga. This seemed to end the fight, with Nicolás agreeing to pay for the damage to the cornfield. But, Nicolás then picked up a rock and threw it at Mateo, again hitting him on the head. In his testimony, Nicolás said he was just teasing Mateo and did not mean to hit him.

When Josefa de la Asención, Mateo's mother, saw Nicolás's father, Francisco Martín Serrano, she told him about his son's behavior and complained about Francisco's previous insults to her. Francisco told her to shut up and raised his hand, telling her that if he hit her it would be for eternity. Other persons witnessed this and commented on it in their testimony.

In response to Josefa's request, Alcalde Juan Esteban García de Noriega returned and took over the case. He noted that it was being heard according to the "real amparo" (royal protection) for which poor widows were entitled. He ordered that Nicolás be arrested and then made an inventory of his land and possessions in order to sequester them for the court costs. Upon approaching Nicolás to make the arrest, the alcalde, however, found that Nicolás had claimed sanctuary in the Nambé church; later, he moved to the Santa Cruz church. Following standard procedure, García de Noriega went to Santa Cruz and asked fray Manuel de Sopena for permission to interview Nicolás. Then, Mateo Martín, Diego Martín Moraga, Francisco Martín Serrano, and other witnesses gave their testimonies. Meanwhile, Pedro Sánchez de Iñigo inspected the cornfield and carefully recorded the damage. He asked each witness to return so he could read their statements to them and they could ratify them.

He then remitted the case to Governor don Gervasio Cruzat y Góngora. By this time Mateo has recovered from his head wound and Josefa had withdrawn her complaint, apparently satisfied with the alcalde's handling of the case. The governor ordered that Nicolás be released from prison, "or wherever he is to be found," and warned him that if he caused further problems then he would be punished. He also ordered Nicolás to pay for the treatment of Mateo's wound and to compensate the public officials and the witnesses for their lost time, which may have been punishment enough. No comment was made about the threat Francisco Martín Serrano made to Josefa.

Although the crime seems minor, the case turns out to be a good example of the way in which the alcaldes executed Spanish Colonial legal procedures on a local level. In the first paragraph, for instance, Pedro Sánchez de Iñigo duly noted Josefa's accusation as the cabeza del proceso (heading) of the hearing document. This was followed by an investigation of the wound and then testimony from witnesses. All testimony was heard by two witnesses and the lieutenant alcalde. Goods were seized for court costs and a site visit made. The alcalde correctly asked permission from the Santa Clara friar to interview Nicolás. Witness statements were ratified and remission to the governor was noted. Perhaps most important, the outcome of the court case was not a punishment; instead, the conflict was worked out among the people involved, all of whom were related, lived close to each other, and saw each other everyday—which they most likely did for the rest of their lives.

TRANSLATION

Charge against Nicolás Martín[2]

At Villa Nueva de Santa Cruz [de la Cañada] on the 10th of September, 1733, I, Pedro Sánchez [de Iñigo],[3] lieutenant to the alcalde mayor and war captain of this villa and its jurisdiction, am acting as presiding judge along with two assisting witnesses due to the absence of our alcalde mayor, Captain Juan [Esteban] García de Noriega,[4] by virtue of Josefa de la Asención[5] having appeared before me seeking that justice be done.

This was due to the fact that one of her sons named Mateo Martín[6] had been injured by the offender named Nicolás Martín, all of them residents of the puesto of Chimayó. Being attentive to the accusation and complying with my obligation according to my job for the royal justice, I proceeded to the house where the injured person was. I took along with me Francisco Xavier Romero,[7] who has seen a number of injuries and has healed them according to orders given by my predecessors. He, knowing what he knows, found an injury to the head above the eyebrow which was three fingers long and one finger in width where the skin had been cut. Finding what appeared to be a break in the skull, he gave the patient a grain of corn for him to crack with his molars or teeth. Not being able to do that, it was assumed that the wound had penetrated the skull.

Upon all of this being seen by me, I, the lieutenant, and my two assisting witnesses who were, Juan Joseph de la Cerda[8] and don Miguel de Quintana,[9] along with Francisco Xavier Romero, attested to the above. This serves as the charge or heading for the proceedings. So that it is all valid, I signed it acting as presiding judge along with my assisting witnesses on the said day, month and year, etc.

Pedro Sánchez [de Iñigo] (rubric)
Presiding Judge
Miguel de Quintana (rubric)
Juan Joseph de la Cerda (rubric)

Statement of Mateo Martín

Continuing, on the same day, month and year, I, the lieutenant to the alcalde mayor, proceeded to take the confession of Mateo Martín, since he was capable of making it, and for which reason I received his sworn statement which he made to God, Our Lord, and to the sign of the Cross, under which he promised to tell the truth as to what he knows and what he was asked.

He was asked who it was that gave him the wound that he has. He stated that it was Nicolás Martín, son of Francisco Martín [Serrano].[10] He was asked what the reasons were for it. He said that upon coming from his cornfield, he met up with Nicolás Martín, and told him that he had seen the damage that the horses of Nicolás had done to his cornfield on three separate occasions. He said that Nicolás answered him by saying that he was a liar. Mateo then said that it was the truth, telling him that he was the liar. Being tired of hearing what was being said, he told Nicolás that he was nothing but a dog. Due to all of this they got into a fight. Then Diego Martín Moraga,[11] his cousin, came at them to separate them. He did separate them giving Mateo a few blows with his hands and giving Nicolás Martín a hard push. After this they all three continued on their way, Nicolás agreeing to pay Mateo for the damages, Diego Martín Moraga walking between the two. After a short distance of walking on the road, Nicolás went to the side and threw a rock at [Mateo] which resulted in giving him the wound that he has from the blow.

Mateo was asked what other persons were present at the time of the fight. He stated that there was no one else other than Diego Martín Moraga. He said that this was the truth as to what happened, asking for justice. Upon his sworn statement being read back to him, he ratified it according to the sworn statement that he has given, stating that he was twenty some years of age, more or less, stating that he did not know how to sign, thus I, the lieutenant, signed it along with my assisting witnesses on the said day, month and year.

 Pedro Sánchez (rubric)
 Presiding Judge
 Miguel de Quintana (rubric)
 Juan Joseph de la Cerda (rubric)

[Statement of Josefa de la Asención]

 Sir, alcalde mayor and war captain, I, Josefa de la Asención, appear before your majesty in my best and most proper form and say that I complain both in a civil and a criminal way against Nicolás Martín for having injured my son. This complaint has been brought before the royal justice due to damages that were caused by the offender's horses and due to what happened when they were in the company of Diego Martín Moraga. As is my maternal right, I am defending my son because of the injury that almost caused my son to become blind, and because of other things that occurred which destroyed or almost destroyed my personal rights. This other thing happened when Francisco Martín [Serrano] told me that if he raised his hand against me it would be to raise his hand forever. To which, sir, I say that the reason for his words were the poor clothes that I wear and because I am a poor widow without any cattle. He was thinking that he could do the same with me as he has done on other occasions. This would mean that I would have to give up my house due to the poverty of my fields, without there being a person that would come to my aid assisting me and my children, as they are alone and orphans.

 We prostrate ourselves at the feet of your majesty so that he may give me the royal protection of His majesty, who God may guard, which he does as a person who represents the real life image of the king, Our Lord. I swear to God and to the sign of the Holy Cross that this, my written document, is not done in malice, but only to acquire its justice according to that which I can argue according to my right and in what is necessary, etc.

 Josefa de la Asención (rubric)

[Case remitted to the alcalde mayor]

 At Villa Nueva de Santa Cruz [de la Cañada] on the 11th of September, 1736, I, Captain Juan Esteban García de Noriega, alcalde mayor and war captain of this villa and its jurisdiction, took the case as it was written. Being reviewed by me, I accepted it as it was according to its proper legal right. Having reviewed it in response to arguments made by Francisco Martín [Serrano], the elder, the father of Nicolás Martín, I told him that it was necessary to present statements from witnesses in order to proceed according to justice, giving him to understand that this procedure was due to the poor widow and according to the real amparo[12] provided for her. He then stated that those who were present were Pedro Romero,[13] resident of El Paso, Antonio Montoya,[14] his stepson, and Diego Martín Moraga. I insert this within this decree so that I might be able to deliver my obligation according to the office of royal justice. The petitioner not knowing how to write, I, the alcalde mayor signed it, acting as presiding judge with my two assisting witnesses. This petition is attached to the proceedings that are being followed according to what may result as finalized, etc.

    Juan Esteban García de Noriega (rubric)
    Miguel de Quintana (rubric)
    Juan Rael de Aguilar[15] (rubric)

Statement of Diego Martín Moraga

At this Villa of Santa Cruz [de la Cañada] on the 12th of September, 1733, I, Captain Juan Esteban García de Noriega, alcalde mayor and war captain of this villa and its jurisdiction, reviewed the previous proceedings that were completed by my lieutenant Pedro Sánchez. It being necessary for its prosecution, I made to appear before me Diego Martín Moraga, cited by Mateo Martín. Upon his being present, I took his sworn statement which he made to God and to the sign of the Cross and under which he promised to tell the truth according to what he knew and what he was asked.

He was asked if he was present at the time of the fight between Mateo and Nicolás Martín. He stated that while he was fixing his *carreta* [cart], and Mateo Martín being in his presence, he saw that Nicolás Martín was approaching riding his horse. Upon getting there Mateo told Nicolás that his horse had done some damage to his cornfield. Nicolás then responded by telling him that his horse did not eat corn and that he was a liar. Mateo then told him that he was the liar and that he was a dog. For this reason, they got into a fight, with Nicolás picking up some rocks. At this point this witness got in between them and broke up the fight, with Nicolás then agreeing to pay for the damages. Under this agreement they all left together and proceeded on their way.

After a short distance, the three of them being together, Nicolás again picked up some rocks and unexpectedly threw one at Mateo, which caused the injury that he acquired. He, Diego, then gave Nicolás a few blows with his fists and left for his home, where he was joined by the brothers of the aggressor and the one who was injured. He added that no one else was present at the time of the fight, and that this was the truth and is what he knows, and nothing else. Upon his statement being read back to him, he ratified it under the sworn statement that he had made, saying that he was a first cousin to both of them, and forty years of age, more or less. He did not sign because he said that he did not know how. I, the alcalde mayor, signed it along with my assisting witnesses on the said day, month and year.

Juan Esteban García de Noriega (rubric)
Miguel de Quintana (rubric)
Juan Joseph de la Cerda (rubric)

Carreta at Las Golondrinas near Santa Fe, New Mexico. Photograph taken by and courtesy of Doug Lindsay and courtesy of El Rancho de Las Golondrinas Living History Museum. 2013

Proceedings

On the said day, month and year, I, the alcalde mayor, questioned Diego Martín Moraga in regard to the enclosed petition and complaint that Josefa de la Asención presented to me, in which she cites him. This was regarding the statement that was made concerning his presence at the time that Francisco Martín [Serrano], the father of Nicolás Martín, told Josefa de la Asención that when he raised his hand it would be for the rest of eternity. Diego responded and said that he did not hear such a thing, that he was not present at the time that he said it, and that he does not know anything else

other then what he has stated. This he said was the truth, which he ratified, and so that it is valid I, the alcalde mayor, signed it along with my assisting witnesses on the said day, etc.
 Juan Esteban García de Noriega (rubric)
 Miguel de Quintana (rubric)
 Juan Joseph de la Cerda (rubric)

Confiscation of goods
 Continuing on the said day, month and year, I, the alcalde mayor, by virtue of the proceedings that I have received, proceeded to the home of Nicolás Martín to confiscate his goods. I did not find him there because he had taken refuge[16] at the church of the Pueblo of San Francisco de Nambé, from where he moved to this one of Villa Nueva de Santa Cruz [de la Cañada]. I completed the inventory of his goods. I did not take his bed because of the laws and royal orders in which it is so stated.
 The inventory was taken in the following manner: First of all, the house, which consists of one room; one adobe mold; a planted cornfield; an *almud* [dry measurement] of corn and two others as was declared by Francisco Martín, the father of Nicolás. In addition, there were some lands which had not been assigned to him as his son and which are legitimately his according to a land grant which Francisco holds in his favor. These were designated as being recognized as his, all of which were accepted as satisfactory. He did not sign these proceedings which will act as a receipt because he did not know how. I, the alcalde mayor, signed it along with my assisting witnesses on the said day, month and year, etc.
 Juan Esteban García de Noriega (rubric)
 Miguel de Quintana (rubric)
 Juan Joseph de la Cerda (rubric)

Statement of Pedro Romero
 On the said day, month and year, I, the alcalde mayor, made to appear before me Pedro Romero, resident of El Paso, cited by Josefa de la Asención. I received his sworn statement which he made to God and to the sign of the Cross, under which he promised to tell the truth as to what he knew and what he was asked.
 He was asked if he was present when Josefa de la Asención asked Francisco Martín why they had done what was done to her son Mateo Martín. He stated that upon seeing that Mateo was hurt, when he was standing at a short distance away, he heard Josefa de la Asención as follows: "Is it possible sir that we should continue to fight during this time?" Francisco Martín, the father of Nicolás, then answered her saying, "Shut your mouth." Josefa de la Asención then told him, "Why should I shut up? Is it because you hate me? When you raised your hand against me, you said it would last for an eternity." This is how he understood what she said to Francisco

Martín. This he says is what he saw and heard and nothing else. He was asked if Diego Martín Moraga was present at the time. He stated shortly after that happened he saw Diego approaching.

This he says is the truth and does not know anything else. He was asked if he was related in any way to any of these parties. He stated that he was in no way related. Upon his sworn statement being read back to him he ratified it under the same oath that he had made. He stated that he was between thirty-three and thirty-four years of age, but did not sign because he said that he did not know how. I, the alcalde mayor, signed along with my assisting witnesses on the said day, month and year, etc.

Juan Esteban García de Noriega (rubric)
Miguel de Quintana (rubric)
Juan Joseph de la Cerda (rubric)

Statement of Antonio Montoya

On the said day, month and year, I, the alcalde mayor, made to appear before me Antonio Montoya, cited by Josefa de la Asención, from whom I took his sworn statement which he made to God and to the sign of the Cross, under which he promised to tell the truth as to what he knew and what he was asked.

He was asked if he was present at the time that Mateo Martín arrived with an injury. He stated that being at the door of his home he saw him walking toward him with Francisco Martín, the father of Nicolás Martín. He was asked what he heard at the time. He said that he had heard Josefa de la Asención say, "Is it possible that they have done that to my son?" Hearing this, Francisco Martín responded by telling her to shut her mouth, "When I raise my hand I will uphold it for an eternity."

This he said is what happened, what he heard, and nothing else, because he immediately went into his home. Upon his sworn statement being read back to him he ratified it under the sworn statement that he had made. He stated that he was thirty years of age, more or less.

He was asked if he was related to any of the parties. He stated that he was not related to anyone. He was raised by Fernando Martín, late husband of Josefa de la Asención, which is the reason they call him a stepson, but he is not related. He did not sign his sworn statement because he said that he did not know how. I, the alcalde mayor, signed it along with my assisting witnesses on the said day, month and year.

Juan Esteban García de Noriega (rubric)
Miguel de Quintana (rubric)
Juan Joseph de la Cerda (rubric)

Recognition of the damage done

Continuing, on the said day, month and year, I, the alcalde mayor, to better understand the substance and merit of these proceedings decided it would be a good thing to go and see the damage that Nicolás Martín did to the cornfield of Mateo. Being guided by Antonio Montoya, above cited, along with my assisting witnesses, I examined the part that was being questioned. Upon seeing it, I saw that there were some ears of corn that had been chewed upon and somewhat eaten and others that were perhaps touched but not totally eaten. In all there were twelve to fourteen ears of corn that were somewhat damaged. So that this proceeding is valid I signed it along with my assisting witnesses on the said day, month and year, etc.

 Juan Esteban García de Noriega (rubric)
 Miguel de Quintana (rubric)
 Juan Joseph de la Cerda (rubric)

Ratification of Mateo Martín
 On the 2nd of October, 1733, I, the alcalde mayor and war captain, in order to continue with the prosecution of these proceedings went to ratify the statement of the parties involved as well as those of the witnesses. The first one to ratify his statement was Mateo Martín, the injured person, and being at his home, I, the alcalde mayor, along with my assisting witnesses, read back to him the sworn statement that he had made. Upon having heard it and understanding it, being certain that it was as he had made it, and not having anything to add or delete, he affirmed and ratified it as being correct according to the sworn statement that he had made. He did not sign because he did not know how, so I, the alcalde mayor, signed it along with my assisting witnesses on the said day, month and year as it was, etc.

 Juan Esteban García de Noriega (rubric)
 Miguel de Quintana (rubric)
 Juan Joseph de la Cerda (rubric)

[*Editor's note*: Ratifications for Diego Martín, Pedro Romero, and Antonio Montoya were also taken using nearly the same language. These are included in the transcription, but are not translated here.]

Statement of Nicolás Martín
 At the Villa Nueva de Santa Cruz [de la Cañada] on the 15th of October, 1733, I, the alcalde mayor, obtained permission from the Reverend Father Preacher fray Manuel de Sopena,[17] minister of Villa Nueva de Santa Cruz, so that I can obtain a sworn statement from Nicolás Martín, who had taken refuge in the church of this villa. Then I, along with my two assisting witnesses, took the sworn statement of Nicolás Martín, which he made under his proper legal right before God, Our Lord and the sign of the Cross, under which he promised to tell the truth about what he knew and what he was asked.
 He was asked why it was that he had taken sanctuary. He responded and said

that it was because of the cracked skull that he had given to Mateo Martín, his cousin. He was asked what the reasons were for doing it. He stated that it was because of some damage that his horse had done to Mateo's cornfield, which resulted in a fight that was stopped by Diego Martín Moraga. Then the three of them were walking together in a friendly manner and having a rock in his hand and without intention of hurting him, he threw it at Mateo, being that they were always teasing each other. Having injured him, without intending to do so, and upon seeing the blood flowing and being afraid of the royal justice, he sought refuge. He stated that he did not do it intentionally, not trying to hurt him.

He stated that this was the truth and was what happened and nothing else. Upon his sworn statement being read back to him he stated that it was properly written and that he did not have anything else to add or to delete, and he ratified once, twice and three times. He was asked how old he was, and he replied saying that he did not know. He did not sign because he did not know how. I, the alcalde mayor, signed it along with my assisting witnesses on the said day, month and year.

 Juan Esteban García de Noriega (rubric)
 Miguel de Quintana (rubric)
 Juan Rael de Aguilar (rubric)

Ratification of Nicolás Martín

On the 16th of October, 1733, I, the alcalde mayor, made known to Nicolás Martín his above sworn statement, word by word. He upon having heard and understood it stated that it was correct according to the way he had made it. He does not have anything to add or to delete and ratifies it according to the sworn statement that he has made. So that it is valid, I, the alcalde mayor, signed it along with my assisting witnesses on the said day.

 Juan Esteban García de Noriega (rubric)
 Miguel de Quintana (rubric)
 Juan Rael de Aguilar (rubric)

Decree of Remission

At Villa Nueva de Santa Cruz on the 17th of October, 1733, I, the alcalde mayor, have entirely completed the investigation of the complaint made by Josefa de la Asención and her son, Mateo Martín. Everything has been received and compiled for these proceedings. Because I have taken the sworn statement of Nicolás Martín along with his ratification, and because Mateo is once again healthy as is seen by the statement of the curandero Francisco Xavier Romero found at the bottom of these proceedings,[18] I submit them to the governor. This is so that upon his review he will order what he decides. So that it is valid I signed as presiding judge along with my assisting witnesses on the said day, month and year, etc.

Juan Esteban García de Noriega (rubric)
Miguel de Quintana (rubric)
Juan Rael de Aguilar (rubric)

[Final determination]
At the Villa of Santa Fe on the 23rd of October, 1733, I, Colonel don Gervasio Cruzat y Góngora,[19] governor and captain general of this kingdom of New Mexico, have reviewed the proceedings of this criminal case against Nicolás Martín made by a complaint from Josefa de la Asención for having injured a son of hers named Mateo Martín. Nicolás having been excused by Josefa de la Asención from her complaint and her son Mateo being found once again healthy and at no risk according to the statement of the *cirujano* [surgeon] who has healed him named Francisco Romero, I should order and do order that Nicolás Martín be released from the prison where he is found. He is to be placed at liberty with the understanding that if he would ever again cause problems for Mateo Martín he will be forced to appear before me and I will impose upon him the penalty that the laws allow.

He will pay the expenses demanded, compensating for that which was attended to including the expenses for the healing as well as any other minor expenses and damages which followed regarding losses to the official work or personal occupation. I thus approve, order and sign this, along with my assisting witnesses due to the lack of a public or royal scribe, there not being one in this kingdom.

Don Gervasio Cruzat y Góngora (rubric)
Gaspar Bitton[20] (rubric)
Juan Antonio de Unanue[21] (rubric)

TRANSCRIPTION

Auto de Cabesa de Proseso Contra Nicolas Martin

En la Villa Nueba de Santa Cruz en diez dias del mes de Septiembre de mill setezientos y treinta y tres años yo Pedro Sanchez, Theniente de Alcalde Mayor y Capitan Aguerra desta dicha Villa y su jurisdiction actuando como Jues Receptor con dos testigos de mi assistenzia en auciensia del Capitan Juan Garcia de Noriega mi Alcalde Maior en virtud de aver comparesido ante mi Josepha de la Asencion, diziendo que pedia justizia.

Por averle erido a un hijo suyo llamado Matheo Martin siendo el transgresor Nicolas Martin vezinos todos del Puesto de Chimayo, y en atension alo delatado por la dicha cumpliendo con mi obligazion segun mi empleo y delato de la Real Justizia pase ala cassa donde se hallaba el erido llebando en mi compania a Francisco Xabier Romero quien ha reconosido otras heridas y curandolas por horden de mis antesesores y reconosiendo esta halle una erida en el rostro ariva dela seja tres dedos de largo la sesura y un dedo de ancho roto el curtiz y segun demuestra agugerado el casco y dandole a el paziente un grano de mais a que lo quebrara con las muelas o dientes no pudo en que parase demuestra ser penetrante la erida que vista y reconosida por mi dicho Theniente y los dos testigos de mi assistensia que lo fueron Juan Joseph de la Zerda y Dn. Miguel de Quintana y el dicho Francisco Xavier Romero conquienes di fee, y esta deligencia sirbe de auto primero de cabesa de proceso que para que conste lo firme acutuando como Juez Receptor con los ynfraescriptos testigos de mi asistenzia en dicho dia, mes y ano fecho ut supra __ Enmendado vale

    Pedro Sanchez (rubric)
    Juez Receptor
    Miguel de Quintana (rubric)
    Juan Joseph de la Serda (rubric)

Declaracion de Mateo Martin

    Y luego yncontinenti en dicho dia, mes y año yo dicho Theniente de Alcalde Mayor pase a tomar su confesion a Matheo Martin por allarle capaz para poderle hazer para cullo efecto le resevi juramento por Dios Nuestro Señor y la Señal dela Cruz devajo de cuyo cargo prometio dezir verdad en lo que supiera y le fuera preguntado.

    Siendole quien le dio la herida que tiene; Dijo que Nicolas Martin hijo de Francisco Martin; Preguntado que motibos ubo; Dijo que biniendo este declarante de su milpa se topo con el dicho Nicolas Martin y que le dijo fueze a ver el daño que le avian echo sus vestias por tres veses en su milpa y que le respondio era un embustero y que a estas razones es verdad que le respondio adolerido de los daños resevidos, que era un perro y que a estas razones se travaron llendose para este declarante el dicho Nicolas Martin Moraga, su primo, y que los aparto dandole a este declarante unos punetes y a el dicho Nicolas Martin un arempujon que aviendose ya avenido el dicho Nicolas a pagarle el daño se binieron todos tres biniendo en medio de los dos pleiteantes, dicho Diego Martin Moraga y que a poca distancia de camino se salio por un lado dicho Nicolas y le tiro una pedrada que lo privo resiviendo la erida que tiene del golpe.

    Preguntado que otras personas se hallaron presentes ala refriega. Dijo que no ubo mas que el dicho Diego Martin Moraga y que esta es la verdad y lo que paso y que pide justizia y leida esta su declaracion se ratifico en ella devajo del juramento que fecho tiene, es de edad de veinte años poco mas o menos y dijo no saber firmar, firmela yo dicho Theniente con los ynfraescriptos testigos de mi assistenzia en dicho dia, mes y año __

    Pedro Sanchez (rubric)
    Jues Receptor
    Juan Joseph de la Serda (rubric)
    Miguel de Quintana (rubric)

Señor Alcalde Mayor y Capitan Aguerra Josepha dela Asension ante Vuestra Magestad paresco en el derecho y lugar y al mio conbenga y digo que me querello sibil y criminalmente de Nicolas Martin por aber enposibilitado a mi hijo como consta ala Real Justizia por un daño que ysieron las bestias del dicho trasgressor y biniendo en compania de Diego Moraga y en causa de aber susedido de la cantelasion del dicho trasgressor defendiendo mi derecho maternal abiendo traydo mi hijo a mi presensia de sega por que lo abien puesto asi la respuesta que resebio fue destrasando mi persona que fue disiendome que cuando alsara la mano para mi fuera para la eternidad a que Señor fue causa el traje tanto que como pobre mujer y desbacuda y buida temorosa de que con migo no se ysiere lo mesmo que a ejecutado y otras beses large mi casa y mi pobresa en los campos sin aber persona que de mi se me la allo Señor y mis criaturas como solos y buerfanos.

Nos postramos a los pies de Vuestra Magestad y me diera el amparo Real de Su Magestad, que Dios Guarde, como a persona que representa la biba ymagen del Rey Nuestro Señor y juro por Dios y la Señal de la Santa Cruz no ser este mi escrito de malicia sino por alcansar su Justicia y en todo lo que alegar puedo en mi derecho y lo nesesario, ut supra.

    Josepha de la Asension (rubric)

En la Villa Nueba de Santa Cruz en onze dias del mes de Septiembre de mil setezientos y treinta y seis años ante mi el Capitan Juan Esteban Garcia de Noriega Alcalde Mayor y Capitan Aguerra desta dicha Villa y su jurisdiccion la presento la contenida en ella y por mi vista la ube por presentada en quanto a luger en derecho y aviendo visto su relatibo alas razones que Francisco Martin, el viejo, padre de Nicolas Martin le dije es nesesario presente ynformazion de testigos para proseder en justizia y aviendole dado a entender este auto reziviendola por pobre vuida en el Real amparo dijo que quien estava presente es Pedro Romero vezino del Paso y Antonio Montoya su entenado y Diego Martin Moraga que con el dolor de ver a su hijo como selo avian puesto no se acuerda de otros cullas razones tube por combeniente expresar y ynsertar en este auto para el descargo de mi obligazion y oficio dela Real Justizia y no sabiendo firmar la suplicante la firme yo dicho Alcalde Mayor autuando como Juez Receptor con dos testigos de mi asistenzia quedando acomulada esta petision a los autos que se estan siguiendo por lo que de ella resulta fecha ut supra.

    Juan Estevan Garcia de Noriega (rubric)
    Juan Rael de Aguilar (rubric)
    Miguel de Quintana (rubric)

Declaracion de Diego Martin Moraga
    En la Villa Nueva de Santa Cruz en dose dias del mes de Septiembre de mill

setezientos treinta y tres años yo el Capitan Juan Estevan Garcia de Noriega, Alcalde Mayor y Capitan Aguerra desta dicha Villa y su jurisdicion aviendo visto las deligencias anteriores echas por mi Theniente Pedro Sanchez y ser nesesario para la prosecucion de ellas tube por combeniente hazer pareser ante mi a Diego Martin Moraga sitado de Matheo Martin y presente le resevi juramento por Dios y la Señal de la Cruz devajo de cullo cargo prometio dezir verdad en lo que supiere y le fuere preguntado.

Siendole si se hallo presente ala reyerta que Mateo y Nicolas Martin tubieron? Dijo que estando componiendo su carreta vido benir a Nicolas Martin a cavallo estando con este declarante Matheo Martin quien dijo al dicho Nicolas hombre mira que tu bestia me ha echo daño y que el dicho Nicolas le respondio que su vestia no comia mais que era un embustero y que estas rasones le dijo Matheo que el era el embustero y que era un perro y que sobre esto se travaron cogiendo piedras Nicolas y que este declarante se metio de por medio y los compuso quedando el dicho Nicolas a pagar el daño a Matheo.

Que en esta fee se vino este declarante con los dos y a poca distanacia biniendo los tres cojio piedras el dicho Nicolas y de ymproviso le tiro con una y le dio la erida que tiene y que no lo pudo remediar que viendo erido al dicho matheo le dio este declarante unas punetes a Nicolas y se bino a su casa este declarante que de alli binieron los hermanos del transgresor, y el erido se fue a su casa que no se hallaron otros ala refriega.

Que esta es la verdad y lo que sabe, y no otra cossa y siendole leida esta su declaracion se ratifico en ella so cargo del juramento que fecho tiene es primer hermano de los dos y de edad de quarenta años poco mas o menos y no firmo por que dijo no saber firmelo yo dicho Alcalde Mayor con los ynfraescriptos testigos de mi assistenzia en dicho dia, mes y año = tachado no vale =deligensia

    Juan Esteban Garcia de Noriega (rubric)
    Miguel de Quintana (rubric)
    Juan Joseph de la Serda (rubric)

En dicho dia mes y año yo dicho Alcalde Mayor sobre el punto dela ynclusa petision y querella que Josepha de la Asencion me presento en que zita al anterior declarante Diego Martin Moraga so cargo del juramento que en su declaracion tiene fecho le exsamine sobre el punto de su se hallo presente cuando Francisco Martin padre de Nicolas Martin dijo ala dicha Josepha dela Asencion que cuando alsara la mano seria para la eternida: Respondio y dijo que ni oyo tales voses ni se hallo presente a el tiempo en que la dicha lo zita y que no sabe ni vido mas que lo que tiene declarado y que esta es la verdad en que se ratifico y para que conste la firme yo dicho Alcalde Mayor con los ynfraescriptos testigos de mi assistenzia en dicho dia, ut supra

    Juan Esteban Garcia de Noriega (rubric)
    Miguel de Quintana (rubric)
    Juan Joseph de la Serda (rubric)

Confisco de bienes y deposito

Y luego yncontinente en dicho dia, mes y año yo dicho Alcalde Mayor en virtud de las diligencias por me rezevidas paze ala casa de Nicolas Martin para confiscar sus bienes, y no enbarque su persona por hallarse refugiada en la yglesia sagrada del Pueblo de San Francisco de Nambe de donde se traspuso a esta dela Villa Nueba de Santa Cruz en cullo virtud hize ynbentario de los vienes, no embargando la cama por leyes y disposicion Real y los expresa en la forma y manera sigiente.

Primeramente la cassa que se compone de una zala; yten una adovera; yten una milpa sembrada en ella; una almud de mais y dos enbosadas segun declaro Francisco Martin padre del contenido como asi mismo no aberle señalado tierras al dicho su hijo delas que por legitima le tocan dela merzed que a su favor tiene, en cuya virtud lo señale por depositario de los reconosidos quedando a dar satisfaction de ellos, y no firmo este auto para que sirbiese de resivo por que dijo no saber, firmelo yo dicho Alcalde Mayor con los ynfraescriptos de mi assistenzia en dicho dia, mes y año ut supra _

    Juan Esteban Garcia de Noriega (rubric)
    Miguel de Quintana (rubric)
    Juan Joseph de la Serda (rubric)

Declaracion de Pedro Romero

En dicho dia, mes y año yo dicho Alcalde Maior hize pareser ante mi a Pedro Romero vezino del Paso sitado de Josepha de la Asencion aquien resevi juramento por Dios y la Señal de la Cruz devajo de cullo cargo prometio dezir verdad en lo que supiera y le fuera preguntado.

Siendole si se hallo presente cuando Josepha de la Asencion dijo a Francisco Martin qur por que le avian puesto a su hijo Matheo Martin de aquella suerte; dijo que viendo benir al dicho Matheo erido estando parado a poca distanzia oyo dezir ala dicha Josepha de la Asencion es posible Señores asta cuando emos de andar en pleitos y que Francisco Martin, padre del dicho Nicolas le dijo calle la voca y que la dicha Josepha de la Asencion le respondio por que tengo de callar por que me tiene amenasada que cuando el lebanto la mano para mi a de ser para la eternidad;

Que esto es lo que vido y oyo y no otra cossa; preguntado si estava alli Diego Martin Moraga? Dijo que no que despues de un rato lo bido benir y que esta es la berdad y no sabe otra cosa; preguntado si toca alas generales alguna de estas partes; Dijo que no que en ninguna. Y siendole leida esta su declaracion se ratifico en ella devajo del juramento que fecho tiene y dijo ser de edad de treinta y tres a treinta y quatro años; y no firmo por que dijo no saber, firmela yo dicho Alcalde Mayor con los ynfraescriptos testigos de mi assistenzia en dicho dia, mes y año fecho, ut supra_

    Juan Esteban Garcia de Noriega (rubric)

Miguel de Quintana (rubric)
Juan Joseph de la Serda (rubric)

Declaracion de Antonio Montoya

En dicho dia, mes y año yo dicho Alcalde Maior hize pareser ante mi a Antonio Montoya zitado de Josepha de la Asencion a quien resevi juramento por Dios y la Señal de la Santa Cruz, devajo de cullo cargo prometio dezir verdad en lo que supiere y le fuere preguntado.

Siendole si se hallo presente a el tiempo que vino erido Matheo Martin? Dijo que estando en la puerta de su casa lo vido benir con los hijos de Francisco Martin, padre de Nicolas Martin. Preguntado que razones o vozes oyo. Dijo que lo que oyo dezir a Josepha de la Asencion fue, es possible que asi me aigan puesto a mi hijo, y que a estas razones respondio el dicho Francisco Martin padre de Nicolas disiendole calla esa voca que si yo levanto la mano la e de echar ala eternidad que esto es lo que paso y oyo y no otra cossa por que luego se metio a su casa y que esta es la verdad y lo que sabe y leida esta su declaracion se ratifico en ella devajo del juramento que fecho tiene es de edad de treinta años poco mas o menos; preguntado si toca alas generales a alguna de las partes; Dijo que a ninguna, que lo crio Fernando Martin esposo que fue de la dicha Josepha de la Asencion por culla causa le llaman entenado pero que no lo es y no firmo esta su declaracion por que dijo no saver firmela yo dicho Alcalde Mayor con los ynfraescritos testigos de mi assistenzia en dicho dia mes y año __

Juan Estevan Garcia de Noriega (rubric)
Miguel de Quintana (rubric)
Juan Joseph de la Serda (rubric)

Reconocimiento del daño

Y luego incontinente en dicho dia, mes y año yo dicho Alcalde Mayor para la substancia y merito destas deligencias tube por combeniente pasar a reconoser el daño que Matheo avia rezevido en su milpa de Nicolas Martin y siendo guiado por Antonio Montoya ariva zitado con los ynfraescriptos de mi asistenzia reconosi por la parte en que seme manifesto solo despartadas unas masorcas y medio comidas otras que mirado en juisio se repute todo por doze o catorze masorcas y para que conste desta deligencia la firme con los dichos testigos de mi asistenzia en dicho dia, mes y año, ut supra

Juan Estevan Garcia de Noriega (rubric)
Miguel de Quintana (rubric)
Juan Joseph de la Serda (rubric)

Ratificasion de Matheo Martin

En dos dias del mes de Octubre de mill setecientos y treinta y tres años yo dicho Alcalde Mayor y Capitan Aguerra para la prosecucion destas diligencias pase ala ratificazion asi ala parte como de los testigos y siendo la primera la de Matheo Martin erido estando en su casa yo dicho Alcalde Mayor con los testigos de mi assistenzia le fue leida la declaracion que tiene fecha ante mi Theniente y aviendola oido y entendido dijo estar segun y como la tiene echa y que no tiene que anadir ni quitar a ella y que en ella se afirma y ratifica so cargo del juramento que fecho tiene y no firmo por no saber firmela yo dicho Alcalde Mayor con los ynfraescriptos testigos de mi assistenzia en dicho dia mes y año fecho ut supra

 Juan Estevan Garcia de Noriega (rubric)
 Miguel de Quintana (rubric)
 Juan Joseph de la Serda (rubric)

Ratificazion de Diego Martin Moraga

Y luego incontinenti en dicho dia, mes y año yo dicho Alcalde Maior hize pareser ante mi a Diego Martin Moraga y presente le hize notoria la declaracion que fecha tiene leyendosela de verbo ad berbum y aviendole oido y entendido dijo estar segun y como la tiene fecha que esta bien escripta que en ella se ratifica y ratifico y que no tiene que anair ni quitar so cargo de el juramento que fecho tiene y no firmo por no saber firmela yo dicho Alcalde Maior con los testigos de mi assistenzia en dicho dia, mes y año.

 Juan Estevan Garcia de Noriega (rubric)
 Miguel de Quintana (rubric)
 Juan Rael de Aguilar (rubric)

Ratificazion de Pedro Romero

En dicho dia, mes y año yo dicho Alcalde Maior hize pareser ante mi a Pedro Romero vezino del Paso y residente en este Reyno y hallandose presente le fue leida la declaracion que fecha tiene y aviendola oido y entendido de verbo ad verbum dijo esta bien escripta y segun y como la tiene echa y en ella se ratifico devajo del juramento que fecho tiene y dijo que no tiene que anadir ni quitar y no firmo por no saber firmela yo dicho Alcalde Mayor con los testigos de mi assistenzia en dicho dia, mes y año __

 Juan Estevan Garcia de Noriega (rubric)
 Miguel de Quintana (rubric)
 Juan Rael de Aguilar (rubric)

Ratificazion de Antonio Montoya

    En dicho dia, mes y año yo dicho Alcalde Mayor hize pareser ante mi a Antonio Montoya aquien presente le hize nottoria la declaracion que fecha tiene y aviendola sido de verbo ad verbum dijo esta bien escripta segun y como la tiene fecha y que no tiene que anadir ni quitar y en ella se afirmo y ratifico so cargo del juramento que fecho tiene y no firmo por no saber firmela yo dicho Alcalde Maior con los testigos de mi assistenzia en dicho dia   Juan Estevan Garcia de Noriega (rubric)

    Miguel de Quintana (rubric)

    Juan Rael de Aguilar (rubric)

Declaracion de Nicolas Martin

    En la Villa Nueba de Santa Cruz en quinse dias del mes de Octubre de mill setesientos y treinta y tres años yo dicho Alcalde Mayor aviendome dado su beneplasito el Reverendo Padre Predicador Fray Manuel de Sopena, Cura Ministro dela Villa Nueva de Santa Cruz para que parase a tomar declaracion a Nicolas Martin refugiado en la Yglesia desta dicha Villa con dos testigos de mi assistenzia pase a dicha deligensia y para este efecto le rezevi juramento a dicho Nicolas Martin en toda forma de derecho que lo hizo por Dios Nuestro Señor y la Señal dela Cruz so cullo cargo prometio desir verdad en lo que supiera y le fuera echo de cargo.

    Siendole por que esta retraido; respondio y dijo que por una descadabradura que dio a Matheo Martin su primo; preguntado que motibos tubo para ello? Dijo que sobre un daño que su bestia hizo en la milpa de dicho Mateo se travaron y que Diego Martin Moraga los compuso y biniendo los tres ya amistados es verdad traia este declarante una piedra en la mano y que sin yntencion danada le tiro a dicho Matheo por que siempre se chansean y que aviendolo erido sin querer viendole la sangre temoroso del brazo de la Real Justizia se retrajo que no lo hizo advertidamene ni con yntenzion de dagnificarlo.

    Que esta es la verdad y lo que paso y no otra cosa y siendole leida esta su declaracion dijo estar bien escrita y que no tiene que anadir ni quitar y en ella se ratifico por una, dos y tres vezes y preguntado que edad tiene, dijo que no sabe quantos años tiene y no firmo por que dijo no saber, firmela yo dicho Alcalde Mayor con los testigos de mi assistenzia en dicho dia, mes y año.

    Juan Estevan Garcia de Noriega (rubric)

    Miguel de Quintana (rubric)

    Juan Rael de Aguilar (rubric)

Ratificazion de Nicolas Martin

    En dies y seis dias del mes de Octubre de mill setezientos y treinta y tres años yo dicho Alcalde Maior hize notaria la declaracion de arriba a Nicolas Martin de verbo ad verbum y aviendola oido y entendido dijo estar segun y como la tiene echa y que no tiene que anadir ni quitar y en ella se ratifico devajo del juramento que fecho tiene y para que conste lo firme yo dicho Alcalde Mayor con los testigos de mi asistenzia en dicho dia

 Juan Esteban Garcia de Noriega (rubric)
 Miguel de Quintana (rubric)
 Juan Rael de Aguilar (rubric)

Auto de Remision
 En la Villa Nueva de Santa Cruz en dies y siete dias del mes de Octubre de mill setezientos y treinta y tres años yo dicho Alcalde Mayor aviendo rezevido la vaja de querella que haze Josepha de la Asencion y su hijo Matheo Martin rezevidola y acomuladala a estas deligencias tomado su declaracion a Nicolas Martin y su ratificazion y estar el dicho Matheo ya bueno como consta por la declaracion que al pie de dicha vaja hizo Francisco Xavier Romero hago remission al Señor Governador para que en su vista provea lo que fuese servido y para que conste la firme como Juez Receptor con los ynfraescriptos testigos de mi assistenzia en dicho dia mes y año fecho ut supra

 Juan Esteban Garcia de Noriega (rubric)
 Miguel de Quintana (rubric)
 Juan Rael de Aguilar (rubric)

 En la Villa de Santa Fee en veinte y tres dias del mes de Octubre de mill setesientos treinta y tres años yo el Coronel Dn. Gervasio Cruzat y Góngora, Governador y Capitan General de este Reyno dela Nueva Mexico en vista de los hautos de esta causa criminal fulminada contra Nicolas Martin por querellas presentadas de Josepha de la Asencion por haverle herido a un hijo suyo llamado Mateo Martin y haviendose apartado que desistido de dicha querella la referida Josepha de la Asencion y hallarse sano y fuera de todo riesgo el dicho Mateo Martin como costa por la declaracion de el sirujano que le ha curado que se llama Francisco Romero devia mandar y mande que dicho Nicolas Martin salga de la prision en que se halla y sea puesto en libertad con apersivimiento de que si en otra occasion tubiere disensiones y causare agravios a dicho Mateo Martin se tendra presente todo lo actuado en este proseso para inponerle la pena que segun leyes del derecho esta dispuesta y pagara las costas prosesales indemnidando ala atendida asi la presento que pudiere inportar la curasion como las menos causos y perjuisios que se le han podido seguir en los ministerios y ocupasiones de su travajo personal. Asi lo provey, mande y firme con los testigos de mi asistensia a falte de Escribano Publico y Real que no lo ay en este Reyno

 Dn. Gervasio Cruzat y Gongora (rubric)
 Gaspar Bitton (rubric)
 Juan Antonio de Unanue (rubric)

Notes

1. Salazar, "1705 New Mexico Muster": 8-21.
2. Nicolás Martín was the son of Francisco Martín Serrano and Juana García de los Rios; the grandson of Luis Martín Serrano II and Antonia de Miranda; and the great-grandson of Luis Martín Serrano I and Catalina Salazar. All were settlers in the Chimayó area before the 1680 Pueblo Revolt. (Chávez, *Origins*: 72-73, 222-25.)
3. Pedro Sánchez de Iñigo II was born about 1695 (or at least before the Pueblo Revolt of 1696). He was the grandson of Juana López and the son of Pedro Sánchez de Iñigo I (who died in 1720) and Leonor Baca. His aunt was Francisca Sánchez de Iñigo, who was the wife of Juan García de Noriega. He was the son-in-law of Miguel de Quintana and Gertrudis Torres, and he was married to Michaela Quintana. In 1745, Pedro Sánchez de Iñigo II is referred to as a captain with a *rancho* in Chimayó. He was still alive in 1764. (Chávez, *Origins*: 279-80; SANM II #468; Moore, "Guaje Canyons": 167-69.)
4. Juan Esteban García de Noriega was the son of Juan García de Noriega and Francisca Sánchez de Iñigo (cited above). He was married to Luisa Gómez Luján (or Gómez de Castillo). In 1735, he petitioned for land in the area, but was denied. He was the alcalde of Santa Cruz in 1736. In the inventory attached to his will, he left, among other things, a mason's trowel and plumb. (Chávez, *Origins*: 182; SANM I #386, SANM I #347, and SANM I #1225, all WPA translations.)
5. Josefa de la Asención (González) was the third wife of Hernán Martín Serrano, the brother of Luis Martín Serrano II. Hernán claimed to have been in New Mexico by 1633, as a captain and encomendero, having returned with Diego de Vargas. Hernán's father (of the same name) came with Governor Juan de Oñate as a sergaent. The younger Hernán operated an *obraje* or weaving shop in pre-revolt Santa Fe. Josefa and Hernán were the parents of Andrés, Mateo, Tomosa, and María. (Chávez, *Origins*: 72, 224; Esquibel, "Thirty-eight Adobe House1608-1699":125.)
6. Mateo Martín was the son of Josefa de la Asención and Hernán Martín Serrano. Mateo was married to Antonia Maese. Together they had twin sons, in 1730, both of whom were named Joaquín. They also had a daughter, perhaps adopted, who was named Inez Griego. (Chávez, *Origins*: 224.)
7. A native of Mexico City, Francisco Xavier Romero married María de la Cruz in 1693. He was in Santa Fe in 1694; later, he moved to Chimayó, where he was a shoemaker and practiced medicine. In 1715, he was called upon to inspect injuries inflicted by Diego Martín on another person from Chimayó. Also, late in November of that year, he was sentenced to work in the obraje or textile mill of former governor Valverde. He escaped, taking sanctuary in a church , probably in Albuquerque. After Albuquerque residents begged that he remain in the villa to cure their wounds and diseases, his sentence was commuted to a two years treating the sick without pay. Late in 1716, a land grant he held in Santa Cruz was revalidated by Governor Felix Martínez. In this case, he is referred to as both a curandero and a surgeon. (Chávez, *Origins*: 273; NMGS, *New Mexico Baptisms*: 23; Tigges and Salazar, *Colonial Lives*: 160, 162; SANM I #320, WPA translation; West, "Right of Asylum": 150-51.)
8. A native of Michoacán, Mexico, Juan Joseph de la Cerda was the son of Juan de la Cerda and María de Chavarria. He was in Santa Cruz in 1721, when he married Antonia Sánchez, the daughter of Pedro Sánchez de Iñigo I and María Luján. Juan and Antonia had one son named Juan and possibly another son, Francisco de la Cerda. (Chávez, *Origins*: 159.)
9. For information on Miguel de Quintana, see Case 23.
10. Francisco Martín Serrano was the son of Luis Martín Serrano II and Antonia de Miranda. He married Juana Laurera and then Juana García de los Rios in 1694. They had twelve children, including Nicolás Martín. In the early eighteenth-century, Francisco and a cousin, Cristóbal Martín Serrano I (another son of Hernán Martín Serrano), were involved in a series of lawsuits over some land in Río Arriba. (Kessell, Hendricks, and Dodge, *Boulders*: 962n76, 1149; SANM I #490, SANM I #496, SANM I #504, SANM I #515, and SANM I #523, all WPA translations.)
11. Diego Martín Moraga was the son of Cristóbal Martín Serrrano I and Antonia Moraga all of whom lived in Chimayó. Diego married Manuela de Vargas in 1714; the following year, he was charged with hitting Joseph Vásquez and biting his finger during a fight in Chimayó. A transcription and translation of the document relating to the latter is found in Tigges and Salazar, *Spanish Colonial Lives*: 160-71, 181n1.
12. The term "real amparo" means "royal protector" (or supporter) of the poor. (*Velasquez Dictionary*: 81; see also Case 10 and Case 12.)
13. To date, no information has been found on Pedro Romero of El Paso. He may have been a relation of Francisco Xavier Romero, mentioned in this document.
14. Antonio Montoya was apparently the stepson of Francisco Martín Serrano. He married Juana Medina in 1718, and together they had twelve children. He may have been the son of Felipe de Montoya and the

grandson of Diego de Montoya. When he wrote his will in 1749, Antonio ordered the sale of a gun, powder flask, and sixty bullets of stone and lead to pay for his funeral. (Chávez, *Origins*: 377; SANM I #528, WPA translation.)
15. Juan Rael de Aguilar was the son of Alfonso Rael de Aguilar I and Josefa Ana García de Noriega. Alfonso, who originally came to New Mexico from Lorca, Spain, was a well-known figure in Santa Fe. He came with don Diego de Vargas in 1692, and he served in serveral offices including secretary of government and war, Santa Fe alcalde, and Protector of the Indians. Juan married Manuela de Sandoval Martínez in 1720. In 1723, he was in Taos where he was a witness to a deed. In 1727, he was a resident of Santa Fe. (Chávez, *Origins*: 263, 385; SANM I #510.)
16. In the Spanish text, the word used is "*refugio.*" In this case, the accused invokes the rights of sanctuary and takes refuge in two different places. We do not know why he did not stay longer at Nambé.
17. Fray Manuel de Sopena was in New Mexico from 1718 to 1746; previously, he served as a notary in El Paso. Among the places he served were Santa Cruz, Picuris, Taos, Nambé, Jémez, San Juan, Abiquiu, and Santa Fe. He seems to have been something of an artist: there are decorations on the flyleaves and borders of the record books used by him. (Chávez, *Archives*: 13, 27, 35, 226, 236, 256.)
18. This item seems to have been lost.
19. For information on Gervasio Cruzat y Góngora, see Case 23.
20. For information on Gaspar Bitton, see Case 23.
21. For information on Juan Antonio de Unanue, see Case 23.

25

MOTHER OF SOLDIER SLAPPED BY SANTA FE TRADER; SON INTERVENES
October 23–December 2, 1722, SANM II #393

Synopsis and editor's notes: In this case, Micaela López appeared in court because she was assaulted by don Salvador Martínez. She was accompanied by the strong (but not entirely effective) backing of her son, Marcial Rael, and two witnesses. In the eighteenth-century Spanish Colonial documents, the appearance of Micaela, a servant woman, was unusual. Most of the women who did appear in the records of this period were wives of officials or military officers or property owners—and, in some instances, the women were property owners themselves.

The quarrel between Micaela López and Salvador Martínez occurred when he discovered that some of his textile trade goods had been stolen, possibly by Micaela, who had been seen wearing a skirt made of the same kind of fabric that had gone missing. When Salvador saw her at the church, where he was making adobes, he asked her tactfully, he said, where she had bought her skirt. Micaela gave a rude response by asking Salvador if he was "crazy," or "dreaming," or "drunk." Offended by her remarks, Salvador responded by lashing out with the bridle reins of his horse, hitting her on the face and "bathing her in blood," as Micaela later stated. As was later revealed in court, immediately after the incident Salvador apologized to Micaela and offered to pay for the costs relating to her injury, and Micaela pardoned him. When a guard from the Albuquerque squadron asked Micaela about her injuries, she explained that all was well, for she had pardoned Salvador.

The situation seemed to have been resolved until Micaela's son, the soldier Marcial Rael, returned home from being out on escort service and saw his mother with her injury. He demanded that Alcalde Juan González Bas II imprison Salvador Martínez. Gonzáles Bas complied with the request, but the imprisonment was lifted after members of the community urged his release. Salvador's wife was, after all, Rosalia García de Noriega, a daughter of Luis García de Noriega, a well-known rancher and the brother of two of Albuquerque's founders. Marcial Rael then withdrew his complaint and the alcalde declared the case ended.

The case, however, continued because Micaela López insisted on a day in court for herself and her two witnesses. She described the altercation, explained that she had accepted Salvador Martínez's apology, and stated that he had agreed to pay her whatever she wanted (or so she said). The two witnesses said that they had not witnessed the assault, but they had seen her later when she was all bloody and her face was swollen.

By this time Salvador Martínez was no longer inclined to be tactful. He responded to the belated testimony by stating that he had given Micaela López two sacks of corn, but that he had never agreed to pay her *diezmo* (church tithe). He scolded the alcalde by pointing out that the correct legal procedure would have been to submit the case to the governor, who would have had Micaela's wounds inspected. Also, the governor would have heard witnesses before a final determination was made. There is no recorded response by alcalde Juan González Bas. The procedures in this case were indeed abbreviated, as compared to other cases that he handled. Perhaps, he had to pay attention to more pressing matters.

The case includes mention of adobes being made and the delivery of corn stalks, probably to be used as a binder in the adobes. These mud and straw bricks were intended for the building or repair of a church, but the church is not identified in the document. It was likely located in Albuquerque, where some of the testimony took place. Or, less likely, it may have been at the puesto of La Purisima Concepción de la Alameda, where later testimony by Micaela and her two witnesses occurred. Alameda was the home of González Bas and his family. He had purchased the Alameda grant in 1712 from Francisco Montes Vigil, and later built the Our Lady of the Concepción Chapel.[1]

This document illustrates yet another example of the theft of textile trade goods finding its way into a court case. As described in Case 20, in 1720 Isidro Sánchez stole textile trade goods from the presidio storehouse in Santa Fe. Some of the fabrics had come from the adjacent house of Felix Martínez, Salvador Martínez's father.

When researching the background of the people involved in this case, it also becomes apparent that violence was a way of life for some New Mexicans. For instance, in a document dating to 1736, Ramón García Jurado accused Salvador Martínez of shooting at Luis García, Salvador's father-in-law, and trying to run him down with a horse.[2] Several years later, according to a court record, Luis García was charged with drawing a knife on a servant in 1743.[3] And, in a 1747 case document, it is recorded that Gregorio Jaramillo, one of the witnesses in the case, was fined thirty pesos for wounding Tadeo Romero at Fuenclara.[4] One explanation for all this violence might be that nearly all of the male residents of New Mexico at that time were either presidio or militia soldiers who were prepared to fight hostile Indians and sometimes each other.

TRANSLATION

Alcalde Mayor

[Complaint by Marcial Rael[5]]

I, Marcial Rael, a soldier in this royal presidio and one of those assigned to guard this Villa of San Felipe de Albuquerque, appear before your honor in my best possible manner. I say that in order to avoid major problems, as they could come about, I ask on my behalf and on behalf of my mother, who is the one who is likely to suffer the most, justice against Salvador Martínez.[6] I ask that he be questioned as to his reasons for mistreating my mother and the reasons that he had for him to give her such a blow to her face without hindrances or wrong statements. This was without any respect and understanding that she was a woman and a poor woman as such. He should state the reasons for doing so because he had no reason to do what he did without any cause given by her.

For all of this I would be satisfied if Salvador [Martínez] is punished for having done what he did, so that he does not continue to go about without being afraid of the royal justice. For all of this I ask of your honor that you be pleased to consider this case according to justice and reason, and upon this being done I will be well served. I swear in my most proper form that it is not done in malice, expenses excluded, and done for the best cause, etc. I petition that this my petition be received as is presented on this paper, being that the sealed type is not found in this kingdom.

Marcial Rael (rubric)

[Copy to Salvador Martínez]

At this Villa of San Felipe de Albuquerque on the 23rd of October of the year of 1733, I, Captain Juan González Bas,[7] alcalde mayor of this villa and of its jurisdiction, received the above as was presented by the aforesaid. Upon being seen by me, I accepted it as presented according to the proper legal right and accordingly I order and did order that a copy be given to Salvador Martínez so that in the time allowed by the law, he can respond to it. As such I decreed, ordered and signed it on the said day, month and year acting as presiding judge due to the lack of a public or royal scribe, being that there are none in this kingdom, etc.

Juan González Bas (rubric)
Witness
 Francisco Antonio González[8] (rubric)
Witness
 Baltasar Romero[9] (rubric)

[Declaration of Salvador Martínez]

Having seen the petition that was presented against me by Marcial Rael in which he asks why it was that I mistreated his mother, I state that I did not mistreat her. What happened was as follows: From my house there were missing five varas of *manta de mimosa*.[10] Upon my being at the church making adobes, I saw the servant Micaela[11] with a new skirt, which my servant told was me was made from the material that had been stolen from me. To this Gregorio Jaramillo[12] responded saying that a few days earlier she had made a skirt that went all the way to the feet.

Making Adobe Bricks. Ernest Knee, *Santa Fe,* Self published, Santa Fe New Mexico, 1942: 40.

Adobe Bricks Drying. Ernest Knee, *Santa Fe,* Self published, Santa Fe, New Mexico, 1942: 41

I approached her and asked her, very politely, who had sold her the material. By doing it this way, I did not accuse her of being a thief nor say that she had stolen it. From my home, the servants steal on a daily basis and the women from the area purchase from them, so it could have happened that way. She could have acquired it in that way, being that she could have been around them. As such she need not have been so suspected. In this way, I asked her, being that she is a servant in a household. To this she responded, asking me if I was crazy, dreaming, or if I was drunk. Because of her being so rude, and being that she is a servant in a household, I threw her a punch. Then upon my recovering my composure I knelt at her feet and asked for her forgiveness, which she did forgive me. She seemed to be satisfied with this, as I had rephrased the whole thing.

Marcial Rael states that I should be punished. I say that I did not hurt or kill anyone. That is the reason that I walk around freely. Up to this time she did not receive any of the Holy Sacraments of Extreme Unction[13] as Marcial did with a servant who was in grave danger in the past year. From that situation no one made a big issue, and now, from a blow to a servant it has been grave. Also, Sir, the patient does not complain. I did not hit anyone for being poor, as this would not have been a reason. If he complains, given the explanation that I have given, then he needs to understand what really happened. But for what happened, I was treated like a dog, I should have none of this. What I have stated are the reasons I petition your honor to look at the reasons for justice. I take responsibility for the expenses and for whatever else that is required. This is not done in malice, and I swear to everything in the proper form, etc.

Salvador Martínez (rubric)

[Copy to Marcial Rael]

On the 28th of October of the year of 1733, I, Captain Juan González [Bas], alcalde mayor of this villa and of its jurisdiction, upon seeing the response given by Salvador Martínez, order that a copy be given to Marcial Rael, a soldier with this squadron, so that he can respond to it within the time allowed by the law. Thus I decreed and ordered it on the said day, month and year. So that it is valid I signed it along with my assisting witnesses due to the lack of a public or royal scribe, there not being one in the kingdom, and it is done etc.

Juan González Bas (rubric)
Witness
Pedro Lucero[14] (rubric)
Witnesss
Juan Julian González[15] (rubric)

Alcalde Mayor and War Captain

[Declaration by Marcial Rael]

I, Marcial Rael, the one who is involved in these proceedings, appear before your honor. Having fully understood the answer given by Salvador Martínez and having understood the whole thing word by word, I respond to it in the following manner. I say that it is true that he did hit my mother, for the reasons that have been given. For which reasons and for his answer, your honor has sufficient reason for him to be held. Accordingly, no one has the right to lay a hand on anyone without being castigated. It is true that his confession showed that there is a cause for him to be held, and for which I ask that he be held. Then he can proceed with the allegations that he brings forth, stating why his servant was hit.

To this I respond, that his allegations are false, illicit and null, because my mother did not deserve it. Accordingly, it should not be done to anyone, not even to punish their servants, and should not be done even to their slaves without a just cause. If Salvador Martínez is used to doing this, I am not obligated to agree to it, but if he agrees to make a declaration, I shall give proof that he has indeed done it. He states that I have acknowledged that the Holy Oils [for the Holy Sacrament of Extreme Unction] were given to a servant, to which I respond, that this has nothing to do with the case. This is because anyone who argues about their rights, property and seniority does not have the right to bring them out in proceedings, but only that item that they are arguing about. For this reason, I am not required to respond to that matter. It is up to the alcalde to do so, who is your honor, who should respond.

He states that from that no such scandal was brought forth. He continues saying that he struck her with a punch (along with what else he confesses), I say that it was not only a punch. Besides having mistreated her with words, he also implied that she was a thief, got her all bloody, and got her face to the point that she was unrecognizable. All of this I saw after I returned from an escort, where I had found myself for eight days. I found her still very ill, which was the reason for me to find out what had occurred, and for this, your honor, I seek justice. He states in his argument that my mother had pardoned him for the sake of God, to which I ask if she really did or did not pardon him. This is something that I do not know, but what I do know is that at that point she did pardon him because he did not have anyone else who would do so. If this was so, I am not ready to consent to this, being that she is my mother and it would be very unjust, bad and disgraceful.

For all of this, your honor should see to it that it is done in justice, and place him under security in order for me to be satisfied and for the public not to be disgraced. After that he should appear before you to give his account. This is so that I can proceed with my proof as to how my mother was totally bathed in blood, her clothes torn, and her face so bad that she could not be recognized. I say that this is not an argument about any fabric, but is a daring and unjust doing, and even without a petition on my part he should be punished. This is what I have to offer and to argue in my favor. Of your honor I ask and petition that you act for the sake of justice and that you proceed to the arguments with his person being held secure so that I shall receive justice. I swear in my proper form that it is not done in malice, but for what is necessary, etc.

Marcial Rael (rubric)

Response to complaint by Marcial Rael

At this Villa of Alburquerque on the 7th of November, 1733, I, the war captain of this villa and of its jurisdiction, upon seeing the response and request of Marcial Rael, a soldier with the guard, I decided to order and did order that it be executed as he requests. I placed Salvador Martínez in prison and ordered that they proceed with their arguments to be received according to justice according to their legal rights and that it be done according to their [paying] expenses. I thus decreed and ordered acting as presiding judge with two assisting witnesses due to the lack of a royal or public scribe, which there is none in this kingdom. So that it is thus valid, I signed it on the said day, month and year.

Juan González Bas (rubric)
Witness
Pedro Lucero (rubric)
Witness
Juan Julian González (rubric)

Alcalde Mayor and War Captain

[Petition of Marcial Rael]

I, Marcial Rael de Aguilar, appear before your honor in the best form possible. I find myself under my legal rights, I state that I desist from the petition that I have presented before your honor against Salvador Martínez being that I have been asked to do so by a number of persons with merit and respect. I only request that he be fined under some penalty so that he becomes warned, your honor, doing this in whatever manner your honor wishes. With this I will be satisfied, and as such I ask your honor that you be pleased to do as I request. I swear in due form that this, my written petition, is not done in malice, but for what is necessary, etc.

Marcial Rael de Aguilar (rubric)

[Release of don Salvador Martínez]

At this puesto de la Purisima Concepción de la Alameda on the 9th of November of year of 1733, I, Captain Juan González Bas, alcalde mayor of this villa, was presented by Marcial Real with the above. Upon it being seen by me, I took it as it was presented according to his legal right and I agreed to the release from prison in which is found don Salvador Martínez. He can still be culpable of the charges and complaint under which he was sentenced, and I impose the costs caused by such upon him. So that it is valid I thus decreed it and signed it with my two assisting witnesses acting as presiding judge due to the lack of a royal or public scribe, there not being one in this kingdom, etc.

    Juan González Bas (rubric)
Witness
Juan Julian González (rubric)
Witness
Joseph González Bas (rubric)

[Declaration of Micaela López]

    At this puesto de la Purisima Concepcíon de la Alameda, on the 2nd of December, 1733, before me, Captain Juan González Bas, alcalde mayor and war captain of this jurisdiction, there appeared Micaela López. She stated that because she is a poor person and has no one who could write for her, she has appeared to present her statement verbally. She stated that in the past days Salvador Martínez approached her and asked her who had sold to her the seven varas of cloth, to which she responded that indeed someone had sold her the cloth. To this Salvador Martínez said that he had witnesses that no one had sold it to her, and that her daughter had made a skirt. To this she responded to Salvador Martínez, asking him if he was dreaming, and who had told him so. Upon saying this, he answered and tried to hit her with the reins, but she did not hear him because the horse whinnied. Then he got off his horse and began hitting her, and he beat her extensively and bathed her in blood.

    Then, being in this way she called the lieutenant Gerónimo Jaramillo[16] and told him to see what Salvador Martínez had done to her. When the lieutenant went to find him, she backed off because Salvador Martínez had already asked her to pardon him and stated that he would pay her whatever it was that she wanted. She responded telling him what she wanted, but desisted and stopped because a number of persons prayed that she would. But she stated she would agree to desist only after she was paid for the damage that was done to her, which is still pending. The reason she is continuing the complaint is because Salvador Martínez goes around saying that he did not hit her but one punch, but it was more likely two or more, and she has witnesses who saw her and will testify how badly she was beaten up. The witnesses are Gregorio Jaramillo and Salvador Durán,[17] who saw the way that she was injured. She states that what she has said is the truth, which she ratified and affirmed, but did not sign because she did not know how. The alcalde mayor signed it along with his two assisting witnesses, acting as presiding judge, and on the present paper because the sealed type does not exist in these parts.

    Juan González Bas (rubric)
Witness
Lugardo Vallejo (rubric)
Witness
Pedro Lucero (rubric)

Declaration of Lieutenant Gerónimo Jaramillo

 Continuing on the said day, month and year, I, the alcalde mayor, made appear before me the lieutenant Gerónimo Jaramillo. I took his sworn statement under his proper legal right before God, Our Lord, and the Holy Cross, and having done this, he promised to tell the truth as to what he was asked. He stated that on the day that this happened he proceeded to call Micaela López to his home. When she came there he saw that she was all bloodied up and had a blow to one side of her jaw and some others on the other side. He asked her if she would make a complaint against Salvador Martínez. She stated that she would not make a complaint against him because he had already asked her to pardon him, telling her that he would care for her and offer her from that time forth whatever he could offer. But even if she had pardoned him, her son Marcial Rael would take revenge and he would be there for her for whatever happened. This he says is the truth according to what he saw and heard, and which he affirmed and ratified according to the testimony that he has made and he signed it along with me and my assisting witnesses.

 Gerónimo Jaramillo (rubric)
 Juan González Bas (rubric)
 Witness
 Lugardo Vallejo[18] (rubric)
 Witness
 Pedro Lucero (rubric)

Declaration of Gregorio Jaramillo

 Continuing, in order to hear more information, I made to appear before me Gregorio Jaramillo, Spanish, and a resident of the Villa of Albuquerque. I took his sworn statement according to his legal right before God Our Lord and to the Holy Cross, and having done this, he promised to tell the truth as to what he was asked, and he was asked what he knew and what he had seen. He stated that on the day on which Micaela López had her quarrel with Salvador Martínez, he, the declarant, was loaded down with a cart full of corn stalks. He saw when Salvador Martínez hit Micaela López with three punches. Upon seeing that she was crying she went to his home and he saw that she was all bloodied and was complaining about her nose, which appeared to be broken. This he states is the truth and he ratified it and affirmed it to be his true statement which he has made. He did not sign because he did not know how, I, the alcalde mayor. signed it along with my assisting witnesses, etc.

 Juan González Bas (rubric)
 Witness
 Lugardo Vallejo (rubric)
 Witness
 Pedro Lucero (rubric)

Declaration of Salvador Durán

Continuing, on the same day, month and year, I, the alcalde mayor, continuing with these proceedings made to appear before me Salvador Durán, resident of this jurisdiction. I took his sworn statement according to his right before God, Our Lord and the Holy Cross, and having done this he promised to tell the truth according to what he was asked. He stated that on the day that this whole quarrel came up, he was working in the convento and saw Micaela López with her face all swollen and her eyes as if they wanted to pop out of her head. He heard her say that Salvador Martínez had hit her, but that he had not seen him do it. This he says is what he knows and is the truth and he affirmed and ratified it according to the sworn statement that he had made. He did not sign because he did not know how. I, the alcalde mayor, signed it along with my assisting witnesses.

Juan González Bas (rubric)
Witness
Pedro Lucero (rubric)
Witness
Lugardo Vallejo (rubric)

[Remission of testimony to Salvador Martínez]

At this Hacienda de la Purisima Concepcíon de la Alameda, on the 2nd day of the month of December, 1733, I, Captain Juan González Bas, alcalde mayor of this jurisdiction, have heard testimony presented by Micaela López in her sworn statement and have heard that which was stated by the witnesses whom she presented. In order to provide the proof and justification, I order and did order that a copy be given to Salvador Martínez so that he can respond to it within the time allowed by the law. I thus decreed, ordered and signed it acting as presiding judge with two assisting witnesses due to the lack of a public or royal scribe, there not being one in this kingdom, etc.

Juan González Bas (rubric)
Witness
Lugardo Vallejo (rubric)
Pedro Lucero (rubric)

[Declaration by Salvador Martínez]

Sir, having seen what Micaela López has given against me, and having seen the statements given by the three witnesses, I say that, as can be seen in these proceedings, everyone has desisted from the complaint, including those whom she presented against me. Thus, it is wrong for Micaela to bring the proceedings up again, being that there is no reason to do so except that they told her to do so. It is not enough that many things are said, but what happened is not as they say. Another thing, she argues that upon paying the church tithe,[19] I would repay her. This is wrong. What I sent to her were two sacks of corn. That this was done, is correct, and it had nothing to do with the tithe, which I did not agree to pay for, and never promised.

Another thing, why did you examine so many witnesses after the quarrel had been desisted? This is one of the first things that should have been done, as this is what happens throughout the world. What I feel that you should have done was to have sent both of us to the villa, to appear before the governor, who is known to have a doctor, to see the harm that was caused by me. No, this was not done by you because you lack the sense of justice, and because you tend to disrupt the sense of the case on a daily basis with so many stories against me about what I do and what I say that are without substance. This is only done so that stories are brought up and damage done, all of which appears bad to everyone, and the justices come to see all men as being bad.

You also say that she called upon the lieutenant to check on her at the time that I hit her, to take her false statement about how she was at the time, and upon being examined by the lieutenant to see if she had a complaint. To this she answered that she did not have a complaint, but only said that there was nothing to it. As such the lieutenant on duty did not accuse me. It is not because of injuries that disagreements come forth, but in some cases the false statements keep the justices from doing their duties. You should be aware that all of this was nothing. She should find herself to be well in a short time, not as is stated above, that it will take months and years.

All of this I state without arguing about all of the hearsay that there was given. I thus petition your honor that you do as I ask above, for the sake of receiving justice and I swear in due form that it is not done in malice but for whatever is necessary, etc.

Salvador Martínez (rubric)

TRANSCRIPTION

Señor Alcalde Mayor

Marsial Rael soldado de este Real Presidio y uno delos senalados en esta escolta dela Villa de San Phelipe de Alburquerque paresco ante Vuestra Merced como major preseda y digo que por obiar o escusar mayor pleyto que como puede susedar pido por mi parte y por mi madre que es la mayor doliente justicia contra Salvador Martines preguntandole los motivos que el dicho tubo para apolear a mi dicha madre y el atrevimiento que tubo para ponerle tanta cara sin otras estorsiones y ynjusticias que le yso a su salvo sin respetar ni attender el que era muger, y muger pobre y que como tal por mucha causa que tubiera era digna de no aber executado tal maldad; dando los motivos que tubo para ello para quedar yo satisfecho y dicho Salvador castigado pues abiendyyo executado lo que yso se anda pasiando sin temor ala Real Justicia por todo lo qual a Vuestra Magestad pido y suplico se sirva de mirar esta causa en justizia y reason que en ello resibire bien y juro en devida forma no ser de malicia costas y en lo nesesario ut supra = Ofresi que se me resiva este suplico en el presente papel por que el sellado no corre en este Reyno =

 Marsial Rael (rubric)

En esta Villa de San Phelipe de Alburquerque en beinte y tres dias de el mes de Octubre de el año de mil setesientos y treinta y tres, yo el Capitan Juan Gonsales, Alcalde Mayor de dicha Villa y su jurisdision la presento el contenido en ella, y por mi bista la ube por presentada en cuanto a lugar y derecho debe mandar y mando sele de traslado a Salbador Martines para que responda en el tiempo premitorio de la ley, asi lo decrete y mande y firme en dicho dia, mes y año, autuando como Jues Resetor a falta de escribano publico y Real que no lo ay en este Reyno ut supra

 Juan Gonsales Bas (rubric)
 Testigo
 Francisco Antonio Gonzales (rubric)
 Witness
 Baltasar Romero (rubric)

Bisto el escrito que Marsial Rael presento contra mi pidiendo que de los motivos por que aporre a su madre, digo que no la aporre, si lo que paso fue que en mi casa faltaron sinco baras de manta de alimoso, y estando asiendo adoves en la yglesia, bido una mosa, ija de la Micaela con una camisa nueba, dijo mi moso Blas, que es la manta que me urtaron. A esto dijo Gregorio Jaramillo el otro dia, yso una camisa hasta los pies quisas sera. Pase yo a preguntarle disiendole que quien le abia bendido la manta; a esto me respondio ablandole con mucho amor que si estaba loco, sonando o borracho; a esto como fue tan pesada, en berdad le tire un punete;

No preguntarle esto fue desirle que era ladrona; ni que ella lo urto; que mi casa todos los dias hurtan las criadas y las mujeres del lugar les compran; pudo ello ser asi, que rodando cayera en su poder los otros; que de otra no lo sintiera tan pesada, respuesta que como sirbiente de casa le di; parese que la parte esta satisfecha, en esta forma, que luego que bolvi de la colera me arodille a sus pies pidiendole perdon, alo cual me perdono; Dise que yo sea castigado; Digo, Señor que yo no eri ni mate; motibo por que me paseo; que asta ora no a resebido ninguno los Santos Sacramentos dela estremunsion como Marsial iso con un moso pues corio gran riesgo el año pasado, desto no ubo tanto estremo. Y de un punete a mi sirbiente a ora le ase: Lo otro Señor que como pasiente no se queja; no por pobre le di; que no fuera rason: Si por lo que llevo dicho como quejarse se puede llegar al conocimiento de lo que fue, o lo que me diria, pues a tanto llego su libiandad que me puso de perro, de esto no tengo nada, estos son los motibos por todo lo cual a Vuestra Merced pido y suplico se sirba de mirar los motibos con justicia; que me asisten ofresco costas, y en lo nesesario, no ser de malisia juro en toda forma, ut supra.

Salvador Martines (rubric)

⁂

En beinte y ocho dias del mes de Octubre del año de mil sietesientos y treinta y tres llo el Capitan Juan Gonsales, Alcalde Mayor de dicha Billa y su jurisdision en bista de la respuesta dada por Salbador Martin mando se le de traslado a Marsial Rael soldado de esta escolta para que responda en el tiempo notorio de la ley, asi lo decreto y mando en dicho dia, mes y año y para que asi conste lo firme con los testigos de mi asistensia a falta de escribano publico y Real que no lo ay en este Reino y es fecho ut supra =

Juan Gonsales Bas (rubric)
Testigo
Pedro Lucero (rubric)
Witness
Juan Julian Gonsales (rubric)

⁂

Señor Alcalde Mayor y Capitan Aguerra

Marsial Rael comprendido en estos autos paresco ante Vuestra Merced y digo que abiendome enterado dela respuesta de Salvador Martines y entendido de verbo a berbo todas sus clausulas alas que responde por su tenor, dise que es berdad aberle dado a su madre y los motivos que tubo para ello, alo qual digo: que con esa respuesta tiene Vuestra Merced suficiente para apremiarlo y asegurarlo pues ninguno tiene mano ni facultad para darle a otro sin que por alguna manera sea castigado; es sierto que el dicho confiesa luego tiene causa para estar en seguro lo cual pido se aga y despues se pase alas aberiguasiones de lo que alega.

Dise que a como su sirbiente le dio; a lo cual digo, que es falso, ylisito y nulo, por que mi madre, ni le sirve, ni le a servido y dado y no consedido, que le sirviera ninguno aquien le sirban los pequenos, por ninguna ley de una, ni humana tiene mano para castigar a sus sirbientes pues es bisto que ni aun alos esclabos es permitido sin justa causa; y si el dicho Salbador Martines lo acostumbra yo ni estoy obligado a saberlo pero si se ofriese dare tambien prueba para que lo aiga hecho; dise que yo esedo causa para que a un moso dieran los Santos Oleos, alo qual digo: que eso no es del caso por que ninguno que alega en derecho propiedad y señorio, no saco atiguydades sino el echo delo en que esta, fuera que ami no me toca responder en ese punto quando al Alcalde, que es Vuestra Merced, le toca responder.

Pues dise que de ello no se yso tanto escandalo; prosigue disiendo que un punete le dio (y fuera de lo que confiesa), digo que no fue solo punete porque amas de aberle maltratado de palabras pues quasi la ymputa de ladrona, la bano en sangre, y le puso la cara que no sele conosia si tenia perfecion de ella dare ynformacion de ello; en su lugar fuera de que yo alcabo de aber benido de una escolta, en donde me allaba que fue alos ocho dias, la alle todavia muy mala, que fue el motivo para que yo lo supiera, y que a Vuestra Merced pidiese justicia. Dise en el sullo aber mi madre perdonadole por Dios, alo qual digo: que si le perdono, o no, le perdono yo, no lo se y lo que se es que entonses pudo perdonarle por no tener persona que de su parte ysiera, y que aunque fuese sierto yo no lo abia de consenter siendo mi madre y lo ysiera muy injusta, mala y con desberguensa.

Con este supuesto, sea de servir Vuestra Merced de mirarlo en justicia y poner en seguro su persona para quedar yo satisfecho y la bendita publica desescandalisado y que despues pase a dar sus ynformasiones, para dar yo las pruebas de como mi madre la bano en sangre, la desgaro de su repaje y le puso la cara que no se conosia, fuera Señor Alcalde Mayor, que esto no es alegato de ninguna propriedad, sino que es un atrebimiento y osadia ynjusta, que sin peticion de parte se debia castigar; por todo lo qual y lo que alegar puedo a mi fabor = A Vuestra Merced pido y suplico sea serbido de obrar en justicia y pasar alas aberiguaciones, estando en seguro su persona, que en ello resebire justicia y juro en debida forma no ser de malisia y en lo nesesario, ut supra =

Marsial Rael (rubric)

En esta Billa de San Felipe de Alburquerque en siete dias del mes de Nobiembre del año de mil setesientos y treinta y tres yo el Capitan Aguerra de dicha Villa y su jurisdicion en bista de la respuesta y pedimento dada por Marsial Rael soldado de esta escolta debo mandar y mando que se ejecute como lo pide la parte poniendo en prision a Salbador Martines y que una parte y otra coran sus pruebas que se las resibiran en justisia que es de derecho y que sea a confiansa de costas, asi lo decrete y mande autuando como Jues Receptor con dos testigos de mi asistenzia a falta de Escribano Publico y Real que no lo ay en este Reyno y por que asi conste lo firme en dicho dia, mes y anñ, ut supra.

Juan Gonsales Bas (rubric)
Testigo
Pedro Lucero (rubric)
Witness
Juan Julian Gonsales (rubric)

Señor Alcalde Mayor y Capitan Aguerra

Marsial Rael de Aguilar paresco ante Vuestra Merced en la major bia y forma que alla lugar en derecho y al mio combenga y digo que me bajo, aparto y desisto del pedimento que ante Vuestra Merced tengo presentado contra Salvador Martin por aber pedido algunas personas de meritos y respecto y solo pido que se multe en alguna pena para escaramiento, la que Vuestra Merced fuese servido de imponerle que en eso quedo satisfecho y por tanto a Vuestra Merced pido y suplico sea servido de aser como pido y juro en devida forma que este mi escrito no es de malicia y lo nesesario, ut supra.

 Marsial Rael de Aguilar (rubric)

Disision bajo de querella a Marsial Rael

 En este Puesto dela Purisima Concepcion dela Alameda en nuebe dias del mes de Nobiembre del año de mil setesientos y treinta y tres años yo el Capitan Juan Gonsales Bas, Alcalde Mayor de dicha Villa la presento el contenido en eya y por mi bista la ube por presentada en cuanto ay lugar en derecho le consedo sele de soltura dela prision en que se aya a Dn. Salbador Martines quien estara siempre a derecho a resebir el cargo de culpa y pena en que fuera penado y costas del proseso causado y por que asi conste lo decreto y firme con dos testigos de mi asistenzia autuando como Jues Receptor de falta de Escribano Publico y Real que no lo ay en este Reino, ut supra.

 Juan Gonsales Bas (rubric)
 Testigo
 Juan Julian Gonsales (rubric)
 Witness
 Joseph Gonsales Bas (rubric)

Pedimento berbal de Micaela Lopes

 En este Puesto de la Purisima Consepcion de la Alameda en dos dias del mes de Diciembre de mill setesientos y treinta y tres años ante mi el Capitan Juan Gonsales Bas, Alcalde Mayor y Capitan Aguerra desta jurisdicion paresio Micaela Lopes quien dijo que por ser una pobre y no tener quien la escribiera bino a representar berbalmente y dise que por cuanto los dias pasados fue Salvador Martines y sobre aberle preguntado ala declarante que quien le avia bendido siete varas de manta, a lo qual le respondio que le abian bendido tal manta, esto dijo el Salbador Martines que el tenia testigos de que se la avian bendido y que su ija dela declarante abia echo una camisa y que a esta rason dijo la declarante al dicho Salbador Martines que si estava sonando el y quien selo abia dicho y a esta razon le quiso dar de rendasos y no oio por que el caballo cillo y que entonses se apeo del caballo y le empeso a dar y que la maltrato mucho y la bano en sangre.

 Estando desta manera llamo al Teniente Geronimo Xaramillo y le dixo que mirara como la abia puesto Salvador Martines a que le pregunto el dicho Teniente que este fue que se allaba y que dijo no se y con ella bajaron entonses por que lla Salbador Martines le avia pedido perdon y prometido que en juntando el fue diciendo que el le pagaria lo cual le abia faltado, abiendo tomado la defensa y presentado el grito y desistio y aparto por ruegos que algunas personas le isieron y que ella quiere y pide sele remunese el daño resivido pues todabia esta estando y que el motibo que tiene para susitar esto es porque el dicho Salbador Martines anda disiendo que no le dio mas que un punete a bien dos y de mucho mas o que sita por testigos de bista de lo maltratado que quedo, a Gregorio Xaramillo y a Salvador Duran quienes la bieron dela manera que estava y que es lo que tiene dicho es la berdad en que se afirmo y la ratifica y no firmo por no saver firmelo dicho Alcalde Mayor con dos testigos de mi asistensia auctuando como Jues Resptor en el presente papel por que el sellado no corre en estas partes =

 Juan Gonsales Bas (rubric)
 Testigo
 Lugardo Ballejo (rubric)
 Witness
 Pedro Lucero (rubric)

Declaracion de Teniente Geronimo Xaramillo

 Luego incontinente en dicho dia, mes y año yo dicho Alcalde Mayor hise pareser ante mi al Teniente Geronimo Xaramillo y le resevi su jurmento en forma de derecho por Dios Nuestro Señor y la Santa Cruz y abiendolo echo prometio desir berdad en lo que le fuere preguntado dise que el dia que le susedio este y en berlo enbio a llamar a su casa a Micaela Lopes y aviendo ido a su llamada ablo a la dicha ensangretada y que tenia una punete de un lado de un carillo y otras mas en el otro y que le pregunto a la doliente que si se querellaba de Salbador Martines y que dijo que no se querellava por que lla le avia pedido perdon que si queria que biera como estava por lo que en adelante se pudiera ofreser por que aunque ella habia perdonado que su ijo Marsial Rael abia de tomar la bengansa y que para lo que se ofresiera lo estava por testigo y que esta es la berdad de lo que bido y ollo en que se afirmo y ratifico so cargo del juramento que fecho tiene y lo firmo con migo y los testigos de mi assistensia =

 Geronimo Jaramillo (rubric)
 Juan Gonsales Bas (rubric)
 Testigo
 Lugardo Ballejo (rubric)
 Pedro Lucero (rubric)

Declaracion de Gregorio Xaramillo

 Luego incontinente para la informasion qual la parte ofrese yse arser ante mi a Gregorio Xaramillo, Espanol y vecino desta Villa de Alburquerque y le resevi juramento en forma de derecho por Dios Nuestro Señor y la Santa Cruz y aviendole echo prometio desir verdad delo que le fuere preguntado y siendole preguntado lo que sabia y abia bisto, dise que el dia que le ante dio Micaela Lopes por el pleito con Salbador Martines benia el declarante con una careta cargada de oja y bido que Salvador Martines le dio a la dicha Micaela Lopes tres punetes y despues biendo que estaba llorando fue a su casa y la bido ensangretada y que se quejava de la narises que parese que las tenia quebradas y que esto es la berdad en que se afirmo y ratifico so cargo del juramento que fecho tiene y no firmo por no saver, firmelo yo dicho Alcalde Mayor con los testigos de mi asistenzia, ut supra =

 Juan Gonsales Bas (rubric)
 Testigo
 Testigo
 Lugardo Ballejo (rubric)
 Pedro Lucero (rubric)

Declaracion de Salvador Duran

 Luego yncontinente en dicho dia, mes y año yo dicho Alcalde Mayor en presecusion destas deligensias hise pareser ante mi a Salvador Duran vesino desta jurisdision y le resevi juramento en forma de derecho por Dios Nuestro Señor y la Santa Cruz y aviendolo echo prometio desir berdad en lo que fuere preguntado y siendole dise que el dia que susedio este ruido estava el declarante trabajando en el conbento y bido a Micaela Lopes con la cara inchada y los ojos que paresia que sele querian rebentar y que ollo desir que Salbador Martines le avia dado que el no lo bido y que esto es lo que save y que es la verdad que se afirmo y ratifica so cargo del juramento que fecho tiene y no firmo por no saver firmelo yo dicho Alcalde Mayor con los testigos de mi assistencia =

 Juan Gonsales Bas (rubric)
 Testigo
 Pedro Lucero (rubric)
 Witness
 Lugardo Ballejo (rubric)

En esta Hacienda de La Purisima Concepcion de la Alameda en dos dias del mes de Disiembre de mill Septecientos treinta y tres años yo el Capitan Juan Gonsales Bas, Alcalde Mayor desta jurisdision por cuanto a representado berbalmente Micaela Lopes lo que consta por su declaracion y los testigos que presento para la prueba y justificasion debo mandar y mando sele de traslado a la parte de Salvador Martin para que responda en el tiempo perenttorio de la lei, asi lo decrete, mande y firme actuando como Jues Receptor con dos testigos de mi assistenzia y falta de escribano publico y real que no lo ai en este Reyno fecho, ut supra =

 Juan Gonsales Bas (rubric)
 Testigo
 Lugardo Ballejo (rubric)

Testigo
Pedro Lucero (rubric)

Señor, bisto la representacion que Micaela Lopes yso contra mi, y echome capaz delas declaraciones de los tres declarantes digo que ya estan bajados dela querella, pues Marsial Rael, que es quien represento contra mi esta bajado dela querella como costa en estos autos; luego es malisia de la dicha, Micaela, el bolber a nueba representacion cuando no ay motibo sin mas que dise que le dijeron; no es bastante que muchas cosas disen, sin ser como suenan; lo otro que alega disiendo que en recojiendo el diesmo, le pagaria, a esto dise mal, que es falso que lo que yo le mande fueron dos costales de mais que a eso, no faltare, y no del diesmo, que yo no compre, para de ay prometer.

Lo otro Señor, que a que tira con esta su sitasion con tanta examinasion de testigos, que segun parese es lo primero, que en el mundo pasa, que lo que yo allo por mejor es que asi ami, como ala dicha nos remita ala Villa, a que comparescamos ante el Señor Governador que se a reconosido por sirujano, aver el daño que tiene resebido de mi, esto digo, no, por que Usted, Señor falta ala justisia sino por que todos los dias no ande inquietando el animo de Usted con tantos cuentos por el lugar contra mi que yo digo, que yo ago, tan sin ninguna sustansia solo porque se sigan daño ala ora que yo le di, que la jusgara como se allaba, y confesada por dicho Teniente que si se querellaba a que respondio, que no, ello solo dise que no seria, nada, toda la bes que el Teniente de ofisio no me castigo; que no por que uno de unas erridas y no ayga querella de partes, dejan las justicias de aser su ofisio, alle Usted, que no seria nada: Pues en tan corto tiempo, no se habia de allar sana, como costa arriba en los escritos meses y años.

Esto digo sin lo alegar puedo delo desbocada que es, sin en tanto a Vuestra Merced pido y suplico se sirba de aser como llebo pedido arriba que resebire justisia y juro en toda forma no ser de malisia costas y en lo nesesario, ut supra.
Salvador Martines (rubric)

Notes

1. See Simmons, *Albuquerque*: 103.
2. See SANM II #343.
3. See SANM II #448.
4. See SANM II #476.
5. [Pedro] Marcial Rael de Aguilar claimed to be the natural son of Alfonso Rael de Aguilar II. Marcial married Isabel Sedillo in 1730 in Alameda. Salvador Martínez refers to the beating of a servant by Marcial, but no documents have been found regarding this. By 1741 Marcial was a soldier with the Albuquerque squadron. In 1742, the members of the squadron, including Marcial, took sanctuary in various churches to avoid a court martial for not preventing the theft of the horse herd by Indians. As a result, all members of the squadron were ordered out of service and their pay stopped. (NMGS, *Aquí*: 156; Christmas, *Military Records*: 54; SANM II #446.)
6. Salvador Martínez claimed to be the son of interim New Mexico governor, Felix Martínez (who served from 1715 to 1717), and doña Catarina de Esparze, who were married in Chihuahua, Mexico. Salvador married Rosalia García de Noriega, the only child of the well-to-do Luis García de Noriega and his first wife, Josefa Valverde. After the marriage, Salvador Martínez was involved in a series of lawsuits regarding Rosalia's inheritance (see Case 31). There were also lawsuits about property he purchased nearby and partly within

Sandia Pueblo. In 1748, he traveled to Mexico City to petition the viceroy for an appointment as head of the military squadron in Albuquerque. In his petition, he substantiated his claim of being the son of Felix Martínez and described his qualifications for the job. He was given the appointment, but he had to return to the viceroy to ask for money so that he and a companion could return to New Mexico. (Tigges and Salazar, *Spanish Colonial Lives*: 470-77; SANM I #532.)

7. Juan González Bas II was the son of Juan González Bas I and Nicolasa Zaldivar Jorge. Juan II returned to New Mexico with his family, settling in Bernalillo and Albuquerque, and by 1710 he was captain of the Albuquerque squadron. Juan II was also alcalde mayor of Albuquerque in 1712, and he served in many administrative positions, including as lieutenant governor. He was married to María López de Castillo. Juan II and María had a son they named Juan. (Barrett, *Conquest*: 176; Chávez, *Origins*: 189; Kessell, Hendricks, and Dodge, *Boulders*: 1173n109.)

8. Francisco Antonio González was the son of Juan González Bas II. In 1711, he was a witness to the baptism of Martín Hurtado's grandson. In 1727, Francisco was the notary of the Albuquerque church. (Chávez, *Origins*: 190; NMGS, *Aquí*: 290; Henrietta Christmas, in email to the author, June 18, 2016.)

9. A Native New Mexican, Baltasar Romero had returned to the province by 1694, and in 1703, he married Francisca Góngora. Together, they were among the first families to found Albuquerque. In 1705, Romero is included in the Santa Fe presidio muster; by 1716 he was the alcalde for Laguna Pueblo; and, he was active in land purchases in Bernalillo and Santa Ana. In 1737, he was accused of "molesting" the Indians. Baltasar died about 1745. (Ebright, "Advocates": 362n83; Ebright, Hendricks, and Hughes, *Leagues*: 54-55; Chávez, *Origins*: 271; NMGS, *Aquí*: 188, 390; SANM II #460; SANM II #681; SANM II #684.)

10. In this document, "manta de mimosa" probably refers to a blanket or a covering of soft cloth. Currently, the term is used for cloths or blankets made for babies and young children.

11. Micaela López was the daughter of Luis López and Ana María Bernal; and, as this document indicates, Micaela was the mother of Marcial Rael. Ana María Bernal was the niece of Melchora González Bas and alcalde Juan González Bas, making Micaela his grandniece. (Chávez, *Origins*: 189.)

12. Gregorio Jaramillo was the son of Cristóbal Varela Jaramillo, a native of New Mexico, and Leonor Luján Domínguez. Gregorio married Francisca Salas y Hurtado in 1727. The extended family lived at Fuenclara/Tomé south of Albuquerque. He was a stepbrother of Gerónimo Jaramillo, who is mentioned above. (Chávez, *Origins*: 198-99; Tigges and Salazar, *Spanish Colonial Lives*: 437-48.)

13. The "Holy Sacrament of the Exteme Unction" is offered when a sick person is in danger of dying. The priest anoints the person with the "holy oils" for the health of the soul and body and repeats a prescribed service. (Addis, *Catholic Dictionary*: 328-29.)

14. Pedro Lucero is probably the son of Nicolás Lucero de Godoy and María Montoya, both of whom returned with the Spanish Reconquest. Nicolás and María were one of the founding families of Albuquerque. Pedro was born about 1690, probably in El Paso. He married María Quintana about 1720, and he was in Albuquerque for the 1750 census. His name also appears in several land transaction records. He died in 1777. (NMGS, *Aquí*: 330-31.)

15. "Juan Julian González" is probably the same person as "Juan González Bas II." In 1752, he and Isabel Baca were godparents for Manuel Paulin Rael, a member of the Sedillo Rico de Rojas family. (NMGS, *Aquí*: 16; Christman, personal communication by email, June 18, 2016.)

16. Gerónimo Jaramillo was the son of Cristóbal Jaramillo and Casilda Sedillo Rico de Rojas, and he was a stepbrother of Gregorio Jaramillo. He married Gertrudis Silva in 1709, and he died in 1777 at Fuenclara/Tomé. (NMGS, *Aquí*: 461-62, 465.)

17. This may be the Salvador Durán who was born about 1675 and escaped with his family to El Paso during the Pueblo Revolt of 1680. He was likely a son of Nicolás Durán. Salvador was an adjutant with the El Paso presidio until 1701. His wife was Ana Márquez (or Luján). However, there is a record dating to 1752 that describes a Salvador Durán marrying an Antonia Torres, but this may be a different Salvador Durán. (Chávez, *Origins*: 170; NMGS, *Aquí*: 130.)

18. Lugardo Vallejo was born in 1707, the son of Manuel González Vallejo, a blacksmith, and Mariana Hurtado, both of whom came to New Mexico in 1694 with the Farfán Expedition. Mariana was a sister of Martín Hurtado, the first alcalde of Albuquerque. Lugardo married Rosa Romero. He died in 1769 in Albuquerque. (Chávez, *Origins*: 271, 303; NMGS, *Aquí*: 79; Esquibel, "Mexico City": 68.)

19. The diezmo is the church tithe used to pay for maintenance of the clergy. At one time, it amounted to one tenth of the increase in goods since the previous year or, alternatively, it was 10 percent of the income of the parishioner. (Velasquez, 2007: 381.)

26

WIFE COMPLAINS TO GOVERNOR ABOUT HUSBAND'S FIFTEEN-YEAR AFFAIR
July 20–September 16, 1744, Source: SANM II #458a

Synopsis and editor's notes: In July 1744, in Santa Fe, Juana Martín decided to assert her legal rights by making a criminal charge against her husband's lover, Gertrudis de Segura, a free, single mulatta. She charged her with having a fifteen-year-long affair with her husband, Joseph de Armijo, and with physical abuse, which Juana suffered at the hands of both Gertrudis and Joseph. Juana Martín was probably part of the Martín Serrano clan of Chimayó. Joseph de Armijo was a nephew of Antonio Durán de Armijo, known as a *maestro barber* (master medic) and a procurador—basically someone who acted as a legal representative for the soldiers and settlers. Antonio and his brother, Vicente, were both Camino Real merchants (as indicated in Case 22). Although Juana Martín does mention her husband's income, his source of income is unclear, for there is no evidence that he was a merchant like his uncles or that he was a presidio soldier.

Juana Martín's complaint was made directly to Governor Joachín Codallos y Rabal and then later it was sent to Alcalde Antonio de Ulibarrí. The complaint began with a statement that her husband spent more time with Gertrudis than he did with his wife and that he spent half of his income on the other woman. Juana further explained that when she complained Joseph hit her; at one point, he beat her with branches from his ramada.[1] She said that she became so afraid that she petitioned the ecclesiastical judge, Santiago de Roybal, for help, and when that came to nothing, she went to the governor. She asked the governor to banish Gertrudis de Segura to some faraway place, and after some investigation by the alcalde, the governor did just that. Gertrudis was banished for four years to either El Paso or another place outside the kingdom. In addition, Juana's husband was ordered to pay Gertrudis's travel costs. When she learned the true cost of the sentence, however, Juana relented and asked the governor to reduce the penalty and allow Gertrudis to remain in New Mexico. The governor complied by sentencing Gertrudis to banishment in Santa Cruz and made no mention of court costs. It may be that she did leave Santa Fe for a while, but in 1747 Gertrudis was listed as being married to Marcial Brito, and three years later, according to the 1750 census, the couple was living in Santa Fe with three children.

It was not uncommon in eighteenth-century New Mexico for a woman to file a complaint against her husband, see him convicted, and then ask for a pardon or reduced sentence that was granted by the governor.[2] In this case, the governor may have expected that the threat of having to pay court costs and going on an extended trip to El Paso would have reunited the couple.

Interestingly, neither the husband, Joseph de Armijo, nor any of his supporters were asked to testify by the governor. This abbreviated case is similar to that of Francisco Gomez de Torres, which occurred almost thirty years earlier (see Case 6). In this instance, it may have been because Armijo's poor behavior was so well-known in Santa Fe that a full investigation was unnecessary. Also, the case had been previously heard by the ecclesiastical judge, who may have solicited testimony.

Joseph de Armijo's lover is described as a "mulatta," which means she was a child of a Spanish parent and a black parent. Although the *casta* or racial mixture of persons in Spanish Colonial times was often described and illustrated, when it related to marriage and other social activities, the use of the term mulatta seems to have been fluid.

TRANSLATION

1744

Criminal complaint by Juana Martín[3] against Joseph de Armijo[4] for cohabitation with Gertrudis de Segura,[5] mulatta, single, before the sergeant major don Joachín Codallos y Rabal,[6] the governor and captain general of this kingdom of New Mexico

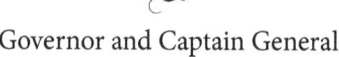

Governor and Captain General

[Complaint of Juana Martín]

I, Juana Martín, legitimate wife of Joseph de Armijo, appear before your honor in order to begin these solemn proceedings according to my legal right, and I state that I present this criminal complaint against Gertrudis de Segura, mulatta, free and single.

This is due to the fact that without fear of God and even less respect to the royal justice, she has been publicly and scandalously cohabitating with my husband for approximately the last fifteen years without any shame whatsoever. He is with her more than with me, not losing an instant of his free time so that from the time of eating his dinner at the hour of the evening prayer, he leaves for her home and returns from there later and later every time. As for his work, when he is employed he takes half of what he makes to her home and leaves the other half for his sustenance and mine and for our children. On various occasions when I have tried to influence him to live according to the law of God, his only response has always been with angry words which I do not wish to repeat to your honor, but adding others that are not as bad.[7] On certain occasions I have been gravely injured. The same is true for the mulatta, as she has on repeated occasions also mistreated me. This can be proven by a scar that I have on my face which she caused by hitting me, from which I suffered for a long period of time.

In summation, sir, my husband has treated me badly many times, one being on Monday of this week. [When I] reproached him about his taking a fanega of corn to the home of the mulatta that your honor had ordered him to give to another for a certain purpose, he hit me with numerous blows and has me so scared that I do not know how to take it any longer. Even though I have consulted with the ecclesiastical judge,[8] and he admonished my husband on various occasions, he has not chosen to do otherwise. So I have no other choice but to consult with your honor, so that [the mulatta] can be banished to a far off place so that my husband cannot be near to her. Thus, in ordering for him this grave punishment there will be no quarrel or revenge to cause me bad treatment either by act or by word.

If your honor orders me to come up with some proof, he should order that the witnesses that I bring forth declare what they know to your honor, because they would most likely not do it solely at my request. From your honor I petition and request that this complaint be honored and order what I have requested to be done according to justice. I swear before God and to the Cross that it is not done in malice, but in what is necessary, etc.

Juana Martín (rubric)

Santa Fe, July 20, 1744

[Proceedings]

Upon reviewing the above written complaint, I, took it as it was presented and I order that this party justify the complaint and that the witnesses that are presented be examined according to the request of this petition. Upon that being done, it is to be brought forth to me so that justice is provided which would have reason. For this purpose, I commission the alcalde mayor [Antonio de Ulibarrí] of this villa, and I thus approve it and rubricate it in my usual manner.

Governor Joachín Codallos y Rabal (rubric)

Statement of Clara de Chávez[9]

At this Villa of Santa Fe on the 29th of July, 1744, I, Antonio de Ulibarrí,[10] alcalde mayor and war captain of this villa, according to the previous decree of the governor of this kingdom and for its justification and proof according to the way it was ordered, I called Clara de Chávez, a resident of this villa, who was offered as a witness by Juana Martín. Upon her being present I received her sworn statement which she made before God, Our Lord and to the sign of the Holy Cross, under which she promised to tell the truth as to what she knew, and was asked to respond to what had been presented by Juana Martín.

She stated that she and her husband have known the complainant for many years as being from here. She knows from seeing it that he has maltreated her because he would much rather be cohabitating with Gertrudis de Segura, mulatta, unmarried.

All this she knows from hearing it from numerous persons as well as from seeing it. She stated that she knew that Joseph de Armijo gave a blow to her face which Juana showed on a certain occasion to the ecclesiastical judge. Even though he tried to do something about it, it did not help at all and the mistreatment has been ongoing to this day. Just a few days prior to this complaint, her husband mistreated her by calling her a whore and hurting her arm with some branches of his own ramada.

She stated that everything that was said in the complaint is certain and well-known throughout the villa and is the truth according to the sworn statement that she has given. She affirmed and ratified this, stating that she was over the age of fifty and that she is not affected by the generalities of the law. She did not sign because she stated that she did not know how. I, the alcalde mayor, signed it along with my two assisting witnesses who heard and saw everything and with whom I act due to the lack of a scribe, there not being one in this kingdom, to which I certify.

Antonio de Ulibarrí (rubric)
Witness
Joseph Romo de Vera[11] (rubric)
Witness
Lucas Miguel de Moya[12] (rubric)

Statement of Sebastián de Apodaca[13]

Continuing on the same day, month and year with the information that is offered by the complainant, Juana Martín brought forth as a witness Sebastián de Apodaca, resident of this villa. Being before me and my witnesses, I took his sworn statement which he made before God, Our Lord and the sign of the Holy Cross, under which he promised to tell the truth as to what he knew and what he was asked according to the tenor of what had been written in the complaint presented by Juana Martín. He stated that according to public knowledge he knows that Joseph de Armijo was cohabitating with Gertrudis de Segura, a single mulatta. He also knows that he had mistreated Juana Martín verbally and physically in order to show that he hated her.

This he said was what he knew and what he stated according to the statement that he has given. He affirmed and ratified this, stating that he was fifty years of age, more or less, and that the generalities of the law did not apply to him. He signed it along with me, acting as presiding judge, due to the known fact there is no scribe in these parts, and which I certified.

Antonio de Ulibarrí (rubric)
Witness
Joseph Romo de Vera (rubric)
Lucas Miguel de Moya (rubric)
Witness
Sebastián de Apodaca (rubric)

Statement of Felipe Tafoya [14]

At this Villa of Santa Fe on the said day, month and year in order to support the information that was given by Juana Martín, wife of Joseph de Armijo, she presented as a witness Felipe Tafoya, also a resident of this villa. He being present before me, the alcalde mayor, I took his sworn statement which he made to God, Our Lord, and to the sign of the Holy Cross, under which he promised to tell the truth as to what he knew and was asked.

Making him aware of the petition presented by Juana Martín, he stated that what she said is the truth being that everyone knows that she has been mistreated both by word as well as by being hurt, being that Joseph de Armijo is cohabitating. He stated that this is the truth regarding the sworn statement that he has made and which he affirmed and ratified. He signed it along with me, the alcalde mayor, and the witnesses who heard and saw it, with whom I act due to the lack of a scribe. Felipe Tafoya stated that he was thirty years of age and that the generalities of the law do not apply to him, which I certified.

 Antonio de Ulibarrí (rubric)
 Felipe Tafoya (rubric)
 Witness
 Joseph Romo de Vera (rubric)
 Witness
 Lucas Miguel de Moya (rubric)

Statement of Juana Gómez[15]

At the Villa of Santa Fe on the 29th of July, 1744, in order to gather more information about which was stated, Juana Martín presented Juana Gómez, resident of the Villa of Santa Fe. Upon her appearing before me I took her sworn statement which she made before God, Our Lord and the sign of the Holy Cross, under which she promised to tell the truth as to what she knew and what she was asked.

Having read to her the petition that was presented before the governor and understanding it, she said that what had been stated was the truth and that she knows that Joseph de Armijo is cohabitating with Gertrudis de Segura, having heard it been said publicly, but not having seen them. She said that it was true that in the year passed this witness saw that Juana Martín had gone to the home of the *vicario*[16] with the evidence shown by the blood flowing from her nose.

She said that this was the truth regarding her sworn statement that she has given and which she affirmed and ratified upon her statement being read back to her. She stated that she was fifty-three years of age and that the generalities of the law do not apply to her. She did not sign because she said that she did not know how. I, the alcalde mayor, signed it along with my two acting witnesses who heard and saw it. I acted as presiding judge due to the known fact of the lack of a public or royal scribe, which there is none in this kingdom to which I certify.

Antonio de Ulibarrí (rubric)
Presiding Judge
Witness
Lucas Miguel de Moya (rubric)
Witness
Joseph Romo de Vera (rubric)

Act of Remission

At the Villa of Santa Fe on the 29th of July, 1744, I, Antonio de Ulibarrí, alcalde mayor and war captain of this villa and its jurisdiction, have seen sufficient information provided by Juana Martín, at whose demand this was done. I have also heard that she has tried to remedy the situation on other various occasions, and which was the reason I heard her complaint. As such I order that these proceedings be returned to the sergeant major don Joachín Codallos y Rabal, governor and captain general of this kingdom, so that his honor upon his review, can determine what has to be done, which always is for the best. I thus signed it along with the witnesses as is done.

Antonio de Ulibarrí (rubric)
Presiding Judge
Witness
Lucas Miguel de Moya (rubric)
Witness
Joseph Romo de Vera (rubric)

Sentence

At the Villa of Santa Fe, New Mexico, on the 6th of August, 1744, I, sergeant major don Joachín Codallos y Rabal, governor and captain general of this kingdom, have reviewed this case and also the act of submission by the alcalde mayor of this villa. I have reviewed this certified document as well the information provided by the complaining party in which she sufficiently proved cohabitation for a number of years, which was the scandal of this kingdom, and the wrongful and bad treatments which he has caused to his wife, along with the rest as is contained herein.

I state that I hereby condemn the cited Gertrudis de Segura to be banished for the time period of four consecutive years from this villa to the presidio of El Paso del Río del Norte or some other place outside this kingdom under the penalty that if she violates this banishment she will be punished in other ways. As for Joseph de Armijo, if he does not treat his wife like he should and she brings forth more complaints against him, he will be punished according to the law. In addition, he is to be punished by having to pay for the expenses of the mulatta, single, for her passage from this Villa of Santa Fe to the presidio El Paso del Río del Norte, who is to be taken there at my say. I thus approved and signed this along with my assisting witnesses with whom I act to

the lack of a scribe there not being one in this kingdom, to which I certify.
    Joachín Codallos y Rabal (rubric)
    Witness
    Joseph Romo de Vera (rubric)
    Witness
    Antonio Aramburu[17] (rubric)

[Notification of Sentence to Gertrudis de Segura]
    At the Villa of Santa Fe on the 18th of August, 1744, I, Antonio de Ulibarrí, alcalde mayor of this villa, being at the house and home of Gertrudis de Segura, mulatta, single, and being a person whom I know, I read to her and made her understand the decree contained on this page as it is found. Upon her having heard it and understanding it, she said that she has heard it and is ready to comply with what is ordered of her, but she is extremely poor and does not have the means to go to her place of banishment. She petitions the governor that when the need arises for him to send her to El Paso she be assisted with whatever is necessary. This is what she gave as her response. I, the alcalde mayor, took the mulatta to the home of don Juan Joseph Moreno[18] so that she remain under his custody until something else is ordered by the governor, and so that it is valid I placed it as a proceeding, to which I certify.
    Antonio de Ulibarrí (rubric)
    Presiding Judge

[Notification of Sentence to Joseph de Armijo]
    At the Villa of Santa Fe on the 20th day of August, 1744, I, Antonio de Ulibarrí, alcalde mayor of this villa, in fulfillment of what was ordered by the sergeant major, don Joachín Codallos y Rabal, governor and captain general, proceeded to notify Joseph de Armijo of the sentence. Upon hearing and understanding it, he said that he had heard it and is informed of its contents and is willing to comply with it, and so that it is valid I signed it with my name.
    Antonio de Ulibarrí (rubric)
    Presiding Judge

    One other thing, I requested of him that he treat his wife kindly as is ordered in the said decree under the penalty of the law that is provided, etc.
    Sergeant Major, Governor and Captain General

[Plea for Revised Sentence]
    I, Juana Martín, resident of this Villa of Santa Fe, prostrated at the feet of your

honor in the best manner possible that there is according to my legal right and say this: That having presented before the graciousness of your honor three written documents in which I asked for the reduction of the complaint that I have filed against my husband Joseph de Armijo and Gertrudis de Segura. I once again petition your grandness saying as I do that the complaint was impetuously filed due to my jealousy of a woman. I did not realize at the time what could come about such as the great expenses that would follow as has been explained above.

Having considered that I am a Christian, and that my husband has not lacked nor is lacking in anything that is needed to meet his obligation for maintenance and clothing and anything else that is needed by providing through his work, all of which I spend in the maintenance of the home, I petition and ask of you sir, that as the kind and generous person that you are, you will allow Gertrudis to return to her home, which is what I expect from your Christian heart.

All of which I ask of your honor, and I petition of your honor, with the most profound rendition of my obligation that you might be pleased to do as I ask. This is so that I might receive all of the mercy and grandness, imploring the goodness, piety and mercy that your honor might consider. I swear that my petition is not done in malice or violence, but for the justice that I seek for what is necessary, etc.

Juana Martín (rubric)

Decree

At the Villa of Santa Fe, New Mexico, on the 23rd of September, 1744, before me, sergeant major don Joachín Codallos y Rabal, governor and captain general of this kingdom, this written document was presented by Juana Martín. Upon being reviewed by me and with attention to the sound reasons that are placed forth for the reduction of the sentence that is herein stated, I took as it was presented and ordered that the banishment for the mulatta Gertrudis [de Segura] be reduced as far as the distance goes with the understanding that the same four years are to be spent at the Villa of Santa Cruz de la Cañada. It is also with the understanding that if she violates [this order] the original order will be executed to the fullest according to the decree that was provided originally. This order is to be verified by the alcalde mayor of this villa, and is to be done as I approved and ordered, acting as I do, to which I certify.

Joachín Codallos y Rabal (rubric)
Witness
Dn. Francisco de Roa y Carrillos[19] (rubric)
Witness
Joseph Romo de Vera (rubric)

[Notice to Gertrudis de Segura]

At this Villa of Santa Fe on the 26th of September, 1744, I, Antonio de Ulibarrí, alcalde mayor of this villa, proceeded to the house of the captain don Juan Joseph Moreno where Gertrudis de Segura, mulatta, single, was being held and personally notified her of the decree of the sergeant major don Joachín Codallos y Rabal, governor and captain general of this kingdom. Upon hearing it and having understood it, she stated that she would obey it. So that it is valid, I signed it along with my assisting witnesses acting as presiding judge, due to the lack of a public and royal scribe, which there is none in this kingdom, to which I certify.

    Antonio de Ulibarrí (rubric)
    Presiding Judge
    Witness
    Juan Manuel de Chirinos (rubric)
    Witness
    Juan Joseph Moreno (rubric)

TRANSCRIPTION

Año de 1744

Causa Criminal por Querella de Juana Martin Contra Joseph de Armijo en razon de el amansavamiento con Getrudes de Segura mulatta soltera. Determinada Por el Sargento Mayor Dn. Joachin Codallos y Rabal Governador y Capitan General de este Reino dela Nueva Mexico.

Señor Governador y Capitan General

Juana Martin muxer legitima de Joseph de Armijo premisas las solemnidades en derecho necesarias paresco ante Vuestra Señoria y digo que me querello criminalmente de Getrudes de Segura mulata libre soltera. En razon de que con poco temor de Dios y en menos precio de la Real Justizia esta publica y escandalosamente amancebada con el dicho mi marido tiempo de quinze años poco mas o menos con tal desberquenza que mas tiempo ha que trata con ella que con migo porque no pierda ynstante que este desocupado de modo que toma desenar ala oracion dela noche y se ba a casa de la dama donde buelbe mas beses mas tarde que otras y delo que adquiere de su trabajo cuando esta ocupado lleba la mitad a casa dela suso dicha dexando la otra mitad para su mantencion y la mia y de nuestros hijos; y por que algunas beses lo e recombenido sobre que biba segun la ley de Dios la respuesta a sido con palabras yndignas de referir ante Vuestra Señoria anadiendo otras de mano de tal manera que muchas beses e quedado lastimada grabemente aciendo lo mismo la dicha mulata en repetidas ocasiones y aun se mantiene de mi rostro una cicatriz que me causo un golpe sullo de que padeci largo tiempo.

En suma Señor son ynnumerables los malos tratamientos que el dicho mi marido me a echo y me ace y a un el dia Lunes desta semana por recombenirlo yo sobre aber llebado a casa de dicha mulata una fanega de mais que Vuestra Señoria le mando dar sierto de manera que mi dio muchos golpes y me tiene tan atemorizada que no soy osada ni lo e sido a solicitor el remedio de tanto mal y aunque ocuri al Señor Juez Eclesiastico y este le hizo varias notificaciones no e concegido por otro medio mas que el que espero de la gran justificacion de mandar desterar ala suso dicha aparte tan distante que no la pueda ber el dicho mi marido ya este en ponerle grabes penas para que no por esta querella ni en su benganza me aga mal tratamiento de obra ni de palabras.

Si Vuestra Señoria mandare que yo de alguna prueba ha de serbir demander tambien que los testigos que yo senalare declaren lo que supieran ante Vuestra Señoria por que me temo que a mi ruego no han de querer aserlo en cuya obligazion, a Vuestra Señoria pido y suplico se sirba de admitir esta querella y demandar hazer y determinar lo que tengo pedido que es de Justicia y juro a Dios y ala Cruz ser cierto y no de malizia en lo necesario, ut supra.

Juana Martin (rubric)

Santa Fee y Julio 20 de 1744 años

Visto el presente escrito lo hube por presentado y mande que esta parte justifique su querella y los testigos que presentare se examinen al thenor de este pedimento, y fecho se trayga para probehir en justicia lo que hubiere lugar, para lo qual se da comission al Alcalde Mayor de esta Villa, y asi lo probehi y rubrique actuando en la forma ordinaria.

(rubric of Governor Joachin Codallos y Rabal)

Declaracion de Clara de Chabes

En la Villa de Santa Fee en beinte y nueve dias del mes de Jullio de mill setesientos y quarenta y quatro años yo Antonio de Ulibarri Alcalde Maior y Capitan Aguerra de esta dicha Villa en conformidad de el decreto antesedente del Señor Governador de el Reyno y para la justificazion y prueba que esta mandada resivir y dio por testigo la dicha Juana Martin a Clara de Chabes vesina de esta dicha Villa a quien estando presente le resevi juramento que yso por Dios Nuestro Señor y la Señal de la Santa Cruz debajo de cuio cargo prometio el desir verdad en lo que supiere y le fuere preguntado y siendolo a el tenor de el escripto presentado por Juana Martin.

Dixo que conose ala querellante de muchos años a esta parte y lo mismo a el dicho su marido y sabe de bista que le a echo muchos tratamientos malos con el motive de estar amancebado con Getrudes de Segura mulatta soltera y esto lo sabe de oidas a muchisimas personas y tanbien de bista sabe que a esta le dio un golpe en la cara ala que la presento con quia occasion a el Señor Juez Eclesiastico y aun que este quiso poner el remedio no basto ninguna deligenzia a ynpedir el amansabemiento en que via prosegido asta el presente.

Pocos dias ha la trato mal de palabra llamandola de puta y lastimandole un braso con unos troncos de su misma ramada y que todo lo contenido en dicho querella es sierto y notorio en toda la Villa y la verdad so cargo de el juramento que fecho tiene en que se afirmo y ratifico y dise ser de edad de mas de sinquenta años y que no le tocan las generales de la ley y no firmo por desir no saber firmelo yo dicho Alcalde Maior con dos testigos de oida y bista siendolos de mi assistenzia con quienes aucto a falta de Escribano que no lo ay en este Reyno de que doi fee =

    Antonio de Ulibarri (rubric)
    Juez Receptor
    Testigo
    Joseph Romo de Vera (rubric)
    Testigo
    Lucas Miguel de Moya (rubric)

Declaracion de Sebastian de Apodaca

Y luego yncontinente en dicho dia mes y año para la ynformazion que ofrese la querellante ofrese por testigo a Sebastian de Apodaca vesino desta Villa a quien estando presente ante mi y los testigos le resevi juramento que yso por Dios Nuestro Señor y la Señal de la Santa Cruz debajo de cuio cargo prometio de desir verdad en lo que supiere y le fuere preguntado y siendole a el tenor de el escrito y querella presentada por Juana Martin dixo que sabe por bos publica estar amansebado Joseph de Armijo con Getrudes de Segura mulata soltera y que sabe aber maltratado de palabra y obras ala dicha Juana Martin el referido Joseph de Armijo por ebitarle esta mala amista y que esto es lo que sabe y declara por el juramento que fecho tiene en que se afirmo y ratifico y dise ser de edad de sinquenta años poco mas o menos y que no le tocan las generales de la ley y lo firmo con migo como dicho es autuando por receptoria por la notoria falta de escribano que no lo ay en este de que doi fee.

    Antonio de Ulibarri (rubric)
    Jues Receptor
    Joseph Romo de Vera (rubric)
    Testigo
    Lucas Miguel de Moya (rubric)
    Testigo
    Sebastian de Apodaca (rubric)

Declaracion de Felipe Tafoya

Esta Villa de Santa Fee en dicho dia mes y año para la ynformasion que ofrese Juana Martin muger de Joseph de Armijo presento por testigo a Felipe Tafoya tanbien besino de dicha Villa a quien es de presente ante mi dicho Alcalde Maior le resevi juramento que yso por Dios Nuestro Señor y la Señal de la Santa Cruz debajo de cuio cargo prometio el desir berdad en lo que supiere y le fuere preguntado.

Asiendole relacion de la petision presentada por Juana Martin, dixo que es berdad todo lo que la referida Juana Martin dise por ser notorio a todos y le consta aberla maltratado de palabra y de obras por estar amansebado el dicho Joseph de Armijo; y que esta es la verdad so cargo del juramento que fecho tiene en que se afirma y ratifica y lo firmo con migo dicho Alcalde Maior y los dos testigos de oida y de bista con quien autuo por la notoria falta de Escribano y dise el dicho Felipe Tafoia ser de edad de treinta años y que no le tocan las generales de la ley que de todo doi fee.

 Antonio de Ulibarri (rubric)
Jues Resepto
Felipe Tafoya (rubric)
Testigo
Joseph Romo de Vera (rubric)
Testigo
Lucas Miguel de Moya (rubric)

Declaracion de Juana Gomez
 En la Villa de Santa Fee en beinte y nueve dias del mes de Jullio de mil setesientos y quarenta y quatro años para la ynformasion que ofrese Juana Martin presento a Juana Gomez vesina de esta Villa de Santa Fee a quien estando presente le resivi juramento que yso por Dios Nuestro Señor y la Señal de la Santa Cruz debajo de cuio cargo prometio de desir berdad en lo que supiere y le fuere preguntado.

Abiendole leydo la petision presentada ante el Señor Governador y enterado de ella dixo que es berdad que lo sabe que esta amansebaado el dicho Joseph de Armijo con Getrudes Segura y que esto lo a oido desir publicamente pero que no los a bisto y que es berdad que el año pasado fue esta declarante la que la bido yr en casa del Señor Vicario con la senal ensima de las narises coriendo sangre y que esta el la berdad so cargo del juramento que fecho tiene en que se afirmo y ratifico siendole leyda su declaracion y dise ser de edad de sinquenta y tres años y que no le tocan las generales de la ley, no firmo por desir no saber firmela yo dicho Alcalde Mayor con dos testigos de oida y bista con los que autuo por receptoria por lo notoria falta de Escribano Publico y Real que no lo ai en este Reyno que de todo doy fee =

 Antonio de Ulibarri (rubric)
Jues Receptor
Testigo
Joseph Romo de Vera (rubric)
Testigo
Lucas Miguel de Moya (rubric)

Auto de Remision

En la Villa de Santa Fee en beinte y nueve dias del mes de Jullio del año de mill setesientos y quarenta y quatro yo Antonio de Ulibarri, Alcalde Maior y Capitan Aguerra de esta dicha Villa y su jurisdision abiendo bisto la plena ynformasion dada por Juana Martin de cuio hecho estas tambien enterado por que diferentes beses e procurado remediarlo en caso nesesario asi lo justifico de pedimento dela querellante y asi mismo mande que debuelban estos autos a el Señor Sargento Maior Dn. Joachin Codallos y Rabal, Governador y Capitan General de este Reyno para que Su Señoria en su bista determine lo que fuere serbido que sera como siempre lo mexor y lo firme con los dichos testigos como dicho es =

 Antonio de Ulibarri (rubric)
 Jues Resepto
 Testigo
 Joseph Romo de Vera (rubric)
 Testigo
 Lucas Miguel de Moya (rubric)

Auto

En la Villa de Santa Fee de la Nueva Mexico en seis dias del mes de Agosto de mill setecientos y quarenta y quatro añnos, el Sargento Maior Dn. Joachin Codallos y Rabal Governador y Capitan General deste dicho Reino haviendo visto esta causa el auto de debolucion del Alcalde Mayor de esta dicha Villa y su aditamento sertificado; y vista assi mismo la informacion dada por la parte querellante en que plenamente se provo el amancevamiento de largos años, el escandalo de este Reino, y la evisia y malos tratamientos que ha hecho ala dicha su muger, con lo de mas que veer combino.

Dixe que devia condenar ala citada Getrudes de Segura a destierro por el tiempo de quattro años continuos de esta Villa para el Presidio del Paso del Rio del Norte, o otra parte para tierra fuera con pena silo quebrantare de que se procedera alo mas que aya lugar = Y al dicho Joseph de Armijo sele apersiva pena del mismo destierro trate bien ala dicha su muger sin dar lugar a otra quexa en que sele atendera y guardara justicia = Y assi mismo sele condena en los costos dela conducion dela dicha mulata, soltera desde esta dicha Villa de Santa Fee para el sitado Presidio del Rio del Passo del Norte el que se regulara ami arbitrio y asi lo probey y firme con los testigos de mi asistenzia con quienes actuo a falta de Escribanao que no lo hay en este Reyno: doy fee … enmendado Joseph Vera. . . .

 Joachin Codallos y Rabal (rubric)
 Testigo
 Joseph Romo de Vera (rubric)
 Testigo
 Antonio Aramburu (rubric)

En la Villa de Santa Fee en dies y ocho dias del mes de Agosto de mil setesientos y quarenta y quatro años yo Antonio de Ulibarri, Alcalde Maior desta Villa estando en la casa de la morada de Getrudes Segura mulata soltera en su persona que conosco le ley y notifique el auto de esta foja como se contiene y abiendolo oido y entendido dixo que lo oie y que esta pronta a cumplir con lo que se le manda pero que es sumamente pobre y no tiene con que yr a su destierro y suplica a el Señor Governador que quando llege el caso de enbiarla a el Paso sel le asista con lo nesesario y esta dio por su repuesta y yo dicho Alcalde Mayor pase a dicha mulata ala casa del Teniente Dn. Juan Joseph Moreno para que este en ella de manifiesto asta que otra cosa se mande por dicho Señor Governador y para que conste lo pongo por diligenzia de que doi fee =
    Antonio de Ulibarri (rubric)
    Juez Receptor

En la Villa de Santa Fee, en beinte dias del mes de Agosto de mill setesientos y quarenta y quatro años yo Antonio de Ulibarri, Alcalde Maior de esta dicha Villa en cumplimiento delo mandado por el Señor Sargento Maior Dn. Joachin Codallos y Rabal, Governador y Capitan General pase a aserle la notificazion a Joseph de Armijo que oida y entendida dixo que la oie y esta enterado de ella y obediente a su cumplimiento y para que conste lo firme de mi nombre.
    Antonio de Ulibarri (rubric)
    Jues Receptor

Otro si le apersebi aga buenos tratamientos ala dicha su muger como en dicho decreto se manda y debajo de la pena que se prebiene ut supra =

Señor Sargento Maior, Governador y Capitan General

Juana Martin vesina de esta Villa de Santa Fee puesta alas plantas de Vuestra Señoria en la mas bastante forma que aya lugar en derecho y digo: Señor que aviendo presentado ante la grandeza de Vuestra Señoria tres escriptos expresando en ellos la vaja de querella que tengo puesta contra mi esposo Joseph de Armijo y Getrudes Segura buelvo a ynplorar su grande begnidad diziendo como digo que la querella fue biolentada del selo de muger, no advirtiendo por entonses cosa alguna en los graves daños que de ella se podian seguir como llevo explicado en el Segundo y terser escripto.

Aviendo considerado el que soy Christiana, y que el dicho mi esposo no me a faltado ni me falta en todo aquello que lo es de obligasion en la mantension y bistuario y todo quanto alcansa con su travajo todo lo gasto yo en casa, y asi Señor buelvo a suplicarle el que como begnino y piadoso se compadesca en que la dicha Getrudes buelva a su casa, que asi lo espero de su Christiano pecho por todo lo qual a Vuestra Señnoria pido y suplico con el mas profundo rendimento de mi obligacion sea mui servido de azer y determiner como llevo pedido que en ello rescivire bien y mersed ymplorando la begninida, piedad y misericordia de Vuestra Señoria y juro no ser de malisia ni biolentada a este pedimento si justisia que pido y en lo nesessario, ut supra =

    Juana Martin (rubric)

Auto
    En la Villa de Santa Fee dela Nueva Mexico en veinte y tres dias del mes de Septiembre de mill setecientos quarenta y quatro años ante mi el Sargento Maior Dn. Joachin Codallos y Rabal, Gobernador y Capitan General de este dicho Reino se presento este escripto por la contenida en el y visto por mi y en atencion a las rasones de utilidad que propone y la vaja de querella que haze la ube por desistida y mande sele relebe el destierro en quanto a la distancia ala mulatta Getrudes, entendiendose por los mismos quattro años en la Villa de Santa Cruz de la Cañada, y con apersevimiento que si lo quebrantare se executara ala letra el auto probeido en los dela materia y este lo notificara el Alcalde Mayor de esta Villa y assi lo probei y mande actuando como dicho es doy fee =

    Joachin Codalllos y Rabal (rubric)
    Testigo
    Dn. Francisco de Roa y Carrillo (rubric)
    Testigo
    Joseph Romo de Vera (rubric)

    En la Villa de Santa Fee en beinte y seis dias del mes de Septiembre del año de mill setesientos y quarenta y quatro yo Antonio de Ulibarri Alcalde Maior de esta Villa pase ala casa del Capitan Dn. Juan Joseph Moreno en donde se alla Getrudes Segura, mulata soltera depositada y en su persona le notifique el auto del Señor Sargento Maior Dn. Joachin Codallos y Rabal, Governador y Capitan General de este Reino quien lo oio y entenido y dixo que lo obedezia y para que conste lo firme con los testigos de mi asistenzia autuando por receptoria por la notaria falta de Escribano Publico y Real que no lo ai en este Reyno de que doi fee.

    Antonio de Ulibarri
    Jues Receptor
    Testigo
    Juan Joseph Moreno (rubric)
    Testigo
    Juan Manuel Chirinos (rubric)

Notes

1. A *ramada* is a lean-to made of branches.
2. See Case 6 and Case 24.
3. Juana Martín was probably part of the Martín Serrano clan, or else she was a widow of a Martín Serrano family member. She married Joseph de Armijo in 1729. To date, no further information on her has been found. (Kessell, Hendricks, and Dodge, *Boulders*: 526n27.)
4. Joseph (Antonio) de Armijo III was the son of José de Armijo II and María Manuela Velásquez (who married in 1710). José II was the son of José Durán de Armijo I and Catalina Durán, who married in Zacatecas, Mexico. José II was the brother of Antonio, Marcus, and Vicente Durán de Armijo. Joseph de Armijo III married Juana Martín in 1729. (Chávez, *Origins*: 136-37; Kessell, Hendricks, and Dodge, *Boulders*: 562n26.)
5. Gertrudis de Segura may have been the daughter of (or a relation of) Pedro Segura, or she may have been related to one of his sons, Cayetano Segura or Tomás Segura. To date, however, no specific mention of her has been found. (For information on Pedro Segura, see Chávez, *Origins*: 286; and SANM II #239d.)
6. Joachín Codallos y Rabal was governor of New Mexico from 1743 to 1749. He was also a major in the Spanish Army. His term as governor was originally supposed to end in 1747, but his appointed successor, Francisco de la Rocha, had to decline the position because of ill health. Tomás Vélez Cachupín was appointed Codallos y Rabal's successor in 1749. (*Wikipedia*, "Governor Joaquín Codallos y Rabal," accessed on August 12, 2016.)
7. See the comments about Clara de Chávez in note 9 below.
8. Father Santiago de Roybal was the ecclesiastical judge and vicar at this time. He was the brother or son of Ignacio de Roybal, who was high sheriff of the Holy Office of the Inquisition and from Galicia, Spain. Father Roybal was educated in Mexico City and was ordained by Bishop Crespo in Durango, Mexico. He served as the vicar and ecclesiastical judge in New Mexico from 1730 to 1774. He was the first native-born priest in New Mexico. (Chávez, *Origins*: 273-75.)
9. Clara de Chávez was a natural daughter of don Fernando Durán y Chávez, who returned to New Mexico with Diego de Vargas and settled on old family lands at Atrisco. Clara was married to Juan de la Mora Piñeda, who was from Guadalajara, Mexico, and came to New Mexico as part of the Spanish Reconquest. He was a secretary to alcalde Martín Hurtado and living in Santa Fe by 1695; he also served as alcalde mayor of Taos from 1715 to 1720. He died in 1727. Clara's name appears in the 1750 census. (Chávez, *Origins*: 160-61, 258, 384; NMGS, *Aquí*: 373, 375.)
10. For information on Antonio de Ulibarrí, see Case 23.
11. Joseph Romo de Vera came from Mexico City and was in New Mexico by 1731. His first wife was María Maldonado y Sais, with whom he had nineteen children, all of whom had died by 1750. His second wife was Angela Francisca Valdéz, with whom Joseph had one child. Joseph's will of 1753 indicates he was a Santa Fe merchant and stock raiser and that he owned, among other things, "a loom with all its equipment except for the spinning wheels." (Chávez, *Origins*: 273; Baxter, *Las Carneradas*: 34; SANM I #1052, WPA translation. See also Esquibel, "Romo de Vera," parts 1 and 2.)
12. Lucas Miguel de Moya was the son of Antonio de Moya and Francisca Antonia Morales (or de Guijosa), both of whom were natives of Mexico City. Lucas was the third husband of Juana de Anaya Almazán and a charter officer in the religious *cofradia* (brotherhood) Our Lady of Light. (Chávez, *Origins*: 240.)
13. Sebastián de Apodaca was a New Mexico native who married Juana Hernández de la Trinidad in 1707. Sebastián was in Santa Fe from 1716 to the 1740s; his name frequently appears as a witness on government documents. (Chávez, *Origins*: 213; SANM I #512, WPA translation.)
14. Felipe Tafoya was the son of Antonio Tafoya Altamirano, who came to New Mexico in 1695. His mother was María Luisa Godines. Felipe married Margarita González de la Rosa in 1728; and, in 1750, he married Teresa Fernández. He was an alcalde of Santa Fe, a lieutenant general of the kingdom, and in 1747, he was appointed church notary. He also acted as a legal representative for the Villa of Santa Fe and was a legal defender for San Ildefonso Pueblo. He died about 1769. (Kessell, Hendricks, and Dodge, *Boulders*: 1169n87; Chávez, *Origins*: 291; SANM I #995; Norris, *Year Eighty*: 117; Cutter, *Legal Culture*: 75-76; Cutter, *Protector de Indios*: 76-77, 83.)
15. The Juana Gómez included in this document may have been Juana María Gómez del Castillo, who was born in 1730 to Francisco Gómez del Castillo and Ursula Guillén. (Chávez, *Origins*: 187.)
16. The "vicario" (vicar) was Santiago de Roybal.
17. Little is known about Antonio Aramburu, except that he frequently acted as a witness for the governor in the 1740s. He was probably a relative of Joseph Aramburu, a Chihuahua merchant who was active in the New Mexican trade. (See SANM II #427 and #506.)
18. For further information on Juan Joseph Moreno, see Case 21.
19. To date, nothing has been found on Francisco de Roa y Carrillos. He may have been the son of (or at last related to) Pedro de Rojas de Liscano, who was a soldier in Santa Fe in 1697. Or, Francisco could be the son of Josef de Royas and Teresa de Los Reyes, or possibly he was the son of Pedro de Sedillo Rico de Rojas. (Chávez, *Origins*: 388.)

27

SANTIAGO RESIDENT ASKS FOR HELP WITH INCORRIGIBLE WIFE; COUPLE ESCORTED TO VALENCIA BY SOLDIERS
July 31–August 4, 1746, Source: SANM II #459

Synopsis and editor's notes: In 1744, Nicolás de Aragon submitted a complaint about his wife's abusive behavior to Lieutenant Alcalde Juan Galván. At that time, Nicolás was living in Santiago, a village near Bernalillo, on the west side of the Río Grande, across from the bulge in the river called Weavers' Bend. His wife of ten years was Margarita Gallegos, the daughter of Antonio Gallegos II and granddaughter of Antonio Gallegos I, a pre-revolt settler.

When Galván went to meet Nicolás de Aragon at his house to review the complaint, he found no one home but then saw Nicolás waving from a small house nearby. When Galván asked him what he was doing, he said he was hiding out and spying on his wife because she had recently been seen with a young man named Jacinto Gutiérrez. After Galván cautioned Nicolás to let him handle it, the two waited until nighttime and then went to the main house where they found the lover, Jacinto Gutiérrez, in bed with Margarita "as if they were husband and wife." Nicolás said that this had happened before, and he also explained that he had wanted to move to land he had purchased in Valencia but his wife refused to leave.

The case went to the ecclesiastical judge, Santiago de Roybal, who did nothing to help Aragon, and then the case was sent to the governor. This was the second complaint by Nicolás about his wife. The governor supported his request to move to Valencia, a decision in line with the expected role of the governor in supporting the stability of families and uniting husbands and wives. The governor sent a message to the lieutenant alcalde of the jurisdiction, Juan Moya, ordering him to take two soldiers and two witnesses to Santiago, and then immediately and without hesitation he was to take Margarita and Nicolás to Valencia. The governor also ordered Lieutenant Alcalde Moya to notify Margarita that she was to live in a married state honestly and quietly with her husband, and if she did not comply she would be punished accordingly. In response to an additional request from Nicolás, Lieutenant Alcalde Moya was also directed to order the alcaldes Antonio Baca and Joseph Baca to not prevent Nicolás from trading or selling his land or purchasing land in Valencia, or they too would be punished. Lieutenant Alcalde Moya then took Margarita, Nicolás, and the two soldiers to Valencia and read the governor's orders to which all of the participants agreed.

Four years later, in the 1750 Spanish Colonial Census for New Mexico, Nicolás, by then age forty-five, and Margarita Gallegos, age forty, were listed as living together with their four children, ages nineteen, seventeen, seven, and three.

It is likely that Nicolás wished to move to Valencia to take advantage of the vacant land made available to settlers because of a channel change in the Río Grande. Santiago, where Nicolás lived previously, was the site of a pre-contact settlement. According to Clay Mathers, prior to Francisco Vázquez de Coronado's arrival, Santiago was a Pueblo Indian village, but it did not retain its pueblo name. Mathers further states that it was at or near the site of Coronado's winter camp. The Spanish removed the Indians, occupied the site, and renamed it Santiago. This village was later abandoned by the Spanish during the Pueblo Revolt, and then it was occupied by colonists who came into the region with the Spanish Reconquest.

As a legal document, the procedures were much abbreviated. The only testimony given was by the husband and the ecclesiastical judge, none by the wife, neighbors, friends, or relatives of the wife. While it was not unusual that the alcalde would go to the home of the complainant, it is unusual that the lieutenant alcalde went with Nicolás at night to spy on his wife. After their testimony, the case immediately went to the governor, who, without any hesitation, pronounced a sentence. Most likely, the governor and the ecclesiastical judge had heard about the situation before. There is no indication as to why Antonio and Joseph Baca would have wished to prevent Nicolás from selling his house and moving to Valencia, or why they would have interfered with Nicolás's trading efforts. The Bacas, however, may have seen Nicolás as being in competition with their own trading activities. The governor must have known something about this, for his order to stop their interference was quite clear.

TRANSLATION

Year of 1744

Denunciation to the lieutenant to the alcalde mayor, Juan Galván,[1] who is from the pueblo of Jémez, regarding some problems that Nicolás de Aragon[2] has with his wife, both residents of the puesto[3] of Bernalillo, in which document they are ordered to live in a married state

[Letter of the complaint]

I, Juan Galván, lieutenant to the alcalde mayor, certify that having arrived at the main house of Nicolás de Aragon, and asking for him, found that neither he or his wife were at home at the large house. Continuing on a distance, I noticed that someone was waving at me from a small house, where I found the said Nicolás hiding out watching his wife. Upon asking him why he was hiding at this house, he answered me saying that he was spying on his wife, being that she had been seen with a young man by the name of Jacinto Gutiérrez.[4] Being that I am presently the lieutenant, and recognizing the danger in which his wife found herself,[5] I ordered Aragon to leave it alone, doing this as a precaution. He responded to me as the official justice, saying that it was all due to the life that his wife was leading while he was living with her, and that he would place the responsibility in my hands. That night I proceeded to the house with Aragon where he found his wife in bed with the young man, Jacinto Gutiérrez, as if they were husband and wife. To all of this I took an oath and gave testimony, and I swear that it is true. So that it is valid I signed it in the year of forty-four.

 I, the lieutenant
 Juan Galván (rubric)

[Letter of the ecclesiastical judge]

Nicolás de Aragon:
 I became aware during the years past of the manner of life of your wife and the many annoyances that she has caused you on the repeated occasions that have come before me and my notaries as legal complaints.[6] We tried to remedy these in the best possible way by bringing the complaints to your majesty as the various notices were given to me by the notary Quintana.[7] This is done understanding the natural disposition, so incorrigible, of Margarita Gallegos,[8] your wife.

 You have represented to me that you no longer have lands in Santiago[9] where you used to have them, rather they are now in Valencia. I also recognize that your wife does not want or intend to go there in your company, but rather for her willfulness insists on remaining at the ranch you previously had at Santiago. Because of her stubbornness and because I do not wish to ignore the many quarrels and unpleasantness which were had at the puesto [of Santiago], I recognize that is not suitable for her to live without you, where it would be convenient for her.

 For all of this I order and did order that you take her [to Valencia] without any further problems for anyone and live a married life as is ordered by God, of whom I ask that he safeguard his majesty's life for many years. Villa of Santa Fe, July 31, 1746.

 At the request of your majesty
 Bachiller Santiago de Roybal[10] (rubric)

Governor and Captain General

[Statement by Nicolás de Aragon]
 I, Nicolás de Aragon, resident of the puesto of Valencia, with all of the solemnity allowed to me by my legal right, appear before your honor. I say that finding myself with reasons that are most sufficient, as can be seen by your honor according to the two notices that were presented before your greatness by the vicario and ecclesiastical judge of this kingdom, and another by the lieutenant to the alcalde mayor of the jurisdiction of Bernalillo, which is the place where I lived. By these your honor can determine whether there is any justification to continue living at the puesto of

Santiago, due to the fact that I have purchased lands at the puesto of Valencia, where I can live in a more comfortable way with fewer problems. For all of this I petition of your honor as father and appeals judge to permit me and not to impede me in selling the place that I have at the puesto de Santiago and allow me to move with my wife and family to that of Valencia, for a more suitable life.

Also I petition your honor to order that I not be prevented from trading or making contracts, as it may be by the alcalde mayor of the jurisdiction the Villa of Albuquerque, or by any one person, for as is well-known by your honor, there are no other means by which I am able to carry on. For all of this I petition and solicit your honor, with the most profound rendering of my obligations that you may be pleased to do as I petition by which I shall receive all of your goodness and mercy. Thus I swear that this, my petition, is not done in malice, but rather for the justice that I seek, and for what is necessary, etc.

Nicolás de Aragon (rubric)

Signature of Nicolas de Aragon with rubric. SANM II #459, roll 8, f 334

Decree

At this Villa of Santa Fe on the 2nd of August 1746, before me, the sergeant major, don Joachín Codallos y Rabal,[11] governor and captain general of this kingdom of New Mexico, this petition was presented. Upon being reviewed by me, along with the attached papers, I ordered that Juan Moya, lieutenant to the alcalde mayor of the Villa of Albuquerque, proceed with two soldiers and two residents and get the married woman from where she is, as is mentioned in the document. In the company of her husband (if he is found present) she is to be taken to the *paraje* [Valencia] that is indicated, immediately and without hesitation on the part of the lieutenant. There he is to notify her that she is to live in a married state, honestly and quietly, with her husband, and if she does not she will be punished accordingly for anything that she does wrong.

The lieutenant is to notify the alcaldes Antonio[12] and Joseph Baca[13] that they are not to stop Aragon in any way from his ability to trade, nor are they to prevent him from selling his lands that he says he has in Bernalillo or to purchase those that he has already agreed to buy at the paraje that is known as Valencia, under the penalty that they will be denied anything that they might have or anything else that can be considered.

Once these proceedings are concluded, the lieutenant is to submit them to this superior government. I thus approved, ordered and signed this along with my assisting witnesses with whom I act due to the lack of a public or royal scribe, as there is not one in this kingdom, to which I certify.

Joachín Codallos y Rabal (rubric)
Witness
Joseph Romo de Vera[14] (rubric)
Witness
Juan Felipe Jacobo de Unanue[15] (rubric)

Notification

On the 4th of August 1746, Juan Moya, lieutenant to the alcalde mayor of this Villa of Albuquerque, under this special commission, proceeded to the puesto of Pajarito[15] as is mentioned above. With the two alcaldes being present, Antonio Baca and Joseph Baca, before two witnesses, I notified both of them in a clear and intelligible voice the contents of the above decree sent by the sergeant major don Joachín Codallos y Rabal, governor and captain general of this kingdom. They together stated that they had nothing to say other than that they would obey, and the alcalde Joseph Baca stated that there was nothing else to say. So that it is valid I placed it as a completed proceeding and signed it along with the assisting witnesses and the two alcaldes, to which I certified, etc.

Juan Moya[16] (rubric)
Presiding Judge
Joseph Baca (rubric)
Antonio Baca (rubric)
Witness
Felipe Varela[17] (rubric)
Witness
Juan Candelaria[18] (rubric)

[Notification at Valencia]

Continuing accordingly and without any delay, I, Juan Moya, lieutenant in the Villa of Albuquerque, as set forth in the above decree issued by the governor of this kingdom, don Joachín Codallos y Rabal, preceded along with two residents and two soldiers, as ordered according to the previous decree stated above in the preceding page. In fulfillment of my obligation proceeded to the paraje of Bernalillo from where I met with the married woman and wife of Nicolás de Aragon and in company of her spouse and the two witness and the two soldiers, I informed them of the notification that was requested of me. This was to order that both of them live a good married life. The woman then stated that she would obey. She said that he was indeed her husband and that she would comply in doing everything that was required in an honest and quiet manner according to what her husband wanted or needed. This was what the woman stated.

Thus the order was completed, and I placed them at the puesto that is known as Valencia, where I then turned her over to her husband, ordering both of them that they live a good married life, quietly and peacefully. They thus promised me that they would both live gracefully and would serve God. This was what they promised to do on this sixth day of August of the present year. And so that it is valid I signed it along with two assisting witnesses and the two soldiers as instrumental witnesses with whom I act due to the lack of a public or royal scribe, which there is none in this kingdom, to which I certify.

    Juan Moya (rubric)
    Presiding Judge
    Witness
    Felipe Varela (rubric)
    Witness
    Juan Candelaria (rubric)

TRANSCRIPTION

Año de 1744

Denuncia del Theniente de Alcalde Mayor Juan Galban, que lo es del Pueblo de Xemes, sobre ynquietudes de marido y muger, Nicolas de Aragon con su esposa vecinos del Puesto de Bernalillo, en que esta mandado hagan vida maridable, ut supra

    Digo yo Juan Galban, Theniente de Alcalde Maior sertifico como biendo llegado ala casa de Nicolas de Aragon y preguntando por su mersed y no abiendolo hayado en la casa grande ni ha el ni a su muger y pasandome de largo bi que me capeaba dela casita Chiquita en donde estaba reculto en desbelo de su esposa y preguntandole por que estaba oculta en la casa, me respondio que estaba espiando a su esposa por que se bia con un mansebo llamado Jacinto Gutierrez y ayandome de actual Theniente y conociendo el peligro que paraba la mujer y mande a dicha Aragon que se dejara de eso que quisas seria precucion a lo qual me respondio asiendome el cargo como justicia que era dela bida en que se allaba su esposa y mela pondria en mis manos y ala noche pase en compania del dicho Aragon en donde allo a la dicha mujer con el dicho mansebo Jacinto Gutierrez en su cama como marido y mujer delo que di fee y testimonio y juro ser berdad y para que conste lo firme el año de quarenta y quatro.

    Yo el Theniente
    Juan Galban (rubric)

Señor Nicolas de Aragon

    Aviendome serciorado por los años pretentos del modo de vida de su muger de un respecto alos mucho disgustos que le a causado a Usted en repetidas ocasiones que

ante mi y mis notorios a corrido por diligensia y hemos mediado componiendolos en el mejor medio que hemos allado por quejas de Vuestra Magestad como por noticias que me a participado el notorio Quintana y conociendo el natural tan irreducible de Margarita Gallegos, su esposa de usted y que me a representado, no tener ya tierras en Santiago, que onde las tiene es en Lo de Balencia y que su dicha esposa se niega a ir en su compania, insistiendo en que se quiere estar en el rancho que antes tenia en dicho Santiago por su contumacia, y los casos que yo no ignoro por las mu querallas y disgustos que ocaciona su estado en dicho Puesto en el que tambien conosco no conviene que viva sino con un, donde tubiere por conveniente, por lo que ordeno a un, y la mando la llebe sin que le balga disculpa a ninguna con un a haser vida maridable segun manda Dios a quien pido guarde a Vuestra Majestad muchos años. Villa de Santa Fee y Julio 31 de 1746 años.
 De Vuestra Magestad
 Bachiller Santiago de Roibal (rubric)

Señor Governador y Capitan General

 Nicolas de Aragon vesino del Puesto de Balencia premises las solemnidades que el derecho me permite paresco ante la grandesa de Vuestra Señoria y digo Señor que allandome con motivos mui suficientes como podra Vuestra Señoria ber por dos pales que ante su grandesa presento el año del Señor Vicario y Jues Eclesiastico de este Reyno, y el otro del Teniente de Alcalde Maior de la jurisdision de Bernalillo, en donde tenia mi avitasion, que en ellos bera Vuestra Señoria si tengo justificada rason para no vivir en el Puesto de Santiago, y por aver comprado tierras en dicho Puesto de Balencia donde puedo vivir con mas comodidad, y menos ynquietudes por lo que suplico a Vuestra Señoria como Padre y Jues de apelasion me permita el que no seme ympida el bender la parte que en dicho Puesto de Santiago tengo y mudarme con mi esposa y familia al de Balensia por combenensia de vivir.
 Como tambien suplico a Vuestra Señoria el que mande que no seme ympida el tratar y contratar, asi por el Alcalde Maior de la jurisdicion dela Villa de Alburquerque como por ninguna persona, pues bien save Vuestra Señoria ya que no ay otro modo para poder pasar; por lo que a Vuestra Señoria pido y suplico con el mas profundo rendimiento de mi obligasion se sirva de haser y mandar como llevo pedido que en ello resivire bien y mersed y juro en devida forma no ser de malisia este mi pedimento, si justisia que pido y en lo nesesario, ut supra =
 Nicolas de Aragon (rubric)

Auto
 En la Villa de Santa Fee en dos dias del mes de Agosto de millsetecientos y quarenta y seis años, ante mi el Sargento Mayor Dn. Joachin Codallos y Rabal, Gobernador

y Capitan General deste Reyno dela Nueba Mexico, se presento esta petizion, que por mi vista, con los dos papeles que expresan; mando a Juan Moya, Theniente de Alcalde Mayor dela Villa de Alburquerque, que passé con dos soldados y dos vecinos, saque a la muger casada que en el escripto se mensiona, y en compania de su marido (si se hallare presente) la llebe al Paraxe que se refiere, luego luego, y sin dilacion, que no permite dicho Theniente con ningun pretestto, y lo notifique haga vida maidable con el dicho su marido honesta y recogidamente, con apersevimentto que se prosedera contra ella por todo rigor de derecho en qualquiera exceso que cometta.

Notificara dicho Theniente a los Alcaldes Antonio y Joseph Baca, que no le impidan a esta parte su trato, y comercio competente; ni el que venda las tierras que dice tiene en Bernalillo, ni el comprar las que tiene trattado en el Paraxe que llaman de Valencia, pena de que seles condenara en el interes dela parte y demas que huviere lugar; y fechas todas estas diligencias las rremitira dicho Theniente a este Superior Govierno; y asi lo probey, mande y firme con los testigos de mi asistenzia con quienes actuo a falta de escribano publico o real que no lo hay en este Reyno: Doy fee =

 Joachin Codallos y Rabal (rubric)
 TestigoTestigo
 Joseph Romo de Vera (rubric)
 Testigo
 Juan Felipe Jacobo de Unanue (rubric)

Notificacion

En quatro dias del mes de Agosto del año de mill setesientos y quarenta y seis años, Juan Moya, Teniente de Alcalde Maior desta Villa de Alburquerque con especial comision pase al Puesto de Pajarito como en el auto arrriba se contiene y juntos los dos Alcaldes Antonio Baca y Joseph Baca ante dos testigos les notifique en bos clara y ynteligible el auto de ariba despedido por el Senor Sargento Mayor Dn. Joachin Codallos y Rabal, Gobernador y Capitan General deste Reino, quienes a su bos no tubieron que desir mas que obedesian y que tenian que presentar esto dijo el Alcalde Joseph Baca y no otra cosa y para que conste lo puse por deligencia y la firme con los testigos de mi asistensia y los dos Alcaldes de que doi fee, ut supra =

 Juan Moya (rubric)
 Jues Receptor
 Joseph Baca (rubric)
 Testigo
 Felipe Barela (rubric)
 Testigo
 Juan Candelaria (rubric)
 Antonio Baca (rubric)

Luego luego en continente y sin dilasion ninguna bisto yo Juan Moya, Teniente dela Villa de Alburquerque el decreto ariba espresado y despedido del Señor Governador deste Reino Dn. Joachin Codallos y Rabal, pase yo dicho Teniente con dos vesinos y dos soldados como es en el auto de la buelta dela foxa seme ordena y cumplimiento de mi obligasion fui al Paraje de Bernalillo de a donde saque ala muger casada y esposa de Nicolas de Aragon y en compania de su esposo y los dos vesinos y los dos soldados le yse la notificasion que seme ordena que entre los dos agan vida maridable y la mujer respondio que obedesia y que era su marido y que aria lo que sele ordenaba onesta y recojidamente como la estimara y quisiera su marido y esto fue lo que respondio la dicha mugger.

Luego luego parase a la egecusion de la orden y la puse en el Puesto que se expresa en el auto que llaman de Balensia a onde sela entregue a su marido ordenandoles a uno y a otro agan vida maridable y en quieta y pacifica quietu, quienes me prometieron ambos dos vibir en gracia y serbisio a Dios y esto fue lo que prometieron oy dia seis de Agosto deste presente año y para que conste lo firme con dos testigos de mi asistensia y los dos soldados por unstrumentales con quienes auto a falta de escribano publico o real que no lo ai en este Reino, doi fee.

Juan Moya
Jues Receptor
Testigo
Philipe Barela (rubric)
Juan Candelaria (rubric)

Notes

1. Juan [Manuel] Galván was the illegitimate son of Juana la Coyota, stepsister to Juana Hurtado y Salas. He served as the lieutenant alcalde of the Zia jurisdiction, which included Bernalillo. His aunt (or step aunt) was the niece of the governor of Zia Pueblo, Juan Checaye. He was accused by alcalde Ramón García Jurado of living a scandalous life for residing with and having four children with a woman to whom he was not married. The accusation ended with the Pueblo supporting Galván. (Chávez, *Origins*: 179-80; SANM II #345; Brooks, *Captives*: 100-02.)
2. Nicolás Aragon was most likely the son of Ignacio Aragon, a weaver, and Sebastiana Ortiz, who were in New Mexico by 1705, having come with the Farfan Expedition in 1694. In 1734, Nicolás was in Bernalillo and involved in a lawsuit having to do with a skirt that his wife wanted to buy. In 1744, Nicolás Aragon and Margarita Gallegos were listed as parents of María Manuela. (NMGS, *Aquí*: 440; SANM II #397.)
3. This should probably read: "the puesto of Valencia in the jurisdiction of Bernalillo," as it does later in the document. By 1746 Bernalillo was much larger than a puesto, which was a small settlement or outpost.
4. Jacinto Gutiérrez was probably part of the pre-revolt Roque Gutiérrez family. In 1773, a Jacinto Gutiérrez is listed as the godfather of Antonio Toribio Sedillo. (NMGS, *Aquí*: 159; Chávez, *Origins*: 194-95.)
5. The lieutenant alcalde may have been concerned about the danger to her reputation or perhaps even her life. In some cases, finding a wife "*en flagrante*" was considered just cause for killing the wife, the lover, or both. (See the introduction.)
6. To date, information about these proceedings or complaints have not been found.
7. Quintana, the notary, may have been Miguel de Quintana from Santa Cruz, who was also known as a poet. This Quintana died in 1748. Or, it could have been José de Quintana, who is listed as being in Bernalillo in 1709 and who held the title of captain in 1722. (Chávez, *Origins*: 261-62.)
8. Margarita Gallegos was born in 1706, the daughter of Antonio Gallegos II and Rosa Montoya. Antonio was a pre-revolt settler and a sergeant at Bernalillo in 1699. (Chávez, *Origins*: 179.)

9. See Mathers, "Tangled Threads": 376-85; Barrett, *Conquest*: 7, 23-33; David Snow, "Santiago to Guache": 161-81)
10. For information on Santiago de Roybal, see Case 26.
11. For information on Governor Joachín Codallos y Rabal, see Case 25.
12. Antonio Baca is most likely the son of Josefa Baca and brother of Joseph Baca. It is known that he was an alcalde for the Zia jurisdiction in 1753. Or, he could be the Antonio Baca who was the son of Manuel Baca. The latter Antonio returned to Santa Fe in 1693 with his wife, María de Salazar. In 1706, upon the death of María de Salazar, he married María de Aragon. From 1715 to 1716, he was an alférez with the Santa Fe presidio. (Chávez, *Origins*: 144; Christmas and Rau, "Una Lista": 196.)
13. Joseph Baca was a son of Josefa Baca and his wife was Josefa Gallegos. Joseph is listed as being a captain on a list of the original petitioners for the Tomé grant. In 1745, he was alcalde of Fuenclara/Tomé, and later he became alcalde and war captain of Albuquerque. He made out his will in 1766. (NMGS, *Aquí*: 243; Alexander, *Among the Cottonwoods*: 32; SANM II #463, WPA translation; SANM I #117, WPA translation.)
14. For information on Joseph Romo de Vera, see SANM II #464; SANM II #467; Chávez, *Origins*: 273.
15. Juan Felipe Jacobo de Unanue was in New Mexico by 1736, acting as a witness. His wife was María Francisca García. By 1746 he was a captain at the Janos presidio. Unanue is a Basque name. He was also a witness in Case 28 and Case 30 in this book. (Rau, "Unanue to Nuanes": 17-20.)
16. The puesto of Pajarito was apparently the residence of Antonio and Joseph Baca.
17. Juan Moya was alcalde of Albuquerque in 1746. In 1763, there were proceedings against him for the theft of a cow. (See SANM I #340 and Case 10.)
18. It is possible that Felipe Varela was a descendent of Cristóbal Varela and Clementa Ortega, who were in Bernalillo in 1699. A Felipe Barela and Monica Varela were mentioned as godparents to Manuel Cristóbal Lucero in 1763. (Chávez, *Origins*: 305; NMGS, *Aquí*: 475; SANM I #340.)
19. Juan Candelaria was the son of Francisco and Feliciana Candelaria, one of the founding families of Albuquerque. Juan was married to Manuela Varela in 1728. In 1776, he wrote a brief history of Albuquerque, in which he listed the families he remembered as being the original settlers. (Chávez, *Origins*: 156.)

28

ISIDRO SÁNCHEZ GIVES LEGAL ADVICE TO JILTED PRESIDIO SOLDIER
August 2–12, 1744, Source: SANM II #459a

Synopsis and editor's notes: Isidro Sánchez Bañares y Tagle (generally referred to in court documents as just Isidro Sánchez) is known to present-day historians and genealogists for his exceptional and sometimes outrageous behavior. Three documents regarding his exploits are published in this book;[1] a fourth can be found in the 2013 publication, *Spanish Colonial Lives*.

In the case of August 1744, Isidro Sánchez appeared before Governor Joachín Codallos y Rabal, representing a jilted soldier, Joseph Varela Jaramillo, with a complaint against the ecclesiastical judge. He began the case by calmly stating that Feliciana Chávez had promised to marry Jaramillo, agreements were made between them, and then the couple had sexual relations. But, Sánchez explained, Feliciana, unexpectedly and without warning, changed her mind and decided to marry someone else.

Even worse, continued Sánchez, the ecclesiastical judge supported Feliciana's decision and gave her a document stating that she did not know Jaramillo, thus refuting the claim of a sexual relationship between herself and Jaramillo. It was the judge's document that Sánchez was challenging. In doing so, he got himself all stirred up and claimed that Feliciana flaunted the document, he argued with Jaramillo's supporters, and he just generally created an uproar. According to Sánchez, because of Feliciana's actions the whole town of Albuquerque was becoming divided, like the medieval-era battles between the "Guelphs and Ghibellines." He further claimed that some of the townspeople were acting "tumultuous," men were being insulted, and there was even talk of Sánchez and Jaramillo being killed.

In response, the governor said that the ecclesiastical judge should not have been involved, that the Alcalde Joseph Baca would manage any unrest in the town, and Isidro Sánchez should moderate his language. The case was immediately returned to the alcalde, who told Isidro that there was no acceptable legal challenge against the ecclesiastical judge, and therefore the case was dismissed.

Records indicate that Feliciana Chávez married Manuel Baca two years later. Manuel may have been a brother of (or was at least a relation of) the aforementioned Alcalde Joseph Baca. Manuel and Feliciana had six children together. No records have been found indicating that Joseph Varela Jaramillo was ever married in New Mexico.

Isidro Sánchez's interest in the law and his knowledge of the warring Italian factions, the Guelphs and the Ghibellines, suggests that he was well educated before arriving in New Mexico. The story of the Guelphs and Ghibellines goes back to the twelfth century, when armed battles occurred between these two factions in Italy. The struggle continued throughout the Renaissance period, mostly in Florence and Rome, and was discussed in the literature of the period by Dante, Boccaccio, and Machiavelli. Sánchez may have learned about the two warring parties from a childhood in Spain, or from one of the Spanish dominions in Italy, or perhaps from the curriculum at the school he attended.

Whatever his background, Isidro Sánchez made a life for himself in New Mexico: he married in 1725, had at least six children, and died in Albuquerque in 1770, at the age of seventy-three. In Albuquerque, he was called "El Patron," indicating that he was held in high esteem.

TRANSLATION

> A petition by Isidro Sánchez,[2] resident of the settlement of Fuenclara: a notice of complaint against the Bachiller don Santiago de Roybal,[3] vicar and ecclesiastical judge of this realm, as explained herein, *ut supra*.

Governor and Captain General

Petition by Isidro Sánchez

I, Isidro Sánchez Bañares y Tagle, resident of the jurisdiction of Albuquerque, placed at the feet of your honor,[4] appear before you to the extent that it may be beneficial to me. Speaking with the utmost respect due to your honor, I state the following:

I have come to this Villa of Santa Fe to represent this case before your honor, the only means of appeal in this realm, on account of the complete injustice that the Vicar and Ecclesiastical Judge has executed against Joseph Varela Jaramillo,[5] soldier of the royal presidio. He, Jaramillo, has requested in writing that he be allowed to prove with witnesses that Feliciana Chávez[6] had given him her promise of marriage during their friendship of three years, and that guarantees had been made. Based on a promise of marriage, illicit sexual relations also preceded this.

All these things were requested by me of the judge on behalf of this soldier as the one who investigates and proves the case. In addition, I ask the reason why she broke her word having been firm for so long and with great enthusiasm up to the present, having abandoned all maternal authority and that of her relatives in order to realize this marriage that she now so unexpectedly does not want. Much more remained to be brought forth, if provided the opportunity which I will request of the judge.

Also, the judicial[7] letter that I provided the judge had other convincing reasons so that he would come to understand the situation. In all this he failed, and has failed justice. In addition, before praising the one defeated and despising the victor,[8] he granted a legal document to Feliciana which stated that she did not know this man, and that her virginity was intact. With this paper she came here making such a racket and uproar, yelling and arguing with the opposing side, that this could have caused uproar between the two parties. This was not only then, but even now it is not far from happening because the whole jurisdiction is like Rome with the Guelphs and

Ghibellines[9] when even those of very young of age go about insulting men and calling them many inflammatory names. This comes on account of the document that the Judge dispatched with everyone saying as one voice that this soldier is cruel, a liar, a perjurer, and incapable of being in the presidio in the royal service.

Due to all the preceding, imagine, your honor, in your great understanding, how dejected and despised we are, for this is the description given to us. I give it to all without yet having witnessed a complete disaster, which I do not wish to see. For this reason, I requested and request, as the life blood of peace and Christian righteousness, that your honor dispatch an order so that these people control themselves and stop going around stirring things up. I can provide reasons (and I shall prove them if granted the opportunity) for making the representation of their wanting to kill this soldier and wanting to kill me, and a witness who will prove our case. Due to these threats, others have refused to tell the truth. The lack of witnesses has delayed my representation to your honor and led to another tribunal having refused us. I only request what I have stated *ut supra*.[10]

I ask and implore your honor with the best of my ability to be willing to affect that which I have requested, for by doing so you will receive the benefits of avoiding further harm. I swear by all means that this is not been done in malice and is necessary. *Ut supra.*

Furthermore, I state that the mother of the said girl, Feliciana Chávez, comes with some claim, as recorded in a letter that the vicar showed me in the handwriting of the Reverend Father Oronzoro.[11] Being that as it is, I will not refuse to represent the right of said solder. *Vale.*

Isidro Sánchez Bañares y Tagle (rubric)

Signature of Isidro Sánchez Bañares y Tagle. SANM II #459a, roll 8, f. 339. Note the difference in length compared to his 1720 signature. (See Case 20.

Santa Fe, August 2, 1744

[Response of governor]
Submitted, as it regards the official procedure, without requiring that the ecclesiastic judge admit to having anything to do with this document which concerns the marriage that the parties dispute.

Regarding the disturbances mentioned therein, the alcalde mayor[12] of the jurisdiction shall proceed justly against those who excessively engage in provocations and insults. Also, Isidro Sánchez shall be advised to moderate the terms with which he speaks toward persons of ecclesiastical rank under penalty of just punishment. In the case of a violation of the above, the alcalde mayor shall notify me with the necessary decrees. Thus I approved, ordered, and signed it with my assisting witnesses in absence of a royal or public notary which does not exist in this realm. To this I attest. *Ut supra.*

    Joachín Codallos y Rabal[13] (rubric)
Witness
 don Francisco de Roa y Carrillos[14] (rubric)
Witness
[Juan] Felipe Jacobo de Unanue[15] (rubric)

[Notification of governor's decree]

    In this Villa of San Felipe de Albuquerque on the 12th day of the month of August, 1744, I, Captain Joseph Baca, alcalde mayor and captain general of war of this villa, the pueblo of San Agustín de la Isleta, and the puesto of Fuenclara and its jurisdiction: by virtue of the decree issued by the sergeant major don Joachín Codallos y Rabal, governor and captain general of this kingdom, I ordered both parties (the petitioner and the counterparty) to appear before me. I notified them of the decree, which was understood and obeyed by Isidro Sánchez, and I order the other party to observe what is contained herein. Not finding any other legal challenge, I put it on record and I signed it acting as acting judge with the accompanying witnesses in absence of a royal or public notary, which does not exist in this realm. Concluded. *Ut supra.*

    Joseph Baca (rubric)
Acting Judge
Isidro Sánchez (rubric)
Witness
Pedro Romero[16] (rubric)
Witness
Francisco Padilla[17] (rubric)

TRANSCRIPTION

Año de 1744

Peticion de Isidro Sanchez, vezino de la poblazon de Fuenclara, en orden a quejas contra el bachiller don Santiago de Roibal, vicario y juez eclesiastico de este reyno, sobre lo que en ella se expressa ut supra

Señor governador y capitan general

Isidro Sanchez Vañares y Tagle, vezino dela jurisdicion de Alburquerque puesto a las plantas de Vuestra Señoria paresco como mejor proseda a mi fabor, y ablando devajo del devido respecto que a Vuesta Señoría es devido digo:

Que abiendo venido a esta villa solo a representar ante Vuestra Señoría por ser el unico recurso a este reyno, en orden ala total ynjusticia que el señor vicario, y juez eclessiastico a executado contra Joseph Varela Xaramillo, soldado de este real presidio, pidiendole en un escripto justificara con testigos como Feliciana Chabes le tenia da[da] palabra de casamiento supuesta amistad de tres años, y prendas de su parte entregadas a mas dela ylisita copula que en fe de la palabra abia presedido.

De todo esto se le pidio a dicho juez, por parte de dicho soldado como el que aberiguara, y justificara la causa, y por que motivos tan aseleradamente quebrava la palabra estando en dicho tiempo tan constante, y con mayor hervor enel presente pues abandonava todo poderio de madre y parientes para executar su casamiento, lo que de ymproviso no quiso de todo lo referido, y mucho mas que quedo reserbado para alegar si se ofresiera se lo suplico a dicho juez.

Por una carta tras judicial le di yo otras mas fuertes causales para que estubiese en el conosimiento de la materia, y en todo falto, y a faltado a la justicia, y antes aplaude al venzido, y desprecia al venzedor dando a dicha Feliciana papel juridico por donde consta no conoser tal hombre y estar yntacta su virginidad con papel de buelta de aqui dicha muger llego hasiendo tal alarde y boseria, tiros de escopeta, y muchas vozes ynfamatorias a las partes contrarias que pudieron estas ser causa de un tumulto entre una, y otra parcialidad, y no tan solo entonces pero aun haora al presente no esta muy fuera de que suseda pues esta toda aquella jurisdicción como allá en Roma Guelfos, y Jevelinos pues asta los de muy pequeña edad andan valdonando a los hombres poniendoles muchos apodos ynfamatorios lo que todos sufren respecto de lo que por dicho juez fue despachado disiendo todos a una vos ser dicho soldado un mordaz, falso, y perjuro yncapas aun de estar en el presidio haziendo el real servicio.

Con todo lo referido discurra Vuestra Señoría en su alta comprehencion como podremos estar los abatidos, y despresiados, que ese titulo me doy, y doy en nombre de todos sin ver puesto ha una total ruyna la que no quiero ver motivo para que suplique como suplico a la entrañas paz y cristiana justificacion de Vuestra Señoría mande despachar mandamiento para que estos se contengan, y no anden provocando; doy causales, y las probare si acaso se ofrese] para haser esta representacion el haber querido matar al dicho soldado, el aber querido mata[r] a mi, y a un testigo de los que provaban la causa, por cullo motivo timidos los otros se an negado a dezir la verdad por culla falta e suspendido representar ante Vuestra Señoría lo que por otro trivunal señor fue negado, y solo suplicar lo que llevo dicho por todo lo qual: =

A Vuestra Señoria pido y suplico con las veras de mi mayor rendimiento sea muy serbido de hazer como llevo pedido pues en ello se rresive el bien de ebitar el mayor daño juro en todo forma no ser de malicia, y en lo necesario. Ut supra.

Otrosi digo biene la madre de la dicha niña a no se que pedimento como consta por una carta que me enseño el dicho vicario de letra del Reverendo Padre Oronzoro con que siendo asi no me escusare de defender el derecho de dicho soldado = Vale =

Isidro Sanchez Vañares y Tagle
(rubric)

Santa Fee y agosto 2 de 1744

Por presentado, en quanto toca al fuero real sin que en el eclesiastico se admite parte ninguna de este escripto y por lo que toca el matrimonio que se controbierte entre las partes que este cita; Y en quanto a los alborotos que se enunzian el alcalde maior de el partido prosedera en justizia contra los que se exsedieren en probocaziones y otros ynsultos, y se le apersiva a dicho Isidro Sanchez, se modere en los terminos quando able de personas de dignidad eclesiastica, pena de que se procedera, al condigno castigo, y en caso de resulta o contrabenzion, me dara quenta, con autos dicho alcalde maior para dar las providenzias que fueren necesarias, y asi lo provei mande y firme con los testigos de mi asistenzia a falta de escrivano real y publico que no ay en este reyno. Doy fee ut supra.
 Yoachin Codallos y Rabal (rubric)
 Testigo
 don Francisco de Roa y Carrillos (rubric)
 Testigo
 Phelipe Jacobo de Unanue (rubric)

En esta Villa de San Phelipe, de Alburquerque que en doze dias del mes de agosto de mill setecientos quarenta y quatro años, yo, el captian Joseph Vaca, alcalde mayor, y capitan aguerra de dicha villa, Pueblo de San Augustin dela Ysleta puesto de Fonclara y su jurisdion, en virtud del avcto proveyd por el señor sargento mayor don Joachin Codallos y Rabal, governador y capitan general de est reyno mande compareser a una y otra parte esto es: suplicante y contrallente, y les yse notorio dicho aucto el que entendio fue por Isidro Sanchez obedesido, y por la otra mando obserbar lo que en el se expreza, y no allando otra contradicion lo puse por diligencia y firme auctuando por receptorio con testigos de asistencia por falta de escribano real y publico que no lo ay en este reyno. fecho ut supra =
 Joseph Baca
 Juez
 Receptor(rubric)
 Isidro Sanchez(rubric)
 Testigo
 Pedro Romero (rubric)
 Testigo
 Francisco Padilla (rubric)

This document translated and transcribed by Aaron Taylor

Notes

1. See also, Case 20 and Case 29.
2. For further information on Isidro Sánchez, see Case 20, especially note 1.
3. For information on Father Santiago de Roybal, see Case 26.
4. The reference to "your honor" refers to Governor Joachín Codallos y Rabal.
5. Joseph Varela Jaramillo was probably the son of Gerónimo Varela Jaramillo and Gertrudis Silva, and he was probably the grandson of Cristóbal Varela Jaramillo and Casilda Sedillo Rico de Rojas. His grandparents returned to New Mexico from El Paso after the 1689 Pueblo Revolt. If this is the correct person, then Joseph was married to Francisca Vallejo (or Hurtado). A Joseph Jaramillo appears with his brother, Xavier Jaramillo, in a petition for land in Fuenclara in 1768. (Chávez, *Origins*: 199; SANM I #420.)
6. Feliciana Chávez was the daughter of Antonio Durán y Chávez and Antonia Baca, and she was the granddaughter of the first-founder don Fernando Durán y Chávez. (Antonia Baca was Antonio's second wife, who he married in 1718). In 1746, Feliciana Chávez married Manuel Baca, who was a son of Josefa Baca (who had several children but did not marry). Josefa's father, Manuel Baca, returned to New Mexico sometime in 1692 or 1693, and for a time he was the alcalde of Cochiti. (Chávez, *Origins*: 144-45, 160-62.)
7. Usually, "judicial" meant that the document was signed by witnesses.
8. The phrase "praising the one defeated and despising the victor" is probably a quotation from a Latin source (though its origins have yet to be found). The following is a translation of a similar Latin quotation of 1831, said by the Roman orator Tacitus: "praising the past while neglecting the present." (Murphy, *Tacitus*: 158.) Of course, there is always the possibility that the flamboyant Isidro Sánchez made up the phrase himself.
9. The Guelphs and Ghibellines established opposing political factions beginning in the twelfth century, with their opposition continuing through the fifteenth century. Generally, the Ghibellines supported the authority of German emperors in Italy and were seen as aristocratic and the Guelphs wanted an independent papacy and independent city republics. Persons from the warring factions within the Guelph faction are associated with Florence and appear in Dante's *Inferno*. (Mandelbaum, *The Divine Comedy, Inferno*: 322-29; Painter, *Middle Ages*: 233.)
10. *Ut supra* is a Latin term meaning "as above."
11. Reverend Father Oronzoro was born in Puebla, New Spain, and was a priest by 1717 and in New Mexico at Santa Clara by 1733. He was the Franciscan's vice-custos (vice administrator) for the province in 1734; and was situated at Pecos Pueblo by 1736. He died sometime after 1763. (Kessell, *Kiva*: 500; Chávez, *Archdiocese*: 33, 252.)
12. The alcalde mayor was Joseph Baca. For more information on him, see Case 27.
13. For more on Joachín Codallos y Rabal, see Case 26.
14. Francisco de Roa y Carrillos was in New Mexico by at least 1733; that year, he donated a portion of a mine near Picuris Pueblo to Francisco Guerrero. In 1744, he was named in the registration for another mine at Picuris. (See SANM I #334; SANM I #760; SANM I #763.)
15. For information on [Juan] Felipe Jacobo de Unanue, see Case 27.
16. Pedro Romero was likely the son of Baltasar Romero and Francisca Góngora. In 1737, he was accused of "molesting" the Indians. In 1767, a document indicates that he sold some land from the Padilla grant in Isleta to Clemente Gutiérrez. In 1748, Governor Joachín Codallos y Rabal ordered "don Pedro Romero," then the alcalde of the Laguna jurisdiction, to Navajo country with fray Menchero for selection of mission sites, but it is not known if this is the same person. In 1753, a Pedro Romero was also one of the grantees in the Ojo Caliente land grant. In 1765, he appeared on a list of the Las Nutrias grant settlers. (Ebright, *Oppressed*: 75, 281; Ebright, Hendricks, and Hughes, *Leagues*: 356n36; Chávez, *Origins*: 271; Ebright and Hendricks, *Witches*: 56; Brooks, *Captives*: 98.)
17. Francisco Padilla is the son of Diego de Padilla and María Marquez, both of whom had arrived in New Mexico by 1706. In 1713, Francisco married María Vasquez Baca of Bernalillo. The 1762 will of his father, Diego, for which Francisco acted as executor, states that Diego lived near Isleta, where he acquired property known as "lo de Padilla." In 1768, Francisco sold some of his inheritance—"one seventh of the Diego Padilla grant"—to Clemente Gutiérrez, who later partnered with the Hubbell family. (Chávez, *Origins*: 253, 332; SANM I, #695.)

29

ISIDRO SÁNCHEZ ORDERED TO STOP GIVING LEGAL ADVICE BY ALCALDE AND GOVERNOR
March 3, 1745, Source: SANM II #463

Synopsis and editor's notes: In a case dated March 3, 1745, Alcalde Joseph Baca and Governor Joachín Codallos y Rabal again reprimanded Isidro Sánchez and ordered him to stop creating disturbances, stirring up litigation, and acting as the local lawyer. Although Sánchez agreed to comply with their requests, it is not certain if he actually did. Historian Charles Cutter, for instance, discovered that by comparing Sánchez's handwriting in previous cases with a June 1745 document it appears that Sánchez did write the 1745 petition for several Albuquerque residents, though he did not sign his name. Presented to the governor, the petition requested permission for the citizens to sell their wool in the colony.

TRANSLATION

Year of 1745

This order was given to Joseph Baca,[1] alcalde mayor and war captain for the Villa of Albuquerque, so that he can notify Isidro Sánchez,[2] resident of this jurisdiction, that under the penalty of a fine of fifty pesos and fifteen days in the stocks, for the first offense, he not get involved in compiling written documents, or assist in doing so. For the second offense he will be banished from this kingdom, etc.

Sergeant Major don Joaquín Codallos y Rabal,[3] the governor and captain general of this kingdom of New Mexico, its presidios, etc. (rubric)

Order given to Joseph Baca

I have been notified that Isidro Sánchez, resident of the pueblo of Fuenclara,[4] jurisdiction of the Villa of Albuquerque, being that he is a very restless, troublesome man, incites some of the poor residents into schemes and petitions by aiding them with written documents and cooperating with them for the profit that they might bring to him. It is desired that the entire kingdom be without problems, and so that no poor individual will suffer from any loss of their poor belongings by what is expressed above, I order Joseph Baca, alcalde mayor and war captain of this jurisdiction, to notify the above mentioned Isidro Sánchez that from this day forth he is not to make written documents for any reasons, nor is he to cooperate in assisting with them, under the penalty of fifty pesos that are to be imposed immediately and fifteen days in the stocks for the first offense. For the second offense, he will be banished from this kingdom. This notification shall be carried out at the time that this order is issued.

Done at this Palace in Santa Fe, March 3, 1745.

Joachín Codallos y Rabal (rubric)

On the 11th day of the month of March, 1745, I, Joseph Baca, alcalde mayor and war captain of the Villa of San Felipe de Albuquerque, in compliance with the order of the governor and captain general of this kingdom of New Mexico, proceeded to the pueblo of Fuenclara and made to appear before me Isidro Sánchez. He was notified of the above said order which was read to him before my assisting witnesses, and he stated that he would obey. So that it is valid he signed it along with the witnesses, to which I certify. Joseph Baca (rubric); at the request of Domingo Sedillo,[5] Bernardo Vallejo[6](rubric); at the request of Marcial,[7] Bernardo Vallejo (rubric).

Having been heard and seen by me, I understood what was contained within it, and so that it is valid and understanding that I would obey it, I signed it.

Isidro Sánchez (rubric)

TRANSCRIPTION

Año de 1745

Orden que se da a Joseph Baca, Alcalde Mayor y Capitan Aguerra de la Villa de Alburquerque para que notifique a Ysidro Sanchez vesino de dicha jurisdicion, que pena de cinquenta pesos y quinze dias de cepo por la primera vez, no haga escritos, ni coopere a ellos, y por la segunda se estrañara de este Reyno, ut supra.

El Sargento Maior Dn. Joachin Codallos y Rabal, Governador y Capitan General de este Reyno del a Nueva Mexico, sus Presidios y fronteras, ut supra.

[*Note in margin*]
Orden que se da a Joseph Baca

Por quanto me hallo notisioso que Ysidro Sanchez vezino del Pueblo de

Fuenclara jurisdicion dela Villa de Alburquerque, es hombre cabiloso, ynquieto que ynsitta a algunos pobres vecinos a que tengan pleitos haciendoles escriptos y cooperando a ellos por las utilidades que se dan; Y deseando toda quietud en el Reyno y que ningun pobre padezca atrazo alguno en sus cortas combenencias por lo expresado arriba; mando a Joseph Baca, Alcalde Maior y Capitan Aguerra de dicha jurisdizion notifique esta orden al mencionado Ysidro Sanchez para que desde el dia dela fecha de esta, no aga escripto por motive alguno, ni tanpoco que coopere a ellos pena de cinquenta pesos que se sacaran yremisiblemente, y quinze dias de cepo por la primera vez y la segunda se extranara de dicho Reyno; cuya notificazion se pondra a continuazion de esta, y despues su obedesimiento. Dada en este Palacio de Santa Fee y Marzo 3 de 1745.

 Joachin Codallos Rabal (rubric)

En onse dias del mes de Marso de mil setesientos y cuarenta y sinco anos yo Joseph Baca Alcalde Mayor y Capitan Aguerra de la Villa de San Felipe de Alburquerque en cumplimento del orden del Senor Gobernador y Capitan General deste Reino de la Nueva Mexico pase al Pueblo de Fonclara y ise compareser ante mi Ysidro Sanchez a quien delante de los testigos de mi asistensia notifique y lei el sitado orden y dijo que obedesia y para que conste lo firmo con migo y los testigoa de que di fee. Joseph Baca a ruego de Domingo Sedillo; a ruego de Marsial, Bernardo Vallejo (rubric); Bernardo Ballejo (rubric).

Bista y oydo por mi la que entendi como en el se contiene y para que conste de que la obedesi y obedesco la firme =
 Ysidro Sanchez (rubric)

Notes

1. For information on Joseph Baca, see Case 27.
2. For more information on Isidro Sánchez, see Case 20.
3. For information on Joachín Codallos y Rabal, see Case 26.
4. Fuenclara was a settlement south of Albuquerque located near Tomé Hill and near the Río Grande. It is sometimes shown on early maps as "Fuenclara/Tomé." The name of the hill probably comes from an early owner of the property: Tomé Domínguez de Mendoza. Following a shift in the course of the Río Grande in the 1740s, vacant land became available in the area for settlers. The name Fuenclara appears to have been given in honor of Viceroy Pedro Cebrián y Agustín, Count of Fuenclara (from 1742–1746). (Wheat, *Mapping*: 84, 119; Kessell and Hendricks, *By Force of Arms*: 375; Kessell, *Kiva*: 509; Jones, "Rescue and Ransom": 132-33.)
5. Domingo [Francisco] Sedillo was the son of Joaquín Sedillo Rico de Rojas, a native of New Mexico, and María Varela. Domingo was born on August 16, 1709; he married Micaela González Bas about 1732; and he died in 1762. (Chávez, *Origins*: 285, 392; NMGS, *Aquí*: 310-11.)
6. Bernardo Vallejo was the natural son of Pedro Durán y Chávez and grandson of don Fernando Durán y Chávez. He married Francisca Silva in 1725. In the 1760s, Bernardo was involved with the Los Quelites land grant near Tomé. (Chávez, *Origins*: 288, 303, 425; NMGS, *Aquí*: 79, 151.)
7. The "Marcial" listed here may be the Marcial Barreras (or Barreda) who married Rosa Trujillo in 1743. In

1751, Marcial Barreras was named in a document as a witness from Belén for Captain don Nicolás de Chávez, in a court case involving the dowry of doña Eduarda Yturrieta, the widow of Nicolás's son, Luis Chávez. (Chávez, *Origins*: 146; SANM II #516.)

30

LOVERS FLEE SANTA CRUZ FOR OUTSIDE THE KINGDOM: WOMAN RETURNED TO HUSBAND
November 29–December 17, 1745, Sources: SANM II #468

Synopsis and editor's notes: In November 1745, two lovers—twenty-five-year-old Francisco Mondragón, a presido soldier, and nineteen-year-old María de Olguín, wife of Juan Joseph Vasquez—attempted to leave New Mexico. Their plans, however, went awry and they missed each other at San Ildefonso where they agreed to meet. Eventually, they were apprehended and the wife was returned to her husband. Limited information exists about her husband, Juan Joseph Vasquez, but it is known that he was about fifty years old at the time.

Testimony from the trial indicates that Francisco Mondragón was part of a military squadron that was leaving the kingdom with Captain Pedro Sánchez de Iñigo II. Francisco's plan was to claim that a part of his saddle was broken so that he would have to be left behind. The strategy worked. He then went to San Ildefonso where he expected María to be waiting for him. But when he arrived, he was told that she had left, so he followed her trail to the home of Joseph Montoya in La Cieneguilla. When he got there, he was told that Montoya had taken María to yet another place, called El Monte, where Francisco finally found her. By then María apparently had second thoughts about the adventure, so Francisco decided to take her back to San Ildefonso. On the way, Francisco met up with Xavier Mestas and asked him for the use of his saddle, because his own saddle was still broken. Mestas agreed but also decided to accompany the two to make sure his saddle was returned. Francisco took María to Pedro Romero's rancho, where Lieutenant Alcalde Juan de Abeytia found them. The alcalde then brought the couple back to Santa Cruz and imprisoned Francisco.

When María de Olguín gave her testimony, she said that she understood that Francisco Mondragón wanted her to go out of the kingdom with him, but she said she did not give her consent to do so. Both Xavier Mestas and Francisco gave testimony and then the case was sent to Governor Joachín Codallos y Rabal in Santa Fe. He then sent María back to her husband and ordered him to treat her kindly. Mondragón, on the other hand, was to be punished more severely: the governor ordered him to be given one hundred lashes with instructions not to disturb María ever again. He was also to pay sixteen pesos to Lieutenant Alcalde Juan de Abeytia for his expenses. In the end, Mondragón appeared before the lieutenant alcalde, agreed to the payment, and was released from jail. The governor took care to caution the husband, Juan Joseph Vasquez, to not do anything that would to cause a legal indemnity—meaning, he was not to mistreat his wife and cause any further legal action.

The reason Captain Pedro Sánchez de Iñigo ordered the squadron to go outside the kingdom is unknown. He may have been providing an escort for a caravan to El Paso or Chihuahua. Or, it is possible that the Spanish troops were planning to join other presidio troops in an attempt to stop the escalating violence of the Comanches, which had resulted in the Indians being banned from the Taos trade fairs in 1746.[1]

Note that Governor Codallos y Rabal requested that this case be filed in the government archives. In doing so, he was following the request made thirty years earlier, by Sergeant Major Alfonso Rael de Aguilar, to have all government cases filed in the archives.[2] Since being deposited, this document has remained in the archives for 271 years.

TRANSLATION

Year of 1745

Criminal proceedings by the office of the royal justice against Francisco Mondragón,[3] resident of the Villa of Santa Cruz de la Cañada, for having illegally taken with him a certain married woman resident of the puesto of Chimayó, jurisdiction of the said villa, etc

[Arrest]

On the 29th day of the month of November, 1745, I, Lieutenant Alcalde Juan de Abeytia[4] of this Villa of Santa Cruz, have been notified that Francisco Mondragón, resident of this villa, has illegally taken with him María de Olguín,[5] wife of Juan [Joseph] Vasquez,[6] resident of the puesto of Chimayó. I was also informed that Mondragón was with her at the rancho of Captain Pedro Sánchez [de Iñigo II].[7]

By virtue of this I, the presiding judge, ordered and did order that he be found. To do this I proceeded along with two assisting witnesses and upon finding María de Olguín and Francisco Mondragón at the said rancho, they were held prisoners under good security. Then I took a sworn statement from Mondragón about the reason he had taken the said woman in his company. Likewise, I ordered that the María de Olguín give her statement about the reasons that she had for leaving her home and for staying with Mondragón. In addition to this, I ordered that María de Olguín be placed under security at the home of Captain Pedro Sánchez. This is until the governor, after receiving these sworn statements, decides to whom these proceedings are to be transmitted. Upon their being reviewed by his honor, the governor, he will determine what he thinks is for the best and most appropriate.

I thus approved, ordered and signed this acting as presiding judge along with my assisting witnesses with whom I act as presiding judge due to the lack of a public or royal scribe, there not being one in this kingdom, and on this common paper because the sealed one is not found here, to which I certify.

Juan de Abeytia (rubric)

Presiding Judge
Witness
Francisco Gómez del Castillo[8] (rubric)
Witness
Vicente Ginzo Rón y Thobar[9] (rubric)

[Statement of Francisco Mondragón]

On the 2nd of December, 1745, I, the lieutenant alcalde of this villa, Juan de Abeytia, made to appear before my court the prisoner, Francisco Mondragón. I took his sworn statement which he made to God, Our Lord and to the sign of the Holy Cross, under which he promised to tell the truth as to what he knew and what he was asked.

I, the judge, asked him who it was that had summoned María de Olguín to leave her home with him or if the woman had arranged to meet him. He said that upon leaving his home to go outside the kingdom with those who were leaving with Captain Pedro Sánchez, he told his companions that a part[10] of his saddle had broken and so he was left behind. Having been told by María that she would wait for him at the pueblo of San Ildefonso, he returned to that place. Upon reaching the pueblo, he asked the Indians if a certain woman was to be found there. They told him that she had left. From there he followed her trail until he found her at La Cieneguilla at the home of Joseph Montoya.[11] He then asked Xavier Mestas[12] to bring her to the pueblo of San Ildefonso. From there he took her to the ranch of Pedro Sánchez where he remained with her until the lieutenant came and took them as prisoners.

This he said was the truth regarding the testimony he has made. His sworn statement being read back to him, he affirmed and ratified it, saying that he was twenty-five years of age, more or less, and he did not sign because he did not know how. I, the presiding judge, signed it along with my assisting witnesses as it is said, to which I certify.

Juan de Abeytia (rubric)
Presiding Judge
Witness
Francisco Gómez del Castillo (rubric)
Witness
Vicente Ginzo Rón y Thobar (rubric)

[Statement of María de Olguín]

On the said day, month and year, I, the lieutenant went to the house and home of Captain Pedro Sánchez [de Iñigo], where I had securely kept María Mondragón, or should I say, Olguín. There I took her sworn statement before my assisting witnesses, which she made to God, Our Lord, and to the sign of the Holy Cross, through which she promised to tell the truth as to what she knew and what she was asked.

I, the judge, asked her if Mondragón had summoned her to leave her home or if she had arranged to meet him. She stated that it was true that he had arranged to meet her in order to take her out of the kingdom, but that she had not consented. She had gone to La Cieneguilla to the home of Joseph Montoya and that from there he took her to El Monte.[13] At the same time, Xavier Mestas arrived at that place, and Mondragón asked him to take her on horseback to the pueblo of San Ildefonso, which he did in the company of Mondragón. From the pueblo Mondragón took her to the rancho of Captain Pedro Sánchez, where she stayed with Mondragón until the lieutenant came to take them prisoners. This she said was the truth regarding her testimony that she has made. Upon it being read back to her, she ratified and affirmed it saying that she was nineteen years of age, more or less. She did not sign because she said that she did not know how. I, the said judge, signed it along with my assisting witnesses with whom I act, and which I certify.

 Juan de Abeytia (rubric)
 Presiding Judge
 Witness
 Francisco Gómez del Castillo (rubric)
 Witness
 Vicente Ginzo Rón y Thobar (rubric)

[Order]

On the said day, month and year, I, the lieutenant, have seen the previous statements of Francisco Mondragón and María de Olguín in which they state that it was Xavier Mestas who brought her up to the pueblo of San Ildefonso. Thus I demand, order and do order that an order be issued against Xavier Mestas to appear before my court within the time period of four hours in order to comply with the good administration of justice. His sworn statement is to be taken according to all rights. I thus approved, ordered and signed it along with my assisting witnesses with whom I act and to which I certify.

 Juan de Abeytia (rubric)
 Presiding Judge
 Witness
 Francisco Gómez del Castillo (rubric)
 Witness
 Vicente Ginzo Rón y Thobar (rubric)

[Statement of Xavier Mestas]

On the 3rd of December of the said year, Xavier Mestas, having appeared before me and within my court, I took his sworn statement which he made before God, Our

Lord and the sign of the Holy Cross about the charges made, he promised to tell the truth as to what he knew and was asked.

He was asked by me if he had brought María de Olguín on horseback up to the pueblo of San Ildefonso, from what place he had brought her, and who the woman was with. He stated that when coming from the presidio horse herd while driving a number of *machos* (male mules), Francisco Mondragón appeared before him at El Monte. Mondragón asked him if he could borrow his saddle so that he could bring a woman that was there and who was fleeing the kingdom. Having loaned him his saddle he, Mestas, continued on his way with his mules. He had gone bareback up to a point, when upon his thinking about it he returned back to where he had left Mondragón, being suspicious that he would flee with his saddle. He, Mestas, told him that he would take the woman. Then, he did take her up to the pueblo of San Ildefonso, with Mondragón coming in company with him. He did not know if the woman was married or single. She had then remained at the pueblo along with Mondragón. After that he did not know where they went.

He stated that what he had said was the truth and upon his statement being read back to him he affirmed and ratified it saying that he was thirty-five years of age, more or less. He did not sign because he stated that he did not know how. I, the said judge, signed it along with my assisting witnesses as is, to which I certify.

 Juan de Abeytia (rubric)
 Presiding Judge
 Witness
 Francisco Gómez del Castillo (rubric)
 Witness
 Vicente Ginzo Rón y Thobar (rubric)

[Remission]

On the said day, month and year, I, Lieutenant Alcalde Juan de Abeytia, of this Villa of Santa Cruz, having completed these proceedings and having placed them in the state of sentencing, submitted them to the governor and captain general of this kingdom of New Mexico, don Joachín Codallos y Rabal.[14] This is so that upon review of them, he can hand down a sentence or determine what he deems is most appropriate. I thus approved and signed it along with my assisting witnesses with whom I act due to the lack of a public or royal scribe, which there is none in this Kingdom to which I certify.

 Juan de Abeytia (rubric)
 Presiding Judge
 Witness
 Francisco Gómez del Castillo (rubric)
 Vicente Ginzo Rón y Thobar (rubric)

[Sentence]

On the 13the of December, 1745, at the Villa of Santa Fe, I, Sergeant Major don Joachín Codallos y Rabal, governor and captain general of this kingdom of New Mexico and of its provinces, have reviewed the criminal case that was presented by the office of the royal justice against Francisco Mondragón and María de Olguín, for intending to flee the kingdom for which they were apprehended. For this along with other issues which are contained in the proceedings found in the two previous pages, I say that I should order and did order the lieutenant Juan de Abeytia to proceed to the puesto of Chimayó and return María de Olguín to her husband, [Juan] Joseph Vasquez, in respect to that which he has said about wanting to make a married life with her. I order him to be careful so as not to cause a juridical indemnity,[15] but rather to treat her kindly so that they can comply with their obligations in good peace and conformity. If not, he will be punished in the most rigorous manner that is allowed.

As for Francisco Mondragón, he is to be notified that he is ordered to be given one hundred lashes and not to disturb María de Olguín in any way, nor is he to solicit her personally or by any one other person under the same penalty. For now, he is to pay sixteen pesos of the land, which are to be given to the lieutenant for his personal expenses for having come and gone various times from [Santa Cruz de] La Cañada to Chimayó. After these proceedings are completed and Mondragón released from jail, these written proceedings are to be returned to this superior government of the governor.

I thus approved, ordered and signed them along with my assisting witnesses due to the lack of a scribe, which there is none in this kingdom, and which I certify.

don Joachín Codallos y Rabal (rubric)
Witness
Joseph Romo de Vera[16] (rubric)
Witness
[Juan] Felipe Jacobo de Unanue[17] (rubric)

[Notification of Juan Joseph Vasquez]

At the new Villa of Santa Cruz on the 17th of December, 1745, I, Juan de Abeytia, the lieutenant to the alguacil mayor of this villa, have received these proceedings against Francisco Mondragón and María de Olguín along with the decree of sentencing submitted to them by the governor and captain general of this kingdom, don Joachín Codallos y Rabal.

In order to comply with what is ordered of me, I mounted my horse and in the company of my assisting witnesses I read and notified Joseph Vasquez of the decree. He, upon understanding its contents, stated that he would obey it and that he would take his wife back. Making the sign of Holy Cross, he swore to God, Our Lord and the Holy Cross to live in a married way with his wife saying that he would proceed to live in peace with her, in union and agreement, from that time forth. Upon this being heard by me, the judge, I turned her over to him in the presence of the witnesses. He did not sign because he said that he did not know how. I, the judge, signed it along with my assisting witnesses with whom I act as presiding judge due to the lack of a public or royal scribe, which there is none in this kingdom, and on this common paper, because the sealed type is not found in this kingdom, which I certify.

 Juan de Abeytia (rubric)
 Presiding Judge
 Witness
 Francisco Gómez del Castillo (rubric)
 Witness
 Vicente Ginzo Rón y Thobar (rubric)

[Notification of Francisco Mondragón]

On the said day, month and year, I, the lieutenant made to appear before me within my court, Francisco Mondragón, prisoner, to whom, in the presence of my assisting witnesses made known and notified him of the sentence imposed by the governor and captain general of this kingdom, don Joachín Codallos y Rabal. Upon understanding it, he stated that he would obey it and would do as his honor ordered him to do and that he is ready to give him the sixteen pesos that are ordered for the expenses.

Upon doing this I released him from jail. He did not sign because he said that he did not know how. I, the judge, along with my assisting witnesses signed and certified it.

 Juan de Abeytia (rubric)
 Presiding Judge
 Witness
 Francisco Gómez del Castillo (rubric)
 Vicente Ginzo Rón y Thobar (rubric)

[Remission]

On the said day, month and year, I, the lieutenant, upon having concluded these proceedings regarding the matter found with them, by virtue of what was ordered of me, state that I will do and did submit them to the governor and captain general don Joachín Codallos y Rabal. So that it is valid I signed it along with my assisting witnesses with whom I act as presiding judge as has been stated, and which I certify.

 Juan de Abeytia (rubric)
 Presiding Judge
 Witness
 Francisco Gómez del Castillo (rubric)
 Witness
 Vicente Ginzo Rón y Thobar (rubric)

Santa Fe, December 19, 1745

Decree

Place these proceedings in the archives of this government so that they are forever valid. I thus approved and rubricated it.

don Joachín Codallos y Rabal (rubric)

TRANSCRIPTION

Año de 1745

Causa criminal de officio de la Real Justicia Contra Francisco Mondragon vecino dela Villa de Santa Cruz dela Canada, sobre el urto de cierta muger casada vecina del Puesto de Chimayo, jurisdicion de dicha Villa, ut supra

En veinte y nuebe dias del mes de Noviembre de mill setezientos quarenta y cinco años yo el Theniente Juan de Beitia desta Villa Nueba de Santa Cruz, aviendo tenido notizia de como francisco Mondragon vezino de dicha Villa se havia urtado a Maria de Olguin muger de Juan Vasquez vesino del Puesto de Chimayo, y que el dicho Mondragon se mantenia con ella en el Rancho del Capitan Pedro Sanchez.

En virtud de lo qual dize quedaria demander mandava, y mande se pase por mi dicho Juez con dos testigos de mi assistenzia y de allarlos en dicho Puesto se aprisionen abuen recuerdo; y sele resiziva juramento al dicho Mondragon en toda forma de derecho, del motive que a tenido detener esta muger en su compania como asi mismo ala dicha Maria de Olguin de que diga las causales que a tenido para salirse de su casa y mantenerse en dicho Puesto con el dicho Mondragon; y asi mesmo mando que ala dicha Maria de Olguin se ponga en deposito en la casa del Capitan Pedro Sanchez asta determiner el Señor Governador a quien despues de rezividos los juramentos mande sele remitan estas delixensias para que en su bista determine Su Señoria lo que alla ser por mas combeniente.

Asi lo provei, mande y firme auctuando como Juez Rezeptor con los testigos de mi asistenzia con quienes auctuo por receptoria a falta de Scribano Publico ni Real que no lo ai en este Reino y en este papel comun por no corer el sellado, doi fee =

Juan de Beytia (rubric
Jues Receptor
Testigo
Francisco Gomez del Castillo (rubric)
Witness
Vizente Ginzo Rón y Thobar (rubric)

~

En dos dias del mes de Diziembre de mill setezientos quarenta y cinco años, yo el Theniente Juan de Beitia de dicha Villa hise compareser ante mi jusgado a Francisco Mondragon, preso, a quien le tome y rezivi juramento que izo por Dios Nuestro Señor y la Señal de la Santa Cruz so cuio cargo prometio de dezir verdad en lo que supiere y le fuere preguntado.

Siendolo por mi dicho Jues de que se havia sitado ala dicha Maria de Olguin para que saliese de su casa con el o de que si la dicha muger la avia zitado a el; dijo que aviendo salido para fuera con la gente del Capitan Pedro Sanchez les dijo a companeros que sele avia caido un lomillo de su silla y que se avia quedado atras; y por averle zitado la dicha muger que en el Pueblo de San Yldefonso lo esperaba rebolivio; y aviendo llegado a dicho Pueblo pregunto alos Yndios de dicho Pueblo de San Yldefonso si se allaba la dicha muger ai y quele dijeron se avia ydo; y que de ai se fue en seguimento de rastro asta allarla en La Sieneguilla en casa de Joseph Montoia y que de ai le rogo a Javier Mestas la trujese asta el Pueblo de San Yldefonso; y que ai se la llevo el dicho Mondragon para el Rancho de Pedro Sanchez donde se mantenia con ella asta que llego el Señor Theniente a aprisionarlos.

Que esta es la verdad del juramento que fecho tiene y siendola leida esta su declaracion se afirmo y ratifico en ella; dijo ser de edad de veinte y zinco años poco mas o menos y que no firmo por no saver firmela yo dicho Juez con los testigos de mi assistenzia como dicho es doi fee = entre renglones vale desde ai =

Juan de Beytia (rubric
Jues Receptor
Testigo
Francisco Gomez del Castillo (rubric)
Witness
Vizente Ginzo Rón y Thobar (rubric)

~

En dicho dia mes y ano yo dicho Theniente pase ala casa y morada del Capitan Pedro Sanchez a donde tengo depositada a Maria Mondragon, digo Olguin, a quien tome y rezivi juramento delante de mis testigos de assistenzia que lo izo por Dios Nuestro Señor y la Seé dela Santa Cruz so cuio cargo prometio de dezir berdad en lo que supiere y le fuere preguntado.

Siendola por mi dicho Jues de que si la avia zitado el dicho Mondragon para que saliese de su casa o de que si ella lo avia zitado a el. Dijo, que es berdad la avia zitado el dicho Mondragon pa llevarsela para afuera, y que ella no avia condescendido y que ella se fue asta La Sieneguilla en casa de Joseph Montoia y que de ai la trujo asta el monte; y que al mismo tiempo llego Xavier Mestas a quien le suplico el dicho Mondragon la trujese a cavallo asta el Pueblo de San Yldefonso, y que el dicho Xavier Mestas la avia traido asta dicho Pueblo en compania de dicho Mondragon, y que de dicho Pueblo dicho Mondragon se la llevo al Rancho del Capitan Pedro Sanchez donde se mantenia con dicho Mondragon asta que el Señor Theniente paso a aprisionarlos, y que esta es la verdad del juramento que fecho tiene y siendole leida esta su declaracion se afirmo y ratifico, dijo ser de edad de diez y nuebe años poco mas o menos, no firmo por que dijo no saver, firmelo yo dicho Juez con los testigos de mi assistenzia con quien auctto como dicho es doi fee =

Juan de Beytia (rubric
Jues Receptor
Testigo
Francisco Gomez del Castillo (rubric)
Testigo
Vizente Ginzo Rón y Thobar (rubric)

En dicho dia, mes y ano yo dicho Theniente aviendo visto las declaraciones que antezedan de Francisco Mondragon y de Maria de Olguin en que zitan a Xavier Mestas que fue el que la trujo asta el Pueblo de San Yldefonso digo que devia demander, mandava y mando se libre mandamiento contra Xavier Mestas a que comparesca en este mi jusgado dentro del termino de quatro oras por combenir asi la buena administrazion de justizia y sele resiva juramento en toda forma de derecho, asi la provei, mande y firme con los testigos de mi assistenzia con quienes auctuo como dicho es doi fee =

Juan de Beytia (rubric
Jues Receptor
Testigo
Francisco Gomez del Castillo (rubric)
Testigo
Vizente Ginzo Rón y Thobar (rubric)

En tres dias del mes de Diciembre de dicho año, aviendo comparesido ante mi y en mu jusgado Xavier Mestas le tome juramento que izo por Dios Nuestro Señor y la Señal de la Santa Cruz so cuio cargo prometio dezir verdad en lo que supiere y le fuere preguntado.

Siendolo por mi dicho Jues de que si avia traido a Maria de Olguin a cavallo asta el Pueblo de San Yldefonso y del la parte donde la trujo y con quien estaba la dicho muger; dijo que viniendo el dela cavallada co unos machos por delante le salio en el monte Francisco Mondragon suplicandole le prestase su silla para traer una muger que estaba alli que iba juida; y que aviendole prestado la silla se vino caminando con sus bestias que bolvia en pelo en un macho asta el paraje de donde lo avia dejado por aver entrado en suspecha de que sele juise con la silla y que asi le dijo no amigo yo llevare la muger y que la trujo asta el Pueblo de San Yldefonso viniendo el dicho Mondragon en su compania sin que el hubiese conozido si era muger casada o soltera y que en dicho Pueblo se quedo y el dicho Mondragon, despues no supo de su paradero.

Que esta es la verdad que fecho tiene, y siendole leida esta su declaracion se afirmo y ratifico dijo ser de edad treinta y sinco años poco mas o menos, no firmo por que dijo no savia firmelo yo dicho Jues con los testigos de mi assistenzia como dicho es doi fee =

Juan de Beytia (rubric
Jues Receptor
Testigo
Francisco Gomez del Castillo (rubric)
Testigo
Vizente Ginzo Rón y Thobar (rubric)

En dicho dia, mes y año yo el Theniente Juan de Beitia desta Villa Nueba de Santa Cruz aviendo puesto en estado de sentenzia estas delixencias dije que devia azer como ago remission de ellas al Señor Governador y Capitan General Dn. Joachin Codallos y Rabal deste Reino dela Nueba Mexico para que bistas por Su Señoria de la sentenzia o determine lo que allare por mas combeniente asi lo provei y firme con los testigos de mi assistenzia con quienes auctto por receptoria a falta de Scribano Publico ni Real que no lo ai en este Reino, doi fee =

Juan de Beytia (rubric
Jues Receptor
Testigo
Francisco Gomez del Castillo (rubric)
Witness
Vizente Ginzo Rón y Thobar (rubric)

Villa de Santa Fee y Diciembre trese de mill setecientos y quarenta y cinco años el Sargento Mayor Dn. Joachin Codallos y Rabal, Governador y Capitan General deste Reyno de la Nueva Mexico y Sus Provinzias, haviendo visto la causa criminal que de oficio dela Real Justizia se sigue contra Francisco Mondragon y Maria de Olguin por la fuga intentada por los suso dichos en que fueron aprehendidos, y lo demas que se contiene en los autos de las dos foxas antecedents = Dixe que devia mandar y mando al Theniente Juan de Beytia pase al Puesto de Chimaio y entregue a la dicha Maria Olguin a Joseph Vasquez su marido; respecto de las instancias que el suso dicho haze sobre querer hazer vida maridable con ella, precediendo causion juratoria de indemnidad, y buenos tratamientos y seles apersiva cumplir con su obligacion en buena paz y conformidad, pena de que seles castigara con la mayores que ubiere lugar en derecho.

Al dicho Francisco Mondragon sele notifique pena de cien azotes no inquiete en ninguna manera a dicha Maria de Olguin ni la solicite por si ni por interpocita persona devajo dela misma pena y por a ora seles sacaran dies y seis pesos a precious de la tierra que aplico al dicho Theniente por las costas personales que ha debengado en repettidos viajes desde La Canada a Chimayo; y fechas dichas diligencias y suelto dela pricion el dicho Mondragon, debolbera esta causa con ellas a este Superior Gobierno.

Asi lo probei, mande y firme con los testigos de mi assistencia a falta de Escribano que no lo ay Publico ni Real en este Reyno = Doy fee =

Dn. Joachin Codallos y Rabal (rubric)
Testigo
Joseph Romo de Vera (rubric)
Testigo
Phelipe Jacobo de Unanue (rubric)

En la Villa Nueba de Santa Cruz en diez y siette dias del mes de Diziembre de mill setezientos quarenta y cinco años, yo el Theniente de Alguacil Mayor de dicha Villa Juan de Beitia haviendo rezevido estas delixencias seguida contra Francisco Mondragon y Maria de Olguin, y el auto de sentenzia ynsertto en ellas del Señor Governador y Capitan General Dn. Joachin Codallos y Rabal deste Reino.

Para el cumplimiento delo que en el seme ordena me puse a cavallo en compania de mis testigos de assistenzia le lei y notifique dicho auctto quien entendido del dijo que obedezia y que rezivia ala dicha su mujer y puesta la Señal dela Santa Cruz juro a Dios Nuestro Señor y la Cruz que puesta tiene de azer vida maridable con la dicha su mujer y que proseguira con ella en paz, union y conformidad de aqui en adelante; que visto por mi dicho ynfraescripto Juez su respuesta sela entreque en presencia delos dichos testigos de assistenzia; no firmo por que dijo no savia firmela yo dicho Jues con los testigos de assistenzia con quienes auctuo por rezeptoria a falta de Scribano Publico ni Real que no lo ai en este Reyno y en este papel comun por no corer el sellado en este Reino, doi fee =

Juan de Beytia (rubric
Jues Receptor
Testigo
Francisco Gomez del Castillo (rubric)
Testigo
Vizente Ginzo Rón y Thobar (rubric)

En dicho dia, mes y año yo dicho Theniente hize comparecer ante mi y en mi jusgado a Francisco Mondragon, preso, a quien en presenzia de los testigos de mi assistenzia le hize saver y notifique el auto de sentenzia expedido por el Señor Governador y Capitan General deste Reyno Dn. Joachin Codallos y Rabal, quien entendido de el dijo que obedezia y que ejecutaria segun y como Su Señoria le ordeno, y que esta pronto ala entriega delos diez y seis pesos que se ordenan de costas; en virtud de lo qual lo puse en libertad de soltura, no firmo por que dijo no sabia firmelo yo dicho Juez con los testigos de mi assistenzia con quienes auccto como dicho es, doi fee =

 Juan de Beytia (rubric
 Jues Receptor
 Testigo
 Francisco Gomez del Castillo (rubric)
 Testigo
 Vizente Ginzo Rón y Thobar (rubric)

En dicho dia, mes y año yo dicho Theniente haviendo concluido estas delixencias sobre la materia que en ellas constan, en birtud de lo que seme ordena dije que devia de azer como ago remission de ellas al Señor Governador y Capitan General Dn. Joachin Codallos y Rabal de este y para que conste lo firme con los testigos de mi assistenzia con quienes auccto por Receptoria como dicho es, doi fee =

 Juan de Beytia (rubric
 Jues Receptor
 Testigo
 Francisco Gomez del Castillo (rubric)
 Testigo
 Vizente Ginzo Rón y Thobar (rubric)

Santa Fee, Diciembre 19 de 1745 años

Decree
 Pongase esta causa en el Archivo deste Govierno para que en todo tiempo conste y assi lo probei y rubrique.
 Dn. Joachin Codallos y Rabal (rubric)

Notes

1. See Jones, *Pueblo Warriors*: 120-21; Hämäläinen, *Comanche Empire*: 41-42; Noyes, *Los Comanches*: 374-75.
2. For further information on this subject, see Case 13.
3. This Francisco Mondragón was probably the Francisco Xavier Mondragón who was born in 1721, the son of Juan Alonso Mondragón and Sebastiana Trujillo Martín, both of whom were living in Pojoaque in 1715 and four years later were residents of Santa Cruz. If this is the same Francisco Mondragón, then his grandparents

were Sebastián Sánchez de Mondragón (or de Monroy) and María Bernal, who were married in 1693 (after returning to New Mexico with don Diego de Vargas). (Chávez, *Origins*: 233.)
4. For information on Juan de Abeytia, see Case 22.
5. María de Olguín was likely a granddaughter of Juan Olguín, who returned to New Mexico with Diego de Vargas in 1692 and was the alcalde at Jémez. Juan was killed in 1696. María was probably born about 1725, and may be the daughter of one of Juan Olguín's sons: Salvador, Antonio, or Tomás. (Chávez, *Origins*: 244.)
6. This Juan Joseph Vasquez is probably the Juan Joseph Vasquez who married Francisca Martín in 1709. The marriage records indicate that at the time of their marriage he was fourteen years old and she was thirty. If this is correct, then he would have been born in 1695, making him fifty years old at the time of this court case of 1745. María de Olguín may have been his second wife. A documented dated 1715 lists him as being twenty years old and the maker of carretas (wagons) and living in Santa Cruz. In 1727, a deed for land in the Las Trampas area was approved for a "Juan Bazquez" and then revoked, but it is not known if this was the same person. (Chávez, *Origins*: 306-07; Chavez, *Roots*: 2081; SANM I #84, WPA translation.)
7. For more information on Pedro Sánchez de Iñigo II, see Case 24. While his main residence was in Santa Cruz, deed records show that he held parcels of land southwest of (and possibly inside of) the boundaries of the San Ildefonso Pueblo land grant. In a 1763 lawsuit, he and his son-in-law, Antonio Mestas (perhaps a brother of Xavier Mestas), are accused of encroaching on San Ildefonso Pueblo lands. A 2001 archaeological study of three sites in the Los Alamos and Guaje Canyon areas identified one of the sites as a house and corral as being owned by Pedro Sánchez. That study indicates that the property was occupied between 1742 and 1763. Deed records show that Pedro Sánchez eventually left the San Ildefonso area and moved further north, though members of his family remained in the area. (Chávez, *Origins*: 79, 218, 280; Ebright, "Oppressed": 19; Moore, *Guaje*: 167-69, 175-79.)
8. Francisco Gómez del Castillo was the natural son of Juana Luján, who was the daughter of Matias Luján and Francisca Romero (who lived near San Ildefonso). It is speculated that Matias's father was one of the Gómez Robledos, a pre-revolt encomendero family originally from Portugal. Francisco married Ursula Guillén. His name appears as a witness in several New Mexico documents, as late as 1752. (Chávez, *Origins*: 187; Jenkins, "Eighteenth-Century New Mexican Women of Property": 338-39; SANM I #546; Barrett, *Spanish Colonial Settlement Landscapes*:31.)
9. Vicente Ginzo Rón y Thobar married Prudencia González Bas in 1743. He was a lieutenant in the Santa Fe presidio under Governor Francisco Antonio Marín del Valle, from 1754 to 1760. Like Francisco Gómez del Castillo, his name appears as a witness in several court cases of the mid-eighteenth century. By 1752 he had resigned from the presidio. (Chávez, *Origins*: 186, 361; SANM I #546; SANM II #537.)
10. In the Spanish text, the word used is *lomillo*, which can mean a pack saddle or the pads on a saddle.
11. A resident of La Cieneguilla, Joseph Montoya was the son of Andrés Montoya and Antonia Lucero de Godoy. Andrés was an alcalde of the Queres pueblos in 1731 and 1732. By 1722 Joseph Montoya was referred to as captain, and by 1729 he was married to Juana Quintana. (Chávez, *Origins*: 236, 376; SANM I #526, WPA translation.)
12. This Xavier Mestas is probably the Francisco Xavier Mestas who was born in 1711, the son of Juan de Mestas Peralta and María Trujillo. A New Mexico native, Juan de Mestas returned in 1693 to Santa Fe, probably with the Farfán Expedition; by 1746 he owned land in Río Arriba. In 1749, a "*parbulo*" (very young child) of Xavier Mestas was buried in Santa Cruz. This family name is sometimes spelled "Maestas." (Chávez, *Origins*: 218; SANM I #413; NMGS, *NMGS Newsletter*, January 2016: 16.)
13. The location of El Monte is unknown. It could be Tetilla Peak.
14. Joachín Codallos y Rabal was governor of New Mexico from 1743 to 1749. For more information on him, see Case 26 .
15. In the Spanish text, the words for "juridical indemnity" are "*causion juratoria de indemnidad*," which means that while the governor did not charge the husband or wife with anything, Juan Joseph Vasquez had to be careful to not jeopardize the governor's leniency by mistreating his wife.
16. For information on Joseph Romo de Vera, see Case 26.
17. For information on [Juan] Felipe Jacobo de Unanue, see Case 27.

31

ROSALIA GARCÍA DE NORIEGA CLAIMS INHERITANCE; RESCINDS HUSBAND'S POWER OF ATTORNEY
February 17, 1746, Source: SANM II #473

Synopsis and editor's notes: In this document Rosalia García de Noriega agreed to grant her husband, Salvador Martínez, power of attorney, thus giving up inheritance rights that were hers under the Spanish law. Rosalia did this so that she could collect the inheritance left by her mother, Josefa Valverde, the first wife of Luis García de Noriega. When Josefa died in 1735, Rosalia was her only child and under Spanish law half of the estate, as well as any amount brought to the marriage by Josefa, was the property of Josefa's only survivor, Rosalia. The other half of the estate went to Josefa's husband, Luis García de Noriega. In 1736, Rosalia and Salvador petitioned Governor Gervasio Cruzat y Góngora, requesting the payment of the inheritance, claiming that Luis García de Noriega had dispersed some of it and even mortgaged some of it.[1] The governor asked for a response from Luis, but apparently none was received. Rosalia explained that when she visited her father she was treated poorly. And during a following visit, Salvador and Luis exchanged harsh words and threats. To complicate matters, sometime around 1736, Luis García de Noriega married Barbara García Jurado, the daughter of Ramón García Jurado, and in the following years the couple had four children.

At some point after 1736 and before 1746, Luis García de Noriega had an accident that resulted in his being unable to speak words and only make noises. There was some disagreement among family members as to whether or not his power of reason had also been affected. As a result, Luis's new father-in-law, Ramón García Jurado, was appointed executor of his estate. A will, inventory, and appraisal were undertaken and the estate was appraised at 6,108 pesos.[2] Under Spanish law, half of this went to Luis's wife, Barbara García, and half was to be divided equally among the children of Barbara and Luis. Rosalia was not named as a beneficiary, because she had supposedly already received her inheritance on the death of her mother. On February 2, 1746, Ramón García Jurado met with Salvador Martínez regarding Rosalia's inheritance claim. They reached a compromise in which Rosalia would receive one third of the estate in property and goods, instead of half, which meant a loss of about 15 percent of the original inheritance.[3] However, under Spanish law the compromise could not be implemented because the inheritance belonged to Rosalia and not Salvador. She needed to give her husband official consent to agree to the compromise. It is not stated why she did not agree to meet with Ramón García Hurado on her own as was allowed under Spanish law.

Shortly thereafter, on February 17, 1746, Rosalia petitioned the alcalde seeking his approval in giving the power of attorney to her husband Salvador. After receiving approval, the compromise described above was validated and Salvador gained control of all her business affairs, including the buying and selling of property, arranging of mortgages, and using her property to pay her debs. Under Spanish law, he did not have the right to undertake these actions until his wife signed the power of attorney. The language used in the document concerning the power of attorney was probably taken from a legal handbook or guide, such as that used in other cases (for example Case 17).

On May 21, 1746, another petition was filed, this time jointly by Ramón García Jurado and Salvador Martínez, in which it was stated that the two ranches described in the inheritance compromise had been turned over to Salvador, but that other goods promised had not been delivered.[4] Later, in an inventory document of April 1747, Ramón García Jurado stated that he had delivered the two ranches and the goods that together made up the one-third share Rosalia was due from the Luis García de Noriega estate.[5]

On April 1747, just when everything seems to have been settled, Rosalia submitted a petition stating that she wished to renounce and make null and void the power of attorney that gave Salvador the control of her affairs. She said that it did a "grave injury and damage to her inheritance" and to her eight children and explained that she had agreed to it because she "found herself in fear" and was "violently urged" to arrange the power of attorney by her husband. It appears that she believed the one-third inheritance compromise should not have been made and she should have received the full half of the estate as provided by law. She may also have lost trust in her husband. Rosalia further stated that the earlier compromise agreement with her father Luis was done improperly, because he was suffering from injuries and did not have the mental capacity to understand such an agreement.[6]

Governor Joachín Codallos y Rabal accepted her petition and ordered the power of attorney be rescinded. Rosalia then signed an agreement with Ramón García Jurado, stating that the estate of Luis García de Noriega did not owe her anything. Rosalia, Ramón García Jurado, and Barbara García renounced their legal actions against each other, pledged their property in support of the agreement, and stated that they considered the matter finished.[7] One can only wonder whether or not Rosalia was being wise in making these decisions.

The case illustrates how Spanish law in eighteenth-century New Mexico protected a woman's dowry and inheritance, leaving both under the control of the woman to whom it applied. The sale of goods, or a contract involving the goods, in these cases needed the woman's legal approval. When Rosalia gave her "legal approval" for the compromise between Ramón García Jurado and Salvador Martínez, she stated that she did so without "pressure, coercion, or fear" from her husband. The power of attorney she gave Martínez enabled him to represent her and, even more importantly, meant that she "waived all the rights regarding the goods that she has from her father and mother."

In approving this legal act, the presiding judge, Antonio de Ulibarrí, was careful to point out to Rosalia that in giving her husband the power of attorney she was giving up the following rights and protections: the Roman "*senatus consultus Velleianum*," the medieval laws of *Las Siete Partidas*, and the sixteenth-century *Leyes de Toro*. As discussed in the introduction, these legal references were made in several New Mexican cases regarding dowries and property ownership of women, and were apparently understood to be a part of the legal process. Ulibarrí also advised Rosalia on the meaning of the protection of these ancient rights that she was renouncing by shifting her control over the estate to her husband.

This obedience to and reference to Spanish law was prevalent throughout the Spanish empire during this period.[8] For example, almost ninety years earlier, in Quito, Peru, in 1656, when Juan Cristóbal de Arce wanted to put a lien on his wife's property to borrow money for a joint business venture, his wife, doña Josefa Zambrano de Rivera, had to give her permission in the form of a legal document. Here is a portion of the document:

"The aforementioned doña Josefa Zambrano de Rivera renounced the Law of the Juris-consult Senator Veleyano which was approved by the Emperor Justinian, the Laws of the Toro, and the [*Las Siete*] *Partidas* of Madrid, which are in favor of women, whose content I, the notary, explained to her, and understanding the laws she renounced their protection, and because she is married she promised in the name of God the Cross to have signed this contract and not to proceed against it to recuperate her dowry or arras or other rights, nor to allege that she was forced by her husband or any other person and declares that she enters into this contract of her own free will because it is to her useful and beneficial.[9]"

TRANSLATION

Year of 1746

Power of attorney granted by doña Rosalia García de Noriega[10] to don Salvador Martínez, her husband, citizens of Villa de Albuquerque, as contained herein

[Power of Attorney]

In the Villa of Santa Fe, capital of this kingdom of New Mexico, on the 17th day of the month of February, 1746, before me, don Antonio de Ulibarrí,[11] alcalde mayor and captain of war of this villa, appeared doña Rosalia García de Noriega, citizen of the Villa of Albuquerque and resident therein. I attest that I know her and that she bestows her power of attorney in full compliance with the law, as required and may be necessary, to be exercised generally by don Salvador Martínez, her legitimate husband of the same community and residence. This is for matters relating to all her lawsuits, trials (civil or criminal) that she may have now or in the future with any person of any status or condition, whether it be related to monies, or other type of moveable goods or property that pertain to the grantor, whether they be due to inheritances, donations, or in any other direct or indirect manner.

Specifically, she also gives and bestows this power so that in her name and representing her person, [Salvador] Martínez may have, receive, demand, and recover from the possession of Captain Luis García de Noriega,[12] the legitimate father of the grantor, the portion of the estate to which, due to the death of doña Josefa Valverde,[13] lawful wife of Luis García. The grantor is sole heiress to the moveable goods and property of doña Josefa Valverde in possession of Luis García. Being aware of what is among this portion of the estate, she grants and bestows whatever letters of payment, receipts, or simple or authenticated balances that may be petitioned. Likewise, he can and may petition in the name of the grantor any agreement, release, or bankruptcy as may be convenient, that in the way, manner or mode in which they are made. She approves and ratifies the aforementioned as if she herself were to make and grant them. In doing so she calls special attention to the agreement that has been granted between Ramón García [Jurado],[14] holder of the power of attorney for Luis García, and Salvador Martínez. In the document it was agreed that he would turn over the third part of the goods, lands, cattle and sheep and all the other items that belonged to the deceased, Luis García, as was related in the document that they have presented in the presence of the sergeant major don Joachín Codallos y Rabál,[15] governor and captain general of this kingdom. It has been seen and read to him by the alcalde mayor.

From this time forward, the grantor ceases and waives all her rights and actions regarding the paternal and maternal goods that she has had and has and shall not request more quantity nor quantities regarding the previously mentioned goods that are beneficial to her person and profit, because of the knowledge that she has that everyday they were decreased and diminished because of the poor administration by Luis García, as is well-known.

She declares that in all of the previously mentioned matter, nothing, neither in part nor in whole, has been made due to pressure, coercion, or fear from her husband. Rather, she bestows this authority from her free and spontaneous will. Concerning this she renounces the law codes of *Senatus Consultus*,[16] [*Leyes de*] *Toro*, Madrid and [*Las Siete*] *Partidas*, and those of the *Velleyano*, along with the others favorable to women, and her general rights, to which effect she was advised by me, the alcalde mayor. Upon fulfilling all the previously mentioned matters, and for greater validation, she pledges her *adventitius paraphernal*[17] property that she presently has or may have in the future, and with them submits herself to the code and jurisdiction of the justices of His Majesty. This is from their lawsuits they may and should know, so that they compel her and force her lawful right. As is most appropriate, likewise, she renounces her *fuero*,[18] residence and community, and the law *si convenerit venerid de jurisdictione*.[19]

In this manner, she bestowed her authority and did not sign because she stated that she does not know how to read or write. So she asked witnesses to sign it, being her wish that Don Joseph Romo de Vera,[20] and Sebastián de Apodaca,[21] and Juan Domíngo Páez,[22] all citizens of this villa, and those of my assistants with whom I act due to the lack of a public or royal scribe, which do not exist in this kingdom, to which I attest.

    Antonio de Ulibarrí (rubric)
    Presiding Judge
    At the request of Rosalia García de Noriega

Witness
Antonio Felix Sánchez[23] (rubric)
Witness
Juan Manuel de Chirinos[24] (rubric)
Witness
Joseph Manuel Garduño[25] (rubric)

TRANSCRIPTION

Año de 1746

Poder Otorgado por Doña Rosalia Garcia de Noriega á don Salvador Martinez, su marido, Vezinos dela Villa de Alburquerque, como dentro se contiene

En la Villa de Santa Fee, Capital de Este Reyno dela Nueva Mexico en dies y siete dias del mes de febrero de mill setesientos quarenta y seis años Ante mi don Antonio de Ulibarri, Alcalde maior y Capitan Aguerra de Esta dhaVilla paresio presente Doña Rosalia Garsia de noriega vesina de la Villa de Alburquerque y Residente En Esta a quien doi fee, que conosco, otorga que da todo su poder Cumplido Bastante en derecho el que se requiere y fuere nesesario mas pueda y deva baler a don Salbador Martines, su marido lexitimo de la misma besinda y Residensia gueneralmente para En todos sus pleitos, cavsas y negosios Sibiles o criminales que ael presente tenga, o tubiere, en lo de adelante con quales quiera persona de quales quiera calidad o condision que sea sobre, pesos, v otro generos de bienes muebles rraises que le pertenescan ala, otorgante por erensias, donasiones o en otra manera directa o ynderectamente =

Tambien le da y otorga este dho, poder, espesialmente para que En su nombre y representando su propia persona, aia, resiba, demande, y cobre de mano de el Capitan Luis Garsia Padre lexitimo de la otorgante, la parte del cavdal que por muerte de doña Josepha balberde muger que Fue lexitima del dho, Luis Garsia de quien Es unica Eredera la otorgante quedo en bienes Muebles y raises En poder del dho, Luis Garsia y persebido que sea de todo ello de y otorge las cartas de pago, resibos y finiquitos sinples o avtenticos que le sean pedidos y asi mismo pueda en nombre de la otorgante aser y aga quales quiera Conbenios, quitas bagas o quiebras como conbiniese que de la suerte forma y manera que las ysiere y otorgare asi las aprueba y ratifica la suso dha, como, si por su propia persona le ysiesen y otorgasen asiendo presente En Espesial, el conbenio que Esta otorgado entre Ramon Garsia poder aviente del dho Luis Garsia y es que se le entriege el tersio de los bienes tierras, Ganados maiores y menores Y todo lo demas que actualmente esiste en poder del dho, Luis Garsia pertenesiente a dha difunta como se refiere en escripto que an presentado ante el Señor Sargento Maior D.n Joachin Codallos y Rabal, Gov.or y Capitan General de Este dho, Reyno el que a bisto y le a sido leydo por dho, Alcalde maior=

Desde aora para siempre se desiste y aparta la otorgante de todos sus derechos y acsiones que alos bienes Paternos y maternos a tenido y tiene a ellos para no pedir mas cantidad ni cantidades, En ninguna Espesie que sea contentandose con lo referido por resultar como resulta en su, pro, y vtilidad por el conosimiento que tiene de que cada dia se ande atrasar y menos cabar por la mala, aministrasion que el dho, Luis Garsia tiene como Es notorio =

Declara que para todo lo referido ni parte de ellos no a sido con quisa apremiada ni atemorisada por el dho, su marido si no que otorga este poder de Su libre e yspontania boluntad, sobre que renunsia las leyes de partida, senatus consultus, Toro, Madrid y Partida, y las de Beleyano con las demas faborables alas mugeres y la general del derecho de quio efecto fue abisado por mi el presente alcalde Maior y al cumplimiento de todo lo referido y para su maior balidasion obliga sus bienes para frenales abentitious que ael presente tiene y tubiese en lo de adelante y con ellos se somete ael fuero y Jurisdision alas Justisias de Su Magestad que de sus causas puedan y devan conoser para que a ello la Conpelan y apremien por todo rigor de derecho y como mas conbenga asimismo renunsia su fuero, domisilio y besindad y la ley si conbenerid de jurisdisiones =

Asi lo otorgo y no firmo por desir no saber ler ni escrebir y rogo a vn testigo lo firmase siendolo de su otorgamiento don Joseph Romo de Vera y sebastian de Apodaca y Juan Domingo Paes Vesinos de Esta Villa y los de mi asistensia con quienes autuo a falta de Escribano Publico, o Real que no lo ai En Este Reyno que de todo doi fee.

Antt.o de Ulibarri (rubric)
Juez Receptor
A Ruego de Rosalia Garzia de Noriega
Juan Rael Chirinos (rubric)
Antonio Felix Sanches (rubric)
Joseph Miguel Garduño (rubric)

Notes

1. See SANM I #1221, WPA translation.
2. See SANM I #341 and SANM I #342, WPA translations.
3. See SANM II #472.
4. See SANM I #414, WPA translation.
5. See SANM I #343, WPA translation.
6. See SANM I #345, WPA translation.
7. See SANM I #345, WPA translation.
8. See Burkholder and Johnson, *Colonial Latin America*: 232-33; Lavrin and Couturier, "Dowries and Wills": 280-88; Rosen, "Women and Property": 358-59.
9. See Gauderman, *Quito*: 43-44.
10. Rosalia García de Noriega was the only daughter of Luis García de Noriega and Josefa Valverde. See notes 12 and 13 below for further information. (Chávez, *Origins*: 304; NMGS, *Aquí*: 291.)
11. For information on Antonio de Ulibarrí, see Case 5.
12. Luis García de Noriega was the son of Captain Alonso García de Noriega II. During the Pueblo Revolt of 1680, Alonso was one of the leaders of the refugees who escaped to El Paso. He returned to New Mexico with the Spanish Reconquest. Another family member, Alfonso García de Noriega I was in New Mexico by 1636. Luis was a soldier with the Albuquerque garrison, and was a captain of the squadron. In 1715, he was

an alcalde of Albuquerque. Luis and his brothers received the large San Antonio land grant near Albuquerque. (Kessell, Hendricks, Dodge, and Miller, *Settling of Accounts*: 222; SANM I #341; SANM II #484; Barrett, *Spanish Colonial Settlement Landscapes*: 139; Chávez, *Origins*: 18; NMGS, *Aquí*: 291.)

13. Josefa Valverde married Luis García in 1703. Her birth name was "Josefa Xaviera Baca," but she was brought up in the Valverde family. (Cháves, *Origins*: 181.)

14. Ramón García Jurado was the son of José García Jurado of Mexico City. José held many positions in New Mexico, including procurado general (attorney) for the Santa Fe cabildo. Ramón was an alférez during the campaign against the Moqui in 1716, and he was alcalde of Bernalillo and nearby pueblos in 1732 when he was accused of mistreating the Indians. He married Bernardina Hurtado, daughter of alcalde Martín Hurtado, in 1710. As this document indicates, Ramón was the father of Barbara García Jurado, the second wife of Luis García de Noriega, and the executor of Luis's estate. (NMGS, *Aquí*: 291; Tigges and Salazar, *Colonial Lives*: 124n4; Chávez, *Origins*: 183-84.)

15. For information on Joachín Codallos y Rabal, see Case 26.

16. The *senatus consultus Velleianum* was a law adopted before AD 31 under the consulship of Velleius. A "*senatus consultus*" was generally a text or law emanating from the Roman Senate. This law was intended to protect women from taking on her husband's debts with the property that she had brought to the marriage. (Van den Bergh, "Roman Women": 113-36; "Imposed Protection": 583.)

17. This Latin phrase, properly spelled "*adventicius paraphernalia*," is a legal term meaning "the personal belongings inherited or brought to the marriage and reserved by law for a married woman in addition to her dowry." (Black, *Dictionary of Law*: 871, 1077; Van den Bergh,: 13; Winkel, : 583).

18. The Spanish word "fuero" can refer to specific laws and exemptions. In this case, the reference is probably to the laws that protect the dowries and inheritance of women.

19. The Latin phrase "*si convenerit de jurisdictione*" means "settled by a legal authority or in a legal context," or "as agreed to by law." (Weskett, *Complete Digest*: 467; Mommsen-Krueger, Weidman, *Corpus Iuris Civilis I*: 47.)

20. For information on Joseph Romo de Vera, see Case 26. For some reason, neither Romo de Vera nor the other two men she recommended acted as witnesses for her in the end, though they may have acted as advisors.

21. For information on Sebastián de Apodaca, see Case 26.

22. Juan Domíngo Páez was the son of Juan Páez Hurado and Teodora García de la Riva. According to Fray Angelico Chavéz, he does not appear in the documents of the Spanish Colonial Archives until his name is mentioned in the will of his brother-in-law, José Terrus, in 1745. He may have been in Santa Fe to arrange affairs after that death and perhaps in relation to his father's death in 1742. (Chávez, *Origins*: 255-56; SANM I #966.)

23. The Antonio Felix Sánchez named here could be the Antonio Sánchez who was a son of Francisco Sánchez and Josefa de Chávez and who married Ana María Alvarez de Castillo in 1756. If this is the same person, then Antonio Felix Sánchez was also a grandson of Jacinto Sánchez de Iñigo and Isabel Telles, both of whom returned to New Mexico after the 1680 Pueblo Revolt. The name "Antonio Felix" does appear frequently in Spanish Colonial documents of the 1750s as a witness. (Chávez, *Origins*: 281.)

24. For information on Juan Manuel de Chirinos, see Case 17.

25. Joseph Manuel Garduño may have been part of the Bartolomé Garduño family who had arrived in New Mexico by 1695. (Chávez, *Origins*: 185-86.)

GLOSSARY

Acequia. Irrigation canal or ditch.

Alguacil mayor. Chief constable or peace officer.

Alcalde ordinario. A member of the town council responsible for administration of justice; usually a person with stature in the community.

Alcalde mayor. In New Mexico, an official appointed by the governor with civil jurisdiction over one of the six to eight *alcaldías*.

Alcaldía. Region of a province overseen by an alcalde mayor; includes both the Indian and Spanish population.

Alférez. Standard bearer, the lowest ranking commissioned officer in the Spanish military.

Almud. Approximately one-twelfth of a *fanega*.

Amancebados. A couple living together without marriage; cohabitation.

Arroba. A dry measure equal to about twenty-five pounds, or a liquid measure equal to about three and one-half to four gallons.

Audiencia real. Highest royal court of appeals; a council of state to the viceroy.

Auto. Judicial or administrative decree.

Ayudante. In military terms, this is loosely translated as an aide; it did not carry the authority of a higher rank.

Ayuntamiento. Town council or governing body of a chartered town. The term was not often used in New Mexico until the Mexican period.

Bachiller. Recipient of the lowest university degree, often a parish priest.

Bando. Proclamation or order.

Bayeta. A course woolen fabric often napped, usually dyed green or red, and used in New Mexico as a trade item. The English word is baise.

Belduque. A short, pointed sword or knife.

Bosque. A wet and woody place.

Bretaña. A linen fabric used for men's and women's clothing, especially for shirts, and a frequent trade item from Brittany.

Cabeza del proceso. An official statement of a complaint presenting the basis for the investigation. It was intended to be placed at the head of legal proceedings.

Cabildo. A town council, with judicial and administrative powers, granted to chartered towns.

Cabo. Corporal, squadron leader.

Cañada. Literally, a valley between mountains; in New Mexico it could also mean a "sheep-walk."

Canoa. A wooden flume used to help the water flow in an acequia.

Capitán de compaña. The temporary head of a military operation during a campaign.

Capitán general. Chief military officer; on the frontier, a position usually filled by the governor.

Capitan vitalicio. Captain for life.

Carcél. Jail.

Carneras. Sheep, sometimes specifically referring to rams.

Carreta. A two-wheeled, wooden cart used for local transport. Another type of wagon, a *carro*, was larger with four wheels, often covered, and used for long distance trade and transport.

Casas Reales. Government offices.

Castellano. Commander, or castellan of a fortification.

Cedula. A decree from the king, a royal order.

Cienega. Marsh, swamp, bog.

Claustro. Cloister or gallery situated around a courtyard.

Coa. A digging stick.

Cofradia. The Catholic lay brotherhood responsible for paying for certain religous services and the maintenance of a church or chapel.

Colcha. In New Mexico, an embroidery stitch using distinctive "couching"; also, a heavily embroidered shawl or bed cover.

Comadre. Godmother, or a special friend.

Comisario. The Inquisition title for the head of a provincial jurisdiction.

Compadre. Godfather, or a special friend.

Convento. Living and administration rooms for religious personnel associated with a church.

Coyote. Racial category referring to the children of mestizo and Indian parents.

Criado. Servant.

Curandero/Curandera. A healer.

Custodia. In the Franciscan order, the name given to a jurisdiction that has not yet attained the status of a province.

Custos. Head of a Franciscan custodia.

Derecho. In legal documents, it means a legal right.

Ecclesiastical Judge. A judge appointed to review church cases. This could have been a priest, or if acting for the bishop, a lay religious person.

Encomienda. In New Mexico, an encomienda was a grant of tribute of corn and woven goods given to the Spanish *encomendero*. In return, the *encomendero* was to provide for the Indians' welfare and instruction in Christianity. By the eighteenth century it had been outlawed.

Espada. Sword.

Español. A person born in Spain, or a person who claims to be part of the Español casta.

Estancia. Grant of land for raising cattle; a livestock ranch.

Fanega. A dry measure roughly equivalent to 1 ½ to 2 ½ bushels, or the amount of grain that fills a bin of about eighteen inches by seven inches by nine inches. There are two fanegas in a *carga* and twelve *almudes* in a *fanega*.

Fray. Member of a religous order; in New Mexico, a member of the Franciscan order.

Fuerte. Military stronghold.

Fuero. Statute, privilege, or exemption; or a compilation of laws.

Generales de la ley. A legal term (usually found in a phrase such as "*no le tocan los generales de la ley*") which meant that the person testifying in a court case was impartial, with no bias regarding the accused.

Genízaro. A detribalized Plains Indian (or member of another Native American tribe) who had been captured and raised in a Hispanic or sometimes Puebloan household.

Gentiles. Indians who had not been converted to Christianity; also referred to as infidels, heathens, *Indios barberos*, or roving, unsettled Indians.

Gobernador. Governor.

Grillos. Fetters, or leg irons.

Hijo Natural. Literally, an illegitimate child; in legal cases, it meant a child recognized by his or her parents as being theirs.

Judicial. A legal proceeding reviewed and signed by witnesses.

Juez comisario. An official given authority in judicial matters.

Juez receptor. In New Mexico, it referred to a temporary presiding judge.

Justicia. Justice, legal right.

Lienza. A type of linen or fabric woven from flax or hemp; sometimes a canvas.

Macho. Male mule.

Mala Vida. General term used for an "unhappy life," usually the result of abuse by one spouse over another. It could also refer to a lack of financial support, desertion, gambling, physical and verbal abuse, and adultery.

Manta. A general term for a cloth used as a blanket for a human or a horse.

Mestizo. Offspring of European and Indian parents.

Moso. Male servant, or a young male.

Mulatto. A person with a mixture of European and African ancestry.

Obraje. Workplace.

Paño. Coarse woolen cloth; or clothes or blankets made of such fabric.

Paraje. A place, campsite, or watering hole; may also be called a *sitio* or *aguaje*.

Plaza de armas. Military parade ground used for campaigns, musters, and drilling of troops; often located in the central plaza of a town.

Poder. In legal cases, *poder* referred to a power of attorney.

Predicador. A priest or friar who preaches.

Procurador. A legal representative, but not an *abogado* (a certified attorney).

Puesto. Small settlement or outpost.

Ramada. A lean-to or other type of structure made of branches.

Ranchería. Cluster of temporary Indian dwellings; Indian encampment.

Real. Coin worth one eighth of a silver peso.

Real de minas. Town or district specializing in mining.

Real de plata. Silver coin.

Real Hacienda. Royal treasury.

Refugio. See *Santuario*.

Regidor. Member of a town council or *cabildo*.

Rescate. Literally, means "ransom." In New Mexico, it refers to the ransoming of Indians or Hispanics who had been captured by Indians and sold at trade fairs (sometimes called *rescate* fairs). An "*Indios de rescate*" was a term for an Indian made part of Spanish society by capture or ransom.

Residencia. Official evelution held at the end of a term by the incoming office holder. In New Mexico, it usually refered to the evaluation/review of the outgoing governor.

Rubric. Unique mark or flourish added to a signature; the Latin term is *rubrica*.

Sallal. Coarse woolen cloth.

Santuario. A place of sanctuary or refuge, usually in a church, where a person accused of a crime was not subject to arrest. With the permission of the priest, however, an interview of the accused was allowed.

Scarleta. An expensive woolen fabric often dyed an intense red with cochineal.

Sirujano (or *cirujano*). Surgeon.

Summaria. Overall term referring to the factfinding steps in a legal case: gathering of testimony, inspection of injuries, and imprisonment of the accused.

Teniente. Lieutenant.

Vara. A Castilian yard of about thirty-three inches; or a staff of office.

Vecino. Householder, resident of a community, or citizen; often used to indicate a property owner.
Verbo ad verbum. The Latin equivalent for verbatim, or "word-for-word."
Vicario. A person who transacted ecclesiatical affairs, as the representative for the bishop or archhishop.
Virrey. Viceroy.
Villa. In New Mexico, this referred to a settlement with royally defined privileges, including the right to have a *cabildo*.

MAPS

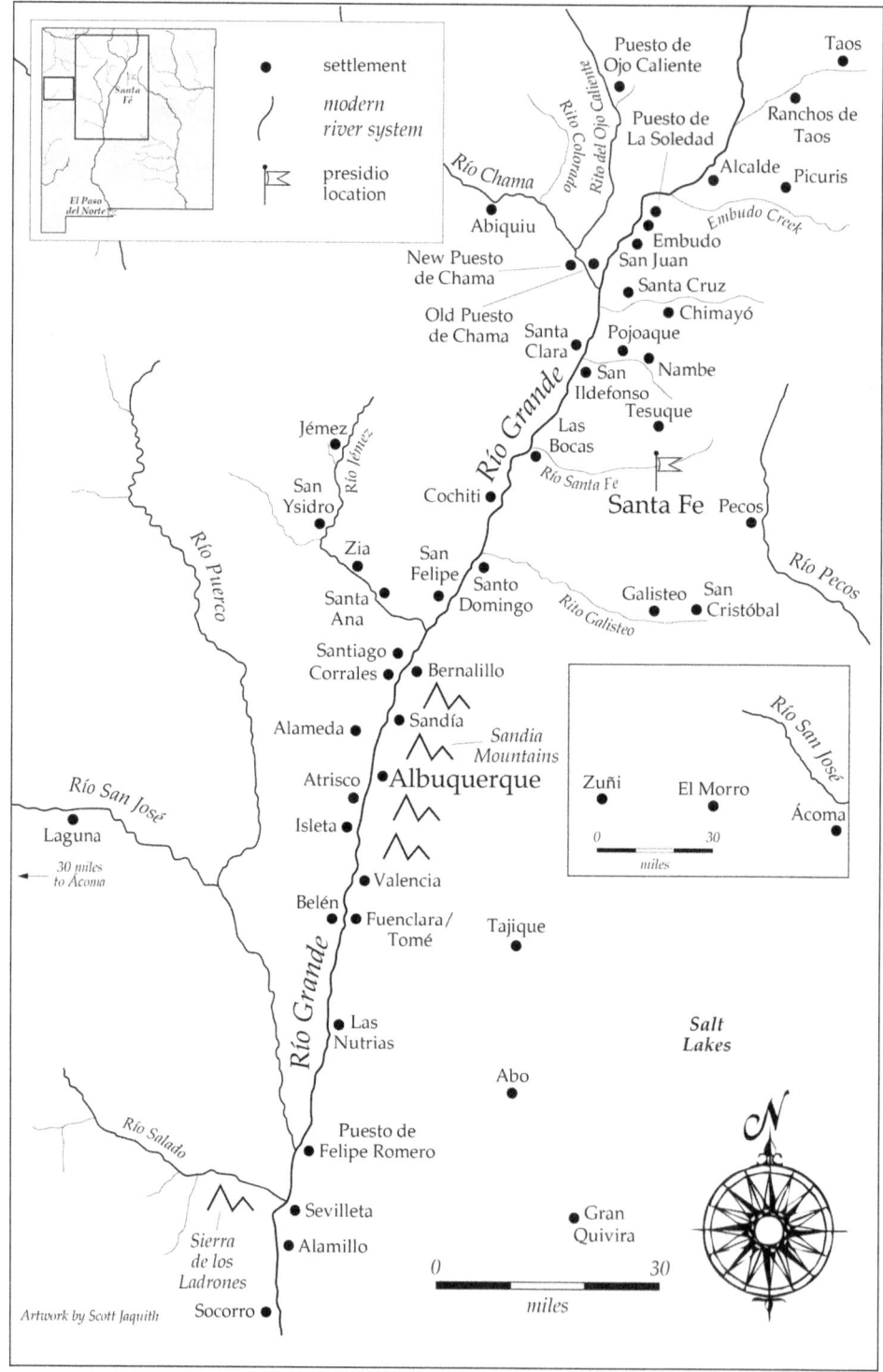

New Mexico in the early and mid-eighteenth century. Map drawn by Scott Jacquith.

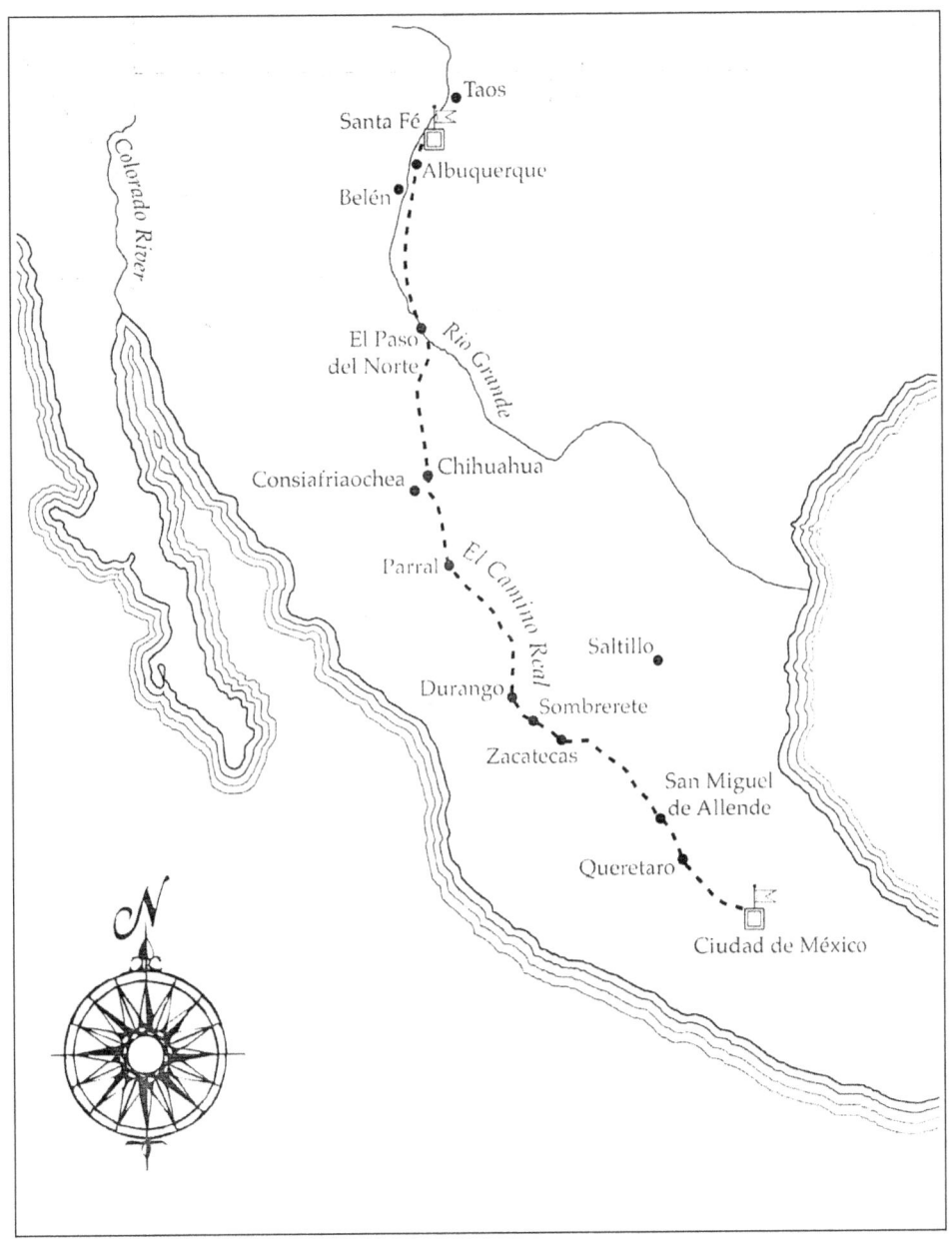

Central and northern New Spain in the eighteenth century. Map drawn by Scott Jacquith.

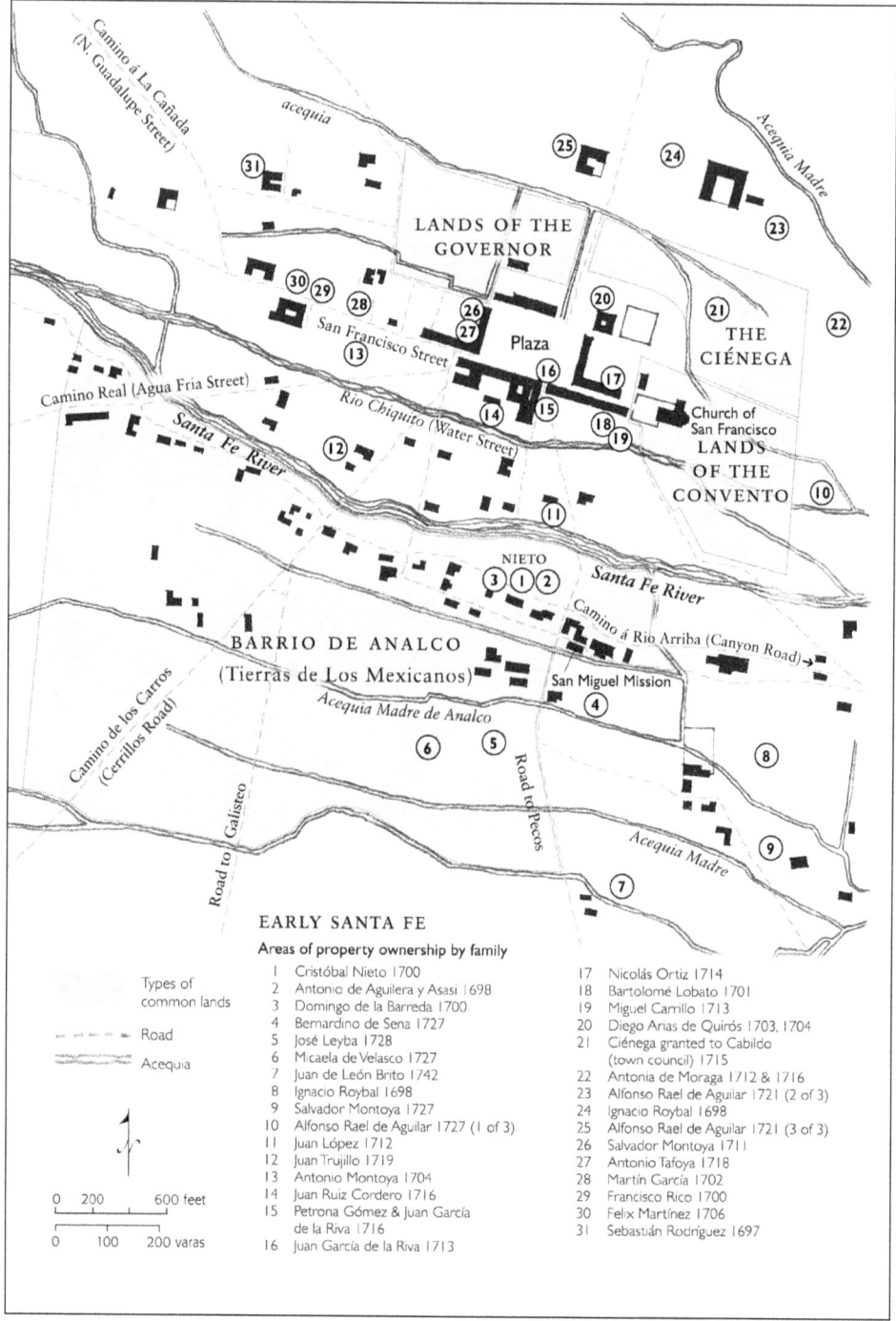

Early Santa Fe, in the eighteenth century. From Malcom Ebright, *Advocates for the Oppressed*:56. Based on information from Malcolm Ebright and Cordelia Thomas Snow. Courtesy of Malcolm Ebright.

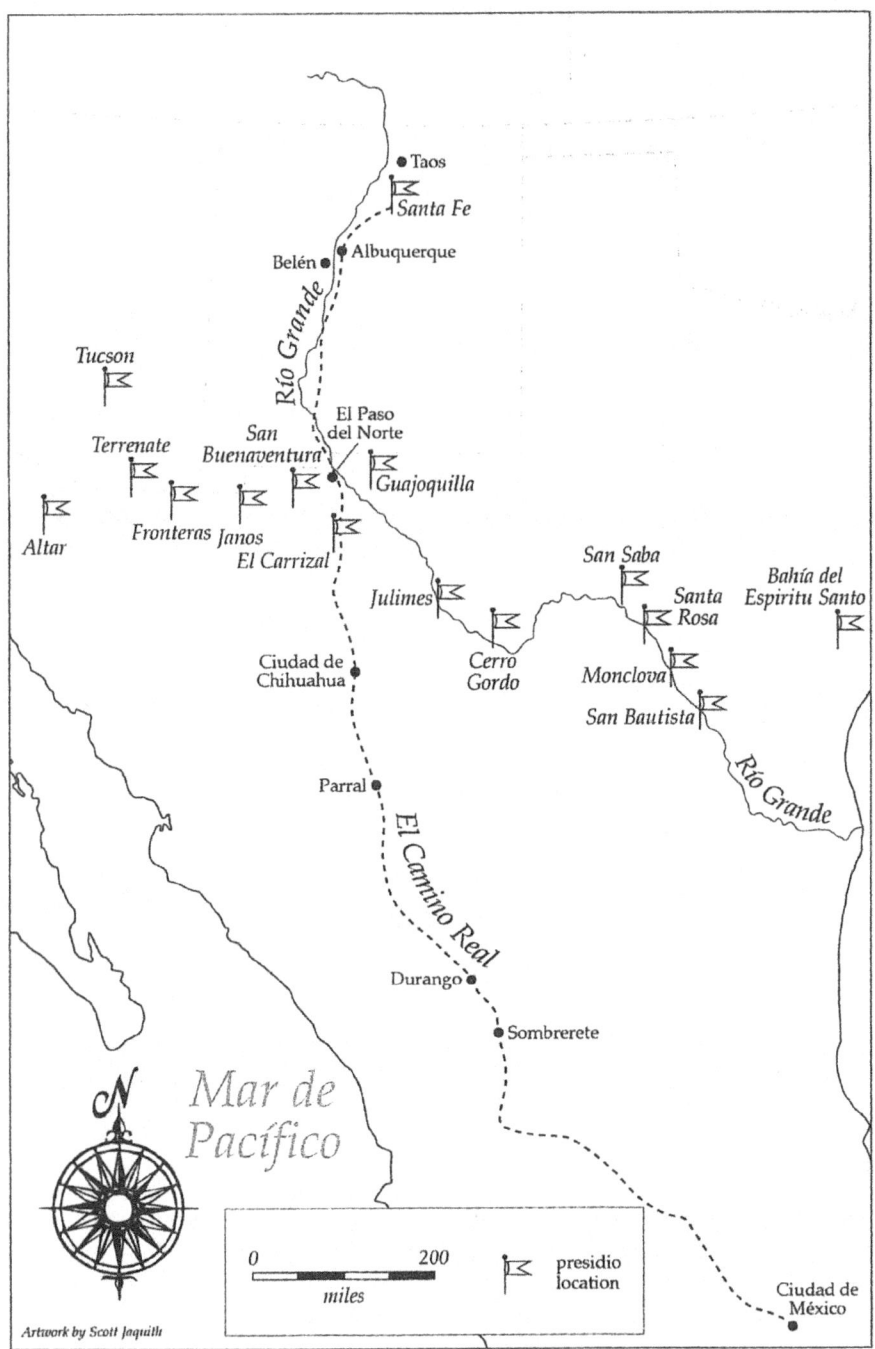

Borderland Presidios in the mid-eighteenth century. Map drawn by Scott Jacquith.

BIBLIOGRAPHY

ARCHIVAL MATERIALS

Archivo General de la Nación, Mexico City, Mexico, in Center for Southwest Research and Special Collections, University of New Mexico, Albuquerque.

Fray Angélico Chávez Collection, Archives and Historical Services Division, State Records Center and Archives, Santa Fe, New Mexico.

Diligencias Matrimoniales, Archives and Historical Services Division, State Records Center and Archives, Santa Fe, New Mexico.

Laws of the Territory of New Mexico, New Mexico Supreme Court Library, Santa Fe, New Mexico.

Ritch Collection, Henry E. Huntington Library, San Marino California, in the Center for Southwest Research and Special Collections, University of New Mexico, Albuquerque.

Spanish Archives of New Mexico, I and II, Archives and Historical Services Division, New Mexico State Records Center and Archives, Santa Fe.

DICTIONARIES

Addis, William Edward, and Thomas Arnold. *Catholic Dictionary: Containing Some Account of the Doctrine, Discipline, Rites, Ceremonies, Councils, and Religious Orders of the Catholic Church.* London: Routledge and Kegan Paul Limited, 1951.

Baretti, Guiseppe Marco Antonio. *A Dictionary, Spanish and English and English and Spanish: containing the signification of words, and their different uses.* London: Luke Hansard, 1800. Facsimile of the first edition, London: British Library and Ecco Print Editions, 2011.

Barron's Spanish English Dictionary. New York: Barnes and Noble, 2006.

Diccionario de Commercial Medieval. Murcia, Spain: Universidad de Murcia, 2016.

Diccionario de la Lengue Española de la Real. 23rd ed. Madrid: Académia Española, 2014.

Oxford Latin Dictionary. Oxford, England: 1968.

Random House Dictionary of English and Spanish. New York: Random House, 1967.

Simon & Shuster International Spanish English Dictionary. 2nd ed. New York: Simon and Shuster, 1977.

Simpson, P. D., ed. *Cassell's Latin Dictionary.* New York: Wiley Publishing, Inc., 1968.

New Velázquez Spanish and English Dictionary. El Monte, CA: Velázquez Press, 2007.

BOOKS, ARTICLES, AND MISCELLANEOUS MATERIALS

Adams, Eleanor, B. and Fray Angélico Chávez, eds. *The Missions of New Mexico 1776: A Description by Fray Francisco Atanasio Domínguez with Other Contemporary Documents.* Albuquerque: University of New Mexico Press, 1975.

Ahlborn, Richard E. "The Will of a New Mexico Woman in 1762." *New Mexico Historical Review* 65, no. 3 (July 1990): 319-55.

Alexander, Francelle E. *Among the Cottonwoods: The Enduring Río Abajo Villages of Peralta & Los Pinos, New Mexico before 1940.* Los Ranchos, New Mexico: Rio Grande Books, 2012.

Arrom, Silvia Marina. *The Women of Mexico City, 1790–1857.* Stanford, California: Stanford University Press, 1989.

Aste, Richard, ed. *Behind Closed Doors.* New York: Brooklyn Museum, in association with Monacelli Press, 2013.

Barahona, Renato. *Sex Crimes, Honour, and the Law in Early Modern Spain: Vizcaya, 1528–1735.* Toronot, Canada: University of Toronto, 2003.

Barrett, Elinore M. *Conquest and Catastrophe: Changing Rio Grande Pueblo Settlement Patterns in the Sixteenth and Seventeenth Centuries.* Albuquerque: University of New Mexico Press, 2002.

_____. *The Spanish Colonial Settlement Landscapes of New Mexico, 1598–1680.* Albuquerque: University of New Mexico Press, 2012.

Basarás, Joaquín Antonio de. *Una Visión del México del Siglo de la Luces: La Codificación de Joaquín Antonio de Basarás: Origen, Costumbres y Estado Presente de Mexicanos y Filipinos, 1763.* México: Americo Arte Editores, 2006.

Baxter, John O. *Las Carneradas.* Albuquerque: University of New Mexico Press, 1987.

Behar, Ruth. "Sexual Witchcraft, Colonialism, and Women's Powers: Views from the Mexican Inquisition." In *Sexuality and Marriage in Colonial Latin America*, edited by Asunción Lavrin, 178-209. Lincoln: University of Nebraska Press, 1989.

Bisson, Thomas. N. *The Medieval Crown of Aragon: A Short History.* Oxford, England: Clarendon Press, 1986.

Black, Georgia D. *Perfect Wives, Other Women: Adultery and Inquisition in Early Modern Spain.* Durham, North Carolina: Duke University, 2001.

Bloom, Lansing B. "Albuquerque and Galisteo, Certificate of Their Founding." *New Mexico Historical Review* 10, no. 1 (June 1935): 48-51.

Boyer, Richard. *Lives of the Bigamists.* Albuquerque: University of New Mexico Press, 2001.

———. "Women, La Mala Vida, and the Politics of Marriage." In *Sexuality and Marriage in Colonial Latin America,* edited by Asunción Lavrin, 253-86. Lincoln: University of Nebraska Press, 1989.

Boyer, Richard, and Geoffrey Spurling, eds. *Colonial Lives: Documents on Latin American History, 1550-1850.* New York: Oxford University Press, 2000.

Brinkerhoff, Sidney, and Odie B. Faulk. *Lancers of the King.* Phoenix: Arizona Historical Foundation, 1965.

Brooks, James F. "This Evil Extends Especially to the Feminine Sex: Negotiating Captivity in the New Mexico Borderlands." *Feminist Studies* 22, no. 2 (Summer 1996): 279-303.

———. *Captives and Cousins.* Chapel Hill: University of North Carolina Press, 2002.

Brown, Tracy. *Pueblo Indians and Spanish Colonial Authority in Eighteenth-Century New Mexico.* Tucson: University of Arizona Press, 2013.

Brugge, David M. "Captives and Slaves on the Camino Real." In *El Camino Real de Tierra Adentro,* Vol. 1, compiled by Gabrielle G. Palmer and Stephen L. Fosberg, 103-10. Santa Fe: Bureau of Land Management, New Mexico State Land Office, 1999.

Burkholder, Mark A., and Lyman L. Johnson. *Colonial Latin America.* 7th ed. Oxford, England: Oxford University Press, 2010.

Burns, Robert, ed., Samuel Parsons Scott, translator. *Las Siete Partidas.* Philadelphia: University of Pennsylvania Press, 2000.

Bustamante, Adrian. "The Matter Was Never Resolved: The *Casta* System in Colonial New Mexico, 1693-1823." *New Mexican Historical Review* 66, no. 2 (April 1991): 143-63.

Cámara, Luis Millet. "Logwood and Archaeology in Campeche." *Journal of Anthropological Research* 40, no. 2 (Summer, 1984): 324-28.

Cambas, Manuel Rivera. *Los Gobernantes de México.* Mexico: Imp. de J. M. Aguilar Ortiz, 1872.

Campbell, Lyle. *Pipil Language of El Salvador.* Berlin: Mouton Grammar Library, 1985.

Candelaria, Juan. "Information Communicated by Juan Candelaria, Resident of this Villa de San Francisco Xavier de Alburquerque." *New Mexico Historical Review* 4, no. 3 (July 1939): 274-97.

Cañeque, Alejandro. *The King's Living Image*. New York: Routledge, 2004.

Chávez, Fray Angélico. *Archives of the Archdiocese of Santa Fe*. Washington, DC: Academy of American Franciscan History, 1957.

_____. "De Vargas's Negro Drumer." *El Palacio* 56 (May 1949): 131-38.

_____. *Cháve.z Distinctive American Clan of New Mexico*. Santa Fe: William Gannon, 1989.

_____. "Genizaros." In *The Handbook of North American Indians, Southwest*, edited by Alonzo Ortiz, 198-200. Washington, DC: Smithsonian Institution, 1979.

_____. *New Mexico Roots, Ltd*. Santa Fe: Museum of New Mexico Press, 1982.

_____. *Origins of New Mexico Families*. Santa Fe: William Gannon, 1975.

_____. "Some Mission Records and Villasur." In *A Moment in Time, The Odyssey of New Mexico's Segesser Hide Paintings*, edited by Thomas E. Chávez, 149-168. Los Ranchos, New Mexico: Rio Grande Press, 2012.

Chávez, Thomas E., ed. *A Moment in Time: The Odyssey of New Mexico's Segesser Hide Paintings*. Los Ranchos, New Mexico: Rio Grande Press, 2012.

Chávez, Tibo J. "Early Witchcraft in New Mexico." *El Palacio* 76, no. 3 (September 1969): 7-9.

Christmas, Henrietta Martinez. "Alcalde Nerio Antonio Montoya." *Herencia* 20, no. 4 (December 2012): 20-233.

_____. *Military Records, Colonial New Mexico, Notas y Revistas*. Albuquerque: Hispanic Genealogical Research Center, 2004.

_____. *The Santa Fe Presidio Soldiers: Their Donation to the American Revolution*. Albuquerque: New Mexico Genealogical Society, 2006.

Christmas, Henrietta Martinez, and Patricia Sanchez Rau. "Una Lista de Soldados – Presidio de Santa Fe, 1712–1719." *New Mexico Genealogist* 42, no. 4 (December 2003): 195, 201.

_____. *The Early Pojoaque Valley, Labradores, Jornaleros y Artesanos*. Albuquerque: Hispanic Genealogical Research Center of Albuquerque, 2004.

_____. *Early Settlers of La Cienega, A Family History*. Albuquerque: Hispanic Genealogical Research Center of Albuquerque, 2008. First published 2004 by Hispanic Genealogical Research Center.

_____. "Santa Fe Tool Distribution, 1704." *New Mexico Genealogist* 53, no. 1 (March 2014): 20.

Christmas, Henrietta Martinez, Jeanette Gallegos, and Patricia S. Rau. *New Mexico Burials, Santa Fe – St. Francis Parish and Military Chapel of Our Lady of Light (La Castrense), 1726–1834*. Albuquerque: New Mexico Genealogical Society, 1997.

Chuchiak, John F., ed. *The Inquisition in New Spain, 1536–1820: A Documentary History.* Baltimore: John Hopkins University Press, 2012.

Cisneros, Jose. *Riders Across the Centuries, Horsemen of the Spanish Borderlands.* El Paso: University of Texas Press, 1984.

Colligan, John B. *The Juan Páes Hurtado Expedition of 1695.* Albuquerque: University of New Mexico Press, 1995.

Coolidge, Grace E. "'A Vile and Abject Women': Noble Mistresses, Legal Power, and the Family in Early Modern Spain. *Journal of Family History* 32, no. 3 (July 2007): 195-214.

Couturier, Edith. "Women and the Family in Eighteenth-Century Mexico: Law and Practice." *Journal of Family History* (Fall 1985): 294-304.

Cutter, Charles. "The Administration of Law in Colonial New Mexico." *Journal of the Early Republic* 18 (Spring 1998): 99-115.

_____. "Judicial Punishment in Colonial New Mexico." *Western Legal History* 8, no. 1 (Winter/Spring 1995): 114-129.

_____. *The Legal Culture of Northern New Spain, 1700–1810.* Albuquerque: University of New Mexico Press, 1995.

_____. *The Protector de Indios in Colonial New Mexico, 1659–1821.* Albuquerque: University of New Mexico Press, 1986.

_____. "The Spanish Borderlands." In *Encyclopedia of the North American Colonies*, Vol. 1, 412-549. New York: Charles Scribner's Sons, 1993.

Cutter, Donald, and Iris Engstrand. *Quest for Empire, Spanish Settlement in the Southwest.* Golden, Colorado: Fulcrum Publishing, 1996.

Davis, Samantha. "Spanish Colonial Lives, Latin Phrases." Unpublished Paper, manuscript held by the editor. December 2015.

De la Concha, Ignacio. *Liber Amicorum: Profesor Don Ignacio de la Concha.* Oviedo, Spain: Universidad de Oviedo, Servicio de Publicacións, 1986.

Downey, Kirstin. *Isabella, The Warrior Queen.* New York: Doubleday, 2014.

Dunmire, William W. *New Mexico's Spanish Livestock Heritage: Four Centuries of Animals, Land, and People.* Albuquerque: University of New Mexico Press, 2013.

Dyer, Abigail. "Seduction by Promise of Marriage: Law, Sex, and Culture in Seventeenth Century Spain." *The Sixteenth Century Journal* 34, no. 2 (Summer 2003): 439-55.

Ebright, Malcolm. *Advocates for the Oppressed: Hispanos, Indians, Genizaros, and Their Land in New Mexico.* Albuquerque: University of New Mexico Press, 2014.

_____. *Land Grants and Lawsuits in Northern New Mexico*. Albuquerque: University of New Mexico Press, 1994.

_____. "Sharing the Shortages: Water Litigation and Regulation in Hispanic New Mexico, 1600–1850." *New Mexico Historical Review* 75, no. 1 (January 2001): 2-45.

Ebright, Malcolm, and Rick Hendricks. *The Witches of Abiquiu: The Governor, the Priest, the Genizaro Indians, and the Devil*. Albuquerque: University of New Mexico Press, 2006.

Ebright, Malcolm, Rick Hendricks, and Richard W. Hughes. *Four Square Leagues: Pueblo Indian Land in New Mexico*. Albuquerque: University of New Mexico Press, 2014.

Eidenbach, Peter L. *An Atlas of Historic New Mexico Maps, 1550–1941*. Albuquerque: University of New Mexico Press, 2012.

Elliott, J. H. *Imperial Spain, 1469–1716*. New York: Penguin Books, 1963.

Ellis, Bruce. "La Garita, Santa Fe's Little Spanish Fort." *El Palacio* 84, no. 2 (Summer 1978):2-22.

_____.*Bishop Lamy's Santa Fe Cathedral*. Albuquerque: University of New Mexico Press, 1985.

Ellis, R. Stewart. "Santa Cruz: Authority and Community Response in the History of New Mexico Town." PhD diss., University of Oklahoma, Norman, 1980.

Engelhardt, Zephyrin. *The Franciscans in Arizona*. Harbor Springs, Michigan: 1899.

Espinosa, Carmine. *Shawls, Crinolines, Filigree: The Dress and Adornment of the Women of New Mexico, 1739–1900*. El Paso: Texas Western Press, 1970.

Espinosa, J. Manuel. *The Pueblo Revolt of 1696 and The Franciscan Missions in New Mexico: Letters of Missionaries*. Norman: University of Oklahoma Press, 1988.

Esquibel, José Antonio. "Descendants of Hernán Martin Serrano in New Mexico, Part I." *New Mexico Genealogist* 51, no. 4 (April 2012): 159-71.

_____. *Early Settlers of Santa Cruz de la Cañada*. New Mexico: José Antonio Esquibel, 2015.

_____. "Mexico City to Santa Fe, Spanish Pioneers on the Camino Real, 1693–1694." In *El Camino Real de Tierra Adentro*, Vol. 2, compiled by Gabrielle G. Palmer and Stephen L. Fosberg, 55-70. Santa Fe: Bureau of Land Management, New Mexico State Office, 1999.

_____. "Residents Traveling from New Mexico, 1712–1716." *New Mexico Genealogist* 35, no. 3 (September 1996): 75-81.

_____. "The Romo de Vera Ancestry, Part I." *Herencia* 20, no. 4 (December 2012): 41-45.

_____. "The Romo de Vera Ancestry, Part II." *Herencia* 21, no. 1 (January 2013): 20-28.

———. "Thirty eight Adobe Houses 1606-1699." In *All Trails Lead to Santa Fe*, 109-129. Santa Fe: Sunstone Press, 2010.

Esquibel, José Antonio and Miguel A. Tórrez. "Martin Serrano Family Genealogy and a Y-DNA Study." *The New Mexico Genealogist 55*, no. 3 (September 2016):137-146.

Flagler, Edward K. "Defensive Policy and Indian Relations in New Mexico during the Tenure of Governor Francisco Cuervo y Valdés, 1705–1707." *Revista Española de Antropologia Americana* 22 (Summer 1992): 89-104

———. "From Asturias to New Mexico: Don Francisco Cuervo y Valdéz." *New Mexico Historical Review* 69, no. 3 (July 1994):249-261.

Flint, Richard. "La Salina of the Estancia Valley, New Mexico." *New Mexico Historical Review* 83, no. 1 (January, 2008): 39-55.

Flint, Richard, and Shirley Cushing Flint, eds. *The Latest Word from 1540: People, Places, and Portrayals of the Coronado Expedition*. Albuquerque: University of New Mexico Press, 2011.

Foote, Cheryl. "Trade along New Mexico's Northern Frontier in the Eighteenth Century." *Journal of the West* 24, no. 2 (April 1985).

Foucault, Michel. *The History of Sexuality: An Introduction*, vol. 1. New York: Vintage Books, A Division of Random House, Inc., 1990.

Franco, John Klingemann. "Blacks in Northern New Spain." *Journal of Big Bend Studies* 16 (June 2004): 47-58.

Frank, Ross. "From Settler to Citizen: Economic Development and the Cultural Change in Late Colonial New Mexico, 1750–1820." PhD diss., University of California, Berkeley, 1992.

Friendly, Henry. "Some Kind of Hearing." *University of Pennsylvania Law Review* 123, no. 6 (June 1995): 1279-95.

Gallegos, Albert, and José Antonio Esquibel. "Alcaldes and Mayors of Santa Fe, 1613–2008." In *All Trails Lead to Santa Fe*, 403-30. Santa Fe: Sunstone Press, 2010.

Garcia Lopez, Ricardo. *Guía de Protocolos de Instrumento Públicos del Siglo XVIII*. San Luis Potosí, Mexico: Universidad Autónoma de San Luis Potosí, Facultad de Derecho, Instituto de Investigaciones Juridicas, 1988.

Gauderman, Kimberly. *Women's Lives in Colonial Quito: Gender, Law, and Economy in Spanish America*. Austin: University of Texas Press, 2003.

Gavin, Robin, Donna Pierce, and Alfonso Pleguezuelo, eds. *Cerámica y Cultura: The Story of Spanish and Mexican Mayolica*. Albuquerque: University of New Mexico Press, 2003.

Gerhard, Peter. *The North Frontier of New Spain*. Norman: University of Oklahoma Press, 1982.

Góngora, Mario. *Studies in the Colonial History of Spanish America*. Cambridge, England: Cambridge University Press, 1975.

Greenfield, Myrtle. *A History of Public Health in New Mexico*. Albuquerque: University of New Mexico Press, 1962.

Greenleaf, Richard E. "Atrisco and Las Ciruelas 1723–1769." *New Mexico Historical Review* 61, no. 1 (January 1987): 5-25.

_____. "The Founding of Albuquerque, 1706." *New Mexico Historical Review* 39, no. 1 (February 1964): 1-15.

_____. "The Inquisition in Eighteenth-Century New Mexico." *New Mexico Historical Review* 60, no. 1 (January 1985): 29-60.

_____. "The Obraje in the Last Mexican Colony." *The Americas* 23, no. 3 (October 1967): 227-50.

Guggino, Patty. "Los Lentes." New Mexico Office of the State Historian, from the internet, October 2, 2012.

Gunn, Giles B. *Early American Writing*. New York: Penguin Classics, Penguin Books, 1994.

Gutiérrez, Rámon A. *When Jesus Came, The Corn Mothers Went Away: Marriage, Sexuality, and Power in New Mexico, 1500–1846*. Stanford, California: Stanford University Press, 1991.

_____. "Women on Top: The Love Magic of the Indian Witches of New Mexico." *Journal of the History of Sexuality* 16, no. 3 (September 2007): 373-90.

Hackett, Charles Wilson. *Historical Documents relating to New Mexico, Nueva Vizcaya, and Approaches Thereto, to 1773*, Vol. 3. Washington, DC: Carnegie Institution of Washington, 1937.

Haggard, J. Villasana. *Handbook for Translators of Spanish Colonial Documents*. Austin: University of Texas, 1941.

Hämäläinen, Pekka. *The Comanche Empire*. New Haven and London: Yale University Press, 2008.

Hammond, George P., and Agapito Rey, eds. *The Rediscovery of New Mexico*. Albuquerque: University of New Mexico Press, 1995.

Hanke, Lewis. *Spanish Viceroys in America*. Houston: University of St. Thomas Press, 1972.

Hendricks, Rick. "Antonio de Valverde Cosio." In *American National Bibliography*, Vol. 22, 148-49. New York: Oxford University Press, 1999.

_____. "The Last Years of Francisco Cuervo y Valdes, 1707–1714." In *Sunshine and Shadows in New Mexico's Past*. Vol. 1, *The Spanish Colonial and Mexican Periods, 1540–1848*, edited by Richard Melzer, 101-10. Los Ranchos, New Mexico: Rio Grande Press, in collaboration with the Historical Society of New Mexico, 2010.

———. "Pedro de Villasur." In *American National Bibliography*, Vol. 22, 365-66. New York: Oxford University Press, 1999

Hendricks, Rick, and Gerald Mandell. "The Apache Slave Trade in Parral." *Journal of Big Bend Studies* 16 (July, 2004): 59-82.

Hendricks, Rick, and John P. Wilson. *The Navajos in 1705: Roque Madrid's Campaign Journal*. Albuquerque: University of New Mexico Press, 1996.

Hernandez, Salomé. "*Nueva Mexicanas* as Refugees and Reconquest Settlers, 1680–1696." In *New Mexico Women, Intercultural Perspectives*, edited by Joan M. Jensen and Darlis A. Miller, 71-93. Albuquerque: University of New Mexico Press, 1986.

Hoberman, Louisa Schell, and Susan Migden Socolow. *The Countryside in Colonial Latin America*. Albuquerque: University of New Mexico Press, 1996.

Hordes, Stanley M. "History of the Santa Fe Plaza, 1610–1720." In *All Trails Lead to Santa Fe*, 133-39. Santa Fe: Sunstone Press, 2010.

Horvath, Steven. "The Social and Political Organization of the Genizaros of the Plaza de Nuestra Señora de los Dolores de Belen, New Mexico, 1740–1812." PhD diss., Brown University, 1979.

Hottz, Gottfried. *The Segesser Hide Paintings*. Santa Fe: Museum of New Mexico Press, 1970.

Jackson, Hal. *Following the Royal Road: A Guide to the Historic Camino Real de Tierra Adentro*. Albuquerque: University of New Mexico Press, 2005.

Jenkins, Myra Ellen. "Some Eighteenth-Century New Mexican Women of Property." In *Hispanic Arts & Ethnohistory in the Southwest*, edited by Marta Weigle, Claudia Larcombe, and Samuel Larcombe, 335-46. Santa Fe: Ancient City Press, 1983.

———. "Spanish Land Grants in the Tewa Area." *New Mexico Historical Review* 47 (1972): 113-34.

———. "Taos Pueblo and Its Neighbors, 1520–1847." *New Mexico Historical Review* 41 (1966): 85-114.

John, Elizabeth A.H., ed. *Views from the Apache Frontier: Report on the Northern Provinces of New Spain by Jose Cortes*. Norman: Oklahoma University Press, 1989.

Johnson, Lyman L., and Sonya Lipsett-Rivera. *Sex, Shame and Violence: The Faces of Honor in Colonial Latin America*. Albuquerque: University of New Mexico, 1998.

Jones, Oakah. *Los Paisanos: Spanish Settlers on the Northern Frontier of New Spain*. Norman: University of Oklahoma Press, 1979.

———. *Pueblo Warriors and Spanish Conquest*. Norman: University of Oklahoma Press, 1966.

———. "Rescue and Ransom of Spanish Captives from the *Indios Bárberos* on the Northern Frontier of New Spain." *Colonial Latin American Historical Review* 4, no. 2 (June 1995): 128-48.

Kagan, Richard L. *Lawsuits and Litigants in Castile, 1500–1700.* Chapel Hill: University of North Carolina Press, 1981.

_____. *Urban Images of the Hispanic World, 1493–1793.* New Haven: Yale University Press, 2003.

Kamen, Henry. *Philip of Spain.* New Haven: Yale University Press, 1997.

Kantor, Deborah E. *Hijos del Pueblo: Gender, Family, and Community in Rural Mexico, 1730–1850.* Austin: University of Texas Press, 2008.

Katzew, Ilona. *Casta Painting, Images of Race in the Eighteenth-Century Mexico.* New Haven and London: Yale University Press, 2005.

_____. *Contested Visions in the Spanish Colonial World.* Los Angeles and New Haven: Los Angeles Museum of Art, distributed by Yale University Press, 2012.

Kelleher, Marie A. *The Measure of Woman: Law and Female Identity in the Crown of Aragon.* Philadelphia: University of Pennsylvania Press, 2010.

Kessell, John. "'Death Delayed': The Sad Case of the Two Marías, 1773–1779." *New Mexico Historical Review* 83, no. 2 (April 2008): 157-70.

_____. *Kiva, Cross, and Crown.* Albuquerque: University of New Mexico Press, 1987.

_____. "A Long Time Coming: The Seventeenth-Century Pueblo-Spanish War." *New Mexico Historical Review* 86, no. 2 (April 2011): 141-56.

_____. *Pueblos, Spaniards, and the Kingdom of New Mexico.* Norman: University of Oklahoma Press, 2008.

_____. *Spain in the Southwest.* Norman: University of Oklahoma Press, 2002.

Kessell, John, and Rick Hendricks, eds. *By Force of Arms: The Journals of don Diego de Vargas, New Mexico.* Albuquerque: University of New Mexico Press, 1992.

Kessell, John L., Rick Hendricks, and Meredith D. Dodge, eds. *Blood on the Boulders: The Journals of don Diego de Vargas, New Mexico, 1694–1697*, vols. 1 and 2. Albuquerque: University of New Mexico Press, 1998.

_____. *To the Royal Crown Restored: The Journals of don Diego de Vargas, New Mexico, 1692–1694.* Albuquerque: University of New Mexico Press, 1995.

Kessell, John L., Rick Hendricks, Meredith D. Dodge, and Larry Miller, eds. *A Settling of Accounts: The Journals of don Diego de Vargas, New Mexico, 1700–1704.* Albuquerque: University of New Mexico Press, 2003.

_____. *That Disturbances Cease: The Journals of don Diego de Vargas, New Mexico, 1697–1700.* Albuquerque: University of New Mexico Press, 2000.

Knauss, Jessica. *Law and Order in Medieval Spain: Alfonsine Legislation and the Cantigas de Santa Maria*. Tucson: Acedrex Publishing, 2011.

Knee, Ernest. *Santa Fe, New Mexico*. Santa Fe:Ernest Knee: 1942.

Korth, Eugene H., and Della H. Flusche. "Dowry and Inheritance in Colonial Spanish America." *Americas* 3 (September 1995): 153-176.

Kubler, George. *The Rebuilding of San Miguel at Santa Fe in 1710*. Colorado Springs, Colorado: The Taylor Museum, 1939.

Lavrin, Asunción, ed. *Sexuality and Marriage in Colonial Latin America*. Lincoln: University of Nebraska, 1989.

Lavrin, Asunción. "Women in Colonial Mexico." In *The Oxford History of Mexico*, edited by William H. Beezley and Michael C. Meyer, 235-62. Oxford, England: Oxford University Press, 2010.

Lavrin, Asuncíon, and Edith Couturier. "Dowries and Wills: A View of Women's Socioeconomic Role in Colonial Guadalajara and Puebla, 1640–1790." *Hispanic American Historical Review* 50, no. 5 (May1979): 280-304.

Lea, Henry Charles. *A History of the Inquisition of Spain*, Vols. 1 and 2. New York: The Macmillan Company, 1906.

Lecompte, Janet. "The Independent Women of Hispanic New Mexico, 1821–1846." In *New Mexico Women, Intercultural Perspectives*, edited by Joan M. Jensen and Darlis A. Miller, 71-93. Albuquerque: University of New Mexico Press, 1986.

Levine, Frances. *Doña Teresa Confronts the Spanish Inquisition: A Seventeenth-Century New Mexican Drama*. Norman: University of Oklahoma Press, 2016.

Lopez, Ricardo Garcia. *Guía de Protocolos de Instrumentos Públicos del Siglo XVIII*. San Luis Potosí, Mexico: Universidad Autónoma de San Luis Potosí, 1988.

Marichal, Carlos. "The Cochineal Commodity Chain: Mexican Cochineal and the Rise of Global Trade." In *A Red Like No Other*, edited by Carmella Padilla and Barbara Anderson: 54-56. New York: Museum of International Folk Art, in association with Skira Rizzoli, 2013.

Marshall, Michael P., and Henry J. Walt. *Río Abajo: Prehistory and History of a Río Grande Province*. Santa Fe: New Mexico Historic Preservation Program, Historic Preservation Division, 1984.

Martinez, Robert D. "Fray Juan Jose Toledo and the Devil in Spanish New Mexico, A Story of Witchcraft and Cultural Conflict in Eighteenth Century Abiquiu." Master's Thesis, Albuquerque: University of New Mexico, 1997.

_____. "Notes on New Mexico Families from Zacatecas." *Herencia* 12, no. 4 (October 2004): 39-42.

_____. "Research Notes from Mexico City." *New Mexico Genealogist* 55, no. 2 (June 2016): 21-22.

Martinez, Robert D., and José Antonio Esquibel, "Villalpando Family Origins." *New Mexico Genealogist* 51, no. 4 (December 2012): 182-91.

Mather, Christine, ed. *Colonial Frontiers: Art and Life in Spanish New Mexico, The Fred Harvey Collection*. Santa Fe: Ancient City Press, 1986.

Mather, Clay. "Tangled Threads." In *The Latest Word from 1540*, edited by Richard Flint and Shirley Cushing Flint, 376-85. Albuquerque: University of New Mexico Press, 2011.

McDonald, Dedra S. "Intimacy and Empire: Indian-African Interaction in Spanish Colonial New Mexico." In *Sunshine and Shadows in New Mexico's Past*, Vol. 1, *The Spanish Colonial and Mexican Periods, 1540–1848*, edited by Richard Melzer, 27-48. Los Ranchos, New Mexico: Rio Grande Press, in collaboration with the Historical Society of New Mexico, 2010.

McDougal, Susan. *Bigamy and Christian Identity in Late Medieval Champagne*. Philadelphia: University of Pennsylvania Press, 2012.

McKnight, Joseph W. "Law without Lawyers on the Hispano-Mexican Frontier." *West Texas Historical Association Year Book* 66 (1990): 51-65.

Medina, José Toribio. *Historias del Tribunal del Santo Oficio de la Inquisición en México*, 2nd ed. Mexico: Cien de Mexico, 2010.

Melzer, Richard, ed. *Sunshine and Shadows in New Mexico's Past*. Vol. I, *The Spanish Colonial and Mexican Periods, 1540–1848*. Los Ranchos, New Mexico: Rio Grande Press, in collaboration with the Historical Society of New Mexico, 2010.

Meschke, Amy. "Women's Lives through Women's Wills in the Spanish and Mexican Borderlands, 1750–1846." PhD diss., Dallas:Southern Methodist University, 2011.

Moore, James, ed. *Prehistoric and Historic Occupation of Los Alamos and Guaje Canyons: Data Recovery at Three Sites Near the Pueblo of San Ildefonso, Archaeology Notes No. 244*. Santa Fe: Museum of New Mexico, Office of Archaeological Studies, 2001.

Moorhead, Max L. *New Mexico's Royal Road: Trade and Travel on the Chihuahua Trail*. Norman: University of Oklahoma Press, 1958.

_____. *The Presidio, Bastion of the Spanish Borderlands*. Norman: University of Oklahoma Press, 1975.

_____. "The Soldado de Cueva: Stalwart of the Spanish Borderlands." *Journal of the West* 8 (1969): 38-55.

Muñoz y Rivero, D. Jesús. *Paleografía Popular, Arte de Leer, Los Documentos Antiguos*. Madrid: Librería de la Vuída de Hernando, 1886.

National Park Service, Long Distance Trails' Group. *El Camino Real de Tierra Adentro National Historic Trail, Draft, Comprehensive Management Plan/Environmental Impact Statement*.

Washington, DC: National Park Service, Bureau of Land Management, United States Department of the Interior, August 2002.

New Mexico Genealogical Society. *Aquí Se Comienza: A Genealogical History of the Founding of La Villa de San Felipe de Alburquerque*. Albuquerque: New Mexico Genealogical Society, 2007.

———. *New Mexico Baptisms, Santa Cruz de la Cañada Church*, Vol. 1: 1710–1794. Albuquerque: New Mexico Genealogical Society, 1994.

Nizza Da Silva, María Beatriz. "Divorce in Colonial Brazil: The Case of São Paulo." In *Sexuality and Marriage in Colonial Latin America*, edited by Asunción Lavrin, 313-40. Lincoln: University of Nebraska, 1989.

Noble, David Grant. *Santa Fe: History of an Ancient City*. Santa Fe: School of American Research Press, 1989.

Norris, Jim. *After "The Year Eighty": The Demise of Franciscan Power in Spanish New Mexico*. Albuquerque: University of New Mexico Press, in cooperation with the Academy of American Franciscan History, 2000.

———. "Franciscans Eclipsed, Church in Spanish New Mexico, 1750–1780." *New Mexico Historical Review* 76, no. 2 (May 2001): 162-73.

Noyes, Stanley. *Los Comanches, The Horse People, 1751–1845*. Albuquerque: University of New Mexico Press, 2001.

Nuñez, Ximena Pulgar. "La Dote como Protección a la Mujer en el Derecho Romano." *Revista Chilena de Historia del Derecho* 16 (1990): 27-32.

Ocaranza, Fernando. *Establecimientos Franciscanos en el Misterioso Reino de Nuevo Mexico*. Mexico: D.F., 1934.

Olmstead, Virginia. "Spanish Enlistment Papers of New Mexico, 1732–1820." *National Genealogical Society Quarterly* 67 (October 1979): 229-36, 294-301.

———. *Spanish and Mexican Censuses of New Mexico, 1750–1830*. Albuquerque: New Mexico Genealogical Society, Inc., 1981.

Ortega, María. "Sorcery and Eroticism in Love Magic." In *Cultural Encounters: The Impact of the Inquisition in Spain and the New World*, edited by Mary Eliza Perry and Anne J. Cruz, 59-92. Berkeley: University of California Press, 1991.

Padilla, Carmella, ed. *Conexiones: Connections in Spanish Colonial Art*. Santa Fe: Museum of Spanish Colonial Art, 2002.

Padilla, Carmella, and Barbara Anderson, eds. *A Red Like No Other: How Cochineal Colored the World*. New York: Museum of International Folk Art, in association with Skira Rizzoli, 2013.

Pagden, Anthony. *Lords of All the World: Ideologies of Empire in Spain, Britain, and France c. 1500–1800*. New Haven: Yale University Press, 1995.

Painter, Sidney. *A History of the Middle Ages, 1284–1500*. New York: Alfred A. Knopf, 1953.

Palmer, Gabrielle, and Donna Pierce. *Cambios: The Spirit of Transformation in Spanish Colonial Art*. Santa Barbara and Albuquerque: Santa Barbara Museum of Art, in cooperation with the University of New Mexico Press, 1992.

Palmer, Gabrielle G, compiler. *El Camino Real de Tierra Adentro*. Vol. 1. Santa Fe: Bureau of Land Management, Department of Interior, New Mexico State Office, 1993.

Palmer, Gabrielle G., and Stephen L. Fosberg, compilers. *El Camino Real de Tierra Adentro II*. Santa Fe: Bureau of Land Management, Department of Interior, New Mexico State Office, 1999.

Payne, Melissa. "Lessons from the Río Abajo: A Colonial Patron's Contested Legacy." *New Mexico Historical Review* 80, no. 4 (November 2005): 397-416.

Perry, Mary Elizabeth, and Anne J. Cruz. *Cultural Encounters: The Impact of the Inquisition in Spain and the New World*. Berkeley: University of California, 1991.

Pierce, Donna, and Marta Weigle. *Spanish New Mexico*. Vol. I, *The Arts of Spanish New Mexico*. Santa Fe: Museum of New Mexico Press, 1996.

Pierce, Donna, and Cordelia Thomas Snow. "A Harp for Playing." In *El Camino Real de Tierra Adentro*, Vol. 2, compiled by Gabrielle G. Palmer and Stephen L. Fosberg, 71-86. Santa Fe: Bureau of Land Management, Department of Interior, New Mexico State Office, 1999.

Pike, Ruth. "Penal Servitude in the Spanish Empire: Presidio Labor in the Eighteenth Century." *Hispanic American Historical Review* 58, no. 1 (February 1978): 21-40.

Porter, Amy M. *Their Lives, Their Wills: Women in the Borderlands, 1750–1846*. Lubbock: Texas Tech University Press, 2015.

Poska, Allyson. "Elusive Virtue: Rethinking the Role of Female Chastity in Early Modern Spain." *Journal of Early Modern History* 8, nos. 1-2 (June 2004): 135-46.

Post, Stephen S. "Crossroads at the Edge of Empire: Economy and Livelihood in Santa Fe during the Spanish Colonial Period." *Chronicles of the Trail* 11, no. 2 (Fall/Winter 2015): 10-15.

Powers, Karen Vieira. *Women in the Crucible of Conquest*. Albuquerque: University of New Mexico Press, 2005.

Prest, Wilfrid, ed. *Lawyers in Early Modern Europe and America*. New York: Holmes and Meier Publishers, Inc., 1981.

Quezada, Noemí. "The Inquisition's Repression of Curanderos." In *Cultural Encounters: The Impact of the Inquisition in Spain and the New World*, edited by Mary Eliza Perry and Anne J. Cruz, 9-92. Berkeley: University of California Press, 1991.

Rau, Patricia Sanchez. "Jose Romo de Vera, Santa Fe Soldier and Grantee." *Herencia* 20, no. 3 (2012): 39-48.

_____. "Marriage Investigations: A Sampling of Originals vs. Extracted Summaries." *New Mexico Genealogist* 55, no. 2 (2016): 69-85.

_____. "Unanue to Nuanes." *Herencia* 23, no. 4 (December 2015): 17-20.

Rawlings, Helen. *The Spanish Inquisition*. Oxford, England: Blackwell Publishing, 2006.

Riley, Carroll L. "Blacks in the Early Southwest." *Ethnohistory* 19, no. 3 (Summer 1972): 247-60.

Riley, James D., ed. *The Inquisition in Colonial Latin America: The Selected Writings of Richard E. Greenleaf*. Berkeley: Academy of American Franciscan History, 2010.

Rock, Rosalind Z. "Pido y Suplico: Women and the Law in Spanish New Mexico, 1697–1763." *New Mexico Historical Review* 65, no. 2 (1990): 145-59.

Roquero, Ana. "Crimson to Scarlet: From American Tradition to European Experimentation." In *A Red Like No Other*, edited by Carmella Padilla and Barbara Anderson: 94-97. New York: Museum of International Folk Art, in association with Skira Rizzoli, 2013.

Rosen, Deborah A. "Women and Property across Colonial America: A Comparison of Legal Systems in New Mexico and New York." *William and Mary Quarterly* 40, no. 2 (April 2003): 353-81.

Rosenmüller, Christoph. *Patrons, Partisans, and Palace Intrigues: The Court Society of Colonial Mexico, 1702–1710*. Alberta, Canada: University of Calgary Press, Alberta Foundation for the Arts, 2008.

Roth, Cecil. *The Spanish Inquisition*. New York: W. W. Norton & Company, 1964.

Rule, William Harris. *History of the Inquisition*, Vol. 1. New York: Scribner, Welford & Co, 1874. Reprint, New York: Bibliobazaar LLC, 2012.

Sáenz Ramírez, Víctor M. *Los Protocolos de la Villa de Nuestra Señora Santa Anna de Camargo, 1762-1809*. Bloomington, Indiana: Palibrio, 2011.

Sanchez, Joseph P. *Between Two Rivers: The Atrisco Land Grant in Albuquerque History, 1692–1968*. Norman: University of Oklahoma Press, 2008.

Scholes, France V., Marc Simmons, and José Antonio Esquibel, eds. *Juan Domínguez de Mendoza: Soldier and Frontiersman of the Spanish Southwest, 1727–1793*. Albuquerque: University of New Mexico Press, 2012.

Scott, Margaret. *Fashion in the Middle Ages*. Los Angeles: The J. Paul Getty Museum, 2011.

Scott, Samuel Partsons. *Visigothic Code*. (*Forum Judicum*) Boston: The Boston Book Company, 1910.

Scurlock, Dan. "The Camino Real at Cerro and Plaza Tome." In *El Camino Real de Tierra Adentro*, Vol. 2, compiled by Gabrielle G. Palmer and Stephen L. Fosberg, 231-40. Santa Fe: Bureau of Land Management, Department of the Interior, New Mexico State Office, 1999.

Seed, Patricia. *To Love Honor and Obey in Colonial New Mexico*. Stanford, CA: Stanford University Press, 1988.

Simmons, Marc. *Albuquerque: A Narrative History*. Albuquerque: University of New Mexico Press, 1982.

_____. *Spanish Government in New Mexico*. Albuquerque: University of New Mexico Press, 1968.

_____. *Witchcraft in New Mexico: Spanish and Indian Supernaturales on the Río Grande*. Lincoln: University of Nebraska Press, 1974.

Sisneros, Francisco. "Ana de Sandoval y Manzañares: A New Mexico Spanish Colonial Woman of Perseverance and Triumph." In *Sunshine and Shadow in New Mexico's Past*. Vol. 1, *The Spanish Colonial and Mexican Periods, 1540–1848*, edited by Richard Melzer, 79-87. Los Ranchos, New Mexico: Rio Grande Books, in collaboration with the Historical Society of New Mexico, 2010.

Smith, Donald E. *The Viceroy of New Spain*. Berkeley: University of California Press, 1913.

Snow, Cordelia Thomas. "A Brief History of the Palace of the Governors and A Preliminary Report on the 1974 Excavation." *El Palacio* 80, no. 3 (September 1974): 1-22.

_____. "A Headdress of Pearls: Luxury Goods Imported Over the Camino Real During the Seventeenth Century." In *El Camino Real de Tierra Adentro*, Vol. 1, compiled by Gabrielle G. Palmer and Stephen L. Fosberg, 69-76. Santa Fe: Bureau of Land Management, Department of the Interior, New Mexico Office, 1993.

_____. "The Plazas of Santa Fe, New Mexico, 1610–1776." *El Palacio* 94, no. 2 (July 1988): 40-51.

Snow, David H. "Santiago to Guache." In *Collected Papers in Honor of Marjorie Ferguson Lambert*, edited by Albert H. Schroeder, 161-81. Albuquerque: Archaeological Society of New Mexico, 1976.

Snow, David H. "Purchased in Chihuahua for Feasts." In *El Camino Real de Tierra Adentro*, Vol. 1, compiled by Gabrielle G. Palmer and Stephen L. Fosberg, 133-46. Santa Fe: Bureau of Land Management, Department of the Interior, New Mexico Office, 1993.

Socolow, Susan Migden. *The Women of Colonial Latin America*. Cambridge, England: Cambridge University Press, 2000.

Stamatov, Suzanne. "Family, Kin, and Community in Colonial New Mexico, 1694–1800." PhD diss., University of New Mexico, 2003.

Stampa, Manuel Carrera. "The Evolution of Weights and Measures in New Spain." *Hispanic American Historical Review* 29 (1949): 2-24.

Steel, Thomas J. "Francisco Xavier Romero: A Hitherto Unknown Santero." In *A Moment in Time: The Odyssey of New Mexico's Segesser Hide Paintings*, edited by Thomas E. Chávez, 169-76. Los Ranchos, New Mexico: Rio Grande Press, 2012.

Stoor, Yvette Cohn, Miguel A. Tórrez, and Ed Silva. "When DNA and Paper Trails Collide: An Identity Crisis in the Silva Family." *The New Mexico Genealogist* 55, no. 2 (September 2016): 112-20.

Stuntz, Jean A. *Hers, His, & Theirs: Community Property Law in Spain and Early Texas*. Lubbock: Texas Tech University Press, 2010.

Swann, Michael M. *Migrants in the Mexican North: Mobility, Economy, and Society in a Colonial World*. Boulder, Colorado: Westview Press, 1989.

Thomas, Alfred Barnaby. *After Coronado*. Norman: University of Oklahoma, 1935.

———. *Forgotten Frontiers: A Study of the Spanish Indian Policy of Don Juan Bautista de Anza, Governor of New Mexico, 1777–1787*. Norman: University of Oklahoma Press, 1932.

———. "Governor Mendiñueta's Proposals for the Defense of New Mexico, 1772–1778." *New Mexico Historical Review* 5 (1931): 21-39.

———. *The Plains Indians and New Mexico, 1751–1778*. Albuquerque: University of New Mexico Press, 1940.

———. *Teodoro de Croix and the Northern Frontier of New Spain, 1776–1783*. Norman: University of Oklahoma, 1941.

Tigges, Linda A. "The Pastures of the Royal Horse Herd of the Santa Fe Presidio." In *All Trails Lead to Santa Fe*, 237-66. Santa Fe: Sunstone Press, 2010.

———. "Santa Fe Brand Registration–1785." *New Mexico Genealogist* 50, no. 3 (September 2011): 121-25.

———. "The Santa Fe Presidial Company, 1712." *New Mexico Genealogist* 50, no. 2 (June 2011): 71-76.

Tigges, Linda A., and J. Richard Salazar. *Spanish Colonial Lives: Documents From the Spanish Colonial Archives of New Mexico, 1705–1774*. Santa Fe: Sunstone Press, 2013.

Torok, George D. *From the Pass to the Pueblos: El Camino Real de Tierra Adentro National Historic Trail*. Santa Fe: Sunstone Press, 2012.

Tórrez, Robert J. "Crime & Punishment in Spanish Colonial New Mexico." Unpublished Paper, New Mexico State Records Center and Archives, Santa Fe, May 20, 1990.

———. "The Presidio of Santa Fe." In *Sunshine and Shadows in New Mexico's Past: The Spanish Colonial and Mexican Periods, 1540-1848*, edited by Richard Melzer, 201-10. Los Ranchos, New Mexico: Rio Grande Books, in collaboration with the Historical Society of New Mexico, 2010.

_____. *UFOs Over Galisteo and Other Stories of New Mexico's History.* Albuquerque: University of New Mexico Press, 2004.

Trigg, Heather B. *From Household to Empire: Society and Economy in Early Colonial New Mexico.* Tucson: University of Arizona Press, 2005.

Tucker, St. George, ed. *Blackstone's Commentaries with notes of reference to the constitution and laws of the federal government of the United States and of the Commonwealth of Virginia.* 5 vols. New Jersey: Rotherman Reprints, Inc., 1969. First published 1803 by William Young Birch and Abraham Small, Philadelphia.

Twinam, Ann. *Public Lives, Private Secrets: Gender, Honor, Sexuality and Illegitimacy in Colonial Spanish America.* Stanford: Stanford University Press, 1999.

Twitchell, Ralph Emerson. *The Spanish Archives of New Mexico*, Vols. 1 and 2. Cedar Rapids, Iowa: The Torch Press, 1914. New Editions. Santa Fe: Sunstone Press, 2008.

_____. *Old Santa Fe, The Story of New Mexico's Ancient Capitol*, Santa Fe, 1925. New Edition. Santa Fe: Sunstone Press, 2007.

Tyler, S. Lyman, ed. *The Indian Cause in the Spanish Laws of the Indies.* Utah: American West Center, University of Utah, 1980.

_____. *Spanish Laws Concerning Discoveries, Pacification, and Settlements among the Indians.* Utah: American West Center, University of Utah, 1980.

Uribe-Uran, Victor M. "Church Asylum and the Law in Spain and Colonial Spanish America." In *Comparative Studies in Society and History* 49, no. 2 (April 2007); 446-472.

Van Kleffens, E. N. *Hispanic Law until the End of the Middle Ages.* Scotland: Edinburgh University Press, 1968.

Vance, John T. *The Background of Hispanic-American Law: Legal Source and Juridical Literature of Spain.* Washington, DC: The Catholic University of America, 1937.

Vance, John T., and Helen L. Clagett. *A Guide to the Law and Legal Literature of Mexico.* Washington, DC: Library of Congress, 1945.

Van den Bergh, Rena. "Roman Women: Sometimes Equal and Sometimes Not." *Fundamina: A Journal of Legal History* 12, no. 2 (May 2006), 113-36.

Vollendorf, Lisa. *The Lives of Women: A New History of Inquisitional Spain.* Nashville: Vanderbilt University, 2005.

Walz, Vina. "History of the El Paso Area, 1680–1692." PhD diss., Albuquerque: University of New Mexico, 1961.

Warner, Ted. J. "Don Felix Martínez and the Santa Fe Presidio." PhD diss., Albuquerque: University of New Mexico, 1963.

Weber, David J. *On the Edge of Empire: The Taos Hacienda of Los Martinez.* Santa Fe: Museum of New Mexico Press, 1996.

———. *The Spanish Frontier in North America.* New Haven: Yale University Press, 1992.

Weigle, Marta, ed. *Hispanic Arts and Ethnohistory in the Southwest.* Santa Fe: Ancient City Press, 1983.

West, Eliza. Howard. "The Right of Asylum in New Mexico in the Seventeenth and Eighteenth Centuries." *New Mexico Historical Review* 41, no. 2 (June 1966): 115-53.

Weskett, John. *A Complete Digest of the Theory, Laws, and Practice of Insurance.* London: Frys, Couchman, & Collier, 1781.

Wheat, I. Carl. *Mapping the Trans-Mississippi West: The Spanish Entrada to the Louisiana Purchase, 1540–1861,* Vol. 1. San Francisco: Institute of Historical Cartography, 1957.

Works, Martha A. "Creating Trading Places on the New Mexico Frontier." *Geographical Review* 82, no. 3 (July 1991): 268-81.

INDEX

abandonment, 24-25, 26, 40, 76, 139n2
abduction, 22-24, 35, 41, 464-69
Abeytia, Antonio de, 22, 238-49, 259n2-3, 260n24, 356n10
Abeytia, Diego (de Vectia), 259n2
Abeytia, Juan de, 324-25, 333, 356n10, 357n18, 464-70
Abeytia, Juana, 357n18
Abeytia (Vectia), Diego de, 356n10
Abiquiu, New Mexico, 271, 407n17
abuse
    physical, 14, 24, 26, 36, 110-18, 122-23, 139n2, 158-65, 427-32
    spousal, 22, 26, 36, 51, 53, 64-65, 110-18, 122-23, 139n2, 158-65, 487
    verbal, 26, 139n2, 158, 160-61, 227, 230, 413, 427, 430-32
    See also mala vida (a bad life)
Acosta, María de, 357n15
Acosta, Simón de, 325, 333, 356n11
adobes
    donations of, 36, 108n24, 170n11, 259n1
    houses of, 31
    making of, 22, 408-11
    molds for, 393
    in Palace of the Governors, 291
adultery
    cases involving, 143, 145, 147, 300, 323, 443-45, 451n5
    charges of, 14, 22-24, 218, 222n6, 285
    and *divorcios*, 36-37
    and illegitimate children, 26-27
    and *mala vida*, 139n2
    as "mortal sin," 22, 34, 156n11
    See also cohabitation
aguacil mayor, 173n3
Aguilera de Ysasi, Antonio, 372, 385n29
Alameda Pueblo, 321n3
Alameda *puesto*, 409, 414-15, 417, 425n5
Alanís, María Antonia de, 282n4
Albizu, Bartolo de, 174-75, 176n5
Albuquerque
    alcaldes mayores of, 226n8, 410, 414, 426n7, 446-48, 459n12, 460-61
    alcaldes of, 43n5, 158, 170n12, 217n16, 223-25, 426n18, 452n13, 452n17, 453, 456, 484n12
    alférez of, 112, 122-24, 139n3, 139n11, 224
    banishment to, 218-20, 227
    cases involving, 159-65, 170n11, 223-25, 408-10, 413, 416, 446-48, 478-81
    church in, 36, 170n11, 409
    early settlers of, 170n13, 226n8, 357n20, 426n7
    founding families of, 13, 43n1, 170n12, 170n17, 217n7, 223-24, 226n1, 408, 426n9, 426n14, 452n19
    Franciscan friars in, 156n6, 157n24-25, 269n22, 357n14
    garrison guardhouse in, 158
    and jilted soldier case, 453-56
    landowners in, 223-24, 226n5, 426n14
    military squadron of, 426n6-7
    militia in, 170n17
    procuradors in, 31, 217n16
    ranchers of, 33
    soldiers in, 41, 170n13, 284-85, 296n1, 408, 414, 425n5, 426n6, 483n12
    squadron captains of, 226n8, 483n12
    surgeons in, 406n7
    traders in, 323
    See also notaries: in Albuquerque
Albuquerque, Duke of, 71-74, 75n1, 208
Alcalá y Escobar, Joseph de Atienza. *See* Atienza, Joseph de (the elder)
alcaldes, 27, 75n2, 139n5, 260n10, 360
    cases heard by, 24, 26, 29, 40, 360-71, 387-88
    and civil/criminal law, 19-20
    daughters of, 40
    gambling of, 41
    give permission to leave, 60-62
    as judges, 186n10
    legal procedures for, 28-34, 409, 444
    petitions to, 11, 13-14, 21-22, 42, 52
    and preserving documents, 210
    uphold Spanish law, 14, 21, 28-29
    See also confinement: in *alcaldes'* home; specific towns
alcaldes mayores, 13, 63n8, 63n11, 107n9, 112, 113, 139n1, 385n28, 485. *See also* specific towns
alcaldes ordinarios, 60-62, 76, 78-92, 171-72, 178, 195, 485. *See also* specific towns
alférez, 212, 217n16, 331-32, 358n36, 484n14, 485. *See also* specific presidios, towns
Alfonso X, King, 15-17, 44n19, 203n28
alguacils, 54, 79-80, 108n14, 485
Almagro, Spain, 331, 334, 357n33
Almazán, Ana María, 82, 85-86, 108n24, 109n31. *See also* Anaya Almazán, Ana
alms, 36, 170n11, 236n2
almud, 393, 485
Alvarez de Castillo, Ana María, 484n23
Álvarez, Juan, 37, 142-47, 149, 156n8, 156n12
amancebados, 86, 109n32, 171-72, 182, 485
amancebamiento, 24, 358n45. *See also* cohabitation
American
    conquest, 20, 44n29
    "due process," 28, 33
    law, 19, 52, 362
    women's rights, 44n29
Anaya Almazán, Ana, 157n28
Anaya Almazán, Francisco de I, 360
Anaya Almazán, Francisco de II, 40, 360-64, 366, 372, 384n4-6, 384n14
Anaya Almazán, Joaquín de, 360-64, 367, 369-73, 384n5-7, 384n14

Anaya Almazán, Juana de, 32, 40, 297n9, 360-73, 384n1, 384n5, 384n6-7, 385n21, 442n12
Anaya Almazán, María Antonia de, 360-62, 364-70, 384n6, 385n15
Anaya Almazán, Salvador de, 360-64, 366-67, 369-70, 384n5-6, 384n8, 385n15, 385n23
Andalusia, Spain, 156n5
Apaches, 275, 321n20
  campaigns against, 176n6, 204n34, 237n12, 260n11
  kill settlers, 385n24
  and love affair case, 299, 301, 303, 305-07, 309, 321n9, 321n23
  as servants, 271
  steal children, 60
  steal goods/livestock, 42
  See also María (Apache woman)
Apodaca, Nicolás de, 191, 203n17
Apodaca, Sebastián de, 430, 442n13, 481
Aragon, Ignacio, 451n2
Aragon, María de, 452n12
Aragon, Nicolás de, 23, 33, 46n110, 443-48, 451n2
Aramburu, Antonio, 433, 442n17
Aramburu, Joseph de, 297n12, 442n17
arancel (judicial fees), 31
Arce, Juan Cristóbal de, 480
Archibeque, Juan de, 41, 173n7, 264-65, 268n19
Archibeque, María de, 173n7
archives
  of the Archdiocese, 11
  of *cabildo*, 205-06, 208-11, 362-63, 367
  government, 242, 465, 471
  See also Spanish Colonial Archive of New Mexico
Archivo General de la Nación (Mexico City), 11
Archuleta, Agustín, 282n10
Archuleta, Juan Joseph de, 274, 282n10, 282n11
Arevalo, Lucas, 149-50, 157n24
Argüello, Juana de, 25-26, 40, 51-55, 58n2, 59n8, 236n12
Arias de Quiros, Diego, 51-52, 54-55, 59n10, 60-62, 89
Armenta, Antonio de, 325, 330, 357n18
Armenta, María de, 218-19
Armenta, Salvador Manuel de, 357n18
Armijo, José de I, 186n9, 297n18. *See also* Durán de Armijo, José I
Armijo, José de II, 321n7, 442n4
Armijo, Joseph de III, 427-34, 442n3-4
Armijo, Vicente de, 204n32, 288, 291, 297n12, 297n18, 326-27. *See also* Durán de Armijo, Vicente
Arranegui, Joseph de, 142, 145, 149, 157n25
arrests, 25, 30-31, 38, 107n10, 110, 171, 173n3, 219, 261, 274, 282n11, 284, 297n16, 388, 465
Arrom, Sylvia Marina, 27
artists, 70n5, 204n34, 407n17
Aspitia, Inez, 37, 142-49, 156n4
assaults, 51, 53, 178-81, 408, 410, 412-13, 415-17. *See also* abuse; physical punishment; whipping
Asturia, Spain, 59n10
Atienza, Joseph de, 111, 114-15, 117, 139n7, 140n15-17
Atienza, Juan de, 71-72, 75n4, 75n6, 114-16, 139n7, 140n15, 140n17

Atienza y Alcalá, Joseph de, 115-16, 139n7, 140n15, 140n17, 302-09, 321n17
Atrisco, New Mexico, 39-40, 158, 160, 170n25, 223, 442n9
audiencia real, 485
ayudante, 70n8, 170n22, 186n11, 195, 203n30, 212, 287, 290, 485
ayuntamiento, 179-80, 485

Baca, Antonia, 36, 170n11, 459n6
Baca, Antonio, 27, 158, 169n7, 443-44, 446-47, 452n12, 452n16
Baca, Bernabé, 43n1, 170n25
Baca, Isabel, 426n15
Baca, Josefa, 27, 43n5, 452n12-13, 459n6
Baca, Joseph
  as *alcalde*, 443-44, 446-47
  as *alcalde mayor*, 13, 453, 456, 459n12, 460-61
  background of, 27, 43n5, 452n12-13, 452n16
  and jilted soldier case, 453, 456
  and Nicolás de Aragon case, 443-44, 446-47
  reprimands Isidro Sánchez, 460-61
Baca, Juana, 141n28
Baca, Leonor, 406n3
Baca, Magalena, 385n19
Baca, Manuel, 452n12, 453, 459n6
Baca, María, 43n3
Baca, María Magdalena, 28
bachiller, 331, 358n49, 445, 454, 485
banishment, 70n7, 429
  to Albuquerque, 218-20, 227
  for cohabitation, 24, 172, 182
  to El Paso, 427, 432-33
  from the kingdom, 24, 460-61
  to Santa Cruz, 23, 54, 65, 188, 427, 434
  sentenced to, 22-26, 28, 32-33, 76-77
  threatened with, 51, 54-55
  to Zuni Pueblo, 188, 217n16
baptisms, 59n11, 70n5, 140n19, 176n3, 259n7, 332, 426n8
Barba, Alonso Martín, 204n32
Barba, Marianna Coronado, 157n26
barbers (medics), 30, 186n9, 238, 248-49, 260n13, 271, 328, 427
Barreras, Marcial, 461, 462n7
Barrios, Juan Antonio, 86, 109n33, 248-49, 260n30
Bejarano, Nicolás de, 59n8
Bejarano, Tomás de, 53, 59n8
belduque, 291, 298n29
Belén, New Mexico, 271, 463n7
Bermúdez, Gabriel, 335, 338
Bernal, Ana María, 426n11
Bernal, Antonio, 302, 305, 321n19
Bernal, Francisco, 321n19
Bernal, Juana, 320n2
Bernal, María, 141n27, 477n3
Bernalillo, New Mexico, 158, 161, 426n9, 451n3
  alcaldes of, 217n16, 223, 451n1, 484n14
  banishment to, 54
  cases involving, 443-48, 451n2
  cemetery in, 170n11

early settlers of, 81-82, 107n2, 170n13, 177n9, 226n8, 426n7, 451n7-8, 452n18
Franciscan friars in, 156n8, 156n12, 157n18-19
marriages in, 140n21, 459n17
muster of, 186n7, 226n5
priests in, 203n18
soldiers in, 139n11
women petitioners in, 40
bienes gananciales, 20
bienes parafernales, 20-21
bigamy
cases involving, 23, 76, 107n4, 261-65, 322-40, 359n72
and Holy Office, 37-39, 107n4, 219, 261-65, 322-40
and *mala vida*, 139n2
Bishop of Durango, 357n29, 358n36, 358n45, 358n49-50
Bisuayn, 224, 226n7
Bitton, Gaspar, 364-65, 373, 384n10, 397
Black Mesa, 141n28
blacksmiths, 41, 59n11, 259n7, 426n18
Blackstone, William, 19
blasphemy, 37, 39
Blea, Salvador Dios, 384n6, 385n15
Bologna, Italy, 15-16, 203n28
Boyer, Richard, 34, 39
breach of promise, 283n12
cases involving, 11, 14, 21, 25, 27, 36, 158, 238-40, 244-49, 259n3, 453-56
explanation of, 21-22
and soldiers, 41, 238-40, 244-49, 453-56
Brito, Juan de León
background of, 259n1, 260n25, 260n29
and gambling, 41, 284, 286, 289
Santa Fe house of, 297n10
seduction/breach of promise case of, 22, 27, 238-41, 243-47, 249, 259n3
Brito, Marcial, 427
Brito, Margarita, 22, 41, 238-40, 243-49, 259n1, 260n24-26
Bueno Bohórques y Corcuera, Francisco Joseph, 270-75, 277, 282n1
burials, 35, 70n11, 190-91, 335, 337, 477n12
Bustamante, Bernardo Antonio de, 13, 43n6
Bustamante, José de, 331, 333, 358n49
Bustamante, Juan Domingo de, 43n6, 282n1, 300, 357n30, 358n49, 384n9
Bustillos, Juan de Paz, 271-76, 282n4

cabildo, 385n20, 385n22
alcalde ordinario of, 218, 364-65, 373
explanation of, 485
inventories of, 222n3
petitions to Viceroy, 64
procuradors of, 217n16, 484n14
See also archives: of *cabildo*; *regidor*; scribes: to *cabildo*; specific towns
Cabrejas, Andrés, 335, 338
Cadena, Francisco, 171-72, 173n4
Cadiz, Spain, 173n7
calderero, 357n15
Camargo, Antonio, 191, 203n18

Camino Real, El, 172, 323, 427
Candelaria, Feliciana, 452n19
Candelaria, Felix, 177n6
Candelaria, Francisco, 452n19
Candelaria, Juan, 447-48, 452n19
canon law, 14-16, 35-37
Canseco, María, 21, 34, 40-41, 43n9, 109n45, 187-95, 202n4-5, 202n7, 203n9
Canseco, Sebastián, 224, 226n11
capital punishment, 23, 28, 33, 77
Caraña, Antonio de, 283n12, 384n8
cárcel, 30, 46n114, 51, 485. *See also* imprisonment; presidio guardhouse; *prisión*
Cardenas, Petrona de, 140n20
carpenters, 156n7
carretas, 158, 164, 391-92, 477n6, 485
Carrillo, Agustín, 109n36
Carrillo, Miguel, 88, 109n36
Carrillo y Biezma, José, 334, 340, 359n55
Carvajal, Alonso de, 107n2
Carvajal, Juan Antonio, 107n2
Carvajal, Lorenzo de, 107n2
Carvajal, María, 321n21
Carvajal, Petrona de
background of, 40, 107n2
commits incest, 77, 82, 107n6, 108n25
rape accusation of, 24-25, 41, 76-78, 81-86, 90-91, 109n42, 261
Casados, Francisco Joseph de, 173n7
Casados, Francisco Lorenzo de, 172, 173n7, 187, 193-95, 203n28, 228-32, 241-42, 264-65
Casas Grandes, Mexico, 107n4, 109n33, 264, 268n14
casas reales, 30, 40, 46n98, 179-80, 186n6, 362, 486
casta (racial mixture), 33, 428
Castaneda, María de, 270, 272-73, 282n5
Castile, Spain, 15, 17-18, 44n19, 107n11, 157n17, 203n28, 322-23, 331, 358n46
Castilian law, 15-18, 44n19
Castillo de la Concepción (Nicaragua), 263, 268n16
Castro, Antonia de, 60-61, 63n9-10
Castro, Cristóbal de, 63n6
Castro, María de, 26, 60-62, 63n4, 63n6, 63n8
Castro Xabalera, Miguel de. *See* Rodarte, Miguel
Catalonia, Spain, 357n23
Catholic Church, 24, 26, 34-37, 143, 171, 264, 326-30, 335, 357n22, 442n12, 486. *See also* Holy Office of the Inquisition
cemeteries, 170n11
Chacón, José, 25
Chama, New Mexico, 139n3, 139n11, 170n23, 321n8
Charles V, King, 17
Chavarria, María de, 406n8
Chávez, Antonia, 170n25
Chávez, Clara de, 259n9, 429-30, 442n9
Chávez, Feliciana, 27, 453-56, 459n6
Chávez, Angélico, 42
Chávez, Isabel de, 161, 163, 170n14, 226n6
Chávez, Josefa de, 484n23
Chávez, Juan de, 145, 156n16
Chávez, Luis de, 173n4, 463n7
Chávez, María de, 177n7
Chávez, Pedro de, 158, 161, 163-64, 170n17, 170n25

Checaye, Juan, 451n1
Chihuahua, Mexico, 188, 268n14, 465
   courts of, 28
   Jesuit plaza in, 326, 357n21
   marriages in, 425n6
   merchants of, 39, 297n12, 442n17
   mines of, 41, 285
   traders in, 186n11, 322-23
children, 40, 71, 73, 158
   captured by Indians, 42, 60, 72, 108n22, 173n4
   and Gertrudis Martín case, 299-301, 305-08
   illegitimate, 22, 26-27, 283n12, 451n1, 486
   and inheritance, 20, 23, 26-27, 187, 205-07
   legal rights of, 26-27
   legitimate, 27, 59n4, 177n6, 207
   and seduction/breach of promise case, 238-40, 244, 247, 249
   testimony by, 321n20
   See also hijos naturales (children born out of wedlock)
chiles, 285
Chimayó, New Mexico, 141n28, 299-300
   cases involving, 31, 40, 282n6, 387-97, 406n11, 465, 469
   curandero in, 406n7
   early settlers of, 389, 406n2, 406n11, 427
   landowners in, 40, 387
   ranches in, 406n3
Chirinos, Juan Manuel de
   background of, 109n35
   as *procurador*, 31, 76, 88-92, 109n37, 109n39
   as scribe to *cabildo*, 172, 179-82, 209, 220
   as witness, 229-30, 242, 271-76, 365-66, 369-71, 373, 435, 482
Chirinos, Lucía, 297n14
Chirinos, María Antonia, 109n35
chocolate, 284, 288
Christians/Christianity, 14-15, 91, 124, 218, 220, 222n8, 334, 434, 455
church
   authorities, 26
   cantors of, 76, 85, 108n30
   forced servitude at, 36
   law, 24, 28, 35-37, 261-65
   tithes, 358n36, 409, 418, 426n19
   See also Holy Office of the Inquisition; *sanctuario* (sanctuary); specific towns
cirujanos (surgeons), 30, 396-97, 406n7, 487
civil law, 19-20, 31, 35
cloisters, 80, 84, 108n18-19, 486
cloth, 297n18
   bayeta, 288, 297n20, 485
   bretaña, 286, 288-89, 297n12, 485
   campeche, 289, 298n25
   cases involving, 149, 284-86, 288-91, 408-10, 412-13, 415, 426n10
   diez y ocheno, 286, 297n8
   escarleta, 286, 289, 297n15
   género, 288, 297n19
   lienza, 487
   manta de mimosa, 410, 426n10, 487
   nanquín, 288, 297n23
   for trade, 408-10
clothing, 191, 297n22, 390, 485
   and battered woman case, 158, 160-61, 164
   cases involving, 451n2
   and divorce case, 143-44, 147-49
   and gambling case, 284, 286, 288-89
   and Indians, 139n9
   petticoats, 301, 305-08, 321n10
   provided by husbands, 434
   and trader case, 408, 410, 414
   typical styles of, 53
Cochiti Pueblo, 60, 63n8, 357n20, 459n6
Codallos y Rabal, Joachín, 43n6
   and adultery cases, 23, 427-29, 432-35, 446-47
   advocates use of archives, 465, 471
   background of, 442n6, 477n14
   and fleeing lovers case, 24, 35, 464-65, 468-71
   and inheritance case, 481
   and jilted soldier case, 453-56, 459n4
   and mission sites, 459n16
   reprimands Isidro Sánchez, 460-61
   rescinds power of attorney, 479
cofradia, 442n12, 486
cohabitation, 22, 26, 451n1
   cases involving, 171-72, 178, 182, 219, 222n6, 300, 306, 358n45, 427-32
   explanation of, 23-24, 40-41
   investigations into, 176n6
   by priests, 37
   See also amancebados; concubinage
Comanches, 42, 465
Commentaries on the Laws of England (Blackstone), 19
concubinage, 24, 109n32, 332-33, 339-40, 358n45, 359n73. *See also* amancebamiento; cohabitation
confession, 38, 83-85, 87-88, 108n26, 261-64, 268n14, 306-07, 389
confinement
   in *alcalde's* home, 30, 51, 110, 112, 115-18
   in guardhouse, 33, 35, 46n98
   in safe home, 30, 299-300, 302, 305, 433, 435, 465-67
   in soldier's home, 274
   See also cárcel; imprisonment; presidio guardhouse; *prisión*
conjugal relations, 110, 114-19, 142-45, 148
contracts, 14, 20, 29, 446, 478-80
convento, 333, 417
   explanation of, 157n20, 486
   sanctuario in, 30-31
   in Santa Fe, 80, 83-84, 88, 108n16, 108n18, 147-48
Coolidge, Grace, 207
Córdova, Antonio de, 140n21
Córdova, Simon de I, 173n5
Córdova, Simon de II, 172, 173n5
Córdova, Tomás de, 119, 140n21
corn, 171, 409, 416-17, 429
cornfields, 31, 387-91, 393, 395-96
Coronado, Francisco Vázquez de, 444
Coronado, Mariana, 141n28, 297n24
Corpus Juris Civilis law, 15-16
Corranza, Juana de, 140n15
Correa, María, 70n2

Cortés del Castillo, José, 321n21
Cortés, Dionisio, 307-09, 321n21
Cortés, Fernando, 75n5
Cortés, Josefa, 75n5
Cortés, Juan, 71-72, 75n3, 75n5
Council of Trent, 34, 239, 335
council of war, 237n12
couriers, 59n7, 139n11
court cases
    costs of, 31, 54, 59n9
    in New Mexico, 17-19
    no determination in, 22, 159, 239, 300, 309-10, 386n33
    See also legal procedures; petitions; sentences: pay court costs
court martial, 425n5
Coyota, Juana la, 451n1
coyote, 107n3, 226n11, 486
coza (pointed hat), 219, 221n1
Crespo, José Benito, 331, 357n29, 442n8
criminal law, 19-22
criollos, 358n39
Cruzat y Góngora, Fausto, 384n9
Cruzat y Góngora, Gervasio, 46n114
    background of, 384n9
    cases heard by, 388, 397
    and inheritance case, 360, 362, 364-65, 373, 478
    land petitions to, 283n12
Cubero, Rodríguez, 59n7, 59n11, 60, 140n19, 170n13, 170n23
Cuervo, Ana María, 205, 217n4
Cuervo, Francisco Antonio, 205, 210-11, 217n1, 217n4
Cuervo y Valdés, Francisco, 70n11, 156n6
    banishes accused, 188
    as governor, 64, 217n7
    and mistress's children, 27, 205-08, 210-11, 217n1, 217n4
Cuidad Real, Spain, 335-36
curanderos/curanderas, 29-31, 186n9, 270, 272, 396-97, 406n7, 486
currency, 20, 187-88, 192-95
    pesos, 202n1, 203n21, 205, 207-11, 363-64, 366-73
    reales, 148, 203n21-22, 363, 487
    tomino, 192, 203n22
    value of, 202n1
Custody of New Mexico, 35, 268n8, 334, 358n47, 486. *See also* custos
customs (local), 32
custos, 37-38, 108n17, 203n18, 268n8, 334, 357n30, 358n39, 358n48, 358n50, 358n53, 486. *See also* Franciscan friars
Cutter, Charles, 29-32, 460

de la Asención, Josefa, 34, 321n4, 387-90, 392-94, 396-97, 406n5-6
de la Candelaria, Feliciano, 43n1, 43n4
de la Candelaria, María, 13, 43n1, 43n4
de la Cerda, Francisco, 406n8
de la Cerda, Juan (father), 406n8
de la Cerda, Juan Joseph (son), 389-90, 392-95, 406n8
de la Concepción, Juana, 170n22
de la Cruz, Agustín, 108n24

de la Cruz, Ana, 172, 173n4
de la Cruz Carajuida, Cristóbal, 119-21, 140n22
de la Cruz, Cristóbal, 109n31
de la Cruz, Felipa, 43n1
de la Cruz, Francisco, 173n4
de la Cruz, Juan, 331
de la Cruz, Juan Antonio, 43n1
de la Cruz, Juana, 109n31
de la Cruz, María, 282n10, 406n7
de la Cruz, María Antonia, 108n24
de la Cruz, María Celestina, 108n14
de la Cueva, Peronila, 156n16
de la Encarnación, Juana, 173n5
de la Encarnación, María, 301-04, 309, 321n13-14
de la Mora Piñeda, Juan, 70n2, 241-42, 259n9, 442n9
de la Palma, Agustín, 41, 109n37
    accused of rape, 24-25, 76-92, 107n6, 109n42
    background of, 107n4, 268n14
    bigamy cases of, 38-39, 107n4, 261-65
    seeks sancturary, 76, 79-80, 83-86, 108n15, 108n18
    See also del Rio, Agustín; Toribio
de la Peñuela, Marqués, 25, 70n8, 73, 78-79, 107n7, 108n17, 139n9, 142, 217n7, 226n5
de la Resa, Simona Bonifacia, 186n7
de la Rocha, Francisco, 442n6
de la Serna, Isabel, 177n8
de la Trinidad, Juana Hernández, 442n13
de la Vega y Coca, Francisca, 260n10
de la Vega y Coca, Miguel, 260n10
de los Reyes Cruz, Isabel, 77, 81, 107n3
de Rosa, Francisco Xavier, 178-82, 185n2, 203n12
debts, 19-20, 187, 190-92, 224, 479, 484n16
del Pino, Juan, 265, 269n23
del Rio, Agustín. *See* de la Palma, Agustín; Toribio
denunciations, 33, 38-39, 156n11, 171-72, 261, 264, 268n8, 322-26, 332, 358n38
diligencias matrimoniales, 36, 142-50
disease, 36, 42, 64, 109n40, 406n7
dishonor, 25, 27, 65-66
divorcio, 22-24, 36-37, 107n6, 139n2, 142-43, 145-47, 149, 156n15, 159
domestic disputes, 51-52, 64-67, 110-25, 142-49, 299. *See also* love affairs
domestic relationships, 15
Domíngo Páez, Juan, 481, 484n22
Domínguez de Mendoza, Antonio, 282n2
Domínguez de Mendoza, José, 260n28
Domínguez de Mendoza, Tomé II, 260n28, 282n2, 462n4
Domínguez, Joseph, 270-73, 282n2
Domínguez, Juan Antonio, 385n24
Domínguez, Juana, 81, 108n22, 157n28, 260n11, 260n28
Domínguez, Manuel, 25, 270-76, 282n2, 282n6
Domínguez, Manuel Antonio, 320n2, 321n22
Domínguez, María, 204n34, 246, 260n27
Domínguez, Petrona, 321n16
doña (honorific), 40
donations, 29, 36
dowries, 174, 203n28, 237n14
    agreements for, 35-36
    cases about, 21, 203n28, 239, 463n7

as compensation, 22, 27, 77
and *divorcios*, 37
and inheritance, 21, 187, 203n28
loss of, 23, 25
non-payment of, 14, 21, 159, 227-28
protection of, 478-80, 484n17-18
and Spanish law, 15-17, 20-21, 187
a woman's right to, 14, 228
Durán, Catalina, 186n9, 297n18, 442n4
Durán de Armijo, Antonio I, 442n4
  background of, 186n9, 260n13
  as barber, 186n9, 238, 248, 260n13, 328, 427
  and bigamy case, 324-25, 328-29, 331, 357n16
  as *procurador*, 22, 31, 186n9, 238-39
  and seduction/breach of promise case, 22, 238-39, 241-46, 248-49, 260n24
  as witness, 180-82
Durán de Armijo, José I, 442n4
Durán de Armijo, Vicente, 427, 442n4
Durán de la Peña, Joseph, 60-61, 63n11
Durán, Felipa, 109n45, 202n5
Durán, Nicolás, 426n17
Durán, Salvador, 415, 417, 426n17
Durán, Ursula, 259n1
Durán y Chávez, Antonio, 36, 46n130, 160-61, 163-64, 169n7, 169n10-11, 170n14, 223-24, 459n6
Durán y Chávez, Fernando, 459n6, 462n6
  background of, 158
  daughters of, 59n7, 170n14, 259n9, 442n9
  large ranch of, 39
  sons of, 158, 169n8, 169n10-11, 170n17, 170n25, 173n4
  wife of, 158, 170n12
Durán y Chávez, Fernando II, 223
Durán y Chávez, Luis, 169n7
Durán y Chávez, María, 59n7
Durán y Chávez, Nicolás, 21, 43n1, 46n130, 158-65, 169n8, 170n14, 223-24, 463n7
Durán y Chávez, Pedro, 31, 462n6
Durango, Mexico, 156n7, 259n2, 357n29, 358n36, 358n45, 358n49, 442n8

ecclesiastical judges, 22, 25, 32, 36-37, 46n110, 142, 328, 331, 333, 340, 358n45, 427, 442n8, 443, 453, 486
economic factors, 23, 39-40, 159, 203n28
Edicts of Faith, 38-39, 156n11, 171, 268n8, 324
El Monte, 464, 467-68, 477n13
El Paso, 142-43, 358n50, 465
  alcaldes mayores of, 203n8, 384n12
  alcaldes of, 357n26
  banishment to, 427, 432-33
  and bigamy case, 322-24, 326-29, 333
  burials in, 173n7
  cabildo of, 108n21, 157n27
  custos of, 358n53
  early settlers of, 51, 59n10, 139n1, 157n27, 203n8, 391, 393-94, 426n14
  Edicts of Faith read in, 39, 324
  Franciscan friars in, 157n18, 324, 326-27, 329-30, 333, 356n11, 357n22, 358n48
  justicia mayor of, 70n6
  lieutenant-governor headquarters in, 285
  marriages in, 236n12, 259n1
  settlers flee to, 360, 426n17, 483n12
  settlers return from, 203n30
  settlers seek cures in, 109n40, 156n14, 204n31
  traders in, 186n11
  See also notaries: in El Paso
El Paso presidio, 157n28
  adjutants of, 426n17
  alférez of, 70n6
  captains of, 59n10, 107n9, 203n8, 285, 384n12
  cases involving, 22, 238-39, 243-46, 248-49
  commander of, 70n8
  muster, 58n2, 63n8, 70n6, 108n14, 139n11, 157n22, 236n10, 260n20, 260n22, 282n10, 320n2, 321n19, 385n20, 385n24
  soldiers of, 40-41, 107n13, 139n3, 140n14, 140n21, 203n20, 218, 220, 238-39, 243, 248-49, 321n8, 385n22
  women work at, 187-90, 203n9
embargo de bienes, 31. *See also* goods: embargoed
Embudo, New Mexico, 176n3, 236n2
encomenderos, 158, 223, 360, 387, 406n5, 477n8
encomiendas, 58n3, 360, 486
England, 11, 19, 43, 52, 75n7, 362
Escobar, Gerónimo de, 60-61, 63n9
Esparze, Catarina de, 425n6
Espejo, María de, 261, 263, 268n10
Espíndola, Antonia de, 217n16
Espinola, Magdalena de, 384n6, 385n15
Esquivel, Antonio de, 384n8
Esquivel, Juan Antonio de, 384n8, 385n23
Esquivel, María de, 283n12, 384n8
Esquivel, María Francisca de, 369-70, 372, 384n6, 384n8, 385n15, 385n23, 385n25
Esquivel, Ventura de, 36, 139n1, 270, 274, 283n12, 360-72, 384n8, 385n22-23, 385n25
estates, 20-21, 29, 139n1, 205, 224, 356n8, 360, 364, 366, 384n1, 478, 481
European countries, 19, 28, 37, 239
Examen and Practica de Escribanos, 29
excommunication, 142-44, 147

family relationships, 14, 19, 26, 139n1, 443-48
famine, 28, 64
fanega, 363, 429, 485-86
Farfán-Velasco Expedition
  militia captain of, 205, 217n6
  recruitment records of, 156n4, 186n9, 204n34
  settlers travel with, 64, 70n2-5, 71, 75n5-6, 75n8, 109n35, 110, 139n6-7, 140n15, 140n17, 140n20, 142, 156n5, 156n7, 156n13, 156n16, 157n26, 170n13, 173n3, 173n7, 185n2, 186n9, 186n11, 217n16, 268n19, 282n4, 297n9, 321n21, 384n8, 385n23, 385n29-30, 426n18, 451n2
farming, 39, 42, 52, 75n9, 81, 110, 123, 158, 160, 203n8, 363, 387-91, 395-96
Ferdinand III, King, 15
Fernández de Avila, Juan, 75n6
Fernández de la Cueva, Francisco, 71-74
Fernández de la Pedrera, Juan, 326-327, 333, 357n20
Fernández de la Pedrera, María Francisca, 357n20
Fernández, José Antonio, 357n18

Fernández, Teresa, 442n14
filigree makers, 75n6
financial assets
    acquired during marriage, 37
    brought to marriage, 20-21, 478, 484n16-17
    division of, 143
financial compensation, 22-23, 25, 27, 31-33, 36, 46n132, 77, 139n1, 205, 239, 388, 397
financial support, 26, 41, 76-77, 123, 139n2, 142-44, 146, 148, 178-79, 181, 207, 427-28, 434
financial transactions, 21
fines, 22-26, 31, 33, 35, 51, 55, 59n12, 171-72, 173n6, 239, 244, 388, 409, 414, 460-61, 464, 469-70
Flores de Valdéz, Antonia, 203n31
Flores Liscano, María, 296n1
Flores Mogollón, Juan Ignacio, 63n8, 139n4, 176n2, 289
    alters Pueblo culture, 139n9
    and domestic dispute cases, 110-19, 123-25, 158-65
    and inheritance petition, 34, 187-93
    and land grants, 363
    orders documents preserved, 210
    and rape case, 76-78
food, 76-77, 81, 85, 149, 285, 368
fornication, 34, 300
Foucault, Michel, 34
Franciscan friars, 108n16, 156n13
    authority of, 357n29
    and bigamy case, 324, 329-30, 332-33
    cases involving, 142-50
    college for, 288
    and denunciations, 322-24
    and Edicts of Faith, 324
    and Holy Office, 37-39, 173n3, 268n8, 322-24, 359n68
    identify sins, 171
    and Indian campaigns, 236n7
    records of, 42
    regulate church law, 35-39
    reports on, 358n50
    in Santa Fe, 108n17, 108n28, 157n18, 157n24, 171, 265, 358n48, 407n17
    vice-custos of, 156n3, 459n11
    as witnesses, 265, 322-24
    See also convento; Custody of New Mexico; *custos*; specific names; specific towns
Franciscan missions, 108n28, 331, 358n46, 358n50, 358n53, 407n17, 459n16. *See also* Pueblo names
Franks, 15
Frequi, María, 107n13
Frequi, Sebastiana, 107n2
friendship, 64-67, 91, 220
Fuenclara, New Mexico, 40, 43n5, 203n30, 409, 426n12, 426n16, 452n13, 454, 456, 459n5, 460-61. *See also* Tomé, New Mexico
fuero, 14-17, 486
funerals, 187, 190-91, 203n19, 407n14. *See also* burials

Galicia, Spain, 15, 70n8, 357n20, 358n37, 442n8
Galisteo Pueblo, 108n28, 269n22
Gallardo, Antonia, 226n9

Gallegos, Antonio I, 443
Gallegos, Antonio II, 443, 451n8
Gallegos, Josefa, 43n5, 452n13
Gallegos, Margarita, 33, 443-48, 451n2, 451n8
Galván, Juan, 443-45, 451n1
Galve, Condé de, 71-73, 75n2, 75n7, 75n9
gambling, 35, 41, 139n2, 187, 239, 284, 286, 288-90
Gamboa, Felipa de, 139n5, 204n32
García de la Mora, Juan
    as *alcalde ordinario*, 373
    bigamy case against, 23, 39, 322-40, 357n34, 358n44-45, 359n72-73
    charges against, 358n38
    hometown of, 323, 331, 357n33
    wives of, 170n25, 322-23, 357n32
García de la Mora, Juan (the elder), 331, 335
García de la Puente, Lucas, 336, 359n61
García de la Riva, Juan, 171-72, 173n3, 177n9, 178-82, 217n6, 217n8, 218-20, 227-29
García de la Riva, Manuela, 177n9
García de la Riva, María Francisca, 27, 205-08, 210-11, 217n4
García de la Riva, Miguel, 173n3, 205, 207, 217n4-6
García de la Riva, Teodora, 356n8, 484n22
García de los Rios, Juana, 387, 406n2, 406n10
García de Noriega, Alfonso/Alonso I, 70n11, 174-75, 176n6, 226n5, 483n12
García de Noriega, Alonso II, 224, 483n12
García de Noriega, Josefa Ana, 43n7, 70n11, 407n15
García de Noriega, Juan Esteban (son), 387-88, 390-97, 406n3, 406n4
García de Noriega, Juan (father), 406n4
García de Noriega, Luis, 223-24, 226n5, 408, 409, 425n6, 478-79, 481, 483n10, 483n12, 484n13-14
García de Noriega, Rosalia, 21, 40, 408, 425n6, 478-81, 483n10
García, Juana, 170n25
García Jurado, Barbara, 226n5, 478-79, 484n14
García Jurado, José, 217n16, 484n14
García Jurado, Margarita, 25, 77
García Jurado, María, 357n20
García Jurado, Ramón, 31, 212, 217n16, 409, 451n1, 478-79, 481, 484n14
García, María, 64-67, 70n3-4, 70n7, 70n10
García, María Francisca, 452n15
García, Nicolás, 70n3
gardens, 108n22, 169n7, 217n5, 231
Garduño, José Gabriel, 384n10
Garduño, Joseph Manuel, 482, 484n24
Garduño, María Diega, 384n10
genízaros, 43n2, 271, 486
Germanic (Gothic) laws, 14, 32
Gerónimo de Mier, Antonio, 338
Gila Indians, 358n46
Giltoméy, Joseph Manuel
    as *ayudante*, 195, 210-12, 287, 290
    background of, 109n40, 156n14, 203n31
    as witness, 89, 145, 195, 208-12, 229-32, 242
Girón, Catalina, 109n45, 202n5
Girón de Tejeda, Nicolás, 64-67, 70n2, 70n5
Girón de Tejeda, Tomás, 70n5, 204n34, 260n27
Godines, María Luisa, 442n14

Godoy, Cristóbal Lucero de, 238
Gómez, Antonio, 263, 268n13
Gómez de Arellano, Luisa, 259n10
Gómez de Chávez, Pedro, 170n25
Gómez de Rivera, María, 71-74, 75n3, 75n5
Gómez de Rivera, Teresa, 71-74, 75n4
Gómez de Torres, Francisca, 26-27, 40, 110-25, 139n3, 139n5, 428
Gómez del Castillo, Francisco, 466-68, 470, 477n8-9
Gómez, Francisca, 358n36
Gómez, Juana, 431-32, 442n15
Gómez Luján, Luisa, 406n4
Góngora, Bartolomé, 156n5
Góngora, Cristóbal de, 109n40, 156n16, 204n31
    background of, 156n4-5
    divorce case of, 23, 37, 142-50, 156n15
    as scribe to *cabildo*, 79-83, 85-90, 92, 108n23, 143, 372
Góngora, Francisca, 426n9, 459n16
Góngora, Gregoria, 226n1
Góngora, Marquis de, 384n9
González Bas, Joseph, 415
González Bas, Juan I, 29, 226n8, 321n3, 426n7
González Bas, Juan II, 224-25, 226n8, 408-10, 412, 414-17, 426n7-8, 426n11, 426n15
González Bas, Melchora, 426n11
González Bas, Micaela, 462n5
González Bas, Prudencia, 477n9
González de Aragon, Josefa, 70n5
González de la Rosa, Margarita, 442n14
González, Francisco, 360-64, 366-73, 384n3, 384n5, 384n7, 385n21
González, Francisco Antonio, 410, 426n8
González, Juan Julian, 412, 414-15, 426n15
González, Manuela, 331, 335, 357n35
González, María, 109n33
González, Sebastián, 81, 85, 108n21, 148, 157n22
goods
    confiscation of, 31, 38, 219, 261, 388, 393
    and dowries, 20-21
    embargoed, 31, 111-12, 300, 302
    fines paid with, 31, 171-72, 173n6, 244, 261
    and inheritance, 187, 193, 195, 362-63, 369, 478-81
    inventories of, 36, 219, 362, 372, 388, 393, 478-79
    owned by women, 139n1
    soldiers paid in, 188
    stolen by Indians, 42
gossip, 14, 22, 26-27, 64-67, 122, 147, 357n17
government funds, 70n8
governors
    authority of, 38
    cases heard by, 24, 32-33, 35-36, 40
    and civil/criminal law, 19-20
    give permission to leave colony, 60, 70n4, 187, 189
    investigation of, 70n8
    legal procedures for, 28-34, 111, 159
    petitions to, 11, 13-14, 21-22, 42, 52
    purchase price of, 107n7
    represent the king, 34, 174, 390
    and rumors/scandal, 26-27
    support the abandoned/needy, 174
    support women, 159, 443-47
    uphold Spanish law, 14, 21, 28-29
    See also real amparo (royal protection); reconciliation; specific names
Granados, José, 337, 359n66
Granillo, Luis, 260n29
Granillo, María, 247, 259n1, 260n25, 260n29
Griego, Inez, 406n6
Griego, Juan, 177n8, 320n2
Guadalajara, Mexico, 185n1, 210, 442n9
Guadalupe, María de, 173n5
Guanajuato, Mexico, 107n3
guardianship, 15, 17, 187-88, 192-95
Guazapares, Mexico, 263, 268n12
Guelphs and Ghibellines, 453-55, 459n9
Guerrero, Francisco, 459n14
Guerrero, José/Joseph Antonio, 171-72, 322-34, 339, 358n39
Guerrero, Juana, 61, 63n4-6, 63n10, 384n3
guías (guides/legal handbooks), 29, 31, 109n39, 238, 260n14, 479
Guido, Juan de, 77, 81, 107n3
Guillén, Ursula, 477n8
gunpowder, 323, 334, 356n2, 358n54, 407n14
Gutiérrez, Antonia, 268n19
Gutiérrez, Antonio, 223-25, 226n1
Gutiérrez, Clemente, 459n16-17
Gutiérrez, Felipe, 226n1
Gutiérrez, Isabel, 385n19
Gutiérrez, Jacinto, 443-45, 451n4
Gutiérrez, María, 226n11

Hacienda de Alamo, 357n20
Havana, Cuba, 323, 334, 337
healers. *See* curanderos/curanderas
health issues, 42, 269n23, 396-97, 426n13, 442n6
hearsay, 38, 306, 322-23, 325-27, 329, 357n17, 418
heresies, 36-37, 39, 171-72, 261-62, 264, 268n8, 324
Herrera, Ana María de, 51-55, 58n3, 59n4
Herrera, Andrés Delgado de, 336, 359n63
Herrera, Eugenia de, 140n21
Herrera, Isabel de, 51-55, 59n4-5
Herrera, Josefa de, 140n14
Herrera, Juan de, 58n3, 59n4
Herrera, Juana (Guerrero). *See* Guerrero, Juana
hides, 70n5, 171, 191, 297n18
hijos naturales (children born out of wedlock), 27, 58n3, 59n4, 107n4, 108n22, 156n16, 207, 210-11, 217n4, 259n9, 260n28, 442n9, 462n6, 477n8, 486
Hinojos, Antonia de, 173n4
Hinojos, Josefa de, 177n9
Holy Office of the Inquisition, 358n52, 359n56, 359n69
    and "abjuration," 261-62, 264-65
    abolishment of, 358n40
    alguacil mayor of, 218-20
    arresting officers of, 173n3
    bigamy cases of, 23, 107n4, 219, 261-65, 322-40, 359n72
    and cohabitation case, 171-72
    comisarios of, 143, 146, 148-49, 157n19, 263-65, 268n8, 322, 324, 333, 339-40, 358n39, 358n50, 486

and denunciations, 33, 38-39
high marshal of, 115-16, 140n17
high sheriff of, 218-20, 268n19, 442n8
inquisitors of, 261-65, 324, 333, 335
and marriage, 171-72
in New Mexico, 38-39, 322-30, 358n37
procedures of, 33, 37-39, 261-62, 322-24, 358n43
and public shaming, 218-20, 221n1
secrecy of, 33, 38, 261, 322-30, 337-38, 356n13
sentences of, 261-64
and slander case, 218-20
in Spain, 37-38, 334-38
See also denunciations; Edicts of Faith; heresies
Holy Sacrament of Extreme Unction, 412-13, 426n13
homes, 434, 477n7
 cases about, 227-28, 230-32, 360, 362-63, 368, 393, 443-46
 owned by Governor Martínez, 289, 298n26
 owned by portion, 227-28, 230-32, 362-63
 owned by women, 40, 70n2, 108n22, 169n7, 217n5, 362-63, 368, 390
 in Santa Cruz, 321n3, 393
 in Santa Fe, 39, 70n2, 108n22, 169n7, 217n5, 227-28, 239, 259n4, 286, 289, 297n10, 298n26
honor, 27-28, 36, 64-67, 122, 224, 244, 247, 259n3
Hopis, 357n14. *See also* Moqui (Hopi) pueblos
Hornero, Josefa, 337, 359n67
Hornero, María de, 323, 331, 335-38, 357n32, 357n34
Hornero, Miguel, 335, 359n60
Hornero, Simón de, 335-36
horses, 111, 176n3, 178, 180, 191
 and broken saddle case, 464, 466-68, 477n10
 cases involving, 387-91, 395-96, 415
 and inheritance, 193
 land for, 363
 presidio herd of, 35, 41, 360, 425n5, 468
 and public shaming, 218-20
 royal herd of, 35, 41, 248
 of soldiers, 107n4, 170n22, 176n6, 189-91, 321n3
 theft of, 60, 425n5
 value of, 36, 46n132, 59n12, 62n1, 202n1
Hurtado, Andrés, 170n12
Hurtado, Bernardina, 217n16, 484n14
Hurtado, Juana, 107n9, 384n12
Hurtado, María, 157n27, 385n28
Hurtado, Mariana, 426n18
Hurtado, Martín, 158, 170n12, 217n16, 223, 260n22, 426n8, 426n18, 442n9, 484n14
Hurtado y Salas, Juana, 451n1
Hurtado y Salas, Lucía
 accused of theft, 223-24
 background of, 158, 170n12
 and daughter-in-law's case, 158-64
 daughters of, 59n7, 170n14, 226n6
 as elite woman, 40
 sons of, 169n8, 169n10-11, 170n17, 170n25

impotence, 36, 143
imprisonment, 31, 107n10, 124, 158, 261, 414
 ordered by Holy Office, 261-64
 in presidio barracks, 284-85, 287-88
 release from, 388, 397, 408, 414, 469-70
 in Santa Cruz, 110, 299, 302, 306, 388, 397, 464-66, 469
 in Santa Fe, 30, 171-72, 178-80, 220
 sentence of, 26, 33, 110, 123
 while awaiting trial, 29-30, 33, 111
 of women, 46n98, 54-55
 See also cárcel; presidio guardhouse; *prisión*
incest, 22, 34, 77, 82, 107n6, 108n25
Indians, 17, 59n7, 222n8, 308, 409
 campaigns against, 41-42, 63n8, 107n7, 170n17, 176n6, 204n34, 236n7, 237n12, 260n11, 297n5, 484n14
 cases involving, 120-21, 140n25, 321n23
 and Franciscan friars, 35, 357n14
 "gentiles," 486
 horses stolen by, 425n5
 hostile tribes of, 25
 languages of, 357n14
 and marriage with settlers, 172, 173n4, 261
 Mexican, 140n22, 259n1
 mistreated by settlers, 217n16, 426n9, 459n16, 484n14
 of mixed race, 107n3
 nomadic tribes of, 41-42, 43n2, 271, 321n20
 "protector" of, 43n7, 140n15
 raids of, 35, 41-42, 64, 107n7
 settlers captured by, 42, 108n22, 173n4
 settlers killed by, 71-72, 75n5-6, 385n24
 taken captive, 170n15
 testimony by, 321n20
 trading by, 39, 41-42, 271, 285, 321n23, 323, 465, 487
 as witnesses, 299, 301, 303, 305-07, 309
 See also María (Apache woman); *rescates*; servants: Indians as; specific tribes, pueblos
inheritance, 23, 25, 159, 202n1
 cases about, 13, 21, 32, 34, 60-62, 187-95, 203n26, 224, 231-32, 360-73, 384n7, 385n21, 386n33, 425n6, 478-82
 collection of, 21, 174-75
 and *divorcios*, 37
 of homes, 360, 362-63, 368
 of land, 13, 43n1, 170n25, 217n6, 223, 360-73, 459n17, 479, 481
 and men, 21, 478-81
 paid in cash, 187-88, 192-95
 paid in goods, 187, 193, 195, 203n24
 protection of, 478-80, 484n17-18
 and Roman law, 14
 and Spanish law, 16-17, 19-21, 187, 478-81
 a woman's right to, 11, 13-14, 187, 478-81
 See also children: and inheritance
injuries
 cases involving, 273-75, 387-91, 393-94, 396-97, 408, 410, 415-18
 cures sought for, 282n1
 examination of, 29-30, 107n10, 159, 270-72, 387-89, 406n7, 409, 418
 sentences for, 33
 and soldiers, 35
 See also abuse: physical; assaults; physical punishment

Inquisition. *See* Holy Office of the Inquisition
insanity, 36
Inscription Rock, 58n3, 107n9, 203n30, 385n18
insults, 11, 25-27, 51, 53, 59n6, 122, 158-61, 270, 275, 387-94, 412-13, 453, 455-56
interpreters, 139n1, 139n5, 204n32, 297n5, 387
Isabella, Queen, 17, 37
Isleta Pueblo, 159, 169n8, 456, 459n16-17

jails/prisons, 33
  in Santa Cruz, 299, 302, 464
  in Santa Fe, 30, 51, 54-55, 171-72, 178-80, 220, 227, 274
  See also cárcel; imprisonment; presidio guardhouse; *prisión*
Janos presidio, 41, 107n4, 261, 264, 268n14, 452n15
Jaramillo, Antonia Tafoya, 59n4
Jaramillo, Cristóbal Varela, 426n12, 426n16, 452n18, 459n5
Jaramillo, Gerónimo Varela, 415-16, 426n12, 426n16, 459n5
Jaramillo, Gregorio, 409-10, 415-16, 426n12, 426n16
Jaramillo, Joseph Varela, 22, 27, 453-56, 459n5
Jaramillo Negrete, José, 140n20
Jaramillo, Roque Jacinto, 119, 140n20
Jaramillo, Teresa Varela, 296n1
Jaramillo, Xavier, 459n5
jealousy, 76, 84, 91, 110, 122, 145, 248-49, 301, 304, 336, 434
Jémez Pueblo, 107n7, 141n28, 407n17, 477n5
Jesús, Teresa de, 384n3
Jews, 15-16, 37, 39
Jiménez de Ancizo, María, 236n2
Jorge de Sotomayor, Isabel, 158, 169n7
Jorge, Nicolasa Zaldivar, 226n8, 426n7
judges, 21, 24, 27-28, 32, 35, 75n2, 88-89, 186n10, 187, 225, 241. *See also* ecclesiastical judges
juez comisario, 70n11, 487
junta, 72-73, 75n2
justicia mayor, 70n6, 274
Justinian law, 15-17, 20-21, 187, 195, 203n28, 480

kings, 27, 34, 37, 174, 205, 210. *See also* specific names
knives, 368

La Ciénega, New Mexico, 206, 217n6
La Cieneguilla, New Mexico, 39, 170n20, 360-63, 371-73, 464, 466-67, 477n11
La Conquistadora Chapel (Santa Fe), 70n11
La Conquistadora confraternity, 177n9, 259n1
La Majada land grant, 357n20
La Soledad, New Mexico, 39
labor, forced, 26, 36, 170n11, 173n7, 406n7
Ladron de Guerrero (Guevara), Josefa, 75n6
Ladron de Guerrero (Guevara), Nicolás Ortiz, 125, 141n28
Laguna Pueblo, 269n22, 426n9, 459n16
land
  agricultural, 39, 41, 363
  cases involving, 443-46
  disputes over, 11, 13, 21, 42, 159, 169n8, 357n15, 360-73, 406n10

  and dowries, 20-21
  inheritance of, 23, 61, 478-81
  inventories of, 388
  managed by women, 299, 320n2
  and ownership, 159, 227-28
  petitions for, 283n12, 459n5
  resettlement of, 58n2, 139n1, 140n20, 385n28, 387, 442n9
  See also specific locations; specific names
land grants, 39, 204n32, 226n1
  in Alameda, 409
  in Albuquerque, 142
  in Atrisco, 223
  in Chama, 139n3, 139n11, 170n23, 321n8
  documents for, 210
  in La Cieneguilla, 360-63
  near Pueblos, 60, 63n8, 236n10, 321n3, 357n20, 477n7
  reaffirmation of, 259n1, 363, 406n7
  in Río Arriba area, 140n20
  in Santa Cruz, 356n7, 385n18, 393, 406n7
  in Santa Fe, 59n10, 140n14, 259n1, 297n18, 320n2
  and Spanish law, 17, 46n120
landowners, 41, 206
  in Bernalillo, 426n9
  in Chimayó, 40, 406n3
  influential, 223-24
  in La Cieneguilla, 360-73
  in Las Trampas, 477n6
  near Ciénaga Pueblo, 217n6
  near Fuenclara/Tomé, 203n30
  near Isleta, 459n17
  near Sandia Pueblo, 426n6
  in Pojoaque, 226n11
  in Río Arriba area, 477n12
  in Santa Cruz, 170n22, 282n4, 321n3, 393
  in Santa Fe, 39, 40, 70n2, 70n5, 141n28, 170n22, 222n3, 227-28, 230-32, 236n2, 236n10, 259n1, 260n21, 297n5, 297n18, 299, 320n2, 357n15, 385n22, 385n28
  in Valencia, 443-48
  women, 36, 40, 70n2, 70n5, 139n1, 217n5, 222n3, 223-24, 299, 320n2, 357n20, 360-73, 408
  See also inheritance: of land; ranches/ranchers
Las Trampas area, 477n6
Laurera, Juana, 406n10
Laws of the Indies, 17-18. *See also* Recopilación de Leyes de los Reinos de las Indias
lawsuits. *See* petitions
Leal, Catalina, 259n2, 356n10
Ledesma, Juan de, 109n31
Ledesma, Juliana de, 335
leg irons/stocks, 35, 76, 284, 460-61. *See also* shackles
legal codes, 14-18
Legal Culture of Northern New Spain, The (Cutter), 29
legal handbooks, 29, 31. *See also* guías (guides/legal handbooks)
legal procedures, 16
  the accusation, 27, 29-31, 33, 37
  for *alcaldes*, 28-34, 270, 299-300, 362-63, 387-88, 409, 444
  auto de cargo, 31

auto de prisión (arrest warrant), 30-31
cabeza del proceso, 30, 111-13, 139n10, 388-89, 485
confesión, 31, 108n26
declaraciónes, 30
embargo de bienes, 31, 111-12
fé de heridas, 30
generales de la ley, 30, 140n13, 260n31, 385n16, 486
   for governors, 28-34, 32, 111
interrogatorio, 31-32
juicio plenario, 31
   in military cases, 35
notificación, 33, 37
ratificación, 32, 108n23, 111, 113-14
remisión, 188
sentencia, 32, 111
summaria, 30-31, 78, 91, 107n10, 108n26, 182, 186n10, 487
   See also sentences; testimony
legal representatives, 29, 31, 33, 70n11, 76, 88-92, 109n37, 186n9, 203n28, 260n14, 284-85, 460-61. *see also* procuradors
legal rights. *See* women's legal rights
León, Juliana de, 337, 359n65
Leyba, Angela de, 139n3, 139n11, 321n8
Leyes de Toro, 17-18, 21, 480-81
licenciados, 333-40, 358n40-42, 359n69
lieutenant governors, 43n6, 64-67, 70n6, 203n8, 226n8, 284-91, 426n7. *See also* specific names
Liñan, Gerónimo de, 265, 269n22
Linares, Viceroy, 70n8
literate persons, 29, 40, 139n6, 142, 284, 357n16
livestock, 20-21, 203n8, 226n7, 390, 485
   branding of, 42, 223-24
   cases about, 33, 223-25, 452n17
   distribution documents for, 75n3, 108n14, 108n24, 140n22, 176n4, 226n11, 260n25, 282n4
   inheritance of, 174-75, 193, 481
   owned by women, 36, 139n1
   petitions for, 109n45, 202n5
   raising of, 363, 442n11
   theft of, 108n28, 452n17
   value of, 36, 46n132
Lobato, Bartolomé, 140n24, 297n14
Lobato, Blas, 120-21, 140n24
Lobato, Juan Cayetano, 70n2, 286, 289, 297n14
lobo, 107n3
López, Alfonso, 259n10
López, Antonia, 58n3, 357n15
López Conejo, María, 385n30
López de Castillo, Ana, 58n3, 59n4
López de Castillo, María, 226n8, 426n7
López de Mendizábal, Bernardo, 38
López Grande, Juan, 24, 178-82, 185n1
López, Isabel, 236n12
López, Juana, 406n3
López, Luis, 426n11
López Merino, Pedro, 336, 359n62
López, Micaela, 408-10, 412-13, 415-18, 426n11
López Nieto, María del Carmen, 207
López Olguín, Juan II, 203n30
López, Pedro, 224, 226n9

López, Petrona, 297n5
López, Salvador, 146, 157n18
Lorca, Spain, 70n11, 407n15
Los Angeles, 75n3
Los Angeles, Catalina de, 109n35
Los Quelites land grant, 462n6
love affairs, 110, 143, 178-82, 205, 207-08, 210, 238, 247-49, 260n24, 299-309, 321n12, 323, 427-35, 443-45, 464-70
Lucero de Godoy, Antonia, 385n28, 477n11
Lucero de Godoy, Antonio, 385n22
Lucero de Godoy, Bernardina, 283n12
Lucero de Godoy, Cristóbal, 41, 243-46, 249, 260n18
Lucero de Godoy, Miguel, 260n18
Lucero de Godoy, Nicolás, 260n18, 426n14
Lucero de Godoy, Rosa, 362, 369-70, 372, 384n8, 385n22-23, 385n25
Lucero, Josefa, 43n3
Lucero, Manuel Cristóbal, 452n18
Lucero, Pedro, 412, 414-17, 426n14
Lucero, Petrona Paula, 243-46, 248-49, 260n19, 260n30
Luján, Agustín, 243, 249, 260n22
Luján, Domingo, 108n22
Luján Domínguez, Leonor, 426n12
Luján, Felix, 110-25, 139n1, 140n26
Luján, José, 259n2
Luján, Juan, 120-21, 139n1, 140n26, 241-42, 260n11, 260n27
Luján, Juan Domingo, 260n11
Luján, Juan Luis, 236n12
Luján, Juana, 36, 40, 139n1, 283n12, 477n8
Luján, María, 357n18, 406n8
Luján, Matias, 139n1, 140n26, 477n8
Luján, Miguel, 28, 33, 110, 139n1
Luján, Pedro, 227, 230, 236n12
Luján, Rosalia, 239, 259n2
Luna, Antonio de, 43n3
Luna, Domingo, 13, 43n1, 43n3
Lutherans, 37, 39

Madrid, Bernardo, 175, 177n8
Madrid, Lorenzo, 108n22, 149, 157n28
Madrid, María, 108n31, 140n22
Madrid, Pedro, 177n8
Madrid, Roque, 108n22, 157n28, 177n8
Madrid, Sebastiana, 259n1
Maese, Alonso, 385n24
Maese, Antonia, 406n6
Maese, Catalina, 297n5, 369, 385n24
Maese, Francisca "La Abuelita," 301-04, 309, 321n6, 321n14
Maese, Juliana, 304, 321n13-15
Maese, María Luisa, 260n22
Maese, Miguel, 385n24
magic, 37
mail carriers, 41
mala vida (a bad life)
   explanation of, 11, 22, 24, 26, 139n2, 487
   and Francisca Gómez de Torres case, 110-11, 113, 116, 119-20, 122

and Juana Montaño de Sotomayor case, 159-61, 163-64
See also abuse
Maldonado y Sais, María, 442n11
Mangado y Clavijo, Diego, 332-33, 339-40, 358n40, 358n42
Manuela, María, 43n1
Manzañares, María de la Rosa, 176n6, 385n18
marca (silver bar), 171-72, 173n6
María (Apache woman), 299, 301, 303, 305-07, 309, 321n9
Marín del Valle, Francisco Antonio, 477n9
Marquez, Ana María (wife of Domingo Valdéz), 259n4
Márquez, Ana (wife of Salvador), 426n17
Marquéz, Juan, 28
Marquez, María, 459n17
marriage, 32, 108n17
   and dispensations, 170n11, 207
   and Germanic law, 14
   gifts given for, 22, 35-36, 239
   and Holy Office, 171-72, 335-37
   and illegitimate children, 26-27
   impediments to, 36, 51, 53, 139n1, 207, 322, 331, 335
   investigations into, 34-36, 139n1, 156n15, 176n6, 322-40
   and "marriage portion," 21, 227-28, 237n14
   permission needed for, 205, 207, 210
   and personal/property rights, 19-21, 478-80
   as a sacrament, 22, 35-36, 39, 143, 171
   and Spanish law, 17
   See also adultery; bigamy; breach of promise; children; *diligencias matrimoniales*; *divorcio*; dowries
Martín, Andrés, 406n5
Martín, Antonio, 176n3
Martín, Cristóbal I, 159, 161, 164-65, 170n21, 282n6, 304. *See also* Martín Serrano, Cristóbal I
Martín, Cristóbal II, 300-304, 320n2, 321n4-5, 321n7, 321n21. *See also* Martín Serrano, Cristóbal II
Martín de Salazar, Francisca, 236n12
Martín, Diego, 31, 140n23, 321n8, 406n7
Martín, Domingo, 114, 118-21, 140n14
Martín, Francisca, 477n6
Martín, Francisco, 139n1, 320n2
Martín, Gertrudis, 177n8, 299-301, 304-05, 308-09, 320n2, 321n5
Martín, Hernán. *See* Martín Serrano, Hernán
Martín, Josefa, 321n21, 322, 325-26, 331-32, 356n12, 359n73, 384n14
Martín, Juan de Dios, 120, 140n23
Martín, Juan Francisco, 176n3
Martín, Juana, 22-24, 299-308, 320n2, 321n7, 321n12, 358n45, 427-34, 442n3-4
Martín, Marcial, 331, 356n12
Martín, María, 308-09, 320n2, 321n22, 406n5
Martín, Mateo, 387-91, 393-97, 406n5-6
Martín Moraga, Diego, 387-92, 394-96, 406n11
Martín, Nicolás, 31, 387-97, 406n2, 406n10
Martín, Pedro, 190, 203n11, 236n12
Martín, Petrona, 170n25
Martín, Sebastiana, 226n9
Martín Serrano, Antonio, 321n21

Martín Serrano, Cristóbal I, 406n10-11
Martín Serrano, Cristóbal II, 321n13-15
Martín Serrano, Francisco, 170n25, 387-94, 406n2, 406n10, 406n14
Martín Serrano, Hernán, 321n4, 387, 406n5-6, 406n10
Martín Serrano, Luis I, 140n14, 387, 406n2
Martín Serrano, Luis II, 140n14, 406n2, 406n5, 406n10
Martín Serrano, María, 260n11
Martín Serrano, Sebastián, 39, 356n12
Martín, Simon, 301, 305-08, 321n16
Martín, Tomasa, 406n5
Martínez Cobo, Juan, 335-37, 359n57, 359n69
Martínez de Agustín, Juan, 337, 359n68
Martínez de Cervantes, Juan Manuel, 109n35
Martínez, Felix
   and 10,000 *pesos* case, 208-09, 211
   background of, 70n8, 425n6
   declaration on weapons, 33
   determines soldier's assets, 187-88, 190-94, 202n1
   as governor, 33, 70n8, 176n2, 206, 236n7
   home of, 289, 298n26, 409
   and land grants, 406n7
   military campaign of, 236n7
   as presidio captain, 64-65, 67, 70n8, 187-88, 190-94
   and seduction/breach of promise case, 238-40, 243-49
   servants of, 178, 180, 182, 203n12
   woman seeks refuge with, 64-65
Martínez, Salvador, 21, 29, 226n5, 408-10, 412-18, 425n5-6, 478-81
Mascareñas, Francisco, 325, 357n15
Mascareñas, José, 357n15
masons, 140n20, 406n4
Mata, Baltazar de, 170n14
Mata, María, 109n45, 202n5
Mata, Miguel, 109n45, 202n5
Matheo, José, 76, 85-86, 108n29
Mathers, Clay, 444
medics, 41, 238, 427. *See also* barbers (medics)
Medina de Cobrera, María, 259n4
Medina, Diego de, 260n21
Medina, Juan Lorenzo de, 286, 288-89, 297n9, 384n1
Medina, Juana de, 156n16, 406n14
Medina, Lugarda de, 331, 356n12
Medina, Ramón de, 243, 248-49, 260n21
Menchero, Juan Miguel, 43n6, 143, 322-23, 333-34, 358n46, 459n16
Menchero Map, 358n46
Mendoza, José Domínguez de, 108n22
merchants, 41, 297n12, 297n18, 322-23, 326-27, 329, 334, 356n2, 358n46, 358n54, 427, 442n11, 442n17
Mestas, Antonio, 477n7
Mestas, Francisco Xavier, 477n12
Mestas, María, 156n7
Mestas Peralta, Juan de, 477n12
Mestas, Xavier, 464, 466-68, 477n7, 477n12
mestizos, 33, 107n3, 186n9, 384n3, 487
Mexico, 139n1, 262-63
Mexico City, 70n2, 70n5, 107n9, 179, 357n15, 384n1, 384n8, 426n6

colonists return to, 71, 73, 205, 207-08, 384n12
diseases in, 42
Farfán-Velasco Expedition leaves from, 139n7
final judgements in, 28, 33
Franciscan friars of, 156n8, 203n18
Governor Cubero travels to, 60
Holy Office in, 37-38, 171, 323-24, 331-35, 339-40, 358n40-42, 359n55
laws of, 24-25
merchants in, 322-23, 358n46
natives of, 75n5, 108n17, 108n28, 139n6, 140n20-21, 140n23, 142, 156n4, 156n6, 156n13, 170n22, 173n3, 217n6, 282n4, 297n24, 324, 385n20, 385n29, 406n7, 442n12
and presidio payroll, 188
prostitution in, 25
public shaming in, 218-19
viceroys in, 43n2
weavers in, 173n3
Michoacán, Mexico, 406n8
midwives, 25, 30, 84, 162
military, 17, 41, 107n11, 141n28, 408
captains, 170n12, 173n7, 237n12, 384n11, 464-65, 485
cases, 31, 35, 284-91
couriers, 59n7
equipment, 186n11, 187-88, 190-91
escorts, 323, 465
expulsion from, 285
leaders, 64, 70n4, 170n17, 176n6
leaves the kingdom, 464-65
in Spain, 14-15, 384n9, 442n6
See also Indians: campaigns against; presidio soldiers; specific presidios
militia, 42, 141n28, 170n17, 173n7, 205, 217n6, 241-43, 245, 259n2, 409
mines, 41-42, 60-61, 63n7, 173n6, 226n11, 268n12, 268n19, 285, 459n14
Mingues, Juan, 142, 144, 146-48, 156n6, 265
ministero doctrinero, 326, 357n22
mints, 63n7, 173n6
Miranda, Antonia de, 406n2, 406n10
Misquia, Francisca de, 384n12
mistresses, 205-08, 210-11
Mondragón, Francisco, 24, 35, 464-70, 476n3
Mondragón, Juan Alonso de, 121, 141n27, 476n3
Mondragón, María, 109n36
Mondragón, Sebastián, 141n27
monogamous women, 27
Montaño, Catalina, 385n24
Montaño de Sotomayor, Juan Antonio, 169n7
Montaño de Sotomayor, Juana, 26, 158-65, 169n7, 169n10, 170n22, 173n4
Montaño, Leonor, 169n7, 172, 173n4
Montaño, Lucas, 384n1
Montaño, María, 320n2
Montaño Moreno, María Magdalena, 160-64, 169n7, 169n10, 170n11
Montaño, Polonia, 170n22
Montes de Oca, Valentina, 260n21
Montes Vigil, Francisco, 236n2, 299-309, 321n3, 321n12, 409

Montes Vigil, Juan, 297n18, 327
Montes Vigil, Pedro, 21, 32, 227-32, 236n2, 321n3
Montoya, Andrés, 360-63, 372-73, 385n20, 385n28, 477n11
Montoya, Antonio, 149, 157n26
  as *alcalde ordinario*, 364-65, 367-69
  background of, 157n27, 385n20, 385n28, 406n14
  and inheritance case, 364-65, 367-69, 372-73
  and Martín cousins case, 391, 394-95
Montoya, Diego de, 157n27, 177n9, 407n14
Montoya, Felipe de, 406n14
Montoya, Joseph, 464, 466-67, 477n11
Montoya, Juana, 109n35, 158, 161, 163-64, 170n17
Montoya, Marcos, 108n24
Montoya, María, 260n10, 321n15, 426n14
Montoya, Rosa, 451n8
Montoya, Salvador, 175, 177n9, 228, 230, 236n11
Monzonga, La, 108n31
Moors, 15, 37, 39, 107n11
Moqui (Hopi) pueblos, 63n8, 139n5, 170n17, 217n16, 228-29, 236n7, 297n5, 484n14
Moraga, Antonia de, 30, 40, 46n98, 282n6, 299-308, 320n2, 321n5, 321n7, 406n11
Moraga, Diego de, 320n2
Moraga, Juan de, 320n2
Morales, Francisca Antonia, 442n12
Morales, Josefa de, 70n4
Morales, Juan Antonio de, 75n10
morals, 19, 37, 77, 171-72
Moran, Miguel, 79-80, 108n14, 179, 220, 222n7, 227, 230
Moreno de Trujillo, Estefania, 114, 117-18, 139n7, 140n16
Moreno, Juan José, 332, 358n36-37, 433, 435
Moreno Trujillo, Gertrudis, 139n6, 156n13
Moreno Trujillo, Nicolás, 140n16
mortgages, 478-79
Moya, Antonio de, 442n12
Moya, Juan, 33, 443, 446-48, 452n17
Moya, Lucas Miguel de, 384n1, 430-32, 442n12
Moya, Manuel and Pedro, 285
mujer mundane, 238, 244, 260n23
mulattas/mulattos, 52, 108n31, 263, 427-30, 432-35, 487
mules, 60, 107n4, 159, 161, 164-65, 468, 487
Muñiz de Castro, Josefa, 204n34
murder, 22-23, 26, 28, 33, 36, 38, 110, 139n1, 323, 328, 334-35, 337-38, 451n5

Nambé Pueblo, 75n5, 203n18, 339, 358n49, 388, 393, 407n16-17
Narváez Valverde, Joseph de, 144-49, 156n9, 265, 268n20
Navajos, 42, 43n6, 107n7, 357n14, 358n46, 459n16
Navarro de Isla, Pedro, 332-35, 339, 358n40
Navarro, María Guadalupe, 109n35
Negrete, Lucía Ana, 140n24, 297n14
New Galicia, 109n36
New Mexico
  first native-born priest in, 442n8
  fleeing from, 24, 223, 464-70
  keeping the peace in, 51-52

natives of, 59n11, 61, 63n8, 84, 107n2, 139n3, 139n11, 141n27, 157n28, 173n4, 203n30, 236n10, 236n12, 260n22, 321n8, 384n4, 426n8, 426n12, 442n13, 462n5, 477n12
  obligation of settlers in, 71, 73, 75n9
  permission to leave, 41, 60-62, 70n4, 71-74, 139n6, 139n7, 178, 182, 208, 282n1
  precarious nature of, 25-26
  settlers recruited for, 63n4, 63n6, 70n8, 321n3
  settlers return to, 139n1, 157n22, 158, 169n8, 223, 320n2, 322
  and Spanish law, 28
  Territorial law of, 20
New Mexico Roots Ltd. (Chávez, Fray Angélico), 34
New Spain colonies, 11, 14, 17-19, 37, 75n7, 139n9
Nieto, Magdalena, 177n7
notaries, 75n9, 260n13, 442n14
  in Albuquerque, 157n24, 170n13, 426n8
  ecclesiastical, 328, 331, 357n14, 357n16
  in El Paso, 140n21, 156n5, 407n17
  Franciscan friars as, 144, 147, 149, 156n9, 265, 269n20, 407n17
  of Holy Office, 325-30, 332-33, 358n37
  in Santa Cruz, 156n8, 156n12, 269n22, 451n7
  in Santa Fe, 144, 157n18, 186n9, 445
  subsitutes for, 29
Nueva Recopilación de Todas las Leyes de Castilla, 17, 44n25
Nueva Vizscaya, 70n4, 285
Nuevo León, 139n9

Ojo Caliente, 322, 459n16
Olavidé y Micheleña, Henrique de, 384n9
Olguín, Juan, 477n5
Olguín, María de, 24, 35, 41, 464-70, 477n5-6
Olguín, Thomas, 195, 203n30
Olivas, Isabel de, 109n40, 156n14, 203n31
Olivas, Juana Bautista, 140n14
Oñate, Juan de, 406n5
Orcasitas, José, 328-30, 357n26
Ordenamiento de Alcalá de Henares, 17
Ordenamiento Real, 17
Order of Saint Dominic, 140n17
Order of Saint Francis, 333
Order of Santiago, 78-79, 107n11, 331
Origins of New Mexico Families (Chávez, Fray Angélico), 42
Ornelas, María de, 331
Oronzoro, Father, 455, 459n11
orphans, 25, 34, 174-75, 390
Ortega, Clementa, 452n18
Ortega, Margarita de, 384n14
Ortiz, Ana, 157n28
Ortiz, Lucía, 108n21, 157n22
Ortiz, Luis, 289, 297n24
Ortiz, Nicolás, 149, 157n26, 238-39, 247, 297n24
Ortiz, Sebastiana, 451n2
Osorio, Sotelo, 30-31
Otermín, Antonio de, 384n4
Our Lady of Light (*cofradia*), 442n12
Oviedo, Spain, 259n4

Pachané (Ponachavé), Magdalena, 120-21, 140n25
Pacheco, Josefa, 59n7
Pacheco y Heridias, Alonso, 38
Padilla, Diego, 84, 108n28, 459n17
Padilla, Francisco, 456, 459n17
Padilla land grant, 459n16
Páez Hurtado, Antonia, 356n8
Páez Hurtado Expedition, 63n4, 70n6, 107n3, 109n45, 140n22, 140n24, 157n17, 202n4-5, 226n11, 259n7, 260n13, 282n5
Páez Hurtado, Juan, 59n7, 217n15, 484n22
  background of, 70n6
  and bigamy case, 324-25, 328
  family of, 217n6, 356n8
  home/land of, 39, 227, 230-32, 356n7-8
  Indian campaigns of, 176n6, 204n34
  and inheritance case, 187-88, 190-95, 203n26
  as lieutenant governor, 64-67, 70n6, 225
  settlers recruited by, 321n3
  and slander case, 32, 64-67
paganism, 36
Pajarito, New Mexico, 447, 452n16
Palace of the Governors (Santa Fe), 41, 59n10, 156n6, 186n6, 242, 284-85, 298n28, 461
Palacio de Hoyo, Francisco Antonio de, 264, 268n17
Palma, Agustín. *See* de la Palma, Agustín
Pamplona, Spain, 384n9
paper, 29, 31, 59n9, 70n10, 242, 270, 276, 465, 470
paraje, 161, 164
pardons, 188, 224
  by governors, 52, 124-25, 427
  of husbands, 110-11, 123-25, 427, 434
  and trader case, 408, 412-13, 415-16
  women ask for, 52, 55, 66-67, 427, 434
Parral, Mexico, 59n8, 170n23, 384n3
peace, 25-26, 51-52, 178, 219, 300, 460, 469
Pecos Pueblo, 76, 81, 84-85, 108n28, 157n25, 260n10, 269n22, 358n36, 385n18, 459n11
Peláez, Jacinta, 43n3
Peláez, Jacinto, 170n14, 357n20
Peláez, María, 357n20
Peñalosa, Diego Dionisio de, 31
penalties. *See* sentences
penance, 34, 36-39, 262, 264
perjury, 291
personal rights, 14, 19-21, 390
petitions, 11, 13-14, 19-22, 30, 40, 42-43, 43n9, 362
Philip II, King, 17, 37
Philippines, 65, 75n7, 109n40, 156n14, 203n31, 358n53, 384n9
physical punishment, 32, 263, 299-301, 303-08, 321n11, 387-91. *See also* abuse; assaults; whipping
Picuris Pueblo, 139n1, 173n4, 269n22, 407n17, 459n14
Pineda, María de, 107n13
Pinto, Roque de, 111, 113-19, 123-25, 139n4, 162, 164-65, 190, 192-93
poets, 139n6, 156n13, 451n7
Pojoaque Pueblo, 118, 177n8, 226n11, 476n3
poor, the, 13, 34, 40, 42, 73, 77, 170n11, 174-75, 187, 193, 195, 240, 388, 390-91, 406n12, 410, 412, 415, 433, 460

Portugal, 140n25, 477n8
power of attorney, 260n12, 487
    and Agustín de la Palma case, 89-90, 109n37
    cases involving, 238, 241-42, 245-46
    and dowry/inheritance case, 21, 187-88, 193, 203n26
    explanation of, 20-21, 109n37, 203n26
    and inheritance case, 478-82
    models for, 29
    in Spain, 337
    and Spanish silver case, 60-62
Powers, Karen Vieira, 25, 27
Pozuelo de Calatrava, Spain, 323, 335-38, 356n1, 357n33, 359n65-67, 359n69
predicador, 84, 108n27, 265, 487
pregnancy, 22, 27, 30, 42, 159, 238-40, 244, 247, 260n24, 299
presidio guardhouse, 30, 33, 35, 46n98, 46n114, 51, 76-77, 79-80, 86-90, 238, 240-41, 243
presidio soldiers, 70n4, 108n22, 109n36, 109n40, 157n17, 176n4, 226n9, 259n4, 259n9, 260n18, 321n3, 321n16, 384n6
    act as escorts, 41, 60, 408, 413
    cases involving, 22, 35, 51, 53, 55, 60-62, 64-67, 70n8, 76-92, 187-95, 202n5, 238-49, 284-91, 325, 362, 371, 453-56, 464-70
    and cohabitation, 40, 172
    equipment of, 188, 190-91
    expelled, 296n1
    killed by Indians, 75n6
    killed on campaigns, 109n45
    legal defense of, 31, 35, 88-92
    legal rights of, 90, 92
    role of, 41-42
    salary of, 41, 187-88, 190-91
    typical sentences of, 35
    and violence, 409
    and widow's insurance, 34
    See also sanctuario (sanctuary); Villasur Expedition
prickly pear cactus, 270, 273, 275
priests, 24-25, 358n51, 359n58, 426n19, 455, 459n11
    assign penance, 34, 36
    cases heard by, 22
    convento of, 30-31
    and the dying, 426n13
    first native-born, 442n8
    and funeral costs, 187, 191
    grant dispensations, 36
    immorality of, 37, 39
    and marriage, 35-36, 239
    and *sanctuario*, 80, 83-84
    on "sins of the flesh," 34
    See also predicador; specific towns
prisión, 30, 46n114, 51. *See also* cárcel; imprisonment; presidio guardhouse
privileges, 14-17, 43
procuradors, 31, 35, 41, 88, 217n16, 238-39, 241, 427, 442n14, 484n14, 487
property
    community, 17, 20, 23
    confiscation of, 31
    contracts for, 29
    ownership, 11, 19, 480
    and Spanish law, 15-17, 19-21, 43, 478-81
    a woman's right to, 13-15, 27
    See also land; landowners
prostitution, 22, 25, 27, 59n6, 260n23
"Protector of the Indians," 140n15, 407n15
protocolos, 29, 238, 260n14
public shaming, 24-26, 32, 39, 218-20, 221n1
Puebla, Mexico, 65, 70n3, 75n3-4, 75n6, 217n16, 269n23, 321n21, 459n11
Pueblo Indians, 39, 43n2, 360
    abandon pueblos, 321n3
    campaigns against, 217n16
    culture/traditions of, 139n9
    displacement of, 444
    and Franciscan friars, 156n8, 156n12, 157n24-25, 357n22, 407n17, 459n11, 459n16
    lands of, 477n7
    legal counsel for, 70n11
    See also specific Pueblos
Pueblo Revolt (1680), 38-39, 51, 58n3, 139n1, 139n5, 223, 360, 384n4, 387, 406n2, 426n17, 444, 483n12, 484n23
Pueblo Revolt (1696), 59n5, 71-73, 75n5-6, 109n40, 156n14, 203n31, 217n7, 236n10, 406n3
purges, 170n16
puta, 32, 59n6
puta alcagueta (*alcahueta*), 25-26

Queres Pueblos, 385n28, 477n11
Querétaro, Mexico, 70n2, 170n13, 226n9, 288, 297n9, 321n21
Quintana, José de, 70n2, 451n7
Quintana, Juana, 477n11
Quintana, María, 426n14
Quintana, Michaela, 406n3
Quintana, Miguel de, 406n3, 445, 451n7
    background of, 139n6, 156n13
    as witness, 111, 113-14, 118-19, 145, 302-09, 389-97
Quiros, María, 186n9, 260n13
Quito, Peru, 480

Rael de Aguilar, Alfonso/Alonso I, 113, 217n6, 407n15
    advocates archive, 206, 363, 465
    as *alcalde ordinario*, 76, 78-92, 208-11
    background of, 43n7, 70n11, 203n28
    cases heard by, 21, 76, 78-92
    and gambling case, 288, 290
    and presidio storehouse robbery, 298n28
    as secretary of government/war, 67, 70n11
    as *sergeanto major*, 195, 205, 208-11, 290
    as witness, 205, 208-11, 391, 396-97
Rael de Aguilar, Alonso II, 385n19, 425n5
Rael de Aguilar, Feliciana, 217n8
Rael de Aguilar, Juan, 391, 396-97, 407n15
Rael de Aguilar, Marcial. *See* Rael, Marcial
Rael, Eusebio, 13, 43n7
Rael, Manuel Paulin, 426n15
Rael, Marcial, 408-10, 412-14, 416, 425n5, 426n11

Ramírez, Gregorio, 76, 79-80, 86-88, 107n13, 191, 203n20
Ramírez, José, 107n13
Ramos, Juan Antonio, 92, 109n45, 187-95, 202n4-5
Ramos, María Manuela, 187-88, 192-95, 202n6, 203n24, 203n28
Ramos y Ruiz, Sebastián, 338
ranches/ranchers, 39, 41, 161, 164, 170n20, 203n9, 223-24, 226n7, 356n8, 406n3, 408, 445, 464-67, 479
rank, 23, 27, 77, 207
rape, 11, 14, 22, 24-25, 30, 41, 76-92, 109n42, 261
Raspeña, Juan, 335, 338
real amparo (royal protection), 34, 46n120, 174, 387-88, 390-91, 406n12
real auxilio (royal kindness), 34, 174, 189
Reaño, José, 39
reconciliation, 64, 67, 110-11, 270
    between couples, 142, 145, 148, 427, 432-33, 443-48, 464-65, 469-70, 477n15
    between friends, 218-20
    ordered by governor, 26, 32-33, 125, 464-65, 469-70, 477n15
Recopilación de Leyes de los Reinos de las Indias, 17-18, 43n2. *See also* Laws of the Indies
refuge. *See* sanctuario (sanctuary)
regidor, 230, 236n11, 487
Rendón, Francisco, 286, 289, 297n5, 298n30, 385n24
reputation, 22, 25, 27, 51, 54, 64-67, 119, 121, 144, 147, 224
rescates, 42, 271, 321n23, 487. *See also* slavery
Riaño Tagle, José, 142-49, 156n3, 263-65, 268n8, 357n20
Rico de Rojas, Felipa Sedillo, 360, 362-63, 372, 384n1, 384n4-6, 384n14
Río Abajo area, 13, 40, 63n8, 170n21, 177n9, 223, 282n2, 321n3
Río Arriba, 140n20, 170n25, 306, 331, 406n10, 477n12
Río Grande, 39, 142, 158-59, 161, 164, 170n18-19, 170n22, 203n30, 204n32, 217n5, 226n1, 443-44, 462n4
Río Puerco, 226n1
Rivera, Juan de, 75n3
Rivera, María de, 75n4
Rivera, Martín de, 75n4
Rivera, Pedro Enriquez de, 195, 204n33, 212, 217n15, 285
Rivera, Ramón de, 207
Rivera, Teresa de, 75n6
Roa y Carrillos, Francisco de, 434, 442n19, 456, 459n14
robbery cases, 41, 226n11, 284-91, 409. *See also* theft
Robledo, Maria Gómez, 59n10
Rodarte, Baltazar, 384n3
Rodarte, Margarita, 109n36
Rodarte, María, 116-18
Rodarte, Miguel, 60-61, 63n4-6, 384n3
Rodríguez de Alba, María, 217n16
Rodríguez, Joseph, 372, 385n30
Rodríguez, Juana, 260n21
Rodríguez, Sebastián, 217n5
Rojas de Liscano, Pedro de, 442n19
Roma, María, 282n10

Roman law, 14-17, 20-21, 28, 32, 187, 195, 203n28, 479-81, 484n16
Romero, Agustina, 59n11, 140n19, 259n7
Romero, Alonso Cadmos, 222n3, 236n10
Romero, Ana María, 40, 236n3
    accused of gossip, 26, 227-30
    background of, 176n4, 222n3
    daughter of, 176n3, 273
    sentences threatened with, 26, 30, 45n98, 218-19
    slander case against, 218-20, 222n6
Romero, Baltasar, 410, 426n9, 459n16
Romero, Francisca, 139n1, 140n26, 477n8
Romero, Francisco Xavier, 387, 389, 396-97, 406n7, 406n13
Romero, Joseph Antonio, 23, 143, 145, 147, 157n17
Romero, Pedro, 391, 393-95, 406n13, 456, 459n16
Romero, Rosa, 426n18
Romero, Tadeo, 409
Romo de Vera, Joseph, 430-34, 442n11, 447, 469, 481, 484n20
Rón y Thobar, Vicente Ginzo, 466-68, 470, 477n9
Rosas, Luís de, 38
Roybal, Ignacio de, 358n36-37, 442n8
Roybal, Juana, 332, 358n36-37
Roybal, Manuela de, 268n19
Roybal, Santiago de, 25, 46n110, 268n19, 427, 431, 442n8, 442n16, 443-45, 453-56
Ruiz Cordero, Juan, 186n11
Ruiz, Francisco (Xavier), 28, 178, 182, 186n11
Ruiz, Gertrudis Tafoya, 59n4
Ruiz, Gregoria, 170n13
rumors, 22, 25-27, 110, 322

sacrilege, 22, 34, 37
sacristans, 246, 260n28
Sáez, Agustín, 285
Salas, Bernardo de, 70n4
Salas, Sebastián de, 64-66, 70n3-4
Salas y Hurtado, Francisca, 426n12
Salas y Orozco, Bernardina de, 170n12
Salazar, Agustín de, 139n5, 204n32
Salazar, Antonio de, 139n5, 195, 204n32
Salazar, Bartolomé de, 139n5
Salazar, Catalina, 406n2
Salazar, Isabel de, 226n1
Salazar, María de, 452n12
Salazar y Villaseñor, Joseph Chacon Medina, 78-79, 107n7
Salveterra, Spain, 109n45, 202n5
Samano, María, 385n30
San Antonio land grant, 226n5, 484n12
San Clemente land grant, 13, 43n1, 43n3
San Felipe Pueblo, 203n18
San Francisco de Conchos presidio, 107n4
San Ildefonso Pueblo
    alcaldes of, 358n37
    case involving, 464, 466-68
    church of, 31, 110, 116, 122
    and Felix Luján case, 31, 110, 116, 120, 122, 124-25
    and Franciscan friars, 156n3, 157n24, 268n8
    legal representatives of, 442n14
    priests in, 203n18, 358n49

settlers' land near, 40, 139n1, 385n18, 477n7-8
    taking sanctuary in, 31, 110, 116, 125
San Juan Pueblo, 111, 158, 160, 331, 407n17
San Luis Potosí, Mexico, 58n2, 107n9, 268n19, 384n12
San Miguel Chapel (Santa Fe), 107n7, 108n24, 170n23, 173n4, 204n34, 236n2, 259n1, 385n28
San Nicolás, María de, 384n8
Sánchez, Antonia, 406n8
Sánchez, Antonio Felix, 482, 484n23
Sánchez Bañales, Alfonso, 296n1
Sánchez Bañales y Tagle, Isidro
    accused of robbery, 239, 284-91, 297n16, 409
    background of, 296n1, 454
    gambling of, 239, 284, 286, 288-90
    as *procurador*, 31, 239
    represents jilted soldier, 27, 239, 453-56
    reprimanded by governor, 460-61
Sánchez de Iñigo, Francisca, 406n3-4
Sánchez de Iñigo, Jacinto, 60-62, 63n4, 63n8, 110-12, 115-18, 121-22, 124-25, 484n23
Sánchez de Iñigo, Pedro I, 406n3, 406n8
Sánchez de Iñigo, Pedro II, 387-91, 406n3, 464-66, 477n7
Sánchez de la Cruz, Juan, 357n30
Sánchez de Mondragón, Sebastían, 477n3
Sánchez, Francisco, 60, 484n23
Sánchez, José, 75n5
sanctuario (sanctuary), 406n7
    and Agustín de la Palma case, 76, 79-80, 83-86, 108n15, 108n18
    explanation of, 30-31, 108n19, 407n16, 487
    and Felix Luján case, 110, 112, 116, 125
    and the Martín cousins case, 388, 393, 395-96, 407n16
    and murder cases, 28
    and soldiers, 30-31, 35, 425n5
Sandia Pueblo, 158, 161, 426n6
Sandoval, Antonio, 282n7
Sandoval y Manzañares, Ana de, 13, 43n1
Santa Ana Pueblo, 156n8, 156n12, 157n18, 426n9
Santa Clara Pueblo, 31, 58n3, 110, 116, 156n3, 236n10, 388, 459n11
Santa Cruz, 230
    alcaldes mayores of, 110-18, 121-22, 124-25, 139n3, 140n15, 390
    alcaldes of, 58n3, 59n11, 60, 63n8, 107n9, 140n19, 157n28, 173n3, 259n7, 357n26, 384n12, 385n18, 406n4, 464-70
    alférez of, 259n2
    banishment to, 54, 65, 188, 427, 434
    baptisms in, 59n11, 140n19, 259n7
    burials in, 477n12
    calderero in, 357n15
    captains of, 259n2, 259n7
    casas reales in, 30, 46n98
    cases involving, 110-25, 145, 240, 299-309, 321n5, 388-91, 395-97, 464-71
    early settlers of, 59n4, 59n11, 63n4, 71, 75n5-6, 107n3, 108n21, 109n35, 109n40, 139n5-6, 140n19-20, 140n23, 156n13-14, 170n13, 203n31, 226n11, 259n7, 282n7, 297n24, 321n4, 321n19, 356n12, 385n30, 476n3

Franciscan friars in, 157n18, 388, 407n17
"Guardian Minister" of, 145
marriages in, 141n27, 357n15, 406n8
priests in, 358n49, 388, 395
refounding of, 217n7
sanctuario in, 388, 393, 395-96, 407n15
soldiers of, 41, 243, 260n17, 298n24, 385n18, 387
traders in, 323
wagonmakers in, 477n6
women petitioners in, 40
See also homes: in Santa Cruz; imprisonment: in Santa Cruz; land grants; landowners
Santa Fe, 217n7
    alcaldes mayores of, 59n10, 270-75, 360-71, 373
    alcaldes of, 21, 43n7, 59n10, 70n6, 70n11, 282n1, 372, 407n15, 427, 442n14
    alcaldes ordinarios of, 52, 54-55, 59n10, 60-62, 78-92, 86-89, 171-72, 173n3, 178-82, 187, 192, 194-95, 208-11, 218-20, 227-32, 241-42, 367-69, 373
    alférez of, 59n10, 161-62, 165, 170n22
    alguacils of, 79-80, 217n16, 385n29
    banishment from, 188, 218-20, 227
    Barrio de Analco of, 259n1, 286, 289, 297n10
    cabildo of, 142, 156n5, 157n28, 177n9, 179, 205-06, 208-11, 217n16, 218, 220, 364-65, 367, 373, 385n29, 484n14
    calderero in, 357n15
    cases involving, 171-72, 205-12, 218-20, 227-32, 238-49, 261-65, 270-77, 324-30, 363-73, 427-35
    cattle distribution in, 226n11
    courtroom in, 179-80
    description of, 178
    early settlers of, 108n24, 156n4, 173n7, 238, 260n11, 442n9, 442n13, 452n12, 477n12
    and Edicts of Faith, 39, 171, 324
    and Holy Office, 171-72, 261
    legal representatives of, 442n14
    marriages in, 107n13, 170n22, 186n9, 204n32, 260n27, 331
    merchants in, 322, 327, 442n11
    ministers/priests in, 145, 147, 171, 358n49
    presidio soldiers' visits to, 41, 238
    prominent citizens of, 407n15
    and Pueblo Revolt, 360, 384n4
    regidor of, 230, 236n11
    sanctuario in, 31, 76, 79-80, 83-86, 108n18-19
    Spanish citizens of, 326-28
    weavers in, 406n5
    women in, 40, 159, 161, 164-65, 187, 189
    See also casas reales; convento: in Santa Fe; land grants; landowners; notaries: in Santa Fe; Palace of the Governors (Santa Fe); San Miguel Chapel (Santa Fe)
Santa Fe Plaza, 70n11, 108n22, 169n7, 186n6, 217n5, 218-20, 239, 259n1, 289-90, 299, 320n2
Santa Fe presidio, 260n17
    alférez of, 43n7, 59n5, 452n12
    captains of, 64-65, 70n8, 70n11, 107n9, 187, 190, 203n30, 261, 282n2, 385n22
    cases involving, 51, 53, 55, 187-95, 238-49, 284-91
    chaplain of, 156n6
    description of, 40-41

and Holy Office cases, 264
imprisonment in, 284-85, 287-88
insurance fund of, 187-88, 190-91, 202n4, 203n15
muster, 70n5, 170n22, 186n7, 260n21, 384n14, 426n9
officers of, 159, 186n9, 477n9
payroll of, 188, 192
sergeants of, 260n13, 384n4
soldiers of, 63n8, 64-67, 70n5, 76-92, 108n20, 145, 156n5, 170n22-23, 174-75, 178-79, 186n7, 203n20, 204n32, 204n34, 222n3, 238-49, 260n21-22, 261, 282n1, 325, 330, 357n18, 442n19
and storehouse robbery, 284-91, 409
See also presidio guardhouse; presidio soldiers
Santa Fe River, 159, 170n19, 178-79, 181, 227, 231, 259n1, 297n5, 297n10, 297n18
Santander, Spain, 43n2, 43n6, 202n8, 203n18
Santiago, New Mexico, 443-46
Santistevan, Andre de, 170n22
Santistevan, Salvador de, 159, 161-62, 165, 170n22-23
Santo Domingo Pueblo church, 31
scandal, 14, 22-23, 25-26, 32, 52, 64-67, 148, 178, 182, 218-20, 413, 427, 432, 451n1
scribes, 29, 70n10, 358n44
  to *cabildo*, 54, 59n11, 79, 85, 92, 109n35, 140n19, 142, 179, 208, 220, 259n7
  comments by, 218
  gambling of, 41
  of Holy Office, 338, 359n71
  receive compensation, 31
  in Santa Fe, 54, 108n23, 109n35, 372
  in Spain, 337
  uphold Spanish law, 21
secrecy, 142. *See also* Holy Office of the Inquisition: secrecy of
secretaries, of government and war, 31, 43n7, 67, 70n11, 78, 113, 139n4, 142, 194, 209, 211-12, 217n15. *See also* specific names
secular court/authorities, 24, 26
Sedaño, Antonia, 297n9
Sedaño, Josefa, 26-27, 40, 64-67, 70n2, 70n5, 70n7, 70n9
Sedaño, Pedro, 70n2
Sedillo, Antonio Toribio, 451n4
Sedillo, Domingo, 461, 462n5
Sedillo, Isabel, 425n5
Sedillo Rico de Rojas, Casilda, 426n16, 459n5
Sedillo Rico de Rojas, Joaquín, 462n5
sedition, 59n7
seduction, 21-22, 24, 34, 41, 205, 208, 238-40, 243-48
Segesser hides, 70n5
Segovia, Spain, 385n30
Seguido, Catalina, 336, 359n64
Segura, Gertrudis de, 23, 427-35, 442n5
Segura, Pedro de, 180, 186n7, 442n5
Sena, Bernardino, 236n2
Senatus Consultus Velleianum, 17, 21, 187, 195, 479-81, 484n16
sentences, 28, 35, 52, 159
  community service, 22, 24, 26, 33, 170n11
  forced marriage, 22, 77, 172, 239
  for men, 22, 26, 32-33, 182

pay court costs, 23, 31, 261, 270, 276, 388, 397, 414, 427, 432
public nudity, 26, 32, 218-20
reduced by governor, 427, 434-35
repair public buildings, 26
for women, 32-33
See also specific types
sergeanto mayor, 158, 195, 205, 210-11, 290, 384n4
Serrano de Salazar, María Martín, 59n8
Serrano de Salazar, Pedro Martín, 58n2, 59n8
servants, 29, 81, 119-20, 190, 384n8, 486-87
  accusations by, 27
  cases involving, 24, 27, 178-82, 203n12, 408-10, 412-18, 425n5
  Indians as, 40, 170n15, 270-71, 299, 301, 303, 305-07, 309, 321n23
  women as, 11, 40, 270-71
  women treated as, 26, 158, 160-61
servitude, enforced, 33, 35, 39, 42, 121, 158, 160-61, 182
Sevillano de Mancilla, Gertrudis, 139n7
Seville, Spain, 70n4, 70n6, 139n9, 323, 337, 357n27, 358n36
sexual behavior, 22, 24-25
  explicit language about, 34
  and honor/dishonor, 27-28
  "illicit", 36, 76-77, 81-82, 85-86, 91, 109n42, 110, 170n11, 177n6, 219, 238, 247-49, 299-300, 302-08, 321n12
  and marriage promises, 453-54
  and married couples, 227, 229
  premarital, 35-36, 51, 171-72, 177n6, 239
  See also conjugal relations; love affairs; rape
shackles, 76, 79, 84, 87, 287. *See also* leg irons/stocks
shame. *See* public shaming
shoemakers, 75n5, 406n7
Siete Partidas law code, 16-17, 21, 203n28, 480-81
signatures, 29, 139n6, 142, 284, 446, 455
Silva, Antonio de, 161-64, 170n13, 224-25
Silva, Francisca, 462n6
Silva, Francisco de, 21
Silva, Gertrudis, 426n16, 459n5
Silva, Salvador, 170n13
silver, 60-61, 62n1, 203n22. *See also* marca (silver bar)
sins
  denunciation of, 156n11
  and dispensations, 170n11
  and Holy Office, 171-72, 218-19
  mortal, 22, 24, 26, 107n6
  against nature, 22, 34, 37
  pecados, 171-72
  penance for, 34
  See also adultery; cohabitation; incest; sacrilege; seduction
Sisneros, María, 385n28
Sitio de Gutiérrrez, 43n1, 226n1
Sixtus IV, Pope, 37
slander, 51, 64-67, 70n7, 121, 218-20, 222n6
slavery, 27, 42, 161, 413. *See also* rescates
soap, 285
social status, 23, 25, 27, 33, 40, 42, 159, 207
society, legalistic, 14, 17-18

Socolow, Susan, 42
Socorro, New Mexico, 157n19
soldiers, 24, 28, 59n5, 59n8, 140n24, 170n13, 237n12.
  See also presidio soldiers; specific presidios; specific towns
Solis, Carlos de, 263, 268n15
Sombrerete, Zacatecas, Mexico, 60-61, 63n4, 63n7, 63n9, 109n45, 202n5, 226n11, 259n9
Sonora, Mexico, 109n45, 202n5
Sopena, Manuel de, 388, 395, 407n17
Sotomayor, María de, 140n20, 219
Spain
  cloth of, 297n12
  legalistic society of, 14-18
  map of, 336
  royal courts of, 16-17, 27, 75n2
  venereal diseases in, 42
  See also Holy Office of the Inquisition
Spanish Colonial Archives of New Mexico, 11, 20-21, 25, 29, 174, 356n8, 363, 408
Spanish Crown, 17, 19, 25, 37, 46n120, 157n17, 157n23, 356n2, 358n54
Spanish law, 193
  history/role of, 14-19
  in New Mexico, 14, 16-21
  procedures for, 28-34, 387-88
  renounced by women, 21, 187, 195, 479-80
  and women's rights, 13-17, 19-21, 44n29, 46n113, 52, 187, 362
Spanish Reconquest, 11, 28, 38-39, 41, 60, 64, 107n9, 108n21, 157n22, 158, 177n7-8, 203n17, 223, 320n2, 384n4, 387, 426n14, 442n9, 444, 483n12
St. Nicolás, María de, 385n23
stocks. *See* leg irons/stocks
superstitions, 37, 218-19
surgeons (*cirujanos*), 156n9, 269n20, 271, 387, 389, 396-97, 406n7, 487

Tafoya Altamirano, Antonio, 442n14
Tafoya Altamirano, Cristóbal, 51, 53, 55, 59n4, 59n5, 59n7
Tafoya Altamirano, Juan de, 59n5
Tafoya, Antonio, 59n5
Tafoya, El Rancho de, 161, 164, 170n20
Tafoya, Felipe, 431, 442n14
Tafoya, Juan de, 53, 59n5, 59n7
Tagle, Pedro Anselmo Sánchez de, 332-34, 339-40, 358n40-41, 358n48
Taguada de Ulloa, Felipa, 59n5
tailors, 185n2
Tamaris, Felipe, 367-71, 373, 385n19
Tamaris, Francisco de, 43n7, 385n19
Taos, New Mexico, 141n28, 407n15
  alcaldes mayores of, 442n9
  alcaldes of, 59n11, 140n19, 259n9
  Franciscan friars in, 157n24, 407n17
  landowners in, 385n22
  pueblo of, 259n7, 384n4
  trading in, 465
Tapia, Francisco de, 175, 177n7
Tapia, María de, 156n7, 222n3, 236n3, 236n10
Telles Girón, Dimas, 195, 204n34

Telles Girón, Isabel, 63n8
Telles Girón, José, 260n20
Telles Girón, María, 260n21
Telles, Isabel, 484n23
Telles, Juan, 243, 248-49, 260n20
Tello, José López, 80, 83-84, 108n17, 326-30, 333, 357n22, 358n48
Tenorio de Alba, Cayetano, 59n11
Tenorio de Alba, Luisa, 357n20
Tenorio de Alba, Manuel, 241-42, 259n10
Tenorio de Alba, Miguel
  background of, 59n11, 140n19, 259n7
  and Francisca Gómez de Torres case, 118-21
  and mistress case, 209, 211-12
  and robbery/gambling case, 286-87, 290-91
  as scribe to *cabildo*, 55
  as secretary of government/war, 194, 209, 211-12, 241, 243-49, 286-87
  and seduction case, 241, 243-49
Terrazas, María Carrillo, 186n11
Terrus, José, 324-28, 356n8, 484n22
testigos. See witnesses
testimony, 13, 19, 28, 30, 32-34, 37, 41, 108n23, 321n20, 358n43, 385n25, 388
Tesuque Pueblo, 108n28, 145, 157n24, 172, 173n4, 203n18
Texas, 44n29
textiles, 408-10, 412-13. *See also* cloth
theft, 14, 31, 35, 41, 60, 108n28, 408-10, 412-18, 425n5, 452n17. *See also* robbery cases
tobacco, 142, 145, 156n10
Toledo, Spain, 15, 17, 37, 140n17, 219, 322-23, 331, 334-38, 359n68-69
Tomé land grant, 43n5, 452n13
Tomé, New Mexico, 462n4, 462n6. *See also* Fuenclara, New Mexico
tools, 58n2
Toribio. *See* de la Palma, Agustín
Torres, Antonia, 426n17
Torres, Antonio de, 299-308, 320n2, 321n5-6, 321n8, 321n12
Torres, Cristóbal de, 40, 112, 115, 122-24, 139n3, 139n11, 301, 305, 307, 321n8
Torres, Diego, 204n32, 323
Torres, Gertrudis, 406n3
Torres, María de, 110-12, 115-16, 139n5, 204n32
torture, 38, 262
trade
  fairs, 42, 158, 160, 271, 321n23, 368, 487
  goods, 171, 186n11, 285, 297n12, 297n20, 408-10, 412
traders/trading, 24, 140n25
  cases involving, 408-10, 443-44, 446
  in El Paso, 186n11
  in Mexico, 186n11, 322-23
  in New Mexico, 39-42, 323, 442n17
  outside the kingdom, 139n6
  in Santa Fe, 172, 327, 408-10
  in Taos, 465
  See also Indians: trading of; merchants
Trujillo, Baltazar, 140n26
Trujillo, Bartolomé de, 321n16

Trujillo, Cristóbal, 385n18
Trujillo, Diego, 333, 358n47
Trujillo, José, 58n3
Trujillo, Joseph, 204n34, 365, 385n18
Trujillo, Juana, 222n3, 227-31, 236n3
Trujillo, María, 140n26, 477n12
Trujillo, Mateo, 21, 222n3, 227-28, 230-32, 236n3, 236n10
Trujillo, Rosa, 462n7
Trujillo, Sebastiana Martín, 141n27, 476n3
Twitchell, Ralph Emerson, 20

Ucles, Castile, Spain, 107n11
Ugarte, Diego de, 322, 324-25, 356n7
Ulibarrí, Antonio de, 21, 224, 360-71, 373, 384n12, 427, 429-35, 479-81
Ulibarrí, Juan de, 78, 107n9, 210-11, 385n18
Unanue, Felipe Jacobo de, 384n11
Unanue, Juan Antonio, 364-65, 373, 384n11, 397
Unanue, Juan Felipe Jacobo de, 447, 452n15, 456, 469
Utes, 42

Valdéz, Angela Francisca, 442n11
Valdéz, Antonia Flores de, 109n40, 156n14
Valdéz, Catalina, 28, 139n1
Valdéz, Domingo "El Tata," 240, 247-48, 259n4
Valdéz, José Luis, 259n4
Valencia, Antonia de, 76-77, 81-86, 91, 107n6, 108n20, 109n42, 203n9
Valencia, New Mexico, 33, 40, 443-48, 451n3
Valero, Marqués de, 285
Valle de San Bartolomé, Mexico, 385n19
Valle, Marín de, 33
Vallejo, Bernardo, 461, 462n6
Vallejo, Francisca, 459n5
Vallejo, Lugardo, 415-17, 426n18
Vallejo, Manuel González, 426n18
Valverde Cossio, Antonio de, 29, 43n6, 187, 189, 202n8, 270, 282n1, 285, 357n30, 406n7
Valverde, Cristóbal de, 142, 156n4
Valverde, Josefa, 425n6, 478, 481, 483n10, 484n13
Valverde, Nicolás, 161, 170n23
varas, 286, 297n7, 297n12, 410, 415, 487
Varela, Ana, 107n2
Varela de Perea, Antonia, 385n22
Varela de Perea, Geronima, 282n2
Varela, Felipe, 447-48, 452n18
Varela, Josefa, 43n1
Varela, Manuela, 452n19
Varela, María, 385n24, 462n5
Varela, Monica, 452n18
Varela, Teresa, 70n11
Vargas, Diego de, 43n7, 44n25, 107n4
  appointments of, 173n3, 205, 217n6
  blind interpreter of, 139n5, 204n32
  death of, 64, 70n6, 109n40, 156n14, 203n31, 217n7
  goods stolen from, 285
  inventory of, 109n40, 156n14, 203n31
  investigation of, 59n7
  land grants given by, 259n1, 297n18, 360, 363
  patron of, 75n7
  petitions to, 109n45, 202n5
  settlers recruited by, 70n8
  settlers return with, 58n2, 110, 140n14, 169n7, 177n9, 202n8, 237n12, 282n10, 360, 384n4, 385n28, 387, 406n5, 407n15, 442n9, 477n3, 477n5
  staff of, 70n8, 70n11, 260n29, 282n2, 360
  testimony against, 59n11, 140n19, 170n13
  valor citation given by, 141n28
Vargas, Manuela de, 406n11
Varo, Andrés, 333, 356n11, 357n29, 358n50
Vasquez Baca, María, 459n17
Vasquez, Joseph, 406n11
Vasquez, Juan Joseph, 464-65, 469-70, 477n6, 477n15
Velasco, Ana, 282n2
Velasco, Cristóbal, 217n6
Velasco, José Ortiz de, 334, 358n53
Velasco, Luis de, 338
Velasco, Micaela de, 40, 43n9, 173n3, 205-09, 211-12, 217n4-6
Velásquez, Joseph, 144-45, 147, 156n7
Velásquez, María Manuela, 442n4
Vélez Cachupín, Tomás, 13, 43n2, 43n6, 297n12, 357n14, 442n6
Vélez de Escalante, Pedro, 335, 338, 359n56
Vera, María de, 157n27
vicario, 427, 431, 442n8, 442n16, 445, 488
viceroys, 43n2, 70n8, 156n5, 217n1, 285, 462n4
  in Mexico City, 426n6
  of New Spain, 59n7, 64, 71-74, 75n1, 75n7, 75n9, 107n9
  petitions to, 27, 71-74
  royal orders of, 33
  uphold Spanish law, 14
vigas, 289-90, 298n26, 385n28
Vigil, Manuel, 321n3
Villa de Leon, 176n4
Villa de Llerena, Mexico, 63n4, 63n7
Villafranca de los Palacios, Seville, Spain, 328, 357n27
Villalpando, Ana María Romero. See Romero, Ana María
Villalpando, Catalina de, 25, 34, 40, 174-75, 176n3-4, 222n3, 270, 273-76
Villalpando, Josefa, 282n7
Villalpando, Juan de, 174-75, 176n3-4, 222n3
Villasur Expedition, 284
  deaths during, 59n11, 70n5, 108n22, 109n31, 140n19, 156n6, 177n7-8, 186n7, 259n7, 260n21, 268n19, 282n2, 357n18
  and massacre investigation, 285
  survivors of, 59n10, 70n5, 109n33, 357n18, 385n19
Villasur, Pedro de, 284-91, 298n28
violence, 19, 24, 38, 139n1, 409, 465
Vique, Spain, 326
virginity, 22, 25, 27, 77, 81-82, 84, 91, 205, 210-11, 240, 243, 248-49, 454. *See also* seduction
Visigothic Code, 14-15

warfare, 25, 42
water supply, 42
wealthy settlers, 11, 20, 26-27, 36, 39-40, 219, 223-24
weapons, 33, 35, 107n4, 139n9, 170n22, 176n6, 190-91, 285, 321n3, 407n14, 486. *See also* belduque

weavers, 173n3, 205, 217n6, 406n5, 406n7, 442n11, 451n2
West Africa, 108n31
whipping, 25, 33, 39, 110, 122, 161-63, 188, 263, 301, 305, 464, 469
widows, 19-20, 24, 27, 34, 40-41
wills, 372, 478
   of Antonio Montoya, 407n14
   of Cristóbal de Tafoya Altamarino, 59n4
   of Cristóbal de Torres II, 321n8
   of Diego de Padilla, 459n17
   of Dimas Girón, 204n34
   of Francisco Anaya de Almazán, 356n12
   of Governor Cuervo y Valdés, 205, 207
   of José Terrus, 356n8, 484n22
   of Joseph Baca, 43n5, 452n13
   of Joseph Romo de Vera, 442n11
   of Juan Francisco Martín, 176n3
   of Juan García de Noriega, 406n4
   of Juan Ruiz Cordero, 186n11
   of Luis García de Noriega, 226n5
   of Miguel Rodarte, 60-61
   of Vicente de Armijo, 297n12, 297n18
   models for, 29
   and Spanish law, 16, 19-20
   and Spanish silver case, 60-61
   of women, 19-20, 260n11, 321n22, 362, 384n1
winegrowing, 203n8
witchcraft, 23, 36-37, 142-43, 145, 148, 156n11, 218-19
witnesses, 14, 22, 25, 28-33, 37, 38, 260n26
women
   "corrected" by men, 26
   death among, 42
   in eighteenth-century New Mexico, 11
   entertain men in homes, 26-27, 64-65
   "house arrest" of, 65-66, 70n9
   independent status of, 14, 19, 43, 52
   lack of opportunities for, 76-77, 159
   Mexican, 44n29
   outspoken, 176n3, 223
   and presidio soldiers, 41
   protection of, 20-21, 164-65, 174, 187, 203n28
   roles of, 42, 362, 372, 408
   sentences for, 32-33, 65
   as separate legal entities, 14, 19, 43, 362
   unmarried, 19-20, 22-23, 27, 205-08, 282n5
   wealthy, 11, 20, 36, 40, 139n1, 219
   work opportunities for, 40, 187-90, 203n9, 228, 230
women's legal rights, 44n29
   in New Mexico, 11, 13-15, 19-22, 43, 71, 159, 362, 427
   protection of, 20-22, 187, 195, 478-81, 484n16-17
   renounced by women, 21, 187, 195, 479-81
   in Spain, 14-22
   stated in documents, 14, 43n9, 52
   See also Spanish law: and women's rights
wood, 368
writers, 156n13. *See also* poets

Xavier y Baca, Josefa, 226n5

Yrigoyen, José, 325-30, 333-34, 357n14

Yturrieta, Eduarda, 463n7

Zabaleta, Juan de, 146, 157n19
Zacatecas, Mexico, 260n13
   marriages in, 442n4
   mines of, 41, 60, 63n7
   natives of, 107n13, 140n19, 140n24, 170n12, 173n5, 186n9, 203n20, 217n16, 236n2, 259n7, 260n13, 260n21, 288, 296n1, 297n18, 321n3, 327-28
   petitioners from, 202n5
   royal treasury of, 217n1
   settlers recruited from, 107n3, 157n17, 356n10
   See also Sombrerete, Zacatecas, Mexico
Zambrano de Rivera, Josefa, 480
Zia Pueblo, 156n8, 156n12, 451n1, 452n12
Zuni Pueblo, 139n5, 188, 217n16, 323

www.ingramcontent.com/pod-product-compliance
Lightning Source LLC
Chambersburg PA
CBHW080802020526
44114CB00046B/2700